Strategies for Leaders in Shifting Cultural and Technological Landscapes

Amdy Diene
Liberty University, USA

Vice President of Editorial	Melissa Wagner
Managing Editor of Acquisitions	Mikaela Felty
Managing Editor of Book Development	Jocelynn Hessler
Production Manager	Mike Brehm
Cover Design	Phillip Shickler

Published in the United States of America by
IGI Global Scientific Publishing
701 East Chocolate Avenue
Hershey, PA, 17033, USA
Tel: 717-533-8845
Fax: 717-533-8661
Website: https://www.igi-global.com E-mail: cust@igi-global.com

Copyright © 2025 by IGI Global Scientific Publishing. All rights reserved. No part of this publication may be reproduced, stored or distributed in any form or by any means, electronic or mechanical, including photocopying, without written permission from the publisher.
Product or company names used in this set are for identification purposes only. Inclusion of the names of the products or companies does not indicate a claim of ownership by IGI Global Scientific Publishing of the trademark or registered trademark.

Library of Congress Cataloging-in-Publication Data

Names: Diene, Amdy editor
Title: Strategies for leaders in shifting cultural and technological
  landscapes / edited by Amdy Diene.
Description: Hershey, PA : IGI Global Scientific Publishing, [2025] |
  Includes bibliographical references and index. | Summary: "This book is
  a comprehensive guide for modern leaders navigating the complex
  interplay of culture and technology in today's rapidly evolving business
  environment. The text explores various topics crucial for effective
  leadership in the 21st century, addressing the challenges and
  opportunities of globalization, digital transformation, and changing
  workforce dynamics"-- Provided by publisher.
Identifiers: LCCN 2024053593 (print) | LCCN 2024053594 (ebook) | ISBN
  9798369355534 hardcover | ISBN 9798369355541 paperback | ISBN
  9798369355558 ebook
Subjects: LCSH: Leadership | Organizational change
Classification: LCC HD57.7 .S781525 2025 (print) | LCC HD57.7 (ebook) |
  DDC 658.4/092--dc23/eng/20250117
LC record available at https://lccn.loc.gov/2024053593
LC ebook record available at https://lccn.loc.gov/2024053594

British Cataloguing in Publication Data
A Cataloguing in Publication record for this book is available from the British Library.

All work contributed to this book is new, previously-unpublished material.
The views expressed in this book are those of the authors, but not necessarily of the publisher.
This book contains information sourced from authentic and highly regarded references, with reasonable efforts made to ensure the reliability of the data and information presented. The authors, editors, and publisher believe the information in this book to be accurate and true as of the date of publication. Every effort has been made to trace and credit the copyright holders of all materials included. However, the authors, editors, and publisher cannot assume responsibility for the validity of all materials or the consequences of their use. Should any copyright material be found unacknowledged, please inform the publisher so that corrections may be made in future reprints.

Table of Contents

Preface v

Introduction xiii

Chapter 1
The Convergence of Culture and Technology: A Crucial Aspect in Reshaping Business in the Digital Age 1

Chapter 2
Leading With Vision and Values 25

Chapter 3
Navigating Cultural Shifts: Strategies for Adaptive Leadership 43

Chapter 4
Embracing Technological Innovation: Leading in the Digital Age 71

Chapter 5
Leveraging Diversity and Inclusion 99

Chapter 6
Strategic Planning in Fluid Environments 121

Chapter 7
Developing Partnerships and Ecosystems 149

Chapter 8
Harnessing Innovation and Emergent Strategy 179

Chapter 9
Engaging Stakeholders: Communication and Collaboration in a Diverse World 195

Chapter 10
Hiring-Reskilling and the Future of Work 215

Chapter 11
Ethical Leadership and Accountability in a Changing World 241

Chapter 12
Maintaining Trust and Transparency 261

Chapter 13
Leveraging Data and Analytics for Strategic Decision-Making 281

Chapter 14
Making Value-Based Decisions 317

Conclusion 353

Compilation of References 355

About the Author 413

Index 415

Preface

SUBJECT MATTER

The book '*Strategies for Leaders in Shifting Cultural and Technological Landscapes*' is a comprehensive guide for modern leaders navigating the complex interplay of culture and technology in today's rapidly evolving business environment. The text explores various topics crucial for effective leadership in the 21st century, addressing the challenges and opportunities of globalization, digital transformation, and changing workforce dynamics. The book examines how technology and culture have converged to reshape the business landscape. It underscores the need for leaders to adapt to a globalized market where cultural diversity and technological advancements are deeply intertwined. Subsequent chapters delve into various aspects of leadership, emphasizing the importance of vision and values in guiding organizations through turbulent times.

A significant portion of the book is dedicated to discussing the cultural aspects of leadership. It extensively explores strategies for navigating cultural shifts, leveraging diversity and inclusion, and engaging stakeholders in a diverse world. These chapters highlight the critical role of adaptive leadership in fostering inclusivity, driving innovation, and unlocking the full potential of a diverse workforce. The book also thoroughly addresses the technological dimension of leadership, equipping leaders with strategies for embracing technological innovation, harnessing emergent strategy, and adapting to the future of work. The book emphasizes the importance of digital transformation, continuous learning, and reskilling in preparing organizations for an increasingly automated and AI-driven future.

Strategic planning and partnerships are also key themes, with the book offering insights into effective planning in fluid environments and developing robust partner ecosystems. These chapters stress the importance of flexibility, scenario planning, and collaborative approaches in creating value and maintaining competitiveness.

Ethical considerations are noticed, with dedicated chapters on ethical leadership, accountability, and maintaining trust and transparency. These sections underscore the importance of integrity and responsible decision-making in building sustainable organizations and navigating the complexities of a globalized economy.

The book offers a holistic approach to leadership in the modern era, combining theoretical frameworks with practical strategies and real-world case studies. It aims to equip leaders with the tools and insights necessary to thrive in an environment characterized by rapid technological change, cultural diversity, and evolving stakeholder expectations.

Where the Topic Fits in the World Today

The topic of leadership strategies in shifting cultural and technological landscapes is highly relevant and timely in today's rapidly evolving global business environment. This subject addresses the critical challenges and opportunities that leaders face in the 21st century, where the pace of change is unprecedented, and the interconnectedness of markets, cultures, and technologies is more significant than ever. In our current era, often called the Fourth Industrial Revolution, we are witnessing a convergence of digital, physical, and biological technologies transforming how we live, work, and interact. This book's focus on navigating these changes is crucial for leaders across all sectors, from multinational corporations to small businesses, non-profits, and government organizations.

The emphasis on cultural shifts and diversity reflects the increasing globalization of markets and workforces. As businesses expand across borders and demographics change within countries, leaders must be adept at managing diverse teams, understanding varied consumer bases, and navigating complex cultural landscapes. This cultural competence is necessary for organizational success and innovation. Simultaneously, the rapid advancement of technologies such as artificial intelligence, machine learning, big data analytics, and the Internet of Things is reshaping industries and business models. The book's coverage of technological innovation and digital transformation speaks directly to the urgent need for leaders to understand and leverage these technologies to remain competitive and relevant.

Topics like ethical leadership, trust, and transparency are particularly pertinent in an age of corporate social responsibility and stakeholder capitalism gaining prominence. In the wake of various corporate scandals and increasing public scrutiny, leaders are expected to navigate complex ethical dilemmas while maintaining accountability and building trust with diverse stakeholders. The book's approach to strategic planning in fluid environments and developing partnerships aligns with the trend toward more agile and collaborative business models. In a world where disruption is the norm, traditional rigid planning methods give way to more flexible, adaptable approaches that allow organizations to pivot quickly in response to changes.

Furthermore, the focus on the future of work, reskilling, and continuous learning addresses one of the most pressing issues of our time: how to prepare workforces for jobs that may not yet exist and how to harness human potential in an increasingly automated world. In essence, this book offers a comprehensive roadmap for leaders navigating the complexities of our current business landscape. It addresses the key challenges of our time, from technological disruption to cultural diversity, from ethical considerations to strategic agility, providing leaders with the tools and insights they need to thrive in an era of constant change and uncertainty.

Target Audience

The target audience for this book is primarily senior leaders, executives, and managers who are navigating complex organizational challenges in today's rapidly changing business environment. However, the breadth and depth of topics suggested that it could be valuable for a broader range of professionals and aspiring leaders.

Specifically, the book seems well-suited for:

C-suite executives and senior management teams who are responsible for setting organizational strategy and vision. The chapters on strategic planning, ethical leadership, and navigating cultural shifts would be particularly relevant to this group.

Mid-level managers and emerging leaders who are looking to develop their skills and prepare for higher leadership roles. The focus on adaptive leadership, diversity and inclusion, and technological innovation would be especially beneficial for this audience.

Human resources professionals and talent development specialists who are involved in workforce planning, skills development, and organizational culture. The chapters on hiring, reskilling, and the future of work would be highly relevant to this group.

Entrepreneurs and business owners who need to navigate the complexities of scaling their organizations in a global, technology-driven marketplace. The insights on partner ecosystems, stakeholder engagement, and digital transformation would be precious.

Consultants and business advisors who work with organizations on strategy, leadership development, and organizational change. The comprehensive coverage of current business challenges and strategies would give them valuable frameworks and insights to apply professionally.

Academic professionals and students in business management, leadership studies, and related fields who are interested in contemporary leadership challenges and strategies.

Board members and corporate governance professionals who need to understand the evolving landscape of business leadership, particularly about ethical considerations, stakeholder engagement, and strategic planning.

Technology leaders and CIOs who are driving digital transformation within their organizations would find the chapters on embracing technological innovation and harnessing emergent strategy especially relevant.

The book's focus on cultural and technological leadership aspects makes it relevant to a diverse audience across various industries and sectors. Its content is tailored for those leading or aspiring to lead in global, multicultural environments where technological disruption is a constant factor. The emphasis on practical strategies and real-world examples suggests that it would be most valuable to those who are actively engaged in or preparing for leadership roles in complex, dynamic organizational settings.

CHAPTER OVERVIEW

Chapter 1. 'Assessing the Winds of Change and the Convergence of Culture and Technology,' explores how technology and culture have merged to reshape the business landscape in the 21st century. It discusses the challenges of navigating a globalized market where cultural diversity and technological advancements are intertwined. The chapter touches on the digital revolution's impact on consumer behavior, the rise of remote work, and the concept of a global market, using examples of successful brands like Airbnb and Coca-Cola to illustrate effective navigation of this new landscape.

Chapter 2. '*Leading With Vision and Values*' focuses on the importance of value-based leadership in creating an ethical corporate culture. It discusses the shift towards this leadership style in response to corporate scandals at the beginning of the millennium. The chapter emphasizes the power of purpose-driven organizations and visionary leaders who recognize that success hinges on financial metrics and the ability to inspire, adapt, and create lasting impact.

Chapter 3. '*Navigating Cultural Shifts*,' delves into the critical role of adaptive leadership in managing the complex dynamics of cultural change within organizations operating in a global marketplace. It emphasizes the importance of fostering inclusivity, leveraging diversity, and driving innovation. The chapter stresses the need for open communication, respect, and continuous learning to unlock the full potential of a diverse workforce and better serve diverse customers.

Chapter 4. '*Embracing Technological Innovation*,' explores digital transformation in modern organizations, focusing on leadership strategies, value alignment, and stakeholder engagement in the digital age. It examines how leaders can craft compelling visions, revolutionize leadership approaches, and leverage digital storytelling for effective communication. The chapter emphasizes the importance of role-modeling digital behaviors, fostering innovation, and continuously evaluating and adapting organizational strategies.

Chapter 5. '*Leveraging Diversity and Inclusion*' discusses the critical importance of diversity and inclusion (D&I) for organizational success. It explores strategies for leveraging D&I to drive innovation, enhance decision-making, and improve performance. The chapter covers approaches such as assessing the current organizational landscape, setting clear D&I objectives, educating leaders on unconscious bias, promoting inclusive communication, and fostering employee resource groups. It concludes by emphasizing that inclusive leadership is a moral and strategic necessity.

Chapter 6. '*Strategic Planning in Fluid Environments*' addresses planning challenges in constantly changing and uncertain business landscapes. It proposes two critical approaches: scenario planning and Agile methodologies. The chapter discusses how integrating these approaches creates a robust framework balancing long-term vision with short-term flexibility. It emphasizes cultivating adaptability, embracing a growth mindset, and developing dynamic capabilities to transform unpredictability into a competitive advantage.

Chapter 7. '*Developing Partnerships and Ecosystems*' explores the transformative power of partner ecosystems in modern business. It examines the critical components of thriving partner ecosystems, from strategy development to implementation and measurement. The chapter discusses emerging trends such as AI integration, cross-sector collaboration, and API-driven integration and emphasizes the importance of embracing an ecosystem mindset to drive innovation and growth.

Chapter 8. '*Harnessing Innovation and Emergent Strategy*' focuses on the critical importance of innovation and adaptability in today's volatile business landscape. It discusses emergent strategy as a flexible approach to planning, contrasting it with traditional rigid methodologies. The chapter explores cultivating an innovation ecosystem, identifying "invisible innovators," and harnessing "productive friction" to drive growth, using case studies of companies like Apple, 3M, and Amazon to illustrate successful implementation.

Chapter 9. '*Engaging Stakeholders: Communication and Collaboration in a Diverse World*' explores effective stakeholder engagement in a diverse global landscape. It emphasizes the importance of cultural competence, trust-building, and adaptive communication strategies. The chapter discusses creating shared value through stakeholder relationships, fostering collaboration and inclusivity, and overcoming challenges in diverse environments.

Chapter 10. '*Hiring - Reskilling and the Future of Work*' examines the rapidly evolving work landscape in the face of technological advancement and societal changes. Emphasis is placed on the growing importance of unique human skills as automation and artificial intelligence reshape industries. The chapter explores the need to rethink hiring practices, the imperative of continuous learning and reskilling, and how organizations can prepare for future jobs that still need to be created.

Chapter 11. '*Ethical Leadership and Accountability in a Changing World*' explores the critical role of ethical leadership in modern organizations. It examines the core components of ethical leadership, including integrity, transparency, fairness, and respect for diversity. The chapter discusses the role of technology in ethical leadership, strategies for developing an ethical organizational culture, and future trends and challenges in ethical leadership.

Chapter 12. '*Maintaining Trust and Transparency*' examines the critical role of trust and transparency in modern business. It explores strategies for cultivating openness, including effective leadership, empowering employees, and leveraging technology. The chapter discusses the balance between transparency and data security, the impact of emerging technologies on transparency initiatives, and offers practical steps for implementing transparency initiatives in organizations.

Chapter 13. '*Leveraging Data and Analytics for Strategic Decision-Making*' This chapter is essential for leaders navigating today's rapidly evolving business landscape, emphasizing the critical importance of leveraging data and analytics for strategic decision-making. It explores various analytical approaches, from descriptive to prescriptive analytics, and highlights the transformative potential of machine learning and AI. The content addresses critical challenges in implementing data-driven approaches, including resistance to change, data quality issues, and skills gaps. It guides leaders in identifying key performance indicators, collecting and cleaning data, and translating insights into actionable strategies. By fostering data literacy and demonstrating the tangible benefits of data-driven decisions, leaders can overcome resistance and create a culture that embraces empirical decision-making. This chapter serves as a roadmap for leaders seeking to harness the full potential of data in shaping their organizations' future, enhancing competitiveness, and driving innovation in shifting cultural and technological landscapes.

Chapter 14. '*Making Value-Based Decisions*' The "Making Value-Based Decisions" chapter is crucial for leaders navigating complex cultural and technological landscapes. It emphasizes the importance of ethical decision-making in organizational leadership, covering key aspects such as recognizing ethical dilemmas, gathering comprehensive information, considering multiple perspectives, and applying ethical frameworks. The chapter highlights how value-based decisions foster trust, enhance organizational culture, and drive long-term success. Providing structured approaches to moral reasoning and transparent communication equips leaders with the tools to make principled choices in rapid change. This content is essential for developing ethical awareness and creating a culture of integrity in modern organizations facing diverse challenges.

CONCLUSION

This book, '*Strategies for Leaders in Shifting Cultural and Technological Landscapes*,' significantly contributes to leadership and organizational management in several ways.

Firstly, it provides a comprehensive and integrated approach to addressing the dual challenges of cultural diversity and technological disruption that define the modern business landscape. By examining these issues in tandem, the book offers a unique perspective that acknowledges the interconnectedness of cultural and technological factors in shaping organizational success. This holistic view is particularly valuable at a time when many leadership texts tend to focus on either cultural or technological aspects in isolation.

The book's emphasis on adaptive leadership and emergent strategies represents a timely contribution to leadership theory and practice. In an era of rapid change and uncertainty, the traditional rigid, top-down leadership models could be more effective. By exploring flexible approaches to strategy and decision-making, the book provides leaders with practical tools to navigate complexity and ambiguity. Furthermore, the text's focus on ethical leadership, trust, and transparency addresses a critical gap in many leadership frameworks. In the wake of corporate scandals and increasing public scrutiny, the book's exploration of these themes offers valuable guidance for leaders seeking to build sustainable, responsible organizations.

The book also makes a notable contribution by addressing the future of work and the implications of technological advancements on workforce development. Discussing topics such as reskilling and the impact of AI on human roles provides forward-thinking insights that can help organizations prepare for impending changes in the workplace. Additionally, the book's exploration of partner ecosystems and stakeholder engagement reflects the growing recognition of the interconnected nature of modern business. The book equips leaders with the skills needed to thrive in an increasingly networked business environment by providing effective collaboration and communication strategies in diverse, global contexts.

The inclusion of case studies and real-world examples throughout the book bridges the gap between theory and practice, making the content more accessible and applicable for leaders at various levels. This practical approach enhances the book's value as a resource for seasoned executives and emerging leaders. This book substantially contributes to the field by offering a multifaceted, forward-looking approach to leadership in the face of cultural and technological shifts. Its comprehensive coverage of key leadership challenges, practical strategies, and ethical considerations positions it as a valuable resource for leaders navigating the complexities of the modern business landscape. By synthesizing insights from various domains - from cultural competence to technological innovation, ethical leadership to strategic agility - the book provides a robust framework for effective leadership in the 21st century, potentially influencing leadership practices and organizational strategies across diverse industries and sectors.

The book concludes with the chapter "Making Value-Based Decisions," synthesizing many preceding themes. This chapter provides a framework for ethical decision-making that aligns with organizational values and builds stakeholder trust. "Strategies for Leaders in Shifting Cultural and Technological Landscapes" represents a significant contribution to leadership in the digital age. Bringing together diverse perspectives on technology, culture, ethics, and strategy offers a holistic approach to leadership that is sorely needed in today's complex business environment. The insights and strategies presented here will equip leaders to navigate challenges while preparing their organizations for future uncertainties. As we move into an era of unprecedented change, the principles outlined in this book will serve as a valuable compass for leaders seeking to create sustainable, ethical, and innovative organizations that thrive amidst the shifting landscapes of culture and technology.

Amdy Diene
Liberty University, USA

Introduction

Leaders face unprecedented challenges and opportunities in an era of rapid technological advancement, cultural evolution, and global interconnectivity. The convergence of digital innovation, shifting societal values, and an increasingly complex business landscape demands a new leadership paradigm. This book aims to help you develop strategies for meeting the challenges of shifting cultural and technological landscapes, offering a comprehensive guide for navigating these tumultuous seas and emerging more substantial on the other side. The traditional boundaries between industries, cultures, and technologies are blurring as we begin a new era. The digital revolution has transformed consumer behavior and redefined the nature of work, organizational structures, and market dynamics.

Remote work, once an exception, has become a norm, challenging leaders to foster cohesion and productivity across virtual teams. Meanwhile, the concept of a truly global market has become a reality, presenting challenges and opportunities for cultural convergence and divergence. In this dynamic environment, successful leadership requires more than just adapting to change; it demands anticipating and shaping it. This book delves into the multifaceted aspects of modern leadership, offering practical advice and exploring how visionary leaders can harness the power of technology while remaining grounded in strong ethical principles and values.

We begin by assessing the winds of change sweeping across industries, exploring how the merger of technology and culture reshapes business. From the influence of social media to the rise of data analytics, we examine how successful brands navigate this new landscape by embracing technology while respecting cultural differences. In an age marked by corporate scandals, we explore the critical importance of value-based leadership. We discuss how visionary leaders can inspire their teams to reach extraordinary heights, guided by a clear sense of purpose and unwavering values. As companies expand globally, adapting to diverse cultural norms becomes crucial. We delve into the concept of adaptive leadership, examining strategies for fostering inclusivity, leveraging diversity, and driving innovation in a multicultural environment.

Digital transformation is no longer optional; it's imperative. We explore leadership strategies for the digital age, from crafting compelling visions to leveraging digital storytelling for effective communication. We also discussed the importance of digital literacy and fostering a culture of experimentation. Diversity and inclusion are not just moral imperatives but strategic necessities. We examine strategies for leveraging D&I to drive innovation, enhance decision-making, and improve performance, illustrated through case studies of successful initiatives from global companies.

Traditional rigid planning methods are increasingly ineffective in today's dynamic landscape. We propose innovative approaches like scenario planning and Agile methodologies, demonstrating how organizations can balance long-term vision with short-term flexibility. In an interconnected world, partner ecosystems have become a transformative force. We explore the critical components of thriving ecosystems, from strategy development to implementation and measurement, and how organizations can create unique value propositions through ecosystem leadership.

Innovation and adaptability are crucial in today's volatile business landscape. We discuss strategies for cultivating an innovation ecosystem, identifying 'invisible innovators,' and leveraging 'productive friction' to drive growth. Effective stakeholder engagement is more critical and more complex than ever. We explore strategies for building trust across cultural boundaries, creating shared value, and leveraging technology to drive sustainable success in a diverse global landscape. As automation and AI reshape industries, we examine the evolving nature of work.

We discuss strategies for rethinking hiring practices, prioritizing soft skills and adaptability, and fostering a culture of continuous learning to prepare for future jobs that don't yet exist. In a rapidly changing world, ethical leadership is not just important; it's paramount. We explore the core components of moral leadership, strategies for developing an ethical organizational culture, and navigating the complex ethical dilemmas posed by technological advancements. Trust and transparency form the foundation of successful organizations.

We delve into strategies for cultivating openness, leveraging technology for transparency, and balancing transparency with data security in an age of increasing privacy concerns. In the age of big data, we explore how organizations can leverage data analytics for strategic decision-making. From cultivating data literacy to implementing data-driven strategies, we provide a roadmap for organizations aiming to thrive in the digital age. We conclude by exploring the critical process of making value-based decisions in organizational leadership. We discuss strategies for recognizing ethical dilemmas, considering multiple perspectives, and effectively communicating decisions to foster a culture of integrity and moral excellence.

Each chapter of this book is packed with practical insights, case studies, and actionable strategies to help leaders navigate the complexities of our rapidly evolving world. From harnessing the power of artificial intelligence to fostering inclusive cultures, from crafting emergent strategies to making value-based decisions, this book presents a complete blueprint for executives who want to succeed in a constantly changing environment. As you progress through the sections below, you will better understand the forces that shape our environment and the skills and mindsets required to lead with vision, flexibility, and integrity.

Whether you're an experienced executive or a budding leader, the insights within will equip you to turn challenges into opportunities and drive your organization toward sustainable success in the digital age. Welcome to the future of leadership, where culture and technology converge, diversity drives innovation, and ethical decision-making forms the bedrock of organizational success. Let us begin this transformative journey together, charting a course through the complexities of modern leadership to create organizations that survive and thrive in the face of change.

Amdy Diene
Liberty University, USA

Chapter 1
The Convergence of Culture and Technology:
A Crucial Aspect in Reshaping Business in the Digital Age

ABSTRACT

This chapter examines the impact of technology and culture on businesses, focusing on company operations, customer interactions, and global market changes. This study uses real-world examples from three books - "The Third Wave," "The Lean Startup," and "Digital Transformation" - to illustrate how technology impacts culture and business. The analysis, supported by NVivo-based qualitative data analysis, reveals that successful organizations must balance technological innovation with cultural sensitivity. Case studies of global brands like Airbnb and Coca-Cola show effective navigation of this convergence. Companies must adapt to change, use modern technology, and understand different perspectives to thrive in the digital age. The chapter argues that culture and technology are intertwined and will keep bringing significant changes to how businesses work, leading to a more active way of managing companies and making plans.

INTRODUCTION

The rapid evolution of digital technologies has transformed how businesses operate, communicate, and create value in the modern economy. This chapter examines the critical intersection of culture and technology in reshaping contemporary business practices, exploring how their convergence drives organizational change, influences consumer behavior, and redefines global market dynamics. As organizations navigate an increasingly digital landscape, understanding the interplay

DOI: 10.4018/979-8-3693-5553-4.ch001

between technological innovation and cultural dynamics has become essential for sustainable business success.

The digital revolution has profoundly affected traditional business paradigms, introducing new challenges and opportunities in organizational management, customer engagement, and market expansion. Data analytics, now a cornerstone of business intelligence, enables organizations to uncover patterns and correlations within vast datasets, informing strategic decision-making processes. Meanwhile, the rise of remote work, accelerated by recent global events, has caused innovative approaches to maintaining company culture and managing employee relationships effectively.

Companies like Airbnb and Coca-Cola exemplify how successful businesses must balance technological capabilities with cultural understanding. Their experiences show that achieving digital success requires more than technical proficiency—it demands a nuanced appreciation of cultural dynamics and their influence on business operations. This understanding becomes relevant as organizations navigate Hofstede's cultural dimensions, revealing how societies vary in decision-making, relationship-building, and technology adoption.

The convergence of technology and culture has catalyzed an unprecedented change in the business environment. Research shows that digital transformation is no longer optional but necessary for maintaining competitive advantage, with technologies such as cloud computing, artificial intelligence, and automation reshaping fundamental business processes. This transformation extends beyond mere technological adoption, encompassing shifts in organizational culture, leadership approaches, and strategic planning methodologies.

This chapter explores these themes through multiple lenses, examining how businesses can effectively harness technological innovation while maintaining cultural sensitivity and adaptability. Drawing on contemporary research and real-world examples, it provides insights into the challenges and opportunities presented by the intersection of culture and technology in modern business operations. The analysis encompasses various aspects of this convergence, from digital workplace management to consumer behavior evolution, offering practical frameworks for understanding and navigating these complex dynamics.

BACKGROUND: THE CONVERGENCE OF CULTURE AND TECHNOLOGY IN BUSINESS

How culture and technology mix is essential for businesses, impacting everything from how companies are organized to how customers shop and how the global market works. This digital transformation has completely changed the way businesses operate. In "The Third Wave," Toffler describes the shift from industrial to digital societies and helps us understand today's technology. Society has undergone three major phases: agriculture, industrial production, and the information age. The digital revolution, characterized by the proliferation of the Internet, mobile devices, and social media platforms, has accelerated cultural convergence, and transformed traditional business paradigms.

Subsequently, digital transformation has caused significant cultural adaptations within organizations. As highlighted in Siebel's "Digital Transformation," successful integration of technologies like cloud computing, artificial intelligence, and the Internet of Things requires more than technical implementation; it demands fundamental shifts in organizational culture and mindset. This cultural evolution has been evident in the rise of remote work, which has challenged traditional workplace norms and necessitated alternative approaches to team collaboration and management.

Considering these cultural shifts, the principles outlined in Ries's "The Lean Startup" have become relevant in this digital landscape. They emphasize prizing rapid iteration, continuous innovation, and data-driven decision-making. Organizations have had to develop new capabilities in agile methodology, digital literacy, and cross-cultural communication to remain competitive. The success of companies like Airbnb and Coca-Cola shows how effectively balancing technological innovation with cultural sensitivity can lead to sustainable growth in diverse markets.

The digital revolution has profoundly impacted consumer behavior and cultural dynamics. More specifically, as explored in Eyal's "Hooked" and Duhigg's "The Power of Habit," technology has created new patterns of consumer engagement and habit formation. Social media platforms have become powerful catalysts for social media cultural exchange and consumer influence, while data analytics has enabled unprecedented insights into consumer preferences and behavior patterns.

The flattening of the global marketplace, as Friedman described and further elaborated in Meyer's "The Culture Map," has created new opportunities and challenges for businesses. Cultural intelligence and adaptability have become crucial competencies for organizations operating in this interconnected environment. The success of global brands increasingly depends on their ability to navigate cultural nuances while leveraging technological capabilities to create consistent yet locally relevant experiences.

Recent developments in artificial intelligence, blockchain technology, and the Internet of Things continue to drive innovation and cultural change. Companies will use new technology while considering the importance of people and their diverse backgrounds. The COVID-19 pandemic has accelerated many of these trends, particularly in remote work adoption and digital transformation, leading to what Microsoft CEO Satya Nadella described as "two years of digital transformation in two months. Businesses must adapt to a connected world by focusing on technology and culture.

Understanding customer behavior, market trends, and the global economy is key to success. *Figure 1* below shows the steps involved with digital transformation.

Figure 1. Digital transformation

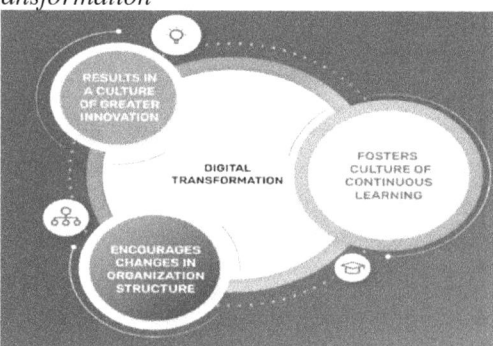

(Source: CloudNow)

LITERATURE REVIEW

The literature review examines the intricate relationship between technological advancement and cultural transformation in the modern business landscape. This analysis draws upon seminal works and contemporary research to explore how the convergence of digital technologies and cultural dynamics reshapes organizational practices, consumer behavior, and global market operations. The review synthesizes perspectives from multiple disciplines, including digital transformation theory, cultural studies, consumer psychology, and organizational management, to comprehensively understand this complex phenomenon.

The theoretical foundation begins with Toffler's "Third Wave" framework, which contextualizes the current digital revolution within the broader scope of societal evolution. This is complemented by more recent works, such as Siebel's analysis of digital transformation and Ries's lean methodology principles, illuminating how organizations navigate technological change while maintaining cultural coherence. The literature reveals a significant shift from traditional business paradigms to more agile, digitally enabled operational models that require careful consideration of cultural implications.

Three primary themes emerge from the literature: the evolution of technology and its cultural implications, the transformation of consumer behavior in the digital age, and the emergence of new organizational paradigms in response to technological change. These themes are examined through various theoretical lenses, including

Meyer's cultural mapping framework, Eyal's habit-forming concepts of product design, and Duhigg's observations on behavioral psychology. This review also considers how global market dynamics and cultural convergence influence the adoption and implementation of new technologies across different business contexts.

This literature review aims to bridge the theoretical understanding of technology-culture interaction with practical business applications, providing insights into how organizations can effectively manage digital transformation while maintaining cultural sensitivity and strategic alignment. The following sections thoroughly explore each theme, examining theoretical foundations and empirical evidence from contemporary business practices.

The Evolution of Technology and Its Cultural Implications

In his book "The Third Wave," Alvin Toffler describes the transition from an Industrial Age society (the "Second Wave") to an Information Age society (the "Third Wave"). The First Wave: Agricultural societies emerged after the Neolithic Revolution, replacing hunter-gatherer cultures. The Second Wave is about mass production and bureaucracy, representing the industrial age. The Third Wave follows and is post-industrial. The Internet and social media have revolutionized cross-cultural communication and globalized culture. Erin Meyer's (2014) "The Culture Map" provides insights into navigating cultural differences.

Companies create ecosystems by connecting customers and providers through marketplaces or industry-specific platforms. A lifestyle brand integrates partners into its banking services, transcending traditional banking boundaries, according to (Wikipedia, 2024). Digital tools empower artists to explore new mediums and techniques, and AI personalization tailors content to individual preferences, fostering inclusivity in the arts (Utah Valley University, 2024). Digital transformation reshapes business models, processes, and strategies; cloud computing, AI, and IoT streamline operations, enhance efficiency, and revolutionize industries. Automation impacts workforce dynamics and organizational structures; digital platforms enable cross-border collaboration, supply chain optimization, and real-time communication, according to Morris (2023). These platforms facilitate global teamwork and international cooperation and impact cultural conflicts within organizations; they balance tradition and innovation crucially for successful digital transformation (Meyer, 2014; Morris, 2023).

Additionally, AI transforms industries with technology by automating tasks, improving decision-making, and enabling personalized experiences. The blockchain revolution ensures secure, transparent transactions, affecting finance, supply chains, and more, and IoT enables associating devices and data and enhances efficiency, safety, and sustainability. This revolution also impacts the workforce and organizational culture. Automation of streamlined processes affects workforce dynamics and allows organizations to adapt to new roles and skill sets. Organizational culture has changed, and technological shifts have accompanied it, balancing tradition, and innovation for the essential and successful digital transformation, according to Morris (2023).

Technological advancements have significantly shaped cultural shifts throughout history. Alvin Toffler's "The Third Wave" delineates three distinct waves of technological advancement and their impact on society. The first wave comprised agricultural societies, the second wave brought industrialization, and the digital revolution characterized the third wave. The Internet and social media have played a pivotal role in globalizing culture by facilitating communication and information exchange across borders. Erin Meyer's "The Culture Map" provides insights into how technology affects cross-cultural communication. Social media platforms like Facebook, Twitter, and Instagram have enabled people from diverse backgrounds to connect and share experiences, thus fostering a more interconnected global culture.

Examples of cultural phenomena born from technology include the rise of e-sports and virtual communities. E-sports and competitive video gaming have gained immense popularity worldwide, attracting millions of viewers and players. Virtual communities, such as online forums and gaming platforms, provide individuals with shared interests a space to connect and interact irrespective of geographical boundaries. Digital transformation has reshaped business models, processes, and strategies. As discussed in works by Vial (2019) and (Davenport & Ronanki, 2018), cloud computing and artificial intelligence have enabled organizations to streamline operations, enhance efficiency, and drive innovation. Automation, a key component of digital transformation, has optimized processes, impacting workforce dynamics and organizational structures.

Technologies like artificial intelligence, blockchain, and the Internet of Things have revolutionized industries by enabling data-driven decision-making, enhancing security, and improving efficiency. Cryptography and decentralized verification make blockchain a secure way to record transactions, benefiting banking and business. Despite its initial promise, blockchain's real-world efficiency is less than expected, causing some banks to reduce their involvement.

Moreover, technology faces ongoing challenges, including high energy consumption, scalability limitations, integration difficulties with existing systems, and regulatory compliance requirements. Despite these hurdles, some successful implementations exist, such as Walmart's use of blockchain for food product tracing and improvements in cross-border payment systems, though traditional systems like SWIFT continue to dominate the financial sector. Research shows that digital platforms make it easier for companies to work together across borders, strengthen their supply chains, and communicate in real time. Technological advances have also influenced cultural conflicts within organizations. New technologies can shake up company culture, leading to clashes between old and new values, say Choudhry et al. (2024). Automation, while streamlining processes, can also disrupt workforce dynamics, causing adaptation and retraining.

Imagine a 45-year-old factory worker who has been with a company for over two decades and has seen the manufacturing industry develop. However, nothing prepared him for the day his employer announced the implementation of a new automated assembly line. Initially, John was apprehensive. He feared his job would become obsolete, as the machines could work faster and more efficiently than he ever could. However, his employer assured him that the goal was not to replace workers but to enhance productivity and remain competitive. Technological advancements have profoundly affected cultural shifts, business practices, and organizational dynamics, and often fear of the unknown. Technology impacts our lives, work, and relationships through the Internet, social media, and automation. Building upon this historical foundation, our discussion focuses on how technology affects business operations.

Digital Workplace Management

The digital transformation of modern businesses is fundamentally reshaping organizational operations, demanding a comprehensive grasp of its implications for optimal results (Haddud & McAllen, 2018). This shift requires a substantial cultural transformation where organizations must cultivate an environment that champions technological advancement and digital proficiency in their workforce. Digital workplaces show significant potential for enhancing productivity and driving innovation, which can only be achieved through strategic management and leadership approaches (Haddud & McAllen, 2018; Murdoch & Fichter, 2021).

Business leaders must develop essential competencies to navigate technological transitions and guide teams in virtual settings effectively. According to Murdoch and Fichter (2021), a notable challenge remains the lag between enterprise and consumer technology adoption, primarily attributed to organizational resistance and slow information dissemination of technological advancements. Organizations can emphasize digital literacy training, implement organized technology adoption programs, and foster a culture that welcomes technological advancement to address these challenges (Murdoch & Fichter, 2021; Haddud & McAllen, 2018).

Technology's Impact on Business Operations

Technology has radically transformed the landscape of business operations, altered the DNA of corporate culture, and catalyzed a shift in business models toward greater agility and innovation. This technology has profoundly impacted business operations, driving significant changes in organizational culture and transforming traditional business models. In his 2011 book, "The Lean Startup," Eric Ries advises changing a business by focusing on flexibility, fast prototypes, and using fewer resources. Ries's (2011) case studies highlight a culture of continuous innovation where failure is a steppingstone to success, a stark contrast to traditional models that favored extensive planning and predictability, and how startups like Dropbox and Intuit have leveraged technology to iterate on their products quickly, gather customer feedback and make data-driven decisions. With a flexible approach, businesses can respond rapidly to market trends, using technology to validate customer behavior and product appeal with limited upfront investment. The rapid advancement of digital technologies enables companies to embrace agility and innovation, as exemplified in the case studies presented in "The Lean Startup" by Eric Ries.

Quick adaptation to customer needs and market changes led to success for these companies. Companies need to embrace technology and change to stay competitive, as Siebel explains in his 2019 book "Digital Transformation." Siebel shows how companies can use innovative technologies such as AI, IoT, and blockchain to create new opportunities and drive innovation. While technology is important, he thinks changing culture is key to real change. To truly benefit from digital change, businesses must encourage trying new things, taking chances, and always learning. The impact of technology on business operations has been profound and multifaceted and has revolutionized how businesses operate, enabling increased efficiency, improved communication, and the ability to reach new customers. This process has made businesses work faster by improving communication worldwide and product development (van Kuiken, 2022). In "The Lean Startup" by Eric Ries, agility and innovation are central themes. The book examines how startups can quickly leverage technology to prototype, test, and iterate their products, enabling accelerated learning and adaptation (Jörissen et al., 2023). Case studies from the book, such as Dropbox and IMVU, illustrate how embracing lean principles and continuous deployment can drive growth and customer engagement.

The rise of remote work is another significant cultural shift driven by technology. The recent surge, driven by new technology and global events like the pandemic, shows how the business world is changing. Employees can work from anywhere worldwide with the proliferation of high-speed Internet, cloud-based collaboration tools, and video conferencing platforms. The spread of this idea has changed how companies think about work-life balance and company culture. Studies on work-life balance and organizational culture in remote work suggest that remote work offers unprecedented flexibility and potential for a better work-life balance. However, remote work also requires significant adjustments to workplace culture and management practices that require companies to adopt digital tools, cultivate trust, and maintain team unity. Although having offices across different regions makes it difficult to establish a strong corporate culture and keep everyone feeling like a single team, recent studies have shown that remote work can boost productivity, improve employee satisfaction, and lower turnover rates.

Remote work has had significant cultural implications, challenged traditional work norms, and encouraged more flexible, purposeful approaches (Morgan, (2023). Recent studies have shown that remote work can emphasize work-life balance, employee autonomy, and mental well-being, posits Morgan. However, this approach makes it harder for employees to build strong relationships at work, considering that cultural adaptability is crucial in the digital transformation era. In his 2019 book "Digital Transformation," Siebel argues that businesses must embrace cloud, big data, AI, and IoT to digitalize, and leaders must guide their teams through these transitions, establishing a climate of adaptability and promoting a growth mindset to ensure the successful integration of technology into business strategies.

The impact of telecommuting goes beyond changing how things are done. As discussed in "Digital Transformation" by Thomas Siebel, adopting digital technologies highlights the need for cultural flexibility in utilizing technology to enhance operational efficiency and as a strategic asset. Siebel argues that digital transformation involves integrating technology into all company operations, changing how companies operate, and delivering customer value. This change requires us to be open to new ideas, flexible, and willing to break tradition. Technology significantly impacts businesses, making them faster, more innovative, and rethinking traditional working methods. According to Siebel, technological and cultural changes are necessary for effective digital transformation. To succeed digitally, businesses need tech savvy, innovation, and adaptability.

Entrepreneurial Ecosystems in the Digital Age

The digital age has transformed entrepreneurial ecosystems, creating a complex landscape where business leaders must adapt to technological imperatives while maintaining personal resilience. Digital technology deployment, particularly in sectors like automotive, has prompted businesses to completely restructure their value chains and operational methodologies (Wiegand & Brautsch, 2022). This technological revolution extends beyond process optimization, as the intricate relationship between project management approaches and digital solutions plays a vital role in establishing sustainable business practices and outcomes across growing industries, posit Wiegand and Brautsch.

The human element remains central to entrepreneurial success, with mounting evidence highlighting the crucial role of entrepreneurs' mental health and well-being (MWB) in shaping their business decisions and drive (Stephan, 2018). While entrepreneurs contribute significantly to economic growth and job creation, their reported high levels of personal satisfaction and happiness in their work have drawn increasing attention across multiple disciplines. According to Stephan, research shows that entrepreneurs who maintain positive mental health display more remarkable persistence and achieve superior performance outcomes. This knowledge has caused the emphasis on changing from only operational indicators to a more comprehensive perspective of entrepreneurial success that encompasses business performance and personal well-being.

Consumer Behavior in the Digital Age

In the digital age, consumer behavior has undergone a significant transformation due to technological advancements. As Nir Eyal discusses in "Hooked: How to Build Habit-Forming Products," technology can create and reinforce habits, shaping consumer expectations and actions (Eyal, 2014). Social media sites like Facebook and Instagram are now a significant force, shaping what people buy and how they act. "The Power of Habit" by Charles Duhigg looks at how habits form and what impact they have, emphasizing the "habit loop" and its influence on consumer choices.

Data analytics have become crucial to businesses in understanding and predicting consumer behavior. In their book "Data Science for Business, " Provost and Fawcett show how companies can use data to make better decisions, highlighting the importance of analyzing customer data to find patterns. By harnessing the power of data analytics, companies can tailor their products, services, and marketing strategies to better meet consumers' growing needs and expectations in the digital age. The digital world gives businesses new ways to connect with customers, leading to difficulties and advantages.

In "Hooked," Nir Eyal describes the Hook Model, a four-step process companies use to create habitual product use (Duhigg, 2012). This model shows how technology has changed people's expectations, leading them to rely on it more and use it constantly. Social media sites use techniques to create habits that strongly influence consumer choices and what is trending. Charles Duhigg's "The Power of Habit" offers insights into the habit loop, cue, routine, and reward that underpin these behaviors. Social media algorithms tailor your feed to make you interact and share, which impacts what others see and fuels cultural trends.

Data analytics has become a cornerstone of understanding and predicting consumer behavior. The book "Data Science for Business" by Foster Provost and Tom Fawcett stresses prizing "data-analytic thinking," which means using data to understand and improve business outcomes. This approach enables businesses to discern patterns in consumer behavior, tailor marketing strategies, and expect future trends, optimizing the consumer experience. The digital age has shifted consumer behavior towards a more interconnected, data-driven, habit-influenced landscape. Habit-forming product design, social media's persuasive power, and data analytics' predictive capabilities combine to shape modern consumerism, creating an environment where businesses must adapt to these evolving dynamics for sustained engagement and growth.

The Global Market and Cultural Convergence

Today's technology makes connecting and doing business globally easier than ever, so the idea of a global market is becoming more common. As Thomas Friedman discusses in "The World is Flat," connectivity has leveled the playing field, enabling businesses to collaborate and compete globally (Whitworth, 2022). However, cultural convergence presents challenges and opportunities for companies operating in diverse markets. Molinsky's "Global Dexterity" shows how to navigate cross-cultural situations with flexibility and understanding.

By using technology and understanding different cultures and brands, businesses can thrive. To illustrate these concepts in action, Airbnb shows successful global expansion. The company has reached over 220 countries by customizing its platform for other places and collaborating with local people. Similarly, Coca-Cola changes its marketing to fit different cultures while maintaining its well-known brand image. Airbnb tailors its user experience of cultural nuances by offering localized content, featuring culturally relevant imagery, and highlighting unique accommodations that reflect the distinct character of each region. The platform also provides personalized recommendations based on user preferences and cultural insights, ensuring travelers can immerse themselves in authentic local experiences.

Coca-Cola, a global beverage giant, adapts its marketing strategies to resonate with diverse audiences worldwide. The company conducts extensive market research to understand cultural preferences, values, and traditions, allowing it to create targeted campaigns that strike a chord with local consumers. Coca-Cola collaborates with local artists, celebrities, and influencers to develop culturally relevant content that strengthens brand affinity. By adapting to each market, Coca-Cola fosters strong global connections and remains a beloved brand. According to a recent McKinsey report, companies with diverse leadership teams are 33% more likely to outperform their peers financially. As the global market evolves, businesses that can balance technological innovation and cultural sensitivity will be well-positioned to thrive in an increasingly interconnected world.

Against this backdrop, in the era of globalization, as Thomas Friedman illustrates in "The World is Flat," technological advancements have flattened the global economic landscape, enabling unprecedented connectivity and competition, according to Whitworth (2022). This shift presents both challenges and opportunities for cultural convergence in business. Companies find it hard to get employees to act appropriately in different cultures without losing authenticity. This convergence offers fertile ground for innovation and growth.

In practice, Starbucks and IKEA show us the good and sides of companies fitting into different cultures. Starbucks' strategic partnerships and respect for local traditions have allowed it to become a global coffeehouse icon. IKEA's easy-to-assemble furniture became a hit because of its efficiency and sustainability, making it popular in various cultures. To succeed in today's dynamic market, businesses must focus on cultural branding and technology. Technology and cultural sensitivity are crucial for companies to grow globally. The constructive interaction of cultural insight and technological prowess can lead to a harmonious global market where diversity is acknowledged and celebrated as a driver of progress and innovation. Successful brands will be those that can navigate this complex terrain with agility and foresight, turning cultural convergence into a competitive advantage.

Digital Entrepreneurship

The digital revolution's impact extends beyond mere technological advancement, reshaping economic and social structures through its deep connection with entrepreneurship (Autio et al., 2024). Digital technologies and infrastructures generate novel opportunities for entrepreneurs, giving rise to digital entrepreneurship (DE) - a transformative approach where businesses strategically leverage digital technologies to drive innovation (Davidson & Vaast, 2010; Hull et al., 2007; Nambisan, 2017). According to Autio and colleagues, these digital entrepreneurs serve as trailblazers, harnessing emerging technological capabilities to revolutionize business models, create value, and boost productivity, influencing the broader entrepreneurial landscape and contributing to enhanced regional and national economic output.

Recent research using the Global Index of Digital Entrepreneurship Systems (GIDES) has revealed significant insights into digitalization's impact on entrepreneurship across developing Asian economies. These regions have strong infrastructure, but Autio's team identified substantial room for cultural and informal institutions to improve. In developing nations, technology is outpacing society's ability to use it effectively.

Mental Health and Wellness Entrepreneurship

The intersection of digital culture and technological advancement has spawned an innovative wave of entrepreneurs dedicated to mental health and wellness initiatives. In the pandemic's wake, social media influencers have emerged as crucial voices addressing psychological well-being, particularly on Instagram, where they function as self-directed entrepreneurs tackling mental health challenges (Mercedes et al., 2023). Research during the COVID-19 crisis has shown that entrepreneurs with previous startup experience maintain better mental wellness, while those with specific entrepreneurial training show enhanced psychological resilience (Yan et al., 2023). However, gender differences have emerged, with women business owners reporting notably poorer mental health outcomes compared to their male peers, posit Yan and colleagues.

The entrepreneurial landscape has witnessed significant adaptation in response to unprecedented challenges. While facing elevated stress and burnout during the pandemic, business owners showed remarkable resilience through support-seeking behaviors, digital technology adoption, and business model innovation (Fernández-Bedoya et al., 2023). Characteristically known for their decisive action and initiative, entrepreneurs confronted complex decisions about operational continuity throughout the crisis. Despite these challenges, entrepreneurship continues to serve as a pathway to enhanced well-being, enabling individuals to pursue work that aligns with their values and aspirations, observe Fernández-Bedoya and colleagues.

DATA ANALYSIS AND METHODOLOGY

In our quest to unravel complex research patterns, we leveraged two powerful digital allies: Citavi and NVivo. Think of Citavi as your research hub, a place to organize your thoughts and work seamlessly. This tool makes research easier by helping researchers manage their sources, keep track of projects, and save their work. Citavi goes beyond storing references. Its collaborative features collapse the traditional walls of solitary research, enabling teams to build upon each other's insights and discoveries.

Complementing this organizational framework, NVivo is our qualitative data transformer, converting raw information into meaningful insights. This sophisticated software peels back the layers of complex data, revealing hidden patterns and relationships that might otherwise remain obscured. As a result of this analysis, NVivo creates vivid visualizations that bring research findings to life, making the abstract concrete and the complex comprehensible. The following word cloud, generated through NVivo's robust word frequency analysis, visualizes our study's key themes and patterns. *Figure 2* below shows a word cloud created with NVivo.

Figure 2. Word cloud

(Source: Dr. Amdy Diene)

NVivo's clustering of items based on word similarity can be seen in the diagram below. Furthermore, the cluster analysis function in NVivo compares files, codes, or cases with similar words, values, or codes to identify patterns. By doing so, researchers can understand the data's structure and meaning and identify relationships between items. It allows them to discover new trends and insights that may not have been apparent previously. This software visually compares items by creating diagrams that show how similar or different they are. We use coding or matrix coding to understand the relationships uncovered by cluster analysis. Research results cannot be obtained by cluster analysis. Diagrams in this chapter were generated using NVivo by the authors.

Figure 3. Diagram

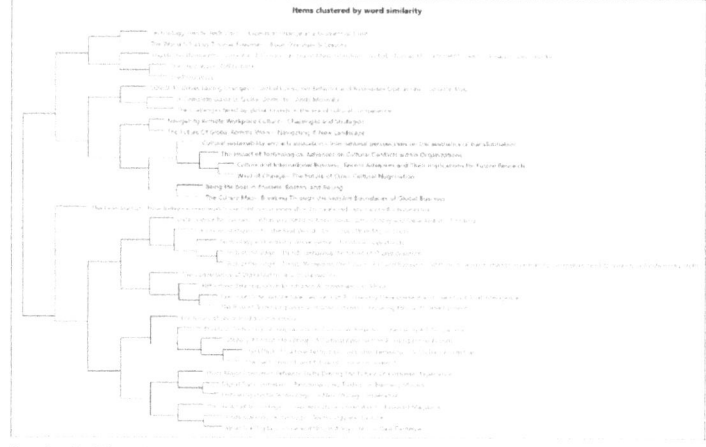

(Source: Dr. Amdy Diene)

CONCLUSION AND SUMMARY

The convergence of culture and technology has emerged as a defining force in reshaping contemporary business practices, fundamentally transforming how organizations operate, compete, and create value in the digital age. This chapter has demonstrated that successful digital transformation requires more than mere technological implementation; it demands a nuanced understanding of cultural dynamics and their influence on organizational change, consumer behavior, and global market operations. Several key findings emerge from this analysis:

First, the digital revolution has catalyzed unprecedented organizational structure and operations changes. Companies that successfully navigate this transformation understand that technological adoption must be accompanied by corresponding shifts in organizational culture, leadership approaches, and strategic planning methodologies. The rise of remote work, accelerated by global events, exemplifies how technological capabilities can reshape traditional workplace paradigms while presenting new challenges in maintaining corporate culture and employee engagement.

Second, consumer behavior has undergone a significant transformation in the digital age. The analysis of habit formation, explored through works like "Hooked" and "The Power of Habit," reveals how technology shapes consumer expectations and actions. Data analytics has become instrumental in understanding and predicting consumer behavior, enabling organizations to create more personalized and compelling customer experiences. Third, the global marketplace has become increasingly interconnected, requiring organizations to balance technological innovation with cultural sensitivity. Successful companies like Airbnb and Coca-Cola demonstrate that effective global expansion requires technological prowess and cultural intelligence. The principles outlined in works such as "The Culture Map" and "Global Dexterity" provide frameworks for navigating these complex cross-cultural dynamics.

Fourth, digital entrepreneurship has emerged as a distinct phenomenon characterized by the strategic leverage of digital technologies for innovation and value creation. The research shows that successful digital entrepreneurs must maintain technological competence and personal resilience, with mental health and well-being emerging as crucial factors in entrepreneurial success. The continued evolution of technologies such as artificial intelligence, blockchain, and the Internet of Things will probably speed up these trends, creating new business opportunities and challenges. Organizations that can effectively integrate technological capabilities while maintaining cultural sensitivity and adaptability will be best positioned to thrive in this dynamic environment.

This research suggests that the future of business success lies not in technology alone but in the thoughtful integration of technological innovation with cultural understanding. As digital transformation continues to reshape the business landscape, organizations must develop frameworks to harness technological advances, while nurturing cultural intelligence and maintaining human connections. The findings underscore the importance of viewing digital transformation as a holistic process encompassing technological and cultural dimensions. Future research might explore how emerging technologies will further influence cultural dynamics in business and how organizations can better prepare for the continuing convergence of these crucial elements.

The technological and cultural imperatives discussed in Chapter 1 naturally intersect with ethical leadership and organizational vision questions. As organizations navigate the complexities of digital transformation, the fundamental challenge extends beyond mere technological implementation to encompass moral stewardship and value-driven leadership. This evolution in organizational dynamics necessitates a deeper examination of how leaders can effectively integrate ethical considerations with technological progress, setting the stage for a comprehensive analysis of vision-driven leadership practices in contemporary business environments.

REFERENCES

Appel, G., Grewal, L., Hadi, R., & Stephen, A. T. (2020). The future of social media in marketing. *Journal of the Academy of Marketing Science*, 48(1), 79–95. DOI: 10.1007/s11747-019-00695-1 PMID: 32431463

Choudhry, T., Sarfraz, M., & Ul Hassan Shah, W. (Eds.). (2024). *Business, Management and Economics. Organizational Culture - Cultural Change and Technology*. IntechOpen., DOI: 10.5772/intechopen.111316

Davenport, T. H., & Ronanki, R. (2018). Artificial Intelligence for the Real World: Don't Start with Moon Shots. *Harvard Business Review*, 96(1), 108–116. https://blockqai.com/wp-content/uploads/2021/01/analytics-hbr-ai-for-the-real-world.pdf

Davidson, E., & Vaast, E. (2010), Digital entrepreneurship and its sociomaterial enactment. *43rd Hawaii International Conference on System Sciences*, IEEE, 1-10.

Dubina, L. (2021). *How brands can navigate cancel culture*. https://www.mintel.com/insights/consumer-research/how-brands-can-use-consumer-identity-and-brand-reputation-to-navigate-cancel-culture/

Duhigg, C. (2012). *The Power of Habit: Why we do what we do in Life and Business*. https://en.wikipedia.org/w/index.php?title=The_Power_of_Habit&oldid=1189068802

Eyal, N. (2014). *Hooked: How to Build Habit-Forming Products: Eyal, Nir, Hoover, Ryan: 9781591847786: Amazon.com: Books*. https://www.amazon.com/Hooked-How-Build-Habit-Forming-Products/dp/1591847788

Fernández-Bedoya, V. H., Meneses-La-Riva, M. E., Suyo-Vega, J. A., & Stephanie Gago-Chávez, J. J. (2023). Mental health problems of entrepreneurs during the COVID-19 health crisis: Fear, anxiety, and stress. A systematic review. *F1000 Research*, 12, 1062. DOI: 10.12688/f1000research.139581.1

Fitzgerald, M., Kruschwitz, N., Bonnet, D., & Welch, M. (2014). Embracing Digital Technology: A New Strategic Imperative. *MIT Sloan Management Review*, (55), 1–16.

Haddud, A., & McAllen, D. K. (Eds.). (2018). *Managing technological entrepreneurship: the engine for economic growth. PICMET'18: Portland International Conference on Management of Engineering and Technology*. Portland State University.

Hassett, E. (2021). The challenges faced by global brands in the era of cultural competence. *Freedman*. https://www.freedmaninternational.com/insights/global-brand-challenges-in-the-era-of-cultural-competence/

Hull, C.E.K., Hung, Y.T.C., Hair, N., Perotti, V. and DeMartino, R. (2007), Taking advantage of digital opportunities: a typology of digital entrepreneurship. *International Journal of networking and Virtual Organizations, 4* (3). 290-303, .DOI: 10.1504/IJNVO.2007.015166

Jörissen, B., Unterberg, L., & Klepacki, T. (Eds.). (2023). *Cultural Sustainability and Arts Education: International Perspectives on the Aesthetics of Transformation.* Springer. DOI: 10.1007/978-981-19-3915-0

Meena, B. S. (2023). The Effect of Cultural Factors on Consumer Behaviour: A Global Perspective. [IJFMR]. *International Journal for Multidisciplinary Research*, 5(6). https://www.ijfmr.com/papers/2023/6/10906.pdf

Mercedes, M. G. Z., Tutivén-Román, C., Cisternas-Osorio, R., Labate, C., Macarena, L., Cantariño, B., Román, T., & Revista, V.A. (2023). Spanish-Speaker Wellness Influencers In The Era Of Care: Trends And Topics In 2023.

Merillot (2023). Navigating Remote Workplace Culture: Challenges and Strategies. *Merillot.* https://www.merillot.com/consulting-insights/navigating-remote-workplace-culture-challenges-and-strategies/

Meyer, E. (2014). *The Culture Map: Breaking Through the Invisible Boundaries of Global Business.* https://erinmeyer.com/books/the-culture-map/

Meyer, E. (2017). Being the employer in Brussels, Boston, and Beijing. *Harvard Business Review*, 95(4), 70–77.

Mishra, R., Singh, S., & Pandey, S. (2023). The Impact of Technological Advances on Cultural Conflicts within Organizations. In T. Choudhry, M. Sarfraz, & W. Ul Hassan Shah (Eds.), *Business, Management and Economics. Organizational Culture - Cultural Change and Technology* (Vol. 16). Pitchpine. DOI: 10.5772/intechopen.113095

MIT Sloan Management Review. (2018). *The Convergence of Digitalization and Sustainability.* https://sloanreview.mit.edu/article/the-convergence-of-digitalization-and-sustainability/

Molinsky, A. (2015). *A Complete Guide to Global Dexterity - Andy Molinsky.* https://www.andymolinsky.com/complete-guide-global-dexterity/

Morgan, B. (2023). The Future of Global Remote Work: Navigating A New Landscape. *Forbes.* https://www.forbes.com/sites/forbesbusinesscouncil/2023/05/30/the-future-of-global-remote-work-navigating-a-new-landscape/?sh=3e9126f25d30

Morris, I. (2023). Digital Transformation: Revolutionizing Traditional Business Models. *J Bus Fin Aff*, 12(4).

Murdoch, D., & Fichter, R. (2021): *From doing digital to being digital. Research Anthology on Digital Transformation, Organizational Change, and the Impact of Remote Work*. In Information Resources Management Association (Ed.): Research Anthology on Digital Transformation, Organizational Change, and the Impact of Remote Work: IGI Global, 23–40.

Nambisan, S. (2017). Digital entrepreneurship: Toward a digital technology perspective of entrepreneurship. *Entrepreneurship Theory and Practice*, 41(6), 1029–1055. DOI: 10.1111/etap.12254

Provost, F., & Fawcett, T. (2013). *Data Science for Business: What you Need to Know About Data Mining and Data-Analytic Thinking*. O'Reilly Media, Inc.

Ries, E. (2011). *The Lean Startup: How today's entrepreneurs use continuous innovation to create radically successful businesses.* https://theleanstartup.com/casestudies

Stephan, U. (2018). Entrepreneurs' mental health and well-being: A review and research agenda. *The Academy of Management Perspectives*, 32(3), 290–322. DOI: 10.5465/amp.2017.0001

Torelli, C. J., & Rodas, M. A. (2024). *Globally Minded Marketing: A Cultural Approach to Building Iconic Brands*. Springer International Publishing; Imprint Palgrave Macmillan. DOI: 10.1007/978-3-031-50812-7

Utah Valley University. (2024). *Understanding Technology: Technology and Culture. Understanding Technology.* https://uen.pressbooks.pub/tech1010/chapter/technology-and-culture/

Van Kuiken, S. V. (2022). *Tech at the Edge: Trends Reshaping the Future of IT and Business: With technological change accelerating, companies must make four fundamental shifts*. McKinsey Digital.

Vial, G. (2019). Understanding digital transformation: A review and a research agenda. *The Journal of Strategic Information Systems*, 28(2), 118–144. DOI: 10.1016/j.jsis.2019.01.003

Whitworth, E. (2022). The World Is Flat by Thomas Friedman: Book Overview & Lessons. *Shortform Books*. https://www.shortform.com/blog/the-world-is-flat-by-thomas-friedman/

Wiegand, T., & Brautsch, C. (2022). Digital Technology Deployment in the German Automotive Industry. In Lee, I., & Wynn, M. G. (Eds.), *Handbook of Research on Digital Transformation, Industry Use Cases, and the Impact of Disruptive Technologies* (pp. 249–267). Advances in E-Business Research. IGI Global., DOI: 10.4018/978-1-7998-7712-7.ch014

Wikipedia. (2024). *The Third Wave (Toffler book)*. https://en.wikipedia.org/w/index.php?title=The_Third_Wave_(Toffler_book)&oldid=1199447222

World Economic Forum. (2020). *The Future of Jobs Report 2020.* https://www.weforum.org/reports/the-future-of-jobs-report-2020

Yakut, E. (2022). Effects of Technological Innovations on Consumer Behavior: Marketing 4.0 Perspective. In Yakut, E. (Ed.), *Industry 4.0 and Global Businesses* (pp. 55–68). Emerald Publishing Limited., DOI: 10.1108/978-1-80117-326-120211004

Yan, J., Zhang, S. X., & Hallak, R. (2023). Research Note Mental Health and Well-being of Tourism Entrepreneurs During Times of Crisis. *Tourism Analysis*, 28(1), 147–153. DOI: 10.3727/108354223X16729590545180

ADDITIONAL READING

Cultural Intelligence and Global BusinessHouse, R. J.. (2014). *Strategic Leadership Across Cultures: GLOBE Study of CEO Leadership Behavior and effectiveness in 24 countries.* SAGE Publications.

Cultural Intelligence and Global BusinessSteers, R. M., Sanchez-Runde, C., & Nardon, L. (2016). *Management Across Cultures: Challenges, Strategies, and Skills.* Cambridge University Press.

Digital Entrepreneurship and InnovationBlank, S., & Dorf, B. (2020). *The Startup Owner's Manual: The Step-by-Step Guide for Building a Great Company.* Wiley.

Digital Entrepreneurship and InnovationGassmann, O., Frankenberger, K., & Csik, M. (2014). *The Business Model Navigator: 55 Models That Will Revolutionize Your Business.* Pearson.

Digital Transformation and Business StrategyRogers, D. L. (2016). *The Digital Transformation Playbook: Rethink Your Business for the Digital Age.* Columbia Business School Publishing. DOI: 10.7312/roge17544

Digital Transformation and Business StrategyWesterman, G., Bonnet, D., & McAfee, A. (2014). *Leading Digital: Turning Technology into Business Transformation.* Harvard Business Review Press.

Emerging Technologies and Future TrendsMcAfee, A., & Brynjolfsson, E. (2017). *Machine, Platform, Crowd: Harnessing Our Digital Future.* W. W. Norton & Company.

Emerging Technologies and Future TrendsParker, G. G., Van Alstyne, M. W., & Choudary, S. P. (2016). *Platform Revolution: How Networked Markets Are Transforming the Economy and How to Make Them Work for You.* W. W. Norton & Company.

Remote Work and Digital Workplace ManagementLarson, B. Z., Vroman, S. R., & Makarius, E. E. (2020). *A Guide to Managing Your (Newly) Remote Workers.* Harvard Business Review Press.

Remote Work and Digital Workplace ManagementNeeley, T. (2021). *Remote Work Revolution: Succeeding from Anywhere.* Harper Business.

Technology and Consumer BehaviorNg, D., & Griffin, P. (2023). *AI-First Healthcare: AI-Powered Digital Transformation Creating the Self-Driving Organization.* Wiley.

Technology and Consumer BehaviorSolomon, M. R. (2023). *Consumer Behavior: Buying, Having, and Being.* Pearson.

KEY TERMS AND DEFINITIONS

Artificial Intelligence (AI): Technology that enables machines to simulate human intelligence processes, including learning, reasoning, and self-correction. In business contexts, AI is used for automation, decision-making, and personalized customer experiences.

Blockchain: A decentralized digital ledger technology that records transactions across multiple computers securely and transparently. While initially promising for various industries, its practical implementation has faced challenges, including energy consumption and scalability issues.

Cross-Cultural Communication: Information exchange between individuals from different cultural backgrounds requires understanding cultural dimensions, communication styles, and local customs.

Cultural Branding: The strategy of building brands that resonate with the cultural contexts of different markets while maintaining consistent global brand identity, as exemplified by companies like Coca-Cola and Airbnb.

Cultural Convergence: The process by which global cultures become more similar due to increased interconnectedness through technology and communication while maintaining distinct local characteristics.

Cultural Intelligence: The capability to relate and work effectively across cultures, including understanding cultural nuances, adapting communication styles, and navigating cross-cultural business situations.

Data Analytics: is the process of examining data sets to determine their information. In business contexts, it is used to understand consumer behavior, predict trends, and inform decision-making.

Digital Entrepreneurship (DE): A transformative approach to business where entrepreneurs strategically leverage digital technologies to drive innovation, create new business models, and enhance value-creation processes.

Digital Transformation: Integrating digital technology into all business areas fundamentally changes how organizations operate and deliver customer value. It encompasses technological, cultural, and operational changes that organizations must undergo to compete effectively in an increasingly digital world.

Digital Wellness: Individuals can achieve optimal health and well-being in a digital environment, including maintaining healthy relationships with technology and managing digital stress.

Digital Workplace Management: The comprehensive approach to managing work environments that integrate digital technologies, remote work capabilities, and virtual collaboration tools while maintaining organizational culture and effectiveness.

Entrepreneurial Mental Health and Well-being (MWB): The psychological and emotional state of entrepreneurs, including their ability to cope with stress, maintain work-life balance, and sustain personal resilience while managing business challenges.

Global Index of Digital Entrepreneurship Systems (GIDES): A measurement framework used to assess and compare digital entrepreneurship ecosystems across different economies, evaluating factors such as infrastructure, cultural institutions, and technological readiness.

Global Market Dynamics: The interplay of economic, cultural, and technological factors influencing how businesses operate across international markets, including adaptation strategies and localization requirements.

Habit Loop: Charles Duhigg described a neurological pattern consisting of three elements: cue, routine, and reward. Understanding this pattern helps businesses create products and services that become habitual to consumers.

Hook Model: A four-step process described by Nir Eyal for creating habit-forming products, consisting of trigger, action, variable reward, and investment phases. Used by companies to develop products that become integrated into users' daily routines.

Internet of Things (IoT): A network of interconnected devices and objects embedded with sensors, software, and other technologies enabling them to collect and exchange data, enhancing efficiency, safety, and sustainability in business operations.

Lean Startup Methodology: An approach to business development popularized by Eric Ries, emphasizes rapid prototyping, customer feedback, and iterative development to create successful businesses with minimal resource waste.

Remote Work Culture: Collective practices, values, and communication patterns that emerge in organizations where employees work from different locations are enabled by digital technologies and require alternative approaches to management and collaboration.

Third Wave: A concept introduced by Alvin Toffler describes the post-industrial society characterized by the information age, following the first wave (agricultural) and second wave (industrial) societies. Marked by the dominance of information technology and digital communication.

Chapter 2
Leading With Vision and Values

ABSTRACT

At the height of corporate scandals at the beginning of this millennium, Chang et al. (2021) report that literature began to pay attention to value-based leadership behavior. This shift was motivated by identifying leadership behaviors that could create an ethical culture and help companies avoid similar scandals. Value-based leadership behavior was seen as an effective way to promote ethical decision-making and prevent unethical behavior. Imagine a world where every organization is driven by a profound sense of purpose, guided by a clear vision, and anchored in unwavering values. In this world, leaders inspire their teams to reach extraordinary heights, navigating the ever-changing landscape with resolute determination and a steadfast commitment to making a positive impact. This is the power of leading with vision and values. Visionary leaders stand out as beacons of purpose and direction. These influential individuals recognize that an organization's success hinges not only on financial metrics but also on its ability to inspire, adapt, and create lasting impact.

INTRODUCTION

In an era where corporate scandals and environmental challenges have heightened the need for ethical leadership, integrating vision and values in organizational leadership has become more crucial. This chapter comprehensively examines how modern leaders can effectively combine psychological, sociological, and economic perspectives to drive organizational success while maintaining ethical practices and social responsibility. Through analysis of transformational leadership principles and case studies of companies like Patagonia and Zappos, the text shows how vision-

DOI: 10.4018/979-8-3693-5553-4.ch002

driven leadership can foster innovation, enhance employee engagement, and create sustainable business practices.

The chapter is timely as it addresses the complex relationship between ethical leadership and employee behavior. It explores how leaders balance Counterproductive Work Behavior (CWB) and Organizational Citizenship Behavior (OCB). Incorporating frameworks like Schein's organizational culture model and the Balanced Scorecard approach provides practical tools for measuring leadership effectiveness and implementing value-based strategies. The discussion extends beyond theoretical concepts to examine emerging trends in sustainable entrepreneurship and digital innovation, offering valuable insights for leaders seeking to align organizational objectives with broader societal needs.

Drawing from recent research and real-world examples, this chapter serves as a theoretical foundation and practical guide for modern leaders who aim to create lasting positive impact through their organizations. It emphasizes that successful leadership in today's business environment requires more than just financial acumen; it demands a sophisticated understanding of how vision and values can be leveraged to drive meaningful organizational transformation while maintaining ethical integrity. This book seeks to answer these questions. Using the latest research and examples from many fields, this chapter gives leaders a practical guide to using their vision and values to improve their organizations and society. Leadership skills improve communication and conflict management for leaders of all experience levels. The chapters of this book will provide you with the tools, frameworks, and insights you need to lead with vision and values in the 21st century. *Figure 1* below shows the relationship between the variables involved in leading with vision and values, underscoring how important it is for leaders to shape workplace behavior and to be accountable for it.

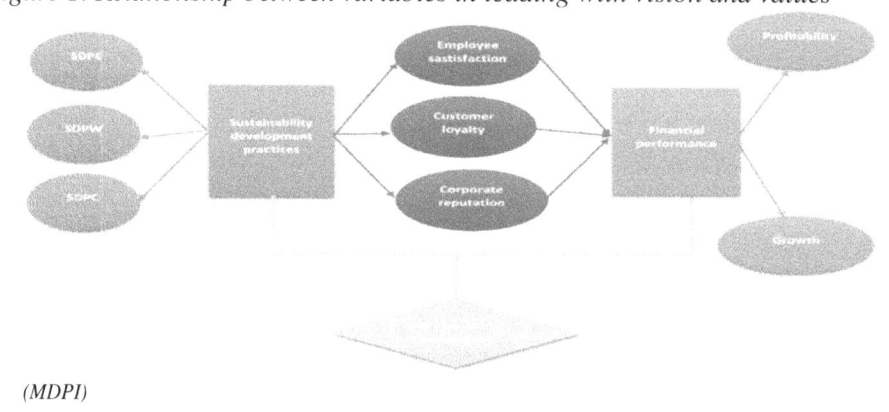

Figure 1. Relationship between variables in leading with vision and values

(MDPI)

INTEGRATING VISION AND VALUES

Modern leadership demands a sophisticated integration of vision and values, combining psychological, sociological, and economic perspectives to propel organizations toward meaningful success. This multifaceted approach recognizes that organizational excellence stems from deliberately aligning corporate objectives with societal needs while nurturing innovation and embedding sustainable practices at every level. Leaders who embrace this framework find themselves better equipped to navigate the complexities of today's business landscape, creating an impact that resonates both within and beyond their organizations (Olurina et al., 2023).

The psychological underpinnings of vision and value-driven leadership reveal its profound impact on workforce dynamics. When leaders communicate an interesting vision while demonstrating unwavering values, they unlock deeper levels of employee involvement and appeal to basic human drives. This alignment with self-determination theory highlights how connecting organizational goals to broader societal impact can enhance employee commitment and satisfaction. The approach proves effective in fostering intrinsic motivation, as team members find greater meaning and purpose in their work, according to Olurina and colleagues.

The sociological dimension of this leadership approach reflects a strengthening business paradigm centered on corporate social responsibility and stakeholder capitalism. Research shows that organizations incorporating social and environmental considerations into their strategic decision-making achieve superior long-term outcomes (Plečko & Hojnik, 2024). This trend shows notable strength in Latin America and the Caribbean, where business leaders consistently show a heightened awareness of conscientious business practices and their broader societal implications.

From an economic standpoint, vision and values-centered leadership catalyzes innovation while unveiling new market opportunities. Combining digital technology with sustainable practices is a powerful way for businesses to perform better and gain a competitive edge. As organizations worldwide navigate regional and cultural variations in leadership approaches, sustainable entrepreneurship increasingly stands out as a crucial engine of economic growth and social advancement. This transformation is evident in the digital realm, where innovative approaches to sustainable entrepreneurship reshape traditional business models and institutional frameworks (Olurina et al., 2023).

Leading With Vision and Values

Studies have begun to focus on ethical leadership because of major corporate scandals. The financial crisis of 2008 highlighted the devastating impact of unethical practices and underscored the need for leaders who prioritize integrity and accountability. This has increased the emphasis on ethical leadership to prevent future crises and restore public trust. This shift was motivated by identifying leadership behaviors that could create an ethical culture and help companies avoid similar scandals. Ethical decisions are easier to make with value-based leadership. Imagine a world where every organization is driven by a profound sense of purpose, guided by a clear vision, and anchored in unwavering values. In this world, inspiring leaders help their teams overcome challenges and achieve great things. Leading with vision and values yields strength and stands out as a beacon of purpose and direction. These leaders understand that a company's success isn't just about finances but also inspiration, adaptation, and long-term impact. Vision and values-based leadership is more than a management buzzword; it is a strategy.

However, how can we lead with vision and values in a constantly changing world of uncertainties? How can we align our teams with a common purpose and foster a culture of trust, collaboration, and innovation? How can we communicate our vision effectively and authentically to all our internal and external stakeholders? Moreover, how can we measure the impact of our vision and values on our organization's performance and society at large? In the following pages, we will try to answer these questions.

The Role of Values: Anchoring Leadership

However, more than a vision is required. The organization's values define its character, drive employee behavior, and foster trust. When employees know what the organization stands for and is expected of them, they are more likely to act with integrity and make decisions that align with the company's objectives. These values create a culture of trust and commitment essential to any successful organization. A culture of trust and loyalty will provide a firm foundation for the organization to build upon, allowing it to achieve its goals. Values are the unwritten rules governing decisions, resolving conflicts, and celebrating success. Whether integrity, collaboration, or innovation, values provide the moral compass for leaders and employees. Imagine a healthcare company committed to patient-centric care. Value permeates every level of the organization, from frontline nurses to boardroom discussions; it influences resource allocation, product development, and even marketing campaigns. Leadership that consistently embodies these values creates a culture of authenticity and purpose.

Honesty, integrity, respect, and accountability are often highlighted as foundational for creating a positive work environment and driving success. Leaders who embody these values can foster a culture of trust, collaboration, and innovation (Barnhill, 2023; Lichtenstein, 2012). This leadership approach ensures that the organization's actions match its goals, leading to lasting success and ethical conduct (Gleeson,

2021). Values are not abstract concepts; they affect organizational life's day-to-day and strategic aspects; they are essential for building a strong, cohesive, and thriving organizational culture. As any manager knows, a generic sounding list of values will only move the culture needle if leadership brings it to life, posit Scott Anthony and Evan Schwartz in a 2017 Harvard Business Review article.

Many firms that have tried to transform have failed. A common reason is that leaders approach the change as one colossal process, during which the old company becomes a new one. According to Anthony and Evan in Harvard Business Review (2017), that does not work for many practical reasons. For instance, an organization that grew up producing newspapers must gain the fundamental skills to build a digital content company. It might resist embracing the news to protect the business it knows and loves. Harvard Business Review says success means updating your primary business and investing in new ones. Apple is the classic "dual transformation" model with the iMac and iBook.

Amazon Web Services (AWS) is another example that addressed a longstanding analyst complaint about Amazon. These successful organizations transform by using culture change to drive engagement, as noted by Scott and Anthony. Microsoft is a case in point; in the four years since Satya Nadella became CEO, he has been credited with transforming Microsoft's cautious, insular culture. Nadella was known for listening, learning, and analyzing. Instead of speeches, he motivated employees through empowering company-wide projects. Microsoft's cloud and AI businesses (32% of revenue) thrived thanks to engaged employees. These examples illustrate the role of employee engagement in successful transformations.

According to Barnhill (2023), organizational transformation is the symbolic integration of values within a company's culture and decision-making processes because a robust organizational culture is founded on shared vision and values. Research shows that individuals who align actions with their values experience reduced stress and anxiety, leading to enhanced emotional well-being, resilience, and overall life satisfaction, posits Barnhill. Values-based leadership leads to ethical decisions and increases team trust and respect, according to Chang et al. (2021). Value-based leadership is commonly considered one of the emerging forms of authentic, ethical, and servant leadership. It focuses on providing value in management (i.e., ethical, moral, responsible, serving, and genuine leadership). This leadership style promotes employee value alignment and company commitment (Lemoine et al., 2019).

In a meta-analysis of research (Peng & Kim, 2020), ethics is tied to follower normative conduct, regardless of job satisfaction. Thus, ethical leadership benefits organizations by increasing or decreasing follower normative and counter-normative behavior. The leader's moral stance raises questions about the norms they will promote. Ethical leadership requires leaders to model the ethical standards they wish their followers to uphold. This can be challenging when the leader has to decide what norms to promote to their followers, as it may be challenging to agree on what those norms will be.

The complex relationships between CWB, OCB, and ethical leadership have been the subject of much research. Traditionally, CWB and OCB are opposite ends of the spectrum, where CWB harms the organization, and OCB benefits it (Sypniewska, 2020). However, according to the author, studies have shown that these behaviors can coexist within individuals and organizations. For example, an employee will show OCB by helping colleagues and engaging in CWB by taking longer breaks than allowed. It is often assumed that ethical leadership will reduce the occurrence of CWB by setting a positive example and creating a moral climate (Searle, 2022). While this is generally supported, there is evidence that ethical leadership alone may not prevent CWB, especially when employees feel unjustly treated or are under significant stress, posits Searle.

Leaders expect that promoting OCB will foster positive follower behaviors. However, the concept of moral licensing suggests that engaging in OCB might lead individuals to feel entitled and later engage in CWB, as they believe they have 'earned' the right to do so after their positive actions (Klotz & Bolino, 2013; Searle, 2022). Researchers have viewed CWB as stemming from individual factors, such as personality traits. Recent perspectives suggest that situational factors, like organizational culture and stressors, play a significant role in the emergence of CWB, according to Searle. OCB is generally seen as beneficial to the organization; however, it can have downsides, leading to burnout among employees who feel pressured to go above and beyond their job requirements, notes Sypniewska (2020). These challenges to traditional assumptions highlight the need for a nuanced understanding of workplace behaviors. They suggest that organizations consider a broader range of factors, including ethical leadership, organizational culture, and employee well-being, for effective management and understanding the dynamics between CWB, OCB, and leadership behaviors.

TRANSFORMATIONAL LEADERSHIP: THE CATALYST

The concept of leading with vision and values finds empirical support in studies like Bass and Avolio's "Transformational Leadership" (1994). Their research underscores the profound impact visionary leaders have on organizational performance. These leaders do not merely manage; they inspire, challenge, and elevate. Their ability to articulate and align an interesting vision with shared values ignites passion and commitment among their teams. Harvard Business Review further illuminates the communication prowess of transformational leaders (Carmine, 2022). Carmine says communication isn't simple words; it's connecting with your audience, so they understand and feel your message. Simple language helps everyone understand, regardless of their job. These transformational leaders excel at distilling complex ideas into simple, relatable language. Instead of jargon-laden monologues, they use short words that resonate across hierarchies. When discussing vision, they evoke emotions, not just intellect. As a result, their messages stick, and their influence endures.

Carmine (2022) notes that transformational leaders are praised for making complex ideas uncomplicated and emotionally resonant. Moreover, the emotional component of communication is crucial. By appealing to emotions, leaders can inspire and mobilize their teams toward a shared vision (Harvard Business Review, 2017). This emotional connection makes the message memorable and the leader's influence lasting. Clear, relatable, and emotional communication makes transformational leaders stand out, says Carmine. According to the Harvard Business Review, such leaders understand that to effect change, they must connect with their followers on a level that transcends mere intellectual understanding and taps into shared human experiences and aspirations.

Hence, their communication style becomes a powerful tool in driving transformation and achieving enduring impact. To change an organizational culture and move into new growth areas, the CEO needs to become "the storyteller in chief," says Aetna's Mark Bertolini. That means telling different aspects of the same transformation narrative to all the company's constituencies and stakeholders (IT Revolution, 2020). In Aetna's case, this meant building a narrative of how the move away from fee-for-service reimbursement to the new business model of value-based care would change the nature of health insurance and render it obsolete one day (Business Intelligence Academy, 2018). "It is easy to underestimate the amount of communication needed," adds Bertolini. It would help if you were tireless about it, consistently, and battering the core messages home weekly. Your leaders must tailor the message to the level of fidelity relevant to each part of the organization.

Transformational leadership builds on transactional leadership, focusing on leader-follower relationships. According to Bass and Avolio, transformational leadership goes beyond mere exchanges or agreements between colleagues and followers, who believe followers identify with leaders who encourage them to follow their example. Transformational leadership is because leaders will be role models, inspiring and motivating their followers to achieve higher goals (Marmerchant, 2023). Transformational leaders challenge their followers to think beyond their self-interests and to focus on the bigger picture. They create a trusting and open communication culture essential for successful organizations. By inspiring and motivating their followers, transformational leaders can help to build successful organizations that embrace collaboration and trust.

Leading by Example

"Leading by Example" is a powerful concept in organizational leadership; it involves leaders showing the core values of their organization through their actions, setting a standard for others to follow. Embodying the values they preach fosters trust, inspires employees, and creates a robust and cohesive culture. Patagonia is a prime example of values-based leadership. Founded by Yvon Chouinard, Patagonia is steadfastly committed to environmental sustainability. The company's mission, "We are in business to save our home planet," is more than just words; it is a guiding principle that influences every decision. For instance, Patagonia has taken significant steps to use sustainable materials, provide on-site childcare, and source food locally for its cafeteria to reduce its carbon footprint (Austin, 2021; Rock, 2024, p. 1). Moreover, Chouinard's decision to transfer company ownership to fight climate change is a testament to living by one's values (Madhosingh, 2022).

On the other hand, Zappos is renowned for its exceptional customer service and company culture. The company's core values, such as "Deliver WOW through service" and "Embrace and drive change," are deeply ingrained in its operations. Zappos encourages a culture of happiness, trust, and innovation, reflected in its approach to customer service and employee engagement (Hall, 2023; Hsieh, 2010; Inc., 2010). In both cases, the leaders of Patagonia and Zappos have not only preached their organizational values but have also lived them out loud. Authentic leaders attract and keep talent, build customer loyalty, and improve long-term organizational success. Leaders who lead by example can drive meaningful change and achieve remarkable results.

Fostering Alignment and Accountability

Understanding how individual and organizational values connect is easier with Schein's framework. According to Schein, organizational culture comprises three layers: artifacts, espoused values, and underlying assumptions (Fripp, 2023; The World of Work Project, 2019). Understanding Schein's (2017) organizational culture layers helps align individual and company values. Besides evaluating the physical environment, dress code, and organization rituals, consider the external aspects. Often, these artifacts can provide insight into the underlying assumptions and values espoused. Aligning these artifacts with the organization's espoused values can reinforce culture. Take a closer look at the underlying assumptions that are often unconscious but significantly affect organizational behavior. These beliefs and attitudes define the organizational culture. A clear understanding of these assumptions can assist with addressing misalignments (Schein (2017).

Clearly articulate the organization's values. These are a set of values and norms that an organization officially endorses. Mission statements, corporate policies, and other formal declarations will convey these values consistently. Thus, the behavior of individuals within the organization can be aligned with these values. Develop a culture of open dialogue where individuals can express their values and beliefs without fear of retribution. Highlighting the conflict between individual and organizational values can be an opportunity to discuss them constructively. Ensure that the organization's practices and policies align with its values. Recruitment, reward, and recognition systems that reinforce the espoused values and underlying assumptions are among these.

Leaders' behavior reflects the organization's values, aligns individual actions with organizational values, and sets a powerful example. It is vital to ensure congruency between the artifacts, espoused values, and assumptions underlying the artifacts. Organizations must ensure that their environment, statements, and beliefs align. If there are discrepancies between these layers, values can become misaligned. By integrating these strategies, organizations can foster a culture that aligns individual values with the values of their organizations, leading to greater accountability and a more cohesive work environment. By incorporating Schein's model into the discussion of alignment and accountability, organizational culture can be examined and structured, and a consistent culture across the various levels of an organization and leadership's role in establishing a shared vision is emphasized (Schein (2017).

POLICY IMPLICATIONS AND BEST PRACTICES FOR ENTREPRENEURS

The evolution of vision and value-driven leadership reshapes organizational policies and governance frameworks. Educational institutions must integrate entrepreneurship and sustainability education across all levels to prepare future leaders (Surono, 2024). This transformation extends to government policy, where incentive structures can be designed to reward businesses showing strong social and environmental performance. Corbett (2024) noted that regulatory frameworks should actively promote corporate social entrepreneurship (CSE) and sustainable business practices, especially as stakeholders increasingly expect businesses to balance financial performance with environmental and social responsibilities.

The institutionalization of corporate social responsibility (CSR) signifies a significant change in how companies conduct their operations and disclose their effects. Companies worldwide now regularly publish comprehensive reports detailing their social and environmental initiatives, with many organizations establishing dedicated departments and executive positions to oversee these efforts (Corbett, 2024). This development reflects a growing recognition that businesses must serve not only their shareholders' financial interests but also address broader societal expectations and challenges.

For entrepreneurs seeking to lead with vision and values, several key practices have emerged as essential for success. These include developing a clear, purpose-driven vision that connects business objectives with societal impact and leveraging digital technologies to enhance sustainability initiatives (Plečko & Hojnik, 2024). Successful entrepreneurs also foster innovative cultures where employees are encouraged to develop solutions addressing business and societal challenges (Corbett, 2024). According to Corbett, this approach requires investing in employee skill development to drive sustainable innovation and implementing robust governance systems that ensure transparency and accountability in all operations (Anggraini et al., 2024).

Measuring Progress and Iterating

Introducing metrics to assess the effectiveness of implementing vision and values in organizations is a strategic approach that aligns with the principles of the Balanced Scorecard. The Balanced Scorecard is a multifaceted framework that translates an organization's vision and strategy into coherent performance measures (Kaplan & Norton, 1992). To measure how well an organization's vision and values are embedded within its operations, consider the following metrics: **Alignment of Goals**: This metric evaluates how individual and team goals support the overarching vision and values. **Behavioral Indicators**: Observe behaviors that reflect the organization's values in daily operations. **Cultural Assessments:** Conduct surveys or interviews to gauge the internal perception of the organization's vision and values. *Figure 2* below shows a balanced scorecard linked to performance measurement.

Figure 2. The balanced scorecard links and performance measurements

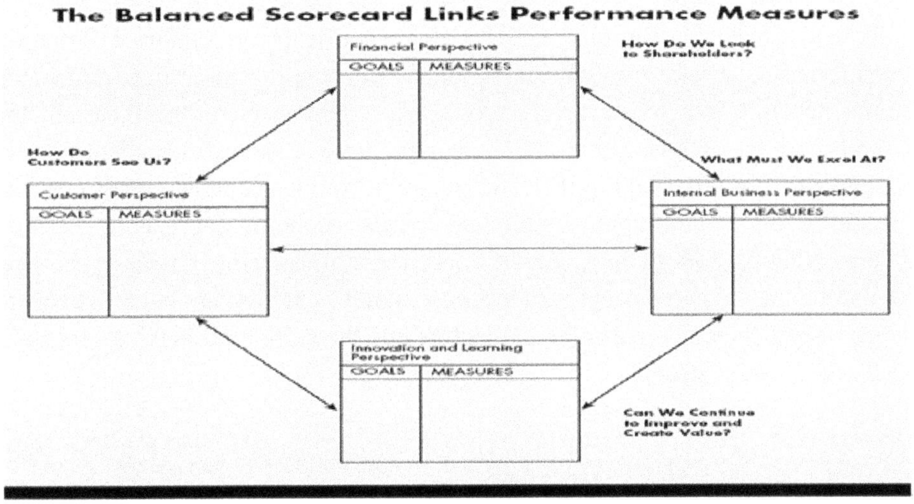

The Balanced Scorecard Links Performance Measures

(Harvard Business School)

According to Cole (2023), the Balanced Scorecard incorporates four comprehensive perspectives on organizational performance, as shown below.

- Financial Perspective: Measures financial success and economic value creation.
- Customer Perspective: Assesses customer satisfaction and perceptions of products and services.
- Internal Process Perspective: Evaluates the efficiency and effectiveness of business processes.
- Learning and Growth Perspective: Focuses on the development and growth of organizational capabilities.

Leaders must set specific and measurable targets for each perspective to implement the Balanced Scorecard effectively. They must choose metrics directly linked to the organization's strategic objectives and vision, set up a system for continuously monitoring and evaluating the metrics, and align initiatives and resources with the identified metrics and goals, posits Cole. By integrating these metrics and the Balanced Scorecard approach, organizations can create a robust framework for evaluating their performance against strategic objectives while ensuring that their vision and values are at the core of their operations. The key is to measure and use these measurements for continuous improvement and strategic alignment.

Recent Studies and Analysis

Recent research has illuminated the evolving landscape of sustainable entrepreneurship through several groundbreaking studies. Engineering innovations in artificial intelligence, IoT, and blockchain are driving fundamental shifts toward sustainable economic models (Olurina et al., 2023); comprehensive analysis has identified six key thematic clusters shaping the field, ranging from sustainable entrepreneurial orientation to green entrepreneurship and circular economy approaches (Ferreira & Ferreira, 2024). These developments are further enhanced by findings showing that entrepreneurs who strategically leverage digital technologies are more likely to incorporate social and environmental factors into their decision-making processes (Plečko & Hojnik, 2024).

CONCLUSION AND SUMMARY

The chapter "Leading with Vision and Values" explores the critical integration of vision and values in modern organizational leadership, particularly emphasizing the importance of ethical practices and sustainable business methods in today's corporate environment. At its core, the chapter examines leadership through three fundamental perspectives. From a psychological standpoint, it demonstrates how vision and values significantly impact workforce engagement and motivation. The sociological perspective emphasizes the growing importance of corporate social responsibility and stakeholder capitalism. Economically, the chapter illustrates how vision-driven leadership catalyzes innovation and creates new market opportunities.

One of the chapter's main ideas is transformational leadership. This leadership approach transcends traditional transactional methods by inspiring and elevating teams through clear, emotional communication that resonates across all organizational levels. The text emphasizes that effective leaders must be skilled communicators who can distill complex ideas into simple, relatable language that intellectually and emotionally connects with their audience.

The chapter presents several compelling case studies illustrating successful vision and values-based leadership. Patagonia exemplifies environmental sustainability commitment, while Zappos shows how strong organizational values can drive exceptional customer service. These examples show how authentic leadership can create a lasting positive impact while maintaining business success. Measurement and accountability receive significant attention when discussing the Balanced Scorecard approach. This framework evaluates performance across financial, customer, internal process, and learning perspectives, emphasizing the importance of continuous improvement and strategic alignment. The chapter explains how organizations can effectively measure progress in implementing their vision and values while keeping long-term sustainability and immediate outcomes in mind.

A notable portion of the text explores the complex relationship between Counterproductive Work Behavior (CWB) and Organizational Citizenship Behavior (OCB), examining how ethical leadership influences these behaviors. Using Schein's organizational culture model, the chapter delves into how organizations can align individual and organizational values through understanding artifacts, espoused values, and underlying assumptions. The chapter also addresses emerging trends in leadership, including integrating digital technology with sustainable practices, the rising importance of sustainable entrepreneurship, and the growing focus on corporate social responsibility. It emphasizes that modern leaders must balance financial performance with social and environmental responsibilities while maintaining strong ethical foundations.

The text consistently emphasizes practical application, providing leaders with actionable frameworks and strategies for implementing vision and values-based leadership in their organizations. The chapter highlights the importance of measuring progress and implementing best practices, suggesting that successful modern leadership requires a sophisticated understanding of how vision and values can drive meaningful organizational transformation while maintaining ethical integrity. This comprehensive analysis serves as both a theoretical foundation and a practical guide for contemporary leaders. It emphasizes that effective leadership in today's business environment demands more than just financial acumen; it requires a deep understanding of how vision and values can be leveraged to create lasting positive impact on organizations.

As organizations implement vision and values-based leadership frameworks, they must simultaneously address the challenges of rapid cultural evolution in an increasingly interconnected world. The principles of ethical leadership and organizational transformation discussed above provide the foundation for understanding how leaders can effectively navigate cultural shifts while maintaining organizational integrity. This intersection of visionary leadership and cultural adaptability represents a critical frontier in contemporary organizational management.

The complex interplay between visionary leadership and cultural adaptability, highlighted in the preceding discussion, sets the stage for a deeper examination of how organizations navigate cultural transformation in our digital age. While the foundational principles of ethical leadership remain constant, their application must evolve to meet the demands of an increasingly interconnected global landscape. This next chapter builds upon these established frameworks by presenting empirical evidence from worldwide organizational case studies, offering insights into how leaders can effectively shepherd their institutions through periods of cultural upheaval while preserving core values and driving innovation.

REFERENCES

Anggraini, A., Kalangi, L., & Warongan, J. D. (2024). The influence of accounting information systems, internal control systems, and human resource competencies on the quality of financial reports with regional government leadership style as a moderation variable (Case study of regency/city regional government in North Sulawesi Province). *The Contrarian: Finance. Accounting and Business Research*, 3(2), 136–153. DOI: 10.58784/cfabr.163

Austin, J. (2021). *How to make values-based leadership your North Star - Work Life by Atlassian.* https://www.atlassian.com/blog/leadership/values-based-leadership-patagonia

Barnhill, A. (2023). Cultivating A Winning Culture: The Role Of Values-Based Leadership. *Forbes.* https://www.forbes.com/sites/forbescoachescouncil/2023/09/18/cultivating-a-winning-culture-the-role-of-values-based-leadership/?sh=5de6820470a7

Bass, B. M., & Avolio, B. J. (1994). *Improving Organizational Effectiveness Through Transformational Leadership* (1st ed.). SAGE.

Business Intelligence Academy. (2018). *Transformational Leadership.* https://www.businessintelligenceacad.com/blog/transformational-leadership

Carmine, G. (2022). *How Great Leaders Communicate.* Harvard Business Review. https://hbr.org/2022/11/how-great-leaders-communicate

Chang, S. M., Budhwar, P., & Crawshaw, J. (2021). The Emergence of Value-Based Leadership Behavior at the Frontline of Management: A Role Theory Perspective and Future Research Agenda. *Frontiers in Psychology*, 12, 635106. DOI: 10.3389/fpsyg.2021.635106 PMID: 34113282

Cole, C. (2023). *What Is a Balanced Scorecard? | HBS Online.* https://online.hbs.edu/blog/post/balanced-scorecard

Corbett, M. F. (2024). Unleashing the power of corporate social entrepreneurship: An emerging tool for corporate social responsibility. *S.A.M. Advanced Management Journal*, 89(2), 122–153. DOI: 10.1108/SAMAMJ-03-2024-0003

Ferreira, N. C., & Ferreira, J. J. (2024). Quo Vadis Sustainable Entrepreneurship? A Systematic Literature Review of Related Drivers and Inhibitors in SMEs. *IEEE Transactions on Engineering Management*, 71, 9644–9660. DOI: 10.1109/TEM.2023.3305475

Fripp, G. (2023). *Schein's Model of Organizational Culture - Organizational Behavior*. https://www.myorganisationalbehaviour.com/scheins-model-of-organizational-culture/

Gleeson, B. (2021). 5 Attributes (And Benefits) Of Values-Based Leadership. *Forbes*. https://www.forbes.com/sites/brentgleeson/2021/07/19/5-attributes-and-benefits-of-values-based-leadership/?sh=1513b18c3d21

Hall, A. (2023). Zappos CEO Tony Hsieh on Self-Organization, Adaptability, and Values. *Aaron Hall*. https://aaronhall.com/insights/zappos-ceo-tony-hsieh-on-self-organization-adaptability-and-values/

Harvard Business Review. (2017). *What the Best Transformational Leaders Do*. https://hbr.org/2017/05/what-the-best-transformational-leaders-do

Hsieh, T. (2010). *How Zappos Infuses Culture Using Core Values*. Harvard Business Review. https://hbr.org/2010/05/how-zappos-infuses-culture-using-core-values

Inc. (2010). The Zappos Core Values. *Inc*. https://www.inc.com/inc-advisor/zappos-managin-people-zappos-core-values.html

Industrial Engineering Website. (2023). Statistical Process Control (SPC). *Industrial Engineering Website*. https://industrial.ienajah.com/statistical-process-control-spc/

Kaplan, R. S., & Norton, D. P. (1992). *The Balanced Scorecard—Measures that Drive Performance*. Harvard Business Review. https://hbr.org/1992/01/the-balanced-scorecard-measures-that-drive-performance-2

Klotz, A. C., & Bolino, M. C. (2013). *Citizenship and Counterproductive work Behavior: A Moral Licensing View*, 38(2). https://www.jstor.org/stable/23416446

Lemoine, G. J., Hartnell, C. A., & Leroy, H. (2019). Taking Stock of Moral Approaches to Leadership: An Integrative Review of Ethical, Authentic, and Servant Leadership. *The Academy of Management Annals*, 13(1), 148–187. DOI: 10.5465/annals.2016.0121

Lichtenstein, S. (2012). The Role of Values in Leadership: How Leaders' Values Shape Value Creation - Integral Leadership Review. *Integral Leadership Review*, 12(1), 1–18.

Madhosingh, S. (2022). 4 Key Leadership Lessons from Patagonia Founder, Yvon Chouinard. *CEOWORLD Magazine*. https://ceoworld.biz/2022/10/14/4-key-leadership-lessons-from-patagonia-founder-yvon-chouinard/

Marmerchant, B. (2023). *Transformational Leadership Strategies: A Comprehensive Overview*. https://www.worldconsulting.group/leadership-strategy-definitions-transformational-leadership-strategy

Olurina, J. O., Gidiagba, J. O., Ehiaguina, V. E., Ndiwe, T. C., Ayodeji, S. A., Banso, A. A., Tula, O. A., & Ojo, G. G. (2023). Engineering Innovations And Sustainable Entrepreneurship: A Comprehensive Literature Review. *Materials & Corrosion Engineering Management*, 4(2), 70–79. DOI: 10.26480/macem.02.2023.70.79

Overton, M. G. (2023). Leadership Strategies to Enhance Communication and Conflict Management. *MedicalTraining.Me*. https://medicaltraining.me/leadership-strategies-to-enhance-communication-and-conflict-management/

Peng, A. C., & Kim, D. (2020). A meta-analytic test of the differential pathways linking ethical leadership to normative conduct. *Journal of Organizational Behavior*, 41(4), 348–368. DOI: 10.1002/job.2427

Plečko, S., & Hojnik, B. B. (2024). Sustainable Business Practices and the Role of Digital. Technologies: A Cross-Regional Analysis. *Systems*, 12(3), 97. DOI: 10.3390/systems12030097

Revolution, I. T. (2020). *The Five Dimensions of Transformational Leadership - IT Revolution*. https://itrevolution.com/articles/the-five-dimensions-of-transformational-leadership/

Schein, E. H. (2017). *Organizational Culture and Leadership*. John Wiley & Sons, Inc.

Searle, R. H. (2022). Counterproductive Work Behaviors. In Searle, R. H. (Ed.), *Oxford Research Encyclopedia of Psychology*. Oxford University Press., DOI: 10.1093/acrefore/9780190236557.013.880

Surono, S. (2024). Enhancing Employability Of Professional Self-Employed. In *Business Management Through Mapping Occupational Standards In Entrepreneurship Within The Indonesian Qualification Framework. Jurnal Ekonomi Teknologi Dan Bisnis*. JETBIS.

Sypniewska, B. (2020). Counterproductive Work Behavior and Organizational Citizenship Behavior. *Advances in Cognitive Psychology*, 16(4), 321–328. DOI: 10.5709/acp-0306-9 PMID: 33500742

The World of Work Project. (2019). Edgar Schein's Organizational Culture Triangle: A Simple Summary. *World of Work Project*. https://worldofwork.io/2019/10/edgar-scheins-culture-triangle/

KEY TERMS AND DEFINITIONS

Balanced Scorecard: A strategic planning and management system that organizations use to communicate what they're trying to accomplish; align day-to-day work with strategy; prioritize projects, products, and services; and measure and monitor progress toward strategic targets.

Corporate Social Entrepreneurship (CSE): Extending an organization's domain of competence and corresponding opportunity set through innovative resource leveraging to address social problems and needs.

Corporate Social Responsibility (CSR): A business approach that contributes to sustainable development by delivering economic, social, and environmental benefits for all stakeholders.

Counterproductive Work Behavior (CWB): Actions that harm or are intended to harm organizations or people in organizations, including behaviors like taking excessive breaks or engaging in workplace deviance.

Cultural Integration: Combining different organizational cultures and value systems into a cohesive whole is often necessary during mergers, acquisitions, or significant organizational changes.

Digital Innovation: The application of digital technologies to transform business processes, culture, and customer experiences to meet changing business and market requirements.

Ethical Leadership: Leadership that shows and promotes normatively appropriate conduct through personal actions, interpersonal relationships, and the promotion of such conduct among followers.

Organizational Citizenship Behavior (OCB): Voluntary employee behaviors that go beyond formal job requirements and contribute positively to the organizational environment. Moral Licensing is when individuals who have demonstrated exemplary behavior feel justified in later engaging in actions that might be considered unethical or problematic.

Schein's Organizational Culture Model: A framework consisting of three levels: - Artifacts: Visible organizational structures and processes - Espoused Values: Strategies, goals, and philosophies - Underlying Assumptions: Unconscious beliefs, perceptions, and feelings

Stakeholder Capitalism: A system in which corporations are oriented to serve the interests of all their stakeholders (customers, suppliers, employees, shareholders, and local communities) instead of only shareholders.

Strategic Alignment: Ensuring that all aspects of an organization (strategy, structure, people, and resources) work together to accomplish organizational objectives.

Sustainable Entrepreneurship: Business practices that integrate environmental and social concerns into business operations while maintaining economic viability.

Transformational Leadership: A leadership approach that goes beyond transactional relationships by inspiring and motivating followers to achieve higher goals through personal example and emotional connection.

Values-Based Leadership: A leadership style that emphasizes making decisions and taking actions based on core organizational and personal values, promoting ethical behavior and sustainable practices.

Vision-Based Leadership: A leadership approach that creates and communicates a clear, compelling picture of the organization's future direction while aligning actions and decisions with this vision.

Chapter 3
Navigating Cultural Shifts:
Strategies for Adaptive Leadership

ABSTRACT

This book chapter explores the critical role of adaptive leadership in navigating the complex dynamics of cultural change within organizations in today's rapidly evolving global marketplace. As companies expand their reach across borders and industries, they face the challenge of adapting to diverse cultural norms, values, and expectations. The ability to anticipate, identify, and respond effectively to these cultural shifts has become crucial in determining an organization's long-term success and competitiveness. The chapter delves into the various aspects of adaptive leadership, including fostering inclusivity, leveraging diversity, and driving innovation. It emphasizes the importance of cultivating a culture of open communication, respect, and continuous learning, which not only enhances employee engagement and satisfaction but also unlocks the full potential of a diverse workforce. Adaptive leaders recognize diversity as a strategic advantage and actively seek out and integrate diverse viewpoints, experiences, and backgrounds to understand better and serve diverse customers.

INTRODUCTION

In this digital era of unprecedented global change and interconnectedness, the ability of organizations to navigate cultural shifts has become paramount to their survival and success. This comprehensive analysis, conducted worldwide, explores the critical intersection of adaptive leadership and cultural transformation in modern organizations. It examines how leaders can effectively guide their institutions through

DOI: 10.4018/979-8-3693-5553-4.ch003

Copyright © 2025, IGI Global Scientific Publishing. Copying or distributing in print or electronic forms without written permission of IGI Global is prohibited.

periods of significant cultural change while maintaining operational excellence and fostering innovation.

The chapter presents a multifaceted examination of adaptive leadership principles, drawing from both theoretical frameworks and practical applications across diverse organizational contexts. These valuable applications are not just theoretical, but they are being used in actual organizations, making the findings of this research highly applicable. Beginning with the foundational work of Ronald Heifetz and Marty Linsky at Harvard Kennedy School, it traces the evolution of adaptive leadership theory and its increasing relevance in today's dynamic business environment. The analysis is timely as organizations worldwide grapple with rapid technological advancement, shifting workforce demographics, and growing societal expectations. Central to this discussion is exploring how adaptive leadership facilitates inclusive cultural change, leverages diversity as a strategic advantage, and builds organizational resilience. By examining recent research and case studies, the chapter illuminates the complex interplay between leadership approaches and cultural dynamics, highlighting the critical role of effective communication and entrepreneurial resilience in successful cultural transformations.

The analysis makes several significant contributions to the field. First, it bridges the gap between theoretical understanding and practical application of adaptive leadership principles in cultural change management. Second, it provides fresh insights into how organizations can build resilience while navigating cultural shifts, particularly in increasingly diverse and global contexts. Finally, it addresses crucial research gaps, especially in non-Western contexts and developing economies, while offering a framework for future investigation in this critical area of organizational development. This work is essential reading for organizational leaders, management scholars, and practitioners seeking to understand and implement effective strategies for cultural transformation in today's complex business environment. Examining the intersection of adaptive leadership and cultural change through multiple lenses provides valuable insights for those guiding organizations through periods of significant cultural transition.

NAVIGATING CULTURAL SHIFTS: STRATEGIES FOR ADAPTIVE LEADERSHIP

Ronald Heifetz and Marty Linsky pioneered adaptive leadership at Harvard Kennedy School. It is a sophisticated approach that helps organizations navigate complex changes and challenges without clear-cut solutions. At its core, this framework emphasizes the crucial distinction between technical and adaptive challenges, with cultural shifts falling firmly into the latter category: requiring fundamental changes in values, beliefs, and behaviors rather than simple technical fixes. The approach encompasses several key strategies: Leaders must continuously assess their organizational environment, maintain a broad perspective to understand patterns of resistance, keep focused attention on complex change issues, empower others in the transformation process, and create safe spaces for diverse voices to emerge from all levels of the organization.

The relevance of adaptive leadership has become increasingly apparent as organizations grapple with unprecedented cultural shifts in the modern workplace. From the widespread adoption of digital transformation and remote work culture to the growing emphasis on diversity, equity, and inclusion initiatives, leaders face complex challenges that demand adaptive solutions. These challenges are further complicated by generational shifts in workplace expectations and the increasing need for effective global and cross-cultural collaboration, making adaptive leadership principles more vital than ever for organizational success.

The intricate relationship between leadership effectiveness and cultural-social contexts has garnered increasing scholarly attention, with recent research emphasizing the critical role of culturally responsive leadership strategies in diverse settings (Taqwiem et al., 2024). The dynamic nature of cultural evolution is exemplified in studies examining Chinese mothers' shifting perspectives on children's shyness, where traditional values favoring reserved behavior are giving way to preferences for assertiveness, reflecting broader societal transformations (Liu et al., 2020). This developing cultural landscape illustrates the complex terrain that adaptive leaders must navigate. It requires them to understand and respond to deep-seated cultural changes while fostering environments that accommodate traditional values and emerging social norms. *Figure 1* below describes the principles of adaptive leadership.

Figure 1. What are the principles of adaptive leadership

(ProofHub)

Effective Communication and Adaptive Leadership

Effective communication is pivotal in navigating cultural shifts and is the cornerstone of adaptive leadership. It plays a crucial role in steering cultural shifts and implementing strategies for adaptive leadership. When an organization undergoes significant changes, clear communication becomes the foundation for a successful transition. Leaders who prioritize open dialogue and actively listen to their team members can foster a culture of trust, empathy, and collaboration. Effective communication in facilitating cultural change requires understanding that can help demystify the reasons behind changes, aligning everyone towards common goals. When leaders communicate openly about changes, it invites feedback and participation, transitioning into a collective effort.

Transparency in communication can reduce uncertainty and fear, often the root causes of resistance to change. Acknowledge the difficulties and uncertainties that come with change. Leaders should be honest about the organization's obstacles and the potential impact on team members. Transparency builds trust and allows employees to prepare for the challenges ahead. Provide platforms for team members to ask questions, share insights, and engage in meaningful discussions. Leaders should be accessible and responsive to their team's concerns, fostering an environment where everyone feels heard and valued. According to researchers, for leaders to communicate transparently and empathetically, they must regularly hold town hall meetings to share updates and progress and address concerns in a public, inclusive setting. Below are practices that can help navigate cultural shifts:

1. **Avoid Misinformation:** To avoid spreading misinformation and rumors, update your teams frequently with these regular updates. Regular, scheduled updates ensure everyone agrees and knows the latest information. This helps ensure that everyone works with the same facts and can make informed decisions. Keep team members informed of the progress of the cultural shift, milestones achieved, and upcoming changes. Regular updates through various channels (e.g., email, newsletters, meetings) help maintain clarity and alignment throughout the transition process.
2. **Explicit Vision Sharing:** In times of transition, it's helpful to articulate a clear and intriguing vision for the future to inspire and motivate teams. A clear vision provides a sense of direction and helps teams understand the purpose of their efforts. It also helps to create a shared understanding of the desired outcomes and goals. Additionally, it allows teams to stay focused and motivated during difficult times. Leaders should articulate a compelling vision for the future that aligns with the organization's values and goals. This vision should be commu-

nicated consistently and frequently to ensure that all team members understand the direction and purpose of the cultural shift.
3. **Practice Open-Door Policies:** Employees are reassured by open-door policies that their leaders are accessible and listen to their concerns. An open-door policy ensures that employees can approach their leaders without fear of judgment or retribution. It also allows leaders to build trust with their employees by showing that their concerns are heard and addressed.
4. **Active Listening:** Active listening is an essential leadership skill, and leaders must acknowledge the emotions and perspectives of their team members. Active listening allows leaders to understand their teams better and identify potential improvement areas. It also helps build trust and mutual respect, which is essential for successful teams. Create opportunities for team members to express their concerns, ideas, and feedback. Regular town hall meetings, focus groups, and open-door policies can encourage honest dialogue and foster a culture of trust. Leaders should listen attentively, validate emotions, and show empathy to show that they value their team's input.

The Dynamics of Cultural Change

Cultural dynamics within organizations reflect the shared values, beliefs, and practices that shape the interactions and behaviors of its members, business operations, and market positioning. They determine how an organization responds to internal and external challenges. As globalization, generational differences, and technological advancements reshape the business landscape, leaders must proactively anticipate and respond to cultural shifts to maintain a competitive edge. According to a Harvard Business Review article, *"The Leader's Guide to Corporate Culture,"* organizational culture encompasses the values, norms, and beliefs that guide employee behavior and decision-making (Groysberg et al., 2018).

However, one can wonder about the persistence of cultural diversity and influence, as Segovia-Martín et al. (2020) explained based on Axelrod's model of dissemination of culture. One can ask how gender and influence are critical drivers of cultural change. Such a question requires much time for reflection. Moreover, if cultural diversity based on Axelrod's model is valid, how can cultural shift maintain an organization's competitive edge when in-group altruism is preferable? Both (Groysberg et al., 2018) and Segovia-Martín et al. (2020) proclaim the same fact that cultural dynamics within organizations reflect shared values that determine our behavior, beliefs, attitudes, and values. One argument on diversity based on identities and the other on cultural diversity leads to the accumulation of cultural variants, as explained by Segovia-Martin and colleagues, which allows in-group altruism, not an inclusive culture in globalization, where it is essential to learn from other cultures.

Globalization has significantly impacted organizational cultural dynamics, as companies face the challenge of navigating cross-cultural communication and adapting to local customs and expectations. An INSEAD case study on the merger between French company Lafarge and Swiss company Holcim emphasizes the importance of cultural integration in the success of international mergers and acquisitions (Knittel et al., 2019). Generational differences also contribute to shifting cultural dynamics. With millennials and Gen Z entering the workforce, organizations must adapt to their values, work preferences, and communication styles. A PwC report found that 61% of millennials value work-life balance over 47% of older generations (PwC, 2021). Leaders must create inclusive cultures that embrace diversity and foster intergenerational collaboration.

The rise of remote work, digital collaboration tools, and data-driven decision-making has shifted organizational culture. A McKinsey study found that companies with solid digital cultures are more likely to achieve better financial performance and customer satisfaction (McKinsey, 2021). The impact of cultural shifts on organizational culture and market dynamics is significant. A study by Bain & Company found that companies with strong, adaptive cultures grow revenue 4.5 times faster than those with weak cultures (Bain & Company, 2020). Leaders who proactively anticipate and respond to cultural changes can create a competitive advantage by aligning their organizational culture with evolving market demands and customer expectations.

In today's interconnected world, leadership success is intrinsically linked to intercultural competence (Moodian, 2013). As organizations operate in a global environment, leaders must possess the ability to interact effectively with individuals from diverse cultural backgrounds. While diversity has often been perceived as a liability within organizations, the capacity to embrace and adapt to cultural differences can yield significant benefits for contemporary leadership, posit Moodian. As the global landscape continues to develop, organizations can no longer afford to view cross-cultural dynamics as a hindrance. Instead, a comprehensive commitment to diversity and inclusion must permeate all echelons of an organization's hierarchy.

This approach starkly contrasts the outdated notion of Axelrod's model of disseminating culture or assimilating individuals into the ideological framework of the majority. Viewing diversity as a liability undermines an organization's potential; conversely, embracing and adapting to cultural differences is helpful for contemporary leaders. A robust commitment to diversity and inclusion is imperative at every tier of an organization, moving beyond mere assimilation towards fostering an environment where diverse perspectives are integral to the organizational ethos. By promoting a culture that celebrates and leverages the strengths of diversity, organizations can unlock the full potential of their workforce and position themselves for success in an increasingly complex and competitive global market.

Besley and Persson (2022) explore the intricate relationship between organizational culture and design, revealing that cultural dynamics are influenced by the expected benefits of various identities within the workplace. These cultural identities, predominant among workgroups, significantly impact project decision-making. The study suggests that the identities of an organization's managers, which are tied to specific values, play a crucial role in mediating the divergent interests of leaders and managers. This amalgamation of group identities makes up the organization's culture. Besley and Persson emphasize that group-based identities extend beyond influencing preference strength; potent in-group motivations can transform the organization's cultural landscape.

Factors driving cultural shifts include globalization, which leads to blending cultures and introducing diverse perspectives in the workplace; generational differences, which bring their values and work expectations that influence organizational culture; and technological advancements that shape communication and work processes, causing cultural adaptation to new working methods. Cultural shifts can lead to changes in organizational structure, employee engagement, and leadership styles. They can affect market dynamics by altering consumer behavior and expectations, requiring businesses to adapt their strategies accordingly. Leaders must be proactive in anticipating cultural changes to maintain a competitive edge. They should foster a culture of adaptability and continuous learning to navigate the complexities of cultural evolution and ensure organizational resilience (Schein & Schein, 2019).

Understanding and managing cultural dynamics is crucial to organizational success. Leaders must be equipped to recognize cultural shifts and guide their organizations through the complexities of change to achieve sustainable growth and market relevance. Various factors, including globalization, generational differences, and technological advancements, shape organizational cultural dynamics. Leaders who recognize the strategic importance of organizational culture and proactively adapt to cultural shifts are better positioned to drive business success in an ever-changing market landscape. By fostering a culture of innovation, inclusivity, and agility, organizations can navigate the complexities of cultural dynamics and maintain a competitive edge.

Research on adaptive leadership has expanded beyond its traditional Western-centric focus to encompass diverse global contexts, revealing nuanced applications and insights across different cultural settings (Chengere & Bekele, 2024). Ethiopia presents an interesting example where successful adaptive leadership manifests through deep community engagement and targeted capacity-building initiatives, demonstrating how leadership effectiveness hinges on careful alignment with local cultural values and norms, said Chengere and Bekele. This emerging global perspective enriches our understanding of adaptive leadership, highlighting how cultural contextualization transforms theoretical frameworks into practical, locally resonant leadership approaches that drive meaningful organizational outcomes.

Fostering an Inclusive Cultural Change

Inclusivity in the workplace refers to creating an environment where all individuals feel valued and integrated into a company's culture, regardless of their background, identity, or perspective. It is about actively inviting the contribution and participation of all employees, which enriches the organization and its work culture. In today's increasingly diverse workforce, embracing inclusivity is no longer optional, but imperative for businesses. According to the U.S. Census Bureau, a crossover of the "majority and minority" populations in the United States is predicted to occur around 2044 (Colby & Ortman, 2015). As Harvard Business Review argues, the case for diversity is already well-established. Companies in the top quartile for gender, racial, and ethnic diversity will probably have financial returns above their industry medians. Ashikali et al. (2021) claim that inclusive leadership is necessary to foster full appreciation and participation of diverse members by positively moderating the negative correlation between team ethnic and cultural diversity and inclusive climate. They argue that inclusive leadership can help to create an environment where diverse members feel valued and accepted.

This leadership style can also help reduce feelings of exclusion and marginalization, leading to greater collaboration and productivity. To reap the benefits of diversity, organizations must create a culture of inclusion where diverse perspectives are actively sought, listened to, and integrated. According to the Harvard Business Review, to fully benefit from increased diversity, organizations must adopt a learning orientation and be willing to change the corporate culture and power structure (Ely & Thomas, 2020).

Strategies for Creating an Inclusive Culture include promoting open communication, which encourages employees to share their thoughts and ideas; ensuring that everyone's voice can be heard; recognizing and respecting the different backgrounds and experiences employees bring to the table; developing hiring strategies that reach a diverse candidate pool and reduce unconscious bias in the selection process. There are consequences for ignoring cultural shifts. A stark example of the negative impacts of neglecting cultural shifts is Kodak's failure to adapt to digital photography. Despite inventing the first digital camera, Kodak clung to its traditional film-based products and failed to invest heavily in digital innovation, leading to its eventual downfall (Harvard Business Review, 2016).

Gallup's research identifies critical requirements for an inclusive culture, including:

1. Promoting open and honest communication
2. Valuing and respecting diverse opinions and experiences
3. Implementing fair hiring and advancement practices
4. Providing resources and support for underrepresented groups
5. Demonstrating commitment to inclusion at the leadership level

Building a truly inclusive organization is a moral and strategic necessity in a world that is only becoming more diverse and interconnected. It is about creating a culture where every voice matters and harnessing the power of different viewpoints and experiences to drive innovation, growth, and positive change. The companies that get this right will be the ones that thrive in the years ahead. Inclusivity is not just a moral imperative but a strategic one, essential for organizations that aim to succeed in a global and diverse marketplace.

Adaptive Leadership

In today's fast-paced, globally connected marketplace, cultural change within organizations and the broader business landscape is occurring at an unprecedented rate. The dynamics of this cultural change in organizations are increasingly influenced by the rapid pace of change in the global marketplace. As companies expand their reach across borders and industries, they face the challenge of navigating a complex web of cultural norms, values, and expectations. As businesses face new challenges and opportunities, adapting quickly becomes critical in determining an organization's success and longevity. Adaptive leadership is pivotal in guiding organizations through these cultural shifts, enabling them to remain competitive and relevant. Adaptive leadership is about understanding the complexities of the modern business environment and responding effectively to change. It involves reacting to changes, anticipating them, and preparing the organization to navigate them successfully (Hollister et al., 2021; Michaels, 2023).

Leaders who adapt their strategies and leadership styles to the evolving cultural landscape are more likely to foster innovation, resilience, and growth within their organizations. Cultural adaptability is essential for organizations because it affects every aspect of business operations, from employee engagement to customer satisfaction. A study by the University of Michigan found that companies with a positive culture outperformed their counterparts by nearly 30% (Abbas, 2022). Organizational cultural change often occurs in response to significant events or shifts in the internal or external environment. To successfully navigate a culture change, it is crucial to clearly define the problem by identifying the symptoms and their impact on the organization; assess the current culture by considering the values, interactions, trust, respect, transparency, and communication within the organization; involve all members of the organization, and reward employees who adopt the new culture to send a coherent message of commitment to the change, posits Abbas.

Moreover, 94% of executives and 88% of employees believe a distinct workplace culture is essential to business success (Lindner, 2023). This finding underscores the significance of having leaders who can cultivate and maintain an adaptive culture. Adaptive leadership plays a crucial role in navigating these cultural shifts. Leaders who can anticipate, identify, and respond to changes in the market and within their organizations are better equipped to steer their companies toward success. A study by the Center for Creative Leadership found that leaders who excel in adapting to change are three times more likely to be high-performing than those who struggle with adaptability.

Another study conducted by the Boston Consulting Group found that companies with adaptive cultures that embrace change and foster innovation achieve five times the revenue growth of their less adaptive counterparts, according to Hollister et al. (2021), and that companies focusing on culture were more likely to achieve breakthrough results in their digital transformation initiatives. The preceding highlights the significant impact that cultural adaptability can have on a company's bottom line. Furthermore, a report by Deloitte revealed that a distinct workplace culture is essential for business success, emphasizing the importance of cultivating a culture that can withstand and thrive in the face of change (Deloitte, 2020).

Moreover, a white paper by McKinsey & Company suggests that organizations with strong, adaptive cultures are more likely to attract and retain top talent, with 82% of employees stating that culture is a potential competitive advantage (McKinsey & Company, 2018). As the war for talent intensifies, companies that can show their ability to adapt and evolve are more likely to attract the best and brightest minds in their respective fields. Research suggests that the rate at which employees adapt as organizational culture changes over time is a powerful predictor of success, according to Corritore et al. (2020). Those prioritizing adaptive leadership and fostering a culture of flexibility and innovation position themselves better to navigate these shifts and achieve long-term success. The rapid pace of cultural change in today's global marketplace demands a flexible, innovative, and adaptive leadership approach. By staying attuned to the changing cultural landscape and empowering their teams to adapt accordingly, leaders can ensure that their organizations remain competitive and relevant in an increasingly dynamic business environment.

Strategies for Adaptive Leadership

Adaptive leadership is a practical framework that enables individuals and organizations to adapt to changing environments and effectively respond to recurring problems. It is a critical approach for navigating modern organizations' complex and rapidly changing landscape. It is about mobilizing people to embrace change, continually learning, and evolving, and empowering others to do the same in today's fast-paced world, where cultural shifts can happen overnight. Leaders must proactively anticipate and respond to these changes to keep their organizations relevant and thriving. Adaptive leaders are open to change and understand that it is a constant and necessary part of growth. They commit to continuous personal and organizational learning and development and foster a culture where everyone can contribute to problem-solving and innovation. Adaptive leadership stays ahead by recognizing trends and preparing for potential shifts. They articulate a vision, communicating the direction and changes needed to align the team with the organization's goals.

Adaptive leadership becomes even more critical in cultural shifts. Leaders must be attuned to their employees, customers, and stakeholders' changing values, beliefs, and expectations. They must challenge their assumptions and biases and create an inclusive environment where diverse perspectives are valued and celebrated (Agent Email List, 2023). In challenging and uncertain times, people want an authentic voice from their leaders. To feel respected and trusted, followers want to know that their leaders listen to and take their concerns seriously, are experts, and are empowered to lead and manage change (McKimm et al., 2022). Leaders can employ several practical strategies to remain adaptable in cultural shifts, including:

1. Active listening: Regularly engage with employees, customers, and stakeholders to understand their needs, concerns, and aspirations. Create open communication channels and be receptive to feedback, even when it is uncomfortable or challenging (Arcand, 2023).
2. Embrace discomfort: Step outside of your comfort zone and be willing to try new things. Encourage experimentation and risk-taking within your organization, and view failures as opportunities to learn and grow (Infozillon, 2023).
3. Experiment with alternative approaches: Be open to testing new ideas, technologies, and working methods. Encourage a culture of innovation and creativity and be willing to pivot when something is not working.
4. Build diverse teams: Surround yourself with people with different backgrounds, perspectives, and skill sets. Diverse teams are more innovative, resilient, and adaptable than homogeneous ones.
5. Invest in continuous learning: Make learning a priority for yourself and your organization. Provide opportunities for employees to develop new skills, attend training and workshops, and pursue personal and professional growth.

By embracing these strategies and principles, leaders can position themselves and their organizations to thrive in an ever-changing world. Adaptive leadership is not about having all the answers, but about being willing to ask the right questions, learn from others, and continuously evolve. It requires humility, curiosity, and a deep commitment to growth and development. With these qualities, leaders can navigate even the most complex cultural shifts and emerge more robust and resilient.

Leveraging Diversity as a Strength

Diversity encompasses a range of dimensions, including race, gender, age, and cultural background. According to Li et al. (2021), age diversity increases organizational performance by developing interpersonal relationships between employees of different age groups that help the organization build a diverse network of internal and external relationships. It is a concept that recognizes the value of differences and the unique perspectives each individual brings. The Society for Human Resource Management in 2021 emphasizes the importance of diversity in fostering a rich organizational culture that can lead to increased creativity, problem-solving, and decision-making capabilities (Graddick-Weir et al., 2021). Globally, diversity is increasingly seen as a competitive advantage.

A Forbes 2020 report highlights that diverse organizations are more likely to outperform their peers financially and are better equipped to attract and retain top talent. They are also more innovative, as they benefit from many perspectives that challenge conventional thinking (Fisk, 2021). Several organizations have successfully harnessed diversity for innovation and growth. For example, companies like Google and IBM have been recognized for their diverse workforce and inclusive culture, linked to their ability to innovate and maintain a competitive edge in the technology sector (Hewlett et al., 2013).

Strategies such as forming diverse teams, providing cross-cultural training, and implementing inclusive decision-making processes are vital to effectively leveraging diversity's power. Harvard Business Review suggests that diverse teams are more innovative and more likely to be successful because they bring different viewpoints and experiences to the forefront, leading to better problem-solving and decision-making (Harvard Business Review, 2016). In summary, diversity is not just a social imperative but a strategic one that can drive organizational success. By embracing and nurturing a diverse workforce, companies can unlock innovation, enhance performance, and secure a competitive position in the global market.

Diversity is a multifaceted concept that encompasses various dimensions such as race, gender, age, cultural background, and more. According to the Society for Human Resource Management, diversity refers to the unique characteristics and experiences that define each individual, including but not limited to race, ethnicity, gender, age, religion, disability, and sexual orientation (Bratton et al., 2021). Embracing and valuing diversity in the workplace has become increasingly important in today's globalized business environment.

Diversity can be a significant competitive advantage for organizations operating globally. As Forbes states, companies with diverse workforces are better equipped to understand and cater to the needs of diverse customer bases, leading to improved market share and profitability. Diverse teams bring together various perspectives, experiences, and skill sets, fostering creativity, innovation, and problem-solving capabilities. Several organizations have successfully leveraged diversity to drive innovation and growth.

For example, as highlighted in the Harvard Business Review (2016), L'Oreal, a global cosmetics company, has significantly promoted diversity and inclusion. The company has implemented diverse hiring practices, employee resource groups, and cross-cultural training programs, increasing innovation, employee engagement, and market share in diverse regions. To build diverse teams, leaders must intentionally create teams with individuals from different backgrounds, experiences, and perspectives, leading to more robust decision-making and innovative solutions.

Implementing cross-cultural training requires providing employees with training on cultural sensitivity and effective communication across diverse groups to foster a more inclusive and cohesive workplace. Encouraging inclusive decision-making processes ensures that diverse voices are heard and valued, leading to more comprehensive and practical solutions. Promoting employee resource groups is necessary for supporting employee-led groups to bring together individuals with shared characteristics or experiences that can provide a sense of community, mentorship opportunities, and a platform for diverse perspectives to be shared.

Regularly assessing diversity metrics, setting goals, and holding leaders accountable for progress can help ensure that diversity and inclusion remain top priorities for the organization. Organizations can foster a more innovative, adaptable, and globally competitive workforce by embracing diversity and implementing strategies to leverage its benefits. Diversity is a moral imperative and a key driver of business success in today's interconnected world.

Building Resilience for Navigating Cultural Shifts

Building resilience is essential for adaptive leadership, especially when navigating cultural shifts that often come with resistance or setbacks. Resilience allows leaders to maintain focus, drive, and optimism in facing challenges, ensuring they can effectively lead their teams through change. In today's rapidly evolving world, leaders face the constant challenge of navigating complex cultural shifts within their organizations. As society progresses and new generations enter the workforce, traditional leadership approaches may encounter resistance or setbacks. To successfully adapt and thrive in this dynamic environment, leaders must cultivate resilience: the ability to bounce back from adversity and maintain a positive outlook in the face of change.

Resilience is not merely a desirable trait but a necessity for adaptive leadership. When confronted with cultural resistance or setbacks, resilient leaders view these challenges as opportunities for growth and innovation. They understand that change is inevitable and embracing it is the key to long-term success. By fostering a culture of resilience within their organizations, adaptive leaders inspire their teams to persevere through difficult times and emerge stronger than before. Cultural shifts can be particularly challenging because they involve altering deeply ingrained beliefs and behaviors, and resistance is a natural response to such changes as people cling to the familiar. Setbacks are common, as not all attempts at change will be successful. Resilience provides the strength to persevere through these difficulties, learn from them, and emerge stronger.

One of the most potent resilience-building techniques comes from the work of renowned psychologist Carol Dweck. In her groundbreaking book, "Mindset: The New Psychology of Success," Dweck introduces the concept of a growth mindset: the belief that abilities and intelligence can be developed through dedication and hard work. Leaders with a growth mindset view setbacks as temporary learning experiences rather than permanent failures. They encourage their teams to embrace challenges, learn from mistakes, and continuously improve. Resilience-building techniques include:

1. Encouraging a growth mindset, emphasizing that skills can be developed through effort and learning from setbacks (Dweck, 2016).
2. Building strong support networks that provide emotional and practical help during change (Cross et al., 2021).
3. Practicing adaptive leadership by staying open to new information, being willing to adjust strategies, and maintaining transparency with their teams, according to Ramalingam et al. (2020).

In psychology, Carol Dweck's concept of a growth mindset is particularly relevant for resilience-building techniques. A growth mindset is a belief that abilities and intelligence can be developed through dedication and hard work (Dweck, 2016). This perspective encourages resilience by viewing challenges as growth opportunities rather than insurmountable obstacles. Organizational behavior literature also offers insights into building resilience. Strong relationships and networks have been shown to enable resilience by providing support and helping individuals see a path forward (Cross et al., 2021).

According to Ramalingam and colleagues, adaptive leadership principles suggest expecting future needs, adapting responses based on continuous learning, and showing accountability. Organizational behavior literature also emphasizes the importance of resilience in leadership. Research has shown that resilient leaders are more effective at managing stress, adapting to change, and inspiring their teams to achieve their goals. They create psychologically safe environments where employees feel comfortable taking risks, expressing ideas, and learning from failures. Adaptive leaders foster a sense of shared purpose and commitment to organizational success by modeling resilience and promoting a culture of continuous learning.

Leaders must also prioritize self-care and emotional intelligence to build resilience in cultural shifts. They must recognize their emotional responses to change and develop strategies for managing stress and maintaining a positive outlook. This may involve practicing mindfulness, seeking support from mentors or peers, and taking time for reflection and self-discovery. Leaders become better equipped to support their teams through challenging times by investing in their resilience. As the world continues to change at an unprecedented pace, resilient leadership is the key to unlocking the full potential of individuals and organizations alike. Resilience is not just about bouncing back; it is about using the experience of adversity to propel oneself and one's organization forward. By embracing a growth mindset and adaptive leadership principles, leaders can navigate cultural shifts successfully and build a resilient organizational culture.

Entrepreneurial Resilience and Growth

In the dynamic landscape of entrepreneurial development, adaptive leadership emerges as a critical factor for fostering business resilience and sustainable growth, which is particularly clear in emerging markets. Research from Nairobi City County, Kenya, demonstrates how entrepreneurial competencies, including risk-taking, leadership acumen, innovative thinking, and networking capabilities, are fundamental drivers of growth within micro and small enterprises (Owino & Namusonge, 2024). This finding aligns with comprehensive studies in Botswana that illuminate how the interplay of entrepreneurial, manufacturing SMEs' growth and sustainability are shaped by both firm-specific and exogenous factors (Munodawafa et al., 2024).

The entrepreneurial path, however, remains marked by significant hurdles that need strategic navigation and resilience. Access to financial resources continues to pose a substantial barrier, particularly in developing economies where capital markets may be less mature (Munodawafa et al., 2024). Entrepreneurs must also contend with complex regulatory environments that frequently evolve, creating additional hurdles for business expansion and strategic planning, according to Munodawafa and colleagues. Furthermore, the intensifying global competition for talent has elevated the challenge of attracting and retaining skilled professionals, requiring entrepreneurs to develop innovative approaches to human capital management (Ali et al., 2023). Entrepreneurial resilience also requires cultivating cultural intelligence.

Cultural intelligence, a pivotal element in adaptive leadership, causes leaders to cultivate a nuanced understanding and adaptability to diverse cultural norms, values, and communication patterns (Iriogbe et al., 2024; Taqwiem et al., 2024). Leaders with robust cultural intelligence are adept at fostering inclusive workplace environments and enhancing team performance in multinational settings. This is primarily achieved through their adeptness in adapting leadership approaches and communication styles, as posited by Iriogbe and coauthors. Research consistently underscores the unique advantages of culturally intelligent leaders in managing the complex dynamics of multinational teams. Their proficiency in leveraging cultural diversity as a catalyst for innovation and organizational success is a testament to their effectiveness, as Iriogbe and colleagues argue. These leaders thrive by nurturing a profound awareness of cultural differences, maintaining flexible leadership styles, and implementing effective cross-cultural communication strategies.

Adaptation and Innovation

Traditional leadership models fall short in an era of turbulence, uncertainty, and rapid change. Hierarchical, command-and-control approaches no longer suffice. Instead, adaptive leadership emerges as a powerful paradigm that enables organizations to thrive amidst cultural shifts. According to Hall (2023; Torres et al., 2010), the trends driving the need for adaptive leadership include:

1. **Continuity and Uncertainty**

In today's world, it is impossible to predict the future, so leaders must chart a course regardless of the outcome. They must decide based on current conditions and trends rather than what they expect to happen in the future. This way, they can adjust their plans and strategies as needed to ensure that the organization remains successful.

2. **A network of interdependent ecosystems**

Companies operate in complex networks, boundaries blur, and collaboration becomes vital; hence, who leads whom in this multifaceted system? Companies rely on each other for resources, expertise, and customers. As such, they need strong relationships and collaborative networks to succeed. Companies must identify who is most capable of leading them in this environment. They must also set clear roles and responsibilities to ensure the network runs smoothly.

3. **Transition to a digital world**

As every business becomes an information business, leaders must be adept at deciphering signals and acting swiftly. As businesses become more reliant on data, they need to quickly analyze and interpret the data to make decisions that will have a lasting impact. This transition requires leaders to be quick on their feet and agile in responding to changes in the business environment.

4. **The impact on the environment and society**

Companies' strategies must align with the concerns of society and the environment at large. They must consider the impact of their actions on the environment and strive to create sustainable solutions that benefit all stakeholders.

5. **Trust Attrition**

Adaptive leadership is essential to restoring society's trust in businesses. This leadership involves understanding the needs of all stakeholders, responding to those needs efficiently and effectively, being transparent about the decisions being made, and allowing firms to rebuild trust by being accountable and responsive to the community's needs.

6. **Diverse Competition**

Adapting leadership approaches to varying challenges is crucial for leaders, wrote Torres et al. (2010). They argue that different leadership styles are appropriate for various situations. For example, a more authoritarian style may be more suitable when faced with a crisis. In contrast, a more inclusive and collaborative style may be more appropriate when dealing with long-term planning.

Adaptive leaders create conditions for dynamic networks to achieve common goals amid uncertainty. They embrace uncertainty, adopt alternative approaches, and read the right signals; they foster cognitive diversity and empathize across boundaries. They collaborate beyond functional silos, influence stakeholders across the ecosystem, enable others to adapt, and encourage experimentation and learning. There are examples of companies that thrive in diverse cultural landscapes. These organizations include General Electric (G.E.), which embarked on a transformational journey and embraced Silicon Valley practices. They prioritize digital transformation, effective change management, and employee engagement. G.E. uses strategies that foster agility, communication, and talent development. Their shift from a traditional corporate culture to an agile, innovative one exemplifies adaptive leadership (Hall, 2023). Apple, under the leadership of Steve Jobs's reinventions, is legendary. Apple consistently adapted to cultural shifts from Macintosh to iPod, iPhone, and iPad. Their commitment to innovation and user-centric design drives success. Jobs himself epitomized continuous learning. His curiosity, creativity, and learning enthusiasm fueled Apple's adaptive journey (Triangle I.P., 2023).

Amazon is a prime example of a company with a culture of innovation that thrives by pushing boundaries. Their relentless focus on customer experience, experimentation, and disruptive technologies exemplifies adaptive leadership. Jeff Bezos prioritizes learning, even in the face of failure. His famous quote, "Your margin is my opportunity," reflects Amazon's adaptive mindset (The Agile Company, 2023). Adaptive leaders must embrace lifelong learning. Continuous growth sharpens their ability to navigate cultural shifts. Whether through formal education, mentorship, or self-reflection, adaptive leaders remain curious, open-minded, and agile.

Adaptive leadership is not about heroism but creating conditions for collective success. As cultural landscapes evolve, adaptive leaders thrive by staying curious and fostering collaboration and change. Adaptation and innovation are not merely business strategies; they are the lifeblood of companies seeking to navigate the ever-shifting cultural landscapes of the global market. Resilience and foresight define adaptive leadership facing constant change. The importance of continuous adaptation and innovation cannot be overstated. They are the engines that drive businesses forward, allowing them to stay ahead of cultural shifts and emerging trends.

Companies that master this art do not just survive; they thrive, setting the pace for others to follow. The path to enduring success in today's dynamic cultural environment is paved with the stones of adaptation and innovation. Companies like Apple show that strong leadership and embracing change allow companies to thrive and transform during cultural shifts. For adaptive leaders, the journey of continuous learning and personal development is not just a professional mandate, but a personal creed that drives them to new heights of achievement.

GAPS IN EXISTING RESEARCH AND CONSEQUENCES OF ADAPTIVE LEADERSHIP

While expanding, the current literature on adaptive leadership and cultural shifts reveals significant research gaps that warrant attention from scholars and practitioners. A notable limitation lies in the scarcity of empirical studies that establish clear connections between specific management practices and performance outcomes within culturally diverse environments (Iriogbe et al., 2024). This gap is particularly pronounced in non-Western contexts and developing economies, where unique cultural dynamics may influence leadership effectiveness differently than in Western settings (Chengere & Bekele, 2024). The absence of comprehensive longitudinal studies further constrains our understanding of how adaptive leadership strategies shape organizational culture and performance over extended periods.

Implementing adaptive leadership approaches during cultural shifts generates multifaceted financial, social, and environmental impacts. Organizations often experience enhanced financial performance through improved team cohesion and productivity, though they must initially invest in leadership development and cultural adaptation programs (Iriogbe et al., 2024). On the social front, diverse work environments led by adaptive leaders typically show higher levels of employee engagement and job satisfaction, fostering stronger multicultural team dynamics (Ali et al., 2023). Additionally, adaptive leaders appear better equipped to champion sustainable business practices that harmonize with varied cultural values and address global environmental concerns, suggesting a broader positive impact beyond immediate organizational boundaries.

CONCLUSION: SUMMARY AND RECOMMENDATIONS

This academic chapter thoroughly examines adaptive leadership's role in managing organizational cultural shifts within an increasingly globalized business landscape. The analysis shows how effective adaptive leadership practices can enhance financial performance, team cohesion, and innovation capabilities while highlighting essential research gaps, particularly in non-Western contexts and developing economies. The chapter emphasizes that organizational cultural dynamics reflect shared values, beliefs, and practices that shape interactions, behaviors, and market positioning. Cultural shifts are driven by multiple factors, including globalization, generational differences, and technological advancement, requiring organizations to adapt continuously to maintain competitiveness. These shifts fundamentally alter how organizations operate and compete in the global marketplace.

Building on the foundational work of Ronald Heifetz and Marty Linsky at Harvard Kennedy School, the chapter outlines how adaptive leadership helps organizations navigate complex changes without clear-cut solutions. The framework emphasizes distinguishing between technical and adaptive challenges, maintaining a broad perspective to understand resistance patterns, creating safe spaces for diverse voices, and empowering others in the transformation process. This approach recognizes that cultural changes require fundamental values and behavior shifts rather than simple technical solutions.

The research strongly emphasizes that inclusivity is both a moral and strategic imperative. Organizations must create environments that promote open communication, value diverse opinions and experiences, and implement fair hiring practices. This includes supporting underrepresented groups and showing consistent leadership commitment to inclusion. The chapter argues that organizations fostering inclusive cultures are better positioned to innovate and compete in the global marketplace.

Organizational resilience emerges as a crucial theme throughout the chapter. The research advocates for encouraging a growth mindset, building strong support networks, and practicing adaptive leadership principles while maintaining team transparency. These elements combine to create organizations capable of weathering cultural shifts and emerging stronger. The emphasis on continuous learning is a fundamental component of building and maintaining this resilience. Recent research from various global contexts, including Ethiopia and Kenya, demonstrates how adaptive leadership manifests differently across cultures. This global perspective highlights the importance of deep community engagement, cultural intelligence, local context adaptation, and cross-cultural communication skills. These findings emphasize the need for leaders to possess advanced cultural understanding and adaptation in their leadership approaches.

The chapter identifies several significant research gaps in the current literature. Limited empirical studies connect management practices to performance outcomes in culturally diverse environments. Additionally, insufficient research exists in non-Western contexts and developing economies, and there is a notable lack of comprehensive longitudinal studies on adaptive leadership impacts. These gaps present opportunities for future research to enhance our understanding of adaptive leadership in various cultural contexts. The research provides valuable practical implications for organizations. It underlines the importance of investing in leadership development and cultural adaptation initiatives to achieve success. Organizations must regularly assess and adjust their cultural initiatives while focusing on short-term adaptation and long-term resilience building. The research strongly advocates continuous learning and development at all organizational levels as a key factor in successful cultural transformation.

The chapter asserts that adaptive leadership is essential for organizational success in today's dynamic environment, though implementation requires substantial investment in leadership development and cultural adaptation programs. Organizations implementing adaptive leadership practices are better positioned to navigate complex cultural transitions, foster innovation and creativity, build resilient teams, maintain competitive advantage, and drive sustainable growth. This comprehensive analysis provides valuable insights for organizational leaders, management scholars, and practitioners seeking to understand and implement effective strategies for cultural transformation in today's complex business environment. This study contributes significantly to understanding how companies can effectively navigate cultural shifts while maintaining operational excellence and fostering innovation. The findings suggest that success in the global marketplace increasingly depends on an organization's ability to adapt to and thrive within changing cultural landscapes, making adaptive leadership an essential capability for modern organizations.

As organizations master the complexities of cultural transformation through adaptive leadership, they simultaneously encounter an equally formidable challenge: the rapid acceleration of technological change. The intersection of cultural adaptability and technological innovation creates a unique leadership imperative, where success depends on navigating organizational culture and embracing digital transformation. This developing landscape demands leaders who can synthesize traditional leadership principles with emerging technological capabilities, creating a foundation for sustainable organizational growth in an increasingly digital world.

REFERENCES

Abbas, T. (2022). What is Culture Change in an Organization and How to Implement it? *Umar Tahir*. https://changemanagementinsight.com/culture-change-in-an-organization/

Agent Email List. (2023). Embrace Experimentation and Learning. *Agent Email List*. https://agentemaillist.com/embrace-experimentation/

Ali, R., Ateeq, A. A., Al Ani, Z., & Ahmed Ali, S. (2023). A Critical Review of Contemporary Trends and Challenges in Human Resource Management. In *IJIHRM* 04 (02), pp. 22–27. DOI: DOI: 10.46988/IJIHRM.04.02.2023.003

Arcand, J. (2023). How To Manage Business Relationships. *Work It Daily*. https://www.workitdaily.com/how-to-manage-business-relationships

Ashikali, T., Groeneveld, S., & Kuipers, B. (2021). The Role of Inclusive Leadership in Supporting an Inclusive Climate in Diverse Public Sector Teams. *Review of Public Personnel Administration*, 41(3), 497–519. DOI: 10.1177/0734371X19899722

Bain & Company. (2020). *The Power of Adaptive Leadership in Times of Crisis*.

Besley, T., & Persson, T. (2022). Organizational dynamics: culture, design, and performance. *The Journal of Law, Economics, and Organization*, Article ewac020. Bratton online publication. DOI: 10.1093/jleo/ewac020

Bratton, J., Gold, J., Bratton, A., & Steele, L. (2021). *Human resource management*. Bloomsbury Publishing.

Chengere, K., & Bekele, M. (2024). Cross-Cultural Leadership and Diversity: A Comprehensive Literature Review. In *SI* 12 (6), Article 2022096, pp. 109–112. DOI: DOI: 10.11648/j.si.20241206.14

Colby, S. L., & Ortman, J. M. (2015). Projections of the Size and Composition of the U.S. Population: 2014 to 2060. Population Estimates and Projections. [*U.S. Census Bureau.*]. *Current Population Reports. Series P-28, Special Censuses*, •••, 25–1143.

Corritore, M., Goldberg, A., & Srivastava, S. B. (2020). *The New Analytics of Culture*. Harvard Business Review. https://hbr.org/2020/01/the-new-analytics-of-culture

Cross, R., Dillon, K., & Greenberg, D. (2021). *The Secret to Building Resilience*. Harvard Business Review. https://hbr.org/2021/01/the-secret-to-building-resilience

Deloitte (2020). *The future of work in the wake of COVID-19*.

Deloitte (2021). *The Culture Imperative: Building a High-Performance Organization*.

Dweck, C. S. (2006). *Mindset: The new psychology of success.* Random House.

Ely, R. J., & Thomas, D. A. (2020). *Getting Serious About Diversity: Enough Already with the Business Case.* Harvard Business Review. https://hbr.org/2020/11/getting-serious-about-diversity-enough-already-with-the-business-case

Fisk, L. (2021). Embracing Diversity And Inclusion As A Sustainable, Competitive Advantage. *Forbes.* https://www.forbes.com/sites/forbesbusinesscouncil/2021/01/04/embracing-diversity-and-inclusion-as-a-sustainable-competitive-advantage/?sh=507c55892642

Graddick-Weir, M., Hakel, M. M., Jacobs, R., & Smart, J. B. (2021). NAHRSIOPDI Themes Key Questions and Research Alternatives_final. https://nahr.shrm.org/sites/default/files/NAHRSIOPDI%20Themes%20Key%20Questions%20and%20Research%20Alternatives_final.pdf

Groysberg, B., Lee, J., Price, J., & Cheng, J. (2018). *The Leader's Guide to Corporate Culture.*

Hall, A. (2023). G.E.'s Cultural Shift: Embracing Innovation and Change. *Aaron Hall.* https://aaronhall.com/insights/ges-cultural-shift-embracing-innovation-and-change/

Harvard Business Review (2016). *Leading a Successful Cultural Transformation at Your Organization.* https://hbr.org/2016/07/kodaks-downfall-wasnt-about-technology

Hewlett, S. A., Marshall, M., & Sherbin, L. (2013). *How Diversity Can Drive Innovation.* Harvard Business Review. https://hbr.org/2013/12/how-diversity-can-drive-innovation

Hollister, R., Tecosky, K., Watkins, M., & Wolpert, C. (2021). *Why Every Executive Should Be Focusing on Culture Change Now.*

Infozillon. (2023). *Mastering Personal Growth but how?!* https://infozillon.com/self-management/118-mastering-personal-growth-but-how.html

Iriogbe, H. O., Ebeh, C. O., & Onita, F. B. (2024). Multinational team leadership in the marine sector: A review of cross-cultural management practices. In *Int. j. manag. entrep. res* 6 (8), pp. 2731–2757. DOI: . v6i8.1416.DOI: 10.51594/ijmer

Knittel, E. M., Berdugo, J. D., Cheevavichawalkul, K., & Imbach, M. (2019). The Lafarge-Holcim merger negotiations. *European Journal of International Management,* 13(5), 612–636. DOI: 10.1504/EJIM.2019.102027

Li, Y., Gong, Y., Burmeister, A., Wang, M., Alterman, V., Alonso, A., & Robinson, S. (2021). Leveraging age diversity for organizational performance: An intellectual capital perspective. *The Journal of Applied Psychology*, 106(1), 71–91. DOI: 10.1037/apl0000497 PMID: 32202816

Lindner, J. (2023). Workplace Culture Statistics: Market Report & Data • MeetingFever. *MeetingFever.Com*. https://meetingfever.com/statistics/workplace-culture/

Liu, J. L., Harkness, S., & Super, C. M. (2020). Chinese Mothers' Cultural Models of Children's Shyness: Ethnotheories and Socialization Strategies in the Context of Social Change. *New Directions for Child and Adolescent Development*, 2020(170), 69–92. DOI: 10.1002/cad.20340 PMID: 32431073

McKimm, J., Ramani, S., Forrest, K., Bishop, J., Findyartini, A., Mills, C., Hassanien, M., Al-Hayani, A., Jones, P., Nadarajah, V. D., & Radu, G. (2023). Adaptive leadership during challenging times: Effective strategies for health professions educators: Amee Guide No. 148. *Medical Teacher*, 45(2), 128–138. DOI: 10.1080/0142159X.2022.2057288 PMID: 35543323

McKinsey (2021). *The Digital Culture Challenge: Closing the Employee-Leadership Gap*.

McKinsey & Company. (2018). *Delivering through diversity*.

Michaels, G. (2023). *What is adaptive leadership: examples and principles: Work Life by Atlassian*. https://www.atlassian.com/blog/leadership/adaptive-leadership

Moodian, M. A. (2013). *Contemporary Leadership and Intercultural Competence: Exploring the Cross-Cultural Dynamics Within Organizations* (1st ed.). SAGE Publications; ProQuest.

Munodawafa, T., Naude, M., & Govender, K. K. (2024): Assuring the Sustainability and Growth of Small and Medium-Sized Manufacturing Enterprises in Botswana: An Exploratory Study. In *IJEFI* 14 (4), pp. 253–266. DOI: DOI: 10.32479/ijefi.16632

Owino, P. O., & Namusonge, M. (2024): Risk-taking, Leadership, Innovation, and Networking as Entrepreneurial Competencies of Growth of Micro and Small Enterprises in Nairobi City County in Kenya. In *theijhss*. DOI: DOI: 10.24940/theijhss/2023/v11/i11/HS2311-002

PwC (2021). *The Workforce of the Future: The Competing Forces Shaping 2030*.

Ramalingam, B., Nabarro, D., Oqubay, A., Carnall, D. R., & Wild, L. (2020). *5 Principles to Guide Adaptive Leadership*. https://hbr.org/2020/09/5-principles-to-guide-adaptive-leadership

Schein, E., & Schein, H. P. A. (2019). *A New Era for Culture, Change, and Leadership*. MIT Sloan Management Review. https://sloanreview.mit.edu/article/a-new-era-for-culture-change-and-leadership/

Segovia-Martín, J., Walker, B., Fay, N., & Tamariz, M. (2020). Network Connectivity Dynamics, Cognitive Biases, and the Evolution of Cultural Diversity in Round-Robin Interactive Micro-Societies. *Cognitive Science*, 44(7), e12852. DOI: 10.1111/cogs.12852 PMID: 32564420

Taqwiem, A., & Arpianto, Y. Faradina, Luthfiyanti, L., & Susanti, P. A. (2024): Cross-Cultural Leadership Models in Global Education Systems Implications for Policy and Practice. In *Intl. J. Rel.* 5 (11), pp. 7343–7353. DOI: DOI: 10.61707/1zwc2a56

The Agile Company. (2023). *Fostering a Culture of Innovation: Lessons from Leading Companies*. https://theagilecompany.org/fostering-a-culture-of-innovation/

Torres, R., Reeves, M., & Love, C. (2010). Adaptive Leadership. *BCG Global*. https://www.bcg.com/publications/2010/leadership-engagement-culture-adaptive-leadership

Triangle, I. P. (2023). *10 Trailblazing Companies Leading the Way in Innovative Culture : Triangle I.P.* https://triangleip.com/companies-leading-innovation-culture/

ADDITIONAL READING

Core Leadership Texts Moodian, M. A. (2013). "Contemporary Leadership and Intercultural Competence: Exploring the Cross-Cultural Dynamics Within Organizations"

Core Leadership Texts Schein, E., & Schein, P. A. (2019). *The Culture Era: A New Era for Culture*. Change, and Leadership.

Harvard Business Review Articles. (2013). *"How Diversity Can Drive Innovation"* by Hewlett. Marshall & Sherbin.

Harvard Business Review Articles. (2020). *"The New Analytics of Culture"* by Corritore. Goldberg & Srivastava.

Bratton, J., Gold, J., Bratton, A., & Steele, L. (2021)… *Human Resource Management*.

Research Reports and Industry Studies Bain & Company (2020). "The Power of Adaptive Leadership in Times of Crisis"

Research Reports and Industry Studies Deloitte (2021). "The Culture Imperative: Building a High-Performance Organization"

Research Reports and Industry Studies PwC (2021). "The Workforce of the Future: The Competing Forces Shaping 2030"

Research Reports and Industry StudiesMcKinsey & Company. (2018). Delivering through. *Diversity*.

KEY TERMS AND DEFINITIONS

Active Listening: A leadership skill involving fully concentrating, understanding, responding, and remembering what is being said while acknowledging the emotions and perspectives of team members.

Adaptive Leadership: A sophisticated leadership approach that helps organizations navigate complex changes without clear-cut solutions, emphasizing the distinction between technical and adaptive challenges while requiring fundamental changes in values, beliefs, and behaviors.

Cross-Cultural Training: Educational programs designed to provide employees with cultural sensitivity awareness and effective communication skills across diverse groups to foster a more inclusive workplace.

Cultural Adaptability: The capacity of an organization to adjust its practices, policies, and approaches in response to changing cultural contexts and requirements.

Cultural Dynamics: The shared values, beliefs, and practices that shape interactions and behaviors within an organization, determining how it responds to internal and external challenges and positions itself in the market.

Cultural Intelligence: The ability of leaders to develop sophisticated awareness and responsiveness to diverse cultural norms, values, and communication patterns across cultural boundaries, enabling effective leadership in multinational contexts.

Cultural Integration: The process of bringing together different cultural elements within an organization, particularly important in international mergers and acquisitions.

Cultural Shift: A fundamental change in organizational values, beliefs, and practices, often driven by factors such as globalization, generational differences, and technological advancement.

Digital Transformation: Integrating digital technology into all business areas, fundamentally changing how organizations operate and deliver customer value while necessitating cultural adaptation.

Diversity Management: The practice of supporting and promoting a diverse workplace through various initiatives, policies, and cultural practices.

Entrepreneurial Resilience: The capacity of business leaders to maintain and grow their enterprises despite challenges, incorporating risk-taking, leadership acumen, innovative thinking, and networking capabilities.

Growth Mindset: A belief system, developed by Carol Dweck, that abilities and intelligence can be developed through dedication, hard work, and learning from setbacks rather than being fixed traits.

Inclusive Culture: An organizational environment where all individuals feel valued and integrated regardless of their background, identity, or perspective, actively inviting contribution and participation from all employees.

In-group Altruism: A preference for helping or favoring members of one's group over others, which can sometimes conflict with the goals of inclusive culture in globalization.

Innovation Capabilities: An organization's ability to consistently create new ideas, products, or processes, often enhanced by diverse perspectives and inclusive cultural practices.

Market Dynamics: The forces and factors influencing market behavior and performance, including cultural shifts affecting consumer behavior and organizational strategies.

Organizational Resilience: An organization's ability to bounce back from adversity and maintain positive momentum while navigating cultural shifts and changes.

Sustainable Growth: A business expansion considering long-term viability, including cultural, social, and environmental factors alongside financial performance.

Team Cohesion: The degree to which team members work together effectively and maintain positive relationships, influenced by cultural factors and leadership approaches.

Chapter 4
Embracing Technological Innovation:
Leading in the Digital Age

ABSTRACT

This chapter explores the critical role of digital transformation in modern organizations, focusing on leadership strategies, value alignment, and stakeholder engagement in the digital age. A comprehensive review of literature and case studies examines how leaders can craft compelling visions, revolutionize leadership approaches, and leverage digital storytelling for effective communication. The chapter emphasizes the importance of role-modeling digital behaviors, fostering innovation, and continuously evaluating and adapting organizational strategies. It highlights the Balanced Scorecard framework as a tool for measuring success in digital transformation. Findings underscore the need for digital literacy, cross-functional collaboration, and ethical considerations in technology adoption. While providing a thorough theoretical overview, the chapter is limited by its lack of primary research. Recommendations include implementing comprehensive digital literacy programs and fostering a culture of experimentation.

INTRODUCTION

With unprecedented technological advancement and digital transformation, organizations face the critical challenge of adapting their leadership approaches while maintaining their core values and vision. This chapter examines the intricate relationship between technological innovation and organizational leadership in the digital age, where the convergence of traditional business principles and digital capabilities has become essential for sustainable success. As organizations navigate this complex landscape, leaders must develop new competencies, foster digital

DOI: 10.4018/979-8-3693-5553-4.ch004

Copyright © 2025, IGI Global Scientific Publishing. Copying or distributing in print or electronic forms without written permission of IGI Global is prohibited.

literacy, and create adaptive frameworks that enable their organizations to thrive amid constant change.

The digital revolution has fundamentally altered how organizations operate, communicate, and deliver value to stakeholders, from artificial intelligence and cloud computing to big data analytics and digital platforms. Technological innovations are reshaping traditional business models and creating new opportunities for growth and invention. However, successful digital transformation requires more than merely adopting new technologies; it demands a holistic approach encompassing strategic alignment, cultural transformation, and stakeholder engagement.

This chapter comprehensively examines how organizations can effectively lead in the digital age while maintaining their organizational values and vision. Through analysis of empirical research, case studies, and emerging trends, it explores various dimensions of digital leadership, including stakeholder management, employee development, and strategic vision implementation. Special attention is given to measuring success through balanced scorecards and iterative improvement processes, as well as the importance of fostering employee engagement and developing digital competencies while maintaining ethical standards. The research presented here shows that successful digital leadership requires a delicate balance between embracing technological innovation and maintaining organizational authenticity, ultimately contributing to our understanding of effective leadership in an increasingly digital world.

CRAFTING A COMPELLING VISION FOR THE DIGITAL AGE

In this era of digital metamorphosis, groundbreaking technologies are reshaping the commercial landscape, unveiling many opportunities for enterprises. To survive and flourish in this dynamic milieu, organizations must cultivate a captivating vision that resonates with the digital era's zeitgeist and harnesses the potential of nascent technologies. This paradigm shift entails the seamless integration of digital technologies across all facets of business operations. From streamlining processes to revolutionizing customer interactions and decision-making protocols, digital transformation is the linchpin of organizational success. By wholeheartedly embracing this shift, enterprises can amplify their efficiency, agility, and innovative prowess, which enables them to pivot swiftly in response to mercurial market conditions and developing consumer demands (Chotipurk et al., 2023; El Badawy et al., 2015; Fang & Gong, 2023).

In this digital renaissance, data reigns supreme as an invaluable asset. It fuels informed decision-making and strategic planning and empowers organizations to gain prescient insights, identify developing trends, and make data-driven decisions that propel growth and competitiveness. Cultivating a data-centric culture is not just important; it is empowering, as it encourages the collection, analysis, and utilization of data from myriad sources, including emergent technologies like the Internet of Things, artificial intelligence, and big data analytics (El Badawy et al., 2015; Fang & Gong, 2023; Sinka, 2024).

The breakneck pace of technological advancement necessitates a culture of innovation and agility within organizations. This approach should encourage trying new things, viewing mistakes as learning opportunities, and enabling employees to be creative. By fostering an innovative and nimble mindset, organizations cannot just stay ahead of the curve but also anticipate and adapt to emerging trends and continuously refine their products, services, and processes, inspiring a sense of motivation and drive (Forster, 2006; Lakkhongkha et al., 2023).

In this digital age, human capital is the cornerstone of success. Organizations must prioritize the development of a skilled and adaptable workforce through investments in training and upskilling programs.

These initiatives should equip employees with the digital acumen to leverage emerging technologies effectively. Moreover, cultivating a learning culture that encourages continuous professional development is crucial for maintaining a competitive edge (Mardiani & Utami, 2023; Sinka, 2024). The digital revolution has ushered in unprecedented levels of connectivity and collaboration. Organizations must capitalize on this interconnectedness by fostering collaborative environments that encourage knowledge sharing, cross-functional teamwork, and partnerships with external stakeholders. This collaborative approach enables organizations to tap into diverse perspectives, leverage collective intelligence, and drive innovation (Gorichanaz, 2021; Rogers, 2011).

As emerging technologies continue to shape the business landscape, organizations must prioritize sustainability and social responsibility. This commitment involves adopting environmentally friendly practices and promoting technology's ethical and responsible use. By embracing sustainability and social responsibility, organizations can build trust with stakeholders, enhance their brand reputation, and contribute to a more equitable future.

Values: The Digital Compass

In the digital landscape, organizational values serve as a lodestar, guiding principles that shape an enterprise's culture, decision-making processes, and overall behavior. These values take on heightened significance as they help organizations navigate the complexities and rapid changes brought about by technological advancements. Organizational values function as an abstract compass, providing a framework for employees at all levels to make choices that align with the company's core beliefs.

This framework is crucial in the digital age, where decisions must be made swiftly and autonomously. Values define what an organization stands for and how stakeholders perceive it, emphasizing each employee's role in maintaining its image in an era of heightened transparency (Williams, 2016).

These values form the bedrock of an organization's culture, influencing how employees interact, collaborate, and approach their work (McNaughton, 2003). This cultural foundation is essential for fostering innovation and adaptability in the digital era, inspiring everyone to embrace the potential of technological advancements. Moreover, values provide an ethical framework, guide behavior, and ensure that actions align with the company's moral standards. This is particularly important in the digital landscape, where ethical considerations around data privacy and AI constantly evolve (Suar & Khuntia, 2010). Aligning organizational values with the digital landscape is critical. Organizations must emphasize values that promote adaptability, innovation, and continuous learning (Purnomo & Sri Pudjiarti, 2024). With increased digital connectivity, Williams (2016) argues that prioritizing values that foster transparency and build stakeholder trust is crucial; they encourage collaboration and connectivity, which are essential in a landscape where teamwork often transcends geographical boundaries.

Organizations should incorporate values that address the ethical use of data and respect for privacy, as these are paramount concerns in the digital age (Wiley, 2021). Digital technologies enable more direct and personalized customer interactions and values, emphasizing customer-centricity and responsiveness and allowing greater awareness of global issues. (Nuijten et al., 2017) argue that organizations should consider values that reflect their commitment to sustainability and social responsibility. Implementing values in the digital landscape requires clear communication across digital platforms, ensuring consistency in messaging and actions, posits Williams (2016). Leaders must embody the organization's values in their digital presence and decision-making, setting an example for employees, according to (McNaughton, 2003). Using digital tools and platforms to reinforce and measure adherence to organizational values is crucial (Gonçalves et al., 2023), as is regularly assessing and updating values to ensure they remain relevant in the rapidly evolving digital landscape, argue Purnomo and Sri Pudjiarti (2024).

Organizational values are guiding principles in the digital landscape, providing a framework for decision-making, ethical behavior, and collaboration. By aligning these values with the demands of the digital era and implementing them effectively, organizations can navigate the complexities of the modern business environment while maintaining their core identity and principles. As the digital landscape continues to strengthen, the role of values in guiding organizational behavior and strategy will only become more critical, serving as a beacon in the ever-changing sea of technological advancement (Carnochan & Austin, 2002).

Revolutionizing Leadership in the Digital Age

In today's rapidly evolving digital landscape, leadership must be pivotal in shaping organizational culture and spearheading digital transformation. The crux of effective leadership lies in embodying the digital mindset and behaviors expected from their teams. This quintessential role modeling is not merely a suggestion, but an imperative. Why is leadership role modeling so crucial? It sets a powerful precedent. When leaders show digital fluency, they cultivate an environment where innovation flourishes. This exemplary behavior engenders credibility and trust, catalyzing team members to embrace digital initiatives wholeheartedly (Arifin & Purwanti, 2022; Azra, 2023; Sari et al., 2023).

Moreover, leaders who embody digital behaviors become the vanguard of organizational change. Their actions serve as a lodestar, illuminating the path towards digital adaptation and accelerating transformation. This leadership approach fosters innovation and empowers team members to explore novel ideas and pioneer solutions in today's volatile business milieu, in which agility is paramount. Leaders who model digital behaviors imbue their organizations with the nimbleness of responding swiftly to change (Arifin & Purwanti, 2022; Azra, 2023; Saeid et al., 2023). McKinsey's research on adaptive leadership underscores the significance of leaders exhibiting agility, curiosity, and adaptability. These attributes are indispensable for navigating the labyrinthine complexities of the digital era. Agility enables leaders to pivot strategies amidst uncertainty, deciding based on incomplete information. Curiosity manifests as an insatiable thirst for knowledge, continuously seeking new perspectives. This intellectual voracity drives innovation and propels organizations to the forefront of their industries. Adaptability, the ability to change course in the face of new challenges or opportunities, is crucial for traversing the ever-shifting digital terrain (Azra, 2023; Coetzee et al., 2020; Han et al., 2022).

By embodying these qualities, leaders forge a culture of perpetual learning and improvement within their organizations. This is especially vital in digital transformation, where technologies and best practices are constantly in flux. Furthermore, leaders with a digital mindset and adaptive behaviors are better equipped to identify and harness emergent technologies that benefit the organization. They excel at dismantling silos and fostering cross-functional collaboration, which is essential for successful digital initiatives (Arifin & Purwanti, 2022; Azra, 2023; Sari et al., 2023). These forward-thinking leaders nurture a culture of experimentation and calculated risk-taking among team members. They skillfully navigate the ethical labyrinth and potential pitfalls associated with digital technologies. Perhaps crucially, they build organizational resilience to withstand disruptions and capitalize on new opportunities (Azra, 2023; Coetzee et al., 2020; Gu & Liu, 2022; Saeid et al., 2023).

In reality, leadership role modeling is the linchpin of successful digital transformation and adaptive leadership. Leaders can effectively steer their organizations through the tumultuous waters of the digital age by personifying the digital mindset and behaviors they expect from their teams and showing agility, curiosity, and adaptability. This approach not only fuels innovation and organizational performance but also engenders a culture of continuous learning and improvement, the bedrock of long-term success in today's mercurial business landscape (Arifin & Purwanti, 2022; Azra, 2023; Saeid et al., 2023; Sari et al., 2023).

Communication Channels with Digital Storytelling

Digital storytelling has revolutionized organizational communication. Social media platforms like Facebook, Twitter, LinkedIn, and Instagram have become indispensable tools for disseminating company visions and values. These dynamic platforms offer unparalleled real-time interaction and feedback opportunities, facilitating interactive content creation that galvanizes employee and stakeholder participation (Zulkifli, 2023). Creating compelling, relevant material that resonates with the audience is at the heart of effective content marketing. Blog posts, infographics, and videos illuminate a company's ethos and provide invaluable insights, fostering appreciation and connection among viewers (Singh & Mathur, 2019). Videos, a particularly potent medium, amalgamate visual and auditory elements to craft an immersive experience. Platforms like YouTube and Vimeo serve as popular conduits for hosting and disseminating video content, engendering a profound sense of empathy and connection with the brand. Narrative videos, in particular, can explain a brand's journey, showcasing its genesis, mission, and core values (Nikolić & Leković, 2023).

The potency of employee narratives cannot be overstated. These personal accounts humanize the brand, forging deeper connections with the audience. These stories bring life into corporate values by highlighting individual experiences, achievements, and contributions to the company's mission (Vu et al., 2019). Blogs provide in-depth storytelling and thought leadership, allowing organizations to share comprehensive narratives, insights, and updates. Companies can position themselves as vanguards in their respective fields by disseminating expert opinions and industry insights, thereby building credibility (Singh & Mathur, 2019). According to Vu and colleagues, encouraging employee contributions to the company blog fosters a sense of ownership and involvement, creating a tapestry of diverse and authentic narratives. Internal campaigns are pivotal in reinforcing the company's vision and values among employees. Vu and colleagues argue that collaborative projects, storytelling workshops, and content creation challenges can enhance engagement and buy-in. Leveraging internal communication channels such as intranets, internal social networks, and email newsletters can effectively disseminate the company's ethos, celebrating achievements and highlighting employee stories (Bui, 2019).

McKinsey & Company underscores the significance of clear and consistent communication in driving organizational success. They advocate for aligning messages with the company's vision and values, engaging employees through interactive methods, and leveraging digital tools to amplify, reach, and impact (Chui et al., 2016). The consultancy firm also emphasizes the role of digital tools and platforms in facilitating communication and engagement. By harnessing the power of social media, videos, and blogs, organizations can craft a cohesive and compelling narrative that resonates with employees and stakeholders (Kaz, 2023). Digital storytelling through various media offers a potent means for organizations to communicate their vision and values. Companies can enhance engagement and forge a robust, unified culture by involving employees in co-creating digital narratives and leveraging internal campaigns.

Embedding Values in the Digital Era: A Leader's Imperative

Leaders are responsible for instilling organizational values in the dynamic digital landscape. They can achieve this through a multifaceted approach, leveraging digital literacy and ethics training, fostering a culture of perpetual learning, and cultivating innovation hubs. This strategic approach paves the way for an engaged, productive workforce primed for innovation and cross-functional synergy. Digital literacy is the bedrock of organizational prowess in the digital era. Leaders must integrate this vital skill into employee development programs, ensuring that staff members are proficient in using digital tools and are aware of their ethical implications. Workshops focusing on data privacy, cybersecurity, and responsible social media use act as strongholds against ethical breaches in the digital realm (Annisa & Widyasari, 2023).

As a vital component of organizational machinery, ethics training equips employees with the moral compass necessary to navigate the complexities of the digital world. By immersing staff in scenarios that underscore the gravity of ethical decision-making in digital interactions, organizations reaffirm their unwavering commitment to integrity, Annisa and Widyasari (2023). The Bahrain Training Institute's agile response to the COVID-19 pandemic exemplifies the power of dynamic strategic planning. Their seamless integration of online education and mobile learning underscores the importance of adaptability in weaving ethics and digital literacy into training programs (Lazer & Binz-Scharf, 2004). Similarly, leading UK construction companies have adopted a holistic approach to Building Information Modeling (BIM) training, emphasizing soft skills and ethical considerations (Srivastava et al., 2021). However, this journey has its pitfalls. According to (Vinod et al. (2023), technological disparities and the digital divide pose significant hurdles for small, micro, and medium-sized enterprises in regions like KwaZulu-Natal, South Africa.

Organizations must implement comprehensive, up-to-date training programs to foster a continuous learning culture. These initiatives, from formal sessions to informal learning opportunities, ensure employees remain at the cutting edge of technological advancements (Juliadi et al., 2023). This investment in employee development yields dividends in enhanced productivity and job satisfaction. Innovation thrives in environments that encourage experimentation. To encourage creativity and risk-taking, leaders set up unique places where people can develop new ideas; this often results in breakthroughs, say Vinod and his team. Cross-functional collaboration, facilitated by tools like asynchronous video-sharing applications, further fuels this innovative spirit by bridging geographical divides and fostering a collaborative ethos, posit Vinod et al. (2023).

According to the authors' research findings, implementing cloud-based screen recording and sharing platforms promotes transparency and continuous improvement, ensuring valuable insights permeate the organization. Leaders who successfully embed values across their organizations through digital literacy, ethics training, constant learning, and innovation spaces enhance employee engagement and productivity and position their organizations at the vanguard of the digital revolution. This holistic approach ensures organizational resilience and competitiveness in an ever-developing digital landscape.

Stakeholder Engagement: A Paradigm for Digital Excellence

The key to triumph in digital transformation lies in an unwavering commitment to stakeholder needs. This ethos, exemplified by Amazon's modus operandi, necessitates placing readers, contributors, and stakeholders at the epicenter of all strategic decisions (Lengyel, n.d.). By delving into the psyche of your audience and unearthing their difficulties, preferences, and problems, you can fuel continuous enhancement and innovation, inspiring and exciting potential outcomes for all involved. Emulate Amazon's reverse-engineering approach. Envision the paragon of reader experience or contributor workflow, then meticulously deconstruct the path to their realization (Slater, 2024).

This methodology ensures that innovation springs from genuine user requirements, not internal conjectures. Build a comprehensive feedback system by conducting regular surveys, user testing sessions, and focus groups segmented by user demographics. Leverage this valuable input to fuel iterative improvements, argue (Nohutlu et al., 2023). Empower your workforce by reorganizing it into agile, specialized units dedicated to customer needs. Consider establishing teams for user experience, content curation, and technology, allowing them to innovate within their domain (Salmon,

2021) to cultivate a culture of experimentation where failure is a steppingstone to innovation, making each member feel valued and integral to the process.

Involve your most passionate readers, contributors, and partners in the development process by creating opportunities for creativity and beta testing to generate valuable insights and foster a sense of ownership and loyalty within your organization. Embrace agile methodologies to speed up feature and content development to enable rapid iteration based on user feedback and the ever-changing digital landscape. By prioritizing long-term value creation over short-term metrics, you can invest in features or content that may not yield immediate returns but will enhance your journey's reputation and user satisfaction over time, according to Slater (2024). This approach instills confidence and reassurance in the process's effectiveness.

Foster cross-pollination between diverse teams and departments involved in the digital journey, a symbiosis that can birth innovative solutions that simultaneously address multiple facets of the user experience. By implementing these strategies, you can craft a more engaging, user-centric digital journey that perpetually develops to meet the needs of stockholder engagement. The key to success lies in maintaining an unyielding focus on your users, nurturing a culture of innovation, and showing readiness for iterating based on feedback, according to Salmon (2021). This approach elevates the quality of your digital journey and forges more robust bonds with your employees and partners to engender a sense of being heard and valued.

These findings are consistent with those of previous studies (Khin & Ho, 2019; Tsou & Chen, 2021; Pal et al., 2022; Zhao et al., 2022; Arias-Pérez et al., 2022; Zahoor et al., 2022; Demir et al., 2022; Liu et al., 2023), and show that digital innovation is a significant construct that supports mediation in developing substantial relationships. This growing body of research emphasizes the pivotal role of digital innovation as a mediating construct in developing and strengthening significant relationships within organizational contexts. The consistency across these studies suggests a robust and generalizable pattern in how digital innovation facilitates and enhances relational dynamics in various settings.

Evaluate and Adapt

In digital metamorphosis, organizational vanguards face the Herculean task of perpetually scrutinizing their ethos and raison d'être. This arduous endeavor ensures congruence with the difficulties of our digital epoch. Digital stewardship is the linchpin in shepherding entities through the labyrinthine process of digital transmutation (Araujo et al., 2021). Leaders can recalibrate organizational stratagems, architectures, methodologies, and ethos by harmonizing internal and external assets via information technology and communication. This recalibration is paramount for survival and prosperity in the nascent digital era (Firmansyah, 2024).

Leadership in this digital environment demands a profound knowledge of digital stratagems and technological acumen (Musaigwa, 2024). The odyssey of digital transformation has become the cornerstone of organizational blueprints, permeating every facet of contemporary business topography (Omol, 2023). To deftly navigate this terrain, leaders must possess digital prowess, sagacity, foresight, and prescience to propel digital metamorphosis and acclimate to the mercurial digital milieu (Senadjki, 2023). Efficacious leadership in this digital epoch necessitates change management strategies commensurate with the breakneck pace of digital evolution, posits Musaigwa; thus, organizational leaders must also contemplate the ramifications of digital change processes on adaptive performance within their cohorts.

As entities develop digitally, digitalization reinforces and molds many dimensions of adaptive performance, crisis management, assimilation of novel tasks, and problem-solving. The pivotal role of leadership in driving organizational value amidst digital transformation is underscored by the criticality of knowledge genesis and stewardship (Rosero-Garcia, 2024). In this digital panorama, organizational culture is the crucible for change and innovation. Digital organizational ethos sets the tempo for digital metamorphosis and influences the embrace of novel technologies and ideations (Wang et al., 2022). Efficacious responses to the gauntlets thrown by the digital landscape require addressing competitive ecosystems and harnessing digital technologies for communicative pursuits (Abdullah et al., 2022).

Forging a robust organizational culture entails a laser focus on values such as corporate empowerment, team stewardship, lucidity of vision, direction, and corporate objectives (Zacharias et al., 2021). To ensure organizational resilience and adaptability, leaders must proactively steer their entities toward sustainable triumph by leveraging digital insights and established leadership theories (Araujo et al., 2021). By embracing digital leadership praxis, organizations can better harness digital capabilities to facilitate digital transformation and engender greater value (Sun et al., 2023).

The digital transformation odyssey necessitates the design of malleable organizational paradigms that allow for ceaseless adaptation to the intricacies of the digital realm (Cosa, 2023). Organizational leaders who evaluate and adapt to the ever-developing digital landscape must prioritize digital leadership, change management, organizational culture, and knowledge stewardship. By aligning organizational vision and values with digital transformation initiatives, leaders can navigate the crucibles of the digital era and catalyze innovation and competitiveness within their organizations.

Fostering Employee Engagement to Drive Organizational Accountability

Aligning an organization's vision with its daily operations is beneficial and imperative; therefore, leaders must employ a multifaceted approach to foster this synergy. Begin by crystallizing and disseminating the company's ethos through town halls, onboarding rituals, and ubiquitous visual reminders. This pervasive communication strategy ensures that the message permeates every echelon of the organization. Next, implement a cascading goal structure. Use frameworks like Objectives and Key Results (OKR) to create a symbiotic relationship between overarching objectives and individual targets. This alignment cultivates a sense of purpose, driving employee engagement to unprecedented heights (Galt Foundation, 2023). However, engagement is not solely about alignment; it is about empowerment by creating conduits for employee input, conducting regular pulse checks, and, crucially, taking visible action on feedback.

Flexibility in work arrangements and a commitment to work-life equilibrium are not just perks but essential components of a thriving organizational ecosystem, a network of interconnected organizations, including suppliers, customers, competitors, and other stakeholders. To truly galvanize your workforce and provide opportunities for meaningful contribution and growth. Assign tasks that instill pride and offer development pathways for all, not just the upper echelons (Klevit, 2016). Recognition should be multifaceted, and programs should be implemented that acknowledge monumental and minute achievements and train managers in positive reinforcement (Moran, n.d.; Wilkinson, 2021). It is about making every employee feel valued and appreciated for their contributions.

Fostering camaraderie is equally crucial. Orchestrate team-building exercises and encourage cross-departmental collaboration. Leaders must be paragons of engagement, embodying the commitment they expect from their teams (Galt Foundation, 2023). It is about leading by example and inspiring your team to engage and collaborate. Set unambiguous performance metrics and conduct regular check-ins to track progress toward objectives (Tripp, 2022).

Empower your employees by granting autonomy and involving them in decision-making processes that engender a sense of ownership and accountability (Wilkinson, 2021). Finally, ensure that your incentive structures fit organizational values, reinforcing desired behaviors and outcomes. By implementing this comprehensive strategy, organizations can forge an environment where employees are aligned, accountable, and engaged. The result? According to the Galt Foundation and Wilkinson, is a surge in productivity, innovation, and overall organizational triumph.

Navigating the Digital Frontier: Measuring Success and Iterating Vision

In today's fast-paced digital landscape, organizations must adopt a multifaceted approach to gauge their triumphs and refine their strategic vision. Enter the Balanced Scorecard (BSC) framework, a paradigm-shifting tool engineered by Kaplan and Norton. This revolutionary methodology empowers enterprises to assess their performance through various perspectives, transcending the limitations of conventional financial metrics (Kaplan & Norton, 1992). The BSC framework's quadripartite structure illuminates four critical dimensions of organizational performance:

1. Economic Perspective: This encompasses traditional fiscal indicators such as revenue augmentation, cost curtailment, and return on investment. These metrics are the bedrock for evaluating an organization's financial health and shareholder value creation.
2. Customer Perspective: The focus shifts to customer contentment and retention. Metrics like customer satisfaction and net promoter scores offer invaluable insights into an organization's ability to meet and exceed customer expectations.
3. Internal Business Processes Perspective: This dimension scrutinizes the efficacy and efficiency of internal operations. Cycle time, quality rates, and process improvement metrics help to identify areas ripe for enhancement.
4. Innovation and Learning Perspective: This forward-looking aspect examines an organization's capacity for growth and innovation. Employee training hours, new product introduction rates, and workforce satisfaction metrics ensure continued investment in future capabilities.

In the digital era, the BSC framework can be adapted to assess the implementation of vision and values by incorporating digital-specific metrics and emphasizing agility and innovation. Organizations must first delineate SMART (Specific, Measurable, Attainable, Responsible, and Time-Bound) strategic objectives that align with their overarching goals to effectively measure and iterate on implementing vision and values. The digital context demands a recalibration of metrics across all BSC perspectives.

For instance, the economic perspective might include digital revenue growth and return on digital investments; customer engagement metrics and digital service adoption rates become paramount from the customer perspective; process automation rates and IT system uptime take center stage from the perspective of internal processes; the innovation and learning perspective might track the number of digital innovation projects and employee digital skills training. Leveraging advanced analytics is crucial for deriving actionable insights from the metrics. This data-driven approach enables organizations to identify trends, forecast future performance, and uncover areas for improvement. Regular performance reviews facilitate strategy refinement and process iteration, ensuring organizations remain agile in the face of digital disruption (Kaplan, 2010).

Effective communication of vision, values, and performance metrics is the linchpin of successful implementation. Transparent dashboards and reports foster stakeholder engagement and cultivate a culture of accountability and continuous improvement. The BSC framework offers a comprehensive methodology for measuring the efficacy of vision and values implementation in the digital age. By integrating multifaceted metrics, organizations can gain a holistic view of their performance and make data-driven decisions to iterate and improve continually. This approach ensures alignment with strategic objectives and adaptability in the ever-evolving digital landscape.

Entrepreneurial Growth and Statistics

The digital revolution has fundamentally reshaped entrepreneurship, leveraging technology as a powerful force for innovation and growth. Digital platforms have created unprecedented opportunities for collaboration between startups, academic institutions, and government bodies, fostering an environment where innovation thrives without traditional barriers (Sánchez-García et al., 2024). This technological integration has democratized the entrepreneurial landscape, enabling emerging startups and established companies to drive technological progress. Success in this digitally transformed environment demands a strategic focus on agile methodologies and customer-centered innovation (Kuteesa et al., 2024), and digital literacy has become essential for navigating the modern business landscape. As startups embrace digital transformation, they gain access to tools and platforms that accelerate growth and enhance their competitive advantage while contributing to broader societal advancement, according to Sánchez-García and colleagues.

Technological innovation has proven instrumental in driving entrepreneurial success across diverse industries, as evidenced by Tesla Inc., Beyond Meat, and Zoom Video Communications, three examples of revolutionary companies. These organizations have shown how technological leverage can revolutionize markets and create lasting societal impact through adaptive strategies and forward-thinking leadership (Daraojimba et al., 2023). The Chinese IT sector further reinforces this pattern, where entrepreneurial leadership and robust digital capabilities have fostered innovation and sustained performance improvements (Sahibzada et al., 2024), highlighting how modern businesses can thrive by embracing technological advancement and maintaining resilience in dynamic market conditions. These companies have successfully navigated challenges by adopting strategies and visionary leadership, showcasing resilience in the face of uncertainties and market dynamics (Daraojimba et al., 2023).

ANALYSIS OF SUCCESSES AND FAILURES

Digital entrepreneurship's successes stem from adaptability to technological shifts and strategic ecosystem integration. Companies that thrive and cultivate innovative environments prioritize digital competencies and leverage ecosystem partnerships effectively (Kuteesa et al., 2024). They understand market dynamics and capitalize on emerging opportunities through agile business practices and strategic positioning. However, significant obstacles persist in the digital entrepreneurship landscape. Technological obsolescence threatens sustainability, while intense market competition and intellectual property disputes create substantial barriers to growth (Daraojimba et al., 2023). Digital infrastructure gaps limit market access, and evolving data security challenges pose critical risks to business operations (Putra et al., 2024). These factors demand careful navigation and robust risk management strategies from digital entrepreneurs.

Evaluation of Research Methodologies

Research into digital entrepreneurship employs diverse empirical methods, combining traditional approaches like surveys and case studies with comprehensive literature reviews (Sarkar & Nath, 2024). These methodologies explore digital transformation strategies and their correlation with startup performance through rigorous gathering and analyzing data (Kuteesa et al., 2024). Advanced analytical techniques have revolutionized our understanding of digital entrepreneurship dynamics. Topic modeling and semantic network analysis reveal complex relationships between entrepreneurial activities, technological advancement, and innovation processes (Singh et al., 2023). These sophisticated methods provide granular insights into how digital ventures develop and interact within their ecosystems.

Policy Implications

Research findings have profound implications for digital entrepreneurship policy development. Policymakers must cultivate environments that promote digital literacy and foster innovation through targeted support of ecosystem partnerships (Kuteesa et al., 2024). Critical focus areas include bridging the digital divide and establishing frameworks for ethical business conduct in digital spaces (Daraojimba et al., 2023). Government intervention plays a vital role in addressing digital entrepreneurs' fundamental challenges. Strategic support for technology infrastructure development and improved access to funding mechanisms enables sustainable growth in the digital sector (Putra et al., 2024). Success in the digital economy requires synchronized efforts between policymakers and entrepreneurs to create resilient ecosystems that drive innovation and economic advancement.

Call to Action

Embracing technological innovation in the digital age is not just a choice but an imperative. Organizations must seize the transformative potential of digital technologies with enthusiasm, fostering a culture of perpetual learning and skill. In this era of lightning-fast digital evolution, every sector of the global economy is being reshaped. Those who embrace these seismic shifts will unlock a treasure trove of opportunities, streamline operations, and catapult themselves toward sustainable growth.

Organizations must deploy a multifaceted strategy to harness the power of innovation - leverage automation, AI, and cloud computing to optimize workflows and boost productivity. Harness the power of data analytics to decipher customer preferences, enabling bespoke interactions that feel effortless. Use real-time data to make proactive strategic decisions and respond to market fluctuations with alacrity. Explore the frontiers of emerging technologies like blockchain, IoT, and augmented reality to pioneer new business models and revenue streams (Fernando, 2023; Growth99, 2023). As organizations embark on this digital odyssey, alignment with core vision and values is paramount. They must clearly articulate the digital transformation vision, ensuring every employee is on board, cultivate a digital-first mindset, encourage staff to embrace change and upskill, and foster cross-pollination of ideas by promoting collaboration across diverse disciplines (Bandura & Burns, 2023; Fitzgerald et al., 2013).

Organizations must regularly audit technological initiatives to fortify vision and values alignment. They should also invest in comprehensive training programs to equip employees with innovative digital skills. By forming cross-functional teams to tackle digital projects, they can create a crucible for innovation and engage key stakeholders in the transformation journey, ensuring their perspectives are woven into the change fabric. By embracing technological innovation and aligning it with their ethos, organizations can position themselves at the vanguard of the digital age. This journey demands an unwavering commitment to continuous learning, collaboration, and a proactive approach to harnessing the transformative power of digital technologies.

CONCLUSION AND SUMMARY

The chapter "*Embracing Technological Innovation: Leading in the Digital Age*" examines how organizations must adapt to the digital landscape while preserving their fundamental values and vision. The text begins by recognizing that businesses face previously unheard-of difficulties in the digital age. It then shows that effective transformation needs more than new technology; it calls for a holistic approach that encompasses strategic alignment, cultural transformation, and meaningful stakeholder engagement. Throughout the chapter, several interconnected themes emerge. The discussion of digital leadership emphasizes that modern leaders must develop new competencies and foster digital literacy while creating adaptive frameworks that enable their organizations to thrive amid constant change. This leadership evolution must carefully balance technological innovation with organizational authenticity, ensuring digital transformation efforts don't compromise ethical standards or core values.

The strategic implementation of digital initiatives receives significant attention. The chapter highlights the critical importance of aligning technological advances with organizational vision and values. This alignment process involves active stakeholder engagement, comprehensive employee development programs, and implementing balanced scorecards for measuring success. The chapter emphasizes that organizations must embrace iterative improvement processes, allowing them to adapt and refine their digital strategies continuously. Organizational culture and values emerge as central pillars of successful digital transformation. Research shows that values are a crucial guiding framework in the digital landscape, helping organizations navigate complex decisions and maintain their identity amid rapid change. Cultural transformation is presented as essential for supporting digital initiatives, with particular emphasis on fostering innovation while preserving organizational authenticity.

The technical aspects of digital transformation are thoroughly addressed, with a detailed discussion of how Cloud computing, data analytics, and artificial intelligence are examples of developing technology that businesses can use to their advantage. However, the chapter consistently returns to the human element, emphasizing that technical implementation must be balanced with digital literacy development and competency building across the organization. Integrating digital tools is a technical challenge and an opportunity to enhance organizational communication and collaboration. The chapter concludes by returning to its opening premises, reinforcing that embracing technological innovation is not optional but imperative in the digital age. This conclusion effectively ties together the various threads of the discussion, emphasizing that successful digital transformation requires a multifaceted approach that combines technological advancement with strong organizational values.

The text argues that organizations must balance embracing digital innovation and preserving their core identity, supported by a clear strategic vision, strong leadership commitment, robust stakeholder engagement, and continuous measurement and adaptation of initiatives. Through this comprehensive examination, the chapter provides valuable insights for organizations seeking to navigate the complexities of digital transformation while maintaining their essential character and values. The coherent progression from introduction to conclusion reinforces that success in the digital age requires technological sophistication and unwavering commitment to organizational principles.

As organizations navigate digital transformation while preserving their core values, they must recognize how technological advancement intersects with workforce evolution. The previous chapter's emphasis on balancing innovation with organizational identity naturally leads to inspecting diversity and inclusion as catalysts for sustainable growth in the digital age. While technology provides the tools for transformation, the diverse perspectives and inclusive practices within an organization unlock their full potential. This connection between digital sophistication and human capital development forms the foundation for understanding how modern organizations can thrive by strategically integrating technological and cultural innovations.

FURTHER READING

For those seeking to delve deeper into this subject, a plethora of resources awaits. Thomas M. Siebel's "Digital Transformation: Survive and Thrive in an Era of Mass Extinction" offers invaluable insights. David L. Rogers' "The Digital Transformation Playbook" provides a comprehensive guide to rethinking business strategies. The MIT Sloan Management Review's "Embracing Digital Technology" explores challenges and opportunities for industry leaders' perspectives. Marc García's "Innovation in the Digital Age" highlights critical strategies for leveraging technology. Consider leadership development programs offered by prestigious institutions like MIT Sloan Executive Education, Harvard Business School Online, and Stanford Graduate School of Business for hands-on learning.

REFERENCES

Abdullah, Z., Anumudu, C., & Raza, S. (2022). Examining the digital organizational identity through content analysis of missions and vision statements of malaysian and singaporean sme company websites. *The Bottom Line (New York, N.Y.)*, 35(2/3), 137–158. Doi.org/10.1108/bl-12-2021-0108. DOI: 10.1108/BL-12-2021-0108

Annisa, F., & Widyasari, W. (2023). Development of Digital Literacy for Teachers. *Proceeding International Conference of Technology on Community and Environmental Development.*

Araujo, L., Priadana, S., Paramarta, V., & Sunarsi, D. (2021). Digital leadership in business organizations. International Journal of Educational Administration Management and Leadership, 5-16. DOI: 10.51629/ijeamal.v2i1.18

Arias-Pérez, J., Coronado-Medina, A., & Perdomo-Charry, G. (2022). Big data analytics capability as a mediator in the impact of open innovation on firm performance. *Journal of Strategy and Management*, 15(1), 1–15. DOI: 10.1108/JSMA-09-2020-0262

Arifin, R., & Purwanti, H. (2022). Examining the Influence of Leadership Agility, Organizational Culture, and Motivation on Organizational Agility: A Comprehensive Analysis. *Golden Ratio of Human Resource Management*, 3(1), 33–54. DOI: 10.52970/grhrm.v3i1.205

Azra, A. (2023). Role of Innovation Management Practices in Enhancing Firm Agility and Adaptability during Times of Crisis in Turkey. *International Journal of Strategic Management*, 2(2), 12–22. DOI: 10.47604/ijsm.2185

Bandura, R., & Burns, C. (2023). A Call to Action: Igniting the Digital Revolution in International Development Studies. https://www.csis.org/analysis/call-action-igniting-digital-revolution-international-development-studies

Bui, T.L. (2019). Internal communication in the digital workplace: digital communication channels and employee engagement.

Carnochan, S., & Austin, M. J. (2002). Implementing Welfare Reform and Guiding Organizational Change. *Administration in Social Work*, 26(1), 61–77. DOI: 10.1300/J147v26n01_04

Chotipurk, A., Nuchniyom, R., & Lakkhongkha, K. (2023). Preparing and Developing the Capabilities of Entrepreneurs in the Digital Age. *International Journal of Professional Business Review*, 8(7), e02864. DOI: 10.26668/businessreview/2023.v8i7.2864

Chui, M., Manyika, J., & Miremadi, M. (2016). Leading in the digital age. McKinsey Quarterly. https://www.mckinsey.com/featured-insights/leadership/leading-in-the-digital-age

Coetzee, M., Bester, M. S., Ferreira, N., & Potgieter, H. (2020). Facets of career agility as explanatory mechanisms of employees' career adaptability. *African Journal of Career*, 2(1). Advance online publication. DOI: 10.4102/ajcd.v2i1.11

Cosa, M. (2023). Business digital transformation: Strategy adaptation, communication, and future agenda. *Journal of Strategy and Management*, 17(2), 244–259. DOI: 10.1108/JSMA-09-2023-0233

Daraojimba, C., Abioye, K., Bakare, A., Mhlongo, N., Onunka, O., & Daraojimba, D. (2023). Technology And Innovation To Growth Of Entrepreneurship And Financial Boost: A Decade In Review (2013-2023). *International Journal of Management & Entrepreneurship Research*. DOI: 10.51594/ijmer.v5i10.593

Demir, M., Yaşar, E., & Demir, Ş. Ş. (2022). Digital transformation and human resources planning: The mediating role of innovation. *Journal of Hospitality and Tourism Technology*, 14(1), 21–36. DOI: 10.1108/JHTT-04-2021-0105

El Badawy, T. A., Marwan, R. M., & Magdy, M. M. (2015). The Impact of Emerging Technologies on Knowledge Management in Organizations. *International Business Research*, 8(5). Advance online publication. DOI: 10.5539/ibr.v8n5p111

Fang, J., & Gong, X. (2023). Application of visual communication in digital animation advertising design using convolutional neural networks and big data. *PeerJ. Computer Science*, 9, e1383. DOI: 10.7717/peerj-cs.1383 PMID: 37346553

Fernando, A. G. M. (2023). In today's rapidly evolving digital landscape, embracing technology has become imperative for businesses seeking to thrive and remain competitive. The digital age presents exciting opportunities for innovation, enabling organizations to transform their operations and enhance customer experiences. d. https://www.linkedin.com/pulse/innovation-digital-age-embracing-technology-business-garc%C3%ADa-marc

Firmansyah, F., Erda, G., & Khurniawan, A. W. (2024). The impact of digital transformation and leadership on organizational resilience in distance education institution: Higher-order set approach. *Turkish Online Journal of Distance Education*, 25(2), 115–129. DOI: 10.17718/tojde.1260433

Fitzgerald, M., Kruschwitz, N., Bonnet, D., & Welch, M. (2013). Embracing Digital Technology. MIT Sloan Management Review. https://sloanreview.mit.edu/projects/embracing-digital-technology/

Forster, N. (2006). The Impact of Emerging Technologies on Business, Industry, Commerce and Humanity during the 21st Century. *The Journal of Business Perspective*, 10(1), 27. DOI: 10.1177/097226290601000401

Galt Foundation. (2023). Nurturing Employees: Fostering Lasting Employee Engagement and Commitment. https://galtfoundation.org/2023/11/01/fostering-lasting-employee-engagement-and-commitment/

Gonçalves, M. L. A., Penha, R., Brandão, A. C. L., Da Costa Filho, J. R., & Galvão, G. S. Junior. (2023). Analyzing The Bibliometric Landscape Of Digital Transformation And Project Management In Organizational Contexts. *Revista Contemporânea*, 3(12), 26396–26419. DOI: 10.56083/RCV3N12-087

Gorichanaz, T. (2021). Sanctuary: An institutional vision for the digital age. *The Journal of Documentation*, 77(1), 1–17. DOI: 10.1108/JD-04-2020-0064

Growth99. (2023). Digitalization: Revolutionizing Businesses In The Modern Age | Growth99. https://growth99.com/digitalization-revolutionizing-businesses-in-the-modern-age/

Gu, F., & Liu, J. (2022). Environmentally Specific Servant Leadership and Employee Workplace Green Behavior: Moderated Mediation Model of Green Role Modeling and Employees' Perceived CSR. *Sustainability (Basel)*, 14(19), 11965. DOI: 10.3390/su141911965

Han, S. J., Xie, L., Beyerlein, M., & Boehm, R. (2022). Examining the mediating role of team growth mindset on the relationship of individual mindsets and shared leadership. *European Journal of Training and Development*. Advance online publication. DOI: 10.1108/EJTD-08-2022-0084

Juliadi, E., Syafri, M., & Hidayati, N. (2023). The Effect of Training and Development on Employee Productivity in the Digital Age. West Science Journal Economic and Entrepreneurship, 1(10).

Kane, G. (2019). The technology fallacy: People are the real key to digital transformation. *Research Technology Management*, 62(6), 44–49. DOI: 10.1080/08956308.2019.1661079

Kaplan, R. S. (2010). *Conceptual Foundations of the Balanced Scorecard*. Harvard Business School, Harvard University. DOI: 10.2139/ssrn.1562586

Kaplan, R. S., & Norton, D. P. (1992). The Balanced Scorecard—Measures that Drive Performance. *Harvard Business Review*. PMID: 10119714

Kaz, H. (2023). Leveling up employee engagement: Uncovering the new pillars of an employee retention blueprint. *Strategic HR Review*, 22(6), 195–200. DOI: 10.1108/SHR-08-2023-0048

Khin, S., & Ho, T. C. (2019). Digital technology, digital capability, and organizational performance. *International Journal of Innovation Science*, 11(2), 177–195. DOI: 10.1108/IJIS-08-2018-0083

Klevit, A. (2016). Eight Tips for Fostering Employee Engagement. Business Success Consulting Group. https://www.bizsuccesscg.com/eight-tips-for-fostering-employee-engagement/

Kuteesa, K., Akpuokwe, C., & Udeh, C. (2024). Navigating the digital transformation journey: strategies for startup growth and innovation in the digital era. *International Journal of Scholarly Research in Multidisciplinary Studies*. DOI: 10.56781/ijsrms.2024.4.2.0031

Lazer, D., & Binz-Scharf, M. C. (2004, May). Managing novelty and cross-agency cooperation in digital government. In *Proceedings of the 2004 annual national conference on Digital government research*, 1-2).

Lengyel, A. (n.d.). *Pushing the Boundaries of Innovation: Speed*. Scale, and Transformation in the Cloud.

Liu, Y., Dong, J., Mei, L., & Shen, R. (2023). Digital innovation and performance of manufacturing firms: An affordance perspective. *Technovation*, 119, 102458. DOI: 10.1016/j.technovation.2022.102458

Mardiani, E., & Utami, E. Y. (2023). The Role of Online Education in encouraging Employee empowerment in the Digital Era: A Study on E-commerce. 4, 1.

McNaughton, D. (2003). The Role of Values and Leadership in Organizational Transformation. *Journal of Human Values*, 9(2), 131–140. DOI: 10.1177/097168580300900204

Moran, K. (n.d.). 10 Great Ways to Foster Authentic Employee Engagement | Recognize. Retrieved June 27, 2024, from https://recognizeapp.com/ways-foster-employee-engagement

Musaigwa, M., & Kalitanyi, V. (2024). Effective leadership in the digital era: An exploration of change management. *Technology Audit and Production Reserves*, 1(4(75)), 6–14. Doi.org/10.15587/2706-5448.2024.297374. DOI: 10.15587/2706-5448.2024.297374

Nikolić, S., & Leković, B. (2023). There is no end to storytelling: Transmedia storytelling in the digital mediation of music. *Zbornik Akademije Umetnosti*, (11), 202–221. DOI: 10.5937/ZbAkU2311202N

Nohutlu, Z. D., Englis, B. G., Groen, A. J., & Constantinides, E. (2023). Innovating With the Customer: Co-Creation Motives in Online Communities. *International Journal of Electronic Commerce*, 27(4), 523–557. DOI: 10.1080/10864415.2023.2255111

Nuijten, E., Messmer, M., & van Lammerts Bueren, E. (2017). Concepts and Strategies of Organic Plant Breeding in Light of Novel Breeding Techniques. *Sustainability (Basel)*, 9(1), 18. DOI: 10.3390/su9010018

Omol, E. (2023). *Organizational digital transformation: from evolution to future trends*. Digital Transformation and Society., DOI: 10.1108/DTS-08-2023-0061

Pal, S. K., Baral, M. M., Mukherjee, S., Chittipaka, V., & Jana, B. (2022). Analyzing the impact of supply chain innovation as a mediator for healthcare firms' performance. *Materials Today: Proceedings*, 56, 2880–2887. DOI: 10.1016/j.matpr.2021.10.173

Purnomo, J., & Sri Pudjiarti, E. (2024). Navigasi Kepemimpinan Di Era Digital: Tantangan Dan Peluang Bagi Generasi Mill. Transformasi: Journal of Economics and Business Management.

Putra, J., Karundeng, D., Gofur, A., Tresnadjaja, R., Suhara, A., Sukmayadi, S., & Sopyan, A. (2024). Entrepreneurship in the era of society 5.0: Navigating digitalization for innovation and growth. *Journal of Sustainable Tourism and Entrepreneurship.* DOI: 10.35912/joste.v6i1.2224

Rogers, D.L. (2011). The Network Is Your Customer: Five Strategies to Thrive in a Digital Age.

Rosero-Garcia, J., & Montano-Salamanca, W. (2024). Conceptual model for establishing the relationship between digital transformation and organizational performance in electrical power companies. *International Journal of Management and Sustainability*, 13(2), 253–277. DOI: 10.18488/11.v13i2.3767

Sahibzada, U., Aslam, N., Muavia, M., Shujahat, M., & Rafi-Ul-Shan, P. (2024). Navigating digital waves: Unveiling entrepreneurial leadership toward digital innovation and sustainable performance in the Chinese IT industry. *Journal of Enterprise Information Management.* Advance online publication. DOI: 10.1108/JEIM-01-2024-0023

Salmon, A. (2021). Inside Amazon's culture of scaling, agility and innovation. Digital Works Consulting. https://digitalworksgroup.com/inside-amazons-culture-of-scaling-agility-and-innovation/

Sánchez-García, E., Martínez-Falcó, J., Marco-Lajara, B., & Gigauri, I. (2024). Building the future through digital entrepreneurship and innovation. *European Journal of Innovation Management.* Advance online publication. DOI: 10.1108/EJIM-04-2024-0360

Sari, E., Anindhita, W., Mulyadi, M., Purwoko, D., Madhakomala, M., & Yatimah, D. (2023). Innovation in Adaptive Leadership Management Model through the Development of Digital Mindset in Activator School Programs. *International Journal of Social Science and Human Research*, 6(12). Advance online publication. https://www.semanticscholar.org/paper/Innovation-in-Adaptive-Leadership-Management-Model-Sari-Anindhita/2091c2d542c06db54415ac421ac4c7a2778bc094. DOI: 10.47191/ijsshr/v6-i12-02

Sarkar, D., & Nath, H. (2024). Embracing Disruption: An Empirical Study On The Accepted Practices And Strategic Responses Of Entrepreneurs To Rapid Technological Advancements. ShodhKosh: *Journal of Visual and Performing Arts.* DOI: 10.29121/shodhkosh.v5.i4.2024.2402

Schwab, K. (2017). *The fourth industrial revolution.* Currency.

Senadjki, A., Au Yong, H. N., Ganapathy, T., & Ogbeibu, S. (2023). Unlocking the potential: The impact of digital leadership on firms' performance through digital transformation. *Journal of Business and Socio-Economic Development*, 4(2), 161–177. DOI: 10.1108/JBSED-06-2023-0050

Singh, A., & Mathur, S. (2019). The Insight of Content Marketing at Social Media Platforms. Adhyayan: A *Journal of Management Sciences*, 9.

Singh, S., Singh, S., & Dhir, S. (2023). The evolving relationship of entrepreneurship, technology, and innovation: A topic modeling perspective. *International Journal of Entrepreneurship and Innovation*, 14657503231179597. Advance online publication. DOI: 10.1177/14657503231179597

Sinka, H. (2024). Talent Management in Digital Age. *Interantional Journal OF Scientific Research IN Engineering AND Management*, 08(06), 1–5. DOI: 10.55041/IJSREM35730

Slater, D. (2024). The Imperatives of Customer-Centric Innovation | AWS Executive Insights. https://aws.amazon.com/executive-insights/content/the-imperatives-of-customer-centric-innovation/

Srivastava, Y. C., Srivastava, A., & Granata, C. (2021). *Digitally Enabled Organizations- Leveraging New Age Technologies. On Day 1, Mon, November 15, 2021*. SPE., DOI: 10.2118/207380-M.S

Suar, D., & Khuntia, R. (2010). Influence of Personal Values and Value Congruence on Unethical Practices and Work Behavior. *Journal of Business Ethics*, 97(3), 443–460. DOI: 10.1007/s10551-010-0517-y

Sun, X., He, Z., & Qian, Y. (2023). Getting organizational adaptability in the context of digital transformation. *Chinese Management Studies*, 18(2), 550–574. DOI: 10.1108/CMS-06-2022-0222

Tripp, D. (2022). Fostering Employee Engagement In The Current Work Environment. Forbes. https://www.forbes.com/sites/forbeshumanresourcescouncil/2022/11/08/fostering-employee-engagement-in-the-current-work-environment/

Tsou, H., & Chen, J. (2021). How does digital technology usage benefit firm performance? digital transformation strategy and organizational innovation as mediators. Technology Analysis &Amp. *Strategic Management*, 35(9), 1114–1127. DOI: 10.1080/09537325.2021.1991575

Vinod, S., Selvanayaki, S., Vimal, V. R., & Sheik Dhanveer, H. (2023). Screen recording and Sharing over the cloud Platform For Remote Teams And Cross-Functional Teams. In *2023 International Conference on Research Methodologies in Knowledge Management, Artificial Intelligence and Telecommunication Engineering (RMKMATE)* (pp. 1–5). IEEE. DOI: 10.1109/RMKMATE59243.2023.10369912

Vu, V., Warschauer, M., & Yim, S. (2019). Digital Storytelling: A District Initiative for Academic Literacy Improvement. *Journal of Adolescent & Adult Literacy*, 63(3), 257–267. DOI: 10.1002/jaal.962

Wang, T., Lin, X., & Sheng, F. (2022). Digital leadership and exploratory innovation: From the dual perspectives of strategic orientation and organizational culture. *Frontiers in Psychology*, 13, 902693. Advance online publication. DOI: 10.3389/fpsyg.2022.902693 PMID: 36176785

Wiley, S. K. (2021). The Grey Area: How Regulations Impact Autonomy in Computational Journalism. *Digital Journalism (Abingdon, England)*, 11(6), 889–905. DOI: 10.1080/21670811.2021.1893199

Wilkinson, J. (2021). Employee Engagement: What It Is and 5 Ways to Foster It. Firespring. https://firespring.com/powered-by-purpose/what-is-employee-engagement-how-to-foster-it/

Williams, A. W. (2016). The Value of Values: The Amplified Role of Authenticity in an Increasingly Transparent World. Journal of Creating Value. https://www.semanticscholar.org/paper/The-Value-of-Values%3A-The-Amplified-Role-of-in-an-Williams/043312b7842b9aa25c386a6161998c70a68e0cf8

Zacharias, T., Rahawarin, M., & Yusriadi, Y. (2021). Cultural reconstruction and organization environment for employee performance. *Journal of Ethnic and Cultural Studies*, 8(2), 296–315. Doi.org/10.29333/ejecs/801. DOI: 10.29333/ejecs/801

Zahoor, N., Khan, Z., Arslan, A., Khan, H., & Tarba, S. Y. (2022). International open innovation and international market success: An empirical study of emerging market small and medium-sized enterprises. *International Marketing Review*, 39(3), 755–782. DOI: 10.1108/IMR-12-2020-0314

Zhao, X., Sun, X., Zhao, L., & Xing, Y. (2022). Can the digital transformation of manufacturing enterprises promote enterprise innovation? *Business Process Management Journal*, 28(4), 960–982. DOI: 10.1108/BPMJ-01-2022-0018

Zulkifli, Z. (2023).. . *Strategies For Enhancing Zakat Fundraising Through The Utilization Of Social Media And Digital Campaigns*, 1(2). Advance online publication. DOI: 10.56910/ictmt.v1i1.119

KEY TERMS AND DEFINITIONS

Artificial Intelligence (AI): Advanced computer systems capable of performing tasks that typically require human intelligence, increasingly important in digital transformation.

Balanced Scorecard (BSC): A performance measurement framework that evaluates organizational success through four perspectives: financial, customer, internal business processes, and innovation/learning.

Big Data Analytics: The process of examining large and varied data sets to uncover patterns, trends, and associations, supporting data-driven decision-making.

Change Management: The structured approach to transitioning individuals, teams, and organizations from current state to desired future state, especially crucial in digital transformation.

Cross-Functional Collaboration: The practice of different departments or expertise areas working together to achieve common goals, enhanced by digital tools and platforms.

Digital Competencies: The skills, knowledge, and capabilities required to effectively operate and innovate in the digital environment.

Cloud Computing: The delivery of computing services over the internet, enabling organizations to scale and adapt their technological capabilities flexibly.

Digital Culture: An organizational environment that embraces technology, encourages innovation, and promotes continuous learning and adaptation to digital changes.

Digital Ethics: The moral principles and guidelines governing digital technologies and data management.

Digital Innovation: The creation and implementation of new ideas, products, or processes enabled by digital technologies.

Digital Leadership: The ability to drive organizational change and innovation through digital technologies while maintaining organizational values and vision, requiring new competencies and strategic thinking in the digital age.

Digital Literacy: The capability to effectively understand, use, and navigate digital tools and technologies, considered essential for organizational success in the modern business landscape.

Digital Maturity: The level of an organization's readiness and capability to adapt, compete, and thrive in an increasingly digital environment.

Digital Platforms: Online frameworks that enable various types of interactions, transactions, and collaborations between different users and stakeholders.

Digital Strategy: A comprehensive plan for integrating and leveraging digital technologies to achieve organizational objectives while maintaining alignment with core values.

Digital Transformation: The comprehensive integration of digital technologies across all business operations, leading to fundamental changes in how organizations operate, deliver value, and interact with stakeholders.

Employee Engagement: Employees' emotional commitment and connection to their organization are particularly important during digital transformation initiatives.

Iterative Improvement: The process of continuously refining and enhancing digital initiatives based on feedback and performance metrics.

Key Performance Indicators (KPIs): Quantifiable measures used to evaluate the success of digital initiatives and organizational performance.

Organizational Values: Guiding principles that shape an organization's culture, decision-making processes, and behavior, serving as a compass for navigating the complexities of the digital age.

Return on Digital Investment (RODI): The measurable value and benefits obtained from investments in digital technologies and transformation initiatives.

Stakeholder Engagement: The process of involving and communicating with all parties affected by organizational decisions, critical in digital transformation initiatives.

Chapter 5
Leveraging Diversity and Inclusion

ABSTRACT

Diversity and inclusion (D&I) are critical for organizational success in today's business landscape. This chapter explores strategies for leveraging D&I to drive innovation, enhance decision-making, and improve performance. Key approaches include assessing the current organizational landscape, setting clear D&I objectives aligned with business goals, educating leaders on unconscious bias, promoting inclusive communication, and fostering employee resource groups. Tailoring D&I strategies to local contexts while maintaining global principles is emphasized. Technology plays a vital role in supporting flexible work arrangements and mitigating bias. Case studies of successful D&I initiatives from companies like Sodexo, Johnson & Johnson, and PepsiCo illustrate best practices. The chapter concludes that inclusive leadership is not just a moral imperative but a strategic necessity for organizations aiming to thrive in an increasingly complex and interconnected world.

INTRODUCTION

In today's rapidly evolving business landscape, diversity and inclusion (D&I) have emerged as critical drivers of organizational success rather than merely aspirational goals. Companies increasingly realize that diversity and inclusion are key to developing new ideas, making better decisions, and competing globally. This chapter explores the comprehensive framework for implementing effective D&I strategies across organizations. Beginning with the essential foundation of understanding and assessing the current organizational landscape, it delves into establishing clear objectives that align with broader business goals. The discussion encompasses crucial elements such as leadership development, policy evaluation,

DOI: 10.4018/979-8-3693-5553-4.ch005

Copyright © 2025, IGI Global Scientific Publishing. Copying or distributing in print or electronic forms without written permission of IGI Global is prohibited.

and cultivating Employee Resource Groups (ERGs) while examining how technology can be leveraged to support these initiatives.

Through analysis of successful implementations at leading organizations like Sodexo, Johnson & Johnson, and PepsiCo, the chapter illustrates how D&I strategies can be tailored to meet local needs while adhering to global principles. It addresses organizations' challenges in creating genuinely inclusive environments and provides practical solutions for overcoming these obstacles. The chapter emphasizes that successful D&I implementation requires structural changes and a fundamental shift in organizational culture, supported by committed leadership and measurable accountability. By examining these various dimensions of D&I strategy, this chapter provides a roadmap for organizations seeking to harness the full potential of a diverse workforce and create an inclusive environment where each worker may flourish and participate in the company's development.

LEVERAGING DIVERSITY AND INCLUSION

In today's variegated business landscape, diversity and inclusion are not mere buzzwords; they are the lifeblood of thriving organizations. Diversity, a multifaceted drapery of human differences, encompasses many attributes: gender, age, ethnicity, physical abilities, sexual orientation, socioeconomic background, education levels, and cognitive styles (McKinsey & Company, 2022). Individuals bring a rich mosaic of experiences, perspectives, and identities to the workplace. On the other hand, inclusion is the alchemical process of creating an environment where all individuals feel valued and empowered to contribute fully. As the saying goes, diversity is invited to the party; inclusion is being asked to dance (Myers, 2015). The imperative for diversity and inclusion in modern leadership is indisputable. It is the responsibility of leaders to foster an environment where all individuals feel valued and empowered to contribute fully. Heterogeneous teams are the crucibles of innovation, birthing creative solutions and encouraging out-of-the-box thinking (The National Society of Leadership and Success, 2022). This cognitive diversity is the sine qua non for staying competitive in an ever-evolving business milieu.

Moreover, inclusive workplaces are bastions of employee engagement and retention, engendering a sense of belonging that transcends mere job satisfaction (Tynes, 2022). The benefits of diversity and inclusion extend far beyond employee contentment. They catalyze enhanced decision-making as diverse teams bring a profusion of perspectives, resulting in more nuanced and comprehensive analyses. Furthermore, organizations that champion diversity and inclusion become magnets for top talent, attracting a diverse pool of skilled professionals and burnishing their reputation as employers of choice (The National Society of Leadership and Success,

2022). The financial impact of diversity and inclusion is significant. Studies have unequivocally shown that organizations with diverse and inclusive cultures outperform their homogeneous counterparts, experiencing heightened productivity, creativity, and overall business success, argues Tynes (2022). Diversity and inclusion are not just moral imperatives but strategic linchpins for organizational prosperity with tangible financial benefits. *Figure 1* below shows the signature of inclusive leaders.

Figure 1. The six signatures of an inclusive leader

The six signatures of an inclusive leader:

Source: Deloitte University Press

- **Cognizance** — Because bias is a leader's Achilles' heel
- **Curiosity** — Because different ideas and experiences enable growth
- **Courage** — Because talking about imperfections involves personal risk-taking
- **Cultural Intelligence** — Because not everyone sees the world through the same cultural frame
- **Commitment** — Because staying the course is hard
- **Collaboration** — Because a diverse-thinking team is greater than the sum of its parts

TestGorilla

(TestGotills)

As we navigate the intricacies of this subject, we will uncover the quintessential role of astute leaders in harnessing the power of diversity and inclusion. These vanguards of organizational change are tasked with architecting a workplace ecosystem that embraces and celebrates human differences. Through a meticulous assessment of the current milieu and the establishment of unambiguous objectives, they lay the groundwork for transformation. The journey continues with the improvement and cultivation of leadership acumen, fostering a culture of inclusive dialogue permeating every organization's echelon. A forensic review of extant policies and practices ensures alignment with diversity goals while nurturing Employee Resource Groups

(ERGs), which provide a platform for underrepresented voices. Progress is not left to chance; it is meticulously measured, and accountability is rigorously enforced. Savvy leaders leverage innovative technology and employ critical strategies to catalyze this paradigm shift. In doing so, they transmute diversity and inclusion from abstract concepts into tangible wellsprings of innovation and growth, propelling their organizations to the vanguard of their respective industries.

Assess the Current Landscape: Navigating the Diversity and Inclusion Terrain

Organizations must meticulously assess their diversity and inclusion landscape in today's changing business environment. This evaluation is not merely superficial; it is a strategic imperative. The first step in this journey of organizational introspection is to scrutinize the existing culture, demographics, and technological milieu (Afridah, 2024). Delve deep and unearth the hidden crevices where diversity and inclusion can catalyze positive transformation. This excavation is particularly crucial in our era of technological upheavals and shifting societal values (Purwoko, 2024). The terrain is fraught with challenges. Entrenched mindsets, ossified and resistant to change, pose formidable obstacles and hidden biases, insidious in their subtlety, warp decision-making processes. Structural inequalities, deeply embedded in organizational DNA, require surgical precision to exercise. To navigate this labyrinthine landscape, companies must jettison the colorblind approach; embrace a more inclusive framework that recognizes and actively celebrates differences (Lightfoote et al., 2014).

This transformation demands boldness. Leaders must become cartographers of change, mapping out new territories of inclusivity (Anggoro, 2024). They must keep pace with the breakneck speed of technological advancements while simultaneously responding to the ever-develop tapestry of social norms and expectations. The complexities of global interconnectedness add another layer of intricacy to this already Gordian knot. However, the rewards for successfully navigating this terrain are immense. Organizations that effectively chart this course stand to reap a bountiful harvest of innovation, enhanced market responsiveness, and a fortified brand reputation (Gill et al., 2018). However, beware of the pitfalls; poorly implemented initiatives can engender issues, such as communication breakdowns, perceived inequities, and potential legal crises. The key lies in meticulous planning and execution. Assess, analyze, and act with precision. By thoroughly assessing the current landscape, organizations lay the groundwork for transformative change. Though challenging, this initial step is crucial in creating an environment that embraces diversity and harnesses its power to drive organizational success. The journey may be arduous, but the destination promises a future of unparalleled innovation, creativity, and excellence.

The challenges are manifold, and leaders must navigate to foster genuinely inclusive environments. The path forward is clear, albeit arduous. Leaders must champion a more inclusive organizational culture that values diversity and promotes equity (Pulugurtha, 2023). By cultivating a welcoming and equitable workplace, organizations can unlock the full potential of their diverse workforce. Assessing the current landscape is not a one-time endeavor but an ongoing process, a continuous recalibration. Only through this persistent effort can organizations hope to harness the transformative power of diversity and inclusion, turning challenges into opportunities and differences into strengths.

Leveraging Diversity and Inclusion with Clear Objectives

In modern organizational dynamics, leaders must adeptly wield the prism of diversity and inclusion (D&I). This is not merely about ticking boxes or meeting quotas but about cultivating a veritable crucible of innovation, engagement, and productivity. True diversity transcends the superficial. It is a tapestry woven from myriad perspectives, experiences, and ideas. To foster this rich mosaic, leaders must embrace cognitive heterogeneity, promote hiring practices, and prioritize eclectic educational and professional backgrounds. This approach engenders a fertile ground for novel problem-solving paradigms and groundbreaking innovations.

Creating an inclusive milieu where employees experience a profound sense of belonging is paramount. This sense of affiliation is the linchpin of employee engagement and performance (Vandenbroucke, 2022). Leaders must orchestrate specific inclusion objectives, nurture trust-based relationships, and implement mentorship programs that symbiotically pair diverse employees with seasoned leaders. Aligning D&I with overarching business goals is not just reasonable but imperative. This relationship ensures that D&I initiatives contribute to the organization's holistic success (Claremont Lincoln University, 2023). Leaders must explain how diverse teams catalyze superior decision-making, innovation, and customer understanding, ultimately driving improved business outcomes.

Accountability is the cornerstone of an effective D&I strategy. Leaders must set specific D&I goals and integrate these objectives into performance evaluations. Case studies from vanguard organizations like Nike and DHL exemplify this approach, implementing fair practices, ensuring representation of all echelons, and addressing diversity across varied dimensions (Barbour, 2024). By setting clear, specific D&I goals that transcend mere demographics and nurture a sense of belonging, leaders can forge a more engaged, innovative, and triumphant organization. When these objectives harmonize with broader business goals, D&I efforts become a powerful catalyst for strategic success.

Educate and Train Leaders

Many efficacious methodologies exist in leadership development to enlighten and illuminate those at the helm about unconscious bias and inclusive leadership. This multifaceted approach aims to cultivate a more encompassing milieu within organizations. Unconscious bias training is a cornerstone of this edifice of enlightenment; it illuminates the nebulous concept of implicit prejudice and its far-reaching twists in decision-making processes. Leaders engage in introspective exercises, unearthing their biases, and acquire techniques to mitigate these cognitive blind spots (Brainard, 2017).

Inclusive leadership development programs serve as tests for honing essential skills and knowledge. These comprehensive curricula explain the exemplary traits of inclusive leaders, strategies for fostering psychological safety, and methods to nurture diverse, innovative teams, posits (Radicioni, 2023). Self-awareness exercises form another critical pillar of this educational framework. Leaders must embark on a journey of self-discovery, soliciting feedback from colleagues, contemplating their sociocultural identities and privileges, and engaging in reflective journaling about diversity-related experiences, according to (Dunne-moses, 2023).

Social awareness training amplifies leaders' capacity to empathize and connect with diverse team members. This training encompasses honing emotional intelligence, exploring various cultural perspectives, and mastering the art of active listening (Rajdeep, 2023). Data-driven decision-making workshops equip leaders with the tools to leverage analytics to counteract unconscious biases. These sessions cover implementing objective criteria for personnel decisions, using analytics to identify systemic biases, and constructing diverse panels for interviews and decision-making processes, notes Rajdeep.

Mentoring and reverse mentoring programs serve as conduits for broadening perspectives and forging meaningful relationships. Traditional mentoring propels underrepresented employees upward, while reverse mentoring offers senior leaders invaluable insights from junior staff about diversity challenges, posits Dunne-moses (2023). According to Radicioni (2023), experiential learning provides immersive opportunities for role-playing exercises, simulations showing bias impact, and cross-cultural immersion experiences.

Ongoing education and resources ensure that inclusion remains at the forefront of organizational consciousness. Regular workshops on specific diversity topics, inclusion-focused book clubs, and access to online toolkits for inclusive leadership provide continuous learning opportunities, according to Dunne-moses. By synthesizing these diverse training and education methods, organizations can arm their leaders with the requisite knowledge, skills, and awareness to foster genuinely inclusive environments. Therefore, according to (Korn, 2023), it is imperative to recognize that the journey towards inclusive leadership is not a finite destination but an ongoing odyssey. It demands unwavering commitment, consistent effort, and an insatiable appetite for growth and learning.

Promoting Inclusive Leadership

In the contemporary business milieu, inclusive communication harnesses the full potential of diversity and inclusion within organizational confines. By fostering an environment ripe for candid discourse and exemplifying communication steeped in respect, enterprises can cultivate an environment where employees feel esteemed, acknowledged, and emboldened to proffer their insights. The gravitas of inclusive communication cannot be overstated because it catalyzes employee engagement, as posited by Scott (2023), who argues that when staff members perceive their voices as both heard and respected, their commitment to their vocational pursuits intensifies. This engagement engenders a wellspring of creativity and innovation. *Figure 2* below describes what HR can do to foster inclusive communication.

Figure 2. What HR can do to foster inclusive communication

(HIHR - Academy to Innovate HR)

Scala's 2023 report suggests that different viewpoints and open discussions lead to better problem-solving and more creative ideas. Leaders who actively absorb and consider viewpoints are better positioned to render judicious and comprehensive decisions (Watts, 2022). The ramifications of inclusive communication extend beyond mere productivity. Scott (2023) contends that it engenders a sense of belongingness and respect among all employees, contributing to a more healthful workplace atmosphere. According to Scala, the literature corroborates this notion, showing that organizations prioritizing diversity and inclusive practices are more likely to witness improved financial returns, attract top-tier talent, and elevate organizational performance.

Organizations can adopt a multifaceted approach to promulgate inclusive communication within the workplace. Developing awareness and empathy is a cornerstone strategy. Leaders and employees should be galvanized to recognize their own inherent biases and cultivate compassion for the experiences of others. This approach can be achieved through several methods: unconscious bias training, active listening exercises, and encouraging perspective-taking (Watts, 2022). The utilization of inclusive language is paramount. Leaders must support respectful and inclusive verbiage for all individuals, irrespective of their background, which entails eschewing gendered language, employing person-first language when discussing disabilities, and remaining cognizant of cultural nuances in communication styles (Scott, 2023; Watts, 2022).

Creating safe spaces for dialogue is crucial. Organizations must establish forums and opportunities for open, honest discussions about diversity and inclusion. These safe spaces can manifest as regular team meetings dedicated to D&I topics, employee resource groups, and anonymous feedback channels (Kaado, 2016). Leadership must model inclusive behavior, setting a precedent through their interactions. This activity involves actively seeking diverse perspectives, acknowledging and valuing different viewpoints, and addressing microaggressions and exclusive behavior promptly (Kaado, 2016; Watts, 2022).

Providing inclusive communication training is essential. Organizations should offer ongoing development opportunities to enhance employees' communication skills, focusing on cultural competence, effective listening techniques, and conflict resolution in diverse teams (Duke University, 2024; Watts, 2022). In short, promoting inclusive communication is indispensable for leveraging the benefits of diversity and inclusion in the workplace. Organizations can forge a more inclusive, innovative, and high-performing work environment by fostering open dialogue, modeling respectful communication, and actively listening to diverse perspectives. This approach benefits individual employees and contributes to the organization's overall success and competitiveness in today's diverse global marketplace.

Evaluating and Adjusting Policies for Inclusivity

The exigency of policy recalibration for inclusivity cannot be overstated in the ever-evolving corporate culture landscape. A systematic approach to identifying extant impediments and implementing diversity-promoting strategies is paramount. Frequent policy audits, ideally conducted triennially, ensure relevance and compliance with current legislative frameworks (Power DMS, 2020). Catalysts for policy reappraisal are multifarious. They encompass corporate amalgamations, leadership transitions, legislative amendments affecting organizational operations, and incidents highlighting policy lacunae (Power DMS, 2020).

These events lead the organization to take a proactive role in its transformation. Inclusivity barriers are manifold and insidious. Unconscious bias, the absence of diverse exemplars in leadership echelons, communication dissonance stemming from cultural divergences, entrenched resistance to change, and systemic prejudices favoring specific demographics are formidable obstacles (Diversity in Tech, 2021; Tulsiani, 2023; Workhuman Editorial Team, 2023). Overcoming these hurdles demands robust, comprehensive strategies.

To foster diversity and inclusion, organizations must implement comprehensive initiatives. These include instituting compelling training programs to illuminate unconscious biases and furnish tools for their mitigation. Using various scenarios and interactive workshops enhances comprehension and engagement. Specialized leadership training focusing on inclusive behaviors, such as active listening and cultural intelligence, ensures that those at the helm are equipped to navigate diverse teams and uphold D&I values, argues Tulsiani (2023). Collaboration between HR and management is crucial in revising policies that may harbor systemic biases. Establishing heterogeneous hiring panels ensures a mixture of perspectives in the recruitment processes. It is vital to create transparent communication channels where employees can vocalize their experiences and suggestions. Employee surveys are other invaluable tools for garnering feedback and identifying areas ripe for improvement (Grossmann, 2024; Tulsiani, 2023).

Implementing mentorship programs supports the career trajectory of underrepresented groups while promoting qualified candidates from diverse backgrounds encourages leadership heterogeneity (Grossmann, 2024). Measuring and monitoring progress through qualitative and quantitative metrics is essential for assessing the impact of D&I initiatives (Tulsiani, 2023). Organizations can create a more inclusive and diverse workplace by fostering a continuous learning and adaptation culture. This ongoing commitment enhances employee satisfaction and innovation and propels organizational success in an increasingly competitive business landscape.

Foster Employee Resource Groups (ERGs)

Employee Resource Groups (ERGs) have emerged as a lodestar for diversity, equity, and inclusion (DEI) initiatives in corporate dynamics. These employee-led collectives, bound by shared attributes and experiences, are the bedrock of workplace inclusivity. ERGs span a kaleidoscope of diversity dimensions, encompassing gender, ethnicity, race, sexual orientation (LGBTQ+), disability status, veteran status, age, parental status, and religious affiliation. Empirical evidence suggests that judicious utilization of ERGs yields many benefits for employees and organizations.

The multifaceted advantages of ERGs are manifold. They serve as sanctuaries where employees can forge connections with kindred spirits, mitigating feelings of alienation and augmenting job satisfaction (Wikipedia, 2024; Catalino et al., 2022). By offering opportunities for networking, mentorship, and professional growth, ERGs elevate employee engagement and retention rates. These groups play a pivotal role in attracting diverse talent and nurturing an inclusive milieu that fosters the retention of underrepresented cohorts (Catalino et al., 2022). The confluence of diverse perspectives within ERGs engenders innovative solutions and enhances decision-making processes (Seramount, 2020). Moreover, Catalino and colleagues argue that ERGs provide a crucible for employees to hone leadership acumen and gain organizational visibility.

Organizations should adopt myriad strategies to harness the full potential of ERGs in propelling diversity and inclusion initiatives. Securing executive sponsorship for each ERG establishes a direct conduit to decision-makers and shows organizational commitment (Hastwell, 2023). According to Catalino and colleagues, aligning ERG objectives with the company's overarching DEI strategy and business goals is paramount. Promoting allyship by encouraging open membership across all ERGs and transcending specific identity groups fosters inclusivity, according to Seramount (2020). Acknowledging and supporting the intersectionality of identities by facilitating collaboration between different ERGs is crucial.

Allocating sufficient funding, time, and resources for ERG activities and initiatives is imperative, posits (Hastwell, 2023). Regular assessments of ERG efficacy through employee surveys and pertinent metrics ensure alignment with inclusion objectives (Catalino et al., 2022; Hastwell, 2023). Leveraging ERGs as talent incubators to identify and nurture diverse potential within the organization maximizes their impact. According to Catalino and colleagues, encouraging ERG participation in external endeavors, such as volunteerism or community outreach, bolsters the organization's brand and social impact.

By embracing these diverse dimensions of diversity and implementing supportive strategies, organizations can unlock the transformative power of ERGs. This approach cultivates a more inclusive work environment and enhances employee satisfaction, innovation, and overall business performance. The judicious cultivation of ERGs is a catalyst for meaningful change in organizational DEI initiatives. Through their strategic implementation, companies can forge a path toward a more equitable and inclusive future, harnessing the full potential of their diverse workforce.

Leveraging Diversity and Inclusion with Technology

Modern workplaces are transforming. Using diverse teams and the latest technology can dramatically improve productivity, new ideas, and employee satisfaction. Visionary leaders possess a plethora of strategies to actualize transformative outcomes. Cloud computing, for instance, serves as a conduit for remote work and flexible schedules. Behemoths like AWS, Google Cloud, and Microsoft Azure empower employees with ubiquitous access to work resources, ensuring minimal friction collaboration and ironclad data security (Owl Labs Staff, 2024).

Project management tools are indispensable for remote teams. Asana, Trello, and Monday.com function as digital orchestrators, harmonizing task organization, progress tracking, and accountability, as described by Owl Labs Staff. Real-time communication and collaboration find their digital avatars in video conferencing platforms like Zoom and Microsoft Teams, while instant messaging apps such as Slack bridge the chasm between remote and in-office employees (Owl Labs Staff, 2024; Tulsiani, 2023).

Accessibility and accommodation for diverse communication styles are paramount. Assistive technology tools, including screen readers like JAWS and NVDA and speech-to-text software like Dragon Naturally speaking, empower employees with disabilities to perform optimally. Unified communication platforms like Microsoft Teams and Google Workspace amalgamate various communication modalities, catering to different preferences and needs. These interfaces offer customizable fonts, colors, and layouts, accommodating diverse visual and cognitive requirements.

AI-powered recruitment and assessment tools are revolutionizing hiring practices. Applied and GapJumpers employ anonymization techniques to mitigate biases, focusing exclusively on skills and qualifications (Forbes Technology Council, 2023). Pymetrics and HireVue leverage AI to evaluate candidates' aptitudes and potential fit, promoting fair hiring practices through data-driven insights, posits Forbes Technology Council. Virtual reality has emerged as a potent tool for empathy training. Platforms like Mursion and Strivr offer VR-based modules simulating real-life scenarios, fostering empathy and understanding among diverse colleagues (Tulsiani, 2023). Tulsiani posits that mastering remote work causes superior technology and behavioral metamorphosis. Immersive VR learning environments facilitate perspective-taking, cultivating a profound comprehension of diversity and inclusion issues.

Data analytics plays a crucial role in identifying gaps and opportunities. HR analytics tools like Visier and ADP Workforce Now provide granular insights into workforce demographics, illuminating diversity gaps and tracking the efficacy of inclusion initiatives. Employee feedback platforms, such as Culture Amp and Qualtrics, harvest and analyze employee sentiments, offering valuable insights for improvement and gauging the impact of diversity programs. Flexible workplace solutions are integral to this technological revolution. Proptech, an intelligent building system, enables the creation of malleable workspaces tailored to diverse teams, enhancing comfort and productivity (Ballejos, 2024). Employee scheduling software (When I Work and Deputy) offers flexible scheduling options, empowering employees to select shifts that align with their personal needs, thus promoting work-life equilibrium (Behnke, 2024). By judiciously implementing these technologies, organizations can forge an inclusive and supportive work ecosystem that harnesses the full potential of a diverse workforce.

Best Practices for Tailoring Diversity and Inclusion Strategies to Local Needs

In today's globalized business landscape, the imperative for diversity and inclusion (D&I) transcends mere moral obligation. It is a strategic imperative, a wellspring of innovation, and a catalyst for organizational success. Trailblazing companies are not just embracing D&I; they are sculpting it to fit local contours, embedding it deep within their organizational DNA. Consider Sodexo's unwavering commitment to gender parity. Their inclusion in Bloomberg's Gender Equality Index is not a coincidence but the fruit of concerted effort (Deady, 2020). With 37% women on their executive committee and a staggering 60% female representation on their board, Sodexo is not just talking the talk. They are following through on their promises.

Johnson & Johnson's approach is equally compelling. Their ambitious targets - 50% women in global management and 35% racial diversity in U.S. management by 2025 - are not pipe dreams. They are meticulously crafted goals underpinned by 12 Employee Resource Groups that serve as crucibles for an inclusive culture, argues Deady (2020). The direct reporting line between the Chief Diversity Officer and the CEO underscores the gravitas accorded to D&I at the highest echelons.

PepsiCo's modus operand is nothing short of revolutionary. Their data-driven approach, allowing employees to self-identify their sexual orientation and gender identity where legally permissible, is a masterclass in cultural sensitivity (World Economic Forum, 2024). By partnering with local legal luminaries, PepsiCo ensures its global D&I strategies are legally compliant and culturally resonant.

Salesforce's DEI initiative is a paragon of personalization. Offering confidential tête-à-têtes with internal coaches, they address the barriers to inclusion at a granular level (World Economic Forum, 2024). With over 2,400 cases supported, the transformative impact is palpable, manifesting in increased participant retention. Baker Hughes' supplier diversity policy is a testament to its commitment to D&I beyond its organizational boundaries. By introducing inclusive language in sourcing documents and establishing Supplier Diversity Champions (SDC), they diversify their supply chain and cultivate a more inclusive industry ecosystem (Hughes, 2022).

McKinsey & Company's global program for returning mothers is a masterpiece of localization. By allowing regional adjustments to accommodate varying leave lengths and parental support structures, they have achieved a remarkable 20% decline in attrition among EU consultant mothers (World Economic Forum, 2024). The correlation between diversity and innovation is irrefutable. Research by Josh Bersin shows that inclusive companies can experience a staggering 1.7-fold increase in innovation levels (Deady, 2020). D&I transcends mere benevolence; it enhances outcomes.

The path to true diversity and inclusion is not a one-size-fits-all proposition. It demands a nuanced approach that respects local nuances while adhering to global principles. By tailoring strategies to local needs, leveraging external partnerships, and embedding D&I practices throughout their organizations, companies can create a more inclusive culture, drive innovation, and ultimately, outperform their peers.

CONCLUSION AND SUMMARY

The chapter begins with an interesting premise: diversity and inclusion (D&I) have developed beyond aspirational goals to become critical drivers of organizational success. This significant change in viewpoint allows us to examine how organizations can effectively use diversity and inclusion programs to improve and compete globally. The foundation of successful D&I implementation lies in thorough organizational assessment. The chapter emphasizes that organizations must carefully evaluate their current landscape, including existing culture, demographics, and technological infrastructure, before implementing any initiatives. This initial assessment is a crucial diagnostic tool, revealing obvious and subtle barriers to inclusion while identifying opportunities for meaningful change.

Leadership development and education emerge as central themes throughout the chapter. The text argues that transformative D&I implementation requires leaders who understand and can address unconscious bias, practice inclusive communication, and show cultural competency. These leaders must champion D&I initiatives, model inclusive behaviors, and create psychological safety within their teams. The chapter particularly emphasizes the importance of ongoing education and training, suggesting that leadership development in D&I is not a one-time effort but a continuous journey of growth and learning. The role of policy evolution and structural change receives significant attention. Organizations must systematically evaluate and adjust their policies to support D&I initiatives and conduct regular audits to ensure alignment with their inclusion goals. This process includes revising hiring practices, promotion criteria, and communication protocols. The chapter illustrates how successful organizations have implemented these changes through detailed case studies of companies like Sodexo, Johnson & Johnson, and PepsiCo, each showing unique approaches to policy transformation.

Employee Resource Groups (ERGs) are vital engines of D&I implementation. The chapter explores how these employee-led collectives serve multiple purposes: providing support networks for underrepresented groups, offering professional development opportunities, contributing to business innovation, and fostering cultural awareness. The text emphasizes that successful ERGs require proper funding, executive sponsorship, and precise alignment with organizational objectives to maximize their impact. Technology emerges as a powerful enabler of D&I initiatives. The chapter details how organizations can leverage modern tools, from AI-powered recruitment platforms that reduce hiring bias to virtual reality systems that enhance empathy training. Data analytics plays a crucial role in tracking progress and identifying areas for improvement, while communication platforms support diverse work styles and facilitate inclusive collaboration.

To work well, programs for diversity and inclusion must follow the best ways of doing things, considering international guidelines and local needs. Through case studies, the text shows how leading organizations have maintained consistent D&I values while adjusting their approaches to accommodate local cultural contexts and legal requirements. This flexibility has proven crucial for organizations operating across different regions and cultures. According to the chapter, the impact of successful D&I implementation manifests in multiple ways. Organizations that effectively implement D&I initiatives experience enhanced innovation, improved decision-making, stronger employee engagement, and superior business performance. These outcomes directly support the chapter's initial premise that D&I are essential drivers of organizational success.

Looking toward the future, the chapter concludes that D&I implementation is an ongoing journey rather than a destination. Organizations must continuously adapt their approaches as workforce demographics evolve, societal expectations shift, and new technologies emerge. The text emphasizes that successful D&I implementation requires sustained commitment, regular assessment, and willingness to adapt strategies based on measured outcomes. This comprehensive exploration effectively bridges theory and practice, providing organizations with a clear roadmap for transforming

D&I from abstract concepts into tangible reality. By maintaining a clear connection between its introduction and detailed implementation strategies, the chapter offers valuable guidance for organizations at any stage of their D&I journey, reinforcing the fundamental importance of these initiatives in modern business success.

Recommendations

Senior Leadership Recommendations

Senior leaders should champion diversity and inclusion as core organizational values and strategic imperatives. They should set clear, measurable D&I objectives aligned with business goals and ensure accountability by integrating these objectives into performance evaluations. Leaders must undergo comprehensive, urgent training on unconscious bias and inclusive leadership practices. They should actively seek diverse perspectives, model inclusive behavior, and address microaggressions promptly. Establishing a direct reporting line between the Chief Diversity Officer and the CEO underscores the importance of D&I at the highest levels.

Manager-Level Recommendations

Managers play a crucial role in fostering an inclusive environment. To equip them for this task, they should receive specialized training on inclusive leadership, active listening, cultural intelligence, and creating psychological safety within their teams. This training is crucial as it prepares them to have tough conversations about diversity and inclusion and to address biases in hiring, promotion, and day-to-day interactions. They should be encouraged to mentor underrepresented employees and support Employee Resource Groups (ERGs).

Recommendations for Underrepresented Groups

Organizations should prioritize creating safe spaces for underrepresented groups to voice their experiences and concerns. It is a crucial step in fostering a sense of belonging and inclusion. These safe spaces can be achieved through Employee Resource Groups (ERGs), which should be adequately funded and supported. Mentorship and sponsorship programs should support career progression for underrepresented employees. Companies should offer leadership development opportunities tailored to these groups to build a diverse pipeline of future leaders.

Integrating Corporate Social Responsibility (CSR)

As Baker Hughes ' supplier diversity policy exemplifies, D&I efforts should be integrated with CSR initiatives to create a holistic approach to social impact, which could involve partnering with diverse suppliers. Companies should engage in community outreach programs that support underrepresented groups, aligning these efforts with their D&I goals. They should also consider how their products and services impact diverse communities and strive for inclusive design and accessibility.

Communication Strategies

Develop a comprehensive communication plan to articulate the organization's commitment to D&I. This plan should include regular updates on progress toward D&I goals, success stories, and lessons learned. To reach all employees, use multiple channels, including company-wide meetings, intranets, and social media. Encourage open dialogue about D&I issues and provide platforms for employees to share their experiences and ideas.

Leveraging Social Capital

Recognize and leverage the social capital of diverse employees to enhance organizational performance. Create networking opportunities across different groups, encourage cross-functional collaboration, and value diverse employees' unique perspectives and connections. ERGs can play a significant role in building social capital within the organization.

Aligning Organizational Systems and Practices

Audits of HR policies and practices are conducted to identify and eliminate systemic biases, which include reviewing recruitment, promotion, and retention processes. Implement AI-powered recruitment tools to mitigate bias in hiring, as shown by companies using platforms like Applied and GapJumpers. Develop flexible work policies that accommodate diverse needs, supported by technology solutions for remote work and collaboration.

Create a data-driven approach to D&I, allowing employees to self-identify various aspects of their identity where legally permissible, as PepsiCo exemplifies. Use this data to track progress and inform decision-making. Implement HR analytics tools to provide insights into workforce demographics and the effectiveness of D&I initiatives. Establish a robust feedback mechanism, such as Salesforce's confidential coaching sessions, to address individual barriers to inclusion. Regularly assess the impact of D&I initiatives through employee surveys and relevant metrics.

Finally, recognize that D&I efforts must be tailored to local contexts while adhering to global principles. This strategy may involve adjusting strategies to accommodate varying cultural norms, legal requirements, and social structures in different regions, as demonstrated by McKinsey & Company's global program for returning mothers. By implementing these multilevel recommendations and aligning organizational systems to support D&I initiatives, companies can create genuinely inclusive environments that drive innovation, enhance decision-making, and ultimately lead to superior business performance in an increasingly diverse and dynamic global marketplace.

As organizations master the integration of digital innovation with their core values, they must equally address the human dimension of organizational excellence through diversity and inclusion. The successful implementation of digital transformation creates a foundation for leveraging diverse perspectives and inclusive practices, enabling organizations to harness technological capabilities and human potential. Integrating digital sophistication with human diversity represents a crucial evolution in organizational development, where technological advancement and inclusive practices converge to drive innovation and sustainable growth.

While digital transformation and inclusive practices establish the internal foundations for organizational excellence, external forces demand equally sophisticated approaches to strategic adaptation. The convergence of technological capabilities with human diversity creates a robust platform from which organizations can address their operating environments' increasing volatility and complexity. This intersection of internal readiness and external challenge frames the next evolution in organizational leadership: developing adaptive strategic methodologies that can harness both technological sophistication and human potential to navigate uncertainty while maintaining strategic coherence.

REFERENCES

Anggoro, A., & Anjarini, A. D. (2024). Building an organizational culture that supports diversity and inclusion. *Productivity*, 1(1), 190–197. DOI: 10.62207/12cjyv77

Ballejos, L. (2024). 4 Ways Technology Supports a Remote Workforce | NinjaOne. https://www.ninjaone.com/blog/4-ways-technology-supports-a-remote-workforce/

Barbour, H. (2024). Examples of Diversity Goals to Measure. https://blog.ongig.com/diversity-and-inclusion/diversity-goals/

Behnke, K. (2024). 18 Best Free Employee Scheduling Software of 2024. Black & White Zebra. https://peoplemanagingpeople.com/tools/best-free-employee-scheduling-software/

Brainard, M. (2017). The Impact Of Unconscious Bias On Leadership Decision Making. Forbes. https://www.forbes.com/sites/forbescoachescouncil/2017/09/13/the-impact-of-unconscious-bias-on-leadership-decision-making/

Catalino, N., Gardner, N., Goldstein, D., & Wong, J. (2022). Effective employee resource groups are key to inclusion at work. Here's how to get them right. McKinsey & Company. https://www.mckinsey.com/capabilities/people-and-organizational-performance/our-insights/effective-employee-resource-groups-are-key-to-inclusion-at-work-heres-how-to-get-them-right

Claremont Lincoln University. (2023). 12 Reasons Why Diversity, Equity, and Inclusion Are Important in Business - Claremont Lincoln. https://www.claremontlincoln.edu/12-reasons-why-diversity-equity-and-inclusion-are-important-in-business/

Deady, D. (2020). 9 Companies Around the World That Are Embracing Diversity in a BIG Way. SocialTalent. https://www.socialtalent.com/blog/diversity-and-inclusion/9-companies-around-the-world-that-are-embracing-diversity

Diversity in Tech. (2021). Barriers to workplace inclusion and diversity - Diversity in Tech. https://www.diversityintech.co.uk/barriers-to-workplace-inclusion-and-diversity/

Duke University. (2024). Culturally Inclusive Communication in the Workplace |. Duke University. https://sites.nicholas.duke.edu/studio/presentation-resources/culturally-inclusive-communication-in-the-workplace/

Dunne-moses, A. (2023). Inclusive Leadership: Steps to Take to Get It Right. Center for Creative Leadership. https://www.ccl.org/articles/leading-effectively-articles/when-inclusive-leadership-goes-wrong-and-how-to-get-it-right/

Forbes Technology Council. (2023). 20 Tips For Tech Leaders Seeking To Build Diverse And Inclusive Teams. Forbes. https://www.forbes.com/sites/forbestechcouncil/2023/08/02/20-tips-for-tech-leaders-seeking-to-build-diverse-and-inclusive-teams/

Gill, G., McNally, M., & Berman, V. (2018). Effective diversity, equity, and inclusion practices. *Healthcare Management Forum*, 31(5), 196–199. DOI: 10.1177/0840470418773785 PMID: 30114938

Grossmann, C. (2024). 8 Proven Strategies to Foster Diversity and Inclusivity in the Workplace. Beekeeper. https://www.beekeeper.io/blog/5-ways-promote-workplace-diversity/

Hastwell, C. (2023). What Are Employee Resource Groups (ERGs)? https://www.greatplacetowork.com/resources/blog/what-are-employee-resource-groups-ergs

Hughes, B. (2022). Forward Together.

Kaado, B. (2016). Promoting Diversity: Why Inclusive Communication and Involvement Matter. Businessnewsdaily.Com. https://www.businessnewsdaily.com/9488-diversity-inclusive-communication.html

Korn Ferry. (2023). The journey to becoming a more inclusive leader. Korn Ferry. https://www.kornferry.com/insights/featured-topics/diversity-equity-inclusion/the-journey-to-becoming-a-more-inclusive-leader

Lightfoote, J., Fielding, J., Deville, C., Gunderman, R., Morgan, G., Pandharipande, P., Duerinckx, A. J., Wynn, R. B., & Macura, K. (2014). Improving diversity, inclusion, and representation in radiology and radiation oncology part 1: Why these matter. *Journal of the American College of Radiology*, 11(7), 673–680. DOI: 10.1016/j.jacr.2014.03.007 PMID: 24993534

Lubis, M. (2024). The Role of Communication and Employee Engagement in Promoting Inclusion in the Workplace: A Case Study in the Creative Industry. *Feedback International Journal of Communication*, 1(1), 1–15.

McKinsey & Company. (2022). What is diversity, equity, and inclusion? Myers, V. (2015). Diversity is being invited to the party; inclusion is being asked to dance. In American Bar Association (Vol. 1, No. 11).

Owl Labs Staff. (2024). The best technology for remote working: 4 essential tools.

Power, D. M. S. (2020). Why it is important to review policies and procedures. https://www.powerdms.com/policy-learning-center/why-it-is-important-to-review-policies-and-procedures

Pulugurtha, N. (2023). Breaking Barriers: The Stride Framework For Advancing Women Of Color In Product Management. *International Research Journal of Modernization in Engineering Technology and Science*. Advance online publication. DOI: 10.56726/IRJMETS41433

Purwoko, B. (2024). Diversity and inclusion initiatives: Influence on organizational performance. *Productivity*, 1(3), 461–471. DOI: 10.62207/w5fsnn95

Radicioni, B. (2023). What Is Inclusive Leadership? Entrepreneurship of All Kinds.

Rajdeep, D. (2023). Unconscious Bias: Navigating its Impact on Leadership in a Hybrid Work Environment | LinkedIn. https://www.linkedin.com/pulse/unconscious-bias-navigating-its-impact-leadership-hybrid-dutta/

Scala, S. A. (2023). Why Inclusive Communication Matters in the Workplace. Associated Industries of Massachusetts. https://aimnet.org/why-inclusive-communication-matters-in-the-workplace/

Scott, C. (2023). Inclusive Communication: What Is It and Why It Matters. AIHR | Academy to Innovate HR. https://www.aihr.com/blog/inclusive-communication/

Seramount. (2020). Inclusive Employee Resource Groups. https://seramount.com/resources/research-report-inclusive-employee-resource-groups/

The National Society Of Leadership And Success. (2022). Why Is Diversity Important in Leadership? https://www.nsls.org/blog/why-is-diversity-important-in-leadership

Tulsiani, R. (2023). Overcoming Barriers To Diversity And Inclusion: A Guide For L&D Pros. ELearning Industry Inc. https://elearningindustry.com/overcoming-barriers-to-diversity-and-inclusion-a-guide-for-ld-pros

Tynes, B. (2022). The Importance Of Diversity And Inclusion For Today's Companies. Forbes. https://www.forbes.com/sites/forbescommunicationscouncil/2022/03/03/the-importance-of-diversity-and-inclusion-for-todays-companies/

Vandenbroucke, H. (2022). Sense of belonging among UGent Faculty of Economics and Business Administration students. https://libstore.ugent.be/fulltxt/rug01/003/158/502/rug01-003158502_2023_0001_ac.pdf

Watts, C. (2022). How to Promote Inclusive Communication in the Workplace. https://www.highspeedtraining.co.uk/hub/inclusive-communication-in-the-workplace/

Wikipedia. (2024). Employee resource group. https://en.wikipedia.org/w/index.php?title=Employee_resource_group&oldid=1198628824

Workhuman Editorial Team. (2023). Barriers to Diversity in the Workplace | Workhuman. https://www.workhuman.com/blog/barriers-to-diversity/

World Economic Forum. (2024). These organizations are scaling impactful corporate diversity, equity, and inclusion initiatives. https://www.weforum.org/agenda/2024/01/organizations-impactful-corporate-dei-initiatives/

KEY TERMS AND DEFINITIONS

AI-Powered Recruitment: Artificial intelligence and machine learning algorithms are used to support unbiased hiring practices and candidate assessment.

Assistive Technology: Tools and software that help people with disabilities perform tasks and participate fully in the workplace.

Chief Diversity Officer (CDO): An executive-level position responsible for developing and implementing an organization's diversity and inclusion strategy, often with direct reporting lines to the CEO.

Compliance Monitoring: The systematic review and evaluation of an organization's adherence to D&I policies, legal requirements, and established guidelines.

Cultural Competence: The ability to understand, communicate, and effectively interact with people from different cultures and backgrounds.

Cultural Intelligence (CQ): The capability to relate and work effectively across cultures, essential for leadership in diverse organizations.

D&I Metrics: Quantitative and qualitative measurements, including demographic data, engagement scores, and retention rates, are used to assess the effectiveness of diversity and inclusion initiatives.

Employee Resource Groups (ERGs): Employee-led collectives within organizations that are formed around shared characteristics, experiences, or interests, serving as platforms for support, professional development, and cultural awareness.

Global D&I Strategy: An organization-wide approach to diversity and inclusion that maintains consistent principles while allowing for local adaptation based on regional needs and cultural contexts.

HR Analytics: The practice of collecting and analyzing HR data to improve an organization's workforce management and performance, particularly about D&I objectives.

Inclusion Index: A composite measure that evaluates the degree to which employees feel included and valued within their organization.

Innovation Dividend: The enhanced creative output and problem-solving capabilities that result from diverse teams and inclusive practices.

Psychological Safety: A shared belief that the team environment is safe for interpersonal risk-taking, allowing members to speak up without fear of negative consequences.

Reasonable Accommodation: Modifications or adjustments to jobs, work environments, or processes that enable individuals with disabilities to perform essential job functions and enjoy equal employment opportunities.

Reverse Mentoring: A practice where junior employees mentor senior leaders to share perspectives on diversity issues and emerging trends.

Social Capital: The networks of relationships among people that enable an organization to function effectively, particularly important in diverse workplace settings.

Supplier Diversity Champions (SDC): Designated individuals or teams responsible for promoting and implementing supplier diversity initiatives within an organization.

Unconscious Bias: Implicit social stereotypes about certain groups of people that individuals form outside their conscious awareness can influence decision-making in the workplace.

Virtual Reality Training: Immersive technology used for diversity and inclusion training, allowing employees to experience different perspectives and scenarios.

Chapter 6
Strategic Planning in Fluid Environments

ABSTRACT

This chapter explores strategic planning in fluid environments of constant change and uncertainty. Traditional rigid planning methods are increasingly ineffective in today's dynamic business landscape. Two key approaches are proposed: scenario planning and Agile methodologies. Scenario planning anticipates potential futures, fostering organizational readiness. Agile methods enable iterative planning and execution, allowing strategies to evolve with real-time feedback. Integrating these approaches creates a powerful framework balancing long-term vision with short-term flexibility. Case studies demonstrate successful implementation across various sectors. Tools like SWOT analysis, Agile roadmaps, and OKRs support this dynamic approach. The chapter emphasizes cultivating adaptability, embracing a growth mindset, and developing dynamic capabilities. Leaders are encouraged to view uncertainty as an opportunity for innovation. By adopting flexible planning, organizations can transform unpredictability into a competitive advantage.

INTRODUCTION

In an era of unprecedented volatility, uncertainty, complexity, and ambiguity, organizations face the critical challenge of maintaining strategic direction while adapting to rapid change. This chapter examines the evolution of strategic planning methodologies as they transform to meet the demands of increasingly fluid business environments. Traditional approaches to strategic planning, characterized by rigid multi-year frameworks and linear execution paths, are giving way to more dynamic, adaptive methodologies that combine the foresight of scenario planning with the flexibility of Agile practices. The text explores how successful organizations develop adaptive capabilities through iterative planning cycles, cross-functional

DOI: 10.4018/979-8-3693-5553-4.ch006

collaboration, and continuous learning processes. By integrating scenario planning's ability to anticipate potential futures with Agile methodologies' emphasis on flexible execution, organizations can better navigate uncertainty while maintaining strategic coherence. This integrated approach enables companies to sense and respond to environmental changes more efficiently, transforming possible setbacks into chances for development and creativity.

This chapter comprehensively analyzes modern strategic planning approaches by exploring theoretical frameworks and practical applications. It begins by examining the limitations of traditional strategic planning methods in today's volatile business terrain, presenting the complementing ideas of Agile strategy and scenario planning methodologies. The discussion includes detailed explorations of specific tools and techniques, including SWOT analysis, Kanban boards, and Objectives and Key Results (OKRs), while emphasizing the crucial role of organizational culture in fostering adaptability. Case studies and success stories illuminate how leading organizations have successfully implemented these dynamic approaches, offering valuable insights for practitioners. The chapter pays particular attention to the critical role of leadership in cultivating an organizational environment that embraces both strategic foresight and operational flexibility. Special consideration is given to the challenges and opportunities presented by technological disruption, changing consumer preferences, and global economic uncertainty.

The chapter concludes by synthesizing key lessons and providing practical guidance for organizations seeking to enhance their strategic planning capabilities in fluid environments. By mastering these dynamic approaches, organizations can develop the resilience and adaptability required to thrive in today's rapidly evolving business landscape while maintaining clear strategic direction and purpose. This comprehensive examination of strategic planning in fluid environments will be valuable for business leaders, strategic planners, and organizational development professionals seeking to enhance their organization's capacity for adaptive strategy development and execution. The chapter combines theoretical rigor with practical applicability, making it an essential resource for academics and practitioners in strategic management.

The Need for Flexibility

In today's tumultuous business landscape, strategic agility is helpful and imperative. The celerity of change demands that organizations cultivate an unparalleled capacity for adaptability. Being able to change plans while keeping your primary goals in mind is key to thriving in today's changing world, and you need to be open to new ideas to do it. Fostering a growth mindset is paramount. It is the bedrock upon which organizations build a culture that not only weathers challenges but thrives on them, transmuting setbacks into invaluable learning experiences (Hall, 2023; Wade et al., 2021). This cognitive framework catalyzes innovation, nurtures creativity, and fortifies adaptability throughout the corporate ecosystem.

Organizational plasticity is crucial and causes flexible structures, processes, and systems that must be engineered to respond enthusiastically to mercurial market demands (Hall, 2023) - cross-functional synergy, decentralized decision-making, and Agile resource allocation support this flexibility. Concurrently, heightened risk awareness coupled with robust mitigation strategies is essential. Comprehensive risk assessments, pinpointing potential Achilles' heel, and crafting contingency plans arm organizations with the tools to navigate turbulent waters, according to Hall. Diversification is the buffer against singularity risk. By broadening product portfolios, customer demographics, and supply chain networks, organizations can better withstand exogenous shocks and adapt to shifting business paradigms, according to Hall (2023). Furthermore, cultivating strategic thinking capabilities across the organizational strata aligns employee development with current strategies while instilling a pervasive strategic mindset, thus mitigating the learning curve when pivots become necessary.

Leadership's role is pivotal. Equipping the workforce with leadership acumen and interdisciplinary skills facilitates seamless collaboration across organizational units, a sine qua non for rapid strategic shifts (Hall, 2023). Hall notes that employee development programs must be pragmatic and immediately applicable, leveraging real-world case studies and strategy-focused curricula and implementing scenario-based learning. The fruits of strategic agility are evident in corporate success stories. Airbnb's nimble pivot during the COVID-19 pandemic culminated in a historic tech IPO (Wade et al., 2021). Netflix's evolution from DVD rentals to streaming content creation exemplifies strategic dexterity (Hastings, 2018). Bosch's restructuring into "cross-functional purpose teams" demonstrates a commitment to enhanced responsiveness, according to Hastings.

These examples underscore how strategic agility empowers organizations to capitalize on emergent opportunities and navigate challenges with unparalleled efficacy. It is a perpetual process, demanding unwavering commitment across all organizational echelons. Leaders must promote this approach, cultivating a milieu that prizes flexibility, continuous learning, and innovation. In doing so, they position their organizations not merely to weather storms but to harness the winds of change, charting a course toward sustained success in an ever-evolving business seascape.

Scenario Planning as a Strategic Tool

Scenario planning in organizations has emerged as a beacon of foresight in the complicated realm of organizational strategy. This potent prognostication tool empowers businesses to visualize a pantheon of potential futures, arming them with the insight to navigate the tumultuous seas of uncertainty. Scenario planning's genesis lies in martial applications, later metamorphosing into a corporate staple through the proactive efforts of Herman Kahn at RAND Corporation in the 1950s. Its ascendancy to prominence was catalyzed by Royal Dutch/Shell's prescient deployment during the 1970s oil crisis (Cabanes, 2023; Bradfield et al., 2005; Burt, 2023). The manifold benefits of this strategic divination are:

1. Engendering strategic plasticity
2. Proactive opportunity and challenge identification
3. Preemptive risk mitigation
4. Structured decision-making paradigms

These advantages coalesce into a formidable competitive edge (Ogilvy, 2015; Saurav, 2023; Mariton, 2016). The alchemic process of scenario crafting adheres to rigorous methodologies, including:

1. Focal issue delineation
2. Data aggregation on salient factors
3. Identification of influential forces
4. Uncertainty prioritization
5. Scenario fabrication (typically 2-5)
6. Impact assessment and strategy formulation
7. Early warning system establishment

This systematic approach ensures a comprehensive exploration of potential futures (Ogilvy, 2015; Cabanes, 2023; Mariton, 2016). *Figure 1* below shows the eight-step scenario planning, a business exercise that helps anticipate problems and consider critical uncertainties for a project, strategy, or organization.

Figure 1. The eight-step scenario planning process

THE EIGHT-STEP SCENARIO PLANNING PROCESS

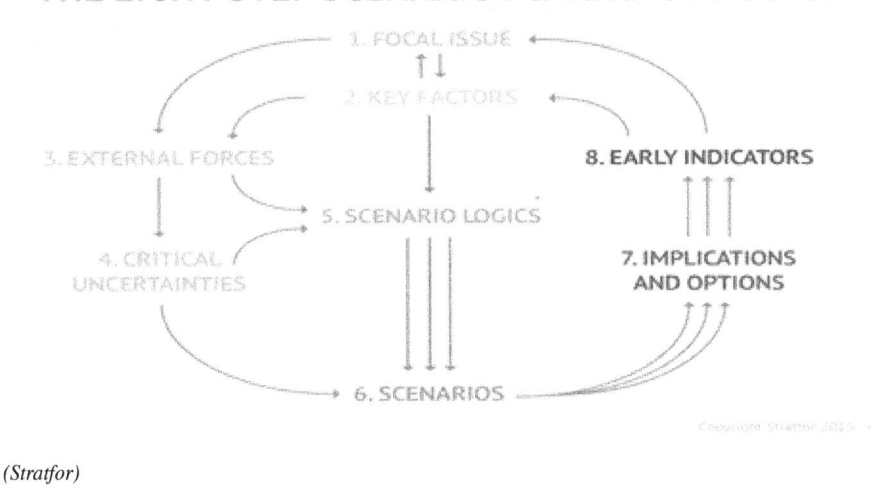

1. FOCAL ISSUE
2. KEY FACTORS
3. EXTERNAL FORCES
4. CRITICAL UNCERTAINTIES
5. SCENARIO LOGICS
6. SCENARIOS
7. IMPLICATIONS AND OPTIONS
8. EARLY INDICATORS

(Stratfor)

Organizations must cultivate a culture of adaptability to harness scenario planning's full potency, developing robust, scenario-agnostic strategies and fostering organizational agility. Vigilant monitoring of critical indicators and regular scenario reassessment enable organizations to maintain their strategic edge. Including diverse stakeholders in the scenario planning process ensures a holistic perspective and engenders widespread support for strategic initiatives (Schoemaker, 1995; Luther & Rami, 2022; Burt, 2023). In the crucible of contemporary business, scenario planning is an indispensable tool for navigating the capricious currents of change.

By embracing this robust methodology, organizations can chart a course through uncertainty, emerging not merely unscathed but poised to capitalize on the myriad opportunities hidden within the mists of the future. Remember, scenario planning provides a competitive advantage by enabling proactive decision-making. By visualizing potential risks and opportunities, your organization can navigate uncertainties effectively and decisively and respond when faced with unexpected events.

The Limitations of Traditional Strategic Planning

In today's unpredictable business landscape, conventional strategic planning methodologies are teetering on the brink of obsolescence. The rapid metamorphosis of markets has rendered these time-honored approaches increasingly inconsistent with contemporary realities. Long-term projections and inflexible plans, often taking months to crystalize, need to be more in sync with the breakneck pace of modern commerce. This disconnect is starkly illuminated by George and Walker's research, which reveals that, while formal strategic planning can bolster organizational performance, it falters in the face of seismic market shifts (Moffitt, 2022). When these strategies are implemented, they are often predicated on antiquated conditions. *Figure 2.* below shows the steps of the old-school strategic planning pyramid.

Figure 2. Old school

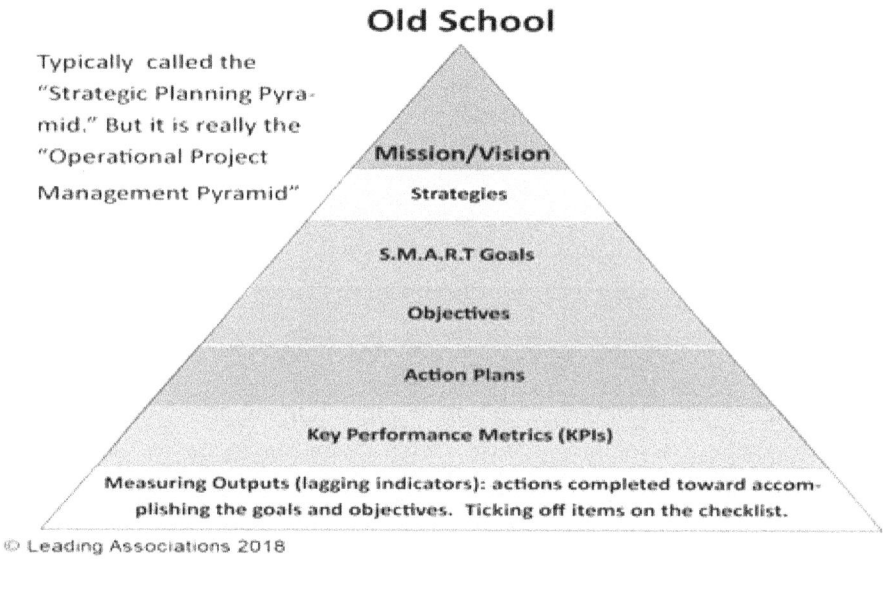

Old School

Typically called the "Strategic Planning Pyramid." But it is really the "Operational Project Management Pyramid"

- Mission/Vision
- Strategies
- S.M.A.R.T Goals
- Objectives
- Action Plans
- Key Performance Metrics (KPIs)

Measuring Outputs (lagging indicators): actions completed toward accomplishing the goals and objectives. Ticking off items on the checklist.

© Leading Associations 2018

(Leading Associations)

More than relying on historical data and past performance to forecast future trends is risky. In the throes of a significant change or rapidly developing market, yesteryear's conditions may be rendered moot. 'We Are Atmosphere' posits that a strategy process predominantly leveraging past knowledge needs to be equipped to navigate the labyrinthine complexities companies face today (Moffitt, 2022). Traditional methods must account for the burgeoning array of viable future scenarios in a volatile environment, a glaring deficiency. The increasing difficulty in selecting a strategy that aligns with a particular anticipated future underscores this complexity (Recklies, 2015). In response to mounting uncertainty, strategists often retreat into myopic internal analysis and near-term futures, potentially overlooking external market forces and disruptive trends.

The relentless march of technological progress presents a formidable challenge to traditional strategic planning. McKinsey's study reveals a stark reality by showing that the average lifespan of S&P 500 companies has plummeted from 61 years in 1958 to 18 years today, primarily because of technological disruption (Assnservices,

2018). This rapid turnover lays bare the futility of long-term planning in industries subject to swift change. The COVID-19 pandemic served as a stark reminder of traditional planning's limitations in the face of unforeseen global events. Gartner's 2020 survey found that 74% of CFOs and finance leaders plan to shift at least 5% of their previously on-site workforce to permanent remote positions post-pandemic (Yancey, 2021). This sudden pivot in work arrangements upended many long-term strategic plans, underscoring the need for more agile approaches.

Traditional strategic planning's need to work on keeping pace with rapidly developing consumer preferences is evident in the disruption of conventional retail strategies by e-commerce and direct-to-consumer models. Deloitte's study found that 58% of consumers altered at least one shopping behavior because of the pandemic, highlighting the imperative for more flexible and responsive strategic approaches (Assnservices, 2018). In response to these limitations, novel approaches to strategic planning are emerging. Companies increasingly embrace more flexible, adaptive strategies, setting shorter delivery timelines and focusing on constant learning and adaptation, posits Moffitt (2022). Advanced scenario planning techniques are gaining traction, incorporating a more comprehensive range of potential futures, and leveraging data analytics.

Some organizations are implementing more iterative and flexible strategic planning processes, borrowing from Agile methodologies in software development. This approach allows for frequent reassessment and adjustment of strategies in response to changing conditions, notes Yancey (2021). In inference, traditional strategic planning methods are floundering in today's volatile business environment. Their reliance on past data, slow adaptation, and limited scenario planning capabilities renders them increasingly ineffective in the face of rapid technological change, market volatility, and shifting consumer behaviors. As a result, organizations are pivoting towards more adaptive and data-driven approaches to strategy formulation to navigate the complexities of the modern business landscape.

TRADITIONAL VS. AGILE STRATEGIC PLANNING

Two divergent strategic planning paradigms have crystallized in modern organizational management's ordeal. While these methodologies aim to propel enterprises toward prosperity, they diverge significantly in their fundamental philosophies and execution. The traditional strategic planning model embodies a top-down, linear trajectory. This modus operandi presupposes a relatively stable business milieu, emphasizing prescience and meticulous forethought (Hanna et al., 2024). Its hallmarks include:

1. Sequential, step-by-step processes
2. Centralized decision-making by upper echelons
3. Expansive, quinquennial to decennial plans
4. Unwavering focus on predictability
5. Immutable resource allocation based on predetermined blueprints (Goetz, 2023).

In stark juxtaposition, Agile strategic planning epitomizes an iterative, adaptable ethos. This methodology acknowledges the mercurial nature of contemporary commerce, prioritizing adaptability above all else (Hanna et al., 2024). Key attributes encompass:

1. Perpetual reassessment and strategic recalibration
2. Collaborative decision-making involving diverse stakeholders
3. Abbreviated planning horizons (often monthly or quarterly)
4. Emphasis on value delivery and change responsiveness
5. Dynamic resource allocation aligned with shifting priorities (Goetz, 2023).

Figure 3. below shows the stark difference between these two methods.

Figure 3. Traditional vs. agile approach

Traditional VS Agile Approach
Software Development

Traditional	Agile
Big & Long	Small & Short
Less Accurate	More & Predictable
Less Flexible	Iterate 2-4 Weeks
Increase Risk Of Failure	Increase Possibility Of Success
Less Management Control	Active Management Control
Wasteful	Eliminate Over Head

(Tech Tammina)

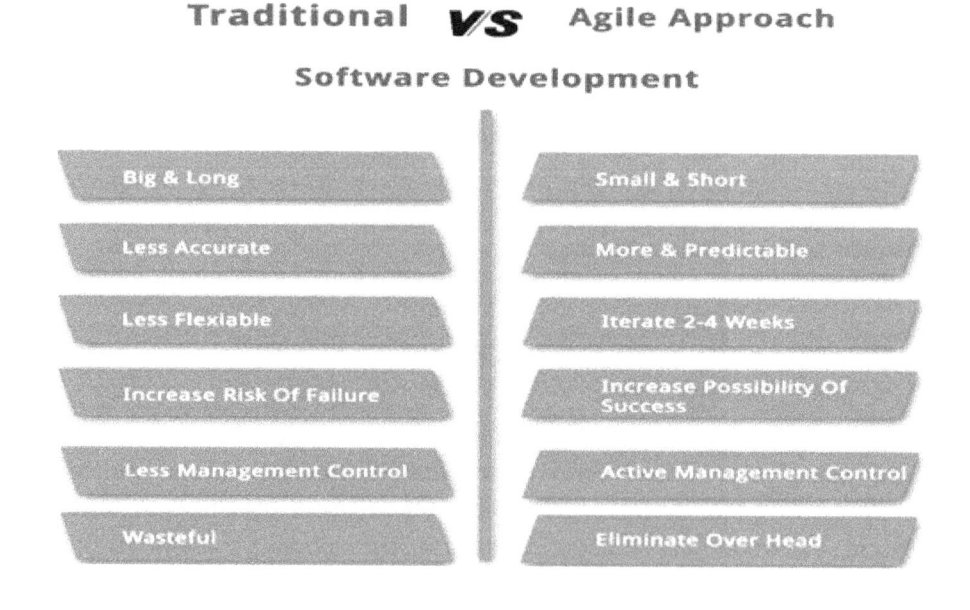

The impetus behind the Agile shift stems from the realization that we cannot plan our way around a world of constant disruption, and any effort to lock in specific execution steps will have gaps and flaws (Hanna et al., 2024). This approach enables organizations to swiftly pivot in response to nascent opportunities or threats, fostering continuous amelioration and erudition (Goetz, 2023).

While traditional planning offers lucid long-term direction and stability, adapting to market vicissitudes can be inflexible and sluggish (Goetz, 2023). Conversely, Agile planning affords greater adaptability but may engender uncertainty because of the need for detailed long-term projections. The selection of these methodologies often hinges on an organization's industry, culture, and specific difficulties. Goetz argues that traditional methods may be more appropriate for stable environments, whereas Agile approaches are frequently favored in dynamic, fast-paced sectors.

In today's rapidly metamorphosing business landscape, many organizations are adopting a hybrid approach, amalgamating traditional and Agile planning elements. This synthesis maintains a pellucid long-term vision while retaining the flexibility to adapt to shifting circumstances (Vizient Newsroom, 2017). Regardless of the chosen methodology, strategic planning's ultimate objective is to give organizations a framework for success in an increasingly labyrinthine and competitive world. By comprehending the strengths and limitations of each approach, leaders can make prudent decisions about the most appropriate planning methodology for their unique context.

Agile Strategic Planning

Agile Strategic Planning is an adaptive, iterative approach to defining and executing organizational strategy. It draws principles from Agile software development, where change is embraced and expected rather than rigidly following a predetermined plan (Writer, 2023). Agile strategic planning revolutionizes organizational flexibility, enabling businesses to pivot quickly in response to real-time feedback and outcomes. This practice confers a plethora of advantages. Metamorphic adaptability stands at the forefront. Agile planning embraces transmutation in a world of flux rather than clinging to ossified strategies, posits Writer. Organizations can swiftly recalibrate in the face of mercurial market dynamics or internal shifts (Hale, 2019). Iterative fluidity sets Agile planning apart. Unlike the linear rigidity of traditional planning, it embodies an adaptable process, establishing a lofty vision while remaining malleable in its pursuit, as described by the Writer. This flexibility allows for continuous refinement of strategies based on emerging insights.

Periodic recalibration forms the heartbeat of Agile planning. Quarterly review cycles validate priorities and ensure imminent endeavors align with overarching strategy, according to Hale (2019). These frequent assessments enable timely course corrections, and value-centric resource allocation drives decision-making. As projects reach fruition and products materialize, value metrics guide investment choices. According to Hale, this laser focus ensures that resources flow to initiatives that yield maximum dividends. Team empowerment flourishes under Agile planning. It decentralizes decision-making, enabling portfolio managers and teams to prioritize projects autonomously. This decentralization catalyzes expeditious execution and fosters accountability. Perpetual synchronization maintains strategic coherence. Continuous dialogue between teams and executives preserves the focus on core priorities while accommodating necessary adjustments, speculates Hale. This ongoing alignment ensures that all efforts remain strategically relevant. The Agile strategic planning process is shown below in *Figure 4*. It shows the iterative nature of the process.

Figure 4. Agile strategic planning process

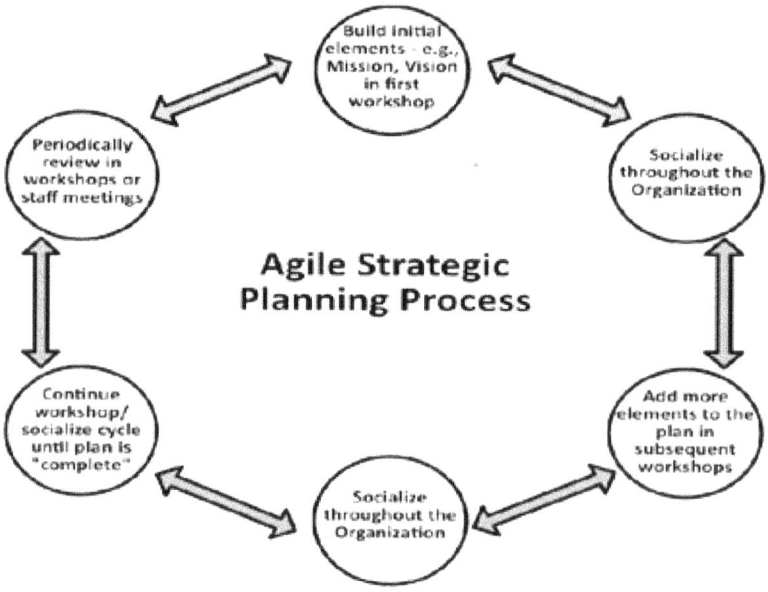

(Gary Rush, IAF CPF)

Rapid threat and opportunity response become second nature. By dissecting strategic initiatives into manageable components, organizations can nimbly navigate emerging market threats or seize nascent opportunities (Premier Agile, n.d.). This agility is paramount in today's volatile business landscape. Enhanced collaborative synergy emerges as a natural byproduct. According to Premier Agile research, cross-functional collaboration and frequent communication foster organizational alignment and spark innovative problem-solving. This synergy drives creativity and efficiency across the enterprise. Outcome-oriented focus sharpens organizational efforts. Agile planning prioritizes achieving desired outcomes over rigid adherence to predefined plans. Teams can pivot their approach as they uncover optimal pathways to strategic objectives, theorizes Writer (2023).

Temporal balance provides both immediate direction and long-term vision. According to Hale (2019), a judicious blend of short-term (quarterly) planning cycles and long-term (12-18 months) scaled planning offers a comprehensive strategic framework. Embracing Agile strategic planning engenders a responsive and adaptive framework. This flexibility empowers organizations to navigate uncertainty, capitalize on emergent opportunities, and maintain a competitive edge in volatile markets. The iterative nature of Agile planning ensures strategies remain relevant and aligned with organizational goals, even as the landscape evolves.

Agile Methodologies

Initially developed for software development, Agile principles can be effectively applied to strategic planning, fostering a culture of flexibility, responsiveness, and adaptability in organizational strategies. This approach, often called 'Agile Strategy Management,' encourages organizations to embrace change and navigate the complexities of the modern business environment with an open mind. This strategic planning revolutionizes traditional approaches by infusing core Agile values into organizational strategy. It prioritizes human interactions over rigid processes, emphasizing stakeholder collaboration (Bydrec, Inc., 2020). This fundamental change favors actionable strategies over verbose documentation, enabling swift implementation and adaptation. Continuous engagement with stakeholders, from customers to employees, becomes paramount in refining strategic direction (ScrumAlliance, 2024). Flexibility reigns supreme, allowing organizations to pivot nimbly in response to market vicissitudes.

The Agile methodology fragments the planning process into manageable iterations. This granular approach facilitates regular recalibration of objectives, heightened responsiveness to market dynamics, and perpetual alignment with organizational aspirations (Z-Stream Blog, 2019). Rapid prototyping has emerged as a crucial tool, permitting expeditious development, and testing of strategic initiatives on a microcosmic scale. These "strategic experiments" yield invaluable insights, informing refinement and scalability decisions (AltexSoft, 2023). At its core, Agile strategy champions ongoing erudition and adaptation. Regular retrospectives scrutinize the efficacy of strategic initiatives, fostering a culture of experimentation and embracing failure as a steppingstone to success, according to the Z-Stream Blog. This iterative learning process permeates the entire strategic planning ecosystem.

Agile methodologies, while diverse, share common threads applicable to strategic planning, including:

1. Rapid iteration
2. Responsive malleability
3. Stakeholder synergy
4. Incremental delivery
5. Empirical process control

In our digital epoch, Agile strategy management assumes even greater significance. It empowers organizations to navigate the tumultuous seas of technological upheaval and digital disruption (ScrumAlliance, 2024). The deluge of real-time data buttresses empirical process control, facilitating data-driven decision-making (Z-Stream Blog, 2019). Agile strategies consider the holistic digital ecosystem, encompassing partners, platforms, and nascent technologies. To successfully implement this avant-garde approach, organizations must:

1. Forge cross-functional teams
2. Leverage visual management tools
3. Institute regular review cycles
4. Cultivate a culture of experimentation
5. Harness cutting-edge technology

By embracing these Agile principles and practices, organizations can craft more responsive, adaptable, and practical strategies. This approach equips them to navigate the labyrinthine complexities of modern business, responding with readiness to change and maintaining strategic alignment with evolving market conditions and stakeholder demands (Altexsolt, 2023; Z-Stream Blog., 2019; ScrumAlliance, 2024). *Figure 5* below describes the 12 Agile principles from the manifesto.

Figure 5. 12 Agile princiles

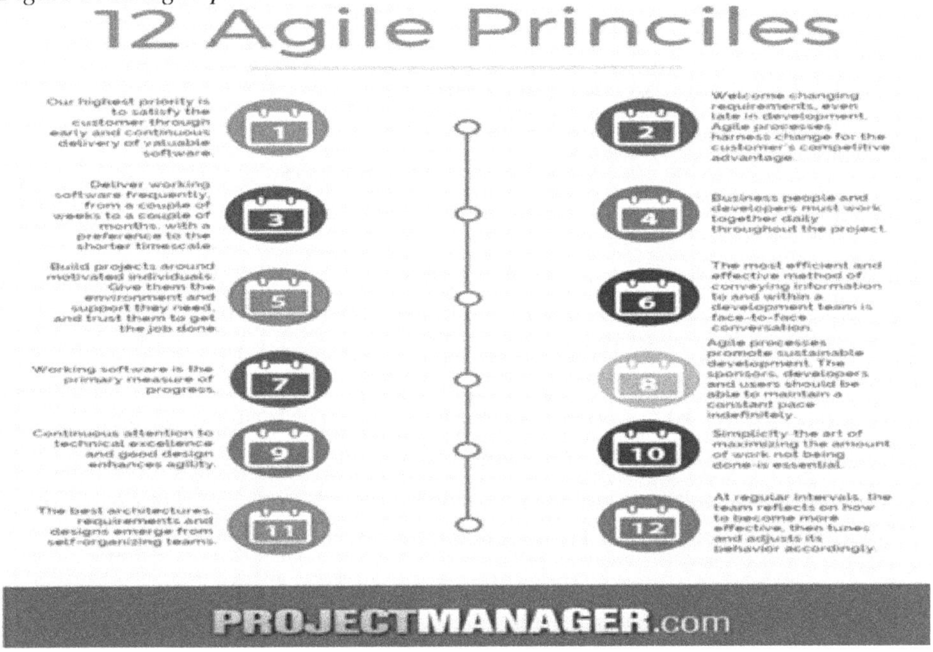

12 Agile Princiles

1. Our highest priority is to satisfy the customer through early and continuous delivery of valuable software.
2. Welcome changing requirements, even late in development. Agile processes harness change for the customer's competitive advantage.
3. Deliver working software frequently, from a couple of weeks to a couple of months, with a preference to the shorter timescale.
4. Business people and developers must work together daily throughout the project.
5. Build projects around motivated individuals. Give them the environment and support they need, and trust them to get the job done.
6. The most efficient and effective method of conveying information to and within a development team is face-to-face conversation.
7. Working software is the primary measure of progress.
8. Agile processes promote sustainable development. The sponsors, developers and users should be able to maintain a constant pace indefinitely.
9. Continuous attention to technical excellence and good design enhances agility.
10. Simplicity—the art of maximizing the amount of work not being done—is essential.
11. The best architectures, requirements and designs emerge from self-organizing teams.
12. At regular intervals, the team reflects on how to become more effective, then tunes and adjusts its behavior accordingly.

PROJECTMANAGER.com

(ProjectManagement.com)

Agile Methodologies for Dynamic Execution

Agile methodology is a dynamic approach to project management and software development that emphasizes iterative development, collaboration, flexibility, and customer satisfaction. This methodology has revolutionized how teams work, particularly in the software industry, by providing a framework that adapts to changing requirements and delivers value quickly. Agile methodology's cornerstone lies in its iterative development approach. Eschewing linear processes, Agile fragments project into manageable iterations or sprints (Simplilearn, 2020). These sprints, typically spanning a fortnight to a month, encompass a comprehensive planning cycle, design, development, and quality assurance (Baker, 2018). The outcome of each sprint yields a potentially shippable product increment. Post-sprint, teams conduct a review to showcase their accomplishments and solicit feedback. This crucial feedback loop serves multiple purposes, including:

1. Aligning the product with customer expectations
2. Preemptive issue identification and resolution
3. Perpetual enhancement of both product and process

Following the review, a retrospective allows for introspection and process refinement (Simplilearn, 2020). This modus operandi facilitates:

- Expeditious and frequent software delivery
- Early and recurrent feedback collection
- Facile adaptation to evolving requirements
- Mitigation of overall project risk

Collaboration is the lifeblood of Agile methodology, both intra-team and with stakeholders. The axiom encapsulates this ethos: "Individuals and interactions over processes and tools" (Agile Alliance, 2015). Cross-functional, self-organizing teams are the norm, fostering close cooperation in problem-solving and decision-making (Simplilearn, 2020). This collaborative milieu, coupled with inherent flexibility, catalyzes team empowerment. Flexibility, another pillar of Agile, acknowledges the mutability of requirements and the emergence of optimal solutions through collaboration and adaptation. This malleability enables teams to:

- Swiftly respond to market fluctuations
- Assimilate nascent ideas and technologies
- Recalibrate priorities based on customer feedback

Customer satisfaction is paramount in Agile methodology. It involves continuous customer engagement, frequent delivery of functional software, feature prioritization based on customer value, and adaptation to evolving customer needs. Agile's prowess lies in its ability to transmute change and uncertainty into strategic advantages through:

1. **Continuous Planning:** Agile teams engage in perpetual planning, adjusting strategies based on the latest intelligence and feedback (Agile Business Consortium, 2024).
2. **Incremental Development:** Regular delivery of small, functional product components allows for rapid pivoting in response to market or customer shifts (Agile Alliance, 2015).
3. **Empirical Process Control:** Agile relies on transparency, inspection, and adaptation to navigate uncertainty (Atlassian, n.d.).
4. **Risk Mitigation:** Prioritizing high-risk or high-value items diminishes overall project risk (Agile Business Consortium, 2024).
5. **Rapid Feedback Loops:** Regular demonstrations and reviews facilitate swift course corrections (Baker, 2018).

In summation, Agile methodology provides a framework for dynamic execution, emphasizing iterative development, collaboration, flexibility, and customer satisfaction. Agile teams can navigate uncertainty and deliver value more effectively than traditional project management approaches by segmenting projects into sprints, gathering regular feedback, and embracing change. The ability to swiftly adapt to changing circumstances is not merely a feature of Agile methodology but a core principle that empowers teams to transmute uncertainty into a competitive edge. *Figure 6* below shows organizations' most popular Agile methodologies for embracing change effectively. These methods use the same principles as described above.

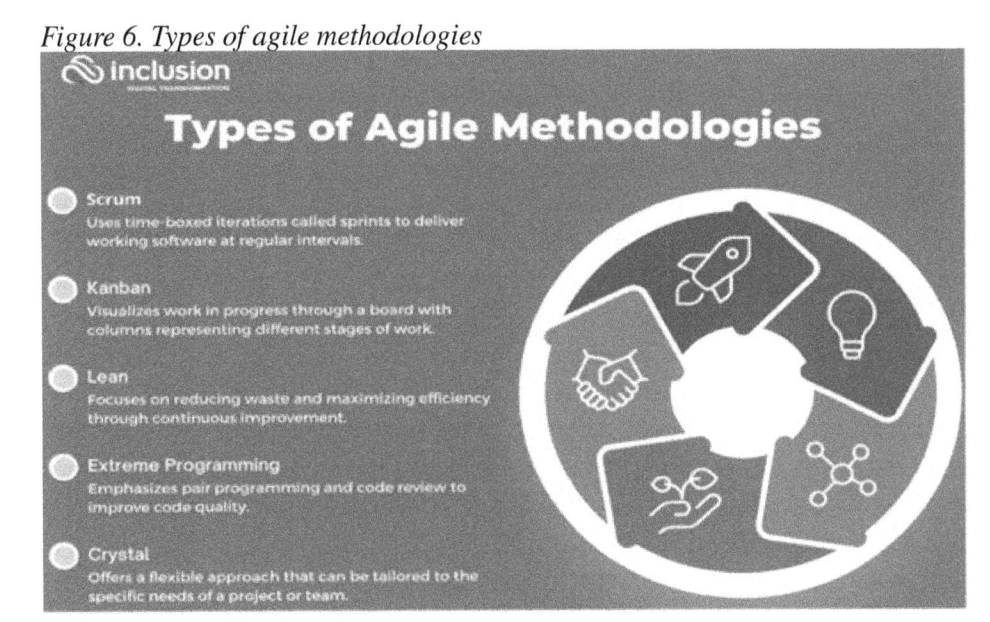

Figure 6. Types of agile methodologies

(Inclusion Digital Transformation)

Combining Scenario Planning with Agile Methodologies

Combining scenario planning with Agile methodologies creates a robust framework for strategic planning in fluid environments by leveraging the strengths of both approaches. This integrated approach allows organizations to expect potential futures while maintaining the flexibility to adapt quickly to changing circumstances. In the complex realm of corporate strategy, a revolutionary symbiosis has emerged, the amalgamation of scenario planning and Agile methodologies. This fusion engenders a formidable framework for strategic planning that is both prescient and malleable, offering solace amidst the tempestuous seas of uncertainty (Mariton, 2016; Atlassian, n.d.).

The quintessential benefits of this union are manifold. Heightened preparedness for capricious futures stands at the forefront, followed closely by augmented decision-making prowess. Amplified organizational plasticity emerges as a crucial advantage, while the synergistic alignment of ephemeral actions with enduring aspirations rounds out the core strengths of this approach. To operationalize this paradigm, astute leaders must embark on a multifaceted journey. They begin by discerning the pivotal catalysts of metamorphosis and critical uncertainties in their commercial milieu (Mariton, 2016). Mariton posits that this foundation enables crafting a quartet of plausible, divergent future scenarios that challenge entrenched assumptions and proffer kaleidoscopic perspectives on potential realities.

The next phase involves assimilating scenario-based cognition into Agile planning processes. During sprint planning, leaders ruminate on the ramifications of disparate scenarios on project priorities and denouements (Wrike, n.d.). Concurrently, they forge cross-functional coalitions that coalesce expertise from varied departments, harmonizing with scenario planning's holistic ethos and Agile's emphasis on interdisciplinary collaboration, posits Wrike. Implementing concise feedback loops leverages Agile's iterative approach to recalibrate scenarios based on nascent information and developing circumstances (Wrike, n.d.). This process merges with cultivating dynamic capabilities that enable swift adaptation to mercurial environments, aligning with Schoemaker, Heaton, and Teece's seminal work (Sa. Global U.S., 2023). The journey culminates in institutionalizing continuous learning through regular retrospectives, distilling insights to refine the strategic planning process (Atlassian, n.d.).

This integrative approach naturally engenders cycles of perpetual learning and adaptation. Organizations can structure this integration through periodic scenario reviews and updates, ideally quarterly or semi-annually. Sprint-based strategy execution focuses on delivering tangible value aligned with the chosen strategic trajectory. Assiduously collecting and analyzing feedback from sprint outcomes and market responses refines scenarios and strategic plans. The continuous honing of dynamic capabilities better navigates emerging scenarios (Sa. Global U.S., 2023).

Throughout this process, leadership's active involvement in the scenario-agile approach proves crucial, providing sagacious guidance and timely decisions based on emergent insights, according to Sa. Global U.S. By embracing this paradigm and maintaining an unrelenting cycle of learning and adaptation, organizations forge a potent framework for strategic planning that is both visionary and responsive. This approach empowers businesses to navigate fluid environments with unprecedented efficacy, striking an optimal balance between long-term vision and short-term agility.

The Key Benefits of Integrating Scenario Planning with Agile in Strategic Planning

Integrating scenario planning with Agile methodologies in strategic planning offers several key benefits that enhance an organization's ability to navigate uncertain and rapidly changing environments, and these include combining scenario planning's forward-looking approach with Agile's iterative processes that allow organizations to expect better and prepare for various potential futures (Forth, 2022). This integration will enable them to develop more robust strategies that withstand market conditions and unexpected challenges. Combining scenario planning's long-term perspective with Agile's short-term focus enhances decision-making processes, posits Forth. By considering immediate needs and potential future outcomes, leaders can make more informed choices, leading to more balanced and effective strategies.

Integrating these methodologies enables companies to respond more quickly and effectively to changes in their business environment (Goldberg & Boyes, 2024). Agile practices facilitate rapid adjustments to strategies based on emerging scenarios, allowing organizations to pivot when necessary and capitalize on new opportunities. According to Goldberg and colleagues, this integrated approach helps organizations bridge the gap between day-to-day operations and long-term strategic objectives. By incorporating scenario-based thinking into Agile sprints and iterations, companies can ensure that their short-term actions consistently contribute to their broader strategic vision. The integration fosters a culture of continuous learning and adaptation (Forth, 2022). As new information becomes available or circumstances change, organizations can quickly adjust their scenarios and strategies, maintaining relevance in dynamic environments.

Organizations can better identify and mitigate risks by exploring multiple potential futures through scenario planning and using Agile methods to test and refine strategies, as suggested by Goldberg and Boyes (2024). This proactive approach to risk management can help companies avoid pitfalls and capitalize on emerging opportunities. The collaborative nature of scenario planning and Agile methodologies encourages greater involvement from diverse organizational stakeholders, posits Forth (2022). This broader participation can lead to more comprehensive strategies and increased support for strategic initiatives. By leveraging these benefits, organizations can create more resilient, flexible, and effective strategic planning processes well-suited to today's complex and rapidly evolving business landscapes.

Case Studies and Success Stories

Dynamic strategic planning has become increasingly important for organizations to navigate uncertain and transforming environments. Several case studies and recent research highlight practical approaches for implementing flexible, adaptive strategic planning processes. In today's erratic business landscape, organizations are abandoning antiquated, inflexible strategic planning models in favor of more dynamic approaches. This significant change is exemplified by McDonald's adopting a rolling 3-year strategic plan, updated annually (Taylor, 2023). This Agile methodology enables the fast-food heavyweight to pivot swiftly in response to mercurial consumer preferences and market vicissitudes. The following case studies highlight successful dynamic strategic planning. Critical components of McDonald's strategic agility include:

1. Lucid, quickly disseminated strategic priorities
2. Inclusive stakeholder engagement throughout the planning process
3. Data-driven decision-making facilitated by pertinent KPIs

The efficacy of Agile strategic planning extends beyond the corporate sphere. An interesting case study involving Region 16 and DEED illustrates how two government educational agencies harmonized their strategic plans using an Agile framework (Taylor, 2023). Despite the challenges posed by the pandemic, they successfully crafted a shared triennial vision through facilitated planning sessions that delineated core customer groups and organizational values. They prioritized three pivotal focus areas: effective communication, process streamlining, and partnership development. Non-profit organizations, too, are reaping the benefits of dynamic strategic planning. According to Taylor, the Hunger Project employs a parsimonious yet potent planning structure comprising unambiguous vision and mission statements, a theory of change model, strategic priorities with quantifiable outcomes, and mutable actions responsive to results and shifting conditions.

Scenario planning has emerged as an indispensable tool for organizations grappling with an uncertain future. Research published in the International Journal of Production Economics corroborates the positive impact of strategic agility enabled by scenario planning on operational and firm performance (Ojha et al., 2020). This approach empowers organizations to envisage potential future scenarios predicated on key uncertainties, formulate strategic options for each scenario, and devise contingency plans for rapid adaptation.

The transplantation of Agile principles from software development has catalyzed a sea change in strategic planning. These salient Agile practices include abbreviated planning cycles with frequent reassessment, cross-functional collaboration in strategy development, and expeditious prototyping and testing of strategic initiatives. The efficacy of developing dynamic capabilities to buttress flexible strategic planning has been empirically validated.

A study in the International Journal of Production Economics advocated a Dynamic Strategic Planning (DSP) scale predicated on this framework (Ojha et al., 2020). The key elements encompass sensing capabilities by identifying and appraising opportunities and threats, seizing capabilities by mobilizing resources to capitalize on opportunities and reconfiguring capabilities for continuous resource alignment and realignment. Another growing body of literature attests to the beneficial effects of dynamic strategic planning approaches.

- A study of Korean SMEs revealed a positive correlation between strategic agility and operational and firm performance (Ojha et al., 2020).
- Research on family businesses showed that flexible planning systems are associated with enhanced innovativeness and firm performance (Ojha et al., 2020).
- A meta-analysis of strategic planning literature concluded that organizations with more comprehensive and adaptive planning processes outperform their rigid, traditional counterparts (Thiyagarajan et al., 2023).

The preponderance of evidence suggests that dynamic strategic planning effectively navigates the tumultuous waters of today's business environment. Organizations that embrace scenario planning, Agile methodologies, and dynamic capabilities are better positioned to adapt to change and seize emergent opportunities. Companies can enhance their strategic agility and overall performance in an increasingly volatile world by implementing flexible, iterative planning processes and fostering a culture of continuous learning and adaptation. *Figure 7* below shows how organizations can plan for achieving a long-term vision and mission using business models strategically.

Figure 7. Business strategy in a nutshell

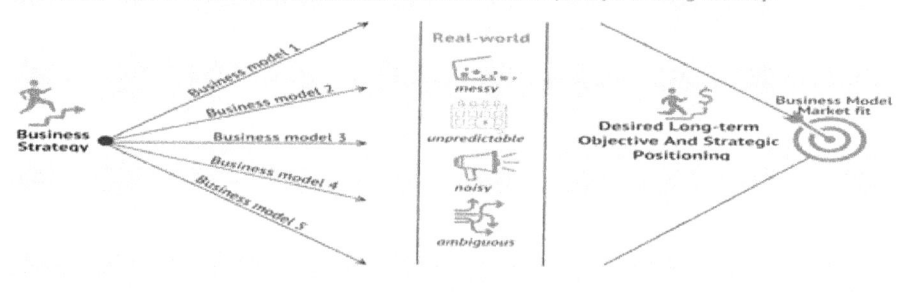

(FourWeekMBA)

TOOLS AND TECHNIQUES FOR LEADERS

Leaders today face an increasingly complex and uncertain business environment. To navigate this landscape effectively, scenario planning and Agile methodologies offer practical tools and methods for strategic planning. These approaches not only help in anticipating and preparing for various future outcomes but also in building a culture that embraces change and continuous improvement. In the labyrinth of corporate strategy, scenario planning emerges as a beacon of prescience. This avant-garde approach empowers organizations to navigate the tumultuous seas of uncertainty with unparalleled aplomb. Let us delve into the quintessential steps and techniques that form the bedrock of this strategic panacea.

> **Unearthing the Catalysts of Change:** The cornerstone of scenario planning is identifying the seismic shifts that could reshape your organizational landscape. This entails comprehensively exploring societal metamorphoses, economic vicissitudes, technological revolutions, and political upheavals.
> **Pinpointing Critical Ambiguities:** It is paramount to zero in on the most impactful uncertainties. In agribusiness, for instance, these might encompass fluctuations in food prices and capricious consumer demands. As Mariton (2016) explains, this crucial step forms the linchpin of effective scenario planning.
> **Crafting Plausible Futures:** Envision a matrix with two critical uncertainties as its axes, spawning four distinct scenarios. This visual representation is a crystal ball, offering glimpses into potential future states.

Deciphering Implications: Scrutinize the ramifications of each scenario and recalibrate strategy accordingly. According to Mariton (2016), this involves setting an organizational compass while considering each possible future trajectory.

To augment this process, practitioners can leverage a triad of analytical tools: SWOT analysis, PESTEL (Political, Economic, Social, Technological, Environmental, and Legal) analysis, and Scenario Matrix. These instruments provide clarity and focus, comprehensively evaluating each scenario's inherent strengths, weaknesses, opportunities, and threats (SWOT). Agile strategic planning offers an elegant, iterative approach to strategy formulation. This methodology provides a lucid, shared vision of strategic objectives, initiatives, and progress. It embraces tools like Agile roadmaps and Kanban boards to facilitate transparency and alignment (Writer, 2023).

The hallmark of Agile planning lies in its frequent reviews and adjustments, typically conducted every quarter. This real-time adaptability empowers organizations to confidently fine-tune their strategy based on tangible results and empirical feedback. Using flexible ways of working helps teams create new things and adjust quickly to changes by prioritizing valuable and strategically important projects (Hale, 2019). Additional Agile tools include Agile Roadmaps and high-level plans delineating the path toward strategic objectives while maintaining flexibility (Writer, 2023). Kanban Boards are visual tools that facilitate workflow management and task prioritization, notes Writer. Objectives and Key Results (OKRs) provide a framework for establishing and tracking measurable goals aligned with the organization's overarching vision, according to Writer.

CONCLUSION AND SUMMARY

The evolution of strategic planning in fluid environments represents a fundamental shift in how organizations approach strategy formulation and execution. This chapter has shown that traditional rigid planning approaches increasingly do not navigate today's volatile, uncertain, complex, and ambiguous business landscape. Integrating scenario planning with Agile methodologies emerges as a robust framework that enables organizations to maintain strategic direction while adapting to rapid change. Several key insights emerge from this analysis. First, the complementarity between scenario planning's long-term perspective and Agile's iterative approach creates a robust foundation for strategic decision-making. Scenario planning provides the strategic foresight needed to anticipate potential futures, while Agile methodologies offer the ability to adapt tactically to changing conditions. This synthesis allows organizations to bridge the gap between long-term vision and short-term execution.

Second, the success of dynamic strategic planning depends heavily on organizational culture and capabilities. Organizations must foster a culture that values ongoing learning, welcomes change, and promotes experimentation. Developing dynamic capabilities - sensing, seizing, and reconfiguring - becomes crucial for executing flexible strategies effectively. Case studies from companies like McDonald's and The Hunger Project show how organizations across different sectors have successfully implemented these approaches. Third, the tools and techniques available to leaders have evolved to support more adaptive planning processes. From SWOT analyzes and scenario matrices to Kanban boards and OKRs, modern strategic planning incorporates diverse instruments that facilitate forward-looking analysis and agile execution. These tools enable organizations to maintain strategic coherence while adapting to changing circumstances.

The evidence presented throughout this chapter suggests that organizations mastering dynamic strategic planning gain significant competitive advantages. They become better equipped to:

- Anticipate and respond to market changes
- Capitalize on emerging opportunities
- Mitigate risks through proactive scenario planning
- Maintain strategic alignment while preserving operational flexibility
- Foster innovation through iterative learning and adaptation

Looking ahead, the importance of dynamic strategic planning is likely to increase as business environments become increasingly complex and unpredictable. Organizations that can effectively combine the foresight of scenario planning with the flexibility of Agile methodologies will be better positioned to navigate future challenges and opportunities. The key to success lies in adopting these approaches and developing the organizational capabilities and culture necessary to execute them effectively. This evolution in strategic planning represents more than just a methodological shift; it signifies a fundamental change in how organizations think about and approach strategy. The future belongs to organizations that can maintain clear strategic direction while remaining adaptable enough to thrive in an ever-changing business landscape. As we move forward, the ability to plan strategically while maintaining operational agility will become an increasingly critical determinant of organizational success.

Cultivating diverse, inclusive organizations provides a robust foundation for addressing an even broader challenge: developing adaptive strategic capabilities in an increasingly volatile business environment. As organizations harness the innovative potential of diverse perspectives, they must simultaneously develop their strategic planning approaches to navigate uncertainty. This convergence of inclusive practices and strategic adaptability represents a critical evolution in organizational capability, enabling institutions to leverage their human capital while developing more resilient and flexible strategic frameworks.

As organizations develop their adaptive capabilities through diversity and strategic flexibility, they must look beyond internal transformations to consider their position within broader value networks. The evolution from self-contained entities to interconnected players reflects a fundamental shift in how modern organizations generate competitive advantage. This transition from focusing on organizational capabilities to ecosystem orchestration represents a natural progression in understanding how businesses can thrive in rapidly evolving technological and market landscapes.

REFERENCES

Agile Alliance. (2015). *What is Iterative Development?* https://www.agilealliance.org/glossary/iterative-development/

Agile Business Consortium. (2024). Chapter 11: *Iterative Development.* https://www.agilebusiness.org/dsdm-project-framework/iterative-development.html

AltexSoft. (2023). *Agile Project Management: Best Practices and Methodologies.* https://www.altexsoft.com/whitepapers/agile-project-management-best-practices-and-methodologies/

Assnservices. (2018). *Don't Attend the Old School of Strategic Planning - World Class Boards.* https://www.worldclassboards.org/dont-attend-the-old-school-of-strategic-planning/

Atlassian. (n.d.). *What is Agile the Agile Methodology.* Retrieved July 16, 2024, from https://www.atlassian.com/agile

Baker, R. (2018). *What Is the Agile Iterative Approach and Where Is It Used?* NTask Manager. https://www.ntaskmanager.com/blog/what-is-agile-iterative-approach/

Bradfield, R., Wright, G., Burt, G., Cairns, G., & van der Heijden, K. (2005). The origins and evolution of scenario techniques in long-range business planning. *Futures*, 37(8), 795–812. DOI: 10.1016/j.futures.2005.01.003

Burt, G. (Ed.). (2023). *Evolution of Scenario Planning: Theory and Practice from Disorder to Order* (1st ed.). Walter de Gruyter GmbH. DOI: 10.1515/9783110792065

Bydrec, Inc. (2020). *What are the 4 Core Principles of Agile Methodology?* https://blog.bydrec.com/core-principles-of-agile-methodology

Cabanes, B. (2023). *The scenario method: an aid to strategic planning* - Polytechnique Insights. Association Polytechnique Insights. https://www.polytechnique-insights.com/en/columns/society/the-scenario-method-an-aid-to-strategic-planning/

Forth, S. (2022). Agile Scenario Planning. *LinkedIn*. https://www.linkedin.com/pulse/agile-scenario-planning-steven-forth/

Goetz, C. (2023). Agile vs. Traditional: Which Method Is Right for You? | *LinkedIn*. https://www.linkedin.com/pulse/agile-vs-traditional-which-method-right-you-carlos-goetz/

Goldberg, E., & Boyes, I. (2024). *Using Scenario Planning to Facilitate Agility in Strategic Workforce Planning*. https://www.shrm.org/executive-network/insights/people-strategy/using-scenario-planning-to-facilitate-agility-strategic-workforce-planning

Hale, D. (2019). *Strategic planning, the agile way* - Work Life by Atlassian. https://www.atlassian.com/blog/jira-align/agile-strategic-planning

Hall, B. (2023). Building Strategic Agility: Navigating Challenges With Strength And Agility. *Forbes*. https://www.forbes.com/sites/forbesbusinesscouncil/2023/06/21/building-strategic-agility-navigating-challenges-with-strength-and-agility/

Hanna, K. T., Bigelow, S. J., & Pratt, M. K. (2024). *What is strategic planning? | Definition from TechTarget*. https://www.techtarget.com/searchcio/definition/strategic-planning

Hastings, R. (2018). *Netflix's success demonstrates the importance of strategic agility*. https://www.worldfinance.com/strategy/netflixs-success-demonstrates-the-importance-of-strategic-agility

Luther, D., & Rami, A. (2022). Scenario Planning: Strategy, Steps and Practical Examples. *Oracle NetSuite*. https://www.netsuite.com/portal/resource/articles/financial-management/scenario-planning.shtml

Mariton, J. (2016). *What is Scenario Planning and How to Use It*. https://www.smestrategy.net/blog/what-is-scenario-planning-and-how-to-use-it

Moffitt, S. (2022). *Why traditional strategy doesn't work now*. We Are Atmosphere Limited. https://weareatmosphere.com/insights/why-traditional-strategy-doesnt-work-now/

Ogilvy, J. (2015). Scenario Planning and Strategic Forecasting. *Forbes*. https://www.forbes.com/sites/stratfor/2015/01/08/scenario-planning-and-strategic-forecasting/

Ojha, D., Patel, P. C., & Sridharan, S. V. (2020). Dynamic strategic planning and firm competitive performance: A conceptualization and an empirical test. *International Journal of Production Economics*, 222, 107509. DOI: 10.1016/j.ijpe.2019.09.030

Premier Agile. (n.d.). *What is Agile Strategic Planning - Process & It's Working*. Retrieved July 15, 2024, from https://premieragile.com/agile-strategic-planning/

Recklies, D. (2015). *Strategy making in the past and today* – Part 2: Problems with the traditional strategy process. Recklies Management Project GmbH. https://www.themanager.org/2015/08/strategy-making-2-problems-traditional-strategy-process/

Sa. Global U.S. (2023). *Scenario Planning For Adaptable HR*. https://www.saglobal.com/en-us/insights/bringing-in-agility-in-hr-with-scenario-planning.html

Saurav, G. (2023). The Power of Scenario Planning in Strategic Decision-Making | *LinkedIn*. https://www.linkedin.com/pulse/power-scenario-planning-strategic-decision-making-saurav-goel-o8bff/

Schoemaker, P. J. H. (1995). (1995). -Schoemaker Scenario Planning-Tool for Strategic Thinking. *Sloan Management Review*.

ScrumAlliance. (2024). *Agile Manifesto Values and Principles*. https://resources.scrumalliance.org/Article/key-values-principles-agile-manifesto

Simplilearn (2020). *What is Agile? Understanding Agile Methodology and Principles in Software Development*. Simplilearn. https://www.simplilearn.com/tutorials/agile-scrum-tutorial/what-is-agile

Taylor, A. (2023). *Strategic Plan Examples: Case Studies and Free Strategic Planning Template*. https://www.smestrategy.net/blog/strategic-plan-examples-case-studies-and-free-strategic-planning-template

Thiyagarajan, S., Saldanha, P. R. M., Govindan, R., Leena, K. C., & Vasuki, P. P. (2023). Effectiveness of agile methodology on metacognitive ability, and clinical performance among nursing students-An interventional study. *Journal of Education and Health Promotion*, 12(1), 283. DOI: 10.4103/jehp.jehp_1798_22 PMID: 37849875

Vizient Newsroom. (2017). *Adopting an Agile Approach to Strategic Planning*. https://newsroom.vizientinc.com/en-U.S./releases/adopting-an-agile-approach-to-strategic-planning

Wade, M., Amit Joshi, A., & Teracino E. A (2021). 6 Principles to Build Your Company's Strategic Agility. *Harvard Business Review*.

Wrike (n.d.). project-management-guide.

Writer, A. S. (/2023). *Agile Strategic Planning*. CIOPages.Com. https://www.ciopages.com/agile-strategic-planning/

Yancey, D. (2021). *How Strategic Planning Is Different in a Post-COVID World*. ASAE. https://www.asaecenter.org/resources/articles/an_plus/2021/july/how-strategic-planning-is-different-in-a-postcovid-world

Z-Stream Blog. (2019). *What is the agile iterative approach and where is it used?* https://www.zstream.io/blog/what-is-the-agile-iterative-approach-and-where-is-it-used

ADDITIONAL READING

Appelbaum, S. H., Calla, R., Desautels, D., & Hasan, L. (2017). The challenges of organizational agility (part 1). *Industrial and Commercial Training*, 49(1), 6–14. DOI: 10.1108/ICT-05-2016-0027

Bennett, N., & Lemoine, G. J. (2014). What a difference a word makes: Understanding threats to performance in a VUCA world. *Business Horizons*, 57(3), 311–317. DOI: 10.1016/j.bushor.2014.01.001

Doz, Y. L., & Kosonen, M. (2010). Embedding strategic agility: A leadership agenda for accelerating business model renewal. *Long Range Planning*, 43(2-3), 370–382. DOI: 10.1016/j.lrp.2009.07.006

McGrath, R. G. (2013). *The end of competitive advantage: How to keep your strategy moving as fast as your business*. Harvard Business Review Press.

Ramirez, R., Churchhouse, S., Palermo, A., & Hoffmann, J. (2017). Using scenario planning to reshape strategy. *MIT Sloan Management Review*, 58(4), 31–37.

Reeves, M., Love, C., & Tillmanns, P. (2012). Your strategy needs a strategy. *Harvard Business Review*, 90(9), 76–83.

Rigby, D. K., Sutherland, J., & Noble, A. (2018). Agile at scale. *Harvard Business Review*, 96(3), 88–96.

Schoemaker, P. J., Heaton, S., & Teece, D. (2018). Innovation, dynamic capabilities, and leadership. *California Management Review*, 61(1), 15–42. DOI: 10.1177/0008125618790246

KEY TERMS AND DEFINITIONS

Agile Strategic Planning: An adaptive, iterative approach to defining and executing an organizational strategy that emphasizes flexibility, rapid iteration, and continuous feedback.

Contingency Planning: The process of identifying potential risks and developing response strategies for different scenarios.

Critical Uncertainties: Key factors in the business environment that could significantly impact an organization's strategy but are difficult to predict.

Dynamic Capabilities: The ability of an organization to integrate, build, and reconfigure internal and external competencies to address rapidly changing environments.

Feedback Loops: Systems for gathering and incorporating feedback to improve strategic planning and execution processes.

Fluid Environment: A business context characterized by constant change, uncertainty, and unpredictability, requiring organizations to be highly adaptable.

Iteration: A cyclic process of refinement and improvement, where each cycle builds upon the lessons learned from the previous one.

Kanban Board: A visual management tool used in Agile planning to visualize work, limit work-in-progress, and ensure continuous flow.

Key Performance Indicators (KPIs): Quantifiable measures used to evaluate the success of an organization in meeting its strategic objectives.

OKRs (Objectives and Key Results): A goal-setting framework that helps organizations set challenging, ambitious goals with measurable results.

Organizational Plasticity: The ability of an organization to adapt its structure, processes, and systems in response to changing circumstances.

PESTEL Analysis: A framework for analyzing macro-environmental factors: Political, Economic, Social, Technological, Environmental, and Legal.

Retrospective: A regular meeting where teams reflect on their work process and identify areas for improvement.

Risk Mitigation: Actions taken to reduce the probability of a risk occurring or its potential impact.

Rolling Forecast: A planning method that involves continuously updating forecasts to reflect changes in the business environment.

Scenario Planning: A strategic planning method that involves developing plausible alternative futures (scenarios) to help organizations prepare for different possible outcomes.

Sprint: A fixed time period (typically 2-4 weeks) during which specific work must be completed and ready for review.

Strategic Agility: The capability of an organization to quickly adapt its strategy in response to changing market conditions while maintaining strategic coherence.

Strategic Coherence: The alignment between an organization's various strategic initiatives and its overall strategic direction.

Strategic Planning: The systematic process of envisioning a desired future and translating this vision into broadly defined goals and a sequence of steps to achieve them.

SWOT Analysis: A strategic planning tool that evaluates an organization's Strengths, Weaknesses, Opportunities, and Threats.

Traditional Strategic Planning: A linear, top-down approach to strategy that typically involves long-term, fixed plans (5-10 years) with predetermined steps and resource allocation.

Chapter 7
Developing Partnerships and Ecosystems

ABSTRACT

Partner ecosystems have emerged as a transformative force in modern business, enabling organizations to create value far beyond what they could achieve alone. This chapter explores the critical components of thriving partner ecosystems, from strategy development to implementation and measurement. Key elements include customer-centricity, clear communication, shared objectives, and mutual accountability. The chapter examines case studies of successful ecosystems, highlighting factors like shared values, strategic clarity, and technological leverage. Emerging trends such as AI integration, cross-sector collaboration, and API-driven integration are reshaping ecosystem dynamics. Measuring success through KPIs and fostering continuous improvement via feedback loops are crucial for ecosystem vitality. The future of business lies in embracing an ecosystem mindset, breaking down industry silos, and leveraging collective strengths to drive innovation and growth. Organizations that master ecosystem leadership can create unique value propositions that are complex for competitors to replicate.

INTRODUCTION

Partner ecosystems have emerged as a transformative force, reshaping how organizations create value, innovate, and compete. This chapter comprehensively examines partner ecosystems, from their conceptual foundations to practical implementation strategies and future trends. As traditional business boundaries blur and digital transformation speeds up, organizations increasingly recognize that success

DOI: 10.4018/979-8-3693-5553-4.ch007

depends not merely on individual capabilities but on their ability to orchestrate complex networks of partnerships that drive collective value creation.

The significance of partner ecosystems cannot be overstated. Research shows that by 2025, ecosystems could capture 30% of global corporate revenue, representing a fundamental shift in how business value is created and distributed. Through carefully cultivated partnerships, organizations can access new markets, accelerate innovation, and deliver comprehensive solutions that address increasingly complex customer needs. The success stories of companies like Microsoft, with 95% of its revenue flowing through partners, and Shopify, whose ecosystem generated $6.9 billion in revenue in 2019, underscore the transformative potential of well-orchestrated partner ecosystems.

This chapter explores the multifaceted nature of partner ecosystems, beginning with their fundamental concepts and evolution from traditional partnerships to dynamic, technology-enabled networks. It examines the critical components of thriving ecosystems, including joint business planning, mutual accountability, and technological integration through Partner Ecosystem Platforms (PEPs). The text delves into practical aspects of ecosystem design, implementation, and scaling while addressing common challenges and providing strategies for measuring success. Special attention is given to emerging trends, particularly the role of artificial intelligence, APIs, and cross-sector collaboration in shaping the future of ecosystem development. This chapter offers practical advice on building and maintaining strong partnerships using theories, data, and real-life examples. As organizations navigate an increasingly interconnected business environment, effectively leveraging partner ecosystems becomes an advantage and a necessity for sustainable growth and competitive success.

UNDERSTANDING PARTNER ECOSYSTEMS

Partner ecosystems have developed significantly from traditional partnerships, transforming into complex networks of relationships that drive value for all participants. This shift represents a fundamental change in how businesses collaborate and create value in the modern economy. In the ever-evolving landscape of commerce, a seismic shift is underway.

The partner ecosystem, a labyrinthine network of symbiotic relationships, redefines how enterprises deliver value while optimizing costs (Abdi, 2023). This paradigm transcends the antiquated one-to-many or many-to-one partnerships, ushering in an era of multifaceted, many-to-many collaborations (Kaur, 2023). Gone are the days of hierarchical, transactional alliances. Kaur argues that today's ecosystems are a crucible of innovation, fostering long-term value creation through unprecedented cooperation. While traditional models fixated on product proliferation, the ecosystem approach pivots towards customer-centricity, orchestrating a harmonious convergence of partners, vendors, and third-party service providers (Kaur, 2023; Rider, 2023).

These ecosystems are not mere assemblages of entities; they are living organisms powered by groundbreaking technologies. Artificial intelligence, machine learning, and data analytics serve as the neural network, driving efficiency and unearthing invaluable insights. Behold the HubSpot App Marketplace, a testament to the ecosystem's transformative potential. This digital agora connects over 1,638 integrated applications with HubSpot's core offerings, exemplifying the ecosystem's ethos (HubSpot, Inc., 2024). It is a bustling bazaar where many-to-many interactions flourish, solutions are crafted with surgical precision, and innovation is the currency of choice.

In a landmark move, PartnerStack's integration with Reveal has set a new benchmark in ecosystem evolution (Tse, 2022). This union of complementary technologies has birthed a powerhouse ecosystem. Partnership teams can now unearth shared opportunities, track deal trajectories from inception to fruition, automate partner remunerations and gain unprecedented visibility into ecosystem dynamics. We stand at the threshold of what Scott Brinker called the "golden age of ecosystems," posits Tse. To thrive in this brave new world, enterprises must transform, shedding the cocoon of traditional partnerships and embracing the ecosystem mindset. This transformation demands a multifaceted approach:

1. Leadership must champion the ecosystem ethos.
2. A robust ecosystem strategy and framework must be meticulously crafted.
3. Partners must be handpicked for their ability to solve customer conundrums (Rider, 2023).
4. Implementation of sophisticated Partner Ecosystem Platforms (PEPs) is crucial to orchestrating these complex relationships.
5. An unwavering focus on customer-centricity and long-term value creation must permeate every facet of the ecosystem (Abdi, 2023; Kaur, 2023).

As we hurtle towards an increasingly interconnected future, partner ecosystems will be the cornerstone of innovation, growth, and customer satisfaction. Those who master nurturing these ecosystems will emerge as the vanguards of the new business frontier. *Figure 1* below shows a map of the network of community partner relationships.

Figure 1. A network map of relationships

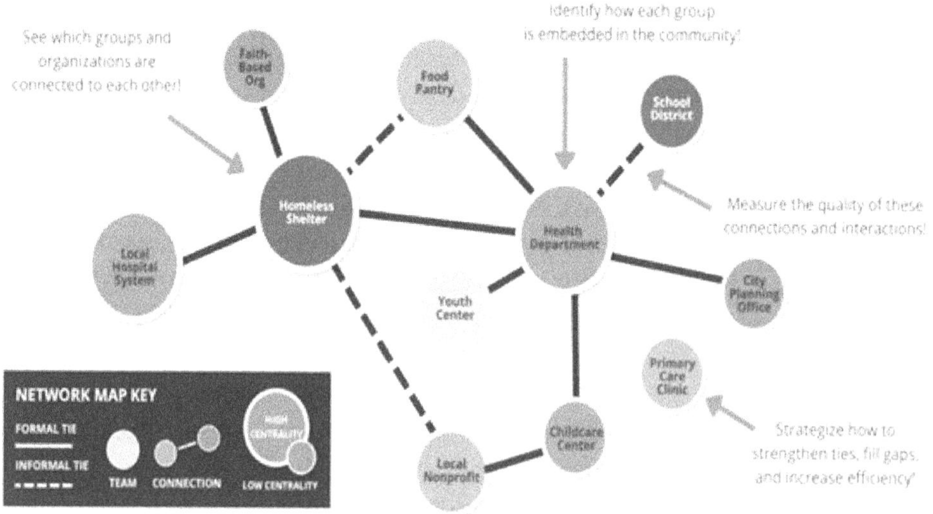

(VisibleNetworkLabs)

Partner ecosystems, interconnected networks of companies, are not just a tool for creating value but a transformative force that can surpass what any organization could achieve alone. In today's complex and rapidly evolving business landscape, these ecosystems are crucial in redefining achievable boundaries in isolation. Partner ecosystems significantly impact modern commerce. Partnerships have become the guiding star in the increasingly labyrinthine commercial landscape, leading firms through uncharted territories. The crucible of diverse perspectives and skills in these partnerships catalyzes breakthroughs at breakneck speeds. Collaborative ventures serve as a springboard, catapulting companies into virgin markets and untapped customer segments. The pooling of resources in these partnerships engenders operational streamlining and fiscal prudence.

These ecosystems offer a monumental potential payoff; McKinsey prophesies that by 2025, ecosystems could confiscate 30% of global corporate revenue, ushering in a new era of prosperity. Accenture's prognostications are even more audacious. They envision a $100 trillion bonanza of businesses and society over the next decade, painting a picture of a thriving global economy. This revenue growth potential exists. Exemplars of triumphant partner ecosystems abound: Microsoft's sprawling network of hardware manufacturers, software developers, and service providers has been instrumental in its PC and enterprise software hegemony (Tan, 2023). Salesforce's AppExchange marketplace, a veritable bazaar of third-party applications, has exponentially amplified the platform's functionality and allure, argues Tan. Amazon

Web Services Partner Network, a global steamroller comprising tens of thousands of organizations, has been pivotal in expanding AWS's capabilities and conquering new markets (Dafydd, 2024).

This burgeoning importance of ecosystems mirrors a global gravitation towards interconnectedness and interdependence. As industry boundaries blur and sectors converge, cross-pollination becomes imperative. Automotive giants now court tech firms for connected car solutions, while healthcare providers tango with data analytics companies to optimize patient outcomes (Tan, 2023; Kiflo, 2023). A new leadership paradigm is crystallizing to navigate this complex ecosystem landscape: ecosystem leadership. This avant-garde approach nurtures a collaborative ethos that prioritizes collective value creation over myopic individual gains (Tan, 2023). Orchestrating diverse partnerships with virtuosic finesse (Kiflo, 2023), cultivating fertile ground for innovation, fostering cross-pollination of ideas, and rampant experimentation, observes Tan. Striking a delicate equilibrium between cooperation and competition, often collaborating with rivals in certain domains while vying in others, posits Kiflo.

In this brave new world of interconnectedness, partner ecosystems have become the sine qua non of business strategy. By harnessing the collective might of diverse allies, companies can drive innovation, expand their sphere of influence, and create value on an unprecedented scale. As this significant change gains momentum, embracing partner ecosystems and mastering the art of ecosystem leadership becomes increasingly urgent for commercial triumph in the 21st century. In this chapter, we will look at understanding partner ecosystems, the benefits of partner ecosystems, critical components of a thriving partner ecosystem, and more.

Partner Ecosystems: A Nexus of Efficiency, Frugality, and Profitability

Partner ecosystems offer significant benefits in efficiency, cost-effectiveness, and revenue generation. These intricate networks of interrelated entities facilitate the seamless dissemination of products and services while curtailing expenses and amplifying value propositions (Abdi, 2023). This reciprocal paradigm empowers enterprises to harness their cohorts' collective prowess, resources, and acumen. The resultant amalgamation yields a cornucopia of benefits, operational efficacy soars, and pecuniary outlays plummet. By forging alliances with complementary ventures, companies can broaden their horizons and infiltrate virgin markets sans substantial capital infusion (Hype, n.d.).

Furthermore, these coalitions unlock access to exclusive expertise and assets that might otherwise prove elusive or financially prohibitive to cultivate in-house. Consider the case of HubSpot's partner ecosystem. This giant, valued at $7.4 billion, is projected to burgeon to $17.9 billion by 2025, posits Abdi (2023). Such meteoric growth is a testament to the exponential potential inherent in strategic partnerships. Conventional project management dogma posits an immutable trilemma: speed, affordability, or quality - pick two. Partner ecosystems, however, defy this axiom. Abdi argues that enterprises can achieve the hitherto impossible trifecta through judicious collaboration. Innovation speeds up time-to-market contracts. Shared resources and streamlined processes engender cost efficiencies. The collective wisdom of the ecosystem elevates product quality to unprecedented heights.

Several key factors underpin the exponential growth potential of these ecosystems. Market expansion in which partners serve as conduits to unexplored customer segments and geographical territories increases the addressable market (Kiflo, 2023). The ordeal of diverse partnerships fosters groundbreaking products, services, and business models. The interconnected nature of ecosystems creates a virtuous cycle where individual triumphs reverberate throughout the network, argues Abdi (2023). As the ecosystem flourishes, it exerts an irresistible gravitational pull-on potential partners and customers (Deeb & Ilesvska, 2023). The collaborative ethos engenders a vested interest in collective success, fostering reciprocal growth and support.

HubSpot's ecosystem epitomizes this phenomenon. Projected to expand from five times the company's size to six and a half times more significant by 2025, it exemplifies the exponential trajectory achievable through astute ecosystem management, posits Abdi (2023). Partner ecosystems represent a fundamental change in business strategy. They offer a potent formula for driving revenue efficiently and cost-effectively while delivering speed, quality, and affordability. By nurturing collaboration, fostering innovation, and leveraging shared resources, these ecosystems cultivate fertile ground for exponential growth and unparalleled success in today's fiercely competitive commercial landscape. *Figure 2* below shows that data, growth, and cost fuel the ecosystems.

Figure 2. Three flywheels fuel business ecosystem success

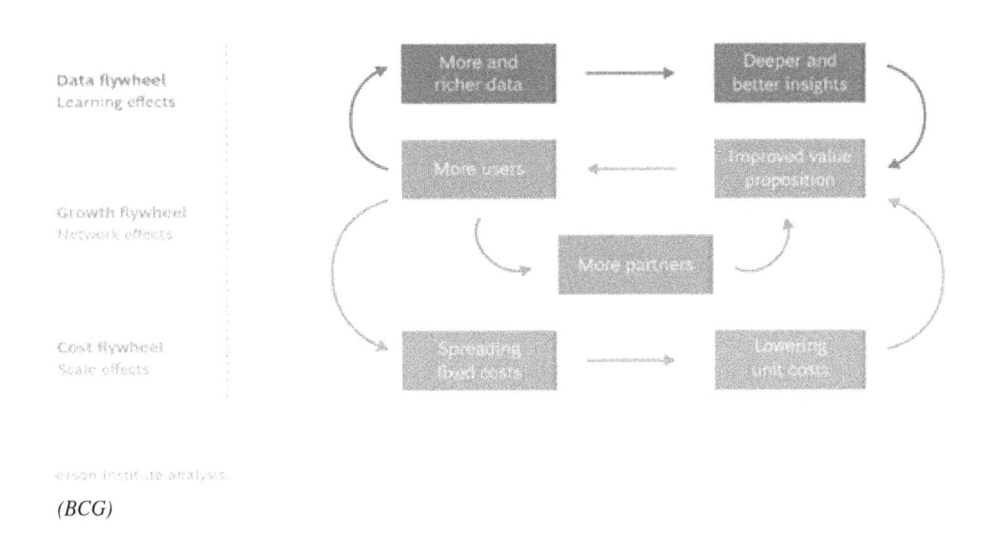

(BCG)

The Components of a Successful Partner Ecosystem

A thriving partner ecosystem is a complex network of relationships that requires careful management, strategic planning, and critical components and tools for building and maintaining a flourishing partner ecosystem. A thriving partner ecosystem is the linchpin of success in today's interconnected business landscape. This intricate web of relationships demands meticulous orchestration and visionary planning. Are you ready to harness its potential? At the heart of this ecosystem lies a shared ethos, a collective understanding of goals and principles that fosters seamless collaboration (Watenpaugh, 2018).

Nevertheless, it does not stop there. Delineating clear roles and responsibilities based on each partner's strengths is paramount to preventing redundancy and amplifying efficiency (Kiflo, 2023). Communication is key and the lifeblood of these partnerships. It is about disseminating information, active listening, and collaborative problem-solving. This symbiotic exchange nurtures trust and transparency, the bedrock of any successful alliance, argues Kiflo.

In our ever-evolving business landscape, adaptability is non-negotiable. The hallmark of long-term success is the ability to pivot in response to market fluctuations and emerging trends. Nevertheless, how do we ensure all parties reap the rewards? The answer lies in value creation. Successful partnerships do not just benefit the involved parties; they extend their positive impact on customers (Watenpaugh, 2018). This holistic approach requires unwavering executive support and a leadership style that supports consensus-building. Trust and mutual benefit are the cornerstones of these relationships. Partners must have the confidence to rely on each other, always acting in the best interest of the collective, argues Watenpaugh. This synergy extends to business planning, transforming abstract ideas into actionable strategies.

Partner Ecosystem Platforms (PEPs) are the technological backbone of modern partnerships. These SaaS marvels offer a plethora of features designed to optimize partner relationships. From real-time customer and lead list comparisons to secure data sharing, these platforms resolve the age-old "partnership dilemma" (Kelly, 2022). However, the innovation does not stop there. PEPs facilitate collaborative sales and marketing efforts, track revenue attribution, and monitor Ecosystem Qualified Leads (EQLs). The integration capabilities of these platforms allow seamless connection with other tools in the partnership tech stack, creating a unified ecosystem, argues Kelly.

Data sharing and collaboration are the lifeblood of a thriving partner ecosystem. Kelly (2022) posits that PEPs offer secure methods for exchanging sensitive information, providing real-time insights into co-selling opportunities and account overlaps. Automated workflows streamline processes for lead sharing, opportunity management, and deal registration (Bowen, 2024). Measuring partnership performance and showing ROI are crucial to long-term success. Bowen notes that connecting partner ecosystem data with other business systems provides a holistic view of partnerships, enabling data-driven decision-making.

While not typically part of PEPs, learning management systems are pivotal in partner enablement. These systems offer a centralized repository for educational materials, structured learning paths, and customized training programs tailored to partner roles and expertise levels (Mercado, 2023). By leveraging these components and tools, organizations can cultivate a thriving partner ecosystem that drives growth, fosters innovation, and ensures mutual success. Fusing strategic management, innovative technology platforms, and comprehensive training systems creates fertile ground for powerful collaborations and expanded market reach. Are you ready to revolutionize your partner's ecosystem? The future of business collaboration awaits.

BUILDING A PARTNER-FIRST STRATEGY

Building a partner-first strategy within an ecosystem involves focusing on clear communication, shared objectives, and mutual growth. This section will provide detailed strategies for joint business planning, coordinated go-to-market approaches, and the importance of enablement and training. The strategies involve several key components, including joint business planning and robust enablement and training programs.

Crafting a successful joint business plan demands a crystal-clear vision and symbiotic objectives. It is imperative to forge a shared trajectory that aligns seamlessly with the strategic aspirations of all parties involved (Natalya & Isaeva, 2021). This synchronization ensures a unified march towards common goals and articulates the alliance's reciprocal advantages. Market penetration, revenue augmentation, or enhanced product portfolios could be the cornerstones of this mutually beneficial relationship, argue Natalya and Isaeva. Orchestrate regular strategic conclaves to assess progress, tackle impediments, and recalibrate strategies as necessary. According to (Feiferytė-Skirienė et al. (2022), these huddles should encompass vital organizational stakeholders.

Construct joint business roadmaps delineating crucial milestones, deliverables, and timelines. These cartographic tools are progress trackers and accountability enforcers (Pietro & Gurpreet, 2021). Harness the power of shared data platforms to illuminate decision-making processes. This data-centric approach, encompassing sales metrics, customer feedback, and market analysis, infuses every decision with empirical gravitas, posit Pietro and Gurpreet. Establish consensus on key performance indicators (KPIs) to gauge partnership efficacy and conduct regular reviews to maintain alignment and implement requisite adjustments.

Synergize marketing strategies to craft cohesive messaging stressing both entities' strengths and value propositions. This unified front reinforces the partnership's image in the customer's mind (Natalya & Isaeva, 2021). Launch joint marketing initiatives, such as co-branded campaigns and webinars, to amplify reach and impact (Pietro & Gurpreet, 2021). Conduct joint sales training sessions to ensure both teams comprehensively understand products, services, and value propositions. This knowledge harmonization delivers a consistent message to customers, posit Pietro and Gurpreet. Implement a lead-sharing mechanism, potentially through a shared CRM system, to ensure fair distribution of new business opportunities.

Partners must use meticulous market segmentation and targeting to pinpoint the most promising customer segments. This strategic focus allows for more precise marketing and sales efforts, posit Natalya and Isaeva (2021). Leverage each partner's geographic strengths to expand into virgin markets, potentially through joint ventures or local partnerships. Develop comprehensive training programs covering product features, benefits, and use cases. Equip sales teams with enablement tools such as playbooks, case studies, and competitive analyses to articulate value propositions effectively and counter objections, according to Pietro and Gurpreet (2021). Implement ongoing training initiatives to keep teams abreast of product developments, market trends, and best practices (Feiferytė-Skirienė et al., 2022).

Successful strategies include establishing feedback loops to gather insights from sales and support teams and using this intelligence to refine training programs and resources continuously. These strategies must also include dedicated support resources, such as a partner portal, seamless access to training materials, marketing collateral, and technical support, remark Feiferytė-Skirienė et al. (2022). Institute incentive programs to galvanize and reward partners for achieving specific benchmarks, such as sales targets or customer satisfaction metrics (Natalya & Isaeva, 2021). By embracing these strategies, organizations can cultivate robust, mutually beneficial partnerships that propel growth and success within their ecosystem. Transparent communication, shared objectives, and robust enablement programs form the bedrock of a cohesive and effective partner-first strategy, according to (Feiferytė-Skirienė et al., 2022; Natalya & Isaeva, 2021; Pietro & Gurpreet, 2021). *Figure 3* below describes building partner-first strategies based on trust and transparency.

Figure 3. Trust and transparency

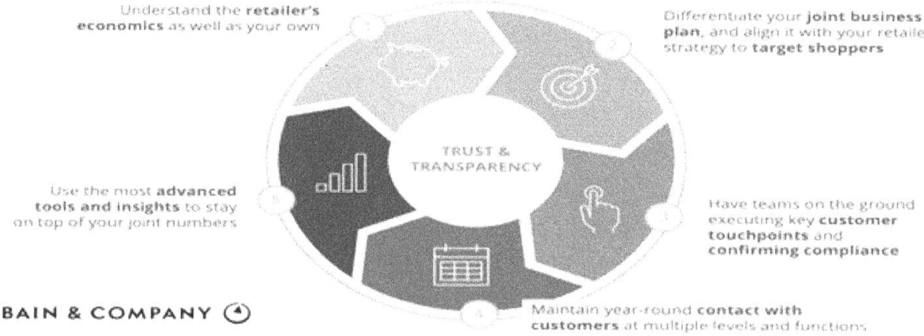

(Bain & Company)

Designing an Ecosystem

Designing an ecosystem involves creating a network of interconnected services, products, and stakeholders to deliver a seamless and integrated experience. This process requires a strategic approach emphasizing customer-centricity and leveraging design thinking methodologies to ensure the ecosystem meets user needs and expectations. A design-led approach to ecosystem development integrates design principles from the very beginning of the planning process. This approach is structured around three key phases: defining the strategy, designing the ecosystem, and building the ecosystem.

Defining the ecosystem strategy involves understanding the market landscape, identifying potential partners, and setting clear objectives for the ecosystem, and requires extensive research and strategic planning to ensure the ecosystem aligns with the company's long-term goals (Niharika et al., 2021). Crafting a meticulous blueprint is paramount to ecosystem design. This intricate process encompasses mapping customer journeys, delineating service blueprints, and ensuring a seamless integration of all touchpoints. The design phase must prioritize user experience, creating an intuitive interface that caters to customer needs with finesse, argue Niharika and colleagues. Customer-centricity lies at the heart of successful ecosystem design. It's integral, not merely trendy, to a unified system. By mapping customer journeys, organizations can pinpoint crucial touchpoints and orchestrate positive experiences at every turn. This holistic approach fosters a seamless user experience that transcends individual interactions (Niharika et al., 2021; Kelton Global, 2021).

A comprehensive roadmap illuminates the ecosystem's inner workings from multiple perspectives. It is a powerful tool that harmonizes customer experiences, business operations, and employee roles. Organizations can identify areas ripe for improvement through this lens and ensure all ecosystem elements function in perfect synchronicity (Niharika et al., 2021). However, the journey does not end there. Continuous refinement is the name of the game. User feedback is the compass, guiding ongoing improvements and ensuring the ecosystem remains in lockstep with developing customer needs (Kelton Global, 2021).

Design thinking emerges as a formidable ally in this quest for integration. This problem-solving approach, steeped in empathy and creativity, comprises five pivotal stages:

1. **Empathize:** Delve deep into users' needs through meticulous research and observation.
2. **Define:** Distill insights into focused problem statements that steer the design process.
3. **Ideate:** Unleash a torrent of ideas, exploring myriad possibilities without constraint.
4. **Prototype:** Breathe life into promising concepts through tangible, cost-effective iterations.
5. **Test:** Subject prototypes to real-world scrutiny, gathering invaluable feedback for refinement (The Innovation Mode, 2022).

Organizations can forge user-centric solutions that deliver unparalleled, integrated experiences by embracing design thinking. This approach elevates customer satisfaction, catalyzes innovation, and cements competitive advantage (Niharika et al., 2021; The Innovation Mode, 2022). The art of ecosystem design demands a strategic, design-led approach that places the customer at its epicenter. By harnessing the power of design thinking and maintaining an unwavering focus on user needs, organizations can craft ecosystems that meet and shatter expectations, delivering extraordinary value and integrated experiences that leave the competition in the dust. *Figure 4* below shows an integrated approach to ecosystem design and the six-step journey of ecosystem design.

Figure 4. The six-step journey of business ecosystem design

EXHIBIT 1 | The Six-Step Journey of Business Ecosystem Design

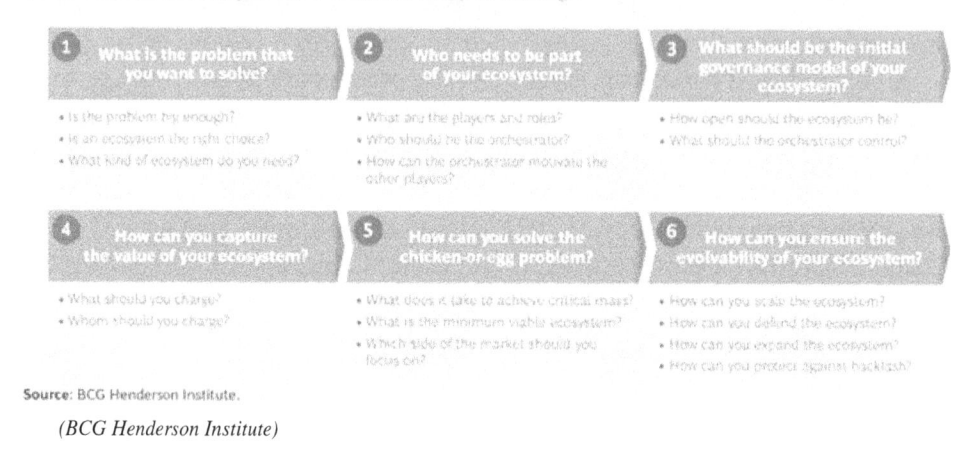

1. What is the problem that you want to solve?	2. Who needs to be part of your ecosystem?	3. What should be the initial governance model of your ecosystem?
• Is the problem big enough? • Is an ecosystem the right choice? • What kind of ecosystem do you need?	• What are the players and roles? • Who should be the orchestrator? • How can the orchestrator motivate the other players?	• How open should the ecosystem be? • What should the orchestrator control?

4. How can you capture the value of your ecosystem?	5. How can you solve the chicken-or-egg problem?	6. How can you ensure the evolvability of your ecosystem?
• What should you charge? • Whom should you charge?	• What does it take to achieve critical mass? • What is the minimum viable ecosystem? • Which side of the market should you focus on?	• How can you scale the ecosystem? • How can you defend the ecosystem? • How can you expand the ecosystem? • How can you protect against backlash?

Source: BCG Henderson Institute.

(BCG Henderson Institute)

Implementing and Scaling the Ecosystem

Implementing and scaling an ecosystem involves a structured approach broken down into three key phases: define, design, and build. Each phase is crucial to successfully adopting an ecosystem strategy and requires a flexible and agile operating model. Additionally, significant cultural shifts are necessary to support this transformation. The path to ecosystem adoption is multifaceted, encompassing distinct phases that demand meticulous attention. Starting with strategy definition, this process requires a profound comprehension of market dynamics, consumer requisites, and organizational strengths. Trend analysis follows suit, delving into the social, economic, and technological undercurrents shaping consumer behavior. Organizations can envision the ecosystem's evolution by forecasting these trends and uncovering novel opportunities. Crystallizing the customer-value proposition is paramount. It is a delicate alchemy of leveraging distinctive advantages, market insights, and corporate aspirations. Co-creation sessions serve as crucibles for generating and evaluating potential value propositions (Joshi et al., 2021).

The design phase is where the ecosystem blueprint takes shape. It is an intricate tapestry woven with interaction and user-interface design principles, ensuring an intuitive ecosystem that resonates with customer needs. Service design plays a pivotal role, transcending industry sectors to forge a seamlessly connected business (Joshi et al., 2021). The ecosystem's architecture, partner roles, information flow, and service integration must be meticulously planned, identifying the technological and operational underpinnings required.

Building the ecosystem is the culmination of this journey. It is a phase of implementation and scalability, marked by pilot projects that serve as trials for testing. These controlled environments are invaluable for identifying potential pitfalls and making necessary course corrections before a full-scale deployment. As the ecosystem expands, constant vigilance is required to ensure all components function harmoniously, delivering the intended value (Joshi et al., 2021). A flexible and agile operating model is essential to ecosystem success. It is the organizational equivalent of a chameleon, adapting swiftly to market fluctuations and growing customer needs. Customer-centricity and collaborative reflexes are the cornerstones of this model, fostering innovation and efficiency.

The 'bias to action' principle is crucial. It cultivates a culture of experimentation and rapid decision-making, enabling organizations to seize fleeting opportunities. Equally important is nurturing a learning mindset and fostering continuous development to stay ahead of market trends and technological advancements (Hollister et al., 2021). Implementing an ecosystem strategy demands seismic cultural shifts within organizations. It requires dismantling silos and nurturing a collaborative milieu. Empowering and holding employees accountable for their ecosystem contributions is vital; leaders must metamorphose into enablers, supporting their teams and acknowledging their efforts, posit Hollister and colleagues.

Sustainable communication is the glue that binds the ecosystem. It is about forging transparent and respectful practices that foster mutual understanding and collaboration. This extends to integrating sustainability into the corporate strategy, ensuring all stakeholders are aligned with the ecosystem's objectives (MHP Blog, 2023). Diversity and inclusivity are not mere buzzwords but are essential to ecosystem success. They create fertile ground for innovation and growth, leveraging varied perspectives and experiences. It is about crafting an environment where every employee feels valued and can contribute meaningfully to the ecosystem's triumph (Shillingford, 2024).

Implementing and scaling an ecosystem is a Herculean task. It demands a structured approach to defining, designing, and building. A malleable and agile operating model is the pivot of success, enabling adaptation to the ever-changing business landscape. Profound cultural metamorphoses are indispensable, embracing change, empowering the workforce, fostering sustainable communication, and supporting inclusivity and diversity.

Navigating Challenges in Ecosystem Development

Mutual accountability and incentives play critical roles in the development and sustainability of ecosystems, particularly in partnerships and collaborative efforts. These elements ensure that all parties involved are committed to shared goals and are motivated to achieve them. Mutual accountability is the lifeblood of successful partnerships. This potent concept drives enhanced performance, aligns goals, and fosters a supportive milieu. When partners hold each other responsible, they cultivate a high-performance ethos that rises above individual achievements (Futcher, 2022; Lo et al., 2021). The glue binds disparate elements into a cohesive whole, ensuring all efforts converge toward a shared vision.

However, accountability alone is not enough. Incentives must be in place to ignite motivation and cement long-term relationships. These judiciously crafted programs are a panacea for retention woes, a springboard for motivation, and the cornerstone of robust partnerships. They transform mundane business interactions into symbiotic ventures, propelling mutual growth and success (Sramek, 2023). Nevertheless, the path to a thriving ecosystem is fraught with obstacles. Problems with shared goals, lack of trust, poor communication, and limited resources can ruin even the best partnerships. These challenges are not insurmountable, however. The right strategies can transform them into steppingstones to success.

Clear communication is paramount. Establish pellucid channels that keep all partners in lockstep. Regular discussions and updates are indispensable for maintaining clarity and coordination. Develop a shared vision that resonates with all stakeholders; the North Star guides every decision and action. Trust-building activities are non-negotiable. Engage in exercises that fortify the bonds between partners. From team-building soirées to collaborative problem-solving sessions, every interaction should reinforce trust. These activities are not just team-building exercises, but crucial investments in the longevity and success of the partnership. Implement efficacious incentive programs tailored to each partner's unique motivations and needs (Sramek, 2023; Brett, 2013). Finally, construct a robust mutual accountability framework. This blueprint should delineate each partner's commitments and the mechanisms for ensuring adherence. It is about setting goals and creating a system for continuous improvement and learning (Lo et al., 2021).

In the tapestry of ecosystem development, mutual accountability and incentives are the warp and weft. By embracing these principles and addressing challenges head-on, partnerships can achieve unparalleled success and longevity. It is about building an ecosystem and nurturing a thriving, dynamic entity that stands the test of time. *Figure 5* below shows a guide to developing incentive programs.

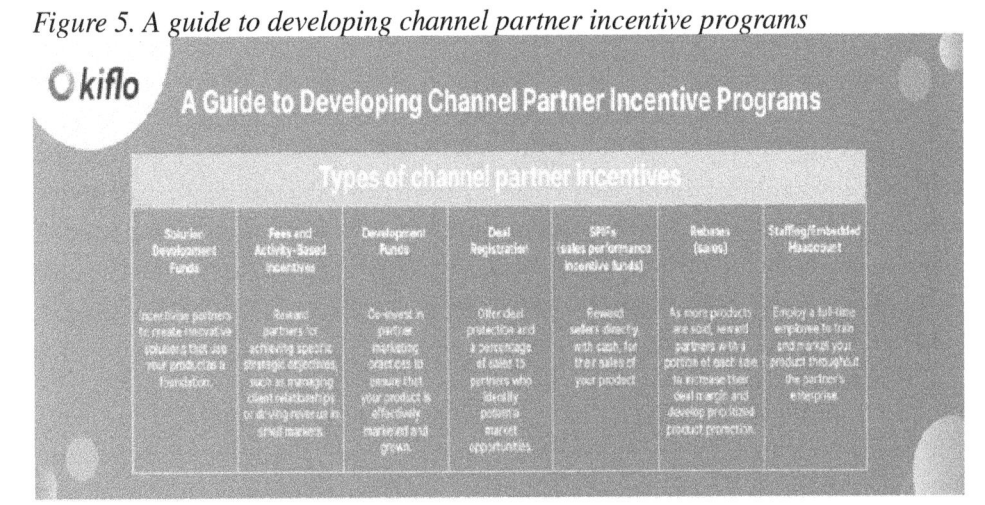

Figure 5. A guide to developing channel partner incentive programs

(Kiflo)

FUTURE TRENDS IN PARTNER ECOSYSTEMS

The landscape of partner ecosystems is evolving rapidly, driven by technological advancements and changing market dynamics (Digital Marketing America, 2023). As we move forward, several key trends and concepts are shaping the future of these ecosystems. The decade of channel ecosystem heralds a transformative partnership era, promising to revolutionize collaboration and innovation. This significant change is characterized by many trends that will reshape the business landscape, as practitioners and researchers predict.

Well-orchestrated partner ecosystems are poised to become veritable goldmines for platform companies. Organizations assiduously cultivating partnerships are projected to reap a wealth of indirect revenue, far outpacing their more passive counterparts (Rider, 2023). The zeitgeist of co-innovation is permeating the industry, with vendors and partners joining forces to forge multi-technology solutions that address customer frustrations. By 2026, a quarter of new application portfolios are expected to emerge from these collaborative crucibles, according to Rider.

In an era of finite resources, vendors and partners are becoming increasingly discerning, gravitating towards symbiotic relationships that yield mutual benefits. This fundamental change underscores the imperative for trusted, efficient collaboration (AchieveUnite, 2023). Emerging technologies are catalyzing the evolution of partner ecosystems, with AI metamorphosing the landscape by enabling bespoke content creation, fortified security measures, and automated customer interactions. These AI-driven solutions enhance decision-making processes and deliver tailor-made client experiences (Devan, 2024).

Seamlessly integrating software via APIs is the lifeblood of thriving partner ecosystems. APIs streamline the integration process, enabling partners to synergize their applications efficiently, reducing development timelines, and eliminating compatibility hurdles (Journeybee, 2024). Concurrently, the proliferation of online marketplaces, particularly in the cloud services domain, is revolutionizing product and service distribution within the channel. Vendors and partners must adapt to this paradigm shift in buying behavior to diversify their routes to market and achieve sustained growth, posits Devan (2024).

Cross-sector collaboration is gaining traction, with Collaborative Ecosystem Product Development (CEPD) emerging as an avant-garde approach involving partnering with multiple, sometimes competing, vendors to develop cost-effective, innovative solutions. CEPD is expected to drive improved business outcomes through collaborative endeavors (Rider, 2023). Thriving partner ecosystems are predicated on reciprocal relationships where both parties bring value. Fostering knowledge sharing, joint strategizing, and maintaining a win-win mindset is paramount for sustainable partnerships, notes Journeybee (2024).

Vendors are striving to achieve heightened operational efficiencies within their partner programs. This approach enhances partner productivity and ensures that partner managers possess the requisite skills to forge and maintain robust relationships (AchieveUnite, 2023). The "decade of channel ecosystem" promises a future replete with opportunities for growth and innovation. This era will witness increased revenue generation, co-innovation, and a laser focus on strategic partnerships. Emerging technologies will drive ecosystem development, while cross-sector collaboration will become the sine qua non for mutual success.

Organizations that embrace these trends and adapt to the growing landscape will be well-positioned to thrive in the years to come (Rajput, 2024). The dawn of the channel ecosystem era represents a seismic shift in partnerships, offering a tapestry of opportunities for those bold enough to seize them. *Figure 6* below describes partner archetypes.

Figure 6. Partner archetypes

Partner archetypes

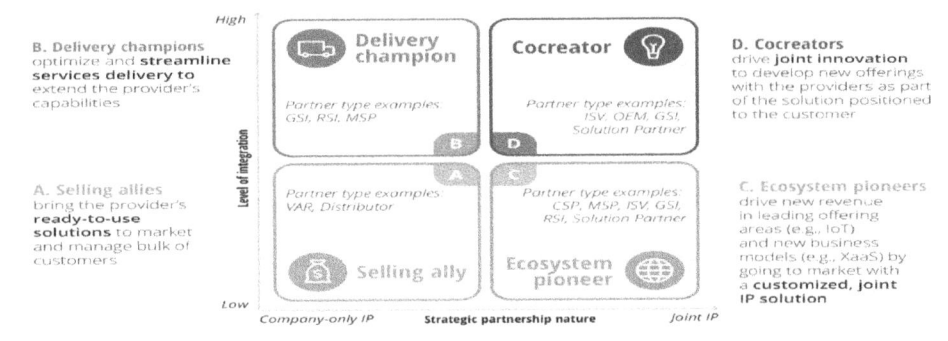

B. Delivery champions optimize and **streamline services delivery to** extend the provider's capabilities	**Delivery champion** *Partner type examples: GSI, RSI, MSP*	**Cocreator** *Partner type examples: ISV, OEM, GSI, Solution Partner*	**D. Cocreators** drive **joint innovation** to develop new offerings with the providers as part of the solution positioned to the customer
A. Selling allies bring the provider's **ready-to-use solutions** to market and manage bulk of customers	**Selling ally** *Partner type examples: VAR, Distributor*	**Ecosystem pioneer** *Partner type examples: CSP, MSP, ISV, GSI, RSI, Solution Partner*	**C. Ecosystem pioneers** drive new revenue in leading offering areas (e.g., IoT) and new business models (e.g., XaaS) by going to market with a **customized, joint IP solution**

Level of integration (Low–High) × Strategic partnership nature (Company-only IP – Joint IP)

Notes: CSP: certified service partner; GSI: global systems integrator; ISV: independent software vendor; MSP: managed service provider; OEM: original equipment manufacturer; RSI: regional systems integrator; VAR: value-added reseller. Solution Partner examples: cloud platform, data management and analytics, IoT.

Source: Deloitte analysis.

(Deloitte)

Emerging Trends

In today's rapidly evolving business landscape, entrepreneurial ecosystems are undergoing profound changes that reshape how innovation emerges and thrives. Recent research by Fernandes and Ferreira (2021) reveals that these ecosystems are increasingly characterized by dynamic interactions between various actors and norms, fostering an environment where adaptability isn't just beneficial; it's essential for survival. This continuous evolution creates a fertile ground where new ideas can take root and flourish.

The intersection of local and global forces has emerged as a crucial factor in ecosystem development. Malecki (2018) and Zhang et al. (2020) highlight this through compelling examples like Suntech, which masterfully orchestrated a liaison between international partnerships and local resources. This strategic approach shows how successful entrepreneurs weave together global opportunities with local strengths, creating resilient networks that span continents while remaining grounded in their communities.

In emerging economies, entrepreneurs face unique challenges that demand innovative solutions. Cao and Shi (2020) point to resource scarcity and institutional voids as significant hurdles that shape entrepreneurial journeys in these regions. Nevertheless, these challenges often spark creative business-building approaches as entrepreneurs develop tailored strategies that work within and sometimes transform their distinctive contexts.

The interconnected nature of ecosystem elements creates a fascinating ripple effect throughout the entrepreneurial landscape. Wurth et al. (2023) describe how these connections can trigger upward causation, where positive developments in one area catalyze growth across the entire ecosystem. This phenomenon underscores the importance of nurturing relationships between different ecosystem components, as each connection has the potential to amplify success across the network.

A critical shift in ecosystem development focuses on addressing gender disparities and promoting inclusivity. Brush et al. (2019) emphasize that the future of entrepreneurial ecosystems depends on ensuring equal access to resources and support for all participants. This isn't just about fairness; it is about unlocking the full potential of human creativity and innovation by removing barriers that have historically limited participation in entrepreneurial endeavors.

Actionable Advice for Entrepreneurs

In this interconnected world, successful entrepreneurs must master the art of building robust ecosystems. As highlighted by Malecki (2018) and Zhang et al. (2020), the key lies in simultaneously cultivating local partnerships while reaching across borders to tap into global opportunities. This dual approach isn't just about expanding reach; it's about creating a rich web of connections that can provide diverse resources, from local market insights to international technological innovations. Imagine a local artisan who partners with nearby suppliers using digital platforms to reach customers worldwide, effectively bridging both worlds.

Business owners are finding creative ways to start and run businesses in areas with limited resources and weak systems. Cao and Shi (2020) emphasize the importance of forging strategic partnerships and collaborating with policymakers to create more supportive business environments. Success stories feature entrepreneurs who have turned limitations into opportunities, like those who have developed mobile payment solutions in areas with limited banking infrastructure, effectively transforming a challenge into a competitive advantage. This trend of mobile payments is prominent in rural Africa, where banking systems are only available in big cities.

The future of entrepreneurship hinges on creating inclusive ecosystems that harness diverse talents and perspectives. Brush et al. (2018) make a compelling case for implementing practices promoting diversity and addressing gender disparities. Forward-thinking entrepreneurs are already leading this charge by establishing mentorship programs, creating inclusive funding mechanisms, and building support networks that ensure all innovators can contribute to the ecosystem's growth.

Adaptation has become the entrepreneur's most valuable skill in our rapidly evolving business landscape. Fernandes and Ferreira (2021) and Wurth et al. (2023) underscore the importance of remaining agile and responsive to emerging opportunities and challenges. Successful entrepreneurs treat change not as a disruption but as a catalyst for innovation, continuously monitoring market trends, embracing new technologies, and pivoting their strategies to stay ahead of the curve. This mindset transforms potential obstacles into steppingstones for growth and innovation.

REAL-WORLD EXAMPLES

Suntech's remarkable journey in the solar PV industry showcases a masterful approach to ecosystem building that many entrepreneurs can learn from. As Zhang et al. (2020) detailed, the company's strategic evolution began with cultivating global partnerships that provided crucial technological expertise and market insights. Like a skilled chess player thinking several moves ahead, Suntech methodically builds strong local relationships, creating a powerful combination of international reach and regional strength. This dual approach transformed them from an industry newcomer into a dominant force in the solar energy sector, demonstrating how thoughtful partnership strategies can catalyze extraordinary growth.

The entrepreneurship landscape in emerging economies reveals interesting patterns of innovation and adaptation. Cao and Shi (2020) point to entrepreneurs turning traditional challenges into opportunities by forging strategic alliances and deeply integrating local knowledge into their business models. These pioneers are writing a new playbook for success in resource-constrained environments, proving that sustainable growth comes from embracing and working within local contexts while maintaining a forward-looking vision. Their experiences underscore a fundamental truth: The future belongs to those who can weave together diverse partnerships, foster inclusive practices, and remain adaptable in the face of change. Through these approaches, entrepreneurs aren't just building businesses but creating resilient ecosystems that can thrive amid complexity and uncertainty.

Case Studies and Success Stories

Partner ecosystems have become increasingly important across various industries, driving innovation, growth, and customer value. Let us explore some notable case studies and success stories and the key factors that contributed to their success. In today's interconnected business landscape, partner ecosystems have emerged as a transformative force, propelling companies to new heights of innovation and growth. The literature abounds with fascinating case studies and success stories that underscore the potency of this collaborative approach.

Consider Spark Biomedical, a fledgling medical device company that catapulted to success through strategic partnerships. By leveraging a synergistic ecosystem, Spark Biomedical brought the groundbreaking Sparrow Therapy System to market in record time (Greenlight Guru, 2021). This wearable neurostimulation device, designed to ease opioid withdrawal symptoms, exemplifies the power of collaborative innovation. The tech behemoth Microsoft stands as a paragon of ecosystem mastery. An astounding 95% of its revenue flows through its vast network of over 400,000 partners worldwide (Tse, 2022). This symbiotic relationship has cemented Microsoft's position as an industry juggernaut.

E-commerce titan Shopify has similarly harnessed the potential of partner ecosystems. In 2019 alone, its ecosystem generated a staggering $6.9 billion in revenue, according to Tse (2022). Meanwhile, Tse argues that Atlassian, a software powerhouse, has cultivated a global partner network that accounts for one-third of its business. What catalyzes these phenomenal success stories? The answer lies in a constellation of crucial factors. Shared values and culture form the bedrock of thriving ecosystems. As Daniel Powell, CEO of Spark Biomedical, astutely observes, "Having partners with common values is just as important as the product or services themselves" (Greenlight Guru, 2021). This axiological alignment fosters robust collaboration and mutual understanding.

Customer-centricity reigns supreme in thriving ecosystems, making the audience feel valued and integral to the business. Thriving networks orbit around the customer, much like planets revolve around the sun. This heliocentric approach ensures that all partners work together to deliver unparalleled value to end-users, reinforcing the importance of our role in the business ecosystem. Strategic clarity guides the path to ecosystem triumph. A well-defined strategy aligned with the ideal customer profile (ICP) is paramount. This strategic lucidity guides partner selection and capability alignment, according to (Blackmon, 2023).

Cross-functional synergy amplifies ecosystem potential. Success demands the involvement of diverse organizational departments. A multidisciplinary team approach ensures comprehensive ecosystem development and implementation (Rider, 2023). Streamlined processes form the backbone of efficient ecosystems. Partner recruitment, onboarding, and support mechanisms must be honed to perfection. According to (Rider, 2023; Blackmon, 2023), providing partners with requisite resources, training, and tools is imperative for ecosystem vitality. Technological leverage accelerates ecosystem growth. Partner Relationship Management (PRM) and through-channel marketing automation solutions can dramatically enhance efficiency and scalability, posits Rider.

Data-driven optimization fuels continuous improvement. Meticulous tracking and analysis of key metrics such as revenue, customer satisfaction, and partner engagement are hallmarks of thriving ecosystems, say Rider and Blackmon. Executive championing paves the way for ecosystem success, and securing C-suite support is critical for managing potential channel conflicts and ensuring consistent strategy implementation. Collaborative synergy amplifies value creation; encouraging partnerships between entities with complementary skills and offerings can magnify value propositions and revenue opportunities for all stakeholders (Tse, 2022; Blackmon, 2023). Adaptive agility ensures ecosystem longevity. Successful networks show remarkable plasticity, swiftly adapting to market conditions and partner needs; moreover, regular strategy reviews and adjustments are essential, posit Rider and Blackmon.

Partner ecosystems have metamorphosed into a robust business paradigm across diverse industries. The triumphant narratives of Spark Biomedical, Microsoft, Shopify, and Atlassian illuminate the transformative potential of well-orchestrated partner ecosystems. By embracing shared values, customer-centricity, strategic clarity, and leveraging cutting-edge technology and data analytics, organizations can cultivate thriving ecosystems that drive sustainable growth and competitive advantage in our increasingly interconnected business realm.

MEASURING ECOSYSTEMS SUCCESS

Partner ecosystems have become increasingly crucial for businesses to drive innovation, expand market reach, and deliver comprehensive solutions to customers. To ensure the success of these ecosystems, it is critical to track and measure specific key performance indicators (KPIs) while fostering a culture of continuous improvement. This section will explore the key performance indicators for partner ecosystems and discuss the importance of feedback loops in driving success. Success in partner ecosystems hinges on a multifaceted performance measurement and enhancement approach. The bedrock of a thriving ecosystem lies in its partner composition, both quantitative and qualitative. Meticulously, track your partner roster, categorizing them by status and type to gauge ecosystem robustness (Hype, n.d.; Kiflo, 2023). Partner activation rates serve as a litmus test for your onboarding efficacy, while engagement metrics offer invaluable insights into ecosystem health (Jose, 2024).

Revenue generation is the quintessential barometer of ecosystem performance. Scrutinize partner-attributed revenue, including monthly sales volume and partner-influenced revenue. These pecuniary indicators explain the fiscal impact of collaborative efforts (Jose, 2024). Equally crucial is the scrutiny of lead generation and conversion rates, illuminating the quality of partner-sourced opportunities.

Partner satisfaction, often overlooked but crucial, demands vigilant monitoring. Regularly assess satisfaction scores for partner-delivered solutions to ensure adherence to quality standards. Concurrently, periodic surveys can gauge partner satisfaction, recognizing that content partners are the linchpin of a productive ecosystem. The time-to-market revenue indicator offers a competitive edge for technology partnerships, measuring the enthusiasm with which joint solutions are integrated and launched.

The pièce de résistance of a flourishing partner ecosystem is its commitment to continuous improvement through robust feedback loops. These mechanisms facilitate rapid adaptation to mercurial market conditions and foster a milieu of collaboration and shared objectives, making every partner feel included in the ecosystem's success (ZINFI Technologies, Inc. 2024). By assiduously gathering and analyzing feedback, organizations can identify and rectify inefficiencies in their partner programs (Hype, n.d.). Implementation of effective feedback loops requires a multi-pronged approach:

1. Institute regular partner check-ins and review sessions
2. Leverage partner management software for real-time communication
3. Conduct periodic surveys to assess partner satisfaction
4. Create forums for partners to exchange best practices and challenges
5. Implement a system to track and address partner suggestions

By embracing these critical performance indicators and fostering a culture of perpetual improvement, organizations can construct resilient, high-performing partner ecosystems. This approach propels business growth and ensures the ecosystem remains agile, innovative, and aligned with evolving market exigencies.

CONCLUSION AND SUMMARY

This comprehensive chapter explores partner ecosystems' evolution, importance, and implementation in modern business environments. The text thoroughly examines how traditional partnerships have transformed into complex, technology-enabled networks that drive value creation and innovation across industries. The chapter begins by establishing the significant impact of partner ecosystems, noting that they are projected to capture 30% of global corporate revenue by 2025. It presents compelling examples of thriving ecosystems, such as Microsoft's partner network, which accounts for 95% of its earnings, and Shopify's ecosystem, which brought in $6.9 billion in 2019.

The content delves into the critical components of thriving partner ecosystems, emphasizing the importance of clear communication, shared objectives, and mutual accountability. It outlines how Partner Ecosystem Platforms (PEPs) are technological backbones for modern partnerships, facilitating data sharing, collaboration, and performance tracking. The chapter also addresses the significance of joint business planning and coordinated go-to-market approaches in building strong partner-first strategies. Much of the text is dedicated to ecosystem design and implementation, presenting a structured approach through three key phases: define, design, and build. It emphasizes the importance of customer-centricity and design thinking methodologies in creating thriving ecosystems. The chapter also tackles common challenges in ecosystem development, offering practical solutions for issues such as trust-building, resource allocation, and alignment of incentives.

Looking toward the future, the chapter examines emerging trends in partner ecosystems, including the increasing role of artificial intelligence, APIs, and cross-sector collaboration. It highlights how these technological advancements are reshaping ecosystem development and creating new opportunities for innovation and growth. The text concludes with a robust discussion of measuring ecosystem success, emphasizing the importance of tracking key performance indicators and maintaining effective feedback loops. It provides practical frameworks for evaluating ecosystem health and performance, ensuring sustainable growth and adaptation to changing market conditions. Throughout the chapter, the author successfully combines theoretical frameworks with practical examples and case studies, offering valuable insights for academics and practitioners in partner ecosystem management. The content shows how well-orchestrated partner ecosystems have become essential for sustainable business growth and a competitive edge in today's linked corporate environment.

The evolution of partner ecosystems, particularly their integration with artificial intelligence and cross-sector collaboration, naturally sets the stage for a deeper examination of innovation management in dynamic business environments. As organizations increasingly rely on ecosystem partnerships to drive growth and maintain competitive advantage, the traditional boundaries between structured strategic planning and emergent adaptation continue to blur. The technological advancements that reshape ecosystem development, discussed extensively in Chapter 7, create opportunities and imperatives for innovation, demanding more sophisticated approaches to strategy formulation and execution. This intersection between ecosystem management and innovation strategy becomes relevant as organizations navigate market volatility and technological disruption. The measurement frameworks and performance indicators established for partner ecosystems provide valuable foundational insights for understanding how organizations can effectively balance structured innovation initiatives with adaptive strategic responses. As we transition from examining the orchestration of partner ecosystems to exploring innovation management and emergent strategy, we observe how these interconnected domains collectively shape organizational success in today's rapidly evolving business landscape.

REFERENCES

Abdi, N. (2023). *The Ultimate Guide to Partnerships for Ecosystems in 2023.* https://partnerstack.com/resources/guides/ultimate-guide-to-partnerships-for-ecosystems

AchieveUnite. (2023). *2024 Trends: Success Through Partnering, Leadership and AI – AchieveUnite.* https://www.achieveunite.com/2024-trends/

Beech, I. (2023). *What is a Partner Ecosystem and Why Should You Want One?* https://breezy.io/blog/partner-ecosystem

Blackmon, K. (2023). *7 Tips for a Successful Partner Ecosystem Strategy.* Zift Solutions. https://ziftsolutions.com/blog/7-tips-for-a-successful-partner-ecosystem-strategy/

Blog, M. H. P. (2023). Implementing Cultural Change in Organizations. *MHP Management- und IT-Beratung.* https://www.mhp.com/en/insights/blog/post/implementing-cultural-change-in-organizations

Bowen, B. (2024). *Best Partner Ecosystem Platforms Software*: User Reviews from July 2024. https://www.g2.com/categories/partner-ecosystem-platforms

Brett, A. B. (2013). Incentives, land use, and ecosystem services: Synthesizing complex linkages. *Environmental Science & Policy*, 27, 124–134. DOI: 10.1016/j.envsci.2012.12.010

Brush, C., Edelman, L. F., Manolova, T., & Welter, F. (2019). A gendered look at entrepreneurship ecosystems. *Small Business Economics*, 53(2), 393–408. DOI: 10.1007/s11187-018-9992-9

Cao, Z., & Shi, X. (2021). A systematic literature review of entrepreneurial ecosystems in advanced and emerging economies. *Small Business Economics*, 57(1), 75–110. DOI: 10.1007/s11187-020-00326-y

Dafydd, L. (2024). [*Partner Ecosystem Benefits for Your Business.* Impartner. https://impartner.com/resources/blog/partner-ecosystem-benefits]. *Top (Madrid)*, 10, •••.

Deeb, T., & Ilesvska, A. (2023). *What Is a Partner Ecosystem and Why Do You Need One?* | Storyblok. https://www.storyblok.com/mp/what-is-a-partner-ecosystem

Devan, A. (2024). *7 Trends to Steer the Channel's Trajectory in 2024.* https://www.channelfutures.com/channel-business/seven-trends-that-will-steer-the-channel-s-trajectory-in-2024

Digital Marketing America. (2023). *PPC - Digital Marketing America*. Digital Marketing America. https://newdma.org/category/ppc/

Feiferytė-Skirienė, A., Draudvilienė, L., Stasiškienė, Ž., Sosunkevič, S., Pamakštys, K., Daniusevičiūtė-Brazaitė, L., & Gurauskienė, I. (2022). Co-Creation Hub Is the First Step for the Successful Creation of a Unified Urban Ecosystem-Kaunas City Example. *International Journal of Environmental Research and Public Health*, 19(5), 2609. Advance online publication. DOI: 10.3390/ijerph19052609 PMID: 35270302

Fernandes, A. J., & Ferreira, J. J. (2022). Entrepreneurial ecosystems and networks: A literature review and research agenda. *Review of Managerial Science*, 16(1), 189–247. DOI: 10.1007/s11846-020-00437-6

Futcher, R. (2022). *The Psychology of Mutual Accountability*. Russellfutcher. Com. https://www.russellfutcher.com/new-blog/2022/4/17/the-psychology-of-mutual-accountability

Greenlight Guru. (2021). Case Study: *How The Partner Ecosystem Has Been Key To Market Success* For Spark Biomedical. https://www.greenlight.guru/blog/spark-biomedical-partner-ecosystem-key-to-market-success

Hollister, R., Tecosky, K., Watkins, M., & Wolpert, C. (2021). Why Every Executive Should Be Focusing on Culture Change Now. *MIT Sloan Management Review*. https://sloanreview.mit.edu/article/why-every-executive-should-be-focusing-on-culture-change-now/

HubSpot, Inc. (2024). PartnerStack HubSpot Integration. *Connect Them Today*. https://app.hubspot.com/ecosystem/46832843/marketplace/apps/sales/partner-relationship-management/partnerstack-490573

Hype. (n.d.). *Partner Ecosystems: What are they and what are the keys to success?* Retrieved July 20, 2024, from https://www.hypeinnovation.com/partner-ecosystems-guide

Jose, L. (2024). *Partner Program KPIs: The Metrics You Should Measure and Optimize*. https://partnerstack.com/articles/partner-program-kpis-metrics-you-should-measure-and-optimize

Joshi, N. H., Khan, H., & Rab, I. (2021). A design-led approach to embracing an ecosystem strategy. *McKinsey & Company*. https://www.mckinsey.com/capabilities/mckinsey-design/our-insights/a-design-led-approach-to-embracing-an-ecosystem-strategy

Journeybee. (2024). *Blooming Partnerships: How to Grow a Successful Partner Ecosystem in 2024*. https://www.journeybee.io/resources/how-to-grow-a-successful-partner-ecosystem

Kaur, S. (2023). Traditional sales ecosystems Vs. Modern sales ecosystems | The channel and sales enablement blog. *The channel and sales enablement blog*. https://channelandsalesenablementblog.mindmatrix.net/traditional-sales-ecosystems-vs-modern-sales-ecosystems/

Kelly, Z. (2022). *Partnerships 101: What is a Partner Ecosystem Platform?* https://insider.crossbeam.com/resources/partnerships-101-what-is-a-partner-ecosystem-platform

Kelton Global. (2021). Experience Innovation: Building a Consumer-Centric Ecosystem - *Kelton Global*. https://www.keltonglobal.com/perspectives/experience-innovation-consumer-centric-ecosystem/

Kiflo (2023). *Managing a Thriving Partner Ecosystem Strategy: From Conception to Execution*. https://www.kiflo.com/blog/managing-a-thriving-partner-ecosystem-from-strategy-to-execution

Lo, L., Aron, L. Y., Pettit, K. L. S., & Scally, C. P. (2021). *Mutual Accountability Is the Key to Equity-Oriented Systems Change*. Marketing, M. 7 Keys to Managing Successful Partner Ecosystems.

Malecki, E. J. (2018). Entrepreneurship and entrepreneurial ecosystems. *Geography Compass*, 12(3), e12359. Advance online publication. DOI: 10.1111/gec3.12359

Mercado, F. (2023). Key Elements of a Thriving Channel-Partner Ecosystem. *LinkedIn*. https://www.linkedin.com/pulse/key-elements-thriving-channel-partner-ecosystem-freddy-mercado/

Natalya, I., & Isaeva, L. (2021). Basic principles of partnership as the factor of sustainable development in the context of business ecosystems. *E3S Web of Conferences*. https://www.semanticscholar.org/paper/Basic-principles-of-partnership-as-the-factor-of-in-Ivashchenko-Isaeva/67517fe8cdf575bee3bdce1f433ebefab633d41f

Niharika Hariharan, N. J., Khan, H., & Rab, I. (2021). A design-led approach to embracing an ecosystem strategy. *McKinsey & Company*. https://www.mckinsey.com/capabilities/mckinsey-design/our-insights/a-design-led-approach-to-embracing-an-ecosystem-strategy#/

Pietro, M., & Gurpreet, M. (2021). The roles of performance measurement and management in developing and implementing business ecosystem strategies. *International Journal of Operations & Production Management*. https://www.semanticscholar.org/paper/The-roles-of-performance-measurement-and-management-Micheli-Muctor/0c675264d4493fe6fc09842acbf36a0b09600f47

Rajput, S. (2024). *Radiating Excellence: Exploring the Top Trends in the Automotive Radiator Market*. https://www.verifiedmarketreports.com/blog/top-7-trends-in-the-automotive-radiator-market/

Rider, C. (2023). Building a Partner Ecosystem? 5 Steps to Drive Your Approach. *Impartner*. https://impartner.com/resources/blog/building-a-partner-ecosystem

Shillingford, A. (2024). *Building the Cultural Power Ecosystem (SSIR)*. https://ssir.org/articles/entry/building_the_cultural_power_ecosystem# Sramek, E. (2023). Partner Incentives: 7 Reward Strategies That Work - *Scaleo Blog*. Scaleo.io. https://www.scaleo.io/blog/partner-incentives-7-reward-strategies-that-work/

Tan, A. (2023). Partner Ecosystems: why we need them. *Future CFO*. https://futurecio.tech/partner-ecosystems-why-we-need-them

Technologies, Z. I. N. F. I. Inc. (2024). *Building a Resilient Partner Ecosystem: Strategies Insights*. https://www.zinfi.com/blog/partner-ecosystem-maximizing-strategies/

The Innovation Mode. (2022). *Design Thinking Grows Up -Welcome to Experience Thinking*. The Innovation Mode. https://www.theinnovationmode.com/the-innovation-blog/design-thinking-grows-up-welcome-to-experience-thinking

Tse, C. (2022). *The Best Partnership Ecosystems Learnings of 2022*. https://partnerstack.com/articles/the-best-partnership-ecosystems-learnings-of-2022

Watenpaugh, N. (2018). Better Together: The 10 Ingredients Of Successful Partnerships. *Forbes*. https://www.forbes.com/sites/forbessanfranciscocouncil/2018/10/24/better-together-the-10-ingredients-of-successful-partnerships/

Wurth, B., Stam, E., & Spigel, B. (2023). Entrepreneurial Ecosystem Mechanisms. *Foundations and Trends® in Entrepreneurship, 19*(3), 224–339. DOI: 10.1561/0300000089

Zhang, W., White, S., & Luo, J. (2020). *How Entrepreneurs Can Build Ecosystems for New Venture Creation*. Social Science Research Network. DOI: 10.2139/ssrn.3713478

KEY TERMS AND DEFINITIONS

API (Application Programming Interface): A set of protocols and tools that enable different software applications to communicate and integrate within the partner ecosystem

Collaborative Ecosystem Product Development (CEPD): An approach involving partnerships with multiple vendors, including competitors, to develop innovative and cost-effective solutions

Cross-sector Collaboration: Partnerships formed between organizations from different industries or sectors to create comprehensive solutions and drive innovation

Design Thinking: A problem-solving methodology comprising five stages (Empathize, Define, Ideate, Prototype, Test) used in ecosystem development

Ecosystem Leadership: A leadership approach focused on orchestrating partnerships, fostering innovation, and maintaining a balance between cooperation and competition

Ecosystem Qualified Leads (EQLs): Potential customers or opportunities identified and qualified through partner ecosystem relationships

Joint Business Planning: The collaborative process of creating shared strategies and objectives between ecosystem partners

Many-to-Many Collaboration: A partnership model where multiple organizations work together simultaneously, replacing traditional one-to-one partnerships

Mutual Accountability: A system where ecosystem partners hold each other responsible for meeting shared objectives and commitments

Partner Ecosystem: A complex network of interconnected businesses, vendors, and service providers working together to create value and drive innovation

Partner Ecosystem Platform (PEP): Technological infrastructure that facilitates partner relationship management, data sharing, and collaboration within the ecosystem

Partner-First Strategy: An approach that prioritizes partnership development and ecosystem growth as core business objectives

Partner Relationship Management (PRM): Tools and processes used to manage and optimize relationships with ecosystem partners

Revenue Attribution: The process of tracking and assigning revenue generation to specific partnership activities within the ecosystem

Service Blueprint: A detailed map of service processes, customer interactions, and backend operations within the ecosystem

Shared Value Creation: The process of generating benefits for all ecosystem participants through collaborative efforts

Strategic Alignment: The harmonization of goals, objectives, and operations among ecosystem partners

Through-Channel Marketing Automation: Technology solutions that help manage and optimize marketing activities across partner networks

Time-to-Market Revenue: A metric measuring how quickly joint solutions are integrated and launched within the ecosystem

Value Proposition: The unique combination of benefits and solutions offered through the partner ecosystem to customers

Chapter 8
Harnessing Innovation and Emergent Strategy

ABSTRACT

This chapter explores the critical importance of innovation and adaptability in today's volatile business landscape. It emphasizes emergent strategy as a flexible approach to planning, contrasting with traditional rigid methodologies. The text discusses cultivating an innovation ecosystem, identifying "invisible innovators," and harnessing "productive friction" to drive growth. Case studies of Apple, 3M, and Amazon illustrate the successful implementation of emergent strategies and innovation processes. The chapter highlights the benefits of these approaches, including enhanced market navigation, seizing new opportunities, and maintaining a competitive edge. It stresses the need for organizations to foster a culture of continuous learning, experimentation, and swift adaptation. The conclusion urges leaders to reassess their strategic approaches, invest in innovation, and nurture creativity at all levels.

INTRODUCTION

In a business environment defined by unprecedented technological advancement and market volatility, organizations face the critical challenge of maintaining competitive advantage through innovation while adapting their strategies to rapidly changing conditions. This chapter explores the vital intersection of innovation management and emergent strategy, examining how successful organizations navigate the delicate balance between structured planning and adaptive response in modern business environments. As traditional rigid planning approaches prove increasingly

DOI: 10.4018/979-8-3693-5553-4.ch008

inadequate in market uncertainty, organizations must develop more flexible and responsive methodologies to survive and thrive.

The chapter advances our understanding of this crucial dynamic through several key focus areas. First, it examines the fundamental role of innovation as a corporate imperative, highlighting how companies like Pixar, Google, and Apple have created cultures that systematically nurture creativity and experimentation. Through cautionary tales of once-dominant companies like Kodak and Blockbuster, we see the existential risks of failing to maintain innovative capacity. The analysis then turns to the critical distinction between emergent strategy and traditional strategic planning, demonstrating how adaptive approaches enable organizations to respond more effectively to environmental changes and unexpected opportunities.

Special attention is given to identifying and nurturing "invisible innovators" - employees who develop novel solutions to organizational challenges but whose contributions often go unrecognized. The chapter also explores the concept of productive friction, showing how constructive disagreement and diverse perspectives can catalyze innovation and organizational growth. We examine successful methodologies for implementing emergent strategies and fostering innovation in practice through detailed case studies of market leaders like Apple, 3M, and Amazon. This comprehensive exploration offers theoretical frameworks and practical insights for organizations seeking to build more adaptive and innovative capabilities. By understanding these dynamics, leaders can better position their organizations to thrive in an increasingly complex and uncertain business environment where continuous learning, experimentation, and swift adaptation have become essential for long-term success.

IGNITING THE SPARK OF INNOVATION: A CORPORATE IMPERATIVE

Innovation is crucial for companies to remain competitive and relevant in today's rapidly growing business. Fostering a culture of creativity and experimentation while providing necessary resources and support is essential for promoting organizational innovation. In today's kaleidoscopic business milieu, encouraging innovation is not merely a luxury, but an existential must. Savvy enterprises must orchestrate a symphony of elements to cultivate an ecosystem ripe for groundbreaking ideas. The genesis of innovation begins with an atmosphere of unbridled collaboration and openness. Pixar's legendary creativity exemplifies this ethos, where cross-pollination of ideas across departmental boundaries has birthed cinematic marvels like Toy Story and Finding Nemo (Sparrow, 2024).

Embracing calculated risks and reframing failures as steppingstones to success is paramount. Google's audacious "20% time" policy, a wellspring of ingenuity that spawned Gmail and Google Maps, is a testament to this philosophy, according to (Sparrow, 2024). However, innovation is not nurtured in a vacuum. It requires ongoing investment in research and development, advanced tools, and continuous learning. According to Sparrow, Apple's relentless pursuit of excellence through substantial R&D expenditures has resulted in fundamental changes in devices like the iPhone and iPad.

Recognition is the lifeblood of sustained innovation. Acknowledging trailblazing contributions is crucial, whether through financial incentives, career advancements, or public accolades. Apple's prestigious "Apple Fellows" program exemplifies this philosophy, immortalizing employees who have left an indelible mark on the company's trajectory. Technological leaps, metamorphosing consumer preferences, and global competitive pressures drive the imperative for ceaseless innovation.

As technology races forward at breakneck speed, it creates a labyrinth of opportunities and challenges across industries. Consumer demands develop in lockstep, convincing businesses to adapt or perish. In this interconnected global village, competition knows no borders, necessitating perpetual innovation to maintain a razor-sharp competitive edge. The annals of business history are littered with cautionary tales of innovation neglect.

Kodak's tragic fall from grace serves as a stark reminder. Despite pioneering the digital camera, Kodak's myopic focus on its traditional film business led to its ignominious bankruptcy in 2012, as (Valuer, 2022) described. Blockbuster's downfall is equally instructive. Clinging to its brick-and-mortar model while Netflix revolutionized content delivery, Blockbuster's intransigence sealed its fate.

These sobering examples underscore the criticality of staying attuned to market undercurrents and embracing self-disruption when necessary. Cultivating a culture of innovation demands a multifaceted approach that nurtures creativity, embraces experimentation, and provides fertile ground for ideas to flourish. By wholeheartedly embracing innovation, enterprises can adroitly navigate the stormy seas of technological upheaval, shifting consumer tastes, and global competition. The cautionary tales of Kodak and Blockbuster serve as stark reminders of the perils that await those who cannot innovate in this dynamic business milieu. In this era of relentless change, innovation is not just a strategy but the difference between thriving and extinction. *Figure 1* below shows what it takes to create a culture of innovation.

Figure 1. Tips to create a culture of innovation

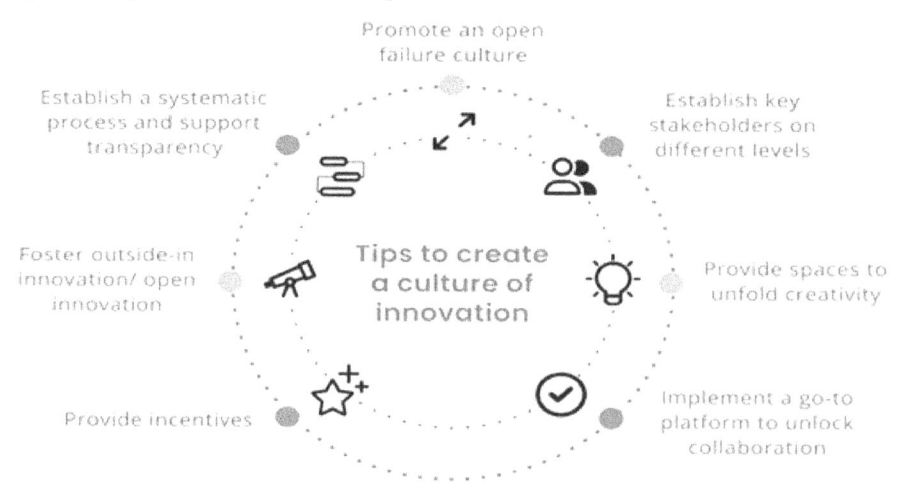

EMERGENT STRATEGY VS. TRADITIONAL STRATEGIC PLANNING

Emergent Strategy is a fundamental change in organizational evolution. This dynamic approach to strategic management eschews the traditional, rigid blueprint in favor of a more supple, adaptive methodology. It is a lucky alchemy of unplanned actions and initiatives that coalesce into a cohesive strategy. Unlike its premeditated counterpart, emergent strategy thrives on real-time responsiveness to environmental vicissitudes and nascent opportunities (Stobierski, 2020; Indeed Editorial team, 2022). Contrast this with the conventional strategic planning process. It is a systematic, deliberate exercise in long-term prognostication. Organizations delineate their objectives and meticulously chart the course to achieve them. This approach leans heavily on exhaustive analysis and forecasting to craft a comprehensive roadmap, according to (Ivory Research, 2019).

The hallmarks of emergent strategy are manifold. Experimentation reigns supreme. Learning is constant. Responsiveness to environmental flux is paramount. Organizations embracing this philosophy cultivate a milieu where employees are encouraged to explore novel ideas and initiatives, often sans a predefined schema. This iterative process engenders rapid adaptation based on empirical outcomes. Failures metamorphose into learning opportunities rather than setbacks (UBC Blog, 2022; Edmondson, 2011). Emergent Strategy's inherent plasticity is its greatest asset. It empowers organizations to remain nimble, adjusting their trajectory based on new intelligence and unforeseen circumstances. This adaptability is crucial in unpredictable industries where market conditions, technological advancements, and competitive landscapes shift with alacrity (Freedman, 2021; Ivory Research, 2019). The benefits of emergent strategy are multifaceted and include:

1. Flexibility: Organizations can pivot swiftly in response to new opportunities or threats, enhancing resilience in volatile markets.
2. Innovation: An emergent strategy often yields innovative solutions and novel business models by fostering spontaneous creativity.
3. Employee Empowerment: All echelons of the workforce are encouraged to contribute to the strategic direction, fostering a sense of ownership and engagement (Stobierski, 2020; Freedman, 2021; UBC Blog, 2022; Mahr & Hendricks, 2023). However, challenges persist and include:

Uncertainty: The absence of a clear, long-term plan can engender ambiguity, potentially unsettling some stakeholders. **Coordination:** Ensuring organizational alignment without a formal plan can be a Herculean task (Mahr & Hendricks, 2023; Ivory Research, 2019).

Emergent Strategy represents a significant change from the inflexible, top-down approach of traditional strategic planning to a more fluid, bottom-up methodology. It values adaptability, experimentation, and perpetual learning. Organizations can more effectively navigate the labyrinthine complexities of the modern business landscape by remaining responsive to environmental changes and learning from triumphs and tribulations. This is a good way to handle fast-changing and uncertain businesses, where adjusting quickly is key to success. *Figure 2* below shows the intended, deliberate, realized, and emergent strategies.

Figure 2. Realized business strategy

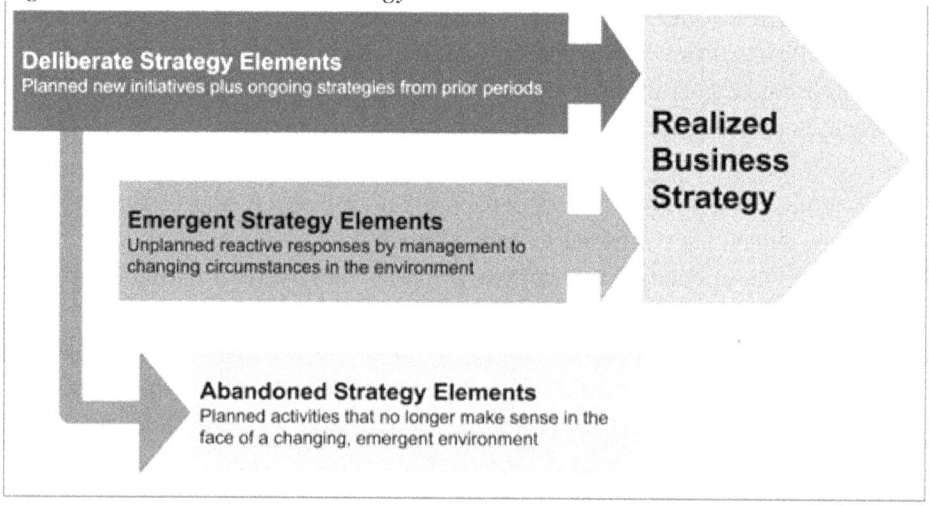

Deliberate Strategy Elements
Planned new initiatives plus ongoing strategies from prior periods

Emergent Strategy Elements
Unplanned reactive responses by management to changing circumstances in the environment

Abandoned Strategy Elements
Planned activities that no longer make sense in the face of a changing, emergent environment

Realized Business Strategy

(Oregon State University)

Identify Invisible Innovators

Within the intricate structures of corporate ecosystems, a group of unsung heroes, the invisible innovators, work tirelessly. These clandestine catalysts are the driving force behind revolutionary solutions that catapult their organizations to unprecedented heights. However, their invaluable contributions often go unnoticed and untapped. Many employees, including the author, experience this unfortunate situation. The genesis of invisible innovation frequently occurs when employees, confronted with quotidian quandaries, concoct novel remedies. This wellspring of creativity, however, remains impeded because of a confluence of factors, including organizational zeitgeist and the innovators' trepidations regarding potential risks or lack of recognition.

Empirical evidence suggests that employees regularly engage in "employee-user innovation," crafting solutions to workplace problems. Paradoxically, these innovations often remain shrouded in secrecy, deliberately concealed by their creators. Such obfuscation may stem from apprehensions about bureaucratic quagmires, a dearth of support, or potential negative ramifications (Fuglsang, 2010; Hartmann & Hartmann, 2023). Hidden teams, those informal coalitions that coalesce organically within organizations, emerge as crucibles of innovation. Operating beyond the confines of formal hierarchies, these fluid and adaptive units are driven by shared aspirations and a thirst for autonomy. Their nimble nature enables rapid and efficacious innovation, as highlighted by (Westover, 2024).

To unmask these invisible innovators, Westover (2024) advocates for strategies that foster transparency and open dialogue. Organizations can illuminate hidden innovations and nurture a culture of creativity by cultivating an environment where goals and achievements are freely discussed. Creative recognition programs are pivotal in identifying and celebrating these unsung heroes. Such initiatives should transcend conventional rewards and embrace personalized and meaningful gestures that resonate with employees. Examples include peer-to-peer accolade platforms, social media encomiums, and small tokens of appreciation like handwritten missives or unexpected treats (Inspirus, 2024). Harnessing technology and connectivity platforms to facilitate the formation and coordination of hidden teams. Internal chat tools and forums enable employees to disseminate their innovations and collaborate more effectively, thus amplifying their contributions, as highlighted by Westover.

Giants like Microsoft and Amazon have successfully leveraged hidden teams to drive innovation in tech. Microsoft's grassroots teams birthed vital products such as OneNote and Cortana, while Amazon's small, autonomous units operate with agility, continuously disrupting industries. In the public sector, innovation often emerges from quotidian practices and problem-solving activities. This form of innovation, known as bricolage, involves employees adapting and creating solutions to unforeseen events. Management can bolster this process by orchestrating experience groups and formalizing the exchange of ideas, ensuring that valuable innovations are preserved and replicated (Fuglsang, 2010). Unveiling and recognizing invisible innovators demands a multifaceted approach that supports transparency, implements ingenious recognition programs, and harnesses technology. By decoding the dynamics of hidden innovation and cultivating a nurturing milieu, organizations can unlock the latent potential of these invaluable contributors, transmuting their clandestine efforts into organizational gold.

Productive Friction: The Catalyst for Innovation and Growth

In today's dynamic business landscape, productive friction emerges as a game-changing paradigm. This revolutionary concept harnesses the power of diverse viewpoints and constructive disagreements to propel organizations toward unprecedented innovation and problem-solving prowess (FasterCapital, 2024). At its core, productive friction thrives on three pivotal elements. Respectful debate is the cornerstone of this approach. Creating a milieu where ideas clash, but personalities are not paramount. This sanctuary of intellectual discourse empowers individuals to voice their thoughts without trepidation, fostering an atmosphere ripe for breakthrough ideation (ADR Times, 2023).

Diverse perspectives form the second crucial component. The amalgamation of varied backgrounds and opinions serves as the crucible for innovation. When eclectic minds converge, they challenge entrenched assumptions and broaden cognitive horizons, leading to more robust decision-making processes (Dansereau, 2022). Constructive disagreements complete this triad. These are the lifeblood of progress. Unlike their destructive counterparts, constructive disagreements focus on ideas rather than individuals, pushing the boundaries of conventional thinking and catalyzing innovation (Hagel, 2005).

The fruits of productive friction are manifold. Innovation incubation stands at the forefront; by fostering an environment where ideas are constantly challenged, organizations create a petri dish for groundbreaking solutions. Enhanced understanding follows closely behind. The collision of diverse viewpoints cultivates empathy and dismantles prejudices, fostering a more harmonious and efficient workplace. Decision-making emerges as another significant benefit. By incorporating multiple perspectives, organizations can transmute raw data into golden decisions, avoiding the pitfalls of groupthink. Perhaps counterintuitively, relationship fortification also results from this process. Navigating conflicts with respect and empathy can strengthen interpersonal bonds, creating a more cohesive team (Hagel et al., 2018).

Organizations must implement specific strategies to cultivate this fertile ground for productive friction. Promoting open communication is crucial. This involves creating a haven for the free exchange of ideas, where active listening is the norm rather than the exception. Nurturing respect is equally important. Organizations must instill a culture that values every team member's input, regardless of their position in the hierarchy. Last, maintaining a focus on issues, not individuals, is essential. This means keeping a laser-like focus on the problem at hand and avoiding ad hominem arguments that can derail productive discourse.

In summary, productive friction is not just a buzzword but a fundamental change in organizational dynamics. By embracing this concept, businesses can unlock their full potential, driving innovation and solving complex problems with unprecedented efficacy. The future belongs to those who can harness the power of productive friction to challenge the status quo and push the boundaries of what is possible. *Figure 3* below shows how diversity spurs unique content and ideas.

Figure 3. How diversity spurs unique content and ideas

Diverse Perspectives Lead to Unique Ideas

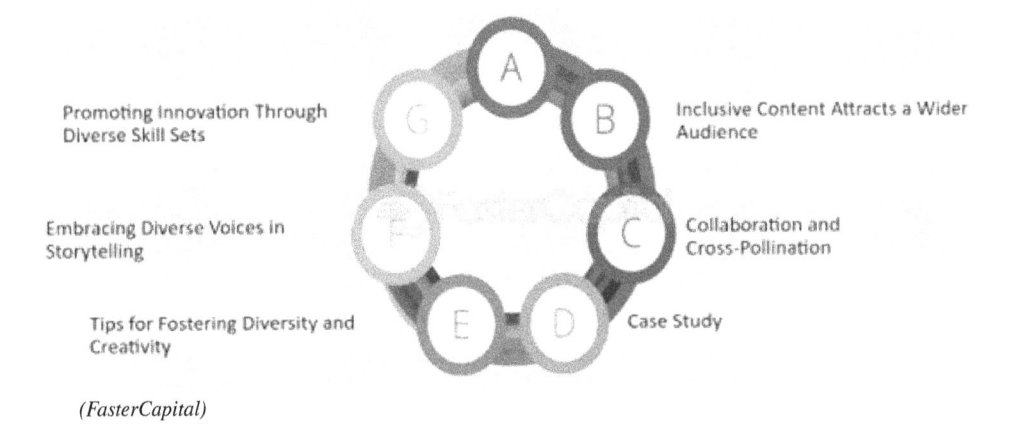

Promoting Innovation Through Diverse Skill Sets

Inclusive Content Attracts a Wider Audience

Embracing Diverse Voices in Storytelling

Collaboration and Cross-Pollination

Tips for Fostering Diversity and Creativity

Case Study

(FasterCapital)

Successful Methodologies and Case Studies

Emergent strategies and innovation processes have become the lifeblood of modern enterprises. In today's unpredictable business landscape, companies must adapt or perish. Let's delve into some compelling case studies that showcase the power of these approaches. Apple stands as a paragon of emergent strategy implementation. Their modus operandi is flexibility in the face of change. The iPhone's genesis exemplifies this approach perfectly. What began as a mere iPod with telephonic capabilities metamorphosed into a revolutionary device that redefined an entire industry (FasterCapital, n.d.). The repercussions were seismic. Apple's market dominance skyrocketed, and its assets swelled exponentially.

3M, another innovation exemplar, has long cultivated a culture of perpetual invention. Their unorthodox "15% time" policy encourages employees to pursue passionate projects, fostering a milieu of experimentation and adaptability (Harpreet, 2023). This approach has yielded myriad breakthroughs, including the ubiquitous Post-it Notes and the indispensable Scotchgard. The fruits of this strategy are manifold: a diverse product portfolio, sustained innovation, and unparalleled employee engagement.

Amazon's trajectory from a humble online bookstore to a global e-commerce monster is a testament to the efficacy of emergent strategies. Their ability to pivot and expand into new markets is remarkable (Spyre Group, 2024). Consider Amazon Web Services (AWS), originally an internal tool that burgeoned into a cloud computing steamroller. Amazon Prime was developed from a simple shipping program into a comprehensive subscription service. These emergent approaches have catapulted Amazon into multiple industries, diversifying their revenue streams and establishing them as frontrunners in fields like cloud computing and artificial intelligence.

The advantages of implementing emergent strategies and innovation processes are irrefutable. Companies employing these methodologies are better equipped to navigate the choppy waters of transforming markets and technologies (Lyons, 2023). They foster a culture of ceaseless innovation, often leading to groundbreaking products and services. By swiftly adapting to new opportunities, these companies can secure first-mover advantages and establish market domination. Moreover, the flexibility inherent in emergent strategies enhances corporate resilience in the face of market disruptions. Cultures that embrace emergent thinking frequently witness elevated employee creativity and satisfaction levels.

Implementing emergent strategies and innovation processes has enabled corporate titans like Apple, 3M, and Amazon to adapt to changing markets and actively shape them. As the pace of market evolution continues to speed up, the ability to implement and refine emergent strategies will undoubtedly become even more crucial for sustained business success. *Figure 4* shows the steps in choosing between an emergent and deliberate strategy.

Figure 4. How to choose between an emergent and deliberate strategy

How to Choose Between an Emergent and Deliberate Strategy

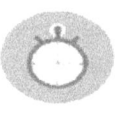

CONSIDER AN EMERGENT STRATEGY IF...
- The future of the company is uncertain
- It's unclear what the right long-term strategy is
- The company is in its early stages
- The industry's competitive landscape is undergoing significant change

CONSIDER A DELIBERATE STRATEGY IF...
- The path to strategic goals is clearly defined
- The company is relatively mature and stable
- Organizational leaders are ready to shift away from survival mode toward growth

Harvard Business School

(Harvard Business School)

CONCLUSION AND SUMMARY

This chapter's exploration of innovation and emergent strategy reveals the critical importance of adaptive, flexible approaches in today's volatile business environment. As organizations navigate increasingly complex market dynamics, the ability to foster innovation while maintaining strategic agility has become paramount to sustained success. The evidence from various case studies and theoretical frameworks shows that traditional rigid planning approaches rarely address rapid market changes and technological disruptions.

The chapter's examination of innovation as a corporate imperative, illustrated through the successes of companies like Pixar, Google, and Apple and the cautionary tales of Kodak and Blockbuster, underscores the existential necessity of maintaining innovative capacity. The contrast between emergent strategy and traditional strategic planning highlights how organizations must balance structured methods that are flexible enough to adjust and react to unforeseen opportunities and difficulties. This dynamic is particularly evident in the success stories of market leaders who have effectively combined clear strategic direction with the ability to pivot and develop their approaches based on changing circumstances.

Identifying and nurturing "invisible innovators" is crucial to organizational success. Working within the fabric of organizations, these unsung heroes often develop novel solutions to complex problems but require recognition and support systems to maximize their contributions. The concept of productive friction, characterized by constructive disagreement and diverse perspectives, catalyzes innovation and organizational growth, demonstrating how managed conflict can drive creative solutions and strategic advancement. The examination of successful methodologies through case studies of companies like Apple, 3M, and Amazon provides practical insights into implementing emergent strategies and innovation processes. These examples illustrate how organizations can successfully balance structure and flexibility, creating environments that foster innovation while maintaining strategic coherence. The importance of continuous learning, experimentation, and swift adaptation emerges as a consistent theme across these successful implementations.

As we look at the future, it becomes clear that organizations must embrace innovation and emergent strategy as fundamental components of their operational DNA. Creating cultures that celebrate successes and failures as learning opportunities while fostering diverse perspectives and constructive disagreement will be crucial for organizations seeking to thrive in an increasingly complex business landscape. The integration of these approaches, supported by recognition systems and technological infrastructure, will be essential for organizations aiming to maintain competitive advantage and drive sustainable growth in an era of continuous change and disruption.

While organizational adaptation and innovation form the bedrock of sustainable growth in today's dynamic business environment, the success of these initiatives hinges heavily on an organization's ability to engage with its diverse stakeholder ecosystem effectively. The technological infrastructure and cultural frameworks that enable innovation must be complemented by sophisticated stakeholder engagement strategies that bridge cultural divides and foster meaningful collaboration. As organizations expand their global footprint and navigate increasingly complex stakeholder networks, building and maintaining robust relationships across cultural boundaries becomes helpful for survival and growth. This interconnection between internal innovation capabilities and external stakeholder engagement represents a critical junction for modern organizations seeking to thrive in unprecedented change and complexity.

REFERENCES

Boyles, M. (2022). *Innovation in Business: What It Is & Why It's So Important.* https://online.hbs.edu/blog/post/importance-of-innovation-in-business

Dansereau, V. (2022). *How Constructive Conflict in the Workplace Can Be Beneficial.* https://pollackpeacebuilding.com/blog/how-constructive-conflict-in-the-workplace-can-be-beneficial/

Edmondson, A. C. (2011). Strategies for Learning from Failure. *Harvard Business Review.* https://hbr.org/2011/04/strategies-for-learning-from-failure

EU Business School Blog post (May2022). What Is Business Innovation and Why Is It Important? Blog EU Business School. https://www.euruni.edu/blog/what-is-business-innovation-and-why-is-it-important/

FasterCapital. (2024). Constructive Dialogue and Debate. *Faster Capital.* https://fastercapital.com/content/Alternative-Opinions--Embracing-Diverse-Perspectives.html#Constructive-Dialogue-and-Debate

FasterCapital. (n.d.). Case Studies Of Successful Innovation Strategies. *FasterCapital.* Retrieved July 26, 2024, from https://fastercapital.com/topics/case-studies-of-successful-innovation-strategies.html

Freedman, J. (2021). Is It Possible to Change? 5 Tips from Emergent Strategy Where Climate Justice and Social Justice Meet. *Six Seconds.* https://www.6seconds.org/2021/08/15/possible-to-change/

Fuglsang, L. (2010). Bricolage and invisible innovation in public service innovation. *Journal of Innovation Economics Management*, 5(1), 67–87. https://www.cairn.info/revue-journal-of-innovation-economics-2010-1-page-67.htm. DOI: 10.3917/jie.005.0067

Hagel, J. (2005). *Productive Friction – A Key to Accelerating Business Innovation.* John Hagel. https://www.johnhagel.com/productive-friction-a-key-to-accelerating-business-innovation/

Hagel, J., III, Brown, J. S., de Maar, A., & Wool, M. (2018). Maximize potential for friction. *Deloitte Insights.* https://www2.deloitte.com/us/en/insights/topics/talent/business-performance-improvement/maximize-potential-for-friction.html

Harpreet, D. (2023). Innovation and Adaptability: Staying Ahead in a Rapidly Evolving Business Landscape | LinkedIn. *LinkedIn.* https://www.linkedin.com/pulse/innovation-adaptability-staying-ahead-rapidly-evolving-dhillon/

Hartmann, M. R., & Hartmann, R. K. (2023). Hiding practices in employee-user innovation. *Research Policy*, 52(4), 104728. DOI: 10.1016/j.respol.2023.104728

Indeed Editorial Team. (2022). *What Is Emergent Strategy? With Benefits and Examples*. https://www.indeed.com/career-advice/career-development/emergent-strategy-definition

Inspirus (2024). The Art of Creative Employee Recognition Programs (2024). https://www.inspirus.com/blog/employee-recognition-programs/

Ivory Research. (2019). The need of emergent Strategy in a Changing Environment | Ivory Research. *Ivory Research*. https://www.ivoryresearch.com/samples/the-need-of-emergent-strategy-in-a-changing-environment/

Lyons, R. (2023). Why Emergent Strategy is the Key to Success. *TopResume*. https://topresume.com/career-advice/why-emergent-strategy-is-the-key-to-success

Mahr, N., & Hendricks, B. (2023). Emergent Strategy | Definition, Advantages & Examples. *study.com*. https://study.com/academy/lesson/emergent-strategy-definition-advantages-disadvantages.html

Sparrow, G. (2024). *10 Ways to Foster Innovation in Your Company: From Ideas to Impact*. https://www.herox.com/blog/1063-10-ways-to-foster-innovation-in-your-company

Spyre Group. (2024). *Examples of Companies with Successful Innovation Strategies*. https://www.spyre.group/post/examples-of-companies-with-successful-innovation-strategies

Stobierski, T. (2020). Emergent vs. Deliberate Strategy: How & When to Use Each. *Harvard Business School*. https://online.hbs.edu/blog/post/emergent-vs-deliberate-strategy

Times, A. D. R. (2023). Constructive Conflict: A Positive Catalyst. *ADR Times*. https://www.adrtimes.com/constructive-conflict/

UBC Blog post (September 2022). Notes on Brown's Emergent Strategy – You're the Teacher. https://blogs.ubc.ca/chendricks/2022/09/10/brown-emergent-strategy/

Valuer (2022). *50 Brands that Failed to Innovate*. https://www.valuer.ai/blog/50-examples-of-corporations-that-failed-to-innovate-and-missed-their-chance

Westover, J. (2024). The Invisible Backbone: Leveraging Hidden Teams to Drive Organizational Success. *HCI Consulting*. https://www.innovativehumancapital.com/post/the-invisible-backbone-leveraging-hidden-teams-to-drive-organizational-success

KEY TERMS AND DEFINITIONS

"15% Time" Policy: Similar to Google's policy, 3M's approach allows employees to dedicate 15% of their time to pursuing passionate projects and innovations.

"20% Time" Policy: An innovation-fostering approach (exemplified by Google) where employees are allowed to spend a portion of their work time on side projects of their choosing.

Bricolage: A form of innovation in the public sector where employees adapt and create solutions to unforeseen events using available resources.

Constructive Disagreement: A form of conflict that focuses on ideas rather than individuals, pushing boundaries of conventional thinking while maintaining respect and professionalism.

Culture of Innovation: An organizational environment that encourages experimentation, accepts calculated risks, and views failures as learning opportunities rather than setbacks.

Emergent Strategy: A dynamic approach to strategic management that favors flexible, adaptive methodologies over rigid planning, allowing strategies to develop through unplanned actions and initiatives in response to environmental changes and opportunities.

Employee-User Innovation: The process where employees create custom solutions to workplace problems, often independently and without formal recognition or support.

Hidden Teams: Informal coalitions that form organically within organizations, operating outside formal hierarchies and driven by shared goals and a desire for autonomy.

Innovation Ecosystem: An organizational environment that systematically nurtures creativity and experimentation through collaboration, resource allocation, and support systems.

Invisible Innovators: Employees who develop novel solutions to organizational challenges but whose contributions often go unrecognized, frequently working outside formal innovation channels.

Innovation Recognition Programs: Formal systems designed to identify, celebrate, and reward innovative contributions within an organization, including peer-to-peer platforms and social recognition.

Market Volatility: The rapid and unpredictable changes in business environments that require organizations to maintain flexible and adaptive strategies.

Productive Friction: The constructive use of diverse viewpoints and disagreements to drive innovation and problem-solving, characterized by respectful debate and focus on ideas rather than individuals.

Self-Disruption: The practice of organizations willingly challenging their existing business models and practices to stay competitive and avoid becoming obsolete.

Traditional Strategic Planning: A systematic, deliberate approach to long-term planning that relies on extensive analysis and forecasting to create comprehensive roadmaps for achieving objectives.

Chapter 9
Engaging Stakeholders:
Communication and Collaboration in a Diverse World

ABSTRACT

This chapter explores the critical role of effective stakeholder engagement in today's diverse global landscape. It emphasizes the importance of cultural competence, trust-building, and adaptive communication strategies in navigating complex stakeholder relationships. Key topics include understanding and valuing cultural diversity, developing effective cross-cultural communication skills, and building trust across cultural boundaries. The chapter discusses strategies for creating shared value through stakeholder relationships, fostering collaboration and inclusivity, and overcoming challenges in diverse environments. It highlights the need for organizations to adapt their engagement approaches continuously, leveraging technology and embracing diverse perspectives to drive innovation and sustainable success. The chapter illustrates how organizations can enhance stakeholder engagement efforts to build stronger, more resilient relationships in an increasingly interconnected world through case studies and practical examples.

INTRODUCTION

Effective stakeholder engagement has become more critical and complex in today's rapidly developing global business landscape than ever. Effective stakeholder involvement has grown increasingly crucial and complex. This chapter, "*Engaging Stakeholders: Communication and Collaboration in a Diverse World,*" examines the complex interactions among stakeholders' relationships across cultural boundaries and presents comprehensive strategies for building meaningful connections in an increasingly diverse business environment. The chapter examines five fundamental

DOI: 10.4018/979-8-3693-5553-4.ch009

aspects: the foundations of stakeholder engagement, the recognition and valuation of cultural diversity, cross-cultural communication strategies, trust-building mechanisms, and methods for creating value through stakeholder relationships.

Drawing from recent research and practical case studies, this chapter illuminates how organizations can navigate the challenges of cultural differences while leveraging diversity as a source of innovation and strength. It shows that successful stakeholder engagement requires more than basic communication skills; it demands cultural competence, adaptability, and a genuine commitment to inclusive practices. The chapter provides practical frameworks and evidence-based strategies for professionals seeking to enhance their stakeholder engagement capabilities in a multicultural context. By examining the challenges and opportunities presented by cultural diversity in stakeholder engagement, this work offers valuable insights for business leaders, project managers, and professionals working in global organizations. The chapter emphasizes that effective stakeholder engagement is not merely a risk management tool but a strategic imperative for creating sustainable value and achieving long-term success in our interconnected world.

ENGAGING STAKEHOLDERS IN A DIVERSE WORLD

Stakeholder engagement is a pivotal force in today's interconnected global business arena. This systematic process identifies, analyzes, plans, and implements actions to involve and influence those affected by an organization's decisions (Association for Project Management, 2024). Why does it matter? Trust-building, risk management, enhanced decision-making, transparency, and shared value creation are all necessary. Aligning stakeholders is imperative. Our ability to connect as a team directly affects our ability to create value (Aha Blog Post, 2023). However, achieving stakeholder alignment can be challenging because of differing priorities and perspectives. Miscommunication or lack of transparency can further complicate the process, leading to misunderstandings and conflicts. Additionally, aligning stakeholders often requires significant time and effort to ensure everyone agrees.

Effective stakeholder engagement is the linchpin of long-term success in a complex, globalized economy. It is about finding growth and innovation opportunities, not managing risks. Organizations can make more robust, sustainable decisions by tapping into stakeholder insights. This commitment to transparency and accountability resonates in our socially conscious business milieu, aligning organizational activities with societal expectations. However, cultural diversity within stakeholder groups presents significant challenges and exciting opportunities. Communication barriers, varying expectations, and power dynamics can complicate matters.

However, this diversity also offers a wellspring of creativity and comprehensive representation if managed effectively. Organizations must adopt a multifaceted approach, such as cultivating cultural competence and tailoring communication strategies to navigate this labyrinth. They must implement inclusive engagement processes and provide cross-cultural training. Above all, they must remain flexible and adaptable. By embracing this kaleidoscope of cultural diversity, organizations can elevate their stakeholder engagement efforts. The result? All parties experience enhanced value creation through more effective communication and stronger collaborations. This approach dovetails with the evolution of stakeholder engagement from a mere risk management tool to a strategic imperative for long-term success in our globalized business landscape (Association for Project Management, 2024). *Figure 1* below depicts stakeholder engagement vs. management and how they create business value.

Figure 1. Stakeholder engagement v. stakeholder management

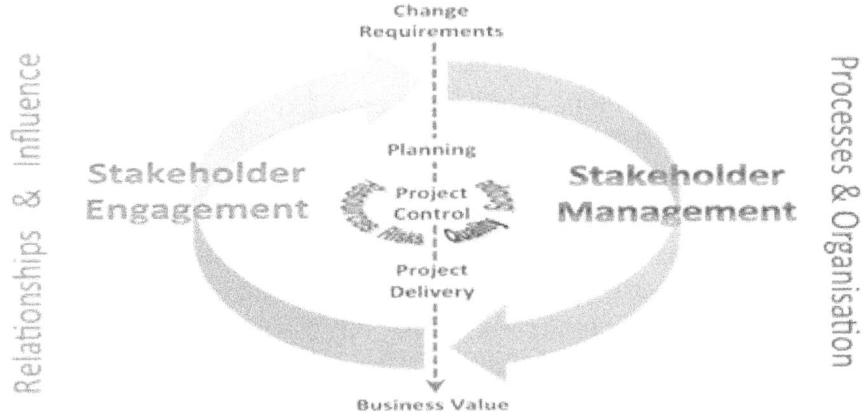

(Association for Project Management)

Understanding Stakeholders: Recognizing and Valuing Cultural Diversity

In the convoluted world of project management and organizational triumph, the identification and prioritization of key stakeholders reign supreme. This intricate tapestry of influence weaves together both internal and external threads. The former encompasses the organization's lifeblood—employees, managers, and shareholders. The latter extends its tendrils to customers, suppliers, regulators, community members, and partners. To navigate this complex web, savvy leaders employ the power-interest matrix, a quintessential tool for categorizing stakeholders based on their clout and investment in the project or organization. Those wielding substantial power and interest demand paramount attention and engagement (Eskafi et al., 2019). *Figure 2* below shows a power-interest matrix for categorizing stakeholders and filling each box based on the stakeholder's characteristics.

Figure 2. Power-interest matrix

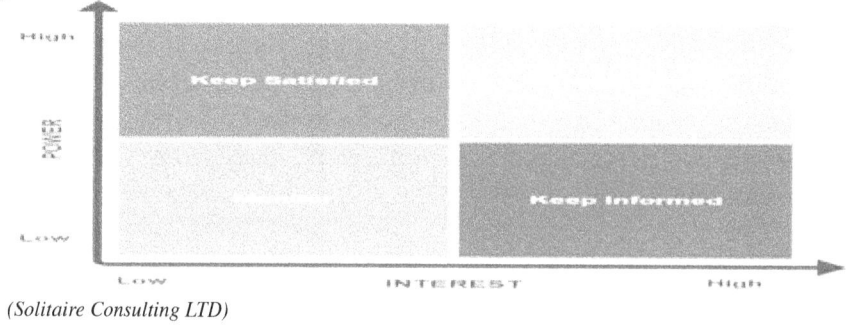

(Solitaire Consulting LTD)

The cultural mixture within organizations presents a formidable challenge to communication and collaboration. This multifaceted prism refracts through language barriers, communication styles, and attitudes toward hierarchical structures. Some cultures embrace forthright discourse, while others circle indirect expression. Mušura (2020) posits that non-verbal cues, subtle gestures, and human dialects can be as enigmatic as ancient hieroglyphs when viewed through different cultural lenses. The decision-making arena further exemplifies this diversity, with some cultures supporting consensus and others contributing to top-down declarations (Katul, 2024).

Cultivating cultural acumen is the cornerstone of effective stakeholder engagement. This enlightened approach yields many benefits, including enhanced trust and cooperation, a crucible for innovation and problem-solving, and a salve for potential conflicts. When stakeholders perceive their cultural essence as acknowledged and revered, trust flourishes, fostering a conducive environment for collaboration (Dirks & Pratt, 2021). The confluence of diverse perspectives ignites the spark of creativity, illuminating novel pathways to resolution, according to Katul (2024). Furthermore, Schmidt et al. (2023) argue that a nuanced understanding of cultural characteristics can effectively defuse conflicts that arise from miscommunication. These benefits underscore the value of investing in cultural insight.

Organizations must deploy many strategies to cultivate this rarefied atmosphere of cultural cognizance. Immersive cultural training programs serve as beacons, illuminating the rich tapestry of global communication styles. Organizations need to integrate inclusive policies into their core values, and they should foster open communication channels that are life-giving. According to Schmidt et al. (2023), as stewards of organizational ethos, leadership must embody culturally sensitive behavior and champion initiatives that elevate cultural awareness. The pinnacle of stakeholder engagement is the recognition and exaltation of cultural diversity. Organizations can deftly identify key players, decipher cultural enigmas, and foster an environment of cultural sensitivity, orchestrating a symphony of enhanced communication, collaboration, and unparalleled success.

Importance of Effective Communication in Diverse Environments

In our increasingly globalized society, communicating effectively across cultures is paramount. This multifaceted skill encompasses far more than mere linguistic proficiency; it demands a nuanced understanding of nonverbal cues, cultural norms, and the art of adaptability. Nonverbal communication, often overlooked, plays a pivotal role in cross-cultural interactions. The subtle nuances of gestures, facial expressions, and body language can make or break a conversation. Gestures can emphasize points, convey emotions, and even replace words when language barriers exist. They add depth to spoken language, making communication more engaging and effective. For example, a simple nod can show agreement, while crossed arms may suggest defensiveness.

An innocent gesture in one culture may be deeply offensive in another. For instance, some Middle Eastern nations could interpret the ubiquitous "thumbs up" sign, a positive affirmation in Western cultures, as an insult (Rcademy, 2023). By honing our awareness of these nonverbal intricacies, we can circumvent misunderstandings, enhance comprehension, and forge stronger connections with individuals from diverse backgrounds.

Open-mindedness serves as the cornerstone of effective cross-cultural communication. It is the key to unlocking cultural immersion, enabling us to delve deeper into the rich global perspectives. This receptivity to new experiences and viewpoints not only sharpens our intercultural communication skills but also helps dismantle stereotypes and preconceptions (Wang et al., 2022). Authenticity thrives when interactions begin with openness. Recognizing and respecting cultural norms and traditions is equally crucial. This knowledge safeguards against unintentional faux pas and fosters a more inclusive environment for all stakeholders (Ollerton, 2023). It allows us to tailor communication strategies with finesse, ensuring the message resonates across cultural boundaries.

Adapting our nonverbal cues shows cultural sensitivity and reinforces our verbal messages. This chameleon-like ability to adjust communication style builds trust and credibility with diverse stakeholders (Rcademy, 2023). It showcases respect for cultural differences and dedication to effective communication. Translation tools can be invaluable in multilingual environments. These resources, which range from professional translation services to real-time interpretation apps, bridge linguistic gaps and ensure the precise conveying of critical information (Harry Clark Translation, n.d.). However, technology alone is not a panacea. One must also employ strategies to overcome language barriers, such as using plain language, incorporating visual aids, and practicing active listening.

Cultural awareness and sensitivity are the bedrock of effective cross-cultural communication. They promote mutual respect, enhance our ability to interpret messages, and allow us to tailor our communication approaches to diverse audiences (Rcademy, 2023). This flexibility is crucial in navigating the complex landscape of global interactions. Communication with non-native speakers often underestimates the importance of patience, despite its inherent virtue. It provides the necessary processing time, reduces stress, and shows respect for the Herculean effort required in cross-cultural communication (Gurmentor, 2021). Effective communication in culturally diverse environments is an intricate dance of awareness, adaptability, and respect. Adopting these strategies can build stronger relationships and minimize misunderstandings. Developing cross-cultural communication skills is essential to fostering understanding and cooperation in an increasingly interconnected world.

The Role of Trust in Stakeholder Engagement

In the intricate needlepoint of stakeholder engagement, trust emerges as the linchpin that binds all elements together. It is the catalyst for autonomous communication, the spark that ignites collaboration, and the fortification of organizational credibility. Trust, in essence, is the "willingness of a party to be vulnerable to the actions of another based on expectations that the other has positive intentions and actions toward the trustor" (Ford et al., 2020, p. 1). When trust permeates stakeholder relationships, it metamorphoses decision-making processes, conflict resolution, and project outcomes. The invisible force emboldens stakeholders to voice their authentic opinions and concerns, fostering an environment ripe for meaningful engagement. Trust is the alchemic agent that transmutes disparate stakeholders into a cohesive unit, working together towards shared objectives. Furthermore, trust is the foundation for building an organization's reputation and securing stakeholder support for future endeavors.

However, the path to trust is fraught with challenges, mainly when traversing cultural divides. The complicated nature of cross-cultural trust-building stems from a mosaic of divergent values, communication styles, and trust-building mechanisms. Leadership must recognize these cultural nuances to navigate this complex terrain successfully. Trust is often based on transparency, reliability, and explicit agreements in the Western hemisphere, particularly in the United States and Canada (Fernandez, 2023). In contrast, rather than formal accords, personal relationships and networks typically cultivate trust in East Asian nations like China and Japan. The German approach to trust-building is characterized by meticulous due diligence and a proven track record of success. Meanwhile, in Brazil, the social fabric plays a crucial role, with trust woven through personal relationships and networks, argues Fernandez.

The hurdles in cross-cultural trust-building are manifold. Communication barriers, divergent trust-building mechanisms, and varying perceptions of actions can create a veritable minefield of misunderstandings. One culture may perceive trust-building as excessive or even offensive in another culture. Nevertheless, there exist universally applicable strategies for cultivating trust across cultural boundaries. These strategies revolve around transparency, consistency, cultural competence, active listening, relationship-building, integrity, and fairness.

Transparency is the cornerstone of trust-building. It involves being forthright in communications and actions, which bolsters stakeholder credibility. Crystal-clear communication, devoid of jargon and convoluted language, is paramount. Regularly disseminating pertinent information keeps stakeholders in the loop and involved in decision-making processes. Consistency in actions and communications engenders reliability and predictability, the twin pillars of trust. Honoring commitments made to stakeholders is non-negotiable (Blomquist, 2022). Establishing consistent communication channels and providing regular updates on progress and changes is crucial, according to (Chandranshu, 2023).

Cultural competence is the compass that guides cross-cultural trust-building; it necessitates a profound comprehension and appreciation of cultural disparities and the ability to adapt engagement strategies accordingly. According to Chandranshu (2023), delving into stakeholders' cultural practices, norms, and values is imperative; demonstrating genuine interest and respect for diverse cultural perspectives fosters goodwill, and tailoring communication styles to align with stakeholders' cultural preferences is a trust-building masterstroke.

Active listening is consuming the speaker's message and responding thoughtfully. It involves showing genuine interest in stakeholders' perspectives by asking insightful questions and summarizing their points to ensure understanding. The author argues that empathy is a powerful trust-building tool when shown through acknowledging stakeholders' emotions and respecting their viewpoints. Investing time in personal relationships is invaluable in cultures where interpersonal connections build trust (Fernandez, 2023). Leveraging existing relationships and networks can serve as a bridge to building trust with new stakeholders (PennState Extension, 2023).

Integrity and fairness form the ethical foundation of trust-building. Stakeholders must believe in the organization's moral compass. Ensuring all actions align with the organization's values is crucial (PennState Extension, 2023); fair treatment of all stakeholders and valuing their contributions is non-negotiable. Building trust in stakeholder engagement is a multifaceted endeavor that demands transparency, consistency, cultural competence, active listening, relationship-building, and unwavering integrity. Organizations can forge stronger, more trusting relationships with their stakeholders by employing these strategies, paving the way for more effective and sustainable engagement outcomes. *Figure 3* below shows how bridging, linking, and bonding networks help stakeholders build trust in social capital.

Figure 3. Efficacy

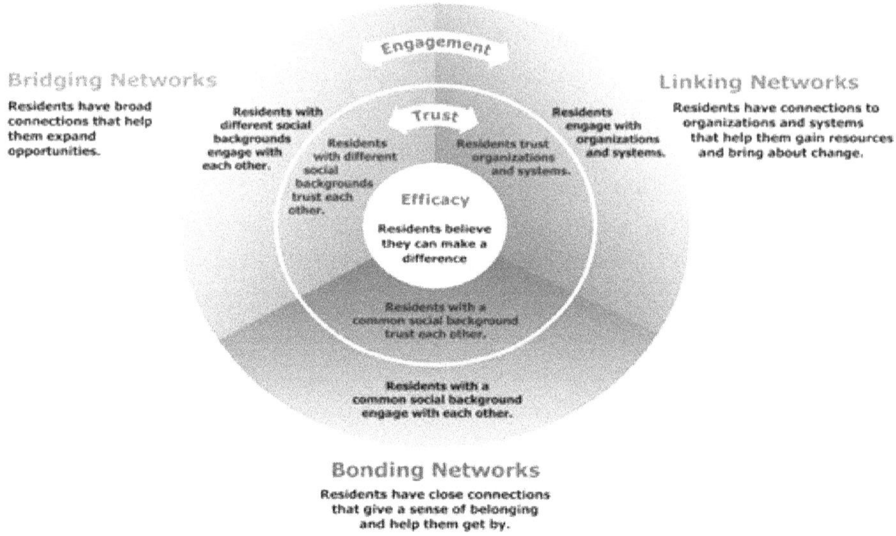

(University of Minnesota Extension)

Creating Value Through Stakeholder Relationships

Stakeholder engagement is the key to shared value creation in our diverse global landscape. It is about aligning interests and orchestrating a symphony of collaboration. When organizations harmonize their objectives with stakeholder needs, magic happens, and they unlock a wellspring of support and innovation (Association for Project Management, 2024). Consider a consumer goods giant that revolutionized its approach to sustainability. How? We engage stakeholders through town halls and surveys. The result? The result was a masterclass in environmental stewardship and brand elevation (FasterCapital Blog Post, June 2024).

However, wait, there is more. Co-creation is not just a buzzword; it is a game-changer. It is about crafting solutions that resonate with everyone involved. This collaboration yields higher-quality outcomes, fosters stakeholder ownership, and cultivates an environment of pellucidity and answerability (BusinessRiskTV, 2023). A local government has transformed a barren plot into a vibrant park. The secret ingredient? Community involvement. Through workshops and consultations, residents became the architects of their recreational haven. The outcome? The result is a park that exemplifies teamwork (FasterCapital Blog Post, June 2024).

Now, let us talk about metrics. Measuring impact is not prudent; it is imperative. It is about defining clear objectives, developing salient KPIs, and gathering feedback with the tenacity of a detective. This process reassures stakeholders and builds confidence. Moreover, do not forget the denouement, which communicates outcomes. It is the thread that weaves trust into the fabric of stakeholder relationships. Consider learning from the non-profit sector. They have mastered the art of impact communication through a multi-channel approach. The result? According to a blog post from FasterCapital, the fundraising goals were shattered, and donor relationships cemented. Effective stakeholder engagement is not just a strategy but an art form. It is about aligning, co-creating, measuring, and communicating. When executed with finesse, it catalyzes trust, sparks innovation, and paves the way for outcomes that benefit all. In our diverse world, it is about creating value and crafting a shared narrative of success.

Fostering Collaboration and Inclusivity

In today's interconnected world, the benefits of collaborative approaches to engaging diverse stakeholders are irrefutable. This modus operandi amplifies understanding and cultivates trust, sparks innovation, mitigates risks, and yields cost efficiencies (Ozdemir et al., 2023). By embracing various perspectives, organizations can craft strategies that resonate with stakeholder needs, fostering a symbiotic relationship that drives success. Practical strategies for promoting collaboration include identifying key stakeholders by pinpointing those most affected by decisions and ensuring their involvement from the outset. Establish an inclusive environment that includes all voices, regardless of background or position. We can achieve this by fostering a culture of trust, respect, and collaboration. We should encourage everyone to express their opinions and participate in decision-making. Set clear objectives by articulating goals unambiguously to align expectations. Provide adequate resources to equip stakeholders with the tools and support for active participation. Maintain transparency by keeping stakeholders apprised of progress and being candid about limitations.

Leverage technology for virtual collaboration. In this digital age, many tools exist to facilitate seamless collaboration. Platforms like Zoom and Microsoft Teams enable virtual meetings, while project management tools such as Trello and Asana ensure accountability. SurveyMonkey and Google Forms serve as efficient conduits for gathering stakeholder input. Host community meetings to disseminate project updates and address concerns. Conduct surveys to inform decision-making and show the value of community feedback. Establish advisory committees or focus groups to involve the public in crucial decision-making. Forge partnerships with organizations, non-profits, and government bodies to leverage expertise and resources. Develop joint initiatives that address shared goals and benefit all parties involved.

Case studies and research on the topic highlight the work of the Body Shop's Community Trade Program, which sources ingredients from marginalized communities, ensuring fair trade practices and supporting local economies (Ozdemir et al., 2023). An urban village renovation in Tianjin, China, leveraged the resource-driving advantages of core stakeholders and established a network-sharing platform, achieving deep cooperation among multiple stakeholders (Zheng et al., 2024). The U.S. Department of Agriculture funded collaborative research in the Walker River Basin, which involved iterative stakeholder engagement throughout the research process, facilitating knowledge co-production (Singletary et al., 2022). Collaborative approaches to engaging diverse stakeholders offer a wealth of benefits. By implementing practical strategies, leveraging technology, and learning from successful case studies, organizations can harness the power of collaboration to drive innovation, mitigate risks, and achieve sustainable outcomes. *Figure 4* below shows stakeholders with different, often competing interests.

Figure 4. Stakeholders with different interests

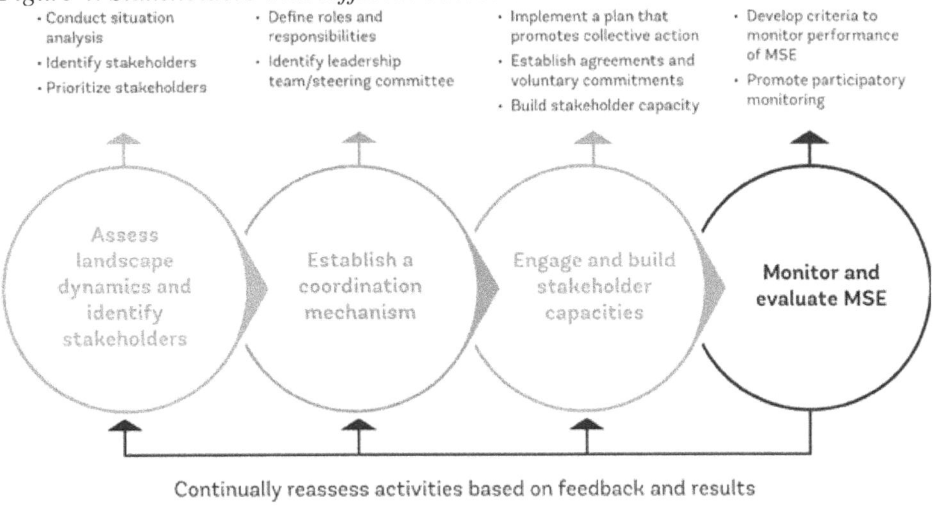

- Conduct situation analysis
- Identify stakeholders
- Prioritize stakeholders

- Define roles and responsibilities
- Identify leadership team/steering committee

- Implement a plan that promotes collective action
- Establish agreements and voluntary commitments
- Build stakeholder capacity

- Develop criteria to monitor performance of MSE
- Promote participatory monitoring

Assess landscape dynamics and identify stakeholders → Establish a coordination mechanism → Engage and build stakeholder capacities → Monitor and evaluate MSE

Continually reassess activities based on feedback and results

(Biocarbon Fund)

Strategies for Effective Stakeholder Engagement

In the complex world of organizational dynamics, the art of stakeholder engagement reigns supreme. It is the key element that can propel an enterprise from mediocrity to magnificence. This intricate dance demands a nuanced approach that combines strategy, empathy, and adaptability. Organizations must embark on a meticulous expedition to map their stakeholder landscape from the rank-and-file to the upper echelons, from patrons to investors, leaving no stone unturned. Tyagi (2023b) meticulously categorizes these entities based on their gravitational pull and vested interests. This stratification will guide you in developing commissioned engagement strategies.

Put on your psychoanalyst's hat and plumb the depths of the stakeholder psyche through a panoply of methodologies—surveys, tête-à-têtes, and feedback loops. Your course of action is proactivity, transparency, responsiveness, and reverence. This chemistry blend will transform skepticism into trust, forming lasting bonds. However, achieving this transformation is not without its challenges. It requires consistent effort, transparency, and open communication from all parties involved. Trust-building is a gradual process that misunderstandings or unfulfilled promises can easily disrupt.

Construct a robust communication edifice, delineating channels, and the cadence of outreach. Make sure that no stakeholder lacks information. Your strategy must be a paragon of inclusivity, acknowledging the display of cultural nuances and perspectives (Tyagi, 2023b; Bangia, 2023). Transcend mere information dissemination; strive for a communication paradigm crucible for diversity and innovation. In our increasingly digitized milieu, championing diversity in virtual realms is non-negotiable. Leverage innovative tools with multilingual capabilities. Cultivate a digital ethos where every voice, regardless of origin, can resonate. This approach catalyzes unparalleled clarity, understanding, and innovation (Grossmann, 2024; Perilli, 2023).

Transform stakeholder input into organizational gold; this process is robust. Your responsiveness to feedback should be swift, transparent, and specific. Tyagi (2023a) asserts that the transformation of words into actions will catalyze the building of stakeholder trust. Be sure the very fabric of your organization embraces diversity and inclusion. Implement comprehensive diversity training programs for all employees and establish clear policies that support equal opportunities. Promote transparent communication and establish employee resource groups to guarantee the inclusion of all perspectives.

Regularly review hiring practices to eliminate biases and promote a diverse workforce. Confront unconscious biases head-on and acknowledge the intricate web of intersectionality. Remember, stakeholder engagement is not a destination but a continuous journey; it demands relentless refinement and adaptation. Your initiatives must be as adaptable as the stakeholders they support, developing with their continually shifting requirements. Master this art and watch your organization become a beacon of stakeholder synergy, collaboration, and enduring success.

Overcoming Challenges

Navigating the web of cultural diversity in the workplace demands finesse and insight. The quintessential challenges that often confound teams include linguistic disparities, entrenched stereotypes, and conflicting mores. Such obstructions can discourage collaborations, however well-meaning. Language, that mercurial medium of exchange, can be a veritable minefield. Misinterpretations lurk in the shadows of unfamiliar dialects and idiomatic expressions. Stereotypes, those harmful cognitive shortcuts, have the potential to contaminate interpersonal relationships even before they start. Furthermore, we must not overlook the clash of values and norms that can transform a straightforward project into a complex network of conflicting expectations.

However, open communication reigns supreme in this arena. It can prevent potential misunderstandings by fostering an environment where team members can share their cultural perspectives openly and honestly. Unlit Leadership (2023) posits that this approach engenders a more inclusive and respectful milieu. When conveying complex information, distillation is vital. Boil down intricate concepts to their essence, ensuring clarity across cultural divides. Encourage probing questions to plumb the depths of diverse viewpoints, which fosters a rapport built on mutual respect and understanding.

Conflict resolution strategies are indispensable in this context. Acknowledge divergent perspectives, analyze root causes, and strive for compromise. The Ontop Team Blog post (2024) encourages us to embrace diversity as a wellspring of innovation rather than a hurdle to overcome. Identify systemic factors contributing to conflicts and address them head-on. Seek common ground by delving into the values and priorities of each team member. Trust-building activities are crucial in forging bonds among team members. Create opportunities for camaraderie to flourish outside the confines of work-related tasks. Transparency in actions and decisions is paramount. Delineate processes for addressing conflicts and ensure all team members are well-versed in these protocols.

Adapting to varying communication styles is an art form. Recognize the distinctions between direct and indirect communication preferences and adjust your approach accordingly (Ontop Team Blog post, 2024; Unlit Leadership, 2023). Remember, overcoming cultural barriers is not a destination but a journey; long-term commitment is essential to sustain these efforts (Newman, 2019). Continuously solicit feedback and iterate on your approach to ensure effective communication and collaboration in a diverse environment (Jangra, 2024). By implementing these strategies, organizations can deftly navigate the complexities of a culturally diverse workplace. The result? The outcome is a setting that fosters inclusivity, innovation, and productivity, embracing diversity as a driving force for success. *Figure 5* below describes the dos and don'ts for engaging stakeholders.

Figure 5. Stakeholder engagement dos and don'ts

(Simplystakeholder)

CONCLUSION AND SUMMARY

This chapter's comprehensive examination of stakeholder engagement underscores the critical importance of effective communication, cultural competence, and trust-building in today's diverse business environment. Several key findings emerge from this analysis that significantly affect organizational practice and success. First, the chapter shows that successful stakeholder engagement requires a sophisticated understanding of cultural diversity and its impact on communication patterns, decision-making processes, and relationship building. Organizations must move beyond simply acknowledging cultural differences to develop nuanced strategies that actively embrace and leverage diversity as a source of innovation and competitive advantage.

Second, the research emphasizes that trust is the foundational element in stakeholder relationships. The chapter reveals how trust-building mechanisms vary significantly across cultures, from the relationship-based approaches prevalent in East Asian societies to the more transaction-focused methods common in Western contexts. This understanding is crucial for organizations operating in global environments, as it informs the development of culturally appropriate engagement strategies. Third, the analysis highlights the transformative potential of collaborative approaches in stakeholder engagement. When organizations successfully facilitate cooperation across diverse stakeholder groups, they can achieve superior outcomes through enhanced innovation, risk mitigation, and value creation. The case studies show how inclusive practices and co-creation lead to more sustainable and mutually beneficial solutions.

Fourth, the chapter identifies several critical challenges in cross-cultural stakeholder engagement, including language barriers, conflicting cultural norms, and varying expectations. However, it also provides practical strategies for overcoming these obstacles through cultural competence training, adaptive communication approaches, and inclusive policies. The results have considerable ramifications for organizational practice. They suggest that organizations must:

1. Invest in developing cultural competence at all levels of the organization.
2. Adapt flexible engagement strategies to different cultural contexts.
3. Build robust communication infrastructures that support diverse stakeholder needs.
4. Establish transparent processes for measuring and communicating impact.
5. Foster an organizational culture that values and promotes diversity and inclusion.

The evolution of stakeholder engagement in an increasingly interconnected world will demand a more significant emphasis on cultural intelligence and adaptive capabilities. Organizations that can successfully navigate the complexities of diverse stakeholder relationships while maintaining authenticity and transparency will be better positioned to achieve sustainable success in the global business landscape. This chapter shows that effective stakeholder engagement in a diverse world is not merely about managing relationships but creating an ecosystem of mutual understanding, respect, and value creation. As organizations continue to operate in increasingly diverse environments, the ability to engage stakeholders across cultural boundaries will become an increasingly critical determinant of organizational success.

The transition between the complex dynamics of stakeholder engagement and the technological transformation of human capital represents a natural progression in understanding modern organizational challenges. As organizations master the intricacies of cross-cultural stakeholder relationships, they face the imperative of technological adaptation and workforce development. The convergence of these domains, cultural intelligence and technological advancement creates a unique intersection where leaders must navigate human and digital transformations. This transition from stakeholder engagement to technological impact on human capital exemplifies the multifaceted nature of contemporary leadership challenges, where success depends on harmonizing human relationships with technological progress.

REFERENCES

Aha Blog Post. (November 2023). Does stakeholder alignment matter? | Aha! Software. https://www.aha.io/blog/does-stakeholder-alignment-really-matter

Association for Project Magement. (2024). *What is Stakeholder engagement?* https://www.apm.org.uk/resources/find-a-resource/stakeholder-engagement/

Bangia, G. (2023). *The Significance of Diversity and Inclusion in P.R. and Communications - Reputation Today*. https://reputationtoday.in/the-significance-of-diversity-and-inclusion-in-pr-and-communications/

Blomquist, B. (2022). *7 Ways to Build Stakeholder Trust*. https://blog.jambo.cloud/7-ways-to-build-stakeholder-trust

BusinessRiskTV. (2023). *Co-creating Solutions with Stakeholders*. https://businessrisktv.com/co-creating-solutions-with-stakeholders/

Chandranshu, S. (2023). Building Trust and Respect with People from Different Cultures. *LinkedIn*. https://www.linkedin.com/pulse/building-trust-respect-people-from-different-cultures-srivastava/

Dirks, L. G., & Pratt, W. (2021). *Technology to Support Collaborative Dissemination of Research with Alaska Native Communities*. AMIA ... Annual Symposium Proceedings. AMIA Symposium, 2021, 398–407. https://pubmed.ncbi.nlm.nih.gov/35308978/

Eskafi, M., Fazeli, R., Dastgheib, A., Taneja, P., Ulfarsson, G. F., Thorarinsdottir, R. I., & Stefansson, G. (2019). View of Stakeholder salience and prioritization for port master planning, a case study of the multi-purpose Port of Isafjordur in Iceland. *European Journal of Transport and Infrastructure Research*, 19(3), 1–47. DOI: 10.18757/ejtir.2019.19.3.4386

FasterCapital Blog Post. (June 2024). Case Studies In Effective Stakeholder Engagement - FasterCapital. https://fastercapital.com/topics/case-studies-in-effective-stakeholder-engagement.html

Fernandez, D. C. (2023). Beyond Borders: How Cultural Differences in Trust Valuation Impact Business Partnerships. *LinkedIn*. https://www.linkedin.com/pulse/beyond-borders-how-cultural-differences-trust-impact-fernandez/

Ford, J. K., Riley, S. J., Lauricella, T. K., & Van Fossen, J. A. (2020). Factors affecting trust among natural resources stakeholders, partners, and strategic alliance members: A meta-analytic investigation. In *Frontiers in Communication*. Frontiers Media S.A. DOI: 10.3389/fcomm.2020.00009

Grossmann, C. (2024). *8 Proven Strategies to Foster Diversity and Inclusivity in the Workplace*. Beekeeper. https://www.beekeeper.io/blog/5-ways-promote-workplace-diversity/

Gurmentor (2021). *What is Language Barrier and How to Overcome It*. Gurmentor. https://gurmentor.com/what-is-language-barrier-and-how-to-overcome-it/

Harry Clark Translation. (n.d.). *7 Tips on How to Overcome Language Barriers*. Retrieved July 28, 2024, from https://harryclarktranslation.co.nz/7-tips-overcome-language-barriers

Improv Success Blog Post. (December 2023). Improv for Business: How Thinking on Your Feet Can Enhance Creativity and Collaboration. Success Improv. https://successimprov.com/improv-for-business-how-thinking-on-your-feet-can-enhance-creativity-and-collaboration/

Jangra, M. (2024). *Managing Global CSR Challenges: Navigating Cultural Differences And Ethical Dilemmas*. https://ruralhandmade.com/blog/managing-global-csr-challenges-navigating-cultural

Katul, Y. (2024). Exploring the impact of cultural diversity in global projects: A comparative analysis of virtual and face-to-face teamwork. *International Journal of Cross-Cultural Management*. https://www.semanticscholar.org/paper/Exploring-the-impact-of-cultural-diversity-in-A-of-Yousef/ce97087c89f75ec82ba52194552858380196b05a

Mušura, G. (2020). The Role of Cultural Dimensions Of Communication And Developing Cultural Awareness In International Business. *In International Scientific Conference ERAZ* - Knowledge Based Sustainable Development, 6th ERAZ Conference Proceedings (part of ERAZ conference collection) (203–206). Association of Economists and Managers of the Balkans, Belgrade, Serbia. DOI: 10.31410/ERAZ.2020.203

Newman, P. (2019). Cultural barriers and how to overcome them in your global company as a global leader. *EURAC - European Academy for Executive Education*. https://eurac.com/cultural-barriers-and-how-to-overcome-them-in-your-global-company-as-a-global-leader/

Ollerton, M. (2023). *Understanding Body Language Across Cultures & the Role of Language Services*. Workplace Languages. https://www.workplacelanguages.com/body-language-cultures/

Ontop Team Blog post. (2024). How to Navigate Conflict Resolution in Diverse Teams. https://www.getontop.com/blog/how-to-navigate-conflict-resolution-in-diverse-teams

Ozdemir, S., Carlos Fernandez de Arroyabe, J., Sena, V., & Gupta, S. (2023). Stakeholder diversity and collaborative innovation: Integrating the resource-based view with stakeholder theory. *Journal of Business Research*, 164, 113955. DOI: 10.1016/j.jbusres.2023.113955

PennState Extension. (2023). *Building Trust with Ecosystem Stakeholders* (Part 3). https://extension.psu.edu/building-trust-with-ecosystem-stakeholders-part-3

Perilli, R. (2023). *Importance of inclusion and diversity in communication in the digital workplace*. https://www.simpplr.com/blog/2021/importance-of-diversity-in-communication-in-the-digital-workplace/

Rcademy. (2023). *Effective Communication in Cross-Cultural and Diverse Environments - Rcademy*. https://rcademy.com/effective-communication-in-cross-cultural-and-diverse-environments/

Schmidt, M., Steigenberger, N., Berndtzon, M., & Uman, T. (2023). Cultural diversity in health care teams: A systematic integrative review and research agenda. *Health Care Management Review*, 48(4), 311–322. DOI: 10.1097/HMR.0000000000000379 PMID: 37615941

Seel, J. (2023). How to build a cross-functional team for custom software development.

Singletary, L., Koebele, E., Evans, W., Copp, C. J., Hockaday, S., & Rego, J. J. (2022). Evaluating stakeholder engagement in collaborative research: Co-producing knowledge for climate resilience. *Socio-Ecological Practice Research*, 4(3), 235–249. DOI: 10.1007/s42532-022-00124-8 PMID: 36036019

Tyagi, S. (2023a). *5 Key Benefits: Why Stakeholder Engagement Drives Success -*. ASKEL. https://askelsustainabilitysolutions.com/5-key-benefits-why-stakeholder-engagement-drives-success/

Tyagi, S. (2023b). *7 Strategies for Strong Stakeholder Engagement*. ASKEL. https://askelsustainabilitysolutions.com/7-strategies-for-strong-stakeholder-engagement/

Unlit Leadership. (2023). *Mastering Communication in a Diverse Workplace*: A Guide. https://unlitleadership.com/communication-in-diverse-workplace/

Wang, C., Wu, S. Y., Nie, Y. Z., Cui, G. Y., & Hou, X. Y. (2022). Open-mindedness trait affects the development of intercultural communication competence in short-term overseas study programs: A mixed-method exploration. *BMC Medical Education*, 22(1), 219. DOI: 10.1186/s12909-022-03281-2 PMID: 35354454

Zheng, X., Sun, C., & Liu, J. (2024). Exploring stakeholder engagement in urban village renovation projects through a mixed-method approach to social network analysis: A case study of Tianjin. *Humanities & Social Sciences Communications*, 11(1), 27. Advance online publication. DOI: 10.1057/s41599-023-02536-7

KEY TERMS AND DEFINITIONS

Co-Creation: A collaborative approach where organizations work directly with stakeholders to develop solutions and create value together.

Cross-Cultural Communication: The exchange of information between individuals from different cultural backgrounds, considering verbal and non-verbal aspects of communication.

Cultural Competence: The ability to understand, appreciate, and interact effectively with people from different cultural backgrounds.

Cultural Diversity: The presence of different cultural perspectives and backgrounds within stakeholder groups, including variations in communication styles, values, and practices.

Cultural Sensitivity: Awareness and respect for cultural differences, including customs, values, and communication preferences.

Inclusive Practices: Strategies and approaches ensure that all stakeholders, regardless of their background, have opportunities to participate and contribute.

Key Performance Indicators (KPIs): Metrics used to measure the effectiveness and impact of stakeholder engagement initiatives.

Power-Interest Matrix: A tool for categorizing stakeholders based on their level of influence (power) and their investment or interest in the project or organization.

Relationship-Based Trust: A form of trust building common in East Asian cultures that emphasizes personal relationships and networks over formal agreements.

Stakeholder Alignment: The process of ensuring that different stakeholders' interests, expectations, and objectives are coordinated and working toward common goals.

Stakeholder Engagement: A systematic process that identifies, analyzes, plans, and implements actions to involve and influence those affected by an organization's decisions.

Trust-Building Mechanisms: Methods and approaches used to establish confidence and reliability between organizations and stakeholders, which can vary significantly across cultures.

Value Creation: The process of generating benefits for the organization and its stakeholders through effective engagement and collaboration.

Virtual Collaboration: The use of digital tools and platforms to facilitate stakeholder engagement across geographical boundaries.

Chapter 10
Hiring-Reskilling and the Future of Work

ABSTRACT

This chapter explores the rapidly evolving work landscape in the face of technological advancement and societal changes. It examines how automation and artificial intelligence are reshaping industries, emphasizing the growing importance of uniquely human skills like creativity, empathy, and critical thinking. The text discusses the need to rethink hiring practices to prioritize soft skills, adaptability, and diversity. It stresses the imperative of continuous learning and reskilling to remain relevant in an ever-changing job market. The chapter delves into how AI can enhance human capabilities rather than replace workers and how organizations can prepare for future jobs that don't yet exist. It emphasizes the importance of strategic planning for human capital, aligning workforce development with long-term business objectives. The conclusion calls for a proactive approach to skill development, fostering a culture of adaptability and lifelong learning. Overall, the chapter paints a picture of a future workplace where human ingenuity and technological advancement coexist harmoniously.

INTRODUCTION

The intersection of technological advancement and human capital development stands at a critical juncture, fundamentally reshaping the modern workplace and demanding a revolutionary approach to skill development and career preparation. This chapter comprehensively examines how organizations and individuals must adapt to an increasingly automated world while emphasizing the enduring value of uniquely human capabilities. As artificial intelligence and automation continue to transform industries, the traditional paradigm of static career paths and finite

DOI: 10.4018/979-8-3693-5553-4.ch010

skill sets has given way to a dynamic landscape where continuous learning and adaptability are paramount.

At its core, this analysis explores several interconnected themes that define the future of work. First, it examines how the rise of automation creates new opportunities while simultaneously challenging traditional employment models. Rather than viewing this technological revolution as a threat to human employment, the chapter positions it as a catalyst for elevating human potential, allowing workers to focus on higher-order tasks that machines cannot replicate. Second, it delves into the critical role of human-centric skills, such as creativity, empathy, and critical thinking, which are gaining importance in an automated world.

The chapter pays particular attention to the imperative of reskilling as a bridge to future relevance. As the half-life of abilities diminishes, businesses must establish comprehensive frameworks for ongoing development, learning, and adaptation. This approach includes technical upskilling and the development of soft skills that enable effective collaboration, innovation, and leadership in exploding work environments. The analysis examines how hiring practices are developing to emphasize adaptability and diversity, recognizing these as key drivers of organizational resilience and innovation.

Moreover, the discussion encompasses the strategic dimension of human capital development, exploring how organizations can align their workforce planning with future needs while maintaining agility in uncertainty. The chapter gives special consideration to artificial intelligence's role as an enhancer of human capabilities, not as a replacement for human workers, highlighting the potential for productive human-machine collaboration. Through this multifaceted examination, the chapter provides valuable insights for business leaders, educators, and professionals seeking to navigate the complex landscape of future work. It offers practical frameworks for understanding and implementing effective reskilling strategies while emphasizing the human elements that will continue to drive organizational success in an increasingly automated world.

THE FUTURE OF WORK: EVOLUTION WITH TECHNOLOGY AND THE VALUE OF HUMAN SKILLS

The workplace is undergoing a seismic shift, propelled by the relentless march of technological progress. This transformation is not merely reshaping our work environments but redefining the essence of human values in the professional sphere. As machines encroach upon tasks once thought to be the exclusive domain of human intellect, our uniquely human attributes are emerging as the linchpin of future success. Consider the trajectory of workplace evolution. Technology has been the catalyst for change, from rudimentary computing to the ubiquity of cloud-based solutions (Ireland, 2022). The COVID-19 pandemic, however, served as an unexpected accelerant, catapulting us into a new era of remote work and digital collaboration.

Remote work has grown from a luxury to a necessity. Innovative project management tools and real-time communication platforms have rendered geographical boundaries obsolete (ArrowCore Group, 2023). Artificial Intelligence, once the stuff of science fiction, now permeates our daily workflows, from sifting through resumes to ensuring round-the-clock business operations, notes Ireland (2022). However, as we embrace this technological revolution, we must not lose sight of our inherent human capabilities. In the face of machine efficiency, we still rely heavily on creativity, that ineffable spark of innovation. While AI excels at pattern recognition, it falters when tasked with true originality. Human ingenuity will continue to drive progress and shape our future (Moioli, 2023).

Empathy, too, is a bastion of human supremacy in the workplace. This quintessential leadership trait, the ability to truly understand and connect with others, is the foundation of high-performing teams and thriving organizational cultures. Superiors and subordinates revere leaders who master this art of emotional attunement (Gentry, 2024). The future demands a delicate equilibrium between technological prowess and human acumen. Our educational systems must rise to this challenge, cultivating technical proficiency and nurturing the soft skills that set us apart. We must hone critical thinking, emotional intelligence, and problem-solving abilities alongside digital literacy (Moioli, 2023).

Organizations promoting the irreplaceable value of human skills will flourish in this nascent work landscape where silicon meets sentience. They will forge dynamic, innovative, and inclusive environments by fostering creativity, empathy, and adaptability. In doing so, they will not merely survive the digital age but thrive in it, charting a course toward unparalleled success and sustainability. *Figure 1* below summarizes what the future of work looks like, and in this chapter, we will explore some of the listed elements.

Figure 1. The evolution of work

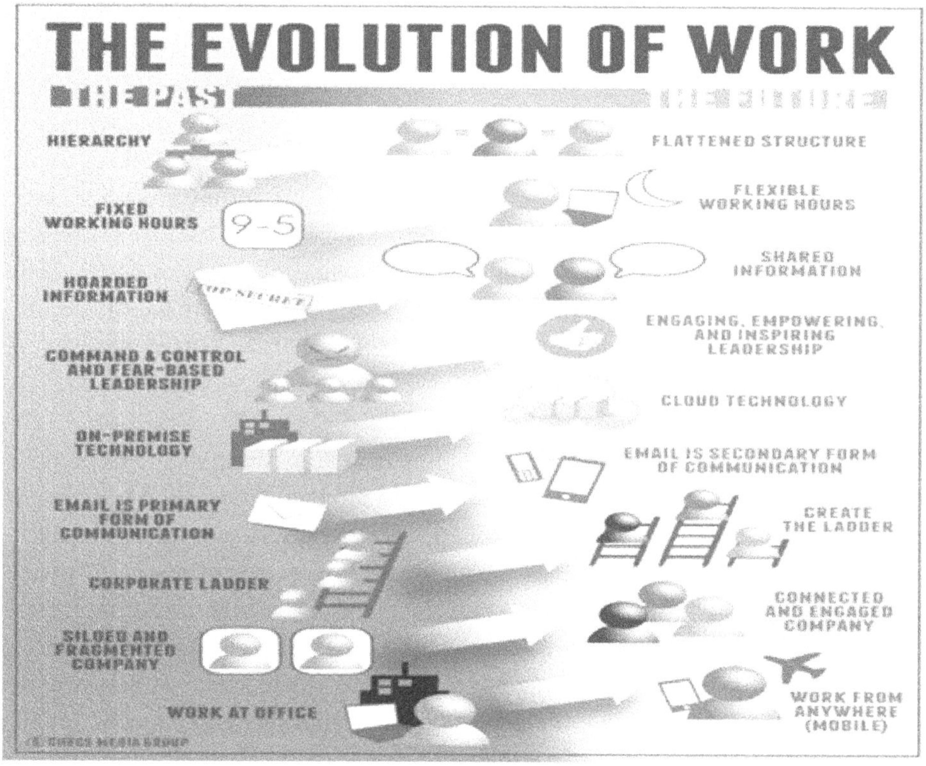

![The Evolution of Work infographic showing past vs future: Hierarchy vs Flattened Structure; Fixed Working Hours vs Flexible Working Hours; Hoarded Information vs Shared Information; Command & Control and Fear-Based Leadership vs Engaging, Empowering, and Inspiring Leadership; On-Premise Technology vs Cloud Technology; Email is Primary Form of Communication vs Email is Secondary Form of Communication; Corporate Ladder vs Create the Ladder; Siloed and Fragmented Company vs Connected and Engaged Company; Work at Office vs Work from Anywhere (Mobile).]

(Jacob Morgan - Chess Media Group)

The Changing Work Landscape with the Rise of Automation

Technological leaps, task automation, and evolving skill requirements are driving a metamorphosis of the work landscape. This seismic shift is recalibrating industries, redefining job roles, and demanding novel approaches to workforce development. However, we must not overlook the inherent adaptability of the human workforce, which can equip itself with the necessary skills to thrive in this innovative world.

Automation, a veritable juggernaut, is leaving no industry untouched. It's revolutionizing sectors by amplifying efficiency, productivity, and profitability. Take the manufacturing realm, for instance. It's undergone a metamorphosis by integrating industrial robots and intelligent manufacturing systems. These technological marvels enable ceaseless production, minimize errors, elevate quality, and safeguard workers by tackling perilous tasks (Michael, 2024; Expert Panel, 2024). However, automation's tentacles extend far beyond manufacturing, reaching into healthcare, finance, transportation, and education, where AI and automated systems optimize operations and elevate service delivery to unprecedented heights (Codeyourcareer, 2023; Manyika et al., 2017).

Work pivots from rote activities to more strategic endeavors as automation subsumes mundane tasks. This significant change manifests in myriad ways: enhancing decision-making, spawning new job opportunities, and facilitating skill transitions. AI now shoulders data processing and basic customer service inquiries, liberating human workers to engage in complex problem-solving and strategic planning (Codeyourcareer, 2023; Expert Panel, 2024). While automation may displace specific roles, it simultaneously births new ones, particularly in technology development, deployment, and maintenance. The job market now teems with positions related to AI, machine learning, and robotics. Concurrently, entirely new industries emerge, such as social media management and app development, as Codeyourcareer, Manyika, and colleagues highlighted.

The need for technological, social, and emotional skills is increasing in this modern world, while the need for physical and manual skills is decreasing. Workers must gain new competencies or hone existing ones to maintain relevance. Advanced IT and programming skills and basic digital literacy are now indispensable. Social and emotional skills, such as empathy and advanced communication, ascend in value as they complement technological advancements, as highlighted in McKinsey (Buchin et al., 2018). Navigating this automated work environment requires a multifaceted approach. Upskilling and reskilling stand at the forefront of this strategy. Workers need autonomous access to training programs that equip them with new skills and adaptability to developing job requirements. We must support lifelong learning to cultivate a resilient and adaptable workforce (Codeyourcareer, 2023; Bughin et al., 2018).

Organizations must reimagine work structures, seamlessly integrating new technologies into workflows, fostering innovation, and supporting employees through this transition. They should focus on crafting roles that leverage uniquely human strengths in areas where machines falter, such as leadership, creativity, and interpersonal communication, posit Bughin et al. (2018). Governments and policymakers are pivotal in orchestrating this transition to an automated economy. Their mandate includes investing in education and training, providing safety nets for displaced workers, and ensuring the fair distribution of automation's benefits across society, as described in an article in McKinsey & Company by (Manyika et al., 2017).

The automation revolution is reshaping industries and recalibrating the work landscape. While it presents challenges like job displacement and skill mismatches, it also unlocks opportunities for growth, innovation, and enhanced productivity. By embracing these changes and preparing for the future, workers and organizations can thrive in an increasingly automated world. The key lies in cultivating a culture of perpetual learning, adapting organizational structures, and supporting workers as they transition to more strategic and fulfilling roles.

Figure 2 below shows three interrelated dimensions: work, workforce, and workplace with technology, including robotics, new talent platforms, and workspaces for co-creation.

Figure 2. Three interrelated dimensions

Workforce

2 Who can do the work?

With new talent platforms and required skills, who can do the work? How do we leverage the continuum of talent from full-time workers, to managed services, to freelancers, gig workers, crowds, and machines?

Workforce options

Work

1 What work can be automated?

With technologies such as robotics, artificial intelligence, and cloud, how is traditional technology work automated, enhanced, and transformed?

Work transformation

Workplace

3 Where is the work done?

With workspaces for cocreation, collaboration tools, and cultures of high performance, how are workplaces and work practices reshaping where and when work is done?

Workplace readiness

Source: Deloitte analysis

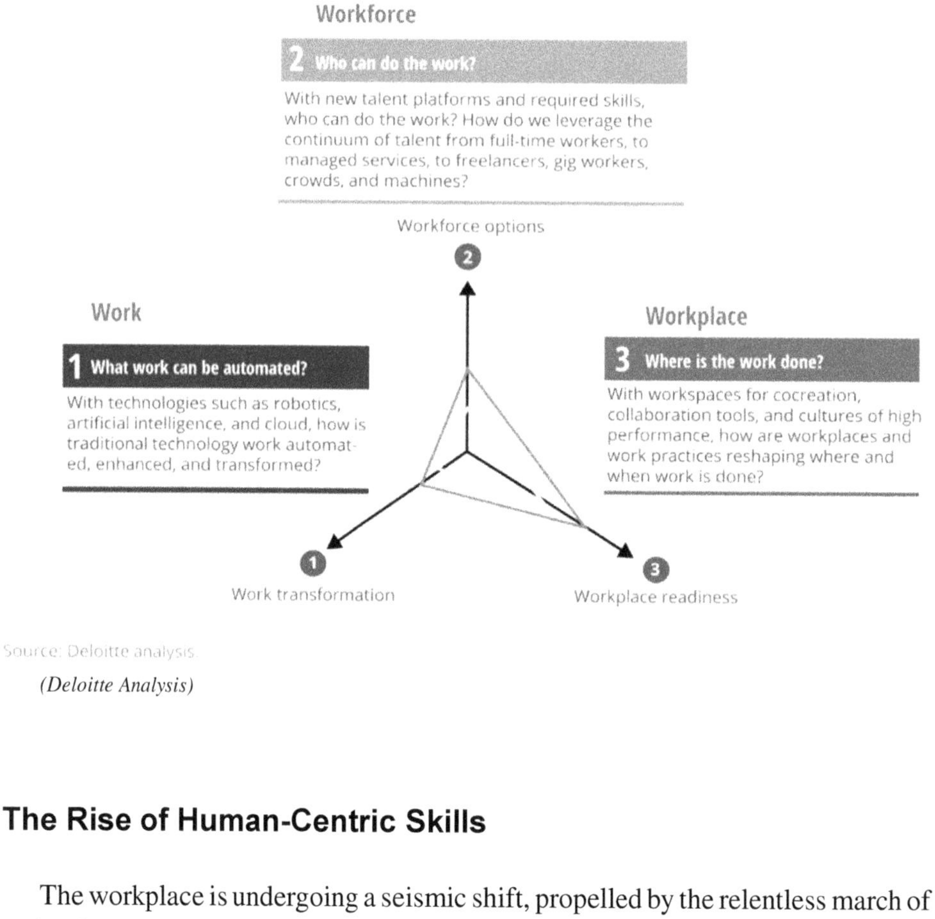

(Deloitte Analysis)

The Rise of Human-Centric Skills

The workplace is undergoing a seismic shift, propelled by the relentless march of technology and the ubiquity of automation. In this brave new world, human-centric skills are ascending to unprecedented heights of importance. These fundamental human skills, such as creativity, empathy, and critical thinking, are increasingly essential for professional success.

Creativity, the wellspring of innovation, is now a coveted commodity in the corporate realm. 70% of companies consider creative thinking an indispensable asset (Wells, 2024b). This cognitive transformation transmutes the mundane into the extraordinary, enabling employees to conjure novel solutions to intractable problems. Creativity has emerged as the ultimate differentiator in an era where machines increasingly relegate rote tasks.

Empathy, the ability to resonate with others' emotions, is the bedrock of a harmonious workplace. Empathic environments foster collaboration, mitigate stress, and elevate morale (Zaki, 2019). This emotional intelligence allows leaders and team members to forge meaningful connections, nurturing a supportive ecosystem that breeds success. Even tech titans like Tim Cook admire empathy, underscoring its pivotal role in shaping future leaders.

Critical thinking, the intellectual scalpel that dissects complex issues, remains an irreplaceable skill in today's business landscape. Despite the proliferation of big data and artificial intelligence, the human capacity for nuanced analysis is unparalleled. Data, no matter how voluminous, is merely a tool; critical thinking wields this tool to identify and address the crux of problems (Gauss, 2022; Wells, 2024c). CEOs recognize critical thinking as the cornerstone of competitive advantage in an increasingly volatile market.

As we hurtle toward an automated future, concerns about technological displacement loom large (Moioli, 2023). However, this technological revolution has paradoxically amplified the demand for soft skills, or "power skills," as they're increasingly known. These uniquely human attributes complement, rather than compete with, artificial intelligence (Wells, 2024a). In response, forward-thinking organizations are investing heavily in cultivating these human-centric skills. They're implementing robust training programs to enhance communication, foster resilience, and promote lifelong learning (Gauss, 2022; Hive Learning, 2024). This proactive approach prepares workforces to survive and thrive in unprecedented change.

The ascendancy of human-centric skills is not a fleeting trend but a fundamental shift in the professional paradigm. As we navigate the uncharted waters of the future, these unique human abilities will serve as our compass. By prioritizing their development, organizations can forge a resilient, adaptable, and innovative workforce capable of steering the ship through the stormy seas of uncertainty and into the calm waters of success. *Figure 3* below describes how human centricity can create user-friendly solutions that meet the specific needs of individuals and communities alike.

Figure 3. Human centricity

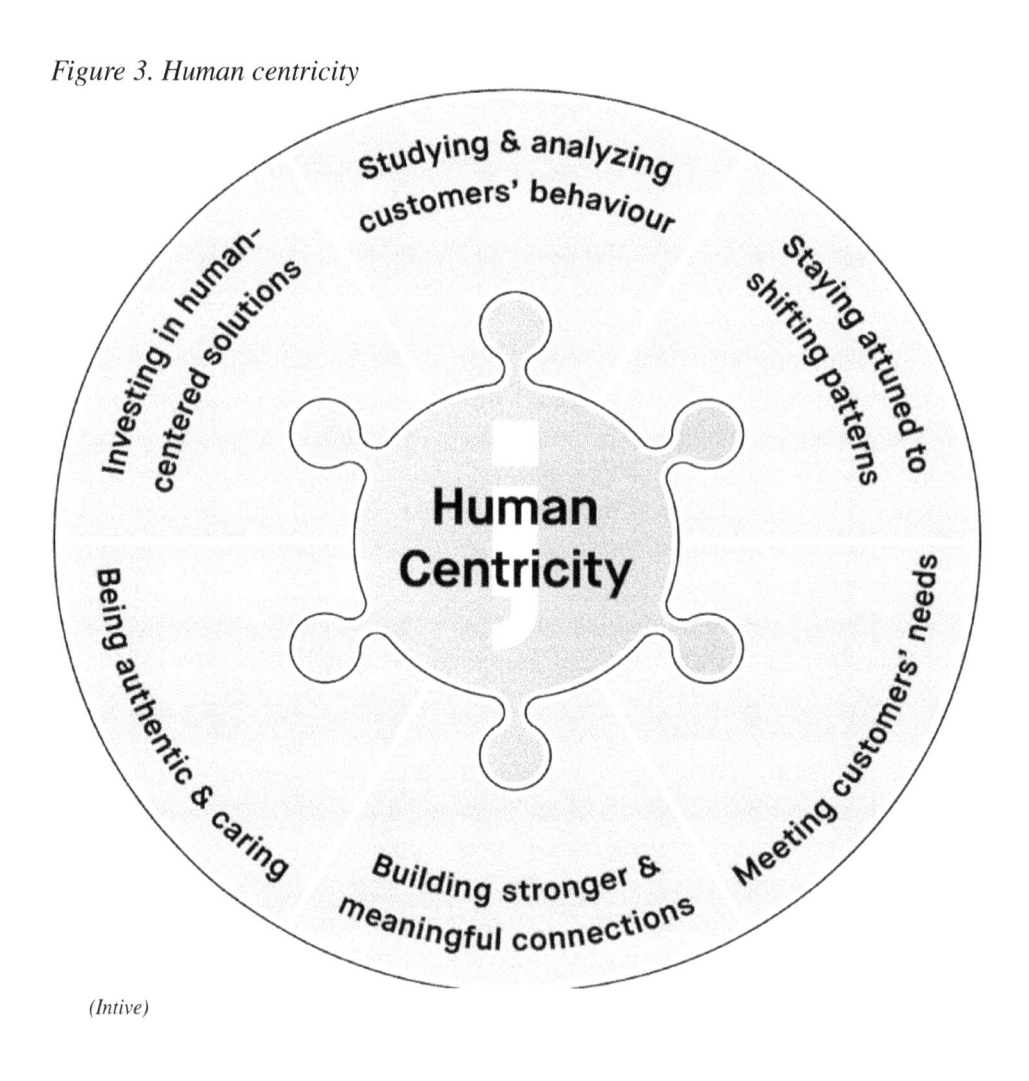

[Figure: Circular diagram labeled "Human Centricity" at center, surrounded by six segments: Studying & analyzing customers' behaviour; Staying attuned to shifting patterns; Meeting customers' needs; Building stronger & meaningful connections; Being authentic & caring; Investing in human-centered solutions.]

(Intive)

Rethinking Hiring Practices: Emphasizing Soft Skills, Adaptability, and Diversity

The evolution of hiring practices has undergone a seismic shift, with organizations now prioritizing soft skills, adaptability, and diversity. This fundamental change is not merely a momentary trend but necessary in today's cutthroat business arena. The days of meticulously crafting resumes and navigating through "seven mountains and seven seas" to submit applications are no longer relevant (LinkedIn Blog Post, February 2024). Soft skills dominate this unfamiliar landscape. These intangible attributes, often called emotional intelligence, encompass many abilities, such as effective communication, seamless teamwork, and innovative problem-solving.

They are the linchpin of a harmonious and productive work environment. One cannot overstate the significance of these skills. They are the bedrock for fostering robust interpersonal relationships, navigating labyrinthine situations, and catalyzing organizational innovation (Partners MBO Blog post, December 2023).

Adaptability, too, has emerged as a coveted trait. In an era of rapid flux, employees who can effortlessly pivot and embrace new challenges are the lifeblood of organizational resilience (St. John's University Blog Post, January 2024). This agility is crucial when engaging with Generation Z, a cohort unlike any that has preceded them. Attracting this demographic requires more than mere linguistic dexterity; it demands an alignment with their core values and a commitment to providing the flexibility and growth opportunities they crave (Kazim, 2024). Diversity and inclusion (D&I) have transcended the realm of mere quota-filling to become strategic imperatives driving business success. The benefits of D&I are manifold and profound. They expand talent pools, infuse organizations with a series of perspectives, and foster an environment of belonging that supercharges employee engagement and retention. Empirical research has proven that diverse teams outperform their homogeneous counterparts in decision-making processes (Wong, 2024; Verlinden, 2018).

The modern employer seeks a synthesis of technical prowess and soft skills. They covet individuals who adapt swiftly, think analytically, and navigate interpersonal dynamics with finesse (Bryan, 2024). Building resilient, innovative, and inclusive teams that navigate the challenges of a constantly changing business landscape requires these attributes, which are both desirable and indispensable. We must recalibrate hiring practices to prioritize soft skills, adaptability, and diversity. By embracing these elements, organizations can forge more resilient, innovative, engaged, and productive teams. This approach will enhance business performance and cultivate a workforce primed for long-term success in an increasingly complex and dynamic global economy.

Reskilling: The Imperative Bridge to Relevance

In today's rapidly developing workplace, reskilling has become a challenging necessity. The cornerstone of this process lies in the meticulous skills gap analysis. This is not merely a superficial exercise but a pivotal undertaking that demands rigorous scrutiny of current employee competencies juxtaposed against future organizational requisites. Employing a multifaceted approach, encompassing surveys, performance evaluations, and market analyses, is paramount (Thinggaard et al., 2023). According to Alireza et al. (2022), the dissonance between academic curricula and job market demands underscores the criticality of perpetual skill refinement. Diverse fields worldwide are not immune to this discrepancy; it permeates them all. For instance, a study of Ethiopian pharmacists unveiled significant lacunae in their smoking cessation knowledge, accentuating the need for suggested training initiatives (Erku et al., 2019).

Presenting reskilling programs as empowering opportunities instead of burdensome obligations is crucial for their productivity. This approach necessitates aligning programs with career trajectories, explaining benefits, and furnishing requisite support and resources. Ensuring congruence between reskilling initiatives and employees' career aspirations can catalyze participation (DeIuliis & Saylor, 2021). By communicating the personal and professional benefits, we can illuminate the value proposition of these programs and inspire our workforce to take charge of their growth (Singh, 2024). A case study on digital transformation in lean and agile organizations emphasized the criticality of upskilling employees and encouraging them to take ownership of their growth as essential to a sustainable digital culture, argues Singh. Moreover, research on the English language needs of cadet officers highlighted the importance of aligning training programs with job performance and personal life benefits to enhance their effectiveness (Rahman et al., 2023).

Fostering a growth mindset is not counterproductive; it is indispensable. This significant change, the conviction that abilities are malleable through dedication and diligence, is the bedrock of successful reskilling endeavors. It is about galvanizing your workforce to perceive challenges as crucibles for growth. As leaders, we can cultivate this mindset by supporting continuous learning, fashioning a supportive milieu, and providing constructive feedback (Lyons & Bandura, 2023; DeIuliis & Saylor, 2021). This responsibility empowers us to shape a culture of growth and adaptability within our organizations.

Equally crucial is creating a culture that venerates learning, innovation, and calculated risk-taking (Singh, 2024; Dufresne & Clair, 2023). Such an ethos encourages employees to embrace new challenges and nurtures creativity and resilience. Studies show that helping employees develop a growth mindset improves their work and job satisfaction. The pressing need for reskilling demands a strategic approach, including addressing skills gaps, nurturing a growth mindset, and framing reskilling programs as empowering opportunities. Organizations can ensure their workforce remains relevant and competitive in an ever-mutating market landscape. This strategic approach prepares us for the future and opens new opportunities and possibilities, instilling a sense of optimism and hope in our workforce. *Figure 4* below describes eight best practices for conducting a skill gap analysis.

Figure 4. 8 Best practices for conducting a skill gap analysis

8 Best practices for Conducting a Skill Gap Analysis
www.zavvy.io | Employee Enablement Platform

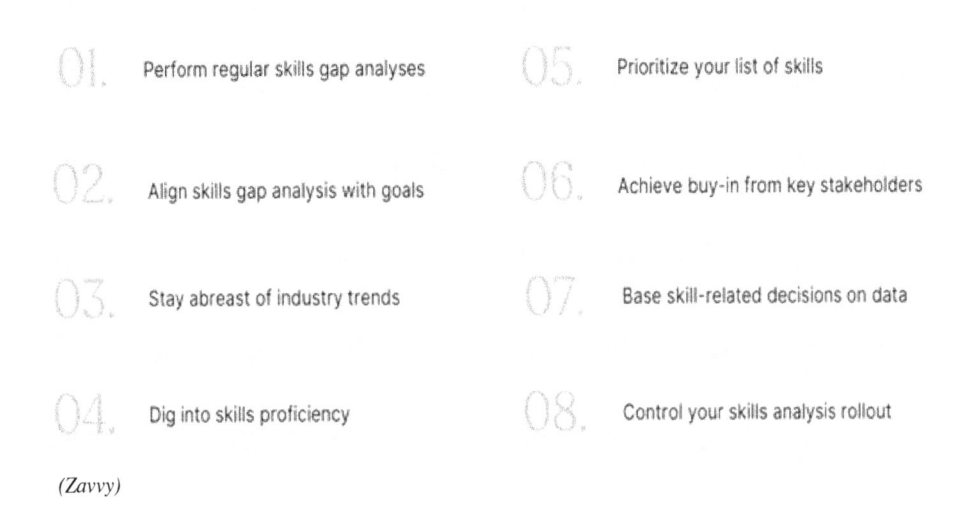

01. Perform regular skills gap analyses
02. Align skills gap analysis with goals
03. Stay abreast of industry trends
04. Dig into skills proficiency
05. Prioritize your list of skills
06. Achieve buy-in from key stakeholders
07. Base skill-related decisions on data
08. Control your skills analysis rollout

(Zavvy)

Human Skills in the Spotlight

Human skills are taking center stage in today's rapidly developing technological landscape. Marr (2023) posits that the most coveted abilities fall into two distinct categories: those that unlock the potential of groundbreaking technology and maximize uniquely human qualities. These technical and soft skills are indispensable for organizations thriving in an increasingly digital world. As automation advances, specific human attributes remain irreplaceable and in high demand. Critical thinking, the cornerstone of problem-solving and decision-making, empowers employees to navigate complex situations and comprehend the far-reaching consequences of their actions, posits Marr. Creativity, the wellspring of innovation, enables businesses to craft distinctive products and services that captivate the market (Taylor, 2023).

Emotional intelligence (EQ) and empathy, the quintessential human traits, foster positive relationships and enhance team dynamics. These attributes are paramount for employee engagement, retention, and overall workplace satisfaction (Brower, 2021). Judgment and complex decision-making, the hallmarks of effective leadership, allow managers to navigate the labyrinthine business landscape with finesse (Marr,

2022). Interpersonal communication, the linchpin of collaboration, ensures teams operate harmoniously and achieve peak productivity, posits Marr.

To flourish in this new paradigm, organizations must cultivate these non-automatable skills. Fostering creativity requires the establishment of psychological safety, where employees can express ideas without trepidation (Taylor, 2023). Encouraging cross-functional collaboration stimulates collective creativity and generates fresh insights. Providing resources and tools equips employees to explore novel concepts and experiment with diverse approaches. Recognizing and rewarding innovative thinking reinforces a culture that values creativity.

Organizations must also spearhead continuous learning, motivating employees to gain new knowledge and skills (Marr, 2022). Conducting workshops and implementing mentorship programs can enhance problem-solving and decision-making abilities. Cultivating empathy through leadership training and establishing open communication channels creates a supportive work environment that considers employees' holistic needs (Brower, 2021).

As technology continues its relentless march forward, the value of distinctly human skills becomes increasingly pronounced. Organizations prioritizing and nurturing creativity, critical thinking, and empathy are better off innovating, adapting, and thriving in an increasingly automated world. Businesses can unlock the full potential of their workforce and achieve sustainable success in this new world by fostering a culture that values and supports these skills. *Figure 5* below shows the top five soft skills sought by employers today.

Figure 5. Top 5 in-demand soft skills in 2024

(Balkan Hire)

Embracing Lifelong Learning from Static Knowledge to Perpetual Growth

The antiquated notion of "learn once, use forever" has become obsolete in unprecedented technological advancement and societal metamorphosis. The zeitgeist (the spirit of the time) demands a more dynamic approach to knowledge acquisition. Once a mere buzzword, lifelong learning has become an indispensable facet of personal and professional development. This shift necessitates a multifaceted approach. We must first nurture an insatiable curiosity. Öz (2022) explains a gender disparity in lifelong learning proclivities, with females exhibiting a greater propensity for continuous education. This finding underscores the imperative to foster curiosity across all demographics, ensuring an inclusive and productive learning ecosystem.

The digital revolution has ushered in a new epoch of educational accessibility. Online platforms have democratized learning, offering various educational opportunities tailored to diverse learning modalities. Tamášová (2015) corroborates the efficacy of e-learning environments, citing high levels of student satisfaction and perceived utility. Integrating pedagogical frameworks, such as the 7E Learning Cycle (Elicit, Engage, Explore, Extend, Elaborate, Explain, Evaluate), further augments the potency of digital education. A holistic approach to continuous learning is paramount. The amalgamation of formal, non-formal, and informal education creates a comprehensive learning tapestry. (Pshembayeva & Pfeifer, 2021) elucidate the symbiosis of these educational modalities for preparing individuals for an ever-evolving landscape.

The exigency of lifelong learning has permeated policy discourses, emerging as a lodestar in educational and employment paradigms (Lavrijsen & Nicaise, 2017). Recognizing the inadequacy of the knowledge and skills gained in formal education for lifelong development underpins this significant change (London, 2011). In the professional sphere, continuous learning has transmuted from a desirable trait to an absolute necessity. Ganie and Jagannathan (2023) emphasize the importance of lifelong learning for educators, emphasizing their need to stay up-to-date with pedagogical innovations and methodologies.

Transitioning from a static educational model to one of perpetual growth is not merely helpful but imperative. By fostering a culture of intellectual voraciousness, harnessing the power of digital platforms, creating diverse learning opportunities, and advocating for continuous education as a professional imperative, we can cultivate an environment where lifelong learning flourishes. This metamorphosis will catalyze personal growth and engender a more adaptable, innovative, and resilient society. *Figure 6*. The word cloud below analyzes researchers' most common words when discussing lifelong learning.

Figure 6. Word cloud

informal frameworks finding ever ecosystem ensuring gender desirable amalgamation demands harnessing facet advantageous **platforms** advancement exigency firstly buzzword across **environment** acquired curiosity cycle **perpetual** females consigned 2023 **must** **imperative** **pedagogical** dynamic integrating augments **elucidate** **continuous** **modalities** culture forever advocating **efficacious** become inclusive insatiable 2021 **creates** **education** **development** criticality ganie citing **knowledge** **learning growth** **shift** catalyze discourses **static** **diverse** **lifelong** **digital** **mere** acquisition holistic engender absolute cultivate exhibiting high courant **foster** **formal** 2017 **innovations** individuals era **paradigm** **professional** **personal** democratized demographics 2022 emerging adaptable **opportunities** accessibility disparity insufficient corroborates **underscore** antiquated epoch jagannathan employment comprehensive embracing intellectual flourishes evolving greater indispensable

(Created with NVivo by Dr. Diene)

The Role of AI in Enhancing Human Capabilities

In today's rapidly developing technological landscape, AI has emerged as a formidable ally in augmenting human capabilities across diverse industries. Far from supplanting human workers, AI serves as a potent catalyst, empowering individuals to transcend mundane tasks and focus on higher-order cognitive functions. This symbiosis between human intellect and machine efficiency revolutionizes decision-making processes, automates quotidian tasks, and unleashes unprecedented creativity and strategic thinking. AI's data analysis and pattern recognition prowess make it an indispensable asset in decision-making. Innovative tools such as Findly AI enhance the skills of analysts, sales agents, and consultants by providing data-driven insights that guide wise decisions (Parker, 2024). The celerity and precision with which AI processes vast troves of data mitigate the risk of human error and bias, fostering a more robust decision-making ecosystem.

AI development is on an exponential trajectory, with its applications permeating an ever-expanding array of sectors (Mauri & Plesset, 2022). We predict that future advancements in AI will revolutionize healthcare, finance, and transportation. The evolution of machine learning algorithms promises to usher in an era of hyper-accurate predictions and suggested experiences. The ethical implications and regulatory frameworks surrounding AI technology will undergo significant recalibration to address the multifaceted challenges posed by this burgeoning field.

One of AI's most salient benefits lies in its ability to emancipate professionals from monotonous tasks. This liberation enables them to engage in more cognitively demanding and value-generative activities. The application of AI in domains such as natural language processing (NLP), computer vision, and robotics exemplifies this paradigm shift. Tools like Grammarly harness the power of NLP to automate grammatical and stylistic proofreading, allowing writers to channel their energies into content creation (Biswal, 2020). In manufacturing, AI-driven robots handle repetitive tasks, such as assembly and quality control, enhancing productivity and safety standards. Integrating AI in autonomous vehicles facilitates visual information processing for safe navigation, minimizing the need for human intervention, posits Biswal.

The synergy between human intuition and AI capabilities often yields results surpassing either entity's performance in isolation. Chess Grandmaster Garry Kasparov's experiments corroborate this phenomenon, demonstrating that a "weak human + machine + better process" can surpass a powerful computer and a strong human with an inferior process (Harvard Business Review, 2021). This symbiotic relationship underscores the importance of seamlessly integrating AI into existing workflows to augment human performance.

As AI continues to permeate various sectors, there is a growing imperative to prioritize responsible AI development, which entails ensuring transparency, fairness, and accountability in AI systems. The AI Index Report underscores the criticality of responsible AI practices, emphasizing the need for developers to adhere to stringent privacy, data governance, and security benchmarks to mitigate risks and foster trust in AI technologies (Stanford University, 2024).

AI's role in amplifying human capabilities is multifaceted and transformative. By serving as a catalyst for enhanced decision-making, automating routine tasks, and augmenting human intelligence, AI empowers individuals and organizations to focus on high-value activities that drive innovation and growth. The key to harnessing AI's potential lies in viewing it as a collaborative partner that complements human strengths rather than as a replacement for human workers. By maximizing productivity and ensuring ethical and responsible deployment, this approach paves the way for a future where artificial intelligence boundlessly amplifies human potential. *Figure 7* below discusses how individuals and organizations use AI in decision-making.

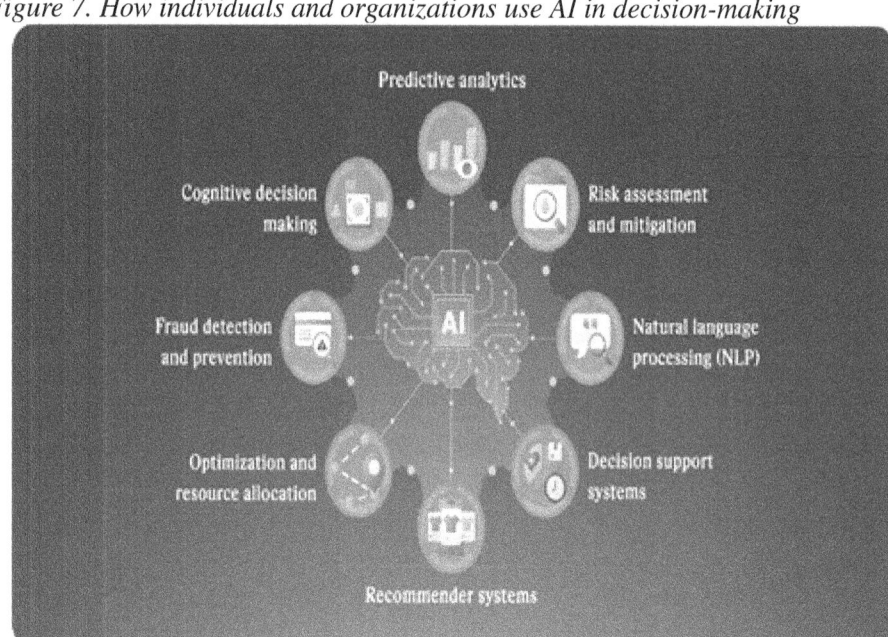

Figure 7. How individuals and organizations use AI in decision-making

(Upwork)

Preparing for Jobs That Do Not Exist Yet

In today's rapidly metamorphosing job landscape, preparing for nonexistent vocations is a herculean task that demands an avant-garde approach to skill cultivation, trend cognizance, and personal malleability. To navigate this labyrinthine challenge, one must embrace many strategies, such as honing transferable aptitudes, maintaining vigilance on emergent trends, and fostering adaptability and resilience.

Transferable skills serve as the cornerstone of this preparatory edifice. These versatile competencies transcend industry boundaries, rendering them invaluable across various roles. Problem-solving prowess, analytical acumen, and critical thinking faculties are the superior cognitive skills essential for success in any professional realm. Leadership, encompassing team stewardship and project propulsion, emerges as a crucial attribute, and interpersonal finesse, facilitating effortless communication and collaboration, becomes paramount as organizational structures evolve toward a more egalitarian paradigm (Pelta, 2020). Vigilance toward technological and societal shifts is imperative for forecasting future job markets. Automation and artificial intelligence loom on the horizon, reshaping industries and redefining skill requirements. The ascendancy of remote work necessitates proficiency in digital tools and virtual collaboration. Sustainability, an increasingly pivotal concern for businesses, heralds a burgeoning demand for environmental management and green technology expertise (Duggal, 2020).

Adaptability and resilience emerge as the twin pillars supporting success in an uncertain job market. Cultivating these traits demands a commitment to continuous learning, an insatiable curiosity, a penchant for experimentation, and the nurturing of a robust professional network. Embracing lifelong learning through formal education or autodidactic pursuits ensures relevance in an ever-shifting landscape: a curious mindset and a willingness to experiment foster innovation and adaptability. Networking across diverse professional spheres yields invaluable insights into emerging trends and opportunities. Mastery of stress management techniques and cultivating a positive outlook bolster resilience (Edwards, 2024).

Practical steps toward preparation involve a meticulous inventory of core skills and leveraging tools like SkillScan to map out strengths. Developing effective learning strategies facilitates rapid skill acquisition. Embracing change as an opportunity rather than a threat cultivates a growth-oriented mindset. Regular skill updates through workshops, certifications, and courses maintain professional relevance. An ecosystem that forges connections across various industries broadens perspectives and insights (Savard, 2024). Success in this ever-evolving professional ecosystem hinges on developing versatile skills, unwavering trend awareness, and cultivating adaptability and resilience. By embracing these strategies, one can position oneself at the vanguard of an uncertain yet exhilarating job market. *Figure 8*. The World Economic Forum lists the top 10 job skills of tomorrow.

Figure 8. Top 10 skills of 2025

Top 10 skills of 2025

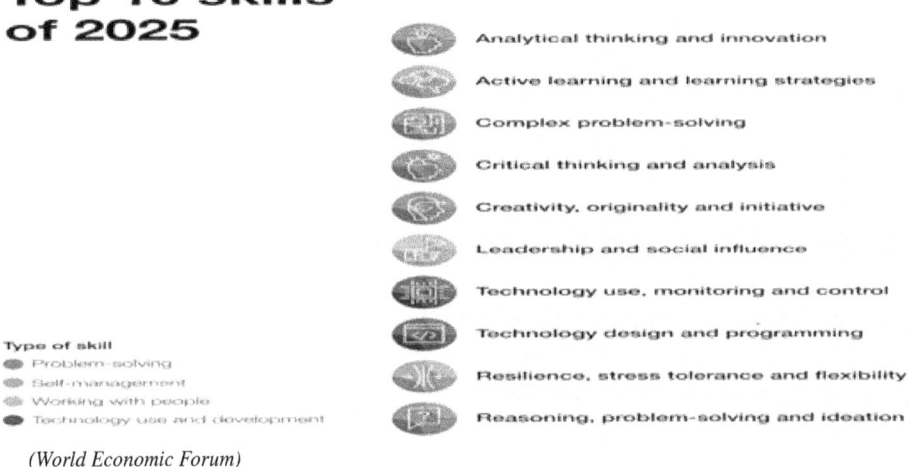

- Analytical thinking and innovation
- Active learning and learning strategies
- Complex problem-solving
- Critical thinking and analysis
- Creativity, originality and initiative
- Leadership and social influence
- Technology use, monitoring and control
- Technology design and programming
- Resilience, stress tolerance and flexibility
- Reasoning, problem-solving and ideation

Type of skill
- Problem-solving
- Self-management
- Working with people
- Technology use and development

(World Economic Forum)

Strategic Planning for Human Capital

In today's rapidly evolving business landscape, the strategic alignment of human capital with overarching corporate objectives is paramount. This symbiosis between business strategies and human resource development is the requirement for organizational success, particularly in talent acquisition, skill enhancement, and future-proofing of the workforce. To achieve this alignment, HR must first immerse itself in the intricacies of the business strategy. This profound comprehension enables the tailoring of HR initiatives to buttress long-term goals (Aldridge, 2023). HR must seamlessly integrate into the strategic planning process, no longer operating in isolation. This integration manifests in myriad ways, from crafting recruitment strategies that align with business objectives to developing training programs that cultivate skills essential for future success.

In this data-driven era, leveraging workforce analytics is non-negotiable. By harnessing the power of data, HR can glean invaluable insights into workforce trends, skill gaps, and employee performance, facilitating informed decision-making that aligns with strategic imperatives (Aldridge, 2023). Moreover, fostering a culture of perpetual learning is crucial; this ethos of continuous development ensures that employees remain agile and adaptable in the face of technological advancements and shifting business needs (HRD Connect, 2024). Scenario planning emerges as a potent tool in navigating the labyrinthine future of work. This strategic approach involves crafting detailed narratives about potential futures, enabling organizations to prepare for a spectrum of possibilities. The process encompasses identifying critical factors shaping future work environments, from technological disruptions to economic upheavals and regulatory metamorphoses (Veldsman, 2022).

HR's pivotal role in this futuristic endeavor encompasses skills-based workforce planning, implementing interventions that support strategic responses to diverse scenarios, and catalyzing organizational change. HR becomes the architect of a future-ready organization by helping leaders grasp their role in nurturing adaptability and continuous learning (Veldsman, 2022; Daley, 2020). Reskilling has become essential for ensuring organizational resilience in constant technological disruption. Forward-thinking companies are creating programs to cultivate skills germane to future needs, exhorting employees to update their competencies ceaselessly. The judicious use of AI-powered tools to match employees with reskilling opportunities and monitor skill development represents the vanguard of this approach (HRD Connect, 2024).

Organizations can navigate the tumultuous waters of future work with aplomb by synergizing business strategies with human resource development and employing perceptive scenario planning. Organizations can create teams that analyze and adapt to changing environments by combining business strategies with human resource development. Thinking ahead about what might happen can help organizations prepare for problems and opportunities. This holistic approach, marrying strategic foresight with human capital development, ensures organizations remain competitive and trailblazers in an ever-evolving business ecosystem.

SUMMARY

The transformation of work in the digital age presents unprecedented challenges and opportunities for organizations and individuals alike. This chapter has shown that success in this developing landscape requires a fundamental shift in how we approach human capital development, skill acquisition, and technology integration in the workplace. The rise of automation and artificial intelligence, rather than diminishing human value, has elevated the importance of human capabilities such as creativity, empathy, and critical thinking. The analysis reveals that the future of work is not characterized by competition between humans and machines but by their synergistic interplay.

Organizations that thrive will leverage technology to augment human capabilities while investing in developing their workforce's unique human skills. The imperative for reskilling emerges as a central theme, highlighting the need for continuous learning and adaptation in response to growing technological and market demands. Examining hiring practices shows a significant shift toward emphasizing soft skills, adaptability, and diversity as key drivers of organizational success. This evolution reflects a deeper understanding that technical competencies alone do not navigate the complexities of modern work environments.

The research underscores that organizations must foster a perpetual learning and growth culture, moving beyond traditional static knowledge acquisition models to embrace lifelong learning as a core organizational value. Strategic human capital planning emerges as a critical factor in preparing for future workforce needs, including jobs that do not yet exist. This requires organizations to develop robust frameworks for continuous skill development while maintaining the agility to adapt to emerging trends and technologies. The role of artificial intelligence in enhancing human capabilities stands out as particularly significant, offering opportunities to automate routine tasks while enabling humans to focus on higher-order thinking and creative problem-solving.

Organizations' success will increasingly depend on their ability to create environments that nurture human potential while effectively integrating technological advances. This includes developing comprehensive reskilling programs, fostering inclusive work cultures, and balancing technical proficiency and human-centric skills. The future workplace will demand individuals who are not only technically competent but also emotionally intelligent, adaptable, and committed to continuous learning.

In conclusion, the future of work represents a significant change that requires a holistic approach to human capital development. Organizations that navigate this transformation will recognize the enduring value of human capabilities while embracing technological advancement as a means of enhancement rather than replacement. The path forward lies in creating synergistic relationships between human and machine capabilities, underpinned by a commitment to continuous learning and adaptation. This approach will drive organizational success and create more fulfilling and sustainable work environments in an automated world.

As organizations adapt to technological transformation through human capital development, they must simultaneously confront the ethical dimensions of leadership in this developing landscape. While integrating human and machine capabilities offers unprecedented opportunities for workplace enhancement, it also introduces complex moral considerations that demand careful navigation. The intersection of technological advancement and ethical leadership presents a critical juncture where organizations must balance innovation with responsibility, examining ethical frameworks and accountability mechanisms relevant to contemporary leadership strategies.

REFERENCES

Aldridge, E. (2023). Align Human Resources (HR) with Business Strategy. *Educate 360 Professional Training Partners*. https://educate360.com/blog/align-human-resources-hr-with-business-strategy/

Alireza, A., Kirsty, K., Marian-Andrei, R., & Katarzyna, M. (Eds.). (2022). *Skills Taught vs Skills Sought: Using Skills Analytics to Identify the Gaps between Curriculum and Job Markets. Zenodo*.

ArrowCore Group. (2023). *Evolution of Work Dynamics: Technology's Reshaping of Traditional Workplace Norms* - ArrowCore Group. https://arrowcore.com/blogs/evolution-of-work-dynamics-technologys-reshaping-of-traditional-workplace-norms/

Biswal, A. (2020). 24 Cutting-Edge [*Simplilearn*. https://www.simplilearn.com/tutorials/artificial-intelligence-tutorial/artificial-intelligence-applications]. *Artificial Intelligence and Applications (Commerce, Calif.)*, 2024, •••.

Brower, T. (2021). Empathy Is The Most Important Leadership Skill According To Research. *Forbes*. https://www.forbes.com/sites/tracybrower/2021/09/19/empathy-is-the-most-important-leadership-skill-according-to-research/

Bryan, R. (2024). 7 Qualities Hiring Managers Seek In 2024 Candidates Looking For High-Paying Jobs. *Forbes*. https://www.forbes.com/sites/bryanrobinson/2024/03/21/7-qualities-hiring-managers-seek-in-2024-candidates-looking-for-high-paying-jobs/

Bughin, J., Hazan, E., Lund, S., Dahlstrom, P., Wiesinger, A., & Subramaniam, A. (2018). *Automation and the workforce of the future*. https://www.mckinsey.com/featured-insights/future-of-work/skill-shift-automation-and-the-future-of-the-workforce

Codeyourcareer. (2023). The Future of Work: How Automation, AI, and Remote Work Are Changing Employment Landscape. *LinkedIn*. https://www.linkedin.com/pulse/future-work-how-automation-ai-remote-changing-landscape/

Connect, H. R. D. (2024). *Reskilling: the imperative strategy for navigating the future of work amidst technological disruption* - HRD. https://www.hrdconnect.com/2024/03/22/reskilling-the-imperative-strategy-for-navigating-the-future-of-work-amidst-technological-disruption/

Daley, L. P. (2020). *Enhancing Inclusive Employee Experiences: Scenario Planning for the Future of Work*. Catalyst. https://www.catalyst.org/research/scenario-planning-future-of-work-covid/

DeIuliis, E. D., & Saylor, E. (2021). Bridging the Gap: Three Strategies to Optimize Professional Relationships with Generation Y and Z. *The Open Journal of Occupational Therapy*, 9(1), 1–13. DOI: 10.15453/2168-6408.1748

Dufresne, R. L., & Clair, J. A. (2023). Courage to Strive: Hypocrisy Monitoring, Integrity Striving, and Ethical Leadership. In By, R. T., Burnes, B., & Hughes, M. (Eds.), *Organizational Change, Leadership and Ethics* (pp. 143–158). Routledge., DOI: 10.4324/9781003036395-11

Duggal, N. (2020). Future Of Work: What Job Roles Will Look Like In 10 Years. *Simplilearn*. https://www.simplilearn.com/future-of-work-article

Edwards, J. (2024). *Resilience and Adaptability: How You Lead Matters*. https://www.nicheacademy.com/blog/resilience-and-adaptability-how-you-lead-matters

Erku, D. A., Hailemeskel, B., Netere, A. K., & Belachew, S. A. (2019). Pharmacist-led smoking cessation services in Ethiopia: Knowledge and skills gap analysis. *Tobacco Induced Diseases*, 17(January), 1. DOI: 10.18332/tid/99573 PMID: 31582913

Expert Panel. (2024). Ways Automation Can (And Will) Impact The Manufacturing Industry. *Forbes*. https://www.forbes.com/sites/forbestechcouncil/2024/03/28/ways-automation-can-and-will-impact-the-manufacturing-industry/

Ganie, I., & Jagannathan, S. (2023). Lifelong Learning Control of Nonlinear Systems with Constraints Using Multilayer Neural Networks with Application to Mobile Robot Tracking. *In 2023 IEEE Conference on Control Technology and Applications (CCTA)*. 727–732. IEEE. DOI: 10.1109/CCTA54093.2023.10252103

Gauss, M. (2022). *5 Human-Centric Skills to "Flex" for Ever-Changing*. WDHB. https://wdhb.com/blog/5-human-centric-skills-to-flex-for-ever-changing-workplaces/

Gentry, B. (2024). The Importance of Empathy in the Workplace. *Center for Creative Leadership*. https://www.ccl.org/articles/leading-effectively-articles/empathy-in-the-workplace-a-tool-for-effective-leadership/

Harvard Business Review. (2021). *AI Should Augment Human Intelligence, Not Replace It*. https://hbr.org/2021/03/ai-should-augment-human-intelligence-not-replace-it

Hive Learning. (2024). *Tackling the Global Skills Gap with Human-Centric Learning*. https://hivelearning.com/resource/resource/tackling-the-global-skills-gap-with-human-centric-learning/

Ireland, J. (2022). *Technology in the workplace: how it's evolving, and how to stay ahead of the curve*. Reed.com. https://www.reed.com/articles/technology-in-the-workplace-advantages-evolution

Lavrijsen, J., & Nicaise, I. (2017). Systemic obstacles to lifelong learning: The influence of the educational system design on learning attitudes. *Studies in Continuing Education*, 39(2), 176–196. DOI: 10.1080/0158037X.2016.1275540

LinkedIn Blog Post. (February 2024). *Recruiting in 2024: Modern Approaches and Techniques*. LinkedIn. https://www.linkedin.com/pulse/recruiting-2024-modern-approaches-techniques-hcmatrix-wb1wf/

London, M. (2011). *The Oxford handbook of lifelong learning*. Oxford University Press. DOI: 10.1093/oxfordhb/9780195390483.001.0001

Lyons, P., & Bandura, R. P. (2023). Stimulating employee work engagement and the growth mindset. *Development and Learning in Organizations: An International Journal*. https://www.semanticscholar.org/paper/Stimulating-employee-work-engagement-and-the-growth-Lyons-Bandura/2b76a2a4d9e0031d7808c565984baea1bd2ed5ce

Manyika, J., Lund, S., Chui, M., Bughin, J., Woetzel, L., Batra, P., Ko, R., & Sanghvi, S. (2017). *What will the future of work mean for jobs, skills, and wages? Jobs lost, jobs gained | McKinsey*. McKinsey & Company. https://www.mckinsey.com/featured-insights/future-of-work/jobs-lost-jobs-gained-what-the-future-of-work-will-mean-for-jobs-skills-and-wages

Marr, B. (2022). Top 16 Essential Soft Skills For The Future Of Work. *Forbes*. https://www.forbes.com/sites/bernardmarr/2022/09/12/top-16-essential-soft-skills-for-the-future-of-work/

Mauri, J., & Plesset, A. (2024). *Biggest AI Developments of 2024 So Far and What's Ahead*. https://ipwatchdog.com/2024/06/19/biggest-ai-developments-2024-far-whats-ahead/id=177950/# Michael (2024). *Robots at Work: How Automation is Transforming Industries*. https://hackernoon.com/robots-at-work-how-automation-is-transforming-industries

Moioli, F. (2023). The Unique Value Of Our Human Skills In An AI-Powered Future. *Forbes*. https://www.forbes.com/sites/forbestechcouncil/2023/07/03/the-unique-value-of-our-human-skills-in-an-ai-powered-future/

Öz, E. (2022a). The Impact of Gender Differences on Lifelong Learning Tendencies in Turkey: A Meta-analysis. *SAGE Open*, 12(2), 215824402210995. DOI: 10.1177/21582440221099528

Parker, H. (2024). 10 AI Tools for Decision-Making to Tackle Problems Efficiently. *ClickUp.* https://clickup.com/blog/ai-tools-for-decision-making/

Partners MBO Blog post. (December 2023). *Soft Skills in the Workplace: Top Skills and How to Improve Them.* https://www.mbopartners.com/blog/how-manage-small-business/why-are-soft-skills-important/

Pelta, R. (2020). *15 Transferable Skills That Companies Want: Examples and Definitions.* https://www.flexjobs.com/blog/post/transferable-skills/

Pshembayeva, E. S., & Pfeifer, N. E. (2021). Lifelong Learning As A Priority Area And A Condition For Successful Personal Career Development. *Bulletin of Toraighyrov University.Pedagogics Series*, (4), 466–472. DOI: 10.48081/HKOS1842

Rahman, N. K. A., Yunus, M., Nasri, N. M., & Abd, R. E. (2023). Proficiency Preparedness in Defence Workforce: A Survey of Cadet Officers' English Language Needs. *International Journal of Learning. Teaching and Educational Research*, 22(11), 96–115. DOI: 10.26803/ijlter.22.11.6

Savard, R. (2024). *Preparing for jobs that don't exist yet.* https://www.andover.edu/news/2024/how-to-prepare-for-jobs-that-dont-exist-yetSingh, M. (2024). Digital culture for lean & agile organization. Brazilian Journal of Development.

Singh, M. (2024). Digital culture for lean & agile organization. Brazilian Journal of Development.

St. John's University Blog Post. (January 2024). *Future-Proof Your Career: The Top 10 Skills Employers are Looking for in 2024.* https://www.stjohns.edu/news-media/johnnies-blog/top-skills-employers-are-looking-for

Standford University. (2024). *Artificial Intelligence Index Report.* Standford University. https://aiindex.stanford.edu/report/

Tamášová, V. (2015). Professional and Career Development of Vocational Subject Teachers as a Trend in the Lifelong Learning of Teachers. *Acta Technologica Dubnicae*, 5(1), 1–20. DOI: 10.1515/atd-2015-0029

Taylor, B. (2023). *Nurturing Creativity: Unleashing Innovation and Problem-Solving Skills in the Workplace | LinkedIn.* https://www.linkedin.com/pulse/nurturing-creativity-unleashing-innovation-skills-workplace-taylor/

Thinggaard, E., Zetner, D. B., Fabrin, A., Christensen, J. B., & Konge, L. (2023). A Study of Surgical Residents' Self-Assessment of Open Surgery Skills Using Gap Analysis. *Simulation in healthcare. Simulation in Healthcare*, 18(5), 305–311. DOI: 10.1097/SIH.0000000000000694 PMID: 36730862

Veldsman, D. (2022). *Scenario Planning: What HR Needs to Know. AIHR | Academy to Innovate HR*. https://www.aihr.com/blog/scenario-planning/

Verlinden, N. (2018). *5 Reasons Why Diversity Hiring Matters (And How to Go about it). AIHR | Academy to Innovate HR*. https://www.aihr.com/blog/diversity-hiring-reasons-hiring-for-diversity-matters/

Wells, R. (2024a). 10+ High-Income Soft Skills You Should Learn In 2024. *Forbes*. https://www.forbes.com/sites/rachelwells/2024/06/28/10-high-income-soft-skills-you-should-learn-in-2024/

Wells, R. (2024b). 70% Of Employers Say Creative Thinking Is the Most In-Demand Skill In 2024. Forbes. https://www.forbes.com/sites/rachelwells/2024/01/28/70-of-employers-say-creative-thinking-is-most-in-demand-skill-in-2024/

Wells, R. (2024c, April 15). 3 Critical Thinking Skills You Need In 2024. Forbes. https://www.forbes.com/sites/rachelwells/2024/04/15/3-critical-thinking-skills-you-need-in-2024/

Wong, K. (2024). Diversity and inclusion in the workplace: Benefits and challenges. *Achievers*. https://www.achievers.com/blog/diversity-and-inclusion/

Zaki, J. (2019). *Making Empathy Central to Your Company Culture*. Harvard Business Review. https://hbr.org/2019/05/making-empathy-central-to-your-company-culture

KEY TERMS AND DEFINITIONS

Artificial Intelligence (AI): Technology that enhances human capabilities rather than replacing them, used for data analysis, pattern recognition, and automation of routine tasks while enabling humans to focus on higher-order thinking.

Critical Thinking: The ability to analyze complex situations, evaluate information objectively, and make reasoned decisions - a skill that remains uniquely human despite technological advancement.

Emotional Intelligence (EQ): The capacity to understand, manage, and effectively express one's emotions while comprehending and responding appropriately to others' emotions - a crucial skill in the modern workplace.

Growth Mindset: The belief that abilities can be developed through dedication, hard work, and continuous learning - crucial for successful reskilling initiatives.

Human-Centric Skills: Abilities unique to humans that cannot be replicated by machines, including creativity, emotional intelligence, complex problem-solving, and interpersonal communication.

Reskilling: The process of learning new skills to transition to a different role or adapt to changing job requirements, considered essential for maintaining employability in an evolving job market.

Scenario Planning: A strategic approach to preparing for various possible futures by creating detailed narratives about potential outcomes and developing appropriate responses.

Skills Gap Analysis: A systematic process of identifying the difference between current employee competencies and future organizational skill requirements.

Soft Skills: Non-technical abilities such as communication, leadership, and teamwork that are increasingly valued in the workplace and complement technical expertise.

Strategic Human Capital Planning: The alignment of human resource development with organizational objectives to ensure workforce capabilities meet current and future business needs.

Technological Disruption: The transformation of traditional business models and work processes through technological innovation, requiring adaptation and new skill development.

Upskilling: Learning new skills within one's current role to enhance job performance and adapt to technological changes.

Workforce Analytics: The use of data analysis to gain insights into workforce trends, skill gaps, and employee performance for informed decision-making in human resource management.

Chapter 11
Ethical Leadership and Accountability in a Changing World

ABSTRACT

This chapter explores the critical role of ethical leadership in modern organizations. It examines the core components of ethical leadership, including integrity, transparency, fairness, and respect for diversity. The chapter emphasizes the importance of accountability mechanisms and navigating ethical dilemmas in a globalized economy. The role of technology in ethical leadership is discussed, focusing on digital transparency, AI-driven decision-making, and cybersecurity. The chapter outlines strategies for developing an ethical organizational culture through exemplary leadership, ethics training, and secure reporting channels. Case studies of ethical successes and failures, such as Johnson & Johnson's Tylenol crisis response and the Wells Fargo scandal, illustrate the real-world impact of ethical leadership decisions. The chapter concludes by looking at future trends and challenges in ethical leadership, including sustainability, technological advancements, and diversity.

INTRODUCTION

In an era of unprecedented global complexity and technological advancement, the imperative for ethical leadership and robust accountability mechanisms has become more critical. This comprehensive study examines the multifaceted dimensions of ethical leadership in contemporary organizations, focusing on how leaders navigate moral challenges while maintaining accountability in an increasingly interconnected world. This research investigates how organizations can foster ethical decision-making while balancing profitability with social responsibility through a detailed analysis

DOI: 10.4018/979-8-3693-5553-4.ch011

of key components, including integrity, transparency, and cultural sensitivity. The study particularly emphasizes the transformative impact of technology on ethical leadership, addressing emerging challenges in digital transparency, artificial intelligence-driven decision-making, and cybersecurity.

This research provides practical insights into developing and maintaining ethical organizational cultures by examining successful and failed ethical leadership instances through case studies. The findings show that establishing and sustaining ethical leadership requires a holistic approach that combines exemplary leadership practices, comprehensive educational initiatives, and secure channels for addressing ethical concerns. This investigation contributes to our understanding of how organizations can effectively implement ethical leadership principles while maintaining accountability in a rapidly developing global business environment.

ETHICAL LEADERSHIP AND ACCOUNTABILITY IN A TURBULENT ERA

In our capricious world, the necessity for ethical leadership and accountability has never been more paramount. Leaders must exemplify and promulgate normatively appropriate conduct as organizations navigate the intricate complexities of cultural and technological metamorphoses. This approach encompasses the embodiment of moral behavior, the exercise of unimpeachable integrity, and the prioritization of equitability and deference in decision-making. The onus of accountability weighs heavily on the shoulders of those at the helm. It demands that leaders stand answerable for their actions and verdicts and ensure congruence with organizational ethos and objectives. Accountable leaders embrace responsibility, communicate clearly, and cultivate trust and ownership within their ranks. Their communication is critical, as it develops confidence and transparency, making their role in maintaining these values significant (Gouldsberry, 2021).

Ethics and accountability form the bedrock of effective stewardship in this interconnected panorama, where the ripple effects of leadership choices can reverberate far and wide. Leaders play a crucial role in promoting ethical conduct and accountability. Those who consistently show integrity and fairness engender trust and loyalty; they craft an organizational zeitgeist that encourages ethical conduct and bolsters employees' readiness to embrace change (Metwally et al., 2019). Accountability is a fortification against malfeasance, promoting transparency and averting unethical practices that could undermine the organization and its stakeholders (Gouldsberry, 2021). Today's leaders face the Herculean task of steering through a sea of cultural diversity and technological advancements. Ethical leadership is pivotal in this navigation by fostering an inclusive ecosystem that venerates diverse perspectives and guides the adoption of nascent technologies. These leaders prioritize human capital over pecuniary gain, ensuring that technological innovations do not compromise ethical standards or exploit the workforce (Terzieva, 2023).

To uphold ethical standards and maintain accountability, leaders must lead by example, communicate honestly, nurture a culture of trust, shoulder responsibility, and champion inclusivity. They must set the ethical bar high through their actions and decisions, establishing a model for others to emulate (Giovanni, 2024). Maintaining transparent communication with teams and stakeholders is crucial to informing all parties about decisions and their implications. Building robust relationships predicated on trust and respect is vital. Leaders should encourage employees to vocalize concerns and contribute to ethical decision-making processes (Terzieva, 2023). Owning up to missteps and implementing corrective measures shows accountability and a commitment to perpetual improvement (Gouldsberry, 2021), and ensuring fair treatment for all individuals and fostering a diverse, inclusive workplace where everyone can flourish is non-negotiable, posits Terzieva.

In this dynamic and interconnected world, ethical leadership and accountability are indispensable. By adhering to ethical standards and cultivating a culture of accountability, leaders can effectively navigate cultural and technological shifts, ensuring long-term success and positive societal impact. These ethical stewards propel organizational triumph and create a more just and equitable global landscape.

The Key Components of Ethical Leadership

Ethical leadership is essential to managerial efficacy and organizational triumph. It is a paradigm that galvanizes others through principled guidance, fostering ethical conduct and decision-making. The crux of this leadership ethos lies in its multifaceted components: purity and moral fortitude, transparency, candid discourse, equitability in judgment, and reverence for diverse perspectives and cultural milieus. Probity forms the foundation of ethical stewardship. Leaders epitomizing this virtue exude veracity, dependability, and steadfastness in their endeavors and verdicts. They cleave to an unimpeachable moral compass, setting a paragon for their subordinates. Moral fortitude augments this integrity, empowering leaders to promote their convictions, even in adversity or unpopular sentiments. According to (Hegarty & Moccia, 2018; Darby, 2024), this amalgamation ensures decisions that transcend mere legal compliance, ascending to ethical eminence.

(Darby, 2024; Schreiner, 2024) assert that clarity in communication entails honestly unveiling the organization's machinations, determinations, and tribulations. Ethical leaders cultivate an ecosystem where information trickles freely, and employees feel encouraged to vocalize their apprehensions and ideas. This candid discourse engenders trust and ensures all stakeholders remain apprised and engaged. It also serves as a defense against misapprehensions and expedites conflict resolution. Equitability plays a crucial role in maintaining trust and unity within an organization. Ethical leaders strive for fair and impartial decision-making. They weigh the impact of their decisions on all stakeholders, ensuring universal respect and equal opportunities. This approach fosters a healthy work environment and enhances the organization's reputation and credibility (Harper Fox Search Partners, 2021; Schreiner, 2024).

Ethical leaders acknowledge and cherish the heterogeneity of their teams. They comprehend that diverse viewpoints can catalyze innovative solutions and superior decision-making. By embracing cultural disparities, these leaders forge an inclusive environment where all employees feel valued and empowered to contribute. This reverence for diversity extends to understanding and addressing various stakeholder cohorts' unique exigencies and challenges (Harper Fox Search Partners, 2021; Valerie Kirk Blog Post, 2024, April).

Ethical leadership is more than just following rules and regulations. It embodies a steadfast commitment to probity, transparency, fairness, and respect for diversity. By embodying these principles, leaders can inspire their teams, foster trust, and guide their organizations toward sustainable success. Ethical leadership seeks to establish a culture of trust and inclusivity that enables all individuals to contribute to the organization's success. *Figure 1* below illustrates what Dr. Lo Lacono describes as the 8 traits of ethical leadership.

Figure 1. Ethical leadership

Ethical Leadership

- **Integrity**: Has the best interests of the company at heart, both financially and morally speaking.
- **Safety**: Develops a psychologically safe workplace for employees.
- **Leads by Example**: With a positive mindset and a good work ethic.
- **Trustworthy**: Someone those you lead can feel that they can trust.
- **EDI**: Is aware of and promotes equality, diversity, and inclusion as a leader.
- **Transparency**: Is transparent and approachable.
- **Empathetic**: Be able to show empathy and compassion.
- **Socially Responsible**: Not only to their organization but also to society at large.

8 Traits of Ethical Leadership

Dr Valeria Lo Iacono (2023)

(Symonds Research)

Accountability Mechanism for Leaders

Accountability in corporate leadership is essential for a flourishing and ethical workplace. The core of leadership accountability is a multifaceted approach that includes self-reflection, stakeholder engagement, performance metrics, and external oversight. The leader's commitment to introspection and personal responsibility is at the core of this accountability paradigm. Leaders must possess the fortitude to engage in unflinching self-assessment, acknowledging their missteps with alacrity. Owning one's errors and gleaning wisdom from them sets a robust standard for the entire organization (Gouldsberry, 2023; Energage, 2023). Moreover, leaders must delineate transparent, attainable objectives and follow through on their pledges, fostering alignment across the organizational spectrum, argues Energage.

Stakeholder engagement emerges as a crucial pillar in the edifice of accountability. By instituting regular feedback mechanisms, leaders can maintain a symbiotic relationship with their teams, gaining invaluable insights into the ramifications of their decisions (Energage, 2023). Transparent communication is the cornerstone of this engagement, with leaders openly discussing their goals, progress, and challenges. This transparency engenders a culture of trust and mutual respect, creating a fertile ground for accountability to flourish, according to Energage. We cannot overstate the nexus between performance metrics and ethical standards. Implementing a robust framework of clear expectations, evaluation mechanisms, and a system of consequences and rewards is paramount. Explicitly defined job descriptions and performance expectations serve as a lodestar for employees, illuminating their responsibilities and amplifying their sense of accountability (Doolittle, 2024). Regular performance appraisals that consider individual and collective contributions help maintain the highest accountability standards, notes Doolittle.

External oversight and regulatory compliance form the last piece of this intricate accountability puzzle. Adherence to industry regulations and standards ensures that organizations operate within the bounds of legality (Yousueng & Hong, 2019). Periodic external audits provide an unbiased assessment of an organization's ethical and performance standards. Yousueng and Hong assert that accountability forums hold leaders accountable to external stakeholders. In the grand needlepoint of organizational leadership, these accountability mechanisms interweave to create a culture of responsibility, transparency, and ethical behavior. Organizations can foster improved organizational performance and a healthier workplace culture by embracing this holistic approach, which holds leaders accountable for their actions and decisions. According to (Metral, 2024), accountability plays a crucial role in fostering thriving enterprises and aligning individual efforts with organizational objectives. He argues that accountability helps to ensure that individuals take ownership of their actions and perform to achieve shared goals. *Figure 2* illustrates the integration of accountability into leadership.

Figure 2. The importance of accountability in leadership

The Importance of Accountability in Leadership

- 01 Builds Trust
- 02 Sets an Example
- 03 Encourages Growth
- 04 Fosters Creativity

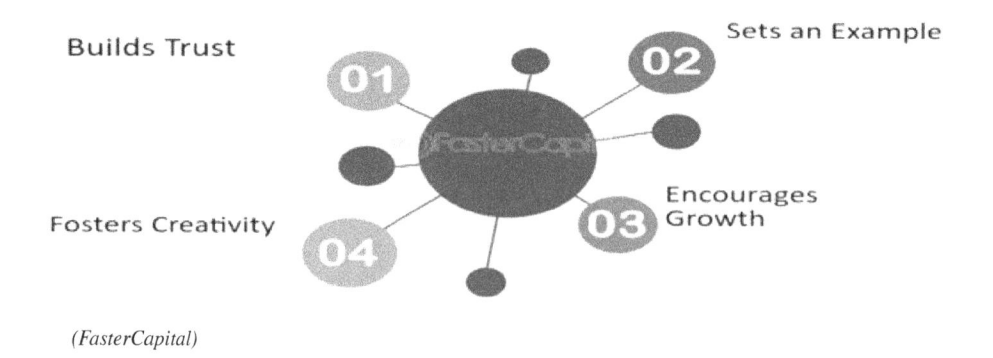

(FasterCapital)

Navigating Ethical Dilemmas in a Globalized Economy

Businesses face a complicated maze of ethical challenges in today's interconnected world. The global economy's intricate tapestry demands a delicate equilibrium between profitability and social conscience while simultaneously grappling with the Herculean task of harmonizing diverse cultural mores and addressing pressing environmental exigencies. This multifaceted challenge necessitates an informed and comprehensive strategy to ensure ethical operations without sacrificing competitiveness. The advent of technological marvels has ushered in an era of unprecedented human influence on our planet's delicate ecosystems (Asgary & Mitschow, 2002). Although this newfound power offers many advantages, it also presents many ethical dilemmas, especially involving the exploitation of natural resources in areas with lax environmental regulations.

The quintessential struggle between profit and social responsibility lies at the heart of these ethical dilemmas. Enter Pieconomics, a paradigm-shifting concept positing that businesses can simultaneously generate profits and social value by creating societal benefits rather than shortsightedly fixating on financial gains (Edmans, 2021). This revolutionary approach abstains from sacrificing profits for charitable endeavors, instead advocating for the generation of wealth through socially responsible practices. Empirical evidence suggests that companies investing in their workforce and maintaining high ethical standards outperform their peers, debunking the myth that social responsibility and profitability are mutually exclusive, asserts Edmans.

The global stage presents a veritable minefield of ethical challenges for multinational corporations. These giants must deftly navigate a patchwork of cultural norms and ethical expectations to preserve their reputations and maintain ethical consistency (Saloome, 2023). Key strategies in this endeavor include emphasizing robust ethical frameworks, cultivating cultural sensitivity, and fostering meaningful stakeholder engagement. Implementing comprehensive ethical guidelines serves as a lodestar for decision-making across diverse cultural contexts. Demonstrating a nuanced understanding and respect for local cultural values and practices is paramount to ethical business operations. Engaging with local stakeholders fosters responsible and respectful business practices, ensuring corporate actions align with community expectations, argues Saloome.

Environmental sustainability is a significant ethical imperative in our globalized economy. Businesses must confront the ecological impact of their operations and adopt sustainable practices to mitigate harm. This Herculean task includes reducing carbon footprints, fostering sustainable supply chains, and supporting corporate social responsibility (CSR). Organizations must reduce emissions and promote energy efficiency to diminish their carbon footprints. Supply chain sustainability ensures that procurement and distribution networks are environmentally conscious and socially responsible. High CSR performance is associated with reduced profit shifting and increased environmental accountability, implying that socially responsible firms are less inclined to participate in environmentally harmful practices (Overesch & Willkomm, 2024).

Successfully navigating the ethical labyrinth of our globalized economy demands a nuanced approach that seamlessly integrates profit-making with social responsibility, cultural sensitivity, and environmental stewardship. By embracing ethical frameworks, fostering stakeholder engagement, and steadfastly committing to sustainable practices, businesses can effectively address these multifaceted challenges while maintaining their competitive edge in the global marketplace. *Figure 3* below denotes how to avoid ethical dilemmas in a decision-making process.

Figure 3. Decision-making process

(Academia World News - image Credit MDPI)

The Role of Technology in Ethical Leadership

In today's digital landscape, technology is a cornerstone of ethical leadership. Digital transparency, AI-driven decision-making, and cybersecurity are the three key components of this technological revolution in leadership ethics. These elements are indispensable for cultivating accountability, ensuring ethical AI practices, and safeguarding stakeholder data. Digital transparency, sharing organizational information and processes, is paramount for accountability. It catalyzes superior decision-making, encourages staff to challenge the current situation, and fosters a culture of continuous experimentation and learning (Bekele, 2023). Organizations can bolster their credibility and trustworthiness by digitizing business processes and embracing transparency. This pellucidity also facilitates monitoring and auditing, preventing fraud and corruption while nurturing an ethical milieu.

York (2024) asserts that workplace transparency garners universal appreciation. Employees often cherish the sense of belonging that stems from inclusion in organizational processes, such as goal-setting or decision-making. Influential leaders, York argues, cultivate a collaborative culture where every voice matters. They explain the rationale behind their decisions, practice active listening, and value diverse inputs. This collaborative leadership approach leaves an indelible mark on teams and organizations. AI and data-driven decision-making have led to a new era of ethical challenges, including privacy concerns, bias, and discrimination. If unchecked, AI systems can perpetuate and amplify existing biases, leading to inequitable treatment in various domains (Parsons, 2020). Ethical leadership in AI necessitates ensuring fairness and justice in the design and application of these systems. This approach encompasses honesty, accountability, bias mitigation, and human judgment.

Leaders must be transparent about AI system usage and ensure accountability for outcomes (Weinstein, 2024). Mitigating biases in AI models and datasets is crucial and often achieved through diverse and inclusive development teams and continuous monitoring. Recognizing AI's limitations and the importance of human oversight in decision-making processes is vital. As described in subsequent chapters, AI should augment human capabilities rather than supplant them entirely (Parsons, 2020).

Cybersecurity, a critical facet of ethical leadership, protects sensitive information from digital threats. Stakeholders, including leaders, play a pivotal role in managing cybersecurity risks by allocating resources and setting an exemplary standard for the organization (Vumetric Blog Post, February 2024). Key measures to enhance cybersecurity include raising awareness, conducting regular audits and penetration testing, and implementing robust security protocols.

Educating employees about common cyber threats, such as phishing attacks, and conducting regular training sessions is essential. Security audits and penetration tests help identify and address system vulnerabilities by simulating potential attacks. Establishing and enforcing robust security protocols, including encryption, multi-factor authentication, and regular software updates, is crucial for protecting data and systems, comments the Vumetric Blog Post.

Integrating technology into ethical leadership involves digital transparency, ethical AI usage, and robust cybersecurity measures. Leaders must ensure their organizations are transparent and accountable, mitigate AI biases, and protect stakeholder information through diligent cybersecurity practices. By doing so, they can cultivate a culture of trust, fairness, and ethical responsibility within their organizations, setting a new standard for leadership in the digital age.

Developing an Ethical Organizational Culture

Cultivating an ethical organizational ethos demands a multifaceted approach that intertwines exemplary leadership, robust educational initiatives, and secure avenues for voicing ethical apprehensions. These pivotal components engender an ambiance where moral conduct becomes second nature, empowering employees to act with unwavering integrity. Leadership, wielding unparalleled influence in molding an organization's moral fabric, is at the helm of this ethical metamorphosis. Ethical leaders must establish a tone of rectitude from the uppermost echelons, embodying moral principles in their quotidian interactions. This includes behavior characterized by honesty, fairness, and transparency, along with a readiness to accept accountability for their actions. The ripple effect of such comportment permeates the entire organizational structure, as employees are accustomed to emulating their superiors, fostering a more ethical milieu (Ethical Systems, 2013; Elharony, 2023; Wizbowski, 2024).

The dividends of ethical leadership are manifold. It engenders trust and loyalty among the workforce, catalyzing heightened productivity, diminished turnover, and enhanced morale. Moreover, organizations helmed by ethical leaders possess a magnetic allure for top-tier talent and enjoy improved customer satisfaction, culminating in augmented sales and profitability (Elharony, 2023; Wizbowski, 2024). Ethics training emerges as a requirement in this ethical edifice, equipping employees with a profound understanding of organizational values and the gravity of ethical conduct. Efficacious training programs transcend mere onboarding rituals, seamlessly integrating into ongoing developmental efforts. These initiatives should encompass experiential training in ethical conundrums, nurture psychological safety in the face of minor lapses, and champion a culture of service through volunteerism and ethical mentorship (Smith & Kouchaki, 2021; Estrada, 2023).

The beneficial effects of regular ethics training are twofold: it fosters individual moral development and furnishes employees with the requisite tools to navigate complex ethical terrains. Furthermore, it underscores the organization's unwavering commitment to ethical behavior and explains the ramifications of moral transgressions (Smith & Kouchaki, 2021; Estrada, 2023). Paramount to maintaining an ethical culture is the establishment of secure and anonymous channels for reporting ethical concerns. Employees must harbor an unshakable conviction that they can flag unethical behavior without fear of reprisal. Implementing clear and accessible reporting mechanisms, like whistleblower hotlines, ensuring serious consideration, and promptly investigating all reports can achieve this (DDI Blog Post, October 2019; Wizbowski, 2024).

Transparency in addressing ethical infractions is equally crucial. Organizations must show a steadfast resolve to penalize unethical conduct while rewarding moral rectitude. This reinforces the primacy of ethics and evinces the organization's steadfast commitment to upholding lofty ethical standards (DDI Blog Post, October 2019; Wizbowski, 2024). In summation, cultivating an ethical organizational culture necessitates a holistic approach that harmonizes ethical leadership, continuous moral education, and secure reporting channels. By setting an exemplary standard, providing ongoing improvement, and fostering open dialogue, organizations can engender an environment where ethical behavior reigns supreme, ultimately yielding enhanced organizational performance, employee contentment, and stakeholder trust. *Figure 4* below shows steps for managing ethical culture to leverage opportunities and build organizational conditions.

Figure 4. Steps for managing ethical culture

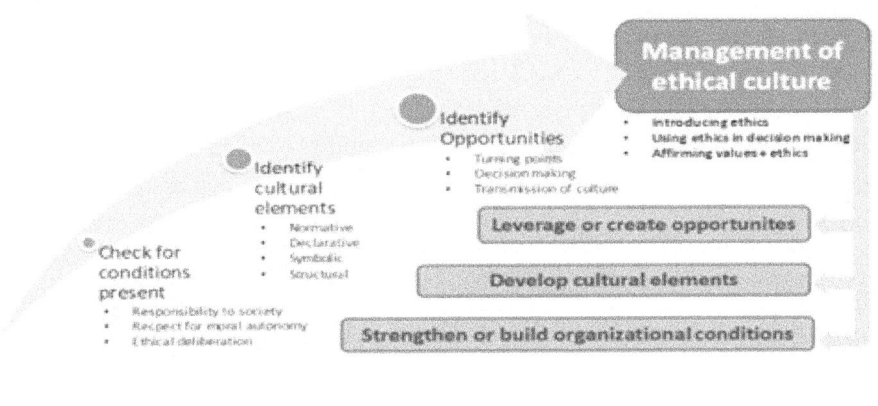

(Semantic Scholar)

The Future of Ethical Leadership

The landscape of ethical leadership is evolving rapidly, presenting both exciting opportunities and formidable challenges. As we venture into uncharted territory, the imperative for ethical guidance has never been more pronounced. Transparency and trust have emerged as linchpins of effective leadership, fostering an environment where collaboration flourishes (Purple, 2024). This newfound openness is not merely a trend but a fundamental shift in organizational dynamics.

In this era of reinforced awareness, sustainability, and corporate social responsibility (CSR) have taken center stage. Ethical leaders are increasingly aware of the long-term ramifications of their environmental and societal decisions. Diverse stakeholders' burgeoning expectations drive this significant change (Wells, 2024). The inexorable march of technological progress has ushered in a new set of ethical sticky situations. The labyrinthine complexities of artificial intelligence and data analytics now require leaders to navigate, ensuring these powerful tools' responsible and ethical use (Quärtápa, 2024). Simultaneously, there is a growing demand for diversity and inclusion. Ethical leadership now requires the creation of inclusive environments where everyone feels valued and respected (The Enterprise World, 2023).

However, there are many obstacles on the path to ethical leadership. Leaders frequently find themselves at the intersection of conflicting values, compelled to make decisions that balance economic viability with ethical soundness (Professional & Executive Development, Harvard DCE, 2024). Maintaining integrity in the face of external pressures requires unwavering commitment and moral fortitude (Wells, 2024). Cultivating an ethical organizational culture is an extraordinary task, demanding consistent modeling of ethical behavior and creating an environment that nurtures ethical decision-making (O'Sullivan, 2023). Moreover, preparing the next generation of moral leaders looms large, necessitating effective mentorship and knowledge transfer (The Enterprise World, 2023).

The future of ethical leadership hinges on our ability to address these emerging trends and challenges head-on. By investing in mentorship, succession planning, and promoting inclusivity, organizations can cultivate leaders who prioritize ethical considerations and drive sustainable success. As we forge ahead, the role of moral leaders in shaping a more equitable and sustainable world becomes increasingly crucial. The time to act is now, for our decisions today will reverberate through the annals of history, shaping the legacy we leave for generations to come.

Case Studies: Ethical Leadership Successes and Failures

Ethical leadership is not just a saying but the cornerstone of organizational integrity and success (Ughulu, 2024). Moral predicaments abound in today's cutthroat business landscape, making ethical leadership more crucial than ever. Look into some riveting case studies illuminating triumphs and tribulations in this arena.

Johnson & Johnson's Tylenol crisis in 1982 stands as a paragon of ethical leadership. When cyanide-laced capsules claimed lives, CEO James Burke did not equivocate. He orchestrated an unprecedented recall of 31 million bottles, hemorrhaging $100 million. This audacious move prioritized consumer safety over the bottom line, setting a new paradigm for product security (Cote, 2023). The lesson? Swift, transparent action can transmute catastrophe into opportunity, fortifying public trust and elevating industry standards.

Fast forward to 2018, and Starbucks faced its ethical crucible. The arrest of two African American men at a Philadelphia outlet ignited a firestorm of public humiliation. CEO Kevin Johnson's response was nothing short of exemplary. He shouldered responsibility, issued a mea culpa, and shuttered 8,000 stores for a day of racial bias training. This bold scheme underscored Starbucks' unwavering commitment to inclusivity and ethical leadership (Tangdall, 2018). Johnson's philosophy of creating "a culture of warmth and belonging" resonated deeply, demonstrating that actions speak louder than words in corporate ethics.

However, for every pinnacle, there is a cautionary tale. The Wells Fargo scandal of 2016 is a stark reminder of what happens when ethical leadership falters. The financial world was rocked by the revelation that employees had fabricated millions of unauthorized accounts to meet draconian sales targets. The leadership's failure to consume these nefarious practices in the bud resulted in criticism, punitive economic sanctions, and an exodus of customer trust (Tangdall, 2018). The takeaway? Ethical lapses can inflict long-term, perhaps irreparable, damage to an organization's reputation and fiscal health.

Perhaps no recent case exemplifies ethical leadership failure more starkly than the Theranos debacle. CEO Elizabeth Holmes, once hailed as the wunderkind of Silicon Valley, promised revolutionary blood-testing technology. The reality was far more sinister. Holmes' web of deceit entangled investors, patients, and partners, ultimately leading to the company's implosion and her criminal indictment (Tangdall, 2018). This cautionary tale underscores the importance of transparency and honesty in maintaining stakeholder trust.

So, how can organizations cultivate ethical leadership? It starts at the top. Leaders should exemplify ethical behavior and set a high standard for their teams. They should foster an environment of open communication where employees feel inspired to voice concerns without fear of reprisal. Regular training on ethical standards and decision-making is non-negotiable. Organizations must also establish and enforce a comprehensive code of ethics, ensuring every employee understands and adheres to these guidelines. Regular audits and reviews of organizational practices are essential to maintaining ethical compliance.

Successes and failures serve as invaluable teachers in pursuing leadership. By learning from triumphs and tribulations, leaders can navigate ethical labyrinths more adeptly, cultivate trust, and forge a sustainable organizational culture. This process of continuous learning and adaptation is the hallmark of genuinely resilient leadership. Ultimately, it is not about avoiding failure altogether but about emerging stronger, wiser, and more ethically grounded from every challenge.

CONCLUSION AND SUMMARY

This comprehensive examination of ethical leadership and accountability in contemporary organizations reveals the intricate interplay between traditional leadership principles and emerging challenges in our rapidly developing global landscape. The research shows that successful ethical leadership requires a sophisticated integration of fundamental components—integrity, transparency, and cultural sensitivity—with robust accountability mechanisms that ensure consistent adherence to moral standards. The findings emphasize that organizations must navigate ethical dilemmas in the globalized economy by reconciling profitability with social responsibility. This is evident in how successful organizations handle cultural differences, environmental concerns, and stakeholder interests while maintaining a competitive advantage.

Technology's transformative impact, especially in digital transparency, AI-driven decision-making, and cybersecurity, has introduced new ethical considerations that leaders must actively address through thoughtful policies and practices. The case studies we examined strongly suggest that creating and maintaining an ethical workplace culture requires a multifaceted approach that includes strong leadership, broad educational programs, and safe ways for employees to voice ethical concerns. Successful organizations show that moral leadership is not merely about compliance but about creating a sustainable culture of integrity that permeates all levels.

Looking to the future, ethical leadership will become increasingly crucial as organizations face more complex challenges in the global business environment. Research suggests that leaders who successfully integrate ethical considerations into their decision-making processes while maintaining strong accountability mechanisms are better positioned to navigate these challenges and create sustainable, thriving organizations. This study contributes to understanding how organizations can effectively implement ethical leadership principles while maintaining accountability in a rapidly evolving global business environment. The findings underscore that ethical leadership is a moral and strategic necessity for long-term organizational success in our interconnected world.

While ethical leadership provides the foundational framework for organizational governance, its practical implementation depends on establishing robust mechanisms of trust and transparency. The interconnected nature of modern business operations, accelerated by technological advancement, has created an environment where ethical decision-making must be visible and verifiable to stakeholders at all levels. As organizations navigate the complexities of digital transformation and global integration, the relationship between ethical leadership principles and transparent business practices becomes increasingly symbiotic. This interdependence manifests most prominently in how leaders build and maintain stakeholder trust through consistent demonstration of moral behavior and open communication. Understanding this crucial intersection between ethical leadership and organizational transparency provides a natural progression into examining how trust dynamics shape contemporary business relationships and organizational success.

REFERENCES

Asgary, N., & Mitschow, M. C. (2002). Toward A Model For International. *Business Ethics (Oxford, England)*, 36(3), 239–246.

Bekele, S. (2023). *The Role Of Transparency And Accountability In Digital Transformation*. Https://Www.Isaca.Org/Resources/News-And-Trends/Industry-News/2023/The-Role-Of-Transparency-And-Accountability-In-Digital-Transformation

Cote, C. (2023). *4 Examples Of Ethical Leadership In Business | Hbs Online*. Harvard Business School. Https://Online.Hbs.Edu/Blog/Post/Examples-Of-Ethical-Leadership

Darby, J. (2024). *What Is Ethical Leadership?* Attributes, Traits, & Examples.

Ddi Blog Post (2019, October). How To Build An Ethical Organizational Culture.

Doolittle, J. (2024). 5 Levers To Create A Culture Of Accountability.

Edmans, A. (2021). The Social Responsibility Of Business Includes Profits. *Pro Market*. Https://Www.Promarket.Org/2021/10/19/Social-Responsibility-Business-Profits-Pieconomics/

Elharony, A. (2023). *Leading By Example: The Power Of Ethical Leadership In Business | Linkedin*. Linkedin. Https://Www.Linkedin.Com/Pulse/Leading-Example-Power-Ethical-Leadership-Business-Amr-Elharony/

Energage (2023). The Importance Of Accountability In Leadership | Top Workplaces.

Estrada, M. (2023). The Importance Of Ethics Training In The Workplace In 2023 And Beyond. *Compliance Training Group*. Https://Compliancetraininggroup.Com/2023/07/17/The-Importance-Of-Ethics-Training-In-The-Workplace-In-2023-And-Beyond/

Ethical Systems. (2013). Corporate Culture - Ethical Systems. Ethical Systems. Https://Www.Ethicalsystems.Org/Corporate-Culture/

Giovanni, G. (2024). Most Important Characteristics Contributing To Ethical Leadership.

Gouldsberry, M. (2021). Leadership Accountability: Why It Matters And How To Fuel It. *Betterworks*. Https://Www.Betterworks.Com/Magazine/Accountability-In-Leadership/

Gouldsberry, M. (2023). Leadership Accountability: How To Build It Into Your Culture - Betterworks.

Harper Fox Search Partners (2021). The Five Principles Of Ethical Leaders - Harper Fox Partners.

Hegarty, N., & Moccia, S. (2018). Components Of Ethical Leadership And Their Importance In Sustaining Organizations Over The Long Term. *The Journal of Values Based Leadership*, 11(1). Advance online publication. Doi.Org/10.22543/0733.111 .1199. DOI: 10.22543/0733.111.1199

Metral, K. (2024). *6 Reasons Why Accountability Is Vital For Business | Cosmico*. Hubspot.

Metwally, D., Ruiz-Palomino, P., Metwally, M., & Gartzia, L. (2019). How Ethical Leadership Shapes Employees' Readiness To Change: The Mediating Role Of An Organizational Culture Of Effectiveness. *Frontiers in Psychology*, 10, 2493. Doi .Org/10.3389/Fpsyg.2019.02493. DOI: 10.3389/fpsyg.2019.02493 PMID: 31798489

O'sullivan, D. (2023). *The Crucial Role Of Ethical Leadership: Reflection Of Honor, Integrity, And Past Actions | Linkedin*. Https://Www.Linkedin.Com/Pulse/Crucial -Role-Ethical-Leadership-Reflection-Honor-Past-O-Sullivan/

Overesch, M., & Willkomm, S. (2024). The Relation Between Corporate Social Responsibility And Profit Shifting Of Multinational Enterprises. *International Tax and Public Finance*. Advance online publication. Doi.Org/10.1007/S10797-024 -09850-Z. DOI: 10.1007/s10797-024-09850-z

Parsons, L. (2020). Ethical Concerns Mount As Ai Takes Bigger Decision-Making Role: Great Promise But Potential For Peril. *Harvard Gazette*. Https://News.Harvard .Edu/Gazette/Story/2020/10/Ethical-Concerns-Mount-As-Ai-Takes-Bigger-Decision -Making-Role/

Professional & Executive Development | Harvard Dce. (2024). *Ethical Leadership - Professional & Executive Development | Harvard Dce*. Https://Professional.Dce .Harvard.Edu/Programs/Ethical-Leadership/

Purple, B. (2024). *Navigating The Future: Ethical Leadership In The New Era – Guiding Principles For 2024 | Linkedin*. Https://Www.Linkedin.Com/Pulse/ Navigating-Future-Ethical-Leadership-New-Era-Guiding-Purple-Group-Z48we/

Quärtápa, T. (2024). *Leadership Reimagined: Navigating The Trends At The Intersection Of Technology, Ethics, And Innovation In 2024 | Linkedin*. Https://Www .Linkedin.Com/Pulse/Leadership-Reimagined-Navigating-Trends-Intersection -Ethics-Qu%C3%A4rt%C3%A1pa-Wk6ic/

Saloome, S. (2023). Ethical Challenges In Global Business: Navigating Cross-Cultural Dilemmas - Academia World News. *Academia World News*. Https://Academiaworldnews.Com/Ethical-Challenges-In-Global-Business-Navigating-Cross-Cultural-Dilemmas/

Schreiner, E. (2024). What Are The Key Elements Of Ethical Leadership In An Organization? Smith, I. H., & Kouchaki, M. (2021). *Building An Ethical Company*. Harvard Business Review. Https://Hbr.Org/2021/11/Building-An-Ethical-Company

Tangdall, S. (2018). *The Ceo Of Starbucks And The Practice Of Ethical Leadership*. Https://Www.Scu.Edu/Leadership-Ethics/Resources/The-Ceo-Of-Starbucks-And-The-Practice-Of-Ethical-Leadership/

Terzieva, K. (2023). The Rise Of Ethical Leadership In Modern Business Enterprises. *Forbes*.

The Enterprise World. (2023). *12 Benefits Of Leadership Roles For Next Generation | The Enterprise World*. Https://Theenterpriseworld.Com/Preparing-Generation-For-Leadership-Roles/

Ughulu, J. (2024). Ethical Leadership In Modern Organizations: Navigating Complexity And Promoting Integrity. *International Journal Of Economics, Business And Management Research, 08*(05), 52–62. Https://Doi.Org/10.51505/Ijebmr.2024.8505

Valerie Kirk Blog Post. (2024, April). What Is Ethical Leadership And Why Is It Important? - Professional & Executive Development | Harvard Dce. Https://Professional.Dce.Harvard.Edu/Blog/What-Is-Ethical-Leadership-And-Why-Is-It-Important/

Vumetric Blog Post. (February 2024). *The Importance Of Cybersecurity For Stakeholders - Vumetric*. Https://Www.Vumetric.Com/Blog/The-Importance-Of-Cybersecurity-For-Stakeholders/

Weinstein, B. (2024). Ai Ethics: 7 Crucial Qualities Of Ethical Leadership. *Forbes*. Https://Www.Forbes.Com/Sites/Bruceweinstein/2024/02/21/Ai-7-Crucial-Qualities-Of-Ethical-Leadership/

Wells, R. (2024, February 15). 8 Leadership Ethics Every Leader Should Live By In 2024. *Forbes*. Https://Www.Forbes.Com/Sites/Rachelwells/2024/02/15/8-Leadership-Ethics-Every-Leader-Should-Live-By-In-2024/

Wizbowski, R. (2024). *Ethical Leadership: Fostering A Culture Of Integrity From The Top Down*. Https://Www.Diligent.Com/Resources/Blog/Ethical-Leadership

York, A. (2024). Transparency In Leadership: Lead Your Team With Class. *Clickup*. Https://Clickup.Com/Blog/Transparency-In-Leadership/

Yousueng, H., & Hong, S. (2019). The Impact Of Accountability On Organizational Performance In The U.S. Federal Government: The Moderating Role Of Autonomy. *Review of Public Personnel Administration*, 39(1), 3–23. Doi.Org/10.1177/0734371x16682816. DOI: 10.1177/0734371X16682816

KEYWORDS TERMS AND DEFINITIONS

Accountability Mechanisms: Systems and processes that ensure leaders are answerable for their actions and decisions, including self-reflection, stakeholder engagement, performance metrics, and external oversight.

AI-Driven Decision-Making: Using artificial intelligence systems in organizational decision-making requires ethical considerations regarding fairness, bias mitigation, and human oversight.

Corporate Social Responsibility (CSR): An organization's commitment to managing its environmental impact, supporting social initiatives, and maintaining ethical business practices while contributing to society.

Cultural Sensitivity: The understanding and respect for diverse cultural perspectives and values in leadership decisions and organizational practices, particularly in a global business context.

Digital Transparency: The practice of openly sharing organizational information and processes through digital means to foster accountability, better decision-making, and trust among stakeholders.

Ethical Leadership: A leadership paradigm that guides others through principled behavior, emphasizing moral conduct, integrity, transparency, and fair decision-making while balancing organizational success with social responsibility.

Moral Fortitude: The strength and courage to maintain ethical principles and promote convictions, even when faced with adversity or unpopular decisions.

Organizational Culture: The collective values, beliefs, and practices that shape behavior within an organization, particularly as they relate to ethical conduct and decision-making.

Pieconomics: A concept suggesting businesses can simultaneously generate profits and social value by creating societal benefits rather than focusing solely on financial gains.

Stakeholder Engagement: The process of involving and communicating with all parties affected by organizational decisions, including employees, customers, investors, and community members.

Chapter 12
Maintaining Trust and Transparency

ABSTRACT

This chapter examines the critical role of trust and transparency in modern business. It emphasizes how these elements form the foundation for successful organizations, shaping stakeholder relationships and driving sustainable performance. The text delves into strategies for cultivating openness, including effective leadership, empowering employees, and leveraging technology. Key topics covered include the psychology of trust, navigating difficult conversations, and the impact of emerging technologies like blockchain and AI on transparency initiatives. The chapter highlights the delicate balance between transparency and data security, especially in the context of increasing privacy concerns and regulations. The discussion extends to the future of trust and transparency, examining how innovations in cloud security, sustainability practices, and data governance reshape business models. The chapter concludes by urging organizations to take immediate action in implementing transparency initiatives, offering practical steps such as conducting audits and developing roadmaps.

INTRODUCTION

Trust and transparency have emerged as the foundational elements of enduring business relationships in the dynamic landscape of 21st-century commerce. These fundamental principles are essential elements that shape the very fabric of successful organizations. Trust and transparency are critical in an era of rapid technological advances and shifting societal expectations. Fostering trust and maintaining transparency has never been more critical because of its multifaceted nature; trust encompasses stakeholders' unwavering confidence in a company's integrity, reliability, and expertise. It is the implicit belief that an organization will prioritize the interests

DOI: 10.4018/979-8-3693-5553-4.ch012

of its constituents and consistently honor its commitments. This intangible asset proves indispensable in nurturing loyalty, facilitating collaboration, and fostering open dialogue within the business ecosystem.

Conversely, transparency is the clarity with which an organization communicates its operations, decisions, and policies to its stakeholders. It involves providing accurate, timely, and accessible information, empowering stakeholders to make informed decisions and feel more confident in their interactions with the company. While some argue that excessive transparency can be counterproductive, balancing its role in establishing credibility and showing accountability is crucial. As we delve deeper into this chapter, we will examine the intricate psychology of trust, examining its construction, maintenance, and occasional erosion in professional settings. We will delve into the crucial role of leadership in fostering an open culture that actively seeks and welcomes employee feedback. We will address the challenges of navigating tough conversations and delivering bad news with empathy and honesty, providing practical strategies for maintaining trust even in trying circumstances.

In our increasingly digitalized world, we cannot overlook the pivotal role of technology in shaping transparency initiatives. From blockchain's promise of immutable record-keeping to the ethical considerations surrounding AI decision-making, we'll examine how groundbreaking technologies revolutionize how organizations approach trust and transparency. Throughout this exploration, we'll confront the delicate balance organizations must strike between openness and security, particularly in an age where data privacy concerns are at the forefront of public consciousness. We will discuss the implementation of robust governance frameworks and the importance of clear communication about data practices in building and maintaining stakeholder trust.

As we stand on the cusp of a new era in business ethics and practices, this chapter comprehensively summarizes the strategies, challenges, and opportunities at the intersection of trust, transparency, and modern commerce. By understanding and implementing these crucial elements, organizations can forge stronger relationships, enhance their reputation, and position themselves for sustainable success in an increasingly complex and interconnected world.

DEVELOPMENT OF TRUST

From our earliest moments, trust shapes who we become and how we connect with others. Consider the fascinating case of Canadian preschoolers, where researchers discovered that children who formed strong friendships at age 5 developed higher levels of trust, leading them to show more kindness and helpfulness by age 6 (Jambon

& Malti, 2022). Like a tiny seed that grows into a mighty tree, these early positive interactions create the foundation for a lifetime of meaningful relationships.

The way trust operates in groups reveals intriguing patterns that affect everything, from how charismatic leaders influence us to how advertising sways our decisions. Researchers using the Trust-Distrust Model found something remarkable: it only takes about 55% agreement among group members to build consensus (Ishii et al., 2021). This highlights the delicate balance of social influence, demonstrating how trust can influence group dynamics and shape collective decisions.

When we enter a classroom, trust becomes the invisible force that shapes learning and connection. A study focusing on students in grades 4-8 revealed how trust weaves through the fabric of classroom life, influencing academic performance and the entire social atmosphere (Bayborodova, 2019). Like a conductor leading an orchestra, trust harmonizes the complex interactions between students and teachers, creating an environment where learning can flourish.

Multiple streams shape our capacity for trust—our unique personality traits, the social environments we navigate, and the repository of our past experiences. Picture someone who has experienced betrayal; their willingness to trust again may be like a delicate flower requiring careful nurturing to bloom. Yet this same person, given the right supportive environment and positive experiences, can rebuild their capacity for trust, demonstrating the remarkable resilience of human nature.

The digital revolution has transformed how we establish and maintain trust. As more of our lives move online, we've had to adapt to building trust without traditional cues like body language or tone of voice. Using personal information as "cryptographic asset data" presents opportunities and challenges in this new frontier, Ishii et al. (2021). Nevertheless, despite these changes, the fundamental importance of trust remains constant—it continues to be the cornerstone of pro-social behavior, social cohesion, and adequate decision-making in both our physical and digital worlds.

Maintaining Trust and Transparency

In commerce, the foundation of enduring relationships is trust and transparency. These quintessential elements are the linchpin for cultivating robust connections within the business ecosystem. Trust, a multifaceted concept, encompasses stakeholders' unwavering confidence in a company's integrity, dependability, and expertise. It is the implicit belief that an enterprise will prioritize the interests of its constituents and honor its commitments firmly. This intangible asset is indispensable for nurturing allegiance, facilitating synergy, and fostering unencumbered dialogue. Consider the plight of managers who need more faith in their subordinates; they are less inclined to furnish the requisite resources or guidance for success. Transparency manifests as the clarity with which an organization disseminates information about its modus operandi, resolutions, and protocols to its stakeholders. It is characterized by providing precise, timely, and accessible data, empowering stakeholders to make informed decisions and feel more confident and in control.

While transparency is crucial to establishing credibility and showing accountability, some contend that excessive transparency can be counterproductive. Researchers argue that it may engender feelings of overwhelm and defensiveness among employees. In industries where data privacy and ethical practices are paramount, trust and transparency are pivotal in bolstering consumer confidence. Take, for instance, AI-powered customer engagement; transparency is crucial in mitigating concerns about bias and fairness, enhancing consumer trust in AI technologies (Dezao, 2024), and making them feel secure and trusting. The symbiotic relationship between transparency and trust forms an integral cycle for achieving sustainable business outcomes. Ashish and Abhijit (2022) propose a framework that integrates these elements to help frontline managers develop competencies that enhance business performance and relationship management.

Software developers revere transparency as a fundamental value that promotes accountability and ethical practices, perceiving it as essential to building trust and maintaining ethical standards of development (Obie et al., 2023). The genetic testing industry is a prime example of the importance of transparency in using customer data for research and commercial purposes. Raz et al. (2020) emphasize that transparency about data usage and getting informed consent are imperative for maintaining customer trust in this domain. Transparency in AI and other technological innovations serves as a bridge between innovative advancements and consumer acceptance. By cultivating a culture of accountability and lucid communication, businesses can align technological development with consumer expectations and ethical considerations, making the audience feel respected and considered, as Dezao (2024) argued.

While trust and transparency are indispensable for business success, their implementation and maintenance require concerted effort. As Hosseini et al. (2016) explain, transparency is essential to businesses and their information systems, often linked to positive ethical and economic attributes, such as accountability and trust. However, the path to transparency is fraught with challenges, including data security concerns and privacy issues. The process can be resource-intensive, demanding significant time and effort to ensure accurate and open communication. Moreover, stakeholders may exhibit resistance to the exposure of sensitive information.

Trust and transparency are indomitable pillars of business success. They augment consumer confidence, optimize business outcomes, ensure ethical practices, and facilitate the acceptance of technological innovations. These intertwined concepts demand unwavering commitment from businesses to implement and sustain them effectively, ultimately shaping the landscape of modern commerce.

Understanding The Psychology of Trust

In the complexity of human relationships, trust stands as an indomitable force, shaping the essence of our personal and professional connections. This fragile yet palpable concept wields immense power, orchestrating the symphony of human interaction with finesse. Cultivating and sustaining trust is a multifaceted endeavor, fraught with opportunities and pitfalls that demand our utmost attention. It reminds us of our significant role in this powerful force that shapes our relationships. At the core of trust-building lies the unwavering commitment to one's word. The consistent fulfillment of promises and obligations serves as the bedrock upon which trust is defined. Over time, this steadfast reliability metamorphoses into an unshakeable foundation of trust (Craig, 2019). Gupta (2021) posits that candid and transparent communication is the lifeblood of trust. It necessitates an unyielding willingness to confront one's missteps and collaborate in their resolution.

To augment one's trustworthiness quotient, individuals must cultivate empathy and invest time in deciphering the emotional surroundings of others (Craig, 2019). This empathetic approach engenders mutual understanding and safety, fostering a deep sense of comfort conducive to trust-building. However, we must exercise discretion when expressing genuine concern, especially in hierarchical relationships, where the impact on one's reputation requires careful consideration. The alignment of values and objectives between parties catalyzes the genesis of trust. This congruence engenders a profound sense of security and mutual comprehension (Hancock et al., 2023). Neuroscientific inquiries have unveiled the role of oxytocin, the bonding hormone, in the trust equation. Research findings reveal that certain managerial behaviors stimulate oxytocin production, enhancing organizational cohesion and productivity (Zak, 2017; Roberts, 2020).

However, the path to trust is fraught with potential pitfalls; inconsistency and unfulfilled promises rank among the most pernicious trust-eroding factors. The failure to deliver on commitments or display consistency in actions can rapidly corrode trust. Even seemingly innocuous breaches can precipitate significant repercussions, according to Craig (2019). Roberts (2020) underscores the detrimental impact of poor communication or information withholding on trust, for clarity and consistency in communication is indispensable for preserving trust. Deception, regardless of its magnitude, can inflict grievous damage to trust. Honesty is the cornerstone of trust, and any transgression can engender skepticism and doubt, posits Craig. Self-aggrandizement and egocentricity represent another treacherous pitfall in the trust landscape. An exclusive focus on personal gain, disregarding others' needs, can significantly diminish trust, said Craig, who believes acknowledging and appreciating others' contributions are pivotal in maintaining trust.

Societal metamorphoses and the proliferation of conflicting information have engendered uncertainty and vulnerability, prompting individuals to retreat from trusting larger institutions and seek validation from familiar sources (Roberts, 2020). As awareness of these trust dynamics permeates individuals and organizations, they can forge stronger, more resilient relationships while remaining vigilant of actions that may undermine trust. For instance, the chronic failure to meet deadlines can erode trust by signaling a lack of reliability and commitment, fostering frustration and impeding team collaboration. Conversely, specific actions that may not ostensibly appear to build trust can bolster it. The open discussion and admission of mistakes, for example, can fortify trust by demonstrating transparency, honesty, and a willingness to assume responsibility for one's actions. Figure 1 below describes the psychology of trust.

Figure 1. Understanding the psychology of trust

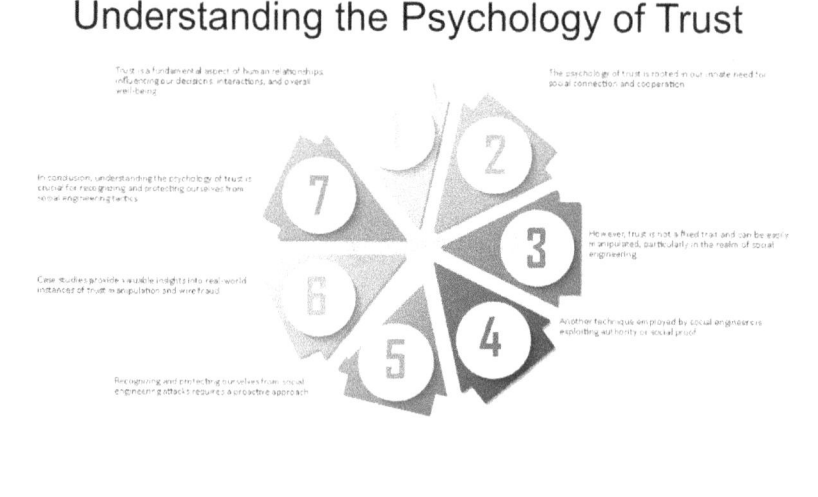

(FasterCapital)

Building a Culture of Openness

Cultivating a culture of openness within the workplace is paramount to nurturing transparency, soliciting employee input, and promoting participation. Leadership is indispensable in this endeavor, setting the tone and establishing the necessary frameworks to support such a culture. Trust and imaginative communication are the bedrock of transparency, exemplary leadership, and employee empowerment. When employees place trust in their leaders, they experience a heightened sense of security and value within the organization. This sense of safety catalyzes morale, augmenting motivation and productivity. It engenders a salubrious work milieu where collaboration and mutual support flourish. During a case study in West Africa, I discovered that relationships build knowledge when employees trust their leaders to develop capabilities. These relationships foster a collaborative environment where employees feel empowered to share ideas and insights. As a result, the organization benefits from enhanced creativity and problem-solving. Additionally, this trust-based dynamic can lead to increased employee engagement and retention.

Transparency germinates through trust. Leaders must cultivate this trust through candid communication, which entails sharing propitious and adverse information with employees and fostering an environment where they feel emboldened to voice their thoughts and concerns. Transparent leaders delineate clear expectations, communicate efficaciously, and prevent unpleasant surprises (Ercanbrack Michelle Blog Post, May 2023; Vyas, 2023). This approach promotes a positive company culture and cements employee loyalty and engagement. Leaders must epitomize the behaviors they wish to see in their employees, which involves being transparent about their vulnerabilities and shortcomings. When leaders share their tribulations and how they surmount them, it humanizes them and encourages employees to follow suit (Chan, 2022). This practice de-stigmatizes failure and fosters a culture that values learning from mistakes.

Empowering teams to act and devolve decision-making to the lowest possible echelon is crucial, as this instills a sense of ownership and accountability among employees, ensuring expeditious decision-making (Defy Expectations, 2024). Leadership also encompasses encouraging employee feedback and participation, including creating safe spaces for feedback, recognizing and celebrating contributions, and fostering continuous improvement and adaptability. Leaders must establish secure environments where employees feel at ease providing honest feedback. Regular tête-à-têtes, anonymous surveys, and open-door policies can achieve this (Ercanbrack Michelle Blog Post, May 2023). Soliciting feedback facilitates swift identification and resolution of issues, leading to more efficient problem-solving and continuous enhancement (Vyas, 2023) and building trust.

Acknowledging and celebrating individual and team contributions is vital for maintaining a positive work environment because recognition bolsters morale and reinforces behaviors and achievements that align with the company's values and objectives (Polly Blog Post, n.d.). This practice helps construct a culture of appreciation and encourages employees to consistently contribute their best efforts, leading to an open organizational culture characterized by continuous improvement and adaptability. Leaders should encourage risk-taking and innovation by creating an environment where employees are not apprehensive about making mistakes (RedHat, 2020). This approach involves being receptive to novel ideas, fostering cross-functional collaboration, adapting to changes, and creating a trustworthy environment.

Organizations must implement systems and processes for transparent decision-making frameworks, regular monitoring, and feedback loops. A transparent decision-making framework allows for collective input and collaboration. It entails disseminating company metrics, performance data, and strategic goals to employees, guaranteeing alignment and informedness (RedHat, 2020). Transparent decision-making builds trust and ensures that employees comprehend the rationale behind decisions.

Monitoring progress and gathering feedback regularly is essential to sustaining a culture of openness. Ongoing dialogues, surveys, and performance reviews can accomplish this process (Defy Expectations, 2024). Research shows leaders can leverage feedback to make necessary adjustments and continuously refine the organizational culture. Building a culture of openness demands intentional efforts from leadership to adopt transparency, encourage employee feedback, and promote participation. By establishing trust, leading by example, empowering employees, and implementing transparent systems and processes, leaders can create a positive work environment where employees feel valued and engaged. This, in turn, leads to heightened employee satisfaction, improved retention, and enhanced organizational performance. *Figure 2* below describes the benefits of openness and the steps involved.

Figure 2. The benefits of openness

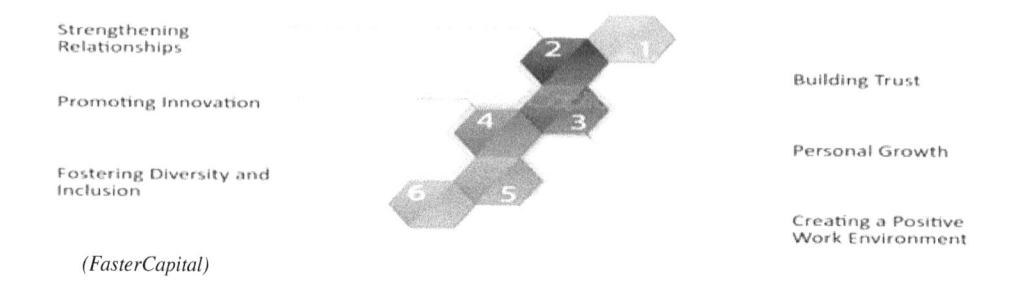

The Benefits of Openness

Strengthening Relationships

Promoting Innovation

Fostering Diversity and Inclusion

Building Trust

Personal Growth

Creating a Positive Work Environment

(FasterCapital)

Navigating Difficult Conversations

Cultivating trust and transparency within organizations requires finesse when dealing with thorny issues, the courage to admit mistakes, and compassion when sharing unpalatable news. However, some contend that excessive openness and honesty can undermine trust and transparency. Consider a scenario where an employee's termination occurs due to factors unrelated to their job performance. In that case, the employer may feel that sharing that information with the rest of the organization is inappropriate. Establishing this trust requires humility and sensitivity, which are essential for creating a solid organizational culture. These pivotal elements are the bedrock of an open, collaborative milieu that engenders a more adaptable and invested workforce. Traversing the treacherous terrain of tough conversations is an inescapable reality in professional spheres. These conversations can range from discussing performance issues to resolving harmful conflicts. Hutchison (2020) posits that transparent communication explains organizational events for employees, aligning their actions accordingly. Town hall gatherings exemplify this approach, where executives explain company performance, impending projects, and obstacles.

The recommendations for successfully navigating these conversations include effective communication strategies, such as active listening, a cornerstone technique that facilitates a comprehensive understanding of another's perspective. This entails not merely hearing words but acknowledging emotions and concerns, defusing tension, and adopting collaborative discourse (Legacy Family Services, Inc., 2024). Empathy, another crucial strategy, enables one to pull on another's metaphorical shoes, engendering trust and connection. This approach catalyzes a more imaginative exchange of ideas, often yielding more fruitful outcomes.

Organizational leaders must address missteps and failures by embracing a culture that views errors as learning opportunities rather than sources of shame and nurtures greater trust and innovation. A tripartite approach can achieve this: acknowledgment and analysis, formulation of a corrective plan, and documentation of lessons learned. Accepting responsibility and dissecting the error is paramount when a faux pas occurs. According to Rainey (2024), this process involves soliciting feedback from team members to unearth the root causes of the failure.

Leadership must also possess the means to deliver adverse news with honesty and empathy. Adhering to several best practices, such as meticulous preparation, lucid and concise communication, expressing empathy, soliciting feedback and questions, and diligent follow-up, can effectively execute this arduous task. Before delivering the news, it is crucial to comprehend its potential impact on the recipient; anticipating their emotional response allows for a more compassionate approach, posits Thompson (2023).

The MindTools Content Team (2024) asserts that honesty, openness, and empathetic communication can preserve rather than damage working relationships when delivering negative news. The Journal of Trauma-Injury Infection & Critical Care published research outlining the characteristics that family members most value when receiving bad news from medical professionals. The study found that four factors are critical from the recipient's perspective: the messenger's attitude, message clarity, privacy, and the ability to address questions. Maintaining trust and transparency within an organization is an ongoing endeavor that requires adept navigation of difficult conversations, open acknowledgment of mistakes, and empathetic delivery of bad news. By adopting a culture of transparent communication, organizations can create circumstances where employees feel valued, engaged, and motivated to contribute to collective success.

The Role of Technology in Transparency

Technology is a potent catalyst for transparency, a cornerstone of trust across myriad sectors in our increasingly digitized world. The integration of innovative digital tools into information dissemination processes has revolutionized organizational and governmental operations, ushering in a new era of opportunities and accompanying challenges. The advent of digital tools has irrevocably transformed the realm of diplomatic negotiations. These technological marvels have become indispensable in fostering trust and facilitating the seamless exchange of information. Nevertheless, this digital metamorphosis necessitates a recalibration of trust boundaries. Although the virtual sphere can sustain trust, its initial cultivation in the digital domain remains an enormous task (Eggeling & Versloot, 2022).

Blockchain technology has emerged as a paragon of transparency, offering unparalleled traceability and accountability without a trusted intermediary. Its utility is particularly pronounced in innovative grid operations, enabling many functionalities, including real-time monitoring and consumption analysis. However, this transparency comes at a cost, raising significant privacy concerns that demand a delicate equilibrium between openness and data security (Loreti et al., 2023). In the agricultural sector, digital data platforms have emerged as game-changers. These platforms enhance decision-making processes by providing unprecedented data sharing and processing transparency. Farmers now wield the power to make informed decisions based on a wealth of data. Nevertheless, these platforms must grapple with data ownership, governance, and transparency (Borrero & Mariscal, 2022).

The delicate balance between transparency and security presents a formidable challenge. While surveillance technology bolsters security and public safety, it raises an alarm about privacy infringement and potential misuse. Determining a balance between the benefits of surveillance and individual rights demands a multifaceted approach encompassing legislative measures, public awareness campaigns, and robust technological safeguards (Suresh, 2023). The deployment of big data analytics in national security and law enforcement necessitates transparency to foster public debate and safeguard individual rights. However, operational secrecy and the obscure complexity of algorithms pose significant impediments to achieving this transparency (Moses & Koker, 2017).

In sectors like agriculture, providing users unfettered access to data can lead to a deluge of information that overwhelms rather than empowers. Effective data-sharing solutions must, therefore, strike a balance between transparency and user control to prevent cognitive overload (Linsner et al., 2022). Cryptographic tools such as secure multi-party computation (SMC) offer a promising avenue for reconciling privacy and transparency in systems like blockchain-based smart grids (Loreti et al., 2023). To ensure transparency and ethical integrity in surveillance and data analytics, it is crucial to establish clear policies and rigorous oversight mechanisms (Suresh, 2023; Moses & Koker, 2017). The design of digital tools with a user-centric focus in mind can enhance transparency while mitigating information overload. This approach involves creating intuitive interfaces that explain data flow comprehensibly (Linsner et al., 2022).

An intriguing case study by Lyutiy et al. (2022) underscores the importance of openness and transparency in Ukrainian defense budgeting. This approach has proven instrumental in combating corruption and, when synergized with other hybrid defense tactics and military provisions, can introduce transparent budgeting standards to the sector. While technology presents many opportunities to enhance transparency, it also presents many challenges that require meticulous management. The quest for equilibrium between transparency and data security remains crucial to fostering trust. Technological innovation, legislative frameworks, and user-centric strategies can synergistically achieve this intricate balance.

The Future of Trust and Transparency

Many cutting-edge technologies and trends are emerging as potent catalysts for change in the rapidly developing organizational trust and transparency landscape. With its indomitable ledger system, blockchain technology is the vanguard of this transformation. This decentralized marvel is revolutionizing supply chain management and financial systems, obliterating the opacity that has long plagued these sectors. Imagine a world where product authenticity is no longer a question but a certainty. Blockchain makes this a reality, infusing stakeholder confidence with an unprecedented robustness. In the financial realm, it's streamlining arduous processes like Know Your Customer (KYC) and Anti-Money Laundering (AML), fortifying security, and bolstering compliance (Girish & Naik, 2024; Nofal et al.,

2024). These standards and the international web of laws, regulations, and procedures protect financial institutions against fraud, corruption, money laundering, and terrorist financing. Yet, the path to blockchain nirvana is not without its thorns. Technical intricacies, regulatory labyrinths, and user adoption hurdles loom, and organizations must navigate these treacherous waters with meticulous planning and stakeholder engagement.

Artificial Intelligence (AI) and its more transparent cousin, Explainable AI (XAI), reshape the decision-making landscape. These cognitive juggernauts are propelling operational efficiencies to stratospheric heights. However, the onus lies on organizations to ensure these systems remain transparent and accountable. XAI, in particular, is pivotal in demystifying the often-opaque world of AI decisions, addressing ethical quandaries, and fostering responsible AI governance (Fahlevi et al., 2023; Muthukrishnan et al., 2024). While AI's potential in risk assessment and operational enhancement is undeniable, it demands robust ethical and privacy frameworks to flourish (Rane et al., 2023).

Cloud security innovations continue to be a linchpin of the trust architecture. As organizations increasingly gravitate toward cloud services, novel security paradigms become indispensable. The "zero trust" model, with its mantra of "never trust, always verify," is redefining access control; this approach is a bulwark against data breaches and unauthorized intrusions (Ragula, 2024). Secure Access Service Edge (SASE) further fortifies this defense, combining network security with wide-area networking to provide a seamless and secure cloud experience. Emerging technologies are catalyzing business model innovation in the realm of sustainability. For instance, blockchain helps track carbon credits and ensures adherence to environmental standards. This technological intervention amplifies corporate social responsibility efforts and fosters sustainable practices (Moiana et al., 2023). Stakeholder involvement in these green initiatives is crucial, serving as a conduit for trust and transparency.

Data privacy concerns have escalated significantly, requiring strong governance frameworks. Compliance with regulations like the General Data Protection Regulation (GDPR) and the California Consumer Privacy Act (CCPA) is no longer optional but imperative. These legal guardrails ensure compliance and build trust with increasingly privacy-conscious stakeholders (Fahlevi et al., 2023; Muthukrishnan et al., 2024). The GDPR is the world's most rigid privacy and security law, and the CCPA of 2018 gives consumers more control over the personal information that businesses collect about them.

Transparent communication about data practices is the cornerstone of this trust-building exercise. Organizations can meet and exceed stakeholder expectancies by embracing these avant-garde trends and technologies. In this complex tapestry of trust and transparency, those who adapt and innovate will undoubtedly lead the charge toward a more accountable and transparent future. *Figure 3* below shows Yee and colleagues' ten technology trends in 2024. McKinsey published a report in 2024 that outlines the expected evolution of technology trends. This report contains a wealth of information, including generative AI, machine learning, quantum computing, etc. Those interested in more information can consult the report by Yee et al. (2024).

Figure 3. 10 Technology trends 2024

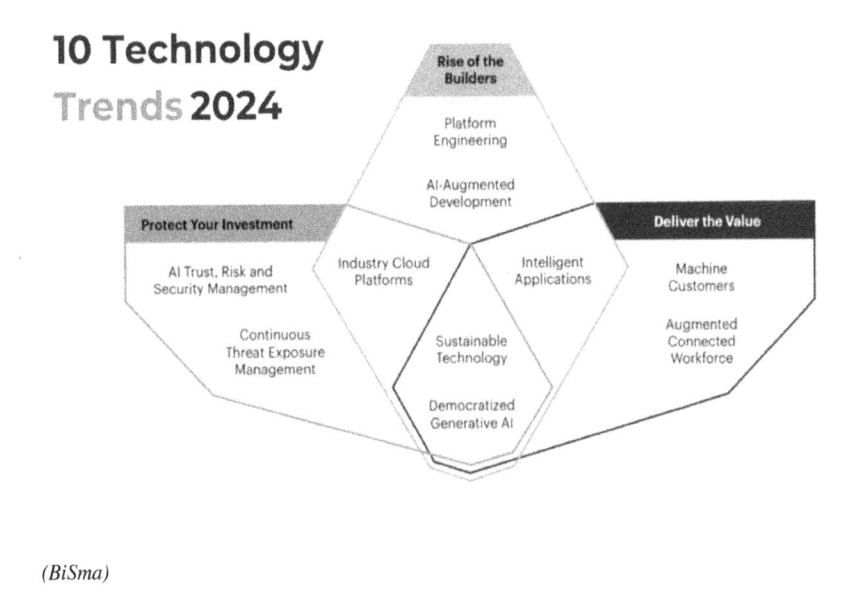

(BiSma)

CONCLUSION AND SUMMARY

Trust and transparency have emerged as critical pillars for sustainable success in today's rapidly evolving business landscape. As explored throughout this chapter, these elements are not just axioms but fundamental principles that shape organizational culture, stakeholder relationships, and overall performance. The key strategies we have discussed form a comprehensive approach to building trust and transparency. Organizations must cultivate a culture of openness by encouraging open communication at all levels, leading by example, and empowering employees through decentralized decision-making. Navigating difficult conversations skillfully is crucial, as well as employing active listening and empathy, viewing mistakes as learning opportunities, and delivering negative news with honesty and compassion.

Leveraging technology for transparency is another vital strategy, which includes implementing blockchain for enhanced traceability, using AI and XAI for efficient and understandable decision-making, and adopting cloud security innovations like the "zero trust" model. However, it's essential to balance transparency with privacy by developing robust data governance frameworks, complying with regulations like GDPR and CCPA, and communicating data practices clearly to stakeholders. Integrating sustainability initiatives, such as using technology to track and ensure adherence to environmental standards and involving stakeholders in green initiatives, further builds trust.

The time to act is now. In an era where trust is a valuable commodity, organizations must proactively implement transparency initiatives to assess the current state through a thorough audit of their organization's transparency practices, identifying gaps and areas for improvement. Develop a transparency roadmap that outlines steps to enhance trust and transparency across all levels of your organization. Investing in technology is crucial. Allocating resources to implement innovative technologies like blockchain, AI, and advanced security systems can bolster your transparency efforts. Equally important is training your workforce, equipping your employees with the skills and knowledge to navigate difficult conversations, and upholding transparency principles.

Engaging stakeholders should be an ongoing process. Regularly communicate your transparency initiatives to all stakeholders, seeking their input and feedback. Finally, measure and iterate on your efforts by establishing a measurement system to track the impact of your transparency initiatives and continuously refine your approach based on results and stakeholder feedback. By embracing these strategies and taking decisive action, organizations can forge stronger relationships, enhance their reputation, and position themselves for long-term success in an increasingly complex and interconnected world. Remember, trust and transparency are not destinations but ongoing journeys that require constant attention and nurturing. Start your journey today and reap the rewards of a more open, accountable, and successful organization tomorrow.

As organizations progress in their transparency journey, the next critical evolution lies in operationalizing these principles through systematic data utilization. The transition from establishing trust through transparency to leveraging data for strategic decision-making represents a natural progression in organizational maturity. While transparency initiatives create the foundation for stakeholder trust, the ability to harness data effectively transforms this thrust into actionable insights that drive organizational success. The interconnected nature of modern business demands that leaders maintain open communication channels and develop sophisticated mechanisms for processing and analyzing the information flowing through these channels. As we shift our focus from building trust frameworks to implementing data-driven decision-making processes, we recognize that transparency and data analytics are complementary forces in the modern leadership toolkit. Organizations that successfully bridge these domains position themselves to maintain stakeholder confidence and leverage this trust for more informed, strategic decision-making in an increasingly digital landscape.

REFERENCES

Ashish, K. T., & Abhijit. P. D. (2022). Relationship Transparency-Trust Cycle: A Matter of Trust and Competency for Frontline Managers.

Bayborodova, E. Y. (2019). The Relationship Of Trust, Personal Characteristics Of Students With The Socio-Psychological Climate Of The Educational Organization. *Bulletin of the Moscow State Regional University (Psychology)*, (4), 6–15. DOI: 10.18384/2310-7235-2019-4-6-15

Borrero, J. D., & Mariscal, J. (2022). A Case Study of a Digital Data Platform for the Agricultural Sector: A Valuable Decision Support System for Small Farmers. *Agriculture*, 12(6), 767. DOI: 10.3390/agriculture12060767

Chan, G. (/2022). How To Develop A Culture Of Openness In The Workplace. *Forbes*. https://www.forbes.com/sites/goldiechan/2022/08/25/how-to-develop-a-culture-of-openness-in-the-workplace/

Craig, H. (2019). 10 Ways To Build Trust in a Relationship. *PositivePsychology. Com*. https://positivepsychology.com/build-trust/

Defy Expectations. (2024). *Culture of Openness*. https://www.defyexpectations.co.uk/culture-of-openness

Dezao, T. (2024). Enhancing transparency in AI-powered customer engagement. *Journal of AI, Robotics & Workplace Automation*. https://hstalks.com/article/8574/enhancing-transparency-in-ai-powered-customer-enga/?business

Eggeling, K. A., & Versloot, L. (2022). Taking Trust Online: Digitalisation and the practice of information sharing in diplomatic negotiations. *Review of International Studies*. https://www.semanticscholar.org/paper/Taking-trust-online%3A-Digitalisation-and-the-of-in-Eggeling-Versloot/6e2c10149530587f4e6ae6c386d5aadce029a2c9

Ercanbrack Michelle Blog Post. (May 2023). *5 Powerful Benefits of Transparency in Business*. BambooHR Blog. https://www.bamboohr.com/blog/creating-transparency-in-workplace

Girish, R. N., & Naik, P. (2024). Transforming Bookstore Dynamics Through Blockchain Integration for Revolutionizing Trust, Transparency and Efficiency. *2024 5th International Conference for Emerging Technology (INCET)*. https://www.semanticscholar.org/paper/Transforming-Bookstore-Dynamics-Through-Blockchain-Naik-Naik/9d2d8a2627f28303dae4da64900a39c300b33d06

Gupta, S. (2021). Why Trust Matters in Your Relationship and How to Build It. *overall Mind*. https://www.verywellmind.com/how-to-build-trust-in-a-relationship-5207611

Halevi, M., Aisjah, S., & Djazuli, A. (2023). Corporate Governance in the Digital Age: A Comprehensive Review of Blockchain, AI, and Big Data Impacts, Opportunities, and Challenges. *E3S Web of Conferences, 448*, 2056. DOI: 10.1051/e3sconf/202344802056

Hancock, P. A., Kessler, T. T., Kaplan, A. D., Stowers, K., Brill, J. C., Billings, D. R., Schaefer, K. E., & Szalma, J. L. (2023). How and why humans trust: A meta-analysis and elaborated model. *Frontiers in Psychology, 14. Frontiers in Psychology*, 1081086, 1081086. DOI: 10.3389/fpsyg.2023.1081086 PMID: 37051611

Hosseini, M., Shahri, A., Phalp, K., & Ali, R. (2016). A Modelling Language for Transparency Requirements in Business Information Systems. In S. Nurcan, P. Soffer, M. Bajec, & J. Eder (Eds.), *LNCS sublibrary. SL 3, Information systems and applications, incl. Internet/Web, and HCI: 9694, Advanced information systems engineering workshops:28th International Conference, CAiSE 2016,Ljubljana, Slovenia,June 13-17, 2016. Proceedings,* 239–254. Springer. DOI: 10.1007/978-3-319-39696-5_15

Hutchison, J. (2020). *Transparent Communication - Toward a Respectful Workplace*. https://workplace.msu.edu/transparent-communication/

Ishii, A., Kawahata, Y., & Okano, N. (2023). Significant Role of Trust and Distrust in Social Simulation. In Peaslee Levine, M. (Ed.), *The Psychology of Trust*. IntechOpen., DOI: 10.5772/intechopen.101538

Jambon, M., & Malti, T. (2022). Developmental Relations between Children's Peer Relationship Quality and Prosocial Behavior: The Mediating Role of Trust. *The Journal of Genetic Psychology*, 183(3), 197–210. DOI: 10.1080/00221325.2022.2030293 PMID: 35088652

Legacy Family Services, Inc. (2024). *Mastering the Art of Navigating Difficult Conversations: Tips and Strategies for Effective Communication - Legacy Family Services, Inc*. https://www.legacyfs.org/mastering-the-art-of-navigating-difficult-conversations-tips-and-strategies-for-effective-communication/

Linsner, S., Steinbrink, E., Kuntke, F., Franken, J., & Reuter, C. (2022). Supporting users in data disclosure scenarios in agriculture through transparency. *Behaviour & Information Technology*, 41(10), 2151–2173. DOI: 10.1080/0144929X.2022.2068070

Loreti, P., Bracciale, L., Raso, E., Giuseppe, B., Sanseverino, E. R., & Gallo, P. (2023). Privacy and Transparency in Blockchain-Based Smart Grid Operations. *IEEE Access*. https://www.semanticscholar.org/paper/Privacy-and-Transparency-in-Blockchain-Based-Smart-Loreti-Bracciale/e32003129c9ac9cb7b600316678585fff19316f7

Lyutiy, I., Petlenko, Y., & Drozd, N. (2022). The Importance Of Openness And Transparency In The Budget Process In The Defense And Security Sector Of Ukraine. *Financial and Credit Activity Problems of Theory and Practice*, 6(47), 99–110. DOI: 10.55643/fcaptp.6.47.2022.3900

Moiana, D., Manotti, J., Ghezzi, A., & Rangone, A. (. (2023). Emerging Technologies: A Catalyst for Sustainable Business Model Innovation.

Moses, L. B., & Koker, L. D. (2017). Open Secrets: Balancing Operational Secrecy and Transparency in the Collection and Use of Data by National Security and Law Enforcement Agencies. *Melbourne University Law Review*, 41(530).

Muthukrishnan, M., Suhas, J., Kapil, K. S., & Gowrisankar, K. (2024). Demystifying Explainable AI: Understanding, Transparency, and Trust. *International Journal for Multidisciplinary Research*. https://www.semanticscholar.org/paper/Demystifying-Explainable-AI%3A-Understanding%2C-and-Muthusubramanian-Jangoan/20e91e6e90bc94b11056cd76094337ac2ede0eb1

Nofal, M. I., Nasim, M., Muaadh, M., Al Khaldy, M., Sowan, B. I., & Almalahmeh, T. M. (2024). A Framework for Using Blockchain-Enabled Supply Chain Management to Enhance Transparency, Traceability, and Trust. *International Conference Control and Robots*. https://www.semanticscholar.org/paper/A-Framework-for-Using-Blockchain-Enabled-Supply-to-Nofal-Matar/fa0a77c09b00e7484c9d84f3267ccbb46a059721

Obie, H. O., Ukwella, J., Madampe, K., Grundy, J., & Shahin, M. (2023). Towards an Understanding of Developers' Perceptions of Transparency in Software Development: A Preliminary Study. DOI: 10.1109/ASEW60602.2023.00010

Polly Blog Post. (n.d.). *8 Ways Employee Feedback Helps Define a Positive Company Culture*. Retrieved August 8, 2024, from https://www.polly.ai/blog/4-ways-employee-feedback-will-help-define-positive-company-culture

Ragula, A. (2024). Emerging Trends in Cloud Security: Zero Trust and SASE. *International Journal for Research in Applied Science and Engineering Technology*, 12(6), 10–17. DOI: 10.22214/ijraset.2024.62457

Rainey, J. (2024). *Embracing Mistakes in Business: A Guide to Turning Setbacks into Success*. https://jennarainey.com/embracing-mistakes-in-business-a-guide-to-turning-setbacks-into-success/

Rane, N., Choudhary, S., & Rane, J. (2023). Blockchain and Artificial Intelligence (AI) integration is needed to revolutionize security and transparency in finance. SSRN *Electronic Journal.* Advance online publication. DOI: 10.2139/ssrn.4644253

Raz, A. E., Niemiec, E., Howard, H. C., Sterckx, S., Cockbain, J., & Prainsack, B. (2020). Transparency, consent and Trust in the use of customers' data by an online genetic testing company: An Exploratory survey among 23andMe users. *New Genetics & Society*, 39(4), 459–482. DOI: 10.1080/14636778.2020.1755636

RedHat. (2020). *Understanding open organizational culture*. RedHat. https://www.redhat.com/en/topics/open-culture

Roberts, N. F. (2020). The Psychology Of Trust Explains How Institutions Can Regain It Once Lost. *Forbes*. https://www.forbes.com/sites/nicolefisher/2020/09/01/the-psychology-of-trust--how-institutions-can-regain-it-once-lost/

Suresh, J. (2023). Surveillance Technology: Balancing Security And Privacy In The Digital Age. *EPRA International Journal of Multidisciplinary Research*. https://www.semanticscholar.org/paper/Surveillance-Technology%3a-Balancing-Security-And-In-Javvaji/a18d82aa246506494a8510be4f07c507ea8e90ba

The MindTools Content Team. (2024). *Delivering Bad News - Communicating Well Under Pressure*. https://www.mindtools.com/a0byhfl/delivering-bad-news

Thompson, S. (2023). *What are the best practices for delivering bad news with empathy and honesty? | LinkedIn*. https://www.linkedin.com/pulse/what-best-practices-delivering-bad-news-empathy-honesty-thompson/

Vyas, D. (2023). *Transparency in the Workplace: What Is It and Why Does It Matter? | LinkedIn*. LinkedIn. https://www.linkedin.com/pulse/transparency-workplace-what-why-does-matter-vyas-l-i-o-n-/

Yee, L., Chui, M., Roberts, R., & Issler, M. (2024). *McKinsey technology trends outlook 2024 | McKinsey*. https://www.mckinsey.com/capabilities/mckinsey-digital/our-insights/the-top-trends-in-tech#/

Zak, P. J. (2017). *The Neuroscience of Trust*. Harvard Business Review. https://hbr.org/2017/01/the-neuroscience-of-trust

Chapter 13
Leveraging Data and Analytics for Strategic Decision-Making

ABSTRACT

This chapter explores how organizations can leverage data analytics for strategic decision-making in today's rapidly evolving business landscape. It emphasizes the importance of data literacy and cultivating a data-driven culture to enhance competitiveness and drive innovation. The text outlines various analytical approaches, from descriptive to prescriptive analytics, and highlights the transformative potential of machine learning and AI in extracting insights from vast datasets. Real-world examples demonstrate how companies like Amazon and Netflix have successfully used data-driven strategies. The chapter also addresses challenges in implementing data-driven approaches, including resistance to change, data quality issues, and skills gaps. It guides the identification of key performance indicators, the collection and cleaning of data, and the translation of insights into actionable strategies. Effective communication and stakeholder engagement are essential in driving organizational change.

INTRODUCTION

In an environment where data has become the lifeblood of modern business, organizations face the critical challenge of transforming vast amounts of information into meaningful strategic decisions. This chapter explores the comprehensive framework of data-driven decision-making, examining how organizations can effectively harness the power of analytics to gain competitive advantages in an increasingly digital world. From establishing robust Key Performance Indicators (KPIs) to implement

DOI: 10.4018/979-8-3693-5553-4.ch013

Copyright © 2025, IGI Global Scientific Publishing. Copying or distributing in print or electronic forms without written permission of IGI Global is prohibited.

advanced analytical methodologies, we delve into the practical aspects of building a data-driven organization that can thrive in today's complex business environment.

The journey toward data-driven excellence is not merely about collecting and analyzing information; it requires a fundamental shift in organizational culture, the development of new capabilities, and the careful balance of technical expertise with business acumen. Examining real-world examples from industry leaders like Amazon, Netflix, and Google, this chapter provides actionable insights into how organizations can overcome common challenges in data implementation while fostering a culture that embraces empirical decision-making.

As we explore the evolution from basic descriptive analytics to sophisticated predictive and prescriptive models, readers will gain a comprehensive understanding of how to translate data insights into tangible business outcomes. At its core, this chapter serves as both a strategic guide and a practical roadmap for organizations seeking to leverage data analytics for improved decision-making. This guide covers the tools and techniques needed to use data successfully to improve a business. It addresses data quality, advanced analysis, and managing change.

DATA-DRIVEN TO TRANSFORM THE BUSINESS LANDSCAPES

The power of data is driving a tremendous transition in the ultramodern commercial landscape. This data-driven revolution reshapes diligence by enabling companies to make informed opinions that enhance competitiveness and drive invention. This section investigates why data-driven decision-making is needed in colorful diligence and provides real-world exemplifications of enterprises that effectively use data for strategic benefit. This metamorphosis is characterized by using data analytics to inform opinions and drive invention.

The Necessity of Data-Driven Decision-Making

In today's dynamic business environment, data-driven decision-making has transformed from a simple tool to a source of empowerment for professionals. It has become imperative for organizations to harness the potency of data, optimize operations, forecast market trends, and deliver revealed customer experiences. This modus operandi empowers professionals to make judicious decisions predicated on empirical evidence, culminating in enhanced performance and a more decisive competitive edge (Inclusion Cloud, 2023). In the rapidly transmuting business landscape, the aptitude for data-driven decision-making has transcended trendiness to become a necessity. Businesses that skillfully use data can quickly adapt to market fluctuations, anticipate customer needs, and position themselves more effectively in the market.

This agility is helpful and pivotal for survival and sustainable growth, enabling businesses to innovate and capitalize on developing opportunities. Data-driven decision-making (DM) uses pertinent data to inform strategic choices and organizational and operational actions. This approach allows businesses to transcend intuition and experiences, prioritizing evidence-based analysis to make informed decisions (Ramadhan & Niam, 2024). According to Cloud Forces (2023), companies can gain profound insights into market trends, customer preferences, and operational performance by leveraging data, facilitating efficiency, enhancing risk management, and crafting personalized customer experiences.

Embracing a Data-Driven Culture

In the relentless pursuit of data mastery, organizations must assiduously cultivate a data-centric ethos to harness its transformative power. This entails fostering data literacy, nurturing collaborative synergies around information, and rendering data accessible and actionable across the organizational hierarchy. Embracing this paradigm allows enterprises to integrate data-driven decision-making into their strategic planning and operational processes, resulting in significant value and positive impact (Tsvetomira, 2022; RIB Software Blog, 2024). A holistic approach is necessary for this transformation, enabling every level of the organization to interpret, analyze, and leverage data effectively. Businesses are experiencing significant changes in problem-solving, risk evaluation, and new idea development as data flow becomes more prevalent. This makes businesses more flexible, quick to respond, and proactive.

Real-World Examples of Data-Driven Success

In the pantheon of data-driven inventions, Amazon is a trailblazer, applying analytics with unequaled dexterity to metamorphose its force chain, craft bespoke client recommendations, and elevate functional efficiency. This data-centric approach has been the linchpin of Amazon's gradual ascent and ascendancy in e-commerce. As the epitome of online retail, Amazon leverages data analytics to anticipate demand, maximize efficiency, and craft client recommendations with precision. This data-driven modus operandi augments functional effectiveness and catalyzes client satisfaction, cementing Amazon's insuperable request position (Leadzen.ai Blog, 2024; Tsvetomira, 2022).

In entertainment, Netflix has orchestrated a veritable revolution through its judicious data analytics operation. The streaming mammoth leverages data to raise the depths of bystander predispositions and curate substantiated joyful recommendations, significantly supplementing stoner engagement and retention (Pothineni, 2023). Netflix's data-driven strategy extends beyond pleased suggestions, informing product opinions and shaping the veritable fabric of its original programming. This adapted approach engenders heightened subscriber engagement and fidelity, buttressing Netflix's preeminence in the fiercely competitive streaming geography (Ilkiu, 2024; Leadzen.ai Blog, 2024). The artificial titan General Electric (GE) has embraced data-driven strategies to metamorphose its operations, while Google and McDonald's have also exercised the power of data to achieve strategic advantages.

GE employs data analytics and Internet of Things (IoT) technologies to call out failures and optimize conservation schedules, yielding substantial reductions in time-out and attendant cost savings (Tawil et al., 2023). Google, a leader in data-driven decision-making, has enhanced directorial effectiveness and reduced energy consumption in data centers by utilizing sophisticated data analysis techniques. Google has achieved advanced platform performance and satisfaction by evaluating directorial traits and implementing feedback systems. Their deployment of machine literacy to optimize data center operations has resulted in fabulous energy savings (reddit, 2023). In a culinary masterstroke, McDonald's uses data perceptivity to tailor menus based on meteorological conditions and unique events, optimizing its low-profit, high-volume business model, particularly in response to demanding demand (Leadzen.ai Blog, 2024).

Challenges and Opportunities

Organizations face a variety of challenges when implementing data-driven decision-making strategies efficiently. Small and medium-sized enterprises (SMEs), in particular, grapple with the Sisyphean task of surmounting resource constraints and bridging the ocean of data wisdom backbones (Tawil et al., 2023). This dearth of coffers and wit frequently relegates SMEs to the fringe of the data revolution, stymying their capability to harness its transformative eventuality. Notwithstanding these impediments, the outlook for invention and growth through data-driven strategies remains vast and irresistible. Enterprises willing to invest in the skills and technologies have many opportunities. The prudent allocation of funds towards data knowledge, structure, and gift acquisition can bring about a significant transformation, enabling resource-constrained associations to transform into agile, data-driven entities capable of navigating the turbulent waters of the ultramodern business landscape with unparalleled agility and foresight.

The data-driven revolution has engendered a seismic shift in the business landscape, empowering organizations to make thoughtful, empirically grounded decisions that catalyze innovation and bolster competitiveness. This paradigm has converted data into a strategic asset of unparalleled value, enabling enterprises to navigate the intricate complexities of the digital age with unprecedented judgment. By assimilating the modus operandi of successful companies and assiduously addressing implementation challenges, businesses can harness the transformative power of data to survive and thrive in an increasingly mercurial market. Adopting data-driven decision-making has grown from a mere strategic advantage to an essential requirement for future success—a fundamental requirement for organizations striving to stay relevant and achieve sustainable growth. As the business world becomes increasingly bifurcated between the data-savvy and the data-naïve, effectively interpreting and operationalizing data insights will emerge as the quintessential differentiator, separating the vanguard of innovation from those consigned to obsolescence.

IDENTIFYING KEY PERFORMANCE INDICATORS (KPIS)

In organizational efficacy, discerning and delineating appropriate Key Performance Indicators (KPIs) is imperative for entities striving to gauge and improve their operational prowess. This sagacious methodology empowers stewards to synchronize their quantitative benchmarks with corporate aspirations, engendering judicious, data-centric determinations that propel triumph. The prudent selection of KPIs furnishes tangible metrics, explaining how an enterprise attains its predetermined objectives (Fone Ng, 2023). When astutely curated, these indicators yield invaluable insight that catalyzes well-informed decision-making processes and fuels organizational ascendancy. By embracing this strategic paradigm, leaders can navigate the labyrinthine landscape of modern commerce with heightened perspicacity, leveraging the power of empirical data to sculpt a trajectory of sustained success and growth. Implementing meticulously chosen KPIs serves as a lodestar, guiding corporations through market volatility and competitive pressures while illuminating areas ripe for enhancement and innovation.

Aligning KPIs with Business Objectives

Finding effective Key Performance Indicators (KPIs) is the first step in the complex process of organizational optimization. It requires careful alignment with the organization's overall goals and strategic plan. This congruence forms the bedrock of a laser-focused, high-impact performance quantification framework (Inamdar et al., 2014). The quintessential first stride in KPI identification necessitates harmonizing with your organization's visionary ethos, raison d'être, and strategic imperatives (LinkedIn Community, 2024a). This mutually beneficial relationship ensures that the inspected measures directly align with the trajectory and purpose of your company. Consider an enterprise that aspires to embody innovation in its industry;

such an entity would be wise to assess factors such as research and development yields, client satisfaction with novel offerings, and market penetration in the early stages of product development.

One must embark upon a tripartite odyssey to orchestrate this alignment with virtuosic precision. First, delineate your organization's strategic objectives, leaving no room for ambiguity or misinterpretation (PsychWeb, 2023). Next, define these objectives with specific, quantifiable outcomes to track progress with scientific rigor. Finally, handpick KPIs that serve as direct barometers of advancement toward these outcomes and act as unfailing guidance in pursuing organizational excellence. This scientific method of KPI selection sharpens the focus of performance monitoring while fostering a data-driven decision-making culture. By establishing an unbreakable link between strategic goals and measurable metrics, organizations can navigate the turbulent waters of modern commerce with unprecedented skill, transforming abstract visions into tangible, actionable insights that propel them to the pinnacle of success in their respective domains.

Choosing Metrics that Truly Matter

In complicated performance management, carefully selecting Key Performance Indicators (KPIs) is a pivotal linchpin. These painstakingly picked measures act as blazing beacons, illuminating the way to organizational success and directing decision-making with unwavering accuracy. The art of KPI curation demands a laser-focused approach, eschewing the temptation of metric proliferation in favor of a curated constellation of truly impactful indicators. People with excellent sense, like Eide Bailly (2023), support this simple strategy because it helps focus mental resources and actions, which makes performance-tracking programs more effective.

An exemplary KPI characterizes its inherent measurability, a feature that (Paredes, 2023) rightly emphasizes as crucial. These quantitative criteria, tracked consistently across temporal dimensions, enable firms to sail the stormy waves of commerce with data-driven aplomb. Moreover, the astute performance architect recognizes the symbiotic relationship between leading and lagging indicators, as explained by the LinkedIn Community (2024a). This dualistic approach, marrying predictive metrics with retrospective gauges, engenders a holistic panorama of organizational health, akin to a financial Janus, gazing into the future and reflecting upon the past.

The availability and quality of data, acting as the foundation of performance metrics, determine the overall effectiveness of KPIs. The LinkedIn Community (2024a) wisely tells businesses to ensure they have access to reliable, timely, and consistent sources of information. Without this fundamental component, even the most effective KPIs become meaningless aspirations that cannot provide businesses with valuable insights. As organizations navigate the Scylla of data overload and the unpredictability of insufficient metrics, the judicious application of these principles serves as a lodestar, guiding them toward a performance management paradigm that is both robust and nuanced. By embracing this sophisticated approach to KPI selection, entities can transmute raw data into strategic gold, forging a path toward sustained excellence in the crucible of modern commerce.

Practical Tips for KPI Selection and Implementation

Identifying and implementing Key Performance Indicators (KPIs) demands a nuanced choreography in the intricate dance of organizational optimization. The savvy performance architect embarks upon this odyssey by enlisting a diverse coterie of stakeholders, as Sivakumar and Dinesh (2023) sagaciously advocated, ensuring a kaleidoscopic perspective on the multifaceted sphere of performance quantification. With wise restraint, one initiates this metric ballet with a carefully curated ensemble of KPIs, typically numbering between five and ten, as counseled by Keck and Ross (2014).

This economical approach is a bulwark against the pernicious specter of metric overload, allowing the organization to pirouette gracefully through the complex steps of performance measurement. As the business landscape undergoes rapid metamorphosis, the astute practitioner continuously reviews and refines the chosen KPIs to align them with developing corporate priorities (Sivakumar & Dinesh, 2023). According to Keck and Ross (2014), data quality is the foundation for performance building, necessitating robust systems and procedures to safeguard the integrity and reliability of the metrics' raw material.

The artful execution of this KPI ballet extends beyond mere selection and measurement, encompassing the crucial act of communication. Inamdar et al. (2014) underscore the imperative of elucidating the chosen KPIs, their significance, and their symbiotic relationship with organizational goals for all pertinent stakeholders, fostering a shared understanding and collective purpose. In this digital age, the thoughtful leveraging of innovative business intelligence and analytics tools serves as a technological deus ex machina, automating the Herculean tasks of data collection, analysis, and reporting, posit Keck and Ross.

For those navigating the labyrinthine corridors of complex, multi-criteria decision-making scenarios, the fuzzy Analytic Hierarchy Process (AHP) emerges as a powerful ally. Ganguly and Rai (2018) demonstrated that this advanced methodology provides a lens for reframing and assessing the perceived significance and satisfaction linked to various KPIs. By adopting this multidimensional approach to KPI selection and execution, businesses can transform the abstract idea of performance into a natural, actionable framework, driving themselves toward the peak of operational excellence in the ever-changing theater of contemporary commerce.

Prioritizing KPIs

Selecting key performance indicators (KPIs) in organizational performance demands a nuanced and strategic approach. A judicious amalgamation of financial, customer-centric, operational, and developmental metrics is paramount for a holistic appraisal of corporate vitality (Inamdar et al., 2014). This multifaceted methodology ensures a panoramic perspective on the organization's well-being and efficacy. By comparing perceived importance to current performance, the Importance-Performance Analysis (IPA) model effectively sets KPI priorities (Ganguly & Rai, 2018).

This matrix-based evaluation illuminates which indicators warrant immediate intervention and which are thriving. The bedrock of KPI selection lies in a crystalline comprehension of the organization's raison d'être, aspirational vision, and strategic imperatives. This foundational understanding facilitates the identification of metrics that genuinely mirror corporate priorities and propel progress toward the overarching objectives. Several salient characteristics in the KPI selection process demand consideration: relevance to organizational goals, quantifiable measurability, actionable insights, and timely information provision for proactive decision-making. The plethora of potential metrics necessitates a discerning approach to KPI prioritization, ensuring a laser focus on the true determinants of organizational success.

The transmutation of strategy into concrete, quantifiable KPIs marks the next crucial phase. This process entails deconstructing lofty objectives into tangible metrics amenable to tracking and analysis (Inamdar et al., 2014). For instance, a corporation aiming to augment customer satisfaction might adopt KPIs, such as customer retention rate, Net Promoter Score (NPS), or mean response time to customer inquiries. The culmination of this process yields a curated set of potential KPIs, which must then undergo further refinement and prioritization based on their criticality to the organization's mission and strategic trajectory.

Strategies for Prioritization

In the intricate shade of organizational strategy, the art of KPI prioritization emerges as a pivotal thread. A prudent approach necessitates alignment with strategic imperatives, ensuring that the identified criteria resonate with the organization's most critical objectives (LinkedIn Community, 2024a). We must weave this strategic concordance with a nuanced consideration of different stakeholder requirements, encompassing the instructional essentials of directors, workers, and external realities. The prioritization process further necessitates a scrupulous assessment of impact and actionability, elevating KPIs that quantify vital business aspects and yield perceptivity conducive to palpable enhancement (Fone Ng, 2023).

Striking a delicate equilibrium between short-term functional extremities and long-term strategic end goals is crucial, ensuring a comprehensive temporal perspective on the named criteria (Poleski, 2023). The capstone of this regular prioritization process yields a refined set of KPIs that transcend bare data collection, instead serving as essential catalysts for organizational success. The essence does not lie in exhaustively monitoring every metric but in a targeted approach that highlights the most valuable insights and drives significant progress.

This strategic curation of KPIs empowers leaders to make more informed decisions, optimize resource allocation, and eventually realize their strategic vision. The accompanying data-driven framework is a pivotal tool for measuring and enhancing organizational performance, fostering a culture of continuous improvement, and aligning collaborative efforts toward achieving crucial business objectives. *Figure 1* shows the best practices for identifying and monitoring KPIs and metrics.

Figure 1. How to choose the right KPIs

How to Choose the Right KPIs

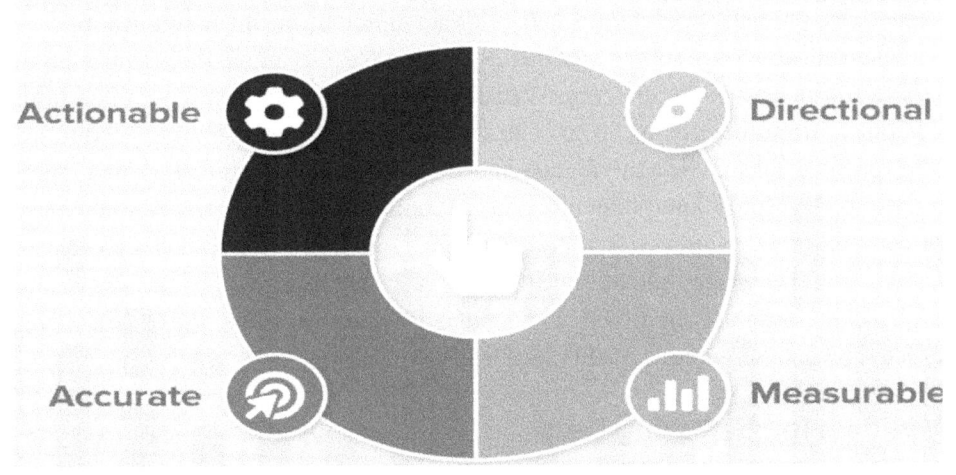

- Actionable
- Directional
- Accurate
- Measurable

(AgencyAnalytics)

COLLECTING AND CLEANING DATA: THE FOUNDATION OF RELIABLE INSIGHTS

Data-driven decision-making often overlooks the critical aspects of data collection and preparation. Inclusion Cloud (2023) states that data quality is paramount to avoid flawed conclusions, misguided strategies, inefficiencies, and financial losses. High-quality data is essential for accurate analyses, predictions, and business decisions (Atlan, 2023). In the following sections, we will discuss the importance of data quality, methods for gathering and cleaning data, and practical advice for maintaining data integrity.

Importance of Data Quality

The essence of data integrity reigns supreme in analytical prowess and strategic insight. The integrity of information, a cornerstone of rational decision-making, stands as an indomitable bulwark against the perils of misguided insights. In this epoch of big data's ascendancy, the triad of volume, velocity, and variety poses a formidable challenge to maintaining the genuineness of our digital assets. The quest for high-caliber data transcends mere aspiration; it is imperative to construct dependable predictive paradigms and cultivate judicious business stratagems.

The ramifications of subpar data quality reverberate throughout the organizational echelons with devastating efficacy. Such deficiencies engender a cascade of harmful outcomes, from the erosion of trust to the inflation of operational expenditures. The repercussions of inaccurate customer data manifest as ineffectual marketing maneuvers and squandered sales prospects (180ops, 2024). Furthermore, the specter of compliance infractions looms considerably, heralding potential legal and fiscal tribulations. The magnitude of this difficulty is starkly illustrated by the staggering $3.1 trillion forfeiture endured by U.S. enterprises, a testament to the excessive toll exacted by data of dubious quality, according to 180ops.

Methods for Gathering Data

The birth of data preparation lies in the art of information harvesting, a multifaceted bid encompassing both primary and secondary sources. This intricate data acquisition process integrates various methodologies, each contributing to a comprehensive understanding. There are many ways to collect data, from structured perceptions gathered through surveys and questionnaires to nuanced stories in qualitative interviews. Experimental studies offer a window into the natural world, while data mining excavates patterns from the bedrock of extensive datasets. Web scraping, a digital rustling fashion, plucks ripe information from the rich fields of the internet, contributing to the bountiful crop of knowledge.

Businesses must tend to their instructional crops with scrupulous care and methodical perfection to cultivate a theater of high-quality data. The process begins with judicious data collection, precisely curating applicable information from a constellation of sources—databases, operations, and the burgeoning ecosystem of IoT bias—all aligned with the organization's strategic objectives (Atlan, 2023; Amazon Web Services, Inc., 2024). We rigorously sanctify this original crop, tagging duplicates and precisely grafting in missing rudiments to enhance the data's usability and trust (LinkedIn Community, 2024b; Tableau, n.d.). Atlan says the last step in the alchemy of data integration turns different data sources into a single, centralized repository. The mysterious trades of ETL (Extract, Transform, Load) usually accomplish this, standardizing formats and structures to create an accessible and harmonious educational symphony.

Data Cleaning Techniques

In data operation, the art of data drawing reigns supreme. This process eradicates inaccuracies and inconsistencies, paving the way for pristine datasets. Complete interpreters use a variety of methods to address their challenges: they identify and eliminate missing values, either by drawing them or attributing them to bias; they identify and eliminate duplicates, ensuring each data point stands out; they strictly correct corruptions and check entries for inaccuracies; they regularize formats with unwavering thickness; and they identify outliers, those cunning data points that deviate significantly from the norm. The capstone of these sweats yields datasets of unequaled quality, ready to repel the adversities of analysis (Castordoc, 2024; Walacor, 2024).

Data integrity, the cornerstone of informed decision-making and stakeholder trust, requires constant vigilance. Organizations must employ a range of effective practices to protect this valuable asset. Automated data confirmation, a powerful tool that detects and corrects errors in real-time, is a bulwark against data corruption (LinkedIn Community, 2024b). A robust data governance framework sets the game's rules, defining roles and responsibilities for data quality and security (Atlan, 2023; Walacor, 2024). Comprehensive training programs teach employees to prevent data offenses and uphold data integrity (Walacor, 2024; Sharma, 2023). Finally, robust backup and recovery procedures are in place to prevent data loss and ensure continuity (Walacor, 2024).

The foundation of effective data operation rests on a solid base. Three essential elements form the foundation. First, a well-conceived data armature and structure provide the scaffolding for flawless integration and storage (Atlan, 2023). Second, a robust data quality operation governance, which includes regular checkups and confirmation processes, guarantees the continuous integrity of data resources (Atlan, 2023; LinkedIn Community, 2024b). Third, the strategic use of analytics and business intelligence tools unlocks the potential within data, providing insights and guiding decision-making processes, according to Atlan (2023) and Walacor (2024). These elements form an impregnable fortress of data excellence, driving organizations toward unparalleled success in the data-driven landscape.

ADVANCED ANALYTICS TECHNIQUES: FROM DESCRIPTIVE TO PRESCRIPTIVE

Data analytics has become essential for ultramodern businesses to gain perceptivity, make informed decisions, and drive success. Organizations can use a variety of crucial approaches and a wide range of data analytics methods, from introductory descriptive styles to more advanced prophetic and conventional models, all to extract valuable insights from vast quantities of data. The following pages will examine several analytical approaches, including machine learning, AI, and more.

Diagnostic Analytics

Diagnostic analytics delves into the intricate web of data connections, unraveling the enigmatic shade of events and issues. This sophisticated approach transcends bare description, piercing the veneer of face-position compliance to expose the underpinning unproductive factors (Miller et al., 2009). Diagnostic analytics illuminates the obscure connections that escape casual scrutiny by employing various methods. Drill-down analysis peels back layers of complexity, revealing hidden patterns and trends. Data discovery, a process of exploratory excavation, unearths precious perceptivity buried within vast instructional geographies. Meanwhile, correlations and retrogression analysis forge essential links between variables, quantifying the strength of their associations and prophetic capabilities. These methodologies merge to form a redoubtable magazine on the hunt for understanding, empowering decision-makers to navigate the complicated pathways of reason with unknown wit.

Descriptive Analytics

Data-driven decision-making illuminates the opaque recesses of the past through descriptive analytics—the foundation of data-driven decision-making. This quintessential approach harnesses a panoply of techniques, including the intrepid exploration of data landscapes and the wielding of statistical weaponry, to distill complex datasets into digestible nuggets of insight (Miller et al., 2009). Picture a retail behemoth unraveling the enigmatic threads of its sales history, unveiling the cyclical rhythms of consumer behavior and the ascendancy of coveted commodities. Such revelations, wrought from the crucible of descriptive analytics, empower organizations to navigate the treacherous waters of market volatility with unprecedented acumen.

Descriptive analytics transmutes raw data into golden insights, offering a panoramic vista of historical performance and emergent trends (Warudkar, 2021). This methodological tour de force employs an arsenal of analytical tools, from aggregating disparate data points to excavating hidden patterns through data mining and statistical sorcery. The fruits of this labor manifest in myriad forms, from the crystallization of key performance indicators in business reportage to the taxonomic categorization of consumer archetypes. Market trend prognostication and the vigilant monitoring of operational efficiency further exemplify the versatility of this approach. To facilitate this alchemical transformation, practitioners wield an array of implements, from the ubiquitous Excel to the more specialized realms of Tableau and Power BI (Warudkar, 2021). Consequently, armed organizations can navigate the turbulent waters of contemporary commerce by transforming the lead of unprocessed data into the gold of actionable intelligence.

Predictive Analytics

Predictive analytics, the oracular seer of the data scope, peers into the murky depths of the future, divining potentialities, and probabilities with uncanny precision. This prophetic discipline harnesses the power of statistical models and machine learning algorithms, transmuting historical data into prognosticative insights (Denton, 2023). Envision a telecommunications titan armed with this prescient methodology, identifying customers teetering on the precipice of defection and orchestrating preemptive maneuvers to secure their loyalty (Kobi & Otieno, 2024).

In predictive analytics, many powerful tools are available: regression analysis examines the complex relationships between variables, time series analysis examines trends over time, and classification and clustering algorithms organize data in meaningful categories. Practitioners of this arcane art wield sophisticated tools such as R, Python, SAS, and IBM SPSS, channeling the raw power of data through these conduits of insight (Stevens, 2023). Through this process, organizations transmute the lead of historical information into the gold of foresight, navigating the treacherous waters of an uncertain future with unprecedented insight.

Prescriptive Analytics

Prescriptive analytics, the magnum opus of data science, transcends mere prognostication to become the ultimate arbiter of strategic action. This paragon of analytical sophistication melds predictive models with optimization algorithms, forging a crucible of decision-making prowess that foresees future landscapes and sculpts them to one's advantage (Denton, 2023). Envision a manufacturing colossus, wielding its Excalibur of data-driven insight as it orchestrates a symphony of efficiency across its labyrinthine supply chain, harmonizing production and distribution with unnatural precision.

Prescriptive analytics is like pseudo-science; it turns raw data into golden opportunities using various mysterious methods. For instance, as optimization algorithms unravel intricate complexities, simulation modeling generates digital representations of real-world scenarios, decision analysis transforms chaos into clarity, and machine learning algorithms endow systems with near-intelligent adaptability. To harness this arcane power, practitioners turn to specialized talismans such as Gurobi and IBM ILOG CPLEX, channeling data's raw potential through these algorithmic magic conduits (GeeksforGeeks, 2024). Organizations transcend reactive paradigms in this rarefied stratum of analytical enlightenment, proactively shaping their destinies with unprecedented insight and foresight.

MACHINE LEARNING AND AI

In the era of data analytics, machine learning, and artificial intelligence have brought a new epoch of technological innovation, revolutionizing the information processing landscape like no other. These arcane disciplines endow computational entities with an almost sentient capacity for self-improvement, enabling them to glean insights from the vast oceans of data that inundate our digital space (Denton, 2023). This pantheon of algorithmic gods reigns supreme, with their omniscient gaze penetrating the opaque veil of complexity to reveal patterns and relationships previously invisible to mortals.

A triad of learning paradigms—supervised, unsupervised, and reinforcement—forms an analytical powerhouse. Supervised learning, the wise mentor guides its digital protégés through labeled data, honing their predictive acumen. In unsupervised learning, the intrepid explorer ventures into uncharted territories of unlabeled data, unearthing hidden treasures of insight. Reinforcement learning, the stern taskmaster, forges resilient algorithms through the crucible of trial and error, tempering their decision-making prowess with each iteration.

In the grand tapestry of artificial intelligence, machine learning emerges as a vibrant thread, weaving a narrative of automated cognition that transcends the boundaries of traditional programming (Austen, 2024). This discipline transmutes raw data into golden insights, unveiling the arcane secrets lurking within vast informational labyrinths. Its applications span a kaleidoscopic array of domains: the proactive identification of customer churn to the vigilant detection of fraudulent activities, from the omniscient curation of personalized recommendations to the preternatural recognition of images and speech.

To harness this eldritch power, practitioners wield sophisticated tools, including the versatile sci-kit-learn, the powerful TensorFlow, and the flexible PyTorch (Austen, 2024). Organizations can chart a course through the turbulent seas of modern commerce and technology with these instruments of digital sorcery, navigating the treacherous waters of big data with unparalleled insight. The convergence of data analytics and machine learning ushers in a new era of cognitive augmentation. This may open up previously unimaginable avenues of insight and innovation as boundaries between human and machine intelligence become increasingly blurred.

Applications of AI in Analytics

Artificial Intelligence, the Prometheus of our digital age, bestows upon data analytics a pantheon of cognitive superpowers, elevating the discipline to Olympian heights of insight and capability. Natural Language Processing, the Hermes of this pantheon, deciphers the cryptic hieroglyphs of human communication, unveiling the hidden sentiments and thematic undercurrents that course through textual data. Computer vision, the all-seeing Argus, casts its penetrating gaze upon the visual empire, transmuting images and video into quantifiable insights with applications spanning from the esoteric depths of medical diagnostics to the pragmatic dominions of quality assurance.

Deep learning, the Daedalus of this digital landscape, constructs labyrinthine neural networks of staggering complexity, conquering Herculean challenges such as speech recognition and the choreography of autonomous vehicles. This AI-driven revolution transcends the mortal limitations of traditional analytics, mimicking—nay, amplifying—human cognition and decision-making prowess (Warudkar, 2021). It automates Sisyphean analytical tasks, conjures natural language insights from the raw ore of data, fabricates synthetic datasets with godlike creativity, and optimizes analytical workflows with Promethean efficiency.

The advent of AI-powered analytics platforms like IBM Watson and Google Cloud AI heralds a new epoch of accessibility, democratizing these arcane powers and ushering in an era where businesses of all sizes can wield the thunderbolts of advanced analytics (Austen, 2024). There will be a symbiotic future in which data-driven insights flow freely, like the nectar of the gods, as the boundaries between machine and human intelligence blur. This harmonious integration could lead to unprecedented advancements in various fields, from healthcare to environmental conservation. Enhanced decision-making processes and personalized solutions will become the norm, improving quality of life and fostering innovation. The seamless collaboration between humans and machines could unlock new creative potential and drive economic growth.

Real-World Applications

The omnipotent triad of data analytics, machine learning, and artificial intelligence has infiltrated the fabric of modern industry, weaving a tapestry of innovation that spans the breadth of human enterprise. In the hallowed halls of healthcare, these digital deities work their arcane magic, conjuring predictive diagnostics from the ether, fashioning bespoke treatment plans with algorithmic precision, and speeding up the alchemical process of drug discovery. Picture, if you will, the omniscient gaze of machine learning algorithms, their cyclopean eye penetrating the mysteries of medical imagery, discerning the first whispers of disease long before mortal senses could perceive them (Denton, 2023).

Meanwhile, in the labyrinthine world of finance, these technologies stand as vigilant sentinels, their algorithmic tentacles probing the chaotic currents of global markets. With supernatural acumen, they unmask the face of fraud, quantify the elusive specter of risk, and orchestrate the frantic dance of algorithmic trading. In this digital colosseum, predictive models emerge as gladiatorial champions, their reflexes honed to a razor's edge, capable of identifying fraudulent transactions with the speed of thought, shielding both institutions and their clientele from the predations of financial malfeasance (Schneeweiß & Glynn, 2018).

In the bustling bazaars of retail, data analytics reigns supreme, a merchant prince wielding the scepter of demand forecasting, the crown of inventory optimization, and the orb of personalized marketing. This omniscient sovereign discovers the capricious whims of consumer desire, tailoring offerings with preternatural precision to sate the insatiable appetite of the marketplace (Ramadhan & Niam, 2024). However, perhaps in the mucky forges of manufacturing, these technologies truly showcase their potential.

Here, amidst the ringing of machinery and the hiss of steam, data analytics and AI stand as tireless sentinels, their watchful gaze never wavering. With foresightful expertise, they expect equipment failures and eliminate the costly threat of downtime with a simple wave of their algorithmic magic. Quality control, once the domain of bleary-eyed human inspectors, now falls under the purview of these digital overseers, their judgment swift, infallible, and incorruptible. According to

Ramadhan and Niam (2024), once a complex logistics network, the supply chain has transformed into a streamlined efficiency model. We are entering an unprecedented efficiency, insight, and innovation age, where the boundaries between physical and digital domains blur. Machine learning, artificial intelligence, and data analytics are the new titans of productivity.

Value in Decision-Making

In the grand dome of corporate governance, data analytics emerges as the omniscient oracle, its digital prophecies illuminating the shadowy recesses of uncertainty and guiding the hands of decision-makers with unnatural acumen. This modern-day Delphic priesthood eschews the capricious whims of intuition, instead anchoring its proclamations in the bedrock of empirical evidence. With a clairvoyant gaze penetrating the opaque veil of complexity, these analytical watchmen unveil hidden patterns and emergent trends, revealing opportunities that otherwise languish in obscurity.

The prescriptive prowess of these digital diviners extends beyond mere insight, offering a Promethean flame of optimization that sears away inefficiencies and kindles the fires of operational excellence. In this brave new world of data-driven decision-making, companies are elevating the customer experience to unprecedented heights by harnessing the protean power of analytics to transform their offerings into bespoke creations tailored with algorithmic precision to their clientele's mercurial desires. Across many industries, data analytics weaves its transformative magic, leaving no sector untouched by its alchemical influence.

In the kingdom of retail, the behemoth Walmart wields predictive analytics like a sorcerer's staff, conjuring forecasts of consumer demand from a mystical brew of historical sales data, meteorological divinations, and the ephemeral whispers of market trends (Team DigitalDefynd, 2024). The hallowed halls of healthcare pulsate with the rhythmic hum of predictive algorithms, their tireless calculations optimizing resource allocation with surgical precision and weaving a prophylactic shield of preventive care around vulnerable populations. In the financial institutions, analytics stands as a vigilant Cerberus, its manifold heads sniffing out the faintest scent of fraud, quantifying the elusive specter of risk, and tailoring financial services with a touch that would make Midas himself envious.

The grim forges of the industry also feel the digital revolution's transformative touch. Siemens, that titan of industry, harnesses the fire of AI and analytics to transmute its operations into paragons of energy efficiency, its factories humming with an almost sentient harmony of productivity and sustainability (Team DigitalDefynd, 2024). Meanwhile, in the ever-shifting battlegrounds of marketing, leviathans like Google deploy big data analytics with the strategic understanding of a chess grandmaster, their personalized ads and content recommendations striking with the precision of Cupid's arrow, accurately finding their mark in the hearts and minds of consumers.

Armed with this pantheon of analytical approaches, business leaders ascend to a quasi-divine state of omniscience, their decisions forged in the crucible of data-driven insight. They discover opportunities and risks from the digital debris of big data, optimize their operations with algorithmic efficiency, and sculpt customer experiences with the finesse of a Renaissance master. In this innovative world, where the distinctions between human intuition and machine intelligence become increasingly blurred, data analytics emerges as the key to modern business, transforming raw information into valuable innovation and competitive advantage.

Challenges and Considerations

Data analytics depicts a chiaroscuro (light-dark) of potential and peril, casting long shadows across the luminous world of insight. In this digital Olympus, the Achilles' heel is its nectar—the data. According to Greek mythology, analytical fruit is only as tasty as the source from which it was derived, its potency inextricably linked to its purity. However, as these digital deities feast upon the personal data of mortals, Pandora's box of ethical quandaries yawns wide, its contents threatening to unleash a torrent of privacy concerns about an unsuspecting world. In this brave new realm, where algorithms reign supreme, the enigmatic pronouncements of advanced models often emerge shrouded in mystery, their inner workings as mysterious as the riddles of the Sphinx.

The "black box" problem casts a pall of uncertainty over the decision-making process, challenging the foundations of transparency and accountability that underpin sound governance. While these challenges are Herculean, the transformative power of data analytics, machine learning, and artificial intelligence continues to reshape corporate decision-making. These digital craftsmen give leaders a clairvoyant vision, penetrating the opaque veils of operational complexity, customer behavior, and market dynamics with unprecedented acuity (Sunitha, 2024). As these technologies develop with Darwinian rapidity, their influence on businesses' strategic and operational realms threatens to eclipse even the most grandiose predictions of futurists and mystics.

However, to harness this creative power, one must approach the altar of analytics with a clear-eyed vision of business objectives, a fanatical devotion to data quality, and a measured approach to capability building that aligns with the unique contours of organizational need. As the analytical understanding of enterprises matures like a fine wine, leaders can embark upon ever more audacious expeditions into the uncharted territories of advanced techniques, unearthing insights of staggering profundity and kindling the flames of business value to heights hitherto unimagined.

In this digital heaven, where the boundaries between human intuition and machine intelligence blur into obscurity, the true masters of the corporate universe will be those who can navigate the treacherous waters of big data with the skill of Odysseus, charting a course through the ethical concerns and the interpretability challenges to reach the promised land of data-driven enlightenment.

TRANSLATING DATA INSIGHTS INTO ACTIONABLE STRATEGIES

Using data insights for tangible business impact requires organizations to transform them into actionable strategies that bridge the gap between analysis and implementation. This process involves interpreting data findings, effectively communicating them to stakeholders, and developing concrete plans to implement data-driven decisions. Our framework comprises several key elements and considerations for translating insights into action.

Data Narration and Storytelling

Data narration emerges as a pivotal conduit, transmuting raw insights into actionable strategies. Amer-Yahia et al. (2023) posit that this process involves exploring, answering questions, structuring answers, and presenting to stakeholders, all while weaving stories from the revealed data. Its efficacy lies in explaining complex insights, captivating decision-makers, and spotlighting the most salient and impactful discoveries. To amplify the resonance of data narration, organizations must craft data stories for distinct stakeholder personas, leverage visualization techniques to render insights more accessible, and integrate next-step recommendations predicated on these revelations.

The art of interpreting insights demands meticulous contextualization of data and identification of key drivers. It is imperative to situate findings within the broader tapestry of business goals, market dynamics, and industry trajectories (Rockborne Graduates, 2023). This panoramic perspective ensures that the strategies conceived are relevant and symbiotically aligned with organizational objectives. Explaining data requires a keen eye for discerning the underlying forces propelling trends or outcomes.

Deciphering these fundamental drivers is quintessential for formulating targeted strategies that address root causes rather than merely easing symptoms (Spector University, 2023). The holistic approach to data interpretation can turn raw data into strategic wisdom for organizations. This metamorphosis of data into actionable intelligence empowers businesses to navigate the labyrinthine complexities of modern markets with unprecedented insight and foresight.

From Insights to Action

Transforming insights into action demands a methodical odyssey, beginning with the distillation of pivotal revelations poised to catalyze business value. This journey traverses the evaluation of each insight's reverberations across organizational aspirations, culminating in the genesis of actionable, quantifiable, and temporally bound recommendations. We rigorously triage these strategic propositions, determining their hierarchy based on their potential impact, feasibility, and alignment with overarching objectives.

The outcome of this process manifests in the form of meticulous implementation blueprints. Concurrently, it becomes imperative to transform data insights into engaging narratives. By harnessing the arcane art of storytelling, one can imbue cold, complex data with a soul that resonates profoundly with stakeholders (Zlojutro, n.d.). Ariadne's thread, the data, guides the audience through a labyrinth of discovery throughout this narrative odyssey, ultimately culminating in a clear call for change.

Organizations must cultivate a data-driven ecosystem within their corporate biosphere to metamorphose insights into potent strategies. This transformation necessitates nurturing data literacy across all echelons of the workforce, empowering employees to decipher, interpret, and wield data with the dexterity of seasoned alchemists (Zaghmout, 2024). This data-centric culture demands a fundamental shift, establishing decision-making processes based on empirical evidence rather than the misleading illusions of intuition or experience. At the apex of this revolution stands the imperative of securing unwavering leadership commitment, ensuring that the upper echelons of management not only support but zealously promote these data-driven crusades, posits Zaghmout.

Translating insights into actionable strategies requires a symbiotic linkage between data revelations and overarching business objectives. This process demands a lucid demonstration of how each data-derived epiphany intertwines with specific corporate goals and priorities, illuminating the path to potential impact for stakeholders (Sankar, n.d.). In this crucible of decision-making, actions born from insights undergo a rigorous triage, their fate determined by a complex calculus of potential impact, feasibility, resource demands, and alignment with the grand tapestry of business strategy (Sopact University, 2023). The ultimate act in this data-driven drama unfolds with the crafting of concrete action plans replete with specific, quantifiable objectives. Rockborne Graduates (2023) assert that these plans steer the organization's path, and they meticulously monitor their progress using carefully calibrated vital performance indicators (KPIs), guaranteeing not just aspiration but methodical pursuit and measurement of success.

Communicating Findings

In data-driven decision-making, the artful selection of visualizations emerges as a cornerstone of effective communication. Like a primary painter choosing the perfect palette, one must discern which charts, graphs, and infographics best illuminate the narrative hidden within the data's intricate tapestry (Pragmatic Institute Resources, 2024). These visual ambassadors must capture the essence of trends, patterns, and relationships and present them in a form that is as lucid as it is compelling. Visual storytelling requires a keen understanding of one's audience, just as a composer tailor an epic to their tastes. This chameleon-like adaptability in presentation style, oscillating between high-level abstractions and granular details, ensures that insights penetrate the minds of stakeholders with surgical precision, regardless of their data literacy (LinkedIn Community, n.d.).

Stakeholder engagement, a delicate and crucial process, forms the foundation of consensus-building. By inviting key players into the chamber of insight interpretation and strategy development, one not only cultivates agreement but also weaves a tapestry rich with diverse perspectives (Shonk, 2024). Consensus-building techniques can further refine this collaborative alchemy, like the unifying power of a single-text document or the shared aspirations ignited by a visioning approach. These methodologies serve as catalysts, fusing disparate viewpoints into a cohesive action plan.

However, objections and concerns often impede reaching a consensus, each presenting a potential obstacle. Data plays a dual role in this situation, protecting recommendations from skepticism and simultaneously refining strategies through feedback (LinkedIn Community, n.d.). This back-and-forth between asserting and adapting ensures that the ultimate strategy is based on data and considers all stakeholders' needs. It is then ready to navigate the complex currents of organizational change with accuracy and resilience.

Overcoming Challenges Leveraging Technology

As organizations struggle to translate insights into actionable strategies, they often face a triad of formidable challenges. Data quality and integration are the first specters looming across the organizational ecosystem, requiring enormous effort to ensure clean and accurate data. Simultaneously, skill gaps emerge, requiring a strategic approach to overcome any deficiencies in analytical or technical skills within the organization.

Nevertheless, perhaps the most insidious foe lurks in the shadows of organizational inertia, manifesting as a pernicious resistance to the clarion call of data-driven decision-making. Organizations must be vigilant to navigate this treacherous terrain, perpetually tracking their progress against the celestial chart of predefined KPIs. This iterative odyssey demands an alacrity to pivot strategies in the face of new data or shifting paradigms, ensuring that the organization's course remains relevant and efficacious (Rockborne Graduates, 2023). Sankar emphasizes the meticulous weaving of each thread in this grand tapestry of action, with clear ownership and realistic timelines acting as the warp and weft of implementation.

The effort to bridge the gap between insight and action becomes a pantheon of powerful allies through technology. At the vanguard stand the oracles of business intelligence tools, their advanced analytics and visualization platforms serving as beacons of clarity in the fog of data complexity. Flanking these are the sage counselors of rule-based expert systems, their algorithms distilling the essence of business intelligence into a nectar of understanding, palatable even to the most data-averse decision-makers (Döppner et al., 2015).

Completing this technological trinity are the swift messengers of real-time data systems, harnessing the might of the Industrial Internet of Things (IIoT) to deliver insights at the speed of thought, enabling decision-making with the rapidity of lightning (Saabye & Powell, 2022). When wielded with skill and purpose, this technological arsenal transforms the once-daunting task of insight translation into a symphony of strategic action, orchestrating a future where data informs and actively shapes the destiny of organizations.

Measuring Impact

Organizations must erect a vigilance, measurement, and adaptability triad to galvanize the efficacy of translated strategies. This triad begins with establishing key performance indicators (KPIs) and meticulously crafted beacons that illuminate the impact of the implemented strategy with the precision of a master cartographer. We scrutinize the outcomes of data-driven decisions with the intensity of an alchemist seeking the philosopher's stone, using these KPIs as the lodestar for a ceaseless vigil. However, a relentless and dynamic process of iteration and refinement leads to true mastery, not mere observation.

The raw materials for refined strategies are feedback and developing insights forged in the crucible of continuous improvement. This way, we bridge the gap between ethereal data insights and tangible business outcomes through a harmonious blend of technical prowess, organizational ethos, and streamlined processes. Through this transformation, organizations transform raw data into the gold of innovation, enhanced decision-making, and, ultimately, excellent business performance. This process perfectly aligns data-driven insights with impactful business actions, ensuring a continuous flow of insights perfectly synced with business operations.

FOSTERING A DATA-DRIVEN CULTURE: OVERCOMING CHALLENGES AND RESISTANCE

Organizations committed to leveraging the power of data in their decision-making processes need to cultivate a data-driven culture; however, resistance to this transformation is expected. As a company, dedicate a lot of time and money to providing comprehensive training programs for your employees. Demonstrating the tangible benefits of data-driven decisions through case studies and pilot projects can also help ease concerns. Transparency and open communication promote employees' involvement in the transformation process by encouraging them to voice their reservations. Below is a comprehensive discussion on overcoming these obstacles and creating a culture that embraces data-driven decision-making.

Resistance to Change

A paradigm change occurs in business decision-making, challenging the status quo of intuition-based tactics. This metamorphosis toward data-driven methodologies often encounters a formidable adversary: the inertia of established practices. The zeitgeist of traditional hierarchies and non-participative cultures proves to be a crucible for innovation, impeding the adoption of empirical approaches (Van der Merwe & Davey, 2024). Employees and management alike, immersed in the cocoon of familiarity, may see this transformation with a critical eye. The threat of employment obsolescence looms large, prompting fears and distrust. Concomitantly, a dearth of comprehension regarding the intrinsic value of data exacerbates this resistance (Talin, 2023; Gerlach, 2023). The crux lies in implementing new systems and orchestrating a seismic shift in organizational ethos. It necessitates a judicious amalgamation of education, persuasion, and strategic realignment to surmount these hurdles and usher in an age of data-driven decision-making.

An employee's resistance to a data-driven utopia requires a multifaceted approach, combining transparency and empathy. The art of clear communication serves as the foundation for understanding how data-driven decisions affect quotidian work processes and roles. Crystallized explanations provide comfort, calming fears and dispelling the haze of uncertainty that often surrounds organizational changes. We should concurrently engineer a significant shift in perception, transforming data analytics from a perceived threat that eliminates jobs to a powerful tool that enhances human cognition and decision-making skills. A symbiotic narrative, rather than one of supplantation, serves as a powerful antidote to technological anxiety. The last thread in this transformational journey is the provision of a robust support ecosystem, resources, and mentorship, empowering employees to confidently and skillfully navigate the unfamiliar terrain of data-driven methodologies.

A pivotal factor in the success of this organization is the leadership's unwavering support. Only a highly motivated executive sponsor can carry out a data-driven crusade (Dykes, 2022). Leading by example, this paragon of empirical decision-making serves as a lodestone, aligning the disparate magnetic fields of organizational resistance toward the true north of data-driven culture. This transformational movement unfolds alongside a strategy of incremental victory, with smaller, manageable data projects providing the vanguard. Using data-centric approaches shows their tangible value through carefully curated and strategically deployed quick wins, which act as catalysts and speed up momentum.

Customized data literacy programs tailored to the diverse skill levels of every organization form the foundation of this cultural metamorphosis (Crabtree, 2022). This educational odyssey, manifesting through a kaleidoscope of workshops, webinars, and hands-on sessions, is a process that transmutes data trepidation into confidence and competence. A culture of experimentation is the ultimate piece of this grand mosaic, a sanctuary where curiosity is currency and innovation is the language. The crucible of creativity nurtures the true potential of a data-driven organization, fostering the flourishing of ideas and the encouragement of questions.

Data Literacy Gap

In the complex world of modern organizations, a profound chasm exists between the availability of data and the understanding required to harness its potential. This dearth of data literacy permeates various echelons of corporate structures, from neophyte employees to seasoned leaders, engendering a milieu ripe for misinterpretation and underutilization of invaluable information (Crabtree, 2024). The complex nature of data analysis and the rapid growth of analytical technologies have resulted in a skills gap of gigantic proportions. This lacuna in expertise hampers the productive implementation of data-driven decision-making and engenders a palpable reluctance to engage with the tools designed to augment organizational efficiency.

The ramifications of this literacy gap are multifaceted and far-reaching. Once heralded as the panacea for corporate ills, data now languishes in digital repositories, its potential untapped due to a shortage of interpretative prowess. This underutilization of resources represents a worthless opportunity of epic proportions, akin to possessing a treasure map without the ability to decipher its cryptic symbols

(Achanta & Boina, 2023). Furthermore, the apprehension around data engagement encourages an avoidance culture in which employees and management alike eschew data-driven operations in favor of the comfort of ancient approaches. This recalcitrance stymies organizational growth and places companies at a significant disadvantage in an increasingly data-centric business landscape.

Organizational Structure and Culture

In the sophisticated areas of organizational evolution, the absence of sophisticated tools, systems, and technologies impedes the seamless integration of data-driven methodologies (Skyone, 2024). This technological lacuna, akin to a craftsman bereft of implements, blocks data's efficacious collection, analysis, and utilization, rendering even the most astute insights impotent. Traditional hierarchies and cultures that don't encourage participation work together like a web of complexity that makes it hard and takes longer to carry out data-centric projects (Van der Merwe & Davey, 202).

This organizational inertia, deeply entrenched in antiquated paradigms, engenders a milieu inimical to the rapid, fluid decision-making processes requisite for data-driven success. Furthermore, the spirit of many corporate cultures, steeped in intuition-based decision-making, presents a formidable bulwark against the incursion of empirical approaches (Panuganty, 2023). The combination of these three issues—inadequate technology, rigid structures, and cultural resistance—creates a significant challenge that necessitates not only the implementation of new systems but also a comprehensive transformation in organizational processes to fully reap the benefits of data-driven decision-making.

In organizational transformation, the transition to a data-driven paradigm demands a nuanced, incremental evolution, not a revolutionary upheaval. Small-scale but mighty in impact, pilot projects initiate this gradual transformation, acting as crucibles to show the precision and potential of data-driven methodologies. These microcosmic endeavors, akin to acorns harboring the DNA of mighty oaks, sow the seeds of confidence and value, gradually eroding the bedrock of skepticism.

Concurrently, choosing the right scalable technologies and processes becomes a strategic imperative. This ensures that the new data infrastructure can grow with the company's evolving goals (Achanta & Boina, 202?). We can construct ever more ambitious data initiatives upon this technological foundation, which is both malleable and robust. The last element of this three-part method is the principle of ongoing enhancement, a relentless dedication to constant development. This relentless pursuit of optimization, akin to the ceaseless polishing of a rough diamond, ensures that data-driven processes remain not static monoliths but dynamic, developing entities, perpetually honed to maintain their cutting edge in the ever-shifting sands of the business landscape.

Developing a Data-Driven Mindset

In the ordeal of organizational transformation, the forging of a data-driven culture demands a multifaceted approach that permeates every corporate hierarchy stratum. At the zenith of this fundamental change stands the imperative of leadership commitment, a beacon of change illuminating the path toward empirical decision-making. These executive luminaries should acknowledge the significance of data and show its transformative power by embodying its ethos. The implementation of continuous education programs becomes essential, serving as a safeguard against the constantly changing landscape of data literacy and analytical proficiency (Hota et al., 2023).

Far from being a one-time activity, this pedagogical attempt must be a continuous voyage, arming employees with the Promethean fire of knowledge to navigate the tortuous universe of data. The ultimate piece of this tripartite strategy involves the judicious deployment of success stories and carefully curated narratives that testify to the efficacy of data-driven methodologies. These stories of victory, woven into the fabric of corporate legend, serve as solid catalysts, kindling the collective imagination and cultivating a zeitgeist in which data reigns supreme in the decision-making pantheon.

Improving Data Accessibility and Quality

Poor data quality in data-driven decision-making poses a significant threat, potentially destroying the fragile trust that forms the foundation of the entire structure. The triumvirate of inaccuracy, inconsistency, and obsolescence can lead even the most astute analysts to misguided conclusions, undermining the foundation of empirical reasoning (Crabtree, 2024). To exorcise these demons of doubt, organizations must abandon the mantle of data stewardship and implement robust governance practices that serve as a crucible for data integrity.

This process transmutes raw information into golden insights, ensuring accuracy and reliability that can withstand the most stringent scrutiny. We must maintain a delicate balance between accessibility and security, akin to a tightrope dancer balancing the gap between open information and secured assets. A three-pronged plan emerges as the lodestar for dismantling the bastions of opposition and ushering in data adoption. First, deploying user-friendly tools and self-service platforms is a powerful lure, drawing even the most technophobic individuals into data analysis (Achanta & Boina, 2023). With their charismatic visualizations, these intuitive interfaces transform the arcane art of data interpretation into a democratic endeavor.

Second, establishing rigorous data validation and cleaning processes is crucial, purifying information and forging unassailable trust in its veracity (Sayogo et al., 2023). This transformation elevates raw data into an organizational gospel impervious to criticism or doubt. Finally, the codification of clear data governance policies emerges as the Magna Carta of the data-driven realm, delineating the rights, responsibilities, and boundaries of data usage (Olaniyi et al., 2023). This constitutional framework, encompassing privacy, security, and ethical considerations, serves as the bedrock upon which a genuinely data-centric culture can flourish, transforming organizations into bastions of empirical decision-making.

Fostering Collaboration and Communication

Data savants and business mavens collaborate on the crucial organizational transformation, transforming raw information into strategic gold. This beneficial collaboration is essential for organizations as it enables data-driven decision-making. This makes sure that empirical projects aren't just academic exercises but rather powerful change agents for businesses (Dykes, 2022). The clarion call for cross-functional teams reverberates through corporate halls, heralding the dawn of a new world where data experts and domain specialists coalesce into a formidable force of innovation (Achanta & Boina, 2023).

Simultaneously, regular data-sharing symposia function as an agora of insights, a marketplace where ideas trade with the enthusiasm of ancient merchants, fostering a culture of intellectual cross-pollination. An ethos of experimentation further enriches this collaborative milieu, promoting the flourishing of data-driven hypotheses, free from the stifling constraints of fear or recrimination. When real-life examples and quick wins are woven into the communication that results, it creates a powerful narrative tool that shows how data-centric methods can change things with the vividness of a master storyteller. Furthermore, by breaking down conventional divisions inside organizations, this comprehensive strategy fosters an atmosphere where data holds the highest authority, driving businesses toward a future where all decisions are based on empirical facts.

Measuring Success

In the Sisyphean task of cultivating a data-driven organizational ethos, the imperative of ceaseless vigilance emerges as the lodestar guiding this transformative odyssey. Regularly assessing data culture initiatives distills progress, transforms challenges into opportunities, and refines strategies to razor-sharp efficacy (Crabtree, 2024). This process of perpetual refinement, fueled by the twin engines of feedback and metrics, serves as a spinner, maintaining the delicate equilibrium between aspiration and reality in the tumultuous seas of organizational change.

Concurrently, aligning performance metrics and incentives with data-driven objectives emerges as the hinge upon which the lever of cultural transformation rests. This symbiosis between individual motivation and organizational goals creates a virtuous cycle, where engagement with data becomes not a burdensome obligation but a quotidian ritual, as natural as respiration in the corporate body. Delineating Key Performance Indicators (KPIs), the quantifiable benchmarks that guide data-driven decision-making, is the first step in the triad of strategies for successful implementation.

Carefully calibrated and judiciously selected KPIs serve as the yardstick for measuring the impact of empirical methodologies, offering tangible evidence of value in the often-intangible realm of data. Regular assessments and a periodic data literacy and usage census are diagnostic tools and progress markers. This organizational pulse-taking identifies areas of strength and weakness and charts the trajectory of the data culture's evolution, providing invaluable insights for course correction and strategic planning. The last element in this tripartite approach is the establishment of robust feedback loops, creating a democratic agora where employees can voice their experiences, concerns, and suggestions regarding data-driven initiatives. This open communication mechanism fosters a sense of ownership and engagement and serves as an early warning system for potential pitfalls and a fountain of grassroots innovation.

SUMMARY

Looking ahead, the role of data analytics in strategic decision-making will probably become even more central as technologies continue to develop and data volumes grow. Integrating artificial intelligence and machine learning capabilities promises to enhance analytical capabilities further, enabling more sophisticated predictive and prescriptive analytics. However, organizations must remain mindful of ethical considerations and balance automated decision-making and human judgment. The success of data-driven transformation ultimately depends on an organization's ability to create a symbiotic relationship between technology, processes, and people. This process requires:

- Constantly invest in data infrastructure and analytical capabilities
- The organization is continuously developing data literacy and analytical skills.
- Regularly assess and refine data strategies and implementations

- Maintaining robust data governance and quality control measures is crucial.
- Encouraging a collaborative culture that values data-driven decision-making

Companies that handle these challenges while focusing on their primary goals will be best able to use data to get ahead of the competition. The future belongs to those who can collect and analyze data effectively and translate those insights into meaningful action that drives business value and innovation. This chapter underscores that the journey to data-driven decision-making is not merely a technological transformation but a holistic organizational evolution that touches every aspect of how businesses operate and compete in the modern world. Success requires a balanced approach that combines technical expertise, strategic thinking, and organizational change management, all while maintaining a clear focus on delivering tangible business value through the power of data analytics.

As organizations increasingly leverage data analytics for strategic advantage, the fundamental question shifts from how to implement these technologies to how to deploy them responsibly and ethically. The preceding chapter established the critical role of data-driven decision-making in modern business operations and highlighted the organizational transformations necessary to harness its potential. However, the sophisticated capabilities of advanced analytics, artificial intelligence, and machine learning introduce complex ethical considerations that leaders must carefully navigate.

The proliferation of powerful analytical tools and vast data repositories creates opportunities and obligations for organizational leadership. While these technologies enable unprecedented insights and predictive capabilities, they raise profound questions about privacy, bias, transparency, and the appropriate balance between automated and human decision-making. Leaders must now extend their focus beyond the technical and operational aspects of data analytics to consider their data-driven strategies' broader implications and ethical dimensions.

This intersection of technological capability and ethical responsibility forms the foundation for the following chapter's examination of value-based decision-making in the modern business environment. As organizations expand their analytical abilities, leaders must develop frameworks integrating ethical considerations into their data-driven decision-making processes, ensuring that technological advancement aligns with organizational values and societal expectations. The evolution from purely data-driven to value-informed decision-making represents a critical maturation in how organizations leverage technology while maintaining their commitment to responsible leadership.

REFERENCES

Achanta, A., & Boina, R. (2023). Evolving Paradigms Of Data Engineering In The Modern Era: Challenges, Innovations, And Strategies. *International Journal Of Science And Research (Ijsr)*, *12*(10), 606–610. Https://Doi.Org/10.21275/Sr231007071729

Amazon Web Services, Inc. (2024). *What Is Data Preparation? - Data Preparation Explained - Aws*. Https://Aws.Amazon.Com/What-Is/Data-Preparation/

Amer-Yahia, S., Marcel, P., & Peralta, V. (2023). Data Narration For The People: Challenges And Opportunities. Https://Doi.Org/10.48786/Edbt.2023.82

Atlan. (2023). *10 Steps To Create An Effective Data Foundation*. Https://Atlan.Com/Data-Foundation/

Austen, C. (2024). *6 Unique Ways To Use Ai In Data Analytics | Datacamp*. Https://Www.Datacamp.Com/Blog/Unique-Ways-To-Use-Ai-In-Data-Analytics

Castordoc. (2024). *7 Data Integrity Best Practices You Need To Know*. Https://Www.Castordoc.Com/Data-Strategy/7-Data-Integrity-Best-Practices-You-Need-To-Know

Cloud Forces. (2023). *Achieving Business Agility Through Cloud Enablement*. Https://Www.Cloudforces.Ca/Post/Achieving-Business-Agility-Through-Cloud-Enablement

Crabtree, M. (2024). *What Is Data Culture? A Comprehensive Guide To Being A More Data-Driven Organization | Datacamp*. Https://Www.Datacamp.Com/Blog/How-To-Create-Data-Driven-Organization

Denton, T. B. (2023). Frontiers Of Medical Decision-Making In The Modern Age Of Data Analytics. *IISE Transactions*, 55, 94–105. Https://Www.Semanticscholar.Org/Paper/Frontiers-Of-Medical-Decision-Making-In-The-Modern-Denton/D93758d4f9d73c40b7e9888e2e5446dcbbf53e97. DOI: 10.1080/24725854.2022.2092918

Döppner, D. A., Schoder, D., & Siejka, H. (2015). Big Data And The Data Value Chain: Translating Insights From Business Analytics Into Actionable Results - The Case Of Unit Load Device (Uld) Management In The Air Cargo Industry. *European Conference On Information Systems*. Https://Www.Semanticscholar.Org/Paper/Big-Data-And-The-Data-Value-Chain%3a-Translating-From-D%C3%B6ppner-Schoder/39458c2fa9f95fd2692ee18640d5054bfdf1b936

Dykes, B. (2022). Why Change Management Skills Are Essential To Data-Driven Success. *Forbes*. Https://Www.Forbes.Com/Sites/Brentdykes/2022/11/29/Why-Change-Management-Skills-Are-Essential-To-Data-Driven-Success/

Eide Bailly. (2023). *How To Prioritize Key Performance Metrics In Your Organization*. Https://Siouxfalls.Business/How-To-Prioritize-Key-Performance-Metrics-In-Your-Organization/

Fone Ng, S. (2023). *Why Kpis Are Important: 10 Reason Key Performance Indicators Stands For? -Meaning, Examples, Template | Linkedin*. Https://Www.Linkedin.Com/Pulse/Why-Kpis-Important-10-Reason-Key-Performance-Indicators-Shone-Fone-Ng/

Ganguly, K., & Rai, S. (2018). Evaluating The Key Performance Indicators For Supply Chain Information System Implementation Using Ipa Model. *Benchmarking: An International Journal*. Https://Www.Semanticscholar.Org/Paper/Evaluating-The-Key-Performance-Indicators-For-Chain-Ganguly-Rai/945f69301a3b1face79fb6ff5064af58df22cf8d

Geeksforgeeks (2024). Comparing Descriptive, Predictive, And Prescriptive Analytics Models. *Geeksforgeeks*. Https://Www.Geeksforgeeks.Org/Comparing-Descriptive-Predictive-And-Prescriptive-Analytics-Models/#

Gerlach, C. (2023). *How Are Data Culture And Change Management Connected?* Https://Www.Statworx.Com/En/Content-Hub/Interview/How-Are-Data-Culture-And-Change-Management-Connected/

Hota, P., Nayak, B., & Mishra, S. K. (2023). Role Of Total Quality Management In Digital Literacy For Management Institutes Of Odisha. *International Journal of e-Collaboration*, 19(1), 1–18. Https://Doi.Org/10.4018/Ijec.316775. DOI: 10.4018/IJeC.316775

Ilkiu, J. (2024). The Data-Driven Revolution: Agile Decision-Making, Exceptional Results - Luby Software. *Felipe Matos*. Https://Luby.Co/Data-Driven/The-Data-Driven-Revolution

Inamdar, S.N., Oke, J.S., & Agashe, A. (2014). *Enterprise Performance Management*.

Inclusion Cloud. (2023). *Data Governance: Ensuring Data Quality And Overcoming Data Bias*. Https://Inclusioncloud.Com/Insights/Blog/Data-Governance-Data-Bias/

Keck, I. R., & Ross, R. J. (2014). Exploring Customer Specific Kpi Selection Strategies For An Adaptive Time Critical User Interface. In T. Kuflik, O. Stock, J. Chai, & A. Krüger (Eds.), *Proceedings Of The 19th International Conference On Intelligent User Interfaces* (Pp. 341–346). Acm. Https://Doi.Org/10.1145/2557500.2557536

Kobi, J., & Otieno, B. (2024). Predictive Analytics Applications For Enhanced Customer Retention And Increased Profitability In The Telecommunications Industry. *International Journal Of Innovative Science And Research Technology (Ijisrt)*, Article Ijisrt24may1148, 1762–1774. Https://Doi.Org/10.38124/Ijisrt/Ijisrt24may1148

Leadzen.Ai Blog (August 2024). Case Studies: Successful Data-Driven Companies. *Leadzen.Ai.* Https://Leadzen.Ai/Blog/Case-Studies-Successful-Data-Driven-Companies

Linkedin Community. (2024a). *How Can You Prioritize Kpis Based On Their Importance To Your Organization?*Https://Www.Linkedin.Com/Advice/1/How-Can-You-Prioritize-Kpis-Based-Importance-Zo6ue

Linkedin Community. (2024b). *What Are The Best Ways To Ensure Data Quality?*Https://Www.Linkedin.Com/Advice/0/What-Best-Ways-Ensure-Data-Quality-Skills-Data-Management

Linkedin Community. (N.D.). *What Are The Best Ways To Present Data Insights And Recommendations To Stakeholders?* Retrieved September 6, 2024, From Https://Www.Linkedin.Com/Advice/0/What-Best-Ways-Present-Data-Insights-Recommendations

Miller, F. P., Vandome, A. F., & Mcbrewster, J. (2009). Data Analysis: Data Analysis, Data, Information, Data Mining, Business Intelligence, Statistics, Descriptive Statistics, Exploratory Data Analysis, Statistical ... Hypothesis Testing, *Predictive Analytics.* Https://Www.Semanticscholar.Org/Paper/Data-Analysis%3a-Data-Analysis%2c-Data%2c-Information%2c-Miller-Vandome/5b73cccb2851253767bbe69f688770994b4d050e

Olaniyi, O. O., Okunleye, O. J., & Olabanji, S. O. (2023). Advancing Data-Driven Decision-Making In Smart Cities Through Big Data Analytics: A Comprehensive Review Of Existing Literature. *Current Journal Of Applied Science And Technology, 42*(25), 10–18. Https://Doi.Org/10.9734/Cjast/2023/V42i254181

180. ops. (2024). *The Impact Of Poor Data Quality On Business: Understanding The Revenue Consequences.* Https://Www.180ops.Com/180-Perspective-Change/Impact-Of-Poor-Data-Quality-On-Business-Understanding-Revenue-Consequences

Panuganty, R. (2023). Data Driven Decision Making: Benefits And Challenges. *Machege.* Https://Www.Macheye.Com/Blog/Challenges-And-Benefits-Of-Data-Driven-Decision-Making/

Paredes, R. (2023). What Is A Key Performance Indicator (Kpi)? | Safetyculture. Https://Safetyculture.Com/Topics/Kpi/

Poleski Danielle Blog Post. (March 2023). Why Are Key Performance Indicators Important? *Klipfolio*. Https://Www.Klipfolio.Com/Blog/Kpi-Importance

Pothineni, S. (2023). The Impact Of Data Strategy And Emerging Technologies On Business Performance. *International Journal of Business Strategy and Automation*, 4(1), 1–19. Https://Doi.Org/10.4018/Ijbsa.334022. DOI: 10.4018/IJBSA.334022

Pragmatic Institute - Resources. (2024). *10 Data Presentation Tips | Pragmatic Institute*. Https://Www.Pragmaticinstitute.Com/Resources/Articles/Data/10-Ways-To-Communicate-Data-Findings-Effectively/

Psychweb. (2023). *Directive*. Https://Psychweb.Com/Directive/

Ramadhan, G. J. M., & Niam, S. (2024). Big Data Analytics: Techniques, Tools, And Applications In Various Industries. *Jurnal Ar Ro'is Mandalika (Armada), 3*(2), 56–65. Https://Www.Semanticscholar.Org/Paper/Big-Data-Analytics%3a-Techniques%2c-Tools%2c-And-In-Ramadhan-Niam/E82406e6f77956b992e7b5ec475897662cfa8d5c

Reddit. (2023). *Data-Driven Decision Making: Case Studies: R/Compsci*. Https://Www.Reddit.Com/R/Compsci/Comments/15pub3z/Datadriven_Decision_Making_Case_Studies/

Rib Software Blog. (2024). *Why Data Driven Decision Making Is Your Path To Busseness Success*. Https://Www.Rib-Software.Com/En/Blogs/Data-Driven-Decision-Making-In-Businesses

Rockborne Graduates. (2023). *Presenting Data Visualisations And Insights To Business-Minded Stakeholders - Rockborne - Graduates*. Https://Rockborne.Com/Graduates/Blog/Presenting-Data-To-Stakeholders/

Saabye, H., & Powell, D. (2024). Fostering Insights And Improvements From Iiot Systems At The Shop Floor: A Case Of Industry 4.0 And Lean Complementarity Enabled By Action Learning. *International Journal of Lean Six Sigma*, 15(5), 968–996. Https://Doi.Org/10.1108/Ijlss-01-2022-0017. DOI: 10.1108/IJLSS-01-2022-0017

Sankar, S. (N.D.). *Design Your Data Strategy In Six Steps | Ibm*. Retrieved September 6, 2024, From Https://Www.Ibm.Com/Resources/The-Data-Differentiator/Data-Strategy

Sayogo, D. S., Yuli, S. B. C., & Amalia, F. A. (2024). Data-Driven Decision-Making Challenges Of Local Government In Indonesia. *Transforming Government: People, Process And Policy, 18*(1), 145–156. Https://Doi.Org/10.1108/Tg-05-2023-0058

Schneeweiß, S., & Glynn, R. J. (2018). Real-World Data Analytics Fit For Regulatory Decision-Making. *American Journal of Law & Medicine*, 44(2-3), 197–217. Https://Doi.Org/10.1177/0098858818789429. DOI: 10.1177/0098858818789429 PMID: 30106649

Sharma, A. (2023). How To Ensure Data Integrity In Your Organization. *Dataversity*. Https://Www.Dataversity.Net/How-To-Ensure-Data-Integrity-In-Your-Organization/

Shonk, K. (2024). Consensus-Building Techniques. *Program On Negotiation At Harvard Law School*. Https://Www.Pon.Harvard.Edu/Daily/Dealing-With-Difficult-People-Daily/Consensus-Building-Techniques/

Sivakumar, P., & Dinesh, E. (2023). Navigating The Modernization Of Legacy Applications And Data: Effective Strategies And Best Practices. *Asian Journal Of Research In Computer Science, 16*(4). Https://Doi.Org/10.9734/Ajrcos/2023/V16i4386

Skyone. (2024). *Data Driven: 4 Challenges In Implementing This Culture*. Https://Skyone.Solutions/En/Blog/Data-Driven-Main-Challenges

Sopact University. (2023). *Actionable Insights: Turning Data Into Dynamic Results*. Https://University.Sopact.Com/Article/Actionable-Insights

Stevens, E. (2021). *The 7 Most Useful Data Analysis Techniques [2024 Guide]*. Https://Careerfoundry.Com/En/Blog/Data-Analytics/Data-Analysis-Techniques/

Sunitha, B. K. (2024). The Impact Of Data Analytics And Mining. In *Transforming The Decision-Making System – Ijsrem*. Interantional Journal Of Scientific Research In Engineering And Management.

Tableau. (N. D.). *Guide To Data Cleaning: Definition, Benefits, Components, And How To Clean Your Data*. Retrieved September 4, 2024, From Https://Www.Tableau.Com/Learn/Articles/What-Is-Data-Cleaning

Talin, B. (2023). 4 Most Common Obstacles To Data-Driven Decision-Making And How To Overcome Them – Morethandigital. *Morethandigital Insights*. Https://Insights.Mtd.Info/4-Most-Common-Obstacles-To-Data-Driven-Decision-Making-And-How-To-Overcome-Them/

Tawil, A. R., Muhidin, M., Schmoor, X., Vlachos, K., & Haidar, D. (2023). *Trends And Challenges Towards An Effective Data-Driven Decision Making In Uk Smes: Case Studies And Lessons Learnt From The Analysis Of 85 Smes*. Http://Arxiv.Org/Pdf/2305.15454

Team Digitaldefynd. (2024). *15 Business Analytics Case Studies*. Https://Digitaldefynd.Com/Iq/Business-Analytics-Case-Studies/

Tsvetomira, P. (2022). *Top Data-Driven Companies You Can Learn From*. Https://Www.Slingshotapp.Io/Blog/Top-Data-Driven-Companies

Van Der Merwe, L., & Davey, C. (2024). The Role Of Organisational Culture And Structure In Data-Driven Green Policy And Decision-Making. *Environmental Science & Sustainable Development, 9*(2), 1–7. Https://Doi.Org/10.21625/Essd.V9i2.1085

Walacor (2024). 6 Best Practices For Maintaining Data Integrity | Walacor Corporation. *Walacor Corporation*. Https://Www.Walacor.Com/2024/01/24/6-Best-Practices-Maintaining-Data-Integrity/

Warudkar, H. (2021). What Is Machine Learning And Machine Learning Techniques: A Complete Guide. *Express Analytics*. Https://Www.Expressanalytics.Com/Blog/Machine-Learning-Techniques-Guide/

Zaghmout, B. (2024). Strategic Decision-Making In Startups: The Role Of Data-Driven Insights In Enhancing Business Innovation. *International Journal Of Entrepreneurship And Business Innovation, 7*(3), 76–91. Https://Doi.Org/10.52589/Ijebi-9joy4tvb

Zlojutro, S. (N.D.). *Actionable Insights: Translating Research Into Data-Driven Decisions*. Retrieved September 6, 2024, From Https://Thrivable.App/Insights/Actionable-Insights-Translating-Research-Into-Data-Driven-Decisions

KEY TERMS AND DEFINITIONS

Data-Driven Culture: An organizational environment where decisions at all levels are based on data analysis rather than intuition alone, characterized by widespread data literacy, analytical thinking, and empirical decision-making processes.

Data-driven decision-making (DDM): Using relevant data to inform strategic choices and organizational actions, moving beyond intuition and experience to prioritize evidence-based analysis for making informed business decisions.

Data Governance: A comprehensive framework of policies, procedures, and standards that ensure data quality, integrity, security, and accessibility while maintaining compliance with regulations and organizational requirements.

Data Literacy: The ability to read, understand, create, and communicate data as information, encompassing skills needed to interpret and analyze data effectively across all levels of an organization.

Data Narration: The process of transforming raw data insights into compelling stories that effectively communicate findings to stakeholders, making complex information accessible and actionable through structured storytelling.

Data Quality: The measure of data's fitness for use, encompassing accuracy, completeness, consistency, timeliness, and reliability, which is fundamental to ensuring trustworthy analysis and decision-making.

Diagnostic Analytics: A form of advanced analytics that examines data to answer "why" something happened, focusing on the root causes of events and issues through techniques like drill-down analysis and correlation studies.

Key Performance Indicators (KPIs): Carefully selected quantifiable metrics that align with an organization's strategic objectives and serve as benchmarks to measure progress toward predetermined goals and assess operational effectiveness.

Predictive Analytics: The use of statistical models and machine learning algorithms to analyze historical data and identify patterns to forecast future trends and outcomes with high probability.

Prescriptive Analytics: The most advanced form of data analytics that combines predictive models with optimization algorithms to forecast future outcomes and recommend specific actions to achieve desired results and shape optimal business strategies.

Chapter 14
Making Value-Based Decisions

ABSTRACT

This chapter explores the critical process of making values-based decisions in organizational leadership. It emphasizes recognizing ethical dilemmas, gathering comprehensive information, considering multiple perspectives, applying ethical frameworks, and effectively communicating decisions. Leaders must develop ethical awareness to identify situations with moral implications. Thorough information gathering from diverse sources is crucial for informed decision-making. Considering multiple viewpoints helps overcome biases and leads to more inclusive solutions. Ethical frameworks like utilitarianism, deontology, and virtue ethics provide structured approaches to moral reasoning. Values-based decisions should align with core organizational principles, even when challenging. Transparent communication of the decision-making process builds trust and reinforces ethical culture. Effective communication includes clarity, context, value alignment, and addressing concerns. This approach to decision-making fosters integrity, stakeholder trust, and employee engagement.

INTRODUCTION

In a complex and rapidly evolving business environment, leaders face unprecedented challenges in making decisions that drive organizational success and uphold ethical principles and core values. This chapter presents a comprehensive framework for value-based decision-making, exploring how leaders can effectively navigate the intricate intersection of ethical considerations and business objectives while maintaining organizational integrity and stakeholder trust. The modern business environment is characterized by increasing stakeholder expectations, regulatory scrutiny, and moral complexities that demand a more sophisticated approach to

DOI: 10.4018/979-8-3693-5553-4.ch014

decision-making. Leaders must balance competing interests while ensuring their choices align with organizational values and societal expectations. The global nature of modern business operations further complicates this challenge, requiring decision-makers to consider cultural differences and diverse value systems.

The chapter addresses these challenges by examining four key components of value-based decision-making. First, it explores the importance of recognizing ethical dilemmas in business contexts. It emphasizes how leaders can develop the awareness and sensitivity to identify potential moral challenges before they escalate into crises. Second, it delves into identifying and articulating core values at individual and organizational levels, demonstrating how they serve as fundamental guides in decision-making.

The third component systematically gathers relevant information, highlighting the importance of comprehensive data collection and stakeholder engagement in ethical decision-making. This section emphasizes the need for leaders to consider multiple perspectives and potential consequences before reaching conclusions. Finally, the chapter examines the crucial aspect of decision implementation and communication, providing strategies for effectively conveying value-based decisions across organizational hierarchies while maintaining transparency and building trust.

Throughout the discussion, the chapter integrates theoretical frameworks with practical applications, drawing on contemporary examples and research to illustrate how leaders can successfully implement value-based decision-making in their organizations. The chapter specializes in the challenges leaders may face, such as time constraints, competing stakeholder interests, and balancing short-term performance with long-term ethical considerations. The chapter also addresses the role of organizational culture in supporting value-based decision-making and the importance of developing systems that reinforce ethical behavior at all levels of the organization.

By providing this comprehensive examination of value-based decision-making, the research aims to equip leaders with the tools and insights necessary to make ethically sound decisions while effectively managing the complex demands of modern business leadership. This framework facilitates improved decision-making procedures. It contributes to building more substantial, resilient organizations that can thrive while maintaining their ethical integrity in an increasingly challenging business environment.

RECOGNIZE THE ETHICAL DILEMMA

Leadership in today's complex business environment requires recognizing ethical dilemmas. A key component of navigating the intricate landscape of modern business ethics is identifying situations where values may conflict or decisions could have significant moral implications. This is a fundamental skill that leaders must develop as organizations face increasing scrutiny and stakeholder expectations around ethical conduct. By sharpening this skill, decision-makers can proactively address potential ethical issues before they escalate.

For instance, a common ethical dilemma in business might involve choosing between maximizing profits and ensuring fair labor practices. Leaders may face pressure to cut costs, which could lead to outsourcing jobs to regions with lower labor standards. Balancing these financial objectives with the ethical responsibility of treating workers fairly is a challenge many leaders encounter. Recognizing an ethical dilemma is the crucial first step in making value-based decisions. This point highlights the importance of ethical awareness and sensitivity, which could have significant moral implications.

The Importance of Recognizing Ethical Dilemmas

In the complicated world of commerce, ethical quandaries crop up when a collision occurs between two or more innocently defensible courses of action, presenting no unambiguous result (Lakacha, n.d.). These mystifications materialize when commercial boundaries or interests disaccord with ethical principles. The intricate shade of ultramodern business operations, global force networks, and fleetly developing technologies engenders new ethical coverings that leaders must cut with finesse (College of Business, 2024). From the difficulties of conflicts of interest to the delicate equilibrium between profit motives and environmental stewardship, these dilemmas permeate commercial geography. Sequestration enterprises, indifferent employment practices, and the tightrope between transparency and confidentiality complicate the ethical terrain.

The spirit of contemporary business, characterized by its global reach and technological complication, has amplified the frequency and intricacy of these moral predicaments (Francis & Murfey, 2015). Those at the helm must keep their wits about discerning these immorally charged situations. This understanding enables them to render reasonable and responsible verdicts harmonizing with their organization's morality and moral marks. A leader's capability to navigate these unfaithful waters isn't simply desirable but an absolute necessity in the moment's turbulent business terrain. As executive leaders exercise this skill, they can steer their companies through the murky waters of ethical nebulosity, cultivating societies of integrity and sustainability.

Ethical Awareness and Sensitivity

Ethical understanding and sensibility are paramount for those who helm the ship of leadership on today's tumultuous business seas. This quintessential skill set encompasses a multifaceted approach to navigating the murky waters of moral quandaries. At its core lies the necessity for leaders to immerse themselves in the labyrinthine world of ethical frameworks, familiarizing themselves with the intricate tapestry of moral theories and decision-making paradigms that serve as beacons in the fog of complex situations (Hughes, 2010). The nurturing of moral imagination complements this intellectual odyssey. This cognitive faculty empowers leaders to envision the potential ethical ramifications of their choices and actions with prescient clarity (Wittrich, 2022).

In our increasingly interconnected global marketplace, the astute leader must also be aware of cultural nuances and their profound impact on ethical perceptions and decision-making processes (Francis & Murfey, 2015). This cultural acumen is a crucial compass in navigating the diverse landscape of international business ethics. Furthermore, the ethical leader must remain vigilant, constantly updating their knowledge repository with emerging ethical conundrums that ripple through their industry and the broader business ecosystem (Wittrich, 2022). Through this commitment to lifelong learning, leadership remains at the forefront of moral discourse and practice.

We cannot overstate the significance of honing ethical awareness and sensitivity, as it confers many benefits to the discerning leader. The most crucial ability is to identify potential ethical pitfalls proactively before they become full-blown crises, enabling leaders to engage in preemptive decision-making and risk mitigation strategies (Schmocker et al., 2021). Moreover, this heightened ethical sensibility allows leaders to align their organizational practices with the ever-evolving expectations of stakeholders, who increasingly demand businesses to be paragons of moral conduct (College of Business, 2024).

The ripple effects of consistent ethical decision-making extend far beyond mere compliance, fostering a bedrock of trust with stakeholders and burnishing the organization's reputation, a valuable currency in the modern business landscape that translates into tangible benefits such as unwavering customer loyalty and enhanced employee retention (Darby, 2022). Ethical awareness is a lodestar in the labyrinthine world of legal and regulatory compliance, guiding organizations through the treacherous waters of potential infractions and costly penalties (Lakacha, n.d.). Perhaps most significantly, when leaders embody and model ethical sensitivity, they become the architects of an organizational culture steeped in integrity, empowering employees at all echelons to voice ethical concerns without trepidation, asserts Darby.

To nurture this invaluable trait, leaders must engage in regular introspection, critically examining personal and organizational values. They must also actively seek diverse perspectives whenever confronted with complex ethical dilemmas, stay abreast of emerging ethical issues within their industry, create an environment conducive to open discussion, and attend rigorous educational and training programs that hone their ethical acumen. By embracing these practices, leaders can forge organizations that not only navigate the moral minefields of modern business but thrive as beacons of integrity in an increasingly complex world.

Frameworks for Ethical Decision-Making

Astute leaders employ analytical frameworks to dissect the predicament when ethical quandaries arise. They begin by pinpointing the salient moral concerns and then contemplate all parties affected by the situation. A reasonable evaluation of diverse courses of action follows, with a meticulous assessment of the ramifications of each potential path. With this comprehensive analysis, decision-makers can render and execute a verdict with unwavering rectitude. The denouement of this process involves introspection on the outcomes and gleaning invaluable insights for future application. This methodical approach empowers leaders to navigate the labyrinthine landscape of ethical decision-making with aplomb and sagacity (Johnson, 2020). By adhering to this framework, executives can ensure that their choices align with organizational values and societal expectations, fostering a culture of integrity and accountability within their spheres of influence.

Challenges in Recognizing Ethical Dilemmas

In the labyrinthine realm of contemporary leadership, many factors can obfuscate the recognition of ethical quandaries. The intricate tapestry of global commerce often veils the full moral ramifications of executive decisions, while the relentless pursuit of ephemeral triumphs can eclipse long-term ethical deliberations. Cognitive biases, those insidious mental shortcuts, have the potential to obscure moral judgment, and the prevailing organizational ethos can either amplify or attenuate ethical cognizance. This confluence of elements creates a formidable challenge for leaders striving to navigate the treacherous waters of moral decision-making in today's fast-paced business milieu (Francis & Murfey, 2015; O'Leary & Stewart, 2006; Hughes, 2010).

Sagacious leaders can employ a multifaceted approach to surmount these obstacles and hone their ability to discern ethical dilemmas. Engaging in formal ethical erudition can augment their moral understanding and decision-making prowess while fostering an environment conducive to candid discourse on ethical matters that promote organizational awareness. Implementing structured ethical decision-making frameworks provides a systematic methodology for identifying and scrutinizing moral issues. By exemplifying ethical conduct, leaders can catalyze the development of ethical awareness in others. Furthermore, actively seeking diverse perspectives from a panoply of stakeholders can broaden ethical understanding and illuminate potential conflicts, ensuring a more comprehensive and nuanced approach to ethical leadership (Chully, 2012; Fahey, 1987; Francis & Murfey, 2015; Pervin, 2023; McCarthy & Puffer, 2008).

Recognizing ethical dilemmas is critical for leaders in today's complex business environment. By developing ethical awareness and sensitivity, leaders can better identify situations where values may conflict and decisions could have significant ethical implications. A strong sense of awareness forms the basis for sound decision-making and ethical leadership, both critical to achieving long-term business success and sustainability. In an era of increased transparency and stakeholder activism, recognizing and navigating ethical dilemmas is a crucial leadership competency. Leaders can make conscientious decisions that balance business objectives with moral imperatives by developing ethical awareness and sensitivity. Organizations and society also build trust, enhance reputation, and create long-term value by minimizing risks.

IDENTIFY CORE VALUES

Through self-reflection and organizational alignment, organizations can create a clear vision of purpose, build trust, and gain credibility by guiding their actions with values, resulting in a more robust organizational culture and effective leadership. Self-reflection allows leaders and employees to understand their values, strengths, and areas for improvement. This deeper understanding helps align personal goals with the organization's mission, fostering a more cohesive and committed workforce. Furthermore, self-reflection promotes constant learning and flexibility, which are necessary for staying aligned in a changing context.

The Importance of Identifying Core Values

Core values, the fundamental foundations of human behavior, serve as a moral compass, directing an individual's behaviors and molding their worldview. These basic tenets influence one's decision-making processes and define the very essence of their character. Identifying and embracing personal core values is an invigorating and transformative experience, enabling leaders to cultivate an authentic and efficacious leadership style (Woliba Market Team, 2024). This profound journey of self-discovery necessitates a thorough analysis of one's psyche, meticulously examining beliefs, experiences, and priorities that have sculpted one's persona.

Unearthing one's core values has many benefits for the individual. It clarifies the essential aspects, offering a transparent perspective to understand the intricacies of life. This newfound clarity is a lodestar, guiding personal and professional decisions with unwavering certainty. Furthermore, it promotes higher self-awareness and sincerity, allowing people to connect their behaviors with their deepest beliefs. This congruence between beliefs and behaviors inevitably leads to more fulfilling relationships and a more harmonious existence.

A leader who undertakes such an introspective journey develops an extensive understanding of their personal moral principles and decision-making principles. Their self-awareness enables them to lead with consistency and authenticity. By engaging in contemplative practices, such as ruminating on life experiences, pondering hypothetical scenarios, and seeking counsel from trusted confidants, leaders can cultivate a leadership style that is both principled and ethical (Westover, 2024). This approach not only engenders trust and respect among followers but also fosters a culture of integrity within the organization, setting a sterling example for others to emulate.

Defining Values Through a Leadership Philosophy

Once leaders have unearthed their core values through introspection, the next crucial step is to articulate these principles in a compelling leadership philosophy statement. This manifesto serves as a beacon, illuminating the leader's ethical framework and guiding their actions in the organizational landscape. A well-crafted statement should encapsulate the essence of one's fundamental values, employing vivid and evocative language that resonates with both the heart and mind. It should transcend mere self-reflection, focusing outwardly on these values' impact on others and the organization. This is a weighty responsibility, as these values will guide the leader's actions and decisions, and they should delineate specific behaviors that the leader commits to embody, thus transforming abstract principles into tangible actions (Westover, 2024).

Core values, those ineffable yet potent forces that shape our very being, serve as the foundation upon which individuals and organizations construct their identities and chart their course through life's tumultuous waters. These fundamental beliefs act as an unwavering compass, guiding us through the labyrinth of complex decisions and helping us maintain our integrity when faced with daunting challenges (Woliba Market Team, 2024). For individuals, identifying and embracing personal core values is a transformative journey. It clearly explains what is truly important in navigating personal and professional domains. This heightened self-awareness fosters authenticity, allowing one to align one's actions with one's deepest convictions and, in turn, cultivate more meaningful and fulfilling relationships.

In organizations, clearly defined core values wield an equally potent influence. They serve as the architectural design for organizational culture, defining its DNA and recruiting personnel with similar values. This unity of personal and business ideals results in a symbiotic connection that fosters employee loyalty and dedication. This affiliation between individual and organizational values creates a reciprocal relationship, fostering employee loyalty and commitment. Moreover, these guiding principles inform strategic planning and decision-making processes, ensuring that every action harmonizes with the organization's fundamental beliefs. The ripple effect of this value-driven approach extends beyond the confines of the company, enhancing brand reputation and fostering customer loyalty. Core values are the invisible yet indomitable force that propels individuals and organizations toward their highest potential, creating a legacy of integrity, purpose, and lasting impact.

Organizational Core Values

Core values are the foundation of corporate ethos, driving employee behavior and influencing strategic decision-making with unwavering clarity. These axioms foster a shared sense of purpose, magnetizing like-minded talent and clientele to the company's orbit. Essentially, they sculpt the DNA of corporate culture, imbuing it with a distinct identity that reverberates through every echelon of the enterprise (Hills, 2023).

When an organization delineates its core values, it unlocks many benefits beyond mere platitudes. These principles guide strategic planning, illuminating the path forward amidst the tumultuous seas of commerce. Moreover, they serve as a crucible for brand reputation, forging an unbreakable bond of loyalty to customers who resonate with the company's ethos. The judicious application of core values can transmute an ordinary business into an extraordinary exemplar of corporate citizenship.

The genesis of organizational core values demands a collaborative approach that harmonizes employees' voices with the company's overarching mission and vision. This transformation process must also consider the industry's unique demands and stakeholders' expectations. The resulting values should be aspirational, actionable, and quantifiable (Hills, 2023). To breathe life into these principles, organizations can employ a variety of methodologies, ranging from employee workshops to leadership retreats and cross-functional teams, ensuring that the values permeate every facet of the corporate ecosystem, assert Gelle-Jimenez & Aguiling (2021).

Articulating and Implementing Core Values

The crystallization of core values demands more than bare identification; it necessitates a profound integration into the veritable fabric of diurnal actuality. For individuals, this transformation may manifest as a particular charge statement or the establishment of objects that reverberate with their natural principles. In the commercial sphere, the dispersion of these values must be unambiguous, woven into the shade of programs and procedures, and corroborated through a judicious system of accolades and impulses (Wong, 2024).

Still, this trip of value articulation isn't without its risks. Organizations and individuals likewise must navigate the unfaithful waters of authenticity, striking a delicate equilibrium between the deficit and superfluity of core values. Conciliating individual and organizational morality is challenging, and maintaining loyalty to these principles in the face of adversity or temptation is a constant challenge (Perry, 2024). When executed with finesse, this hermetic process of value integration transforms abstract ideals into palpable guideposts illuminating the path to individual and organizational excellence.

Benefits of Aligning with Core Values

Benefits resonate throughout the commercial ecosystem when individuals and associations harmonize their conduct with their core values. This alignment fosters a remarkable depth in decision-making, establishing an unbreakable foundation of trust and credibility that endures. The enterprise's ethical address gets a notable upswing, mollifying the threat of misbehavior and fortifying the veritable foundations of organizational integrity (Qualtrics, 2023).

The convergence of individual and organizational values catalyzes a metamorphosis in the plant terrain, bearing a cohesive and immorally predicated commercial culture (Gelle-Jimenez & Aguiling, 2021).

When leadership's moral compass aligns with the organization's guiding principles, it ignites a vital community that propels reality toward unknown heights of success. This harmonious alignment enhances employee engagement and satisfaction while sharpening the organization's decision-making skills. The outcome is a noticeable boost in organizational performance and the development of a strong ethical framework that permeates every level of the company. Human Resource Management (HRM) practices foster this critical value consonance within the organizational circle (Gelle-Jimenez & Aguiling, 2021).

By enforcing judicious strategies, HRM can seamlessly integrate individual and commercial values, creating a sphere where ethical considerations aren't bare tropes but lived accomplishments. This alignment gives the organization an enhanced capacity to navigate the challenges and conflicts that inescapably arise in the commercial world (Ainomugisha, 2022). The attendant community between persuasions and organizational morality galvanizes tender morale and sculpts a redoubtable brand identity that resonates with stakeholders across the diapason.

Impact on Decision-Making and Leadership

The crystallization and articulation of core values by leaders and organizations serve as the foundation of ethical decision-making, erecting an overwhelming buffer against moral nebulosity (Westover, 2024). This axiological foundation engenders a remarkable thickness in conduct and choices, forging an untouchable fortification of trust and credibility that withstands the metal glove of time. The commercial pantheon's core behaviors on integrity serve as examples of this value-driven leadership paradigm. Westover argues that Amazon's obsession with client satisfaction and Southwest Airlines' unyielding commitment to customer satisfaction shows the power of core values that transform businesses. These commercial titans have skillfully exploited their guiding principles to revolutionize their organizational societies, sparking a revolution in business issues that permeate every level of their enterprises. Therefore, the reasonable operation of core values emerges as the alchemical process by which quotidian commercial realities convert into models of ethical leadership and functional excellence.

Individuals and organizations must identify and articulate their core values. A solid ethical foundation, a moral compass for decision-making, and authentic leadership form the foundation of organizational culture. Leaders can strengthen their credibility and trust by reflecting on their values and aligning them with their organizations' values. It is important to continually revisit and reaffirm core values to ensure their relevance and effectiveness as guides for ethical conduct and decision-making throughout the organization and an individual's life. Gather relevant information when making value-based decisions.

Gathering relevant information is an essential part of making ethical opinions. By comprehensively understanding the situation, leaders can make more informed and morally sound opinions. This due diligence process can avoid unintended adverse issues and hasty judgments. Considering multiple perspectives and implicit consequences will also help ensure well-informed opinions.

COMPREHENSIVE INFORMATION GATHERING

In the intricate shade of ethical decision-making, a structured approach serves as the underpinning and weft, weaving together the vestments of morality and pragmatism. This methodology begins with the scrupulous gathering of material information, a foundational step that lays the bedrock for a comprehensive analysis of the situation (Freire, 2021). This original data collection phase is akin to assembling the pieces of an elaborate mystification, enabling decision-makers to paint a holistic picture of ethical characteristics.

By engaging in this thorough surveillance, leaders can identify all stakeholders bogged down, sound the implicit ramifications of colorful courses of action, fete the maze of legal and nonsupervisory considerations, and unearth covert factors that may sway the outgrowth. This total information-gathering process is a bulwark against the threats of deficient analysis, an unfaithful pitfall that can lead to myopic judgments and defective opinions. Pursuing comprehensive data in ethical decisions isn't simply an academic exercise but a pivotal safeguard against the insidious pitfalls of partial information.

Neglecting this vital step can cause oversights, from disregarding vital stakeholder perspectives to undervaluing implicit hazards or negative consequences. Also, it can impede the exploration of indispensable results, constraining the decision-making process within narrow confines. By assiduously amassing all applicable data, leaders can fortify themselves against these risks, constructing a robust foundation for their ethical reflections (Kooli, 2023). This conscientious approach not only enhances the quality of opinions but also imbues the decision-making process with a sense of integrity and thoroughness, fostering trust among stakeholders and bolstering the overall ethical climate of the organization. This systematic approach fosters opinions with integrity and thoroughness and strengthens the ethical climate among stakeholders.

The complicated ethical decision-making process demands a profound comprehension of the contextual situation, the intricate web of stakeholders, and the far-reaching ramifications of potential actions. Without this panoramic view, leaders risk going recklessly into the abyss of hasty judgments, their decisions tainted by the myopia of incomplete or prejudiced perspectives (Gitbook, 2023). The well-judged accumulation of comprehensive information is a panacea to this predicament, unfurling a tapestry of insights illuminating the ethical quandary. This meticulous reconnaissance not only unveils the multifaceted nature of the dilemma but also brings to light the oft-overlooked viewpoints of various stakeholders, their voices echoing through the corridors of ethical deliberation.

Moreover, it functions as a predictive tool, anticipating the potential outcomes and repercussions that could arise from various decisions and enabling a more sophisticated assessment of alternatives. This exhaustive fact-finding mission also serves as a compass, guiding decision-makers toward relevant ethical principles, legal statutes, and organizational policies that may inform their judgment. In essence, this thorough information-gathering process transforms ethical decision-making from a mere exercise in intuition to a rigorous, analytical endeavor, fortifying leaders against the siren call of simplistic solutions and empowering them to navigate the complex waters of moral uncertainty with confidence and clarity.

Key Elements to Consider in Gathering Information

In ethical decision-making, leaders must embark on a comprehensive odyssey of information gathering, akin to assembling a multifaceted mosaic of knowledge. This intellectually rigorous process necessitates a voracious appetite for diverse perspectives and a keen eye for nuanced details. Leaders must delve into the complex depths of the situation, unearthing facts from many sources, each offering a unique vantage point. They must attune their ears to the cacophony of stakeholder voices, discerning the subtle harmonies and dissonances that shape the ethical landscape.

Leaders must meticulously map the legal and organizational terrain, navigating the intricate web of laws, regulations, and policies that form the bedrock of ethical conduct. Foresight becomes paramount as they peer into the crystal ball of consequences, envisioning the immediate ripples and the distant tsunamis that their decisions may precipitate. Ethical frameworks and principles serve as a compass, guiding leaders through the moral maze, while the echoes of similar past situations provide valuable lessons from the annals of history. Finally, we must seek the wisdom of experts in specialized domains, their insights illuminating the dark corners of technical complexity. This harmonious approach to information gathering transforms ethical decision-making into a rich tapestry of knowledge, empowering leaders to navigate the treacherous waters of moral ambiguity with wisdom, foresight, and an unwavering commitment to ethical integrity.

Methods for Comprehensive Information Gathering

In the intricate needlepoint of ethical decision-making, the thread of stakeholder engagement weaves a pattern of paramount importance. This critical process demands a meticulous identification of all parties whose lives may be touched by the ripples of the impending decision. It necessitates a symphony of voices, orchestrated through interviews and surveys, each contributing its unique timbre to the collective understanding. Open forums become crucibles of insight, where hidden concerns and novel ideas bubble to the surface, enriching the decision-makers' perspective with a kaleidoscope of viewpoints. This immersive engagement serves as a lens, magnifying the nuanced intricacies of the situation and illuminating the far-reaching tendrils of potential consequences, according to (Zaki et al., 2021).

In navigating the complexities of ethical quandaries, the Multi-Criteria Decision Analysis (MCDA) framework emerges as a beacon of structured reasoning. This analytical lighthouse guides decision-makers through the fog of competing priorities, helping them chart a course amidst a sea of diverse considerations. It enables leaders to distill the essence of pertinent criteria and weigh them according to their importance. The MCDA approach becomes the tightrope walker's balancing pole, aiding in evaluating trade-offs between conflicting objectives. Furthermore, it functions as a catalyst, effectively integrating stakeholders' diverse preferences into the decision-making process. According to (Linkov et al., 2004), this methodology effectively addresses environmental issues or situations where ethical considerations intertwine with technical and economic considerations.

The quest for comprehensive information in ethical decision-making unfolds as a multifaceted expedition, employing a diverse arsenal of investigative techniques (Borges, 2024). It begins with the art of conversation, as leaders engage in probing dialogues with stakeholders and subject matter experts, mining their experiences and insights. The journey then proceeds through the knowledge archives, scrutinizing relevant documents, data, and records discerningly.

Firsthand observation becomes crucial, allowing decision-makers to immerse themselves in relevant processes or environments, absorbing unspoken truths and subtle nuances. Ethical guidelines and professional codes of conduct serve as compasses, offering direction in the moral landscape. We explore the annals of history, where similar cases and precedents provide valuable lessons from the past. Finally, we seek the wisdom of ethics committees and advisors, their collective expertise illuminating the path forward. This symphonic approach to information gathering transforms ethical decision-making from a mere cognitive exercise into a rich, multidimensional exploration of moral complexity.

Challenges in Information Gathering

While indispensable, pursuing comprehensive information in ethical decision-making is not without its moral quandaries. In the delicate healthcare ecosystem, for instance, collecting patient outcome data becomes a high-wire act, balancing the imperative for thorough analysis against the sacrosanct principles of privacy and confidentiality (Mellien, 1992). This ethical tightrope demands that decision-makers pace with the utmost care, guided by profound respect for individual rights and an acute awareness of the potential ramifications of data mishandling. Leaders must test their mettle as they navigate the treacherous waters between information sufficiency and privacy protection, using the process as a crucible to forge ethical decision-making.

In this intricate dance of information gathering, time emerges as both ally and adversary. Leaders must temper the siren call of comprehensive data collection with the pragmatic recognition that decisions often unfold in a temporal paradox, where the pursuit of exhaustive information collides with the imperative for timely action. The failure to act, born from an insatiable appetite for more data, can metamorphose into an ethical transgression of omission. Thus, ethical decision-making demands a finely tuned judgment, an almost alchemical ability to discern the precise moment when the scales of information sufficiency tip in favor of action (Lee, 2024). This delicate equilibrium requires leaders to cultivate a heightened sensitivity to the rhythms of their contexts, recognizing the subtle cues that signal the transition from information gathering to decisive action.

Obstacles frequently litter the path to thorough information gathering, each posing a unique challenge to the ethical decision-maker (Gitbook, 2023). The constant tick of the clock applies continual pressure, forcing rapid judgments that may trade depth for speed. In the shadows of the mind, cognitive biases lurk, filtering information through the lens of preexisting preconceptions. Cognitive biases lurk in the mind's shadows, insidiously filtering information through the prism of preconceived notions. Organizational architectures may become labyrinths, with silos becoming insurmountable obstacles to the free flow of critical information.

Stakeholders who defend sensitive information, like dragons hoarding gold, may hesitate to offer critical insights. The sheer intricacy of specific topics can make them opaque without specialist knowledge, resulting in islands of competence amid an ocean of ambiguity. However, faced with these challenges, leaders are not powerless. They can carve out sanctuaries of time for due diligence, employ structured approaches as shields against cognitive biases, and cultivate a fertile soil of transparency where information can flourish. Leaders may turn these impediments into stepping stones by fostering trust with stakeholders and accepting various viewpoints.

The Role of Technology in Information Gathering

In the ever-evolving landscape of information gathering, artificial intelligence, and chatbots emerge as double-edged swords, offering tantalizing prospects for rapid data accumulation and analysis while unfurling Pandora's box of ethical quandaries. These technological marvels, with their ability to sift through vast oceans of information at lightning speed, promise a revolution in research methodologies. However, their integration into academic and research spheres has its perils. The specter of bias looms large over AI-generated information, casting shadows of doubt on the objectivity of its outputs.

The thorny issue of authorship and intellectual property rights becomes a labyrinthine puzzle, challenging traditional notions of creative ownership. Moreover, we must temper the seductive allure of AI-driven analysis by acknowledging the indispensable role of human expertise and judgment in the delicate art of result interpretation. As these technologies continue their inexorable march forward, the imperative to forge ethical guidelines for their deployment in decision-making becomes increasingly urgent (Kooli, 2023). The task at hand is nothing short of Herculean: to harness the immense potential of AI while safeguarding the integrity and ethics of research and decision-making.

The culmination of the information-gathering odyssey marks not an end but a beginning—the genesis of a complex process of analysis and integration that breathes life into the raw data (FasterCapital, 2024). This alchemical transformation demands a discerning eye capable of critically evaluating the reliability and relevance of each informational nugget. It requires the keen perception to discern patterns and trends amidst the noise and the wisdom to recognize conflicts that may lurk beneath the surface. The decision-maker must put on the mantle of a philosopher, contemplating how diverse ethical frameworks intersect with the situation. Potential consequences weigh against ethical principles in this moral crucible, and each decision is a delicate balancing act on the high wire of morality.

The process unfolds like a grand strategic game, with multiple options and courses of action developed and scrutinized, each a potential path through the ethical maze. We build ethically sound decisions upon this comprehensive information-gathering and analysis approach. It acts as a buffer against unintended consequences, fostering a climate of trust among stakeholders. Ultimately, this rigorous process yields decisions that are not merely defensible but truly effective—ethical choices that stand as beacons of integrity in the complex landscape of modern leadership.

Gathering applicable information is critical in forming ethical opinions based on a comprehensive understanding of the situation. By engaging in thorough due diligence, leaders can avoid hasty judgments, consider multiple perspectives, and expect the implicit consequences of their conduct. While this process can be challenging and time-consuming, it's essential for making sound choices that stand up to scrutiny and lead to positive outcomes for all stakeholders involved.

CONSIDER MULTIPLE PERSPECTIVES

When making values-grounded opinions, leaders must consider multiple perspectives to develop comprehensive, compassionate, and effective results. They should hear and feel everyone involved in the decision-making process. This approach allows decision-makers to transcend their impulses and consider their opinions' broader consequences. Impulses can significantly distort decision-making by causing leaders to favor particular groups or results over others, frequently unconsciously. This can cause the dismissal of valuable input and lead to opinions that cannot adequately address all stakeholders' needs. Therefore, biased opinions might erode trust and result in practical problems.

The Importance of Multiple Perspectives in Decision-Making

The Value-Based Decision-Making (VBDM) model stands as a paragon of perspicacious leadership, illuminating the indispensability of diverse viewpoints in elevating decision-making processes and fortifying organizational memory (Hall et al., 2003). This multifaceted approach engenders a holistic comprehension of complex issues, unveiling potential cognitive gaps that might otherwise remain obscured. By embracing this pluralistic methodology, decision-makers cultivate more empathetic and inclusive solutions while simultaneously fostering robust support for their ultimate determinations.

Empirical evidence corroborates the efficacy of heterogeneous teams in business decision-making, with an astounding 87% success rate (Arden Coaching, 2023). This significant shift toward cognitive diversity empowers leaders to transcend the limitations of conventional thinking, unearthing a profusion of options and potential outcomes. Such an approach catalyzes innovation, challenging established assumptions and stimulating creative problem-solving. Moreover, it enables the identification of latent risks and opportunities that might elude a more homogeneous group.

Soliciting input from a panoply of stakeholders engenders widespread support for the final decision. This inclusive process shows a commitment to considering myriad perspectives, engendering a sense of value and acknowledgment among participants. Enhancing transparency in decision-making fosters trust and aligns with broader needs and values. Thus, the resulting decisions gain greater legitimacy and are more likely to receive enthusiastic endorsement from diverse constituencies.

Leaders who embrace this multifaceted approach find themselves better equipped to navigate the labyrinthine complexities of modern decision-making. By examining issues through various lenses, they can recognize and mitigate their unconscious biases, ensuring a fairer consideration of underrepresented groups. This comprehensive evaluation facilitates a more thorough examination of ethical implications and enables leaders to balance competing priorities. The VBDM model is a lodestar for enlightened leadership, guiding organizations toward more informed, inclusive, and productive decision-making processes.

Challenges and Benefits of Incorporating Multiple Perspectives

While incorporating diverse perspectives is indisputable, astute leaders must navigate a veritable minefield of potential pitfalls in their pursuit of inclusive decision-making. The difficulties of modern business often demand swift action, creating a tension between thoroughness and practicality. This temporal pressure can exacerbate personal biases and preconceptions, compelling leaders to make hasty judgments without fully assimilating the wealth of viewpoints. The challenge of reconciling conflicting priorities and opinions further complicates this delicate balance, potentially leading to decision paralysis or a false consensus that merely echoes the majority view. Vigilant leaders must guard against tokenism, avoiding superficial inclusion efforts in favor of meaningful engagement with diverse stakeholders.

Notwithstanding these challenges, the benefits of embracing multifaceted perspectives are manifold and transformative. Hall et al. (2003) explain the profound impact on decision quality and organizational memory, while Renz et al. (2013) underscore the enhanced stakeholder engagement and support that result from inclusive practices. Chen's (2019) research illuminates the critical role of diverse viewpoints in comprehensive risk assessment and mitigation strategies. Perhaps most crucially, this approach engenders a nimble organizational mindset, fostering increased adaptability in the face of ever-shifting business landscapes. By deftly navigating the complexities of inclusive decision-making, leaders can harness these benefits, propelling their organizations towards unprecedented heights of success and resilience.

Strategies for Incorporating Multiple Perspectives

In value-based decision-making, leaders must employ various strategies to consider multiple perspectives effectively. Stakeholder engagement emerges as a cornerstone of this approach, with Graff et al. (2024) highlighting its particular significance in medical settings. Leaders can tap into a rich tapestry of values, preferences, and concerns that might remain obscured by actively involving diverse stakeholders. This comprehensive engagement process is a crucible for insights, forging more robust and inclusive decisions. Concurrently, as elucidated by Plack and Greenberg (2005), reflective introspection empowers decision-makers to scrutinize their assumptions and biases. This metacognitive exercise cultivates fertile ground for considering alternative viewpoints, fostering a more expansive decision-making paradigm.

Using structured decision-making models, like the Rehabilitation Evidence-Based Decision-Making (READ) Model (Novak et al., 2021), makes combining different information in a planned way easier. This approach integrates client preferences, family support, and external factors into decision-making. Diversity-based weighting methods, such as the entropy-weighting method (EWM) and variation coefficient method (VCM), complement these structured models by providing objective mechanisms for evaluating the relative importance of disparate perspectives in risk assessment and decision-making (Chen, 2019). These quantitative tools lend rigor and impartiality to the inherently subjective process of balancing diverse viewpoints.

The concept of decision coaching, as explored by Berger-Höger et al. (2023), emerges as a powerful facilitator of informed, value-based decision-making. This non-directive approach gives patients and stakeholders the tools and confidence to participate actively in decision-making, guaranteeing the genuine integration of diverse perspectives. By fostering diversity of thought through diversifying decision-making teams and committees (HCI Consulting, 2023), leaders can create a fertile environment for innovation and comprehensive problem-solving. The systematic consideration of different stakeholder views, facilitated by structured processes like the Perspective Circle (Capucine, 2023), further enriches this ecosystem of ideas.

To fully harness the power of multiple perspectives, leaders must cultivate a suite of interpersonal skills and organizational practices. The art of active listening and empathy serves as a foundation, enabling leaders to truly comprehend the lived experiences and contexts of others. Leaders can develop the cognitive flexibility necessary to view issues from various angles by challenging their mental models and engaging in role-playing exercises. The creation of an environment that not only tolerates but celebrates diverse views is paramount. This necessitates encouraging open dialogue, acknowledging different perspectives, and modeling vulnerability by admitting knowledge gaps. Through these multifaceted approaches, leaders can orchestrate a symphony of diverse voices, resulting in more comprehensive analyses and, ultimately, more reasonable and impactful decisions.

When considering multiple perspectives, it's essential to address potential ethical dilemmas that may arise. In conservation efforts, for example, balancing scientific knowledge with stakeholder concerns can lead to more effective decision-making (Yee et al., 2021). Leaders must be prepared to navigate conflicting values and priorities while committing to ethical principles. Incorporating multiple perspectives in value-based decision-making is a powerful approach that challenges leaders to broaden their understanding and develop more inclusive solutions. By actively seeking diverse viewpoints, decision-makers can uncover potential blind spots, build more vigorous support for their choices, and ultimately make more effective and empathetic decisions. While this approach may require additional time and effort, improved decision quality, stakeholder engagement, and adaptability make it a valuable investment for leaders across various fields.

APPLYING ETHICAL FRAMEWORKS IN ORGANIZATIONAL DECISION-MAKING

In organizational leadership, value-based decision-making reigns supreme, with established ethical frameworks serving as indispensable tools for navigating the labyrinthine corridors of moral quandaries. Far from theoretical constructs, these frameworks provide a robust platform for leaders to construct more rational and defensible choices (Fayayola & Olorunfemi, 2023). The utilitarian approach, a cornerstone of ethical deliberation, compels decision-makers to engage in a meticulous calculus of good and harm, quantifying the potential ramifications of various options for all stakeholders involved (Phukan, 2023).

In juxtaposition, deontological frameworks spotlight the sacrosanct nature of moral rules and duties, urging leaders to contemplate their myriad obligations to diverse stakeholders and the ethical tenets their organizations have pledged to uphold (Phukan, 2023). Virtue ethics, focusing on cultivating moral character, serves as a crucible for introspection, challenging leaders to align their actions with quintessential virtues such as integrity, compassion, and courage (KingdomDweller, 2024). Through the systematic application of these multifaceted ethical lenses, leaders can unlock a panoramic view of a decision's moral dimensions, elevating the caliber of their decision-making processes and, by extension, the ethical fiber of their organizations.

Key Ethical Frameworks

Utilitarianism emerges as a beacon of pragmatic benevolence in the intricate embroidery of organizational ethics, illuminating the path to maximize collective well-being. With its focus on making the most people happier, this philosophical paradigm forces leaders to do a complex calculus of consequences, carefully weighing the effects of their choices on a wide range of stakeholders (Fayayola & Olorunfemi, 202 3). Astute leaders use utilitarian thinking to quantify the multifaceted impact of various options when faced with complex decision-making, which is an effective strategy for resource allocation and policy metamorphosis affecting diverse groups (Ghezal, 2024). This rigorous and compassionate approach enables organizations to navigate the treacherous waters of ethical dilemmas with a compass calibrated to the true north of collective prosperity.

Compared to utilitarianism, which is based on the idea that actions have consequences, deontological ethics is based on moral absolutes and says that actions are right or wrong, no matter what happens. With its unwavering focus on adherence to moral imperatives and duties, this ethical framework provides a robust foundation for leaders seeking to establish and maintain ethical bastions within their organizational ecosystems (Fayayola & Olorunfemi, 2023). Being honest, having integrity, and protecting individual rights are like Scylla and Charybdis in the real world, and leaders must choose between them. Deontological principles help them find their way. By embracing this ethical paradigm, organizations can forge a culture of moral decision-making that transcends the capricious winds of circumstance, anchoring their actions in the bedrock of moral certainty.

Virtue ethics, the third pillar in this triumvirate of ethical frameworks, shifts the locus of moral consideration from actions or consequences to the essence of the decision-maker's character. This approach, emphasizing the cultivation of cardinal virtues such as wisdom, justice, courage, and temperance, offers a transformative lens through which organizations can view their ethical responsibilities (Fayayola & Olorunfemi, 2023). In organizational dynamics, virtue ethics is most potent in deliberately fostering a culture that values and actively rewards ethical behavior. Forward-thinking organizations, recognizing the profound impact of virtuous leadership, are increasingly integrating this ethical framework into their leadership development programs, nurturing a new generation of leaders steeped in the timeless virtues that form the bedrock of ethical decision-making (Adolph et al., 2024). Through this process of character development, companies may transform the base metal of simple compliance into the gold of authentic, ethical leadership, leaving a legacy of integrity reverberating throughout the corporate hierarchy.

Benefits of Applying Ethical Frameworks

Implementing ethical frameworks in organizational decision-making yields many benefits, transforming the often-nebulous realm of moral deliberation into a structured analysis and transparent governance. These frameworks systematically guide leaders through complex ethical dilemmas, offering a methodology for meticulous dissection and scrutinizing multifaceted issues (Fayayola & Olorunfemi, 2023). This structured approach illuminates the rationale underpinning decisions and fosters an environment of trust and lucidity within the organizational ecosystem (Shadbad et al., 2017). According to Fayayola and Olorunfemi, consistently applying these ethical paradigms creates a predictable and fair decision-making landscape that transcends departmental boundaries and situational vagaries.

Furthermore, these frameworks encourage a comprehensive view, forcing leaders to think about how their decisions will affect a wide range of stakeholders, from the daily concerns of employees to the more significant effects on shareholders and society as a whole (Ghezal, 2024)}. These frameworks facilitate systematic ethical analysis in risk management, revealing potential pitfalls and unintended consequences in decision-making. This empowers leaders to preemptively address these latent threats with strategic acumen (Shadbad et al., 2017).

Clarifying Values and Priorities

Within organizational ethics, frameworks are crucial for problem-solving, guiding leaders through the intricate psychological terrain of moral dilemmas with unmatched clarity and accuracy. These ethical supports compel decision-makers to engage in a Socratic dialogue with their values, explicitly articulating and hierarchizing the principles at stake in any scenario, illuminating the decision-making process with the bright light of clarity, and ensuring a harmonious symphony between professed organizational ethos and tangible choices (Vincent, 2023). The deployment of these established frameworks engenders consistency and equity across the organizational landscape, transcending the capricious nature of individual intuition and anchoring decisions in a shared ethical bedrock (Secker, 2013).

Furthermore, these frameworks give leaders a lexicon of ethical discourse—a Rosetta Stone that deciphers the often-abstruse rationale behind thorny decisions, thus fostering an environment of transparency and enabling stakeholders to comprehend the delicate balance struck between competing interests (Faster Capital, 2024). This alchemical process of applying ethical frameworks not only sharpens the moral judgment of leaders but also serves as a crucible for cultivating ethical awareness throughout the organizational hierarchy, reinforcing the paramount importance of consciously weaving ethical considerations into the very fabric of decision-making at all echelons (Bonde & Firenze, 2019).

Challenges and Considerations

In organizational ethics, the application of moral frameworks, while undeniably potent, often unveils a Pandora's box of challenges that demand the Solomonic wisdom of leaders. The clash of ethical paradigms, each a siren song of moral certainty, can lead to a cacophony of conflicting conclusions, engaging decision-makers to navigate treacherous waters with the finesse of Odysseus, judiciously prioritizing principles in the face of situational complexity (Fayayola & Olorunfemi, 2023). The imperative to tailor these frameworks to the Procrustean bed (a scheme or pattern that forces someone to fit into an unnatural or arbitrary pattern) of organizational context further complicates this ethical odyssey, molding them to fit the unique contours of corporate culture, industry idiosyncrasies, and the Damoclean sword of regulatory oversight (Adolph et al., 2024).

In this high-stakes balancing act, leaders must perform a feat: transmute the base metal of ethical considerations into the gold of business objectives, forging a symbiosis between moral imperatives and the relentless pursuit of profitability and growth (Alabdullah & AL-Qallaf, 2023). Implementing these ethical frameworks is not a mere academic exercise but herculean labor, demanding substantial investment in cultivating leaders' moral wisdom through rigorous training and praxis (Taylor, n.d.). However, in the burden of decision-making, these ethical frameworks reveal their true potency, serving as a philosophical lodestone guiding leaders through the moral miasma of complex choices. They necessitate a dual-faceted examination, examining the present and the future simultaneously, shedding light on the maze of potential effects and unexpected outcomes using the lens of foresight (HyperWrite, 2024).

In scenarios where ethical principles battle conflicting interests, frameworks like the principle of double effect emerge as arbiters, providing a compass to navigate the treacherous straits between intended and unintended adverse outcomes (Cote, 2023). Although these ethical frameworks may not cure all moral issues, their strategic implementation can significantly enhance an organization's ability to make values-based decisions. The key lies in equipping leaders with a diverse arsenal of ethical tools, encouraging their deployment in the crucible of high-stakes decisions where moral implications loom. Through this complex process of ethical deliberation, organizations can transmute the lead of mere compliance into the gold of genuine moral leadership, forging a legacy of integrity that resonates through every stratum of the corporate hierarchy.

In organizational decision-making, ethical frameworks emerge as alchemical tools, transmuting the base metal of moral ambiguity into the gold of principled governance. This philosophical guidance offers a Promethean gift to leaders, illuminating the convoluted corridors of ethical complexity with the torch of structured analysis, transparency, and holistic stakeholder consideration (Fayayola & Olorunfemi, 2023; Adolph et al., 2024). However, implementing these frameworks is a daunting task that requires commitment, a training approach, and Solomon's wisdom to navigate through the perils and pitfalls of real-world ethical dilemmas. Leaders need to develop the ability to wield these frameworks expertly, avoiding moral ambiguity and making decisive, value-based decisions.

Organizations must cultivate a culture of inquiry in this ongoing journey of ethical enlightenment, where the pursuit of moral excellence not only elevates to a lofty ideal but also serves as the foundation for building corporate integrity. In this process, the accurate measure of success lies not in the mere adoption of ethical frameworks but in their seamless integration into the DNA of organizational decision-making, creating a legacy of moral leadership that resonates through every corporate hierarchy.

MAKE AND COMMUNICATE YOUR DECISION

Decision-making and communication are pivotal aspects of value-grounded decisions. In this process, one must arrive at a conclusion based on ethical leadership principles and company values, articulate the decision's rationale to stakeholders, and make tough decisions that align with the company's core values. For illustration, an executive decision may stop a successful product line when discovered to be ecologically dangerous. Though financially grueling, this decision aligns with the company's commitment to sustainability and environmental responsibility. By transparently communicating the reasons behind this decision, the company reinforces its fidelity to its core values.

The Importance and Impact of Making Value-based Decisions

In the labyrinthine realm of organizational leadership, executives often navigate a swamp of intricate scenarios demanding scrupulous contemplation. The multifaceted nature of these situations necessitates an informed appraisal of myriad factors, not least of which are the ethical ramifications and accordance with fundamental principles. Empirical evidence suggests that the axiological foundations of managers wield considerable sway over executive decision-making, molding their prioritization of ethics, interpersonal dynamics, and outcomes (Barnett & Karson, 1989). Leaders can engender a tapestry of consistency and integrity by anchoring their judgments with established values.

The variegated hues of cultural values further enrich the decision-making tapestry. These cultural nuances can profoundly influence the decision-making process and the subsequent interpretation of those choices. Scholarly investigations have illuminated managers' propensity for diverse cultural milieus to accord varying degrees of importance to different facets of performance in their evaluations (Jiao & Hardie, 2009). A salient exemplar of this phenomenon is the tendency of Chinese managers to ascribe greater significance to organizational citizenship behavior compared to their Canadian counterparts. This cultural heterogeneity underscores the imperative for leaders to cultivate cultural understanding and embrace a kaleidoscope of perspectives when formulating and disseminating decisions within the global organizational arena.

The role of leadership is challenging, requiring a solid spirit to make tough decisions based on careful analysis and organizational ethos. Craft (2013) explains that value-based decision-making involves examining options through core values and prioritizing those that best align with the organization's ethical principles (Copeland, 2022). This approach may sometimes lead to short-term difficulties, but it ultimately upholds the foundation of integrity. Leaders can use systematic frameworks to evaluate options against values with precision. One such approach involves a three-part analysis: How do the possibilities align with our core values? Can we compromise on any values? Which option best upholds our most important values? This clarity of value-based decision-making can help leaders stay focused and purposeful.

Leaders must go on a path of discernment in the heat of value-based decision-making. This voyage begins with crystallizing the problem and diligently collecting relevant facts and various views. The next phase involves a rigorous analysis of potential solutions juxtaposed against the organization's values and ethical guidelines. A critical juncture in this process is assessing stakeholder impact and weighing the possible repercussions of different options for various constituencies within and beyond the organizational sphere. The outcome of this process is selecting the option that most faithfully mirrors the organization's core values and ethical standards. By subjecting decisions to this systematic, values-centric scrutiny, leaders can cultivate confidence in their choices, fortifying their resolve to navigate the stormy seas of organizational leadership.

Communicating the Decision Transparently

In the wake of a momentous decision, the art of effective communication assumes paramount importance. Leaders must balance transparency and discretion, clearly articulating their reasoning and showing that the decision aligns with the company's values. This clarity forms the foundation of trust, creating an environment where ethical leadership can thrive without hindrance (Jiao & Hardie, 2009). The explanation of the decision-making process serves as a beacon, illuminating the path for others to emulate in their decision-making endeavors. Leaders create a deep understanding that resonates throughout the organizational hierarchy by aligning decisions with core values and principles.

This transparency accomplishes many objectives: It engenders trust through a demonstration of integrity and honesty, serves as a didactic tool for applying values in decision-making, underscores the centrality of ethics and values to the organizational ethos, and provides a proactive forum for addressing potential concerns. The Harvard Business Review posits that transparency is a critical leadership attribute; it helps build trust and is a prerequisite for building a constructive, high-performance culture (Moore, 2023). This transparent approach to decision-making and communication serves as a crucible that forges ethical behavior and reinforces organizational principles.

Leaders who embrace this paradigm of openness create a reciprocal relationship between decision-making and organizational culture. Leaders show their commitment to ethical leadership and encourage stakeholder dialogue and engagement by clarifying the process of evaluating options and potential effects. This inclusive approach generates a sense of communal ownership and accountability for the decision's results. Moreover, it provides a platform for proactive problem-solving, allowing leaders to address concerns and mitigate potential issues before they escalate. In essence, the transparent communication of value-based decisions catalyzes organizational growth and fosters a culture of trust, ethical behavior, and continuous improvement. It also provides a sense of security, making the audience feel reassured and confident in decision-making.

Critical Elements of Effective Decision Communication

Successful communication skills emerge as a critical fulcrum in the complex world of corporate decision-making, determining the balance of success. The quintessential elements of this communicative alchemy comprise a tapestry of clarity, context, value alignment, concern mitigation, and forward-looking directives. Clarity, the lodestar of this process, demands the elucidation of decisions in both pellucid and concise language, eschewing obfuscation in favor of crystalline comprehension. Context, the crucible of deliberation, provides the background information and illuminates the factors under consideration. The alignment of choices with organizational values and ethical standards acts as a beacon, guiding stakeholders through the often-tumultuous waters of transformation.

Anticipating and addressing potential objections or trepidations shows foresight and empathy, preemptively easing concerns that might otherwise fester and undermine the decision's implementation. Finally, delineating the following steps and implementation strategies charts a rational course forward, providing a roadmap for translating decisions into tangible actions. The fruits borne of this communicative labor are manifold and far-reaching. The transparency inherent in this approach cultivates trust, the most precious and elusive of organizational currencies. Lifting the veil of opacity imbues stakeholders with a sense of inclusion and respect, fostering mutual understanding and cooperation.

This clarity of communication creates comprehension, enabling employees and other stakeholders to grasp the underlying rationale that has shaped the decision-making process. By demonstrating a commitment to value-based decision-making, leaders set a paradigmatic example for others within the organizational hierarchy, encouraging the proliferation of ethical behavior throughout the corporate ecosystem. This strategy also simplifies implementation; when individuals comprehend the reasoning behind a decision, they are more inclined to lend their support and exertion toward its realization. Over time, consistent, value-based decision-making and open communication strengthen and improve the organization's ethical standards and culture, resulting in a virtuous cycle of integrity and trust.

One cannot overstate the power of exemplary leadership in this domain. When leaders navigate the treacherous waters of decision-making with transparency and a steadfast commitment to values, they cast a long shadow of influence across the organizational landscape. This exemplary behavior acts as a catalyst for developing an ethical culture, with values serving as the cornerstone that guides the behavior of all levels of the corporate hierarchy. As Wagner (2024) astutely observes, decision-making requires more than skill; it demands courage.

It's not only about blending data, intuition, and understanding consequences; it's about standing firm in one's convictions and values. Consistently showing this courage through actions and communications inspires others, motivating them to align their choices with organizational principles. The cumulative effect of this approach is the gradual permeation of a "value-based decision-making" ethos throughout the company, as elucidated by Craft (2013), creating a harmonious symphony of ethical conduct resonating from the boardroom to the shop floor.

The resonance of effective value-based decision communication extends beyond mere operational efficacy, penetrating the very core of employee engagement and organizational purpose. This approach transmutes abstract corporate values into tangible guideposts that inform and direct critical organizational choices. As Forbes illuminates, aligning decision-making with values creates a feeling of purpose, which leads to increased engagement and a sense of belonging (Barnhill, 2023). Employees who witness and understand the application of organizational values in critical decisions are more likely to experience a profound connection to the company's mission and overarching purpose. This alignment between individual and organizational values emerges as a potent catalyst for engagement, acting as a gravitational force that attracts and keeps talent while propelling performance to unprecedented heights. In essence, transparent communication of value-based decisions forms a shared sense of purpose, binding individuals to the organization's mission with bonds far more substantial than mere financial incentives could ever hope to achieve.

In this discussion on leadership wit, the essence of decision-making based on values and its accompanying communication becomes a symbol of administrative prowess. This multifaceted skill, necessitating an alchemical blend of strength, simplicity, and a deep understanding of organizational morality, forms the foundation for exemplary leadership. By adhering to a structured decisional framework and clearly articulating the underlying explanation, leaders foster a multitude of positive outcomes; they foster trust, which is essential for organizational cohesion; they articulate ethical conduct, starting a righteous cycle of integrity; and they shape an organizational culture that aligns harmoniously with core values and principles.

This paradigm of leadership, characterized by the fearless navigation of complex ethical geographies and the transparent explication of decision-making processes, becomes a lamp of integrity that illuminates the entire commercial edifice. The ripple effect of this approach is far-reaching, percolating every stratum of the organization and igniting a participatory sense of purpose that transcends bare professional obligation. This approach to decision-making and communication not only aspires to organizational excellence but also actualizes it, fostering a collaborative morality that was previously robust, ethical, and naturally motivating.

CONCLUSION AND SUMMARY

This chapter examines value-based decision-making, highlighting its importance in modern organizational leadership. Through careful analysis of its core components, recognizing ethical dilemmas, identifying core values, gathering relevant information, considering multiple perspectives, and communicating decisions effectively, we see how this approach creates a robust framework for leadership success in today's complex business environment. The integration of ethical awareness with practical decision-making processes enables leaders to navigate challenging situations while maintaining organizational integrity and stakeholder trust. The chapter shows that successful value-based decision-making requires more than mere ethical principles; it demands a sophisticated understanding of how values interact with organizational objectives and stakeholder interests. Leaders must develop the capacity to recognize ethical dilemmas early, cultivate sensitivity to moral implications, and maintain an unwavering commitment to organizational values even when faced with competing pressures. The systematic gathering of information and consideration of multiple perspectives emerge as crucial for making well-informed decisions that withstand ethical scrutiny and serve long-term organizational interests.

Furthermore, the research highlights the critical role of transparent communication in implementing value-based decisions. When leaders clearly articulate their choices' reasoning and align with organizational values, they foster trust and engagement throughout the organization. This transparency supports successful implementation, reinforces the organization's ethical culture, and strengthens stakeholder relationships. The chapter's examination of various ethical frameworks, utilitarian, deontological, and virtue ethics, provides leaders with practical tools for analyzing complex situations and making decisions that balance multiple considerations.

The value-based decision-making framework presented here becomes increasingly relevant as organizations face increasing scrutiny and expectations regarding ethical conduct. The research suggests that organizations implementing these practices develop stronger ethical cultures, enhance stakeholder trust, and improve long-term performance. The framework's emphasis on systematic analysis, stakeholder engagement, and transparent communication provides a practical roadmap for leaders seeking to make decisions that align with organizational values while meeting business objectives.

In conclusion, value-based decision-making emerges as a critical competency for modern leaders, requiring continuous development and careful attention to processes and outcomes. The framework presented in this chapter offers a comprehensive approach that integrates ethical considerations with practical business needs, providing leaders with the tools they need to navigate complex decisions while maintaining organizational integrity and fostering sustainable success. As business environments become more complex and stakeholder expectations continue to develop, the ability to make and communicate value-based decisions will become increasingly central to effective leadership and organizational success.

REFERENCES

Adolph, C., Groenewald, Groenewald, E.S., Uy, F.T., Osiaskit, T., Kilag, Carafrances, K., Abendan, Berhnvincent, C., & Dosdos (2024). Philosophy Of Management Ethical Leadership And Organizational Integrity, *1*(3).

Ainomugisha, G. (2022). How To Identify Company Core Values. *6q*. Https://6q.Io/Blog/Identify-Company-Core-Values

Alabdullah, T. T. Y., Al-Qallaf, A. J. M., Alabdullah, T. T. Y., & Al-Qallaf, A. J. M. (2023). The Impact Of Ethical Leadership On Firm Performance In Bahrain: Organizational Culture As A Mediator. Cashflow // The Impact Of Ethical Leadership On Firm Performance In Bahrain: Organizational Culture As A Mediator: Current Advanced Research On Sharia Finance And Economics Worldwide. *Cashflow: Current Advanced Research On Sharia Finance And Economic Worldwide, 2*(4), 482–498. Https://Doi.Org/10.55047/Cashflow.V2i4.736

Arden Coaching. (2023). *Decision-Making Process - Ensuring Diverse Perspectives*. Https://Ardencoaching.Com/Diverse-Perspectives-In-Decision-Making-Process/

Barnett, J., & Karson, M. J. (1989). Managers, Values, And Executive Decisions. *An Exploration Of The Role Of Gender, Career Stage, Organizational Level, Function, And The Importance Of Ethics, Relationships, And Results In Managerial Decision-Making*, 8(10), 747–771.

Barnhill, A. (2024, August 12). *Council Post: Cultivating A Winning Culture: The Role Of Value-Based Leadership*. Https://Www.Forbes.Com/Councils/Forbescoachescouncil/2023/09/18/Cultivating-A-Winning-Culture-The-Role-Of-Value-Based-Leadership/

Berger-Höger, B., Lewis, K. B., Cherry, K., Finderup, J., Gunderson, J., Kaden, J., Kienlin, S., Rahn, A. C., Sikora, L., Stacey, D., Steckelberg, A., & Zhao, J. (2023). Determinants Of Practice For Providing Decision Coaching To Facilitate Informed Value-Based Decision-Making: Protocol For A Mixed-Methods Systematic Review. *BMJ Open*, 13(11), E071478. Https://Doi.Org/10.1136/Bmjopen-2022-071478. DOI: 10.1136/bmjopen-2022-071478 PMID: 37968011

Bonde, S., & Firenze, P. (2019). *A Framework For Making Ethical Decisions. Society And Business Anthology*. Https://Open.Maricopa.Edu/Societyandbusiness/Chapter/A-Framework-For-Making-Ethical-Decisions/

Borges, E. (2024). *What Is Information Gathering?* Tools And Techniques.

Capucine, B. (2023). Seeing The Whole Picture: Why Perspective-Taking Is A Powerful Tool For Sustainable Decision-Making. *I By Imd*. Https://Www.Imd.Org/Ibyimd/Strategy/Seeing-The-Whole-Picture-Why-Perspective-Taking-Is-A-Powerful-Tool-For-Sustainable-Decision-Making/

Chen, P. (2019). On The Diversity-Based Weighting Method For Risk Assessment And Decision-Making About Natural Hazards. *Entropy (Basel, Switzerland)*, 21(3), 269. Https://Doi.Org/10.3390/E21030269. DOI: 10.3390/e21030269 PMID: 33266984

Chully, A. A. (2012). Business Ethics Course And Ethical Sensitivity Among Budding Management Graduates. Https://Www.Semanticscholar.Org/Paper/Business-Ethics-Course-And-Ethical-Sensitivity-Chully/921e68b5ce4b6ade339f5ca6313b571b381dabd7

College Of Business. (2024). *Understanding The Top 10 Ethical Dilemmas In The Workplace*. Https://Blog.Utc.Edu/Business/2024/05/01/Top-10-Ethical-Dilemmas-In-The-Workplace/

Copeland, M. K. (2022). *The Emerging Significance Of Value-Based Leadership: A Literature Review*. Regent University. Https://Www.Regent.Edu/Journal/International-Journal-Of-Leadership-Studies/Significance-Of-Value-Based-Leadership/

Cote, K. (2023). *4 Examples Of Ethical Leadership In Business | Hbs Online*. Harvard Business School. Https://Online.Hbs.Edu/Blog/Post/Examples-Of-Ethical-Leadership

Craft, J. L. (2013). *Mind The Gap: A Case Study Of Value-Based Decision Making In A Nonprofit Organization*. Https://Conservancy.Umn.Edu/Items/97835ad8-70d6-438f-B3ac-5388b846698d

Darby, J. (2022). What Is Ethical Leadership? Attributes, Traits, & Examples. *Thomas International*. Https://Www.Thomas.Co/Resources/Type/Hr-Blog/What-Ethical-Leadership-Attributes-Traits-Examples

Fahey, C. (1987). Corporate Ethical Decision Making In Health Care Institutions. *Hospital Administration Currents*, 31(4), 19–26. Https://Pubmed.Ncbi.Nlm.Nih.Gov/10284887/ PMID: 10284887

Fastercapital. (2024). *Effective Decision Making: Information Gathering: Knowledge Is Power: The Role Of Information Gathering In Decision Making - Fastercapital*. Https://Fastercapital.Com/Content/Effective-Decision-Making--Information-Gathering--Knowledge-Is-Power--The-Role-Of-Information-Gathering-In-Decision-Making.Html

Fayayola, O. A., & Olorunfemi, O. L. (2023). Ethical Decision-Making In It Governance: A Review Of Models And Frameworks. *International Journal Of Science And Research Archive*. Https://Www.Semanticscholar.Org/Paper/Ethical-Decision-Making-In-It-Governance%3a-A-Review-Fayayola-Olorunfemi/F8b16298b126c7341e22aea19c0d257417ed2a04

Francis, R., & Murfey, G. (2015). Global Business Ethics: Responsible Decision Making In An International Context. Https://Www.Semanticscholar.Org/Paper/Global-Business-Ethics%3a-Responsible-Decision-Making-Francis-Murfey/053e32342e474a1a97e3ae018d036741fdec294a

Freire, A. (2021). Towards A Comprehensive Understanding Of Agile Teamwork: A Literature-Based Thematic Network. In *International Conferences On Software Engineering And Knowledge Engineering, Proceedings Of The 33rd International Conference On Software Engineering And Knowledge Engineering* (Pp. 223–228). Ksi Research Inc. Https://Doi.Org/10.18293/Seke2021-106

Gelle-Jimenez, M. & Hector Aguiling (2021). Leveraging Human Resources Management (Hrm) Practices Toward Congruence Of Values. *International Journal Of Research In Business And Social Science*. Https://Www.Semanticscholar.Org/Paper/Leveraging-Human-Resources-Management-(Hrm)-Toward-Gelle-Jimenez-Aguiling/Ef92cb46fdc67a684145061073e2ec58c6356b35

Ghezal, R. (2024). Determinants Of Engagement With And Of Stakeholders In Csr Decision-Making: A Stakeholder Perspective. *European Business Review*, 36(5), 771–790. Https://Doi.Org/10.1108/Ebr-03-2023-0085. DOI: 10.1108/EBR-03-2023-0085

Gitbook. (2023). *Pitfalls In Ethical Decision-Making | Digital Ethics For Tech Professionals*. Https://Www.Ethics-For-Tech.Org/Part-1-Ethical-Decision-Making/Pitfalls-In-Ethical-Decision-Making

Graff, S., Freeman, E., Roach, M., Wilson, R., Fairley, R., Gullatte, M., . . . May-Slater, S. (2024). Abstract Po1-10-06: Understanding Clinical Meaningfulness In Metastatic Breast Cancer Treatment Decision-Making: Experiences And Perspectives Of Patients, Caregivers, And Clinicians. *Cancer Research, 84*(9_Supplement), Po1-10-06-Po1-10-06. Https://Doi.Org/10.1158/1538-7445.Sabcs23-Po1-10-06

Hall, D., Guo, Y., & Davis, R. A. (Eds.). (2003). *Proceedings Of The 36th Annual Hawaii International Conference On System Sciences: 6 - 9 January 2003, Big Island, Hawaii; Abstracts And Cd-Rom Of Full Papers; [Hicss-36.* Ieee Computer Soc. Hci Consulting. (2023). *Embracing Diversity: Navigating Challenges In Implementing Inclusive Decision-Making Processes.* Https://Www.Innovativehumancapital.Com/Article/Embracing-Diversity-Navigating-Challenges-In-Implementing-Inclusive-Decision-Making-Processes

Hills, L. (2023). Value-Based Leadership: Developing And Using Core Leadership Values. *Healthcare Administration Leadership & Management Journal.* Https://Www.Semanticscholar.Org/Paper/Value-Based-Leadership%3a-Developing-And-Using-Core-Hills/218c39a11d487b7b0f20917f6bf526f33d0abb13

Hughes, P. (2010). Decision-Making Processes In The Context Of Ethical Dilemmas: A Study Of Accountants In Training. Https://Www.Semanticscholar.Org/Paper/Decision-Making-Processes-In-The-Context-Of-Ethical-Hughes/236276423a2da88e9224c5c3cb03cdd5af09890a

Hyperwrite. (2024). *Case Studies And Ethical Decision-Making Frameworks | Medical Ethics Study Guide By Hyperwrite.* Https://Www.Hyperwriteai.Com/Guides/Case-Studies-And-Ethical-Decision-Making-Frameworks-Study-Guide

Jiao, C., & Hardie, T. (2009). Nationality, Cultural Values And The Relative Importance Of Task Performance And Organizational Citizenship Behaviour In Performance Evaluation Decisions. *Journal Of Comparative International Management*, 12(17). Https://Www.Semanticscholar.Org/Paper/Nationality%2c-Cultural-Values-And-The-Relative-Of-In-Jiao-Hardie/Db6f86fe65adfa0a6af6855622b4cf267def3b66

Johnson, C. E. (2020). *Organizational Ethics: A Practical Approach* (3rd ed.). Sage.

Kingdomdweller (2024). Deontology, Utilitarianism, And Virtues Ethical Theories. *Kingdomdweller.* Https://Www.Heartforkingdom.Com/2024/05/05/Deontology-Utilitarianism-And-Virtues-Ethics/

Kooli, C. (2023). Chatbots In Education And Research: A Critical Examination Of Ethical Implications And Solutions. *Sustainability (Basel)*, 15(7), 5614. Https://Doi.Org/10.3390/Su15075614. DOI: 10.3390/su15075614

Lakacha, A. (N D). *Ethical Dilemmas In Business And How To Address Them.* Https://Sites.Suffolk.Edu/Ccpe/Ethical-Dilemmas-In-Business/

Lee, Y. (2024). Consciously Choosing Unconsciousness. *Voices In Bioethics, 10.* Https://Doi.Org/10.52214/Vib.V10i.12500

Linkov, I., Varghese, A., Jamil, S., Seager, T. P., Kiker, G., & Bridges, T. (2004). Multi-criteria decision analysis: a framework for structuring remedial decisions at contaminated sites. In *Comparative risk assessment and environmental decision making* (pp. 15–54). Springer Netherlands.

Mccarthy, D. J., & Puffer, S. M. (2008). Interpreting The Ethicality Of Corporate Governance Decisions In Russia: Utilizing Integrative Social Contracts Theory To Evaluate The Relevance Of Agency Theory Norms. *Academy of Management Review*, 33(1), 11–31. Https://Www.Semanticscholar.Org/Paper/Interpreting-The-Ethicality-Of-Corporate-Governance-Mccarthy-Puffer/5c88ba936c331e39adf114ebad94304df6d57bcf. DOI: 10.5465/amr.2008.27745006

Mellien, A. C. (1992). Ethical Dilemmas In The Care Of Premature Infants. *Clinical Nurse Specialist CNS*, 6(3), 130–134. Https://Doi.Org/10.1097/00002800-199200630-00002. DOI: 10.1097/00002800-199200630-00002 PMID: 1393963

Moore, M. G. (2023). *How Transparent Should You Be With Your Team?* Harvard Business Review. Https://Hbr.Org/2023/01/How-Transparent-Should-You-Be-With-Your-Team

Novak, I., Velde, A. T., Hines, A., Stanton, E., Namara, M. M., Paton, M. C. B., & Morgan, C. (2021). Rehabilitation Evidence-Based Decision-Making: The Read Model. *Frontiers in Rehabilitation Sciences*, 2, 726410. Https://Doi.Org/10.3389/Fresc.2021.726410. DOI: 10.3389/fresc.2021.726410 PMID: 36188787

O'leary, C., & Stewart, J. (2006). Factors Affecting Internal Auditors' Ethical Decision-Making Other Corporate Governance Mechanisms And Years Of Experience. Https://Www.Semanticscholar.Org/Paper/Factors-Affecting-Internal-Auditors'-Ethical-Making-O'leary-Stewart/A0a7bac0725304b80c32dc38e43644c360e5285e

Perry, M. (2024). Why Core Values Are Important. *Cooleaf*. Https://Www.Cooleaf.Com/Blog/Why-Core-Values-Are-Important

Pervin, S. (2023). Investigating The Impact Of Ethical Leadership On Student Perceptions Of Ethical Decision-Making In Business Management: Evidence From Bangladesh. *Journal Of Business And Management Studies*. Https://Www.Semanticscholar.Org/Paper/Investigating-The-Impact-Of-Ethical-Leadership-On-Pervin/Ff3676823501f005c9a7f761c679380ab060c2a1

Phukan, P. K. (2023). *Value-Based Decision Making: A Strategic Guide For Executives | Linkedin*. Https://Www.Linkedin.Com/Pulse/Value-Based-Decision-Making-Strategic-Guide-Dr-Pranjal-Kumar-Phukan/

Plack, M. M., & Greenberg, L. (2005). The Reflective Practitioner: Reaching For Excellence In Practice. *Pediatrics*, 116(6), 1546–1552. Https://Doi.Org/10.1542/Peds.2005-0209. DOI: 10.1542/peds.2005-0209 PMID: 16322184

Qualtrics. (2023). *Organizational Core Values: Definition, Benefits, And Examples*. Https://Www.Qualtrics.Com/Experience-Management/Employee/Organizational-Core-Values/

Renz, A., Conrad, D. A., & Watts, C. (2013). Stakeholder Perspectives On The Implementation Of Shared Decision Making: A Qualitative Data Analysis. *International Journal of Healthcare Management*, 6(2), 122–131. Https://Doi.Org/10.1179/2047971912y.0000000027. DOI: 10.1179/2047971912Y.0000000027

Schmocker, D., Tanner, C., Katsarov, J., & Christen, M. (2023). Moral Sensitivity In Business: A Revised Measure. *Current Psychology (New Brunswick, N.J.)*, 42(12), 10277–10291. Https://Doi.Org/10.1007/S12144-021-01926-X. DOI: 10.1007/s12144-021-01926-x PMID: 37215736

Secker, B. (2013). The Purpose Of The Idea: Ethical Decision-Making Framework.

Shadbad, M. Z., Hasani, M. T., & Alishahi, A. G. (2017). The Role Of Professional Ethics In Individual And Organizational Outcomes. *Medical Ethics Journal, 11*(40), 53–62. Https://Doi.Org/10.21859/Mej-114053

Vincent, T. (2023). Virtue, Utilitarianism, & Deontological Ethics: What Are The Differences? *Just Weighing*. Https://Justweighing.Com/Blogs/Wisdoms-Many-Facets/Virtue-Utilitarianism-Deontological-Ethics-What-Are-The-Differences

Wagner, M. (2024). *Leading With Courage: Navigating Decisions With Confidence And Integrity | Linkedin*. Linkedin. Https://Www.Linkedin.Com/Pulse/Leading-Courage-Navigating-Decisions-Confidence-Integrity-Wagner-Npkgc/

Westover, J. (2024). Finding Your True North: How To Identify And Apply Your Core Values In Leadership. *Human Capital Leadership Review*. Https://Www.Semanticscholar.Org/Paper/Finding-Your-True-North%3a-How-To-Identify-And-Apply-Westover/27816cc440f24916d48dc9866d3af4e3dd162590

Wittrich, A. (2022). Ethical Decision-Making In The Work Of Project Leaders – Why Ethics Gains Importance In Future Project Management. In J. Stankevičienė & V. Skvarciany (Eds.), *International Scientific Conference "Business And Management ", 12th International Scientific Conference "Business And Management 2022"*. Vilnius Gediminas Technical University. Https://Doi.Org/10.3846/Bm.2022.820

Woliba Market Team. (2024). Why Do Company Core Values Matter? *Woliba*. Https://Woliba.Io/Blog/Company-Core-Values

Wong, K. (2024). Company Core Values: 25 Inspiring Examples. *Achievers*. Https://Www.Achievers.Com/Blog/Company-Core-Value-Examples/

Yee, N., Shaffer, L. J., Gore, M. L., & Harrell, R. M. (2021). Expert Perceptions Of Conflicts In African Vulture Conservation: Implications For Overcoming Ethical Decision-Making Dilemmas. *The Journal of Raptor Research*, 55(3), 359–373. Https://Doi.Org/10.3356/Jrr-20-39. DOI: 10.3356/JRR-20-39

Zaki, A. M., El-Gohary, H., & Edwards, D. J. (2021). Ethical And Sme Internationalisation Determinants. *International Journal of Customer Relationship Marketing and Management*, 12(1), 1–27. DOI: 10.4018/IJCRMM.2021010101

KEY TERMS AND DEFINITIONS

Core Values: The fundamental beliefs and principles guiding an organization's or individual's behavior and decision-making. They serve as a moral compass and form the foundation for organizational culture and ethical conduct.

Ethical Awareness: Recognizing and identifying situations with moral implications or potential ethical conflicts before they escalate into crises. It includes understanding ethical frameworks and maintaining sensitivity to moral considerations in business contexts.

Ethical Frameworks: Structured approaches to analyzing moral decisions, including utilitarianism, which focuses on maximizing benefits for the most significant number; deontology, which emphasizes moral rules and duties; and virtue ethics, which concentrate on character and moral excellence

Ethical Leadership: A leadership approach that demonstrates and promotes appropriate conduct through personal actions, interpersonal relationships, and decision-making that prioritizes ethical considerations and organizational values.

Moral Sensitivity: The capacity to recognize ethical implications in situations and understand how different actions might affect various stakeholders. It includes the ability to anticipate potential moral consequences of decisions.

Multi-Criteria Decision Analysis (MCDA): A structured methodology for evaluating multiple competing criteria in decision-making, helping leaders balance various considerations, including ethical, financial, and operational factors.

Organizational Culture: The collective values, beliefs, and practices that characterize an organization, including its approach to ethical decision-making and how values are integrated into daily operations.

Stakeholder Engagement: The process of involving and considering all parties affected by a decision, including employees, customers, shareholders, and the community. It ensures comprehensive input and builds implementation support.

Transparent Communication: The clear and honest sharing of information about decisions, including the rationale, process, and alignment with organizational values. It builds trust and facilitates implementation.

Value-Based Decision-Making (VBDM): A systematic approach to making choices that align with core organizational and personal values while balancing ethical considerations with business objectives. It involves recognizing ethical dilemmas, identifying core values, gathering information, considering multiple perspectives, and communicating decisions effectively.

Conclusion

As we conclude our exploration of leadership strategies in the rapidly evolving landscape of culture and technology, it becomes clear that the 21st century demands a new breed of leader: adaptable, visionary, and deeply committed to ethical practices. The convergence of culture and technology has reshaped the business world, creating challenges and opportunities. Leaders must navigate a globalized market where cultural diversity and technological advancements are inextricably intertwined. The digital revolution has transformed consumer behavior, necessitating innovative engagement strategies and a deep understanding of data analytics.

Throughout this book, we've delved into various facets of modern leadership, each crucial for success in today's complex environment. We've seen how successful leaders inspire their teams with a clear vision and unwavering values, creating a culture of purpose and ethical decision-making. As organizations expand across borders, cultural adaptability has become paramount. Leaders must foster inclusivity, leverage diversity, and drive innovation by embracing cultural shifts. The technological landscape demands more than just adopting new tools; it requires a revolution in leadership approaches.

Digital transformation necessitates fostering a culture of experimentation and continuous learning. Hand in hand with this technological shift is the critical importance of diversity and inclusion. Beyond being a moral imperative, D&I has emerged as a strategic necessity for driving innovation and enhancing organizational performance. Leaders must cultivate strategic agility in fluid environments, balancing long-term vision with short-term flexibility. Tools like scenario planning and Agile methodologies have become essential in this regard.

The future of business lies increasingly in developing partnerships and ecosystems, breaking down industry silos to drive innovation and growth. This ecosystem thinking, combined with an emphasis on innovation and emergent strategy, allows organizations to seize new opportunities and maintain a competitive edge in rapidly changing markets. Effective communication and collaboration across diverse stakeholders have proven crucial for building trust and driving sustainable success.

As we look to the future of work, leaders must prepare for its changing nature by prioritizing reskilling, embracing AI as an enhancer of human capabilities, and fostering a culture of lifelong learning. Maintaining trust through ethical leadership and accountability has become paramount in an increasingly transparent world.

The power of data cannot be overstated in today's business landscape. Leveraging data and analytics is crucial for strategic decision-making, requiring leaders to cultivate data literacy across their organizations. However, this emphasis on data must be balanced with a commitment to value-based decision-making. To foster integrity and stakeholder trust, leaders must make decisions that align with core organizational values, even when challenging. As we look to the future, it's clear that the most successful leaders will be those who can navigate the complex interplay between cultural shifts and technological advancements.

These leaders must embrace continuous learning and adaptation, foster inclusive and diverse environments that drive innovation, and leverage technology while maintaining a human-centric approach. Making ethical, value-based decisions in the face of rapid change, building and nurturing ecosystems that create value beyond organizational boundaries, and using data-driven insights while maintaining transparency and trust will be critical competencies for future leaders. The path forward is not without challenges, but it is rich with opportunities for those leaders who can effectively blend cultural intelligence with technological savvy. By embracing the strategies outlined in this book, leaders can guide their organizations to thrive in unprecedented change, creating sustainable value for all stakeholders and positively impacting the world.

As we conclude, it's important to remember that leadership in this new landscape is not about having all the answers but about asking the right questions, fostering a culture of curiosity and innovation, and being willing to adapt and evolve. The future belongs to those who can see the winds of change not as a threat but as an opportunity to sail toward new horizons of success and significance. In this ever-shifting cultural and technological landscape, the leaders who will genuinely make a difference remain committed to growth, empathy, and the courage to chart new courses in uncharted waters.

Amdy Diene
Liberty University, USA

Compilation of References

180. ops. (2024). *The Impact Of Poor Data Quality On Business: Understanding The Revenue Consequences*. Https://Www.180ops.Com/180-Perspective-Change/Impact-Of-Poor-Data-Quality-On-Business-Understanding-Revenue-Consequences

Abbas, T. (2022). What is Culture Change in an Organization and How to Implement it? *Umar Tahir*. https://changemanagementinsight.com/culture-change-in-an-organization/

Abdi, N. (2023). *The Ultimate Guide to Partnerships for Ecosystems in 2023*. https://partnerstack.com/resources/guides/ultimate-guide-to-partnerships-for-ecosystems

Abdullah, Z., Anumudu, C., & Raza, S. (2022). Examining the digital organizational identity through content analysis of missions and vision statements of malaysian and singaporean sme company websites. *The Bottom Line (New York, N.Y.)*, 35(2/3), 137–158. Doi.org/10.1108/bl-12-2021-0108. DOI: 10.1108/BL-12-2021-0108

Achanta, A., & Boina, R. (2023). Evolving Paradigms Of Data Engineering In The Modern Era: Challenges, Innovations, And Strategies. *International Journal Of Science And Research (Ijsr), 12*(10), 606–610. Https://Doi.Org/10.21275/Sr231007071729

AchieveUnite. (2023). *2024 Trends: Success Through Partnering, Leadership and AI – AchieveUnite*. https://www.achieveunite.com/2024-trends/

Adolph, C., Groenewald, Groenewald, E.S., Uy, F.T., Osiaskit, T., Kilag, Carafrances, K., Abendan, Berhnvincent, C., & Dosdos (2024). Philosophy Of Management Ethical Leadership And Organizational Integrity, *1*(3).

Agent Email List. (2023). Embrace Experimentation and Learning. *Agent Email List*. https://agentemaillist.com/embrace-experimentation/

Agile Alliance. (2015). *What is Iterative Development?* https://www.agilealliance.org/glossary/iterative-development/

Agile Business Consortium. (2024). Chapter 11: *Iterative Development*. https://www.agilebusiness.org/dsdm-project-framework/iterative-development.html

Aha Blog Post. (November 2023). Does stakeholder alignment matter? | Aha! Software. https://www.aha.io/blog/does-stakeholder-alignment-really-matter

Ainomugisha, G. (2022). How To Identify Company Core Values. *6q*. Https://6q.Io/Blog/Identify-Company-Core-Values

Alabdullah, T. T. Y., Al-Qallaf, A. J. M., Alabdullah, T. T. Y., & Al-Qallaf, A. J. M. (2023). The Impact Of Ethical Leadership On Firm Performance In Bahrain: Organizational Culture As A Mediator. Cashflow // The Impact Of Ethical Leadership On Firm Performance In Bahrain: Organizational Culture As A Mediator: Current Advanced Research On Sharia Finance And Economics Worldwide. *Cashflow: Current Advanced Research On Sharia Finance And Economic Worldwide, 2*(4), 482–498. Https://Doi.Org/10.55047/Cashflow.V2i4.736

Aldridge, E. (2023). Align Human Resources (HR) with Business Strategy. *Educate 360 Professional Training Partners*. https://educate360.com/blog/align-human-resources-hr-with-business-strategy/

Ali, R., Ateeq, A. A., Al Ani, Z., & Ahmed Ali, S. (2023). A Critical Review of Contemporary Trends and Challenges in Human Resource Management. In *IJIHRM* 04 (02), pp. 22–27. DOI: DOI: 10.46988/IJIHRM.04.02.2023.003

Alireza, A., Kirsty, K., Marian-Andrei, R., & Katarzyna, M. (Eds.). (2022). *Skills Taught vs Skills Sought: Using Skills Analytics to Identify the Gaps between Curriculum and Job Markets. Zenodo.*

AltexSoft. (2023). *Agile Project Management: Best Practices and Methodologies*. https://www.altexsoft.com/whitepapers/agile-project-management-best-practices-and-methodologies/

Amazon Web Services, Inc. (2024). *What Is Data Preparation? - Data Preparation Explained - Aws*. Https://Aws.Amazon.Com/What-Is/Data-Preparation/

Amer-Yahia, S., Marcel, P., & Peralta, V. (2023). Data Narration For The People: Challenges And Opportunities. Https://Doi.Org/10.48786/Edbt.2023.82

Anggoro, A., & Anjarini, A. D. (2024). Building an organizational culture that supports diversity and inclusion. *Productivity*, 1(1), 190–197. DOI: 10.62207/12cjyv77

Anggraini, A., Kalangi, L., & Warongan, J. D. (2024). The influence of accounting information systems, internal control systems, and human resource competencies on the quality of financial reports with regional government leadership style as a moderation variable (Case study of regency/city regional government in North Sulawesi Province). *The Contrarian: Finance. Accounting and Business Research*, 3(2), 136–153. DOI: 10.58784/cfabr.163

Annisa, F., & Widyasari, W. (2023). Development of Digital Literacy for Teachers. *Proceeding International Conference of Technology on Community and Environmental Development.*

Appel, G., Grewal, L., Hadi, R., & Stephen, A. T. (2020). The future of social media in marketing. *Journal of the Academy of Marketing Science*, 48(1), 79–95. DOI: 10.1007/s11747-019-00695-1 PMID: 32431463

Araujo, L., Priadana, S., Paramarta, V., & Sunarsi, D. (2021). Digital leadership in business organizations. International Journal of Educational Administration Management and Leadership, 5-16. DOI: 10.51629/ijeamal.v2i1.18

Arcand, J. (2023). How To Manage Business Relationships. *Work It Daily*. https://www.workitdaily.com/how-to-manage-business-relationships

Arden Coaching. (2023). *Decision-Making Process - Ensuring Diverse Perspectives.* Https://Ardencoaching.Com/Diverse-Perspectives-In-Decision-Making-Process/

Arias-Pérez, J., Coronado-Medina, A., & Perdomo-Charry, G. (2022). Big data analytics capability as a mediator in the impact of open innovation on firm performance. *Journal of Strategy and Management*, 15(1), 1–15. DOI: 10.1108/JSMA-09-2020-0262

Arifin, R., & Purwanti, H. (2022). Examining the Influence of Leadership Agility, Organizational Culture, and Motivation on Organizational Agility: A Comprehensive Analysis. *Golden Ratio of Human Resource Management*, 3(1), 33–54. DOI: 10.52970/grhrm.v3i1.205

ArrowCore Group. (2023). *Evolution of Work Dynamics: Technology's Reshaping of Traditional Workplace Norms* - ArrowCore Group. https://arrowcore.com/blogs/evolution-of-work-dynamics-technologys-reshaping-of-traditional-workplace-norms/

Asgary, N., & Mitschow, M. C. (2002). Toward A Model For International. *Business Ethics (Oxford, England)*, 36(3), 239–246.

Ashikali, T., Groeneveld, S., & Kuipers, B. (2021). The Role of Inclusive Leadership in Supporting an Inclusive Climate in Diverse Public Sector Teams. *Review of Public Personnel Administration*, 41(3), 497–519. DOI: 10.1177/0734371X19899722

Ashish, K. T., & Abhijit. P. D. (2022). Relationship Transparency-Trust Cycle: A Matter of Trust and Competency for Frontline Managers.

Assnservices. (2018). *Don't Attend the Old School of Strategic Planning - World Class Boards.* https://www.worldclassboards.org/dont-attend-the-old-school-of-strategic-planning/

Association for Project Magement. (2024). *What is Stakeholder engagement?* https://www.apm.org.uk/resources/find-a-resource/stakeholder-engagement/

Atlan. (2023). *10 Steps To Create An Effective Data Foundation.* Https://Atlan.Com/Data-Foundation/

Atlassian. (n.d.). *What is Agile the Agile Methodology*. Retrieved July 16, 2024, from https://www.atlassian.com/agile

Austen, C. (2024). *6 Unique Ways To Use Ai In Data Analytics | Datacamp.* Https://Www.Datacamp.Com/Blog/Unique-Ways-To-Use-Ai-In-Data-Analytics

Austin, J. (2021). *How to make values-based leadership your North Star - Work Life by Atlassian.* https://www.atlassian.com/blog/leadership/values-based-leadership-patagonia

Azra, A. (2023). Role of Innovation Management Practices in Enhancing Firm Agility and Adaptability during Times of Crisis in Turkey. *International Journal of Strategic Management*, 2(2), 12–22. DOI: 10.47604/ijsm.2185

Bain & Company. (2020). *The Power of Adaptive Leadership in Times of Crisis.*

Baker, R. (2018). *What Is the Agile Iterative Approach and Where Is It Used?* NTask Manager. https://www.ntaskmanager.com/blog/what-is-agile-iterative-approach/

Ballejos, L. (2024). 4 Ways Technology Supports a Remote Workforce | NinjaOne. https://www.ninjaone.com/blog/4-ways-technology-supports-a-remote-workforce/

Bandura, R., & Burns, C. (2023). A Call to Action: Igniting the Digital Revolution in International Development Studies. https://www.csis.org/analysis/call-action-igniting-digital-revolution-international-development-studies

Bangia, G. (2023). *The Significance of Diversity and Inclusion in P.R. and Communications - Reputation Today.* https://reputationtoday.in/the-significance-of-diversity-and-inclusion-in-pr-and-communications/

Barbour, H. (2024). Examples of Diversity Goals to Measure. https://blog.ongig.com/diversity-and-inclusion/diversity-goals/

Barnett, J., & Karson, M. J. (1989). Managers, Values, And Executive Decisions. *An Exploration Of The Role Of Gender, Career Stage, Organizational Level, Function, And The Importance Of Ethics, Relationships, And Results In Managerial Decision-Making*, 8(10), 747–771.

Barnhill, A. (2023). Cultivating A Winning Culture: The Role Of Values-Based Leadership. *Forbes*. https://www.forbes.com/sites/forbescoachescouncil/2023/09/18/cultivating-a-winning-culture-the-role-of-values-based-leadership/?sh=5de6820470a7

Barnhill, A. (2024, August 12). *Council Post: Cultivating A Winning Culture: The Role Of Value-Based Leadership*. Https://Www.Forbes.Com/Councils/Forbescoachescouncil/2023/09/18/Cultivating-A-Winning-Culture-The-Role-Of-Value-Based-Leadership/

Bass, B. M., & Avolio, B. J. (1994). *Improving Organizational Effectiveness Through Transformational Leadership* (1st ed.). SAGE.

Bayborodova, E. Y. (2019). The Relationship Of Trust, Personal Characteristics Of Students With The Socio-Psychological Climate Of The Educational Organization. *Bulletin of the Moscow State Regional University (Psychology)*, (4), 6–15. DOI: 10.18384/2310-7235-2019-4-6-15

Beech, I. (2023). *What is a Partner Ecosystem and Why Should You Want One?* https://breezy.io/blog/partner-ecosystem

Behnke, K. (2024). 18 Best Free Employee Scheduling Software of 2024. Black & White Zebra. https://peoplemanagingpeople.com/tools/best-free-employee-scheduling-software/

Bekele, S. (2023). *The Role Of Transparency And Accountability In Digital Transformation*. Https://Www.Isaca.Org/Resources/News-And-Trends/Industry-News/2023/The-Role-Of-Transparency-And-Accountability-In-Digital-Transformation

Berger-Höger, B., Lewis, K. B., Cherry, K., Finderup, J., Gunderson, J., Kaden, J., Kienlin, S., Rahn, A. C., Sikora, L., Stacey, D., Steckelberg, A., & Zhao, J. (2023). Determinants Of Practice For Providing Decision Coaching To Facilitate Informed Value-Based Decision-Making: Protocol For A Mixed-Methods Systematic Review. *BMJ Open*, 13(11), E071478. Https://Doi.Org/10.1136/Bmjopen-2022-071478. DOI: 10.1136/bmjopen-2022-071478 PMID: 37968011

Besley, T., & Persson, T. (2022). Organizational dynamics: culture, design, and performance. *The Journal of Law, Economics, and Organization*, Article ewac020. Bratton online publication. DOI: 10.1093/jleo/ewac020

Biswal, A. (2020). 24 Cutting-Edge [*Simplilearn*. https://www.simplilearn.com/tutorials/artificial-intelligence-tutorial/artificial-intelligence-applications]. *Artificial Intelligence and Applications (Commerce, Calif.)*, 2024, •••.

Blackmon, K. (2023). *7 Tips for a Successful Partner Ecosystem Strategy*. Zift Solutions. https://ziftsolutions.com/blog/7-tips-for-a-successful-partner-ecosystem-strategy/

Blog, M. H. P. (2023). Implementing Cultural Change in Organizations. *MHP Management- und IT-Beratung*. https://www.mhp.com/en/insights/blog/post/implementing-cultural-change-in-organizations

Blomquist, B. (2022). *7 Ways to Build Stakeholder Trust*. https://blog.jambo.cloud/7-ways-to-build-stakeholder-trust

Bonde, S., & Firenze, P. (2019). *A Framework For Making Ethical Decisions. Society And Business Anthology*. Https://Open.Maricopa.Edu/Societyandbusiness/Chapter/A-Framework-For-Making-Ethical-Decisions/

Borges, E. (2024). *What Is Information Gathering?* Tools And Techniques.

Borrero, J. D., & Mariscal, J. (2022). A Case Study of a Digital Data Platform for the Agricultural Sector: A Valuable Decision Support System for Small Farmers. *Agriculture*, 12(6), 767. DOI: 10.3390/agriculture12060767

Bowen, B. (2024). *Best Partner Ecosystem Platforms Software*: User Reviews from July 2024. https://www.g2.com/categories/partner-ecosystem-platforms

Boyles, M. (2022). *Innovation in Business: What It Is & Why It's So Important*. https://online.hbs.edu/blog/post/importance-of-innovation-in-business

Bradfield, R., Wright, G., Burt, G., Cairns, G., & van der Heijden, K. (2005). The origins and evolution of scenario techniques in long-range business planning. *Futures*, 37(8), 795–812. DOI: 10.1016/j.futures.2005.01.003

Brainard, M. (2017). The Impact Of Unconscious Bias On Leadership Decision Making. Forbes. https://www.forbes.com/sites/forbescoachescouncil/2017/09/13/the-impact-of-unconscious-bias-on-leadership-decision-making/

Bratton, J., Gold, J., Bratton, A., & Steele, L. (2021). *Human resource management*. Bloomsbury Publishing.

Brett, A. B. (2013). Incentives, land use, and ecosystem services: Synthesizing complex linkages. *Environmental Science & Policy*, 27, 124–134. DOI: 10.1016/j.envsci.2012.12.010

Brower, T. (2021). Empathy Is The Most Important Leadership Skill According To Research. *Forbes*. https://www.forbes.com/sites/tracybrower/2021/09/19/empathy-is-the-most-important-leadership-skill-according-to-research/

Brush, C., Edelman, L. F., Manolova, T., & Welter, F. (2019). A gendered look at entrepreneurship ecosystems. *Small Business Economics*, 53(2), 393–408. DOI: 10.1007/s11187-018-9992-9

Bryan, R. (2024). 7 Qualities Hiring Managers Seek In 2024 Candidates Looking For High-Paying Jobs. *Forbes*. https://www.forbes.com/sites/bryanrobinson/2024/03/21/7-qualities-hiring-managers-seek-in-2024-candidates-looking-for-high-paying-jobs/

Bughin, J., Hazan, E., Lund, S., Dahlstrom, P., Wiesinger, A., & Subramaniam, A. (2018). *Automation and the workforce of the future*. https://www.mckinsey.com/featured-insights/future-of-work/skill-shift-automation-and-the-future-of-the-workforce

Bui, T.L. (2019). Internal communication in the digital workplace: digital communication channels and employee engagement.

Burt, G. (Ed.). (2023). *Evolution of Scenario Planning: Theory and Practice from Disorder to Order* (1st ed.). Walter de Gruyter GmbH. DOI: 10.1515/9783110792065

Business Intelligence Academy. (2018). *Transformational Leadership*. https://www.businessintelligenceacad.com/blog/transformational-leadership

BusinessRiskTV. (2023). *Co-creating Solutions with Stakeholders*. https://businessrisktv.com/co-creating-solutions-with-stakeholders/

Bydrec, Inc. (2020). *What are the 4 Core Principles of Agile Methodology?* https://blog.bydrec.com/core-principles-of-agile-methodology

Cabanes, B. (2023). *The scenario method: an aid to strategic planning* - Polytechnique Insights. Association Polytechnique Insights. https://www.polytechnique-insights.com/en/columns/society/the-scenario-method-an-aid-to-strategic-planning/

Cao, Z., & Shi, X. (2021). A systematic literature review of entrepreneurial ecosystems in advanced and emerging economies. *Small Business Economics*, 57(1), 75–110. DOI: 10.1007/s11187-020-00326-y

Capucine, B. (2023). Seeing The Whole Picture: Why Perspective-Taking Is A Powerful Tool For Sustainable Decision-Making. *I By Imd*. Https://Www.Imd.Org/Ibyimd/Strategy/Seeing-The-Whole-Picture-Why-Perspective-Taking-Is-A-Powerful-Tool-For-Sustainable-Decision-Making/

Carmine, G. (2022). *How Great Leaders Communicate*. Harvard Business Review. https://hbr.org/2022/11/how-great-leaders-communicate

Carnochan, S., & Austin, M. J. (2002). Implementing Welfare Reform and Guiding Organizational Change. *Administration in Social Work*, 26(1), 61–77. DOI: 10.1300/J147v26n01_04

Castordoc. (2024). *7 Data Integrity Best Practices You Need To Know*. Https://Www.Castordoc.Com/Data-Strategy/7-Data-Integrity-Best-Practices-You-Need-To-Know

Catalino, N., Gardner, N., Goldstein, D., & Wong, J. (2022). Effective employee resource groups are key to inclusion at work. Here's how to get them right. McKinsey & Company. https://www.mckinsey.com/capabilities/people-and-organizational-performance/our-insights/effective-employee-resource-groups-are-key-to-inclusion-at-work-heres-how-to-get-them-right

Chan, G. (/2022). How To Develop A Culture Of Openness In The Workplace. *Forbes*. https://www.forbes.com/sites/goldiechan/2022/08/25/how-to-develop-a-culture-of-openness-in-the-workplace/

Chandranshu, S. (2023). Building Trust and Respect with People from Different Cultures. *LinkedIn*. https://www.linkedin.com/pulse/building-trust-respect-people-from-different-cultures-srivastava/

Chang, S. M., Budhwar, P., & Crawshaw, J. (2021). The Emergence of Value-Based Leadership Behavior at the Frontline of Management: A Role Theory Perspective and Future Research Agenda. *Frontiers in Psychology*, 12, 635106. DOI: 10.3389/fpsyg.2021.635106 PMID: 34113282

Chengere, K., & Bekele, M. (2024). Cross-Cultural Leadership and Diversity: A Comprehensive Literature Review. In *SI* 12 (6), Article 2022096, pp. 109–112. DOI: DOI: 10.11648/j.si.20241206.14

Chen, P. (2019). On The Diversity-Based Weighting Method For Risk Assessment And Decision-Making About Natural Hazards. *Entropy (Basel, Switzerland)*, 21(3), 269. Https://Doi.Org/10.3390/E21030269. DOI: 10.3390/e21030269 PMID: 33266984

Chotipurk, A., Nuchniyom, R., & Lakkhongkha, K. (2023). Preparing and Developing the Capabilities of Entrepreneurs in the Digital Age. *International Journal of Professional Business Review*, 8(7), e02864. DOI: 10.26668/businessreview/2023.v8i7.2864

Choudhry, T., Sarfraz, M., & Ul Hassan Shah, W. (Eds.). (2024). *Business, Management and Economics. Organizational Culture - Cultural Change and Technology*. IntechOpen., DOI: 10.5772/intechopen.111316

Chui, M., Manyika, J., & Miremadi, M. (2016). Leading in the digital age. McKinsey Quarterly. https://www.mckinsey.com/featured-insights/leadership/leading-in-the-digital-age

Chully, A. A. (2012). Business Ethics Course And Ethical Sensitivity Among Budding Management Graduates. Https://Www.Semanticscholar.Org/Paper/Business-Ethics-Course-And-Ethical-Sensitivity-Chully/921e68b5ce4b6ade339f5ca6313b571b381dabd7

Claremont Lincoln University. (2023). 12 Reasons Why Diversity, Equity, and Inclusion Are Important in Business - Claremont Lincoln. https://www.claremontlincoln.edu/12-reasons-why-diversity-equity-and-inclusion-are-important-in-business/

Cloud Forces. (2023). *Achieving Business Agility Through Cloud Enablement*. Https://Www.Cloudforces.Ca/Post/Achieving-Business-Agility-Through-Cloud-Enablement

Codeyourcareer. (2023). The Future of Work: How Automation, AI, and Remote Work Are Changing Employment Landscape. *LinkedIn*. https://www.linkedin.com/pulse/future-work-how-automation-ai-remote-changing-landscape/

Coetzee, M., Bester, M. S., Ferreira, N., & Potgieter, H. (2020). Facets of career agility as explanatory mechanisms of employees' career adaptability. *African Journal of Career*, 2(1). Advance online publication. DOI: 10.4102/ajcd.v2i1.11

Colby, S. L., & Ortman, J. M. (2015). Projections of the Size and Composition of the U.S. Population: 2014 to 2060. Population Estimates and Projections. [*U.S. Census Bureau*.]. *Current Population Reports. Series P-28, Special Censuses*, •••, 25–1143.

Cole, C. (2023). *What Is a Balanced Scorecard? | HBS Online*. https://online.hbs.edu/blog/post/balanced-scorecard

College Of Business. (2024). *Understanding The Top 10 Ethical Dilemmas In The Workplace*. Https://Blog.Utc.Edu/Business/2024/05/01/Top-10-Ethical-Dilemmas-In-The-Workplace/

Connect, H. R. D. (2024). *Reskilling: the imperative strategy for navigating the future of work amidst technological disruption - HRD.* https://www.hrdconnect.com/2024/03/22/reskilling-the-imperative-strategy-for-navigating-the-future-of-work-amidst-technological-disruption/

Copeland, M. K. (2022). *The Emerging Significance Of Value-Based Leadership: A Literature Review.* Regent University. Https://Www.Regent.Edu/Journal/International-Journal-Of-Leadership-Studies/Significance-Of-Value-Based-Leadership/

Corbett, M. F. (2024). Unleashing the power of corporate social entrepreneurship: An emerging tool for corporate social responsibility. *S.A.M. Advanced Management Journal*, 89(2), 122–153. DOI: 10.1108/SAMAMJ-03-2024-0003

Corritore, M., Goldberg, A., & Srivastava, S. B. (2020). *The New Analytics of Culture.* Harvard Business Review. https://hbr.org/2020/01/the-new-analytics-of-culture

Cosa, M. (2023). Business digital transformation: Strategy adaptation, communication, and future agenda. *Journal of Strategy and Management*, 17(2), 244–259. DOI: 10.1108/JSMA-09-2023-0233

Cote, C. (2023). *4 Examples Of Ethical Leadership In Business | Hbs Online.* Harvard Business School. Https://Online.Hbs.Edu/Blog/Post/Examples-Of-Ethical-Leadership

Cote, K. (2023). *4 Examples Of Ethical Leadership In Business | Hbs Online.* Harvard Business School. Https://Online.Hbs.Edu/Blog/Post/Examples-Of-Ethical-Leadership

Crabtree, M. (2024). *What Is Data Culture? A Comprehensive Guide To Being A More Data-Driven Organization | Datacamp.* Https://Www.Datacamp.Com/Blog/How-To-Create-Data-Driven-Organization

Craft, J. L. (2013). *Mind The Gap: A Case Study Of Value-Based Decision Making In A Nonprofit Organization.* Https://Conservancy.Umn.Edu/Items/97835ad8-70d6-438f-B3ac-5388b846698d

Craig, H. (2019). 10 Ways To Build Trust in a Relationship. *PositivePsychology.Com*. https://positivepsychology.com/build-trust/

Cross, R., Dillon, K., & Greenberg, D. (2021). *The Secret to Building Resilience.* Harvard Business Review. https://hbr.org/2021/01/the-secret-to-building-resilience

Dafydd, L. (2024). [*Partner Ecosystem Benefits for Your Business.* Impartner. https://impartner.com/resources/blog/partner-ecosystem-benefits]. *Top (Madrid)*, 10, •••.

Daley, L. P. (2020). *Enhancing Inclusive Employee Experiences: Scenario Planning for the Future of Work.* Catalyst. https://www.catalyst.org/research/scenario-planning-future-of-work-covid/

Dansereau, V. (2022). *How Constructive Conflict in the Workplace Can Be Beneficial.* https://pollackpeacebuilding.com/blog/how-constructive-conflict-in-the-workplace-can-be-beneficial/

Daraojimba, C., Abioye, K., Bakare, A., Mhlongo, N., Onunka, O., & Daraojimba, D. (2023). Technology And Innovation To Growth Of Entrepreneurship And Financial Boost: A Decade In Review (2013-2023). *International Journal of Management & Entrepreneurship Research.* DOI: 10.51594/ijmer.v5i10.593

Darby, J. (2022). What Is Ethical Leadership? Attributes, Traits, & Examples. *Thomas International.* Https://Www.Thomas.Co/Resources/Type/Hr-Blog/What-Ethical-Leadership-Attributes-Traits-Examples

Darby, J. (2024). *What Is Ethical Leadership?* Attributes, Traits, & Examples.

Davenport, T. H., & Ronanki, R. (2018). Artificial Intelligence for the Real World: Don't Start with Moon Shots. *Harvard Business Review*, 96(1), 108–116. https://blockqai.com/wp-content/uploads/2021/01/analytics-hbr-ai-for-the-real-world.pdf

Davidson, E., & Vaast, E. (2010), Digital entrepreneurship and its sociomaterial enactment. *43rd Hawaii International Conference on System Sciences*, IEEE, 1-10.

Ddi Blog Post (2019, October). How To Build An Ethical Organizational Culture.

Deady, D. (2020). 9 Companies Around the World That Are Embracing Diversity in a BIG Way. SocialTalent. https://www.socialtalent.com/blog/diversity-and-inclusion/9-companies-around-the-world-that-are-embracing-diversity

Deeb, T., & Ilesvska, A. (2023). *What Is a Partner Ecosystem and Why Do You Need One?* | Storyblok. https://www.storyblok.com/mp/what-is-a-partner-ecosystem

Defy Expectations. (2024). *Culture of Openness.* https://www.defyexpectations.co.uk/culture-of-openness

DeIuliis, E. D., & Saylor, E. (2021). Bridging the Gap: Three Strategies to Optimize Professional Relationships with Generation Y and Z. *The Open Journal of Occupational Therapy*, 9(1), 1–13. DOI: 10.15453/2168-6408.1748

Deloitte (2020). *The future of work in the wake of COVID-19.*

Deloitte (2021). *The Culture Imperative: Building a High-Performance Organization.*

Demir, M., Yaşar, E., & Demir, Ş. Ş. (2022). Digital transformation and human resources planning: The mediating role of innovation. *Journal of Hospitality and Tourism Technology*, 14(1), 21–36. DOI: 10.1108/JHTT-04-2021-0105

Denton, T. B. (2023). Frontiers Of Medical Decision-Making In The Modern Age Of Data Analytics. *IISE Transactions*, 55, 94–105. Https://Www.Semanticscholar.Org/Paper/Frontiers-Of-Medical-Decision-Making-In-The-Modern-Denton/D93758d4f9d73c40b7e9888e2e5446dcbbf53e97. DOI: 10.1080/24725854.2022.2092918

Devan, A. (2024). *7 Trends to Steer the Channel's Trajectory in 2024*. https://www.channelfutures.com/channel-business/seven-trends-that-will-steer-the-channel-s-trajectory-in-2024

Dezao, T. (2024). Enhancing transparency in AI-powered customer engagement. *Journal of AI, Robotics & Workplace Automation*. https://hstalks.com/article/8574/enhancing-transparency-in-ai-powered-customer-enga/?business

Digital Marketing America. (2023). *PPC - Digital Marketing America*. Digital Marketing America. https://newdma.org/category/ppc/

Dirks, L. G., & Pratt, W. (2021). *Technology to Support Collaborative Dissemination of Research with Alaska Native Communities*. AMIA … Annual Symposium Proceedings. AMIA Symposium, 2021, 398–407. https://pubmed.ncbi.nlm.nih.gov/35308978/

Diversity in Tech. (2021). Barriers to workplace inclusion and diversity - Diversity in Tech. https://www.diversityintech.co.uk/barriers-to-workplace-inclusion-and-diversity/

Doolittle, J. (2024). 5 Levers To Create A Culture Of Accountability.

Döppner, D. A., Schoder, D., & Siejka, H. (2015). Big Data And The Data Value Chain: Translating Insights From Business Analytics Into Actionable Results - The Case Of Unit Load Device (Uld) Management In The Air Cargo Industry. *European Conference On Information Systems*. Https://Www.Semanticscholar.Org/Paper/Big-Data-And-The-Data-Value-Chain%3a-Translating-From-D%C3%B6ppner-Schoder/39458c2fa9f95fd2692ee18640d5054bfdf1b936

Dubina, L. (2021). *How brands can navigate cancel culture*. https://www.mintel.com/insights/consumer-research/how-brands-can-use-consumer-identity-and-brand-reputation-to-navigate-cancel-culture/

Dufresne, R. L., & Clair, J. A. (2023). Courage to Strive: Hypocrisy Monitoring, Integrity Striving, and Ethical Leadership. In By, R. T., Burnes, B., & Hughes, M. (Eds.), *Organizational Change, Leadership and Ethics* (pp. 143–158). Routledge., DOI: 10.4324/9781003036395-11

Duggal, N. (2020). Future Of Work: What Job Roles Will Look Like In 10 Years. *Simplilearn*. https://www.simplilearn.com/future-of-work-article

Duhigg, C. (2012). *The Power of Habit: Why we do what we do in Life and Business*. https://en.wikipedia.org/w/index.php?title=The_Power_of_Habit&oldid=1189068802

Duke University. (2024). Culturally Inclusive Communication in the Workplace |. Duke University. https://sites.nicholas.duke.edu/studio/presentation-resources/culturally-inclusive-communication-in-the-workplace/

Dunne-moses, A. (2023). Inclusive Leadership: Steps to Take to Get It Right. Center for Creative Leadership. https://www.ccl.org/articles/leading-effectively-articles/when-inclusive-leadership-goes-wrong-and-how-to-get-it-right/

Dweck, C. S. (2006). *Mindset: The new psychology of success*. Random House.

Dykes, B. (2022). Why Change Management Skills Are Essential To Data-Driven Success. *Forbes*. Https://Www.Forbes.Com/Sites/Brentdykes/2022/11/29/Why-Change-Management-Skills-Are-Essential-To-Data-Driven-Success/

Edmans, A. (2021). The Social Responsibility Of Business Includes Profits. *Pro Market*. Https://Www.Promarket.Org/2021/10/19/Social-Responsibility-Business-Profits-Pieconomics/

Edmondson, A. C. (2011). Strategies for Learning from Failure. *Harvard Business Review*. https://hbr.org/2011/04/strategies-for-learning-from-failure

Edwards, J. (2024). *Resilience and Adaptability: How You Lead Matters*. https://www.nicheacademy.com/blog/resilience-and-adaptability-how-you-lead-matters

Eggeling, K. A., & Versloot, L. (2022). Taking Trust Online: Digitalisation and the practice of information sharing in diplomatic negotiations. *Review of International Studies*. https://www.semanticscholar.org/paper/Taking-trust-online%3A-Digitalisation-and-the-of-in-Eggeling-Versloot/6e2c10149530587f4e6ae6c386d5aadce029a2c9

Eide Bailly. (2023). *How To Prioritize Key Performance Metrics In Your Organization*. Https://Siouxfalls.Business/How-To-Prioritize-Key-Performance-Metrics-In-Your-Organization/

El Badawy, T. A., Marwan, R. M., & Magdy, M. M. (2015). The Impact of Emerging Technologies on Knowledge Management in Organizations. *International Business Research*, 8(5). Advance online publication. DOI: 10.5539/ibr.v8n5p111

Elharony, A. (2023). *Leading By Example: The Power Of Ethical Leadership In Business | Linkedin.* Linkedin. Https://Www.Linkedin.Com/Pulse/Leading-Example-Power-Ethical-Leadership-Business-Amr-Elharony/

Ely, R. J., & Thomas, D. A. (2020). *Getting Serious About Diversity: Enough Already with the Business Case.* Harvard Business Review. https://hbr.org/2020/11/getting-serious-about-diversity-enough-already-with-the-business-case

Energage (2023). The Importance Of Accountability In Leadership | Top Workplaces.

Ercanbrack Michelle Blog Post. (May 2023). *5 Powerful Benefits of Transparency in Business.* BambooHR Blog. https://www.bamboohr.com/blog/creating-transparency-in-workplace

Erku, D. A., Hailemeskel, B., Netere, A. K., & Belachew, S. A. (2019). Pharmacist-led smoking cessation services in Ethiopia: Knowledge and skills gap analysis. *Tobacco Induced Diseases*, 17(January), 1. DOI: 10.18332/tid/99573 PMID: 31582913

Eskafi, M., Fazeli, R., Dastgheib, A., Taneja, P., Ulfarsson, G. F., Thorarinsdottir, R. I., & Stefansson, G. (2019). View of Stakeholder salience and prioritization for port master planning, a case study of the multi-purpose Port of Isafjordur in Iceland. *European Journal of Transport and Infrastructure Research*, 19(3), 1–47. DOI: 10.18757/ejtir.2019.19.3.4386

Estrada, M. (2023). The Importance Of Ethics Training In The Workplace In 2023 And Beyond. *Compliance Training Group*. Https://Compliancetraininggroup.Com/2023/07/17/The-Importance-Of-Ethics-Training-In-The-Workplace-In-2023-And-Beyond/

Ethical Systems. (2013). Corporate Culture - Ethical Systems. Ethical Systems. Https://Www.Ethicalsystems.Org/Corporate-Culture/

EU Business School Blog post (May2022). What Is Business Innovation and Why Is It Important? Blog EU Business School. https://www.euruni.edu/blog/what-is-business-innovation-and-why-is-it-important/

Expert Panel. (2024). Ways Automation Can (And Will) Impact The Manufacturing Industry. *Forbes*. https://www.forbes.com/sites/forbestechcouncil/2024/03/28/ways-automation-can-and-will-impact-the-manufacturing-industry/

Eyal, N. (2014). *Hooked: How to Build Habit-Forming Products: Eyal, Nir, Hoover, Ryan: 9781591847786: Amazon.com: Books*. https://www.amazon.com/Hooked-How-Build-Habit-Forming-Products/dp/1591847788

Fahey, C. (1987). Corporate Ethical Decision Making In Health Care Institutions. *Hospital Administration Currents*, 31(4), 19–26. Https://Pubmed.Ncbi.Nlm.Nih.Gov/10284887/ PMID: 10284887

Fang, J., & Gong, X. (2023). Application of visual communication in digital animation advertising design using convolutional neural networks and big data. *PeerJ. Computer Science*, 9, e1383. DOI: 10.7717/peerj-cs.1383 PMID: 37346553

FasterCapital Blog Post. (June 2024). Case Studies In Effective Stakeholder Engagement - FasterCapital. https://fastercapital.com/topics/case-studies-in-effective-stakeholder-engagement.html

FasterCapital. (2024). Constructive Dialogue and Debate. *Faster Capital*. https://fastercapital.com/content/Alternative-Opinions--Embracing-Diverse-Perspectives.html#Constructive-Dialogue-and-Debate

Fastercapital. (2024). *Effective Decision Making: Information Gathering: Knowledge Is Power: The Role Of Information Gathering In Decision Making - Fastercapital*. Https://Fastercapital.Com/Content/Effective-Decision-Making--Information-Gathering--Knowledge-Is-Power--The-Role-Of-Information-Gathering-In-Decision-Making.Html

FasterCapital. (n.d.). Case Studies Of Successful Innovation Strategies. *FasterCapital*. Retrieved July 26, 2024, from https://fastercapital.com/topics/case-studies-of-successful-innovation-strategies.html

Fayayola, O. A., & Olorunfemi, O. L. (2023). Ethical Decision-Making In It Governance: A Review Of Models And Frameworks. *International Journal Of Science And Research Archive*. Https://Www.Semanticscholar.Org/Paper/Ethical-Decision-Making-In-It-Governance%3a-A-Review-Fayayola-Olorunfemi/F8b16298b126c7341e22aea19c0d257417ed2a04

Feiferytė-Skirienė, A., Draudvilienė, L., Stasiškienė, Ž., Sosunkevič, S., Pamakštys, K., Daniusevičiūtė-Brazaitė, L., & Gurauskienė, I. (2022). Co-Creation Hub Is the First Step for the Successful Creation of a Unified Urban Ecosystem-Kaunas City Example. *International Journal of Environmental Research and Public Health*, 19(5), 2609. Advance online publication. DOI: 10.3390/ijerph19052609 PMID: 35270302

Fernandes, A. J., & Ferreira, J. J. (2022). Entrepreneurial ecosystems and networks: A literature review and research agenda. *Review of Managerial Science*, 16(1), 189–247. DOI: 10.1007/s11846-020-00437-6

Fernandez, D. C. (2023). Beyond Borders: How Cultural Differences in Trust Valuation Impact Business Partnerships. *LinkedIn*. https://www.linkedin.com/pulse/beyond-borders-how-cultural-differences-trust-impact-fernandez/

Fernández-Bedoya, V. H., Meneses-La-Riva, M. E., Suyo-Vega, J. A., & Stephanie Gago-Chávez, J. J. (2023). Mental health problems of entrepreneurs during the COVID-19 health crisis: Fear, anxiety, and stress. A systematic review. *F1000 Research*, 12, 1062. DOI: 10.12688/f1000research.139581.1

Fernando, A. G. M. (2023). In today's rapidly evolving digital landscape, embracing technology has become imperative for businesses seeking to thrive and remain competitive. The digital age presents exciting opportunities for innovation, enabling organizations to transform their operations and enhance customer experiences. d. https://www.linkedin.com/pulse/innovation-digital-age-embracing-technology-business-garc%C3%ADa-marc

Ferreira, N. C., & Ferreira, J. J. (2024). Quo Vadis Sustainable Entrepreneurship? A Systematic Literature Review of Related Drivers and Inhibitors in SMEs. *IEEE Transactions on Engineering Management*, 71, 9644–9660. DOI: 10.1109/TEM.2023.3305475

Firmansyah, F., Erda, G., & Khurniawan, A. W. (2024). The impact of digital transformation and leadership on organizational resilience in distance education institution: Higher-order set approach. *Turkish Online Journal of Distance Education*, 25(2), 115–129. DOI: 10.17718/tojde.1260433

Fisk, L. (2021). Embracing Diversity And Inclusion As A Sustainable, Competitive Advantage. *Forbes*. https://www.forbes.com/sites/forbesbusinesscouncil/2021/01/04/embracing-diversity-and-inclusion-as-a-sustainable-competitive-advantage/?sh=507c55892642

Fitzgerald, M., Kruschwitz, N., Bonnet, D., & Welch, M. (2013). Embracing Digital Technology. MIT Sloan Management Review. https://sloanreview.mit.edu/projects/embracing-digital-technology/

Fitzgerald, M., Kruschwitz, N., Bonnet, D., & Welch, M. (2014). Embracing Digital Technology: A New Strategic Imperative. *MIT Sloan Management Review*, (55), 1–16.

Fone Ng, S. (2023). *Why Kpis Are Important: 10 Reason Key Performance Indicators Stands For? -Meaning, Examples, Template | Linkedin*. Https://Www.Linkedin.Com/Pulse/Why-Kpis-Important-10-Reason-Key-Performance-Indicators-Shone-Fone-Ng/

Forbes Technology Council. (2023). 20 Tips For Tech Leaders Seeking To Build Diverse And Inclusive Teams. Forbes. https://www.forbes.com/sites/forbestechcouncil/2023/08/02/20-tips-for-tech-leaders-seeking-to-build-diverse-and-inclusive-teams/

Ford, J. K., Riley, S. J., Lauricella, T. K., & Van Fossen, J. A. (2020). Factors affecting trust among natural resources stakeholders, partners, and strategic alliance members: A meta-analytic investigation. In *Frontiers in Communication*. Frontiers Media S.A. DOI: 10.3389/fcomm.2020.00009

Forster, N. (2006). The Impact of Emerging Technologies on Business, Industry, Commerce and Humanity during the 21st Century. *The Journal of Business Perspective*, 10(1), 27. DOI: 10.1177/097226290601000401

Forth, S. (2022). Agile Scenario Planning. *LinkedIn*. https://www.linkedin.com/pulse/agile-scenario-planning-steven-forth/

Francis, R., & Murfey, G. (2015). Global Business Ethics: Responsible Decision Making In An International Context. Https://Www.Semanticscholar.Org/Paper/Global-Business-Ethics%3a-Responsible-Decision-Making-Francis-Murfey/053e32342e474a1a97e3ae018d036741fdec294a

Freedman, J. (2021). Is It Possible to Change? 5 Tips from Emergent Strategy Where Climate Justice and Social Justice Meet. *Six Seconds*. https://www.6seconds.org/2021/08/15/possible-to-change/

Freire, A. (2021). Towards A Comprehensive Understanding Of Agile Teamwork: A Literature-Based Thematic Network. In *International Conferences On Software Engineering And Knowledge Engineering, Proceedings Of The 33rd International Conference On Software Engineering And Knowledge Engineering* (Pp. 223–228). Ksi Research Inc. Https://Doi.Org/10.18293/Seke2021-106

Fripp, G. (2023). *Schein's Model of Organizational Culture - Organizational Behavior*. https://www.myorganisationalbehaviour.com/scheins-model-of-organizational-culture/

Fuglsang, L. (2010). Bricolage and invisible innovation in public service innovation. *Journal of Innovation Economics Management*, 5(1), 67–87. https://www.cairn.info/revue-journal-of-innovation-economics-2010-1-page-67.htm. DOI: 10.3917/jie.005.0067

Futcher, R. (2022). *The Psychology of Mutual Accountability*. Russellfutcher. Com. https://www.russellfutcher.com/new-blog/2022/4/17/the-psychology-of-mutual-accountability

Galt Foundation. (2023). Nurturing Employees: Fostering Lasting Employee Engagement and Commitment. https://galtfoundation.org/2023/11/01/fostering-lasting-employee-engagement-and-commitment/

Ganguly, K., & Rai, S. (2018). Evaluating The Key Performance Indicators For Supply Chain Information System Implementation Using Ipa Model. *Benchmarking: An International Journal*. Https://Www.Semanticscholar.Org/Paper/Evaluating-The-Key-Performance-Indicators-For-Chain-Ganguly-Rai/945f69301a3b1face79fb6ff5064af58df22cf8d

Ganie, I., & Jagannathan, S. (2023). Lifelong Learning Control of Nonlinear Systems with Constraints Using Multilayer Neural Networks with Application to Mobile Robot Tracking. *In 2023 IEEE Conference on Control Technology and Applications (CCTA)*. 727–732. IEEE. DOI: 10.1109/CCTA54093.2023.10252103

Gauss, M. (2022). *5 Human-Centric Skills to "Flex" for Ever-Changing*. WDHB. https://wdhb.com/blog/5-human-centric-skills-to-flex-for-ever-changing-workplaces/

Geeksforgeeks (2024). Comparing Descriptive, Predictive, And Prescriptive Analytics Models. *Geeksforgeeks*. Https://Www.Geeksforgeeks.Org/Comparing-Descriptive-Predictive-And-Prescriptive-Analytics-Models/#

Gelle-Jimenez, M. & Hector Aguiling (2021). Leveraging Human Resources Management (Hrm) Practices Toward Congruence Of Values. *International Journal Of Research In Business And Social Science*. Https://Www.Semanticscholar.Org/Paper/Leveraging-Human-Resources-Management-(Hrm)-Toward-Gelle-Jimenez-Aguiling/Ef92cb46fdc67a684145061073e2ec58c6356b35

Gentry, B. (2024). The Importance of Empathy in the Workplace. *Center for Creative Leadership*. https://www.ccl.org/articles/leading-effectively-articles/empathy-in-the-workplace-a-tool-for-effective-leadership/

Gerlach, C. (2023). *How Are Data Culture And Change Management Connected?* Https://Www.Statworx.Com/En/Content-Hub/Interview/How-Are-Data-Culture-And-Change-Management-Connected/

Ghezal, R. (2024). Determinants Of Engagement With And Of Stakeholders In Csr Decision-Making: A Stakeholder Perspective. *European Business Review*, 36(5), 771–790. Https://Doi.Org/10.1108/Ebr-03-2023-0085. DOI: 10.1108/EBR-03-2023-0085

Gill, G., McNally, M., & Berman, V. (2018). Effective diversity, equity, and inclusion practices. *Healthcare Management Forum*, 31(5), 196–199. DOI: 10.1177/0840470418773785 PMID: 30114938

Giovanni, G. (2024). Most Important Characteristics Contributing To Ethical Leadership.

Girish, R. N., & Naik, P. (2024). Transforming Bookstore Dynamics Through Blockchain Integration for Revolutionizing Trust, Transparency and Efficiency. *2024 5th International Conference for Emerging Technology (INCET)*. https://www.semanticscholar.org/paper/Transforming-Bookstore-Dynamics-Through-Blockchain-Naik-Naik/9d2d8a2627f28303dae4da64900a39c300b33d06

Gitbook. (2023). *Pitfalls In Ethical Decision-Making | Digital Ethics For Tech Professionals*. Https://Www.Ethics-For-Tech.Org/Part-1-Ethical-Decision-Making/Pitfalls-In-Ethical-Decision-Making

Gleeson, B. (2021). 5 Attributes (And Benefits) Of Values-Based Leadership. *Forbes*. https://www.forbes.com/sites/brentgleeson/2021/07/19/5-attributes-and-benefits-of-values-based-leadership/?sh=1513b18c3d21

Goetz, C. (2023). Agile vs. Traditional: Which Method Is Right for You? | *LinkedIn*. https://www.linkedin.com/pulse/agile-vs-traditional-which-method-right-you-carlos-goetz/

Goldberg, E., & Boyes, I. (2024). *Using Scenario Planning to Facilitate Agility in Strategic Workforce Planning*. https://www.shrm.org/executive-network/insights/people-strategy/using-scenario-planning-to-facilitate-agility-strategic-workforce-planning

Gonçalves, M. L. A., Penha, R., Brandão, A. C. L., Da Costa Filho, J. R., & Galvão, G. S.Junior. (2023). Analyzing The Bibliometric Landscape Of Digital Transformation And Project Management In Organizational Contexts. *Revista Contemporânea*, 3(12), 26396–26419. DOI: 10.56083/RCV3N12-087

Gorichanaz, T. (2021). Sanctuary: An institutional vision for the digital age. *The Journal of Documentation*, 77(1), 1–17. DOI: 10.1108/JD-04-2020-0064

Gouldsberry, M. (2021). Leadership Accountability: Why It Matters And How To Fuel It. *Betterworks*. Https://Www.Betterworks.Com/Magazine/Accountability-In-Leadership/

Gouldsberry, M. (2023). Leadership Accountability: How To Build It Into Your Culture - Betterworks.

Graddick-Weir, M., Hakel, M. M., Jacobs, R., & Smart, J. B. (2021). NAHRSIOPDI Themes Key Questions and Research Alternatives_final. https://nahr.shrm.org/sites/default/files/NAHRSIOPDI%20Themes%20Key%20Questions%20and%20Research%20Alternatives_final.pdf

Graff, S., Freeman, E., Roach, M., Wilson, R., Fairley, R., Gullatte, M., . . . May-Slater, S. (2024). Abstract Po1-10-06: Understanding Clinical Meaningfulness In Metastatic Breast Cancer Treatment Decision-Making: Experiences And Perspectives Of Patients, Caregivers, And Clinicians. *Cancer Research, 84*(9_Supplement), Po1-10-06-Po1-10-06. Https://Doi.Org/10.1158/1538-7445.Sabcs23-Po1-10-06

Greenlight Guru. (2021). Case Study: *How The Partner Ecosystem Has Been Key To Market Success* For Spark Biomedical. https://www.greenlight.guru/blog/spark-biomedical-partner-ecosystem-key-to-market-success

Grossmann, C. (2024). 8 Proven Strategies to Foster Diversity and Inclusivity in the Workplace. Beekeeper. https://www.beekeeper.io/blog/5-ways-promote-workplace-diversity/

Growth99. (2023). Digitalization: Revolutionizing Businesses In The Modern Age | Growth99. https://growth99.com/digitalization-revolutionizing-businesses-in-the-modern-age/

Groysberg, B., Lee, J., Price, J., & Cheng, J. (2018). *The Leader's Guide to Corporate Culture*.

Gu, F., & Liu, J. (2022). Environmentally Specific Servant Leadership and Employee Workplace Green Behavior: Moderated Mediation Model of Green Role Modeling and Employees' Perceived CSR. *Sustainability (Basel)*, 14(19), 11965. DOI: 10.3390/su141911965

Gupta, S. (2021). Why Trust Matters in Your Relationship and How to Build It. *overall Mind*. https://www.verywellmind.com/how-to-build-trust-in-a-relationship-5207611

Gurmentor (2021). *What is Language Barrier and How to Overcome It*. Gurmentor. https://gurmentor.com/what-is-language-barrier-and-how-to-overcome-it/

Haddud, A., & McAllen, D. K. (Eds.). (2018). *Managing technological entrepreneurship: the engine for economic growth. PICMET'18: Portland International Conference on Management of Engineering and Technology*. Portland State University.

Hagel, J. (2005). *Productive Friction – A Key to Accelerating Business Innovation*. John Hagel. https://www.johnhagel.com/productive-friction-a-key-to-accelerating-business-innovation/

Hagel, J., III, Brown, J. S., de Maar, A., & Wool, M. (2018). Maximize potential for friction. *Deloitte Insights*. https://www2.deloitte.com/us/en/insights/topics/talent/business-performance-improvement/maximize-potential-for-friction.html

Hale, D. (2019). *Strategic planning, the agile way* - Work Life by Atlassian. https://www.atlassian.com/blog/jira-align/agile-strategic-planning

Halevi, M., Aisjah, S., & Djazuli, A. (2023). Corporate Governance in the Digital Age: A Comprehensive Review of Blockchain, AI, and Big Data Impacts, Opportunities, and Challenges. *E3S Web of Conferences, 448*, 2056. DOI: 10.1051/e3sconf/202344802056

Hall, A. (2023). G.E.'s Cultural Shift: Embracing Innovation and Change. *Aaron Hall*. https://aaronhall.com/insights/ges-cultural-shift-embracing-innovation-and-change/

Hall, A. (2023). Zappos CEO Tony Hsieh on Self-Organization, Adaptability, and Values. *Aaron Hall*. https://aaronhall.com/insights/zappos-ceo-tony-hsieh-on-self-organization-adaptability-and-values/

Hall, B. (2023). Building Strategic Agility: Navigating Challenges With Strength And Agility. *Forbes*. https://www.forbes.com/sites/forbesbusinesscouncil/2023/06/21/building-strategic-agility-navigating-challenges-with-strength-and-agility/

Hall, D., Guo, Y., & Davis, R. A. (Eds.). (2003). *Proceedings Of The 36th Annual Hawaii International Conference On System Sciences: 6 - 9 January 2003, Big Island, Hawaii; Abstracts And Cd-Rom Of Full Papers; [Hicss-36*. Ieee Computer Soc. Hci Consulting. (2023). *Embracing Diversity: Navigating Challenges In Implementing Inclusive Decision-Making Processes*. Https://Www.Innovativehumancapital.Com/Article/Embracing-Diversity-Navigating-Challenges-In-Implementing-Inclusive-Decision-Making-Processes

Hancock, P. A., Kessler, T. T., Kaplan, A. D., Stowers, K., Brill, J. C., Billings, D. R., Schaefer, K. E., & Szalma, J. L. (2023). How and why humans trust: A meta-analysis and elaborated model. *Frontiers in Psychology, 14. Frontiers in Psychology*, 1081086, 1081086. DOI: 10.3389/fpsyg.2023.1081086 PMID: 37051611

Hanna, K. T., Bigelow, S. J., & Pratt, M. K. (2024). *What is strategic planning? | Definition from TechTarget*. https://www.techtarget.com/searchcio/definition/strategic-planning

Han, S. J., Xie, L., Beyerlein, M., & Boehm, R. (2022). Examining the mediating role of team growth mindset on the relationship of individual mindsets and shared leadership. *European Journal of Training and Development*. Advance online publication. DOI: 10.1108/EJTD-08-2022-0084

Harper Fox Search Partners (2021). The Five Principles Of Ethical Leaders - Harper Fox Partners.

Harpreet, D. (2023). Innovation and Adaptability: Staying Ahead in a Rapidly Evolving Business Landscape | LinkedIn. *LinkedIn*. https://www.linkedin.com/pulse/innovation-adaptability-staying-ahead-rapidly-evolving-dhillon/

Harry Clark Translation. (n.d.). *7 Tips on How to Overcome Language Barriers*. Retrieved July 28, 2024, from https://harryclarktranslation.co.nz/7-tips-overcome-language-barriers

Hartmann, M. R., & Hartmann, R. K. (2023). Hiding practices in employee-user innovation. *Research Policy*, 52(4), 104728. DOI: 10.1016/j.respol.2023.104728

Harvard Business Review (2016). *Leading a Successful Cultural Transformation at Your Organization*. https://hbr.org/2016/07/kodaks-downfall-wasnt-about-technology

Harvard Business Review. (2017). *What the Best Transformational Leaders Do*. https://hbr.org/2017/05/what-the-best-transformational-leaders-do

Harvard Business Review. (2021). *AI Should Augment Human Intelligence, Not Replace It*. https://hbr.org/2021/03/ai-should-augment-human-intelligence-not-replace-it

Hassett, E. (2021). The challenges faced by global brands in the era of cultural competence. *Freedman*. https://www.freedmaninternational.com/insights/global-brand-challenges-in-the-era-of-cultural-competence/

Hastings, R. (2018). *Netflix's success demonstrates the importance of strategic agility*. https://www.worldfinance.com/strategy/netflixs-success-demonstrates-the-importance-of-strategic-agility

Hastwell, C. (2023). What Are Employee Resource Groups (ERGs)? https://www.greatplacetowork.com/resources/blog/what-are-employee-resource-groups-ergs

Hegarty, N., & Moccia, S. (2018). Components Of Ethical Leadership And Their Importance In Sustaining Organizations Over The Long Term. *The Journal of Values Based Leadership*, 11(1). Advance online publication. Doi.Org/10.22543/0733.111 .1199. DOI: 10.22543/0733.111.1199

Hewlett, S. A., Marshall, M., & Sherbin, L. (2013). *How Diversity Can Drive Innovation*. Harvard Business Review. https://hbr.org/2013/12/how-diversity-can-drive-innovation

Hills, L. (2023). Value-Based Leadership: Developing And Using Core Leadership Values. *Healthcare Administration Leadership & Management Journal*. Https://Www.Semanticscholar.Org/Paper/Value-Based-Leadership%3a-Developing-And-Using-Core-Hills/218c39a11d487b7b0f20917f6bf526f33d0abb13

Hive Learning. (2024). *Tackling the Global Skills Gap with Human-Centric Learning*. https://hivelearning.com/resource/resource/tackling-the-global-skills-gap-with-human-centric-learning/

Hollister, R., Tecosky, K., Watkins, M., & Wolpert, C. (2021). *Why Every Executive Should Be Focusing on Culture Change Now*.

Hollister, R., Tecosky, K., Watkins, M., & Wolpert, C. (2021). Why Every Executive Should Be Focusing on Culture Change Now. *MIT Sloan Management Review*. https://sloanreview.mit.edu/article/why-every-executive-should-be-focusing-on-culture-change-now/

Hosseini, M., Shahri, A., Phalp, K., & Ali, R. (2016). A Modelling Language for Transparency Requirements in Business Information Systems. In S. Nurcan, P. Soffer, M. Bajec, & J. Eder (Eds.), *LNCS sublibrary. SL 3, Information systems and applications, incl. Internet/Web, and HCI: 9694, Advanced information systems engineering workshops:28th International Conference, CAiSE 2016,Ljubljana, Slovenia,June 13-17, 2016. Proceedings,* 239–254. Springer. DOI: 10.1007/978-3-319-39696-5_15

Hota, P., Nayak, B., & Mishra, S. K. (2023). Role Of Total Quality Management In Digital Literacy For Management Institutes Of Odisha. *International Journal of e-Collaboration*, 19(1), 1–18. Https://Doi.Org/10.4018/Ijec.316775. DOI: 10.4018/IJeC.316775

Hsieh, T. (2010). *How Zappos Infuses Culture Using Core Values*. Harvard Business Review. https://hbr.org/2010/05/how-zappos-infuses-culture-using-core-values

HubSpot, Inc. (2024). PartnerStack HubSpot Integration. *Connect Them Today*. https://app.hubspot.com/ecosystem/46832843/marketplace/apps/sales/partner-relationship-management/partnerstack-490573

Hughes, B. (2022). Forward Together.

Hughes, P. (2010). Decision-Making Processes In The Context Of Ethical Dilemmas: A Study Of Accountants In Training. Https://Www.Semanticscholar.Org/Paper/Decision-Making-Processes-In-The-Context-Of-Ethical-Hughes/236276423a2da88e9224c5c3cb03cdd5af09890a

Hull, C.E.K., Hung, Y.T.C., Hair, N., Perotti, V. and DeMartino, R. (2007), Taking advantage of digital opportunities: a typology of digital entrepreneurship. *International Journal of networking and Virtual Organizations, 4* (3). 290-303, .DOI: 10.1504/IJNVO.2007.015166

Hutchison, J. (2020). *Transparent Communication - Toward a Respectful Workplace*. https://workplace.msu.edu/transparent-communication/

Hype. (n.d.). *Partner Ecosystems: What are they and what are the keys to success?* Retrieved July 20, 2024, from https://www.hypeinnovation.com/partner-ecosystems-guide

Hyperwrite. (2024). *Case Studies And Ethical Decision-Making Frameworks | Medical Ethics Study Guide By Hyperwrite*. Https://Www.Hyperwriteai.Com/Guides/Case-Studies-And-Ethical-Decision-Making-Frameworks-Study-Guide

Ilkiu, J. (2024). The Data-Driven Revolution: Agile Decision-Making, Exceptional Results - Luby Software. *Felipe Matos*. Https://Luby.Co/Data-Driven/The-Data-Driven-Revolution

Improv Success Blog Post. (December 2023). Improv for Business: How Thinking on Your Feet Can Enhance Creativity and Collaboration. Success Improv. https://successimprov.com/improv-for-business-how-thinking-on-your-feet-can-enhance-creativity-and-collaboration/

Inamdar, S.N., Oke, J.S., & Agashe, A. (2014). *Enterprise Performance Management*.

Inc. (2010). The Zappos Core Values. *Inc*. https://www.inc.com/inc-advisor/zappos-managin-people-zappos-core-values.html

Inclusion Cloud. (2023). *Data Governance: Ensuring Data Quality And Overcoming Data Bias*. Https://Inclusioncloud.Com/Insights/Blog/Data-Governance-Data-Bias/

Indeed Editorial Team. (2022). *What Is Emergent Strategy? With Benefits and Examples*. https://www.indeed.com/career-advice/career-development/emergent-strategy-definition

Industrial Engineering Website. (2023). Statistical Process Control (SPC). *Industrial Engineering Website*. https://industrial.ienajah.com/statistical-process-control-spc/

Infozillon. (2023). *Mastering Personal Growth but how?!* https://infozillon.com/self-management/118-mastering-personal-growth-but-how.html

Inspirus (2024). The Art of Creative Employee Recognition Programs (2024). https://www.inspirus.com/blog/employee-recognition-programs/

Ireland, J. (2022). *Technology in the workplace: how it's evolving, and how to stay ahead of the curve*. Reed.com. https://www.reed.com/articles/technology-in-the-workplace-advantages-evolution

Iriogbe, H. O., Ebeh, C. O., & Onita, F. B. (2024). Multinational team leadership in the marine sector: A review of cross-cultural management practices. In *Int. j. manag. entrep. res* 6 (8), pp. 2731–2757. DOI: . v6i8.1416.DOI: 10.51594/ijmer

Ishii, A., Kawahata, Y., & Okano, N. (2023). Significant Role of Trust and Distrust in Social Simulation. In Peaslee Levine, M. (Ed.), *The Psychology of Trust*. IntechOpen., DOI: 10.5772/intechopen.101538

Ivory Research. (2019). The need of emergent Strategy in a Changing Environment | Ivory Research. *Ivory Research*. https://www.ivoryresearch.com/samples/the-need-of-emergent-strategy-in-a-changing-environment/

Jambon, M., & Malti, T. (2022). Developmental Relations between Children's Peer Relationship Quality and Prosocial Behavior: The Mediating Role of Trust. *The Journal of Genetic Psychology*, 183(3), 197–210. DOI: 10.1080/00221325.2022.2030293 PMID: 35088652

Jangra, M. (2024). *Managing Global CSR Challenges: Navigating Cultural Differences And Ethical Dilemmas*. https://ruralhandmade.com/blog/managing-global-csr-challenges-navigating-cultural

Jiao, C., & Hardie, T. (2009). Nationality, Cultural Values And The Relative Importance Of Task Performance And Organizational Citizenship Behaviour In Performance Evaluation Decisions. *Journal Of Comparative International Management*, 12(17). Https://Www.Semanticscholar.Org/Paper/Nationality%2c-Cultural-Values-And-The-Relative-Of-In-Jiao-Hardie/Db6f86fe65adfa0a6af6855622b4cf267def3b66

Johnson, C. E. (2020). *Organizational Ethics: A Practical Approach* (3rd ed.). Sage.

Jörissen, B., Unterberg, L., & Klepacki, T. (Eds.). (2023). *Cultural Sustainability and Arts Education: International Perspectives on the Aesthetics of Transformation.* Springer. DOI: 10.1007/978-981-19-3915-0

Jose, L. (2024). *Partner Program KPIs: The Metrics You Should Measure and Optimize.* https://partnerstack.com/articles/partner-program-kpis-metrics-you-should-measure-and-optimize

Joshi, N. H., Khan, H., & Rab, I. (2021). A design-led approach to embracing an ecosystem strategy. *McKinsey & Company.* https://www.mckinsey.com/capabilities/mckinsey-design/our-insights/a-design-led-approach-to-embracing-an-ecosystem-strategy

Journeybee. (2024). *Blooming Partnerships: How to Grow a Successful Partner Ecosystem in 2024.* https://www.journeybee.io/resources/how-to-grow-a-successful-partner-ecosystem

Juliadi, E., Syafri, M., & Hidayati, N. (2023). The Effect of Training and Development on Employee Productivity in the Digital Age. West Science Journal Economic and Entrepreneurship, 1(10).

Kaado, B. (2016). Promoting Diversity: Why Inclusive Communication and Involvement Matter. Businessnewsdaily.Com. https://www.businessnewsdaily.com/9488-diversity-inclusive-communication.html

Kane, G. (2019). The technology fallacy: People are the real key to digital transformation. *Research Technology Management*, 62(6), 44–49. DOI: 10.1080/08956308.2019.1661079

Kaplan, R. S., & Norton, D. P. (1992). *The Balanced Scorecard—Measures that Drive Performance.* Harvard Business Review. https://hbr.org/1992/01/the-balanced-scorecard-measures-that-drive-performance-2

Kaplan, R. S. (2010). *Conceptual Foundations of the Balanced Scorecard.* Harvard Business School, Harvard University. DOI: 10.2139/ssrn.1562586

Kaplan, R. S., & Norton, D. P. (1992). The Balanced Scorecard—Measures that Drive Performance. *Harvard Business Review.* PMID: 10119714

Katul, Y. (2024). Exploring the impact of cultural diversity in global projects: A comparative analysis of virtual and face-to-face teamwork. *International Journal of Cross-Cultural Management.* https://www.semanticscholar.org/paper/Exploring-the-impact-of-cultural-diversity-in-A-of-Yousef/ce97087c89f75ec82ba52194552858380196b05a

Kaur, S. (2023). Traditional sales ecosystems Vs. Modern sales ecosystems | The channel and sales enablement blog. *The channel and sales enablement blog.* https://channelandsalesenablementblog.mindmatrix.net/traditional-sales-ecosystems-vs-modern-sales-ecosystems/

Kaz, H. (2023). Leveling up employee engagement: Uncovering the new pillars of an employee retention blueprint. *Strategic HR Review*, 22(6), 195–200. DOI: 10.1108/SHR-08-2023-0048

Keck, I. R., & Ross, R. J. (2014). Exploring Customer Specific Kpi Selection Strategies For An Adaptive Time Critical User Interface. In T. Kuflik, O. Stock, J. Chai, & A. Krüger (Eds.), *Proceedings Of The 19th International Conference On Intelligent User Interfaces* (Pp. 341–346). Acm. Https://Doi.Org/10.1145/2557500.2557536

Kelly, Z. (2022). *Partnerships 101: What is a Partner Ecosystem Platform?* https://insider.crossbeam.com/resources/partnerships-101-what-is-a-partner-ecosystem-platform

Kelton Global. (2021). Experience Innovation: Building a Consumer-Centric Ecosystem - *Kelton Global.* https://www.keltonglobal.com/perspectives/experience-innovation-consumer-centric-ecosystem/

Khin, S., & Ho, T. C. (2019). Digital technology, digital capability, and organizational performance. *International Journal of Innovation Science*, 11(2), 177–195. DOI: 10.1108/IJIS-08-2018-0083

Kiflo (2023). *Managing a Thriving Partner Ecosystem Strategy: From Conception to Execution.* https://www.kiflo.com/blog/managing-a-thriving-partner-ecosystem-from-strategy-to-execution

Kingdomdweller (2024). Deontology, Utilitarianism, And Virtues Ethical Theories. *Kingdomdweller.* Https://Www.Heartforkingdom.Com/2024/05/05/Deontology-Utilitarianism-And-Virtues-Ethics/

Klevit, A. (2016). Eight Tips for Fostering Employee Engagement. Business Success Consulting Group. https://www.bizsuccesscg.com/eight-tips-for-fostering-employee-engagement/

Klotz, A. C., & Bolino, M. C. (2013). *Citizenship and Counterproductive work Behavior: A Moral Licensing View*, 38(2). https://www.jstor.org/stable/23416446

Knittel, E. M., Berdugo, J. D., Cheevavichawalkul, K., & Imbach, M. (2019). The Lafarge-Holcim merger negotiations. *European Journal of International Management*, 13(5), 612–636. DOI: 10.1504/EJIM.2019.102027

Kobi, J., & Otieno, B. (2024). Predictive Analytics Applications For Enhanced Customer Retention And Increased Profitability In The Telecommunications Industry. *International Journal Of Innovative Science And Research Technology (Ijisrt)*, Article Ijisrt24may1148, 1762–1774. Https://Doi.Org/10.38124/Ijisrt/Ijisrt24may1148

Kooli, C. (2023). Chatbots In Education And Research: A Critical Examination Of Ethical Implications And Solutions. *Sustainability (Basel)*, 15(7), 5614. Https://Doi.Org/10.3390/Su15075614. DOI: 10.3390/su15075614

Korn Ferry. (2023). The journey to becoming a more inclusive leader. Korn Ferry. https://www.kornferry.com/insights/featured-topics/diversity-equity-inclusion/the-journey-to-becoming-a-more-inclusive-leader

Kuteesa, K., Akpuokwe, C., & Udeh, C. (2024). Navigating the digital transformation journey: strategies for startup growth and innovation in the digital era. *International Journal of Scholarly Research in Multidisciplinary Studies*. DOI: 10.56781/ijsrms.2024.4.2.0031

Lakacha, A. (N D). *Ethical Dilemmas In Business And How To Address Them*. Https://Sites.Suffolk.Edu/Ccpe/Ethical-Dilemmas-In-Business/

Lavrijsen, J., & Nicaise, I. (2017). Systemic obstacles to lifelong learning: The influence of the educational system design on learning attitudes. *Studies in Continuing Education*, 39(2), 176–196. DOI: 10.1080/0158037X.2016.1275540

Lazer, D., & Binz-Scharf, M. C. (2004, May). Managing novelty and cross-agency cooperation in digital government. In *Proceedings of the 2004 annual national conference on Digital government research*, 1-2).

Leadzen.Ai Blog (August 2024). Case Studies: Successful Data-Driven Companies. *Leadzen.Ai*. Https://Leadzen.Ai/Blog/Case-Studies-Successful-Data-Driven-Companies

Lee, Y. (2024). Consciously Choosing Unconsciousness. *Voices In Bioethics, 10*.Https://Doi.Org/10.52214/Vib.V10i.12500

Legacy Family Services, Inc. (2024). *Mastering the Art of Navigating Difficult Conversations: Tips and Strategies for Effective Communication - Legacy Family Services, Inc.* https://www.legacyfs.org/mastering-the-art-of-navigating-difficult-conversations-tips-and-strategies-for-effective-communication/

Lemoine, G. J., Hartnell, C. A., & Leroy, H. (2019). Taking Stock of Moral Approaches to Leadership: An Integrative Review of Ethical, Authentic, and Servant Leadership. *The Academy of Management Annals*, 13(1), 148–187. DOI: 10.5465/annals.2016.0121

Lengyel, A. (n.d.). *Pushing the Boundaries of Innovation: Speed*. Scale, and Transformation in the Cloud.

Lichtenstein, S. (2012). The Role of Values in Leadership: How Leaders' Values Shape Value Creation - Integral Leadership Review. *Integral Leadership Review*, 12(1), 1–18.

Lightfoote, J., Fielding, J., Deville, C., Gunderman, R., Morgan, G., Pandharipande, P., Duerinckx, A. J., Wynn, R. B., & Macura, K. (2014). Improving diversity, inclusion, and representation in radiology and radiation oncology part 1: Why these matter. *Journal of the American College of Radiology*, 11(7), 673–680. DOI: 10.1016/j.jacr.2014.03.007 PMID: 24993534

Lindner, J. (2023). Workplace Culture Statistics: Market Report & Data • MeetingFever. *MeetingFever.Com*. https://meetingfever.com/statistics/workplace-culture/

LinkedIn Blog Post. (February 2024). *Recruiting in 2024: Modern Approaches and Techniques*. LinkedIn. https://www.linkedin.com/pulse/recruiting-2024-modern-approaches-techniques-hcmatrix-wb1wf/

Linkedin Community. (2024a). *How Can You Prioritize Kpis Based On Their Importance To Your Organization?* Https://Www.Linkedin.Com/Advice/1/How-Can-You-Prioritize-Kpis-Based-Importance-Zo6ue

Linkedin Community. (2024b). *What Are The Best Ways To Ensure Data Quality?* Https://Www.Linkedin.Com/Advice/0/What-Best-Ways-Ensure-Data-Quality-Skills-Data-Management

Linkedin Community. (N.D.). *What Are The Best Ways To Present Data Insights And Recommendations To Stakeholders?* Retrieved September 6, 2024, From Https://Www.Linkedin.Com/Advice/0/What-Best-Ways-Present-Data-Insights-Recommendations

Linkov, I., Varghese, A., Jamil, S., Seager, T. P., Kiker, G., & Bridges, T. (2004). Multi-criteria decision analysis: a framework for structuring remedial decisions at contaminated sites. In *Comparative risk assessment and environmental decision making* (pp. 15–54). Springer Netherlands.

Linsner, S., Steinbrink, E., Kuntke, F., Franken, J., & Reuter, C. (2022). Supporting users in data disclosure scenarios in agriculture through transparency. *Behaviour & Information Technology*, 41(10), 2151–2173. DOI: 10.1080/0144929X.2022.2068070

Liu, J. L., Harkness, S., & Super, C. M. (2020). Chinese Mothers' Cultural Models of Children's Shyness: Ethnotheories and Socialization Strategies in the Context of Social Change. *New Directions for Child and Adolescent Development*, 2020(170), 69–92. DOI: 10.1002/cad.20340 PMID: 32431073

Liu, Y., Dong, J., Mei, L., & Shen, R. (2023). Digital innovation and performance of manufacturing firms: An affordance perspective. *Technovation*, 119, 102458. DOI: 10.1016/j.technovation.2022.102458

Li, Y., Gong, Y., Burmeister, A., Wang, M., Alterman, V., Alonso, A., & Robinson, S. (2021). Leveraging age diversity for organizational performance: An intellectual capital perspective. *The Journal of Applied Psychology*, 106(1), 71–91. DOI: 10.1037/apl0000497 PMID: 32202816

Lo, L., Aron, L. Y., Pettit, K. L. S., & Scally, C. P. (2021). *Mutual Accountability Is the Key to Equity-Oriented Systems Change*. Marketing, M. 7 Keys to Managing Successful Partner Ecosystems.

London, M. (2011). *The Oxford handbook of lifelong learning*. Oxford University Press. DOI: 10.1093/oxfordhb/9780195390483.001.0001

Loreti, P., Bracciale, L., Raso, E., Giuseppe, B., Sanseverino, E. R., & Gallo, P. (2023). Privacy and Transparency in Blockchain-Based Smart Grid Operations. *IEEE Access*. https://www.semanticscholar.org/paper/Privacy-and-Transparency-in-Blockchain-Based-Smart-Loreti-Bracciale/e32003129c9ac9cb7b600316678585fff19316f7

Lubis, M. (2024). The Role of Communication and Employee Engagement in Promoting Inclusion in the Workplace: A Case Study in the Creative Industry. *Feedback International Journal of Communication*, 1(1), 1–15.

Luther, D., & Rami, A. (2022). Scenario Planning: Strategy, Steps and Practical Examples. *Oracle NetSuite*. https://www.netsuite.com/portal/resource/articles/financial-management/scenario-planning.shtml

Lyons, P., & Bandura, R. P. (2023). Stimulating employee work engagement and the growth mindset. *Development and Learning in Organizations: An International Journal*. https://www.semanticscholar.org/paper/Stimulating-employee-work-engagement-and-the-growth-Lyons-Bandura/2b76a2a4d9e0031d7808c565984baea1bd2ed5ce

Lyons, R. (2023). Why Emergent Strategy is the Key to Success. *TopResume*. https://topresume.com/career-advice/why-emergent-strategy-is-the-key-to-success

Lyutiy, I., Petlenko, Y., & Drozd, N. (2022). The Importance Of Openness And Transparency In The Budget Process In The Defense And Security Sector Of Ukraine. *Financial and Credit Activity Problems of Theory and Practice*, 6(47), 99–110. DOI: 10.55643/fcaptp.6.47.2022.3900

Madhosingh, S. (2022). 4 Key Leadership Lessons from Patagonia Founder, Yvon Chouinard. *CEOWORLD Magazine*. https://ceoworld.biz/2022/10/14/4-key-leadership-lessons-from-patagonia-founder-yvon-chouinard/

Mahr, N., & Hendricks, B. (2023). Emergent Strategy | Definition, Advantages & Examples. *study.com*. https://study.com/academy/lesson/emergent-strategy-definition-advantages-disadvantages.html

Malecki, E. J. (2018). Entrepreneurship and entrepreneurial ecosystems. *Geography Compass*, 12(3), e12359. Advance online publication. DOI: 10.1111/gec3.12359

Manyika, J., Lund, S., Chui, M., Bughin, J., Woetzel, L., Batra, P., Ko, R., & Sanghvi, S. (2017). *What will the future of work mean for jobs, skills, and wages? Jobs lost, jobs gained* | McKinsey. McKinsey & Company. https://www.mckinsey.com/featured-insights/future-of-work/jobs-lost-jobs-gained-what-the-future-of-work-will-mean-for-jobs-skills-and-wages

Mardiani, E., & Utami, E. Y. (2023). The Role of Online Education in encouraging Employee empowerment in the Digital Era: A Study on E-commerce. 4, 1.

Mariton, J. (2016). *What is Scenario Planning and How to Use It*. https://www.smestrategy.net/blog/what-is-scenario-planning-and-how-to-use-it

Marmerchant, B. (2023). *Transformational Leadership Strategies: A Comprehensive Overview*. https://www.worldconsulting.group/leadership-strategy-definitions-transformational-leadership-strategy

Marr, B. (2022). Top 16 Essential Soft Skills For The Future Of Work. *Forbes*. https://www.forbes.com/sites/bernardmarr/2022/09/12/top-16-essential-soft-skills-for-the-future-of-work/

Mauri, J., & Plesset, A. (2024). *Biggest AI Developments of 2024 So Far and What's Ahead*. https://ipwatchdog.com/2024/06/19/biggest-ai-developments-2024-far-whats-ahead/id=177950/# Michael (2024). *Robots at Work: How Automation is Transforming Industries*. https://hackernoon.com/robots-at-work-how-automation-is-transforming-industries

Mccarthy, D. J., & Puffer, S. M. (2008). Interpreting The Ethicality Of Corporate Governance Decisions In Russia: Utilizing Integrative Social Contracts Theory To Evaluate The Relevance Of Agency Theory Norms. *Academy of Management Review*, 33(1), 11–31. Https://Www.Semanticscholar.Org/Paper/Interpreting-The-Ethicality-Of-Corporate-Governance-Mccarthy-Puffer/5c88ba936c331e39adf114ebad94304df6d57bcf. DOI: 10.5465/amr.2008.27745006

McKimm, J., Ramani, S., Forrest, K., Bishop, J., Findyartini, A., Mills, C., Hassanien, M., Al-Hayani, A., Jones, P., Nadarajah, V. D., & Radu, G. (2023). Adaptive leadership during challenging times: Effective strategies for health professions educators: Amee Guide No. 148. *Medical Teacher*, 45(2), 128–138. DOI: 10.1080/0142159X.2022.2057288 PMID: 35543323

McKinsey & Company. (2018). *Delivering through diversity*.

McKinsey & Company. (2022). What is diversity, equity, and inclusion? Myers, V. (2015). Diversity is being invited to the party; inclusion is being asked to dance. In American Bar Association (Vol. 1, No. 11).

McKinsey (2021). *The Digital Culture Challenge: Closing the Employee-Leadership Gap*.

McNaughton, D. (2003). The Role of Values and Leadership in Organizational Transformation. *Journal of Human Values*, 9(2), 131–140. DOI: 10.1177/097168580300900204

Meena, B. S. (2023). The Effect of Cultural Factors on Consumer Behaviour: A Global Perspective. [IJFMR]. *International Journal for Multidisciplinary Research*, 5(6). https://www.ijfmr.com/papers/2023/6/10906.pdf

Mellien, A. C. (1992). Ethical Dilemmas In The Care Of Premature Infants. *Clinical Nurse Specialist CNS*, 6(3), 130–134. Https://Doi.Org/10.1097/00002800-199200630-00002. DOI: 10.1097/00002800-199200630-00002 PMID: 1393963

Mercado, F. (2023). Key Elements of a Thriving Channel-Partner Ecosystem. *LinkedIn*. https://www.linkedin.com/pulse/key-elements-thriving-channel-partner-ecosystem-freddy-mercado/

Mercedes, M. G. Z., Tutivén-Román, C., Cisternas-Osorio, R., Labate, C., Macarena, L., Cantariño, B., Román, T., & Revista, V.A. (2023). Spanish-Speaker Wellness Influencers In The Era Of Care: Trends And Topics In 2023.

Merillot (2023). Navigating Remote Workplace Culture: Challenges and Strategies. *Merillot*. https://www.merillot.com/consulting-insights/navigating-remote-workplace-culture-challenges-and-strategies/

Metral, K. (2024). *6 Reasons Why Accountability Is Vital For Business | Cosmico*. Hubspot.

Metwally, D., Ruiz-Palomino, P., Metwally, M., & Gartzia, L. (2019). How Ethical Leadership Shapes Employees' Readiness To Change: The Mediating Role Of An Organizational Culture Of Effectiveness. *Frontiers in Psychology*, 10, 2493. Doi .Org/10.3389/Fpsyg.2019.02493. DOI: 10.3389/fpsyg.2019.02493 PMID: 31798489

Meyer, E. (2014). *The Culture Map: Breaking Through the Invisible Boundaries of Global Business*. https://erinmeyer.com/books/the-culture-map/

Meyer, E. (2017). Being the employer in Brussels, Boston, and Beijing. *Harvard Business Review*, 95(4), 70–77.

Michaels, G. (2023). *What is adaptive leadership: examples and principles: Work Life by Atlassian*. https://www.atlassian.com/blog/leadership/adaptive-leadership

Miller, F. P., Vandome, A. F., & Mcbrewster, J. (2009). Data Analysis: Data Analysis, Data, Information, Data Mining, Business Intelligence, Statistics, Descriptive Statistics, Exploratory Data Analysis, Statistical ... Hypothesis Testing, *Predictive Analytics*. Https://Www.Semanticscholar.Org/Paper/Data-Analysis%3a-Data-Analysis%2c-Data%2c-Information%2c-Miller-Vandome/5b73cccb28 51253767bbe69f688770994b4d050e

Mishra, R., Singh, S., & Pandey, S. (2023). The Impact of Technological Advances on Cultural Conflicts within Organizations. In T. Choudhry, M. Sarfraz, & W. Ul Hassan Shah (Eds.), *Business, Management and Economics. Organizational Culture - Cultural Change and Technology* (Vol. 16). Pitchpine. DOI: 10.5772/intechopen.113095

MIT Sloan Management Review. (2018). *The Convergence of Digitalization and Sustainability*. https://sloanreview.mit.edu/article/the-convergence-of-digitalization-and-sustainability/

Moffitt, S. (2022). *Why traditional strategy doesn't work now*. We Are Atmosphere Limited. https://weareatmosphere.com/insights/why-traditional-strategy-doesnt-work-now/

Moiana, D., Manotti, J., Ghezzi, A., & Rangone, A. (. (2023). Emerging Technologies: A Catalyst for Sustainable Business Model Innovation.

Moioli, F. (2023). The Unique Value Of Our Human Skills In An AI-Powered Future. *Forbes*. https://www.forbes.com/sites/forbestechcouncil/2023/07/03/the-unique-value-of-our-human-skills-in-an-ai-powered-future/

Molinsky, A. (2015). *A Complete Guide to Global Dexterity - Andy Molinsky*. https://www.andymolinsky.com/complete-guide-global-dexterity/

Moodian, M. A. (2013). *Contemporary Leadership and Intercultural Competence: Exploring the Cross-Cultural Dynamics Within Organizations* (1st ed.). SAGE Publications; ProQuest.

Moore, M. G. (2023). *How Transparent Should You Be With Your Team?* Harvard Business Review. Https://Hbr.Org/2023/01/How-Transparent-Should-You-Be-With-Your-Team

Moran, K. (n.d.). 10 Great Ways to Foster Authentic Employee Engagement | Recognize. Retrieved June 27, 2024, from https://recognizeapp.com/ways-foster-employee-engagement

Morgan, B. (2023). The Future of Global Remote Work: Navigating A New Landscape. *Forbes*. https://www.forbes.com/sites/forbesbusinesscouncil/2023/05/30/the-future-of-global-remote-work-navigating-a-new-landscape/?sh=3e9126f25d30

Morris, I. (2023). Digital Transformation: Revolutionizing Traditional Business Models. *J Bus Fin Aff*, 12(4).

Moses, L. B., & Koker, L. D. (2017). Open Secrets: Balancing Operational Secrecy and Transparency in the Collection and Use of Data by National Security and Law Enforcement Agencies. *Melbourne University Law Review*, 41(530).

Munodawafa, T., Naude, M., & Govender, K. K. (2024): Assuring the Sustainability and Growth of Small and Medium-Sized Manufacturing Enterprises in Botswana: An Exploratory Study. In *IJEFI* 14 (4), pp. 253–266. DOI: DOI: 10.32479/ijefi.16632

Murdoch, D., & Fichter, R. (2021): *From doing digital to being digital. Research Anthology on Digital Transformation, Organizational Change, and the Impact of Remote Work*. In Information Resources Management Association (Ed.): Research Anthology on Digital Transformation, Organizational Change, and the Impact of Remote Work: IGI Global, 23–40.

Musaigwa, M., & Kalitanyi, V. (2024). Effective leadership in the digital era: An exploration of change management. *Technology Audit and Production Reserves*, 1(4(75)), 6–14. Doi.org/10.15587/2706-5448.2024.297374. DOI: 10.15587/2706-5448.2024.297374

Mušura, G. (2020). The Role of Cultural Dimensions Of Communication And Developing Cultural Awareness In International Business. *In International Scientific Conference ERAZ* - Knowledge Based Sustainable Development, 6th ERAZ Conference Proceedings (part of ERAZ conference collection) (203–206). Association of Economists and Managers of the Balkans, Belgrade, Serbia. DOI: 10.31410/ERAZ.2020.203

Muthukrishnan, M., Suhas, J., Kapil, K. S., & Gowrisankar, K. (2024). Demystifying Explainable AI: Understanding, Transparency, and Trust. *International Journal for Multidisciplinary Research*. https://www.semanticscholar.org/paper/Demystifying-Explainable-AI%3A-Understanding%2C-and-Muthusubramanian-Jangoan/20e91e6e90bc94b11056cd76094337ac2ede0eb1

Nambisan, S. (2017). Digital entrepreneurship: Toward a digital technology perspective of entrepreneurship. *Entrepreneurship Theory and Practice*, 41(6), 1029–1055. DOI: 10.1111/etap.12254

Natalya, I., & Isaeva, L. (2021). Basic principles of partnership as the factor of sustainable development in the context of business ecosystems. *E3S Web of Conferences*. https://www.semanticscholar.org/paper/Basic-principles-of-partnership-as-the-factor-of-in-Ivashchenko-Isaeva/67517fe8cdf575bee3bdce1f433ebefab633d41f

Newman, P. (2019). Cultural barriers and how to overcome them in your global company as a global leader. *EURAC - European Academy for Executive Education*. https://eurac.com/cultural-barriers-and-how-to-overcome-them-in-your-global-company-as-a-global-leader/

Niharika Hariharan, N. J., Khan, H., & Rab, I. (2021). A design-led approach to embracing an ecosystem strategy. *McKinsey & Company*. https://www.mckinsey.com/capabilities/mckinsey-design/our-insights/a-design-led-approach-to-embracing-an-ecosystem-strategy#/

Nikolić, S., & Leković, B. (2023). There is no end to storytelling: Transmedia storytelling in the digital mediation of music. *Zbornik Akademije Umetnosti*, (11), 202–221. DOI: 10.5937/ZbAkU2311202N

Nofal, M. I., Nasim, M., Muaadh, M., Al Khaldy, M., Sowan, B. I., & Almalahmeh, T. M. (2024). A Framework for Using Blockchain-Enabled Supply Chain Management to Enhance Transparency, Traceability, and Trust. *International Conference Control and Robots*. https://www.semanticscholar.org/paper/A-Framework-for-Using-Blockchain-Enabled-Supply-to-Nofal-Matar/fa0a77c09b00e7484c9d84f3267ccbb46a059721

Nohutlu, Z. D., Englis, B. G., Groen, A. J., & Constantinides, E. (2023). Innovating With the Customer: Co-Creation Motives in Online Communities. *International Journal of Electronic Commerce*, 27(4), 523–557. DOI: 10.1080/10864415.2023.2255111

Novak, I., Velde, A. T., Hines, A., Stanton, E., Namara, M. M., Paton, M. C. B., & Morgan, C. (2021). Rehabilitation Evidence-Based Decision-Making: The Read Model. *Frontiers in Rehabilitation Sciences*, 2, 726410. Https://Doi.Org/10.3389/Fresc.2021.726410. DOI: 10.3389/fresc.2021.726410 PMID: 36188787

Nuijten, E., Messmer, M., & van Lammerts Bueren, E. (2017). Concepts and Strategies of Organic Plant Breeding in Light of Novel Breeding Techniques. *Sustainability (Basel)*, 9(1), 18. DOI: 10.3390/su9010018

O'leary, C., & Stewart, J. (2006). Factors Affecting Internal Auditors' Ethical Decision-Making Other Corporate Governance Mechanisms And Years Of Experience. Https://Www.Semanticscholar.Org/Paper/Factors-Affecting-Internal-Auditors'-Ethical-Making-O'leary-Stewart/A0a7bac0725304b80c32dc38e43644c360e5285e

O'sullivan, D. (2023). *The Crucial Role Of Ethical Leadership: Reflection Of Honor, Integrity, And Past Actions | Linkedin*. Https://Www.Linkedin.Com/Pulse/Crucial-Role-Ethical-Leadership-Reflection-Honor-Past-O-Sullivan/

Obie, H. O., Ukwella, J., Madampe, K., Grundy, J., & Shahin, M. (2023). Towards an Understanding of Developers' Perceptions of Transparency in Software Development: A Preliminary Study. DOI: 10.1109/ASEW60602.2023.00010

Ogilvy, J. (2015). Scenario Planning and Strategic Forecasting. *Forbes*. https://www.forbes.com/sites/stratfor/2015/01/08/scenario-planning-and-strategic-forecasting/

Ojha, D., Patel, P. C., & Sridharan, S. V. (2020). Dynamic strategic planning and firm competitive performance: A conceptualization and an empirical test. *International Journal of Production Economics*, 222, 107509. DOI: 10.1016/j.ijpe.2019.09.030

Olaniyi, O. O., Okunleye, O. J., & Olabanji, S. O. (2023). Advancing Data-Driven Decision-Making In Smart Cities Through Big Data Analytics: A Comprehensive Review Of Existing Literature. *Current Journal Of Applied Science And Technology*, 42(25), 10–18. Https://Doi.Org/10.9734/Cjast/2023/V42i254181

Ollerton, M. (2023). *Understanding Body Language Across Cultures & the Role of Language Services*. Workplace Languages. https://www.workplacelanguages.com/body-language-cultures/

Olurina, J. O., Gidiagba, J. O., Ehiaguina, V. E., Ndiwe, T. C., Ayodeji, S. A., Banso, A. A., Tula, O. A., & Ojo, G. G. (2023). Engineering Innovations And Sustainable Entrepreneurship: A Comprehensive Literature Review. *Materials & Corrosion Engineering Management*, 4(2), 70–79. DOI: 10.26480/macem.02.2023.70.79

Omol, E. (2023). *Organizational digital transformation: from evolution to future trends*. Digital Transformation and Society., DOI: 10.1108/DTS-08-2023-0061

Ontop Team Blog post. (2024). How to Navigate Conflict Resolution in Diverse Teams. https://www.getontop.com/blog/how-to-navigate-conflict-resolution-in-diverse-teams

Overesch, M., & Willkomm, S. (2024). The Relation Between Corporate Social Responsibility And Profit Shifting Of Multinational Enterprises. *International Tax and Public Finance*. Advance online publication. Doi.Org/10.1007/S10797-024-09850-Z. DOI: 10.1007/s10797-024-09850-z

Overton, M. G. (2023). Leadership Strategies to Enhance Communication and Conflict Management. *MedicalTraining.Me*. https://medicaltraining.me/leadership-strategies-to-enhance-communication-and-conflict-management/

Owino, P. O., & Namusonge, M. (2024): Risk-taking, Leadership, Innovation, and Networking as Entrepreneurial Competencies of Growth of Micro and Small Enterprises in Nairobi City County in Kenya. In *theijhss*. DOI: DOI: 10.24940/theijhss/2023/v11/i11/HS2311-002

Owl Labs Staff. (2024). The best technology for remote working: 4 essential tools.

Ozdemir, S., Carlos Fernandez de Arroyabe, J., Sena, V., & Gupta, S. (2023). Stakeholder diversity and collaborative innovation: Integrating the resource-based view with stakeholder theory. *Journal of Business Research*, 164, 113955. DOI: 10.1016/j.jbusres.2023.113955

Öz, E. (2022a). The Impact of Gender Differences on Lifelong Learning Tendencies in Turkey: A Meta-analysis. *SAGE Open*, 12(2), 215824402210995. DOI: 10.1177/21582440221099528

Pal, S. K., Baral, M. M., Mukherjee, S., Chittipaka, V., & Jana, B. (2022). Analyzing the impact of supply chain innovation as a mediator for healthcare firms' performance. *Materials Today: Proceedings*, 56, 2880–2887. DOI: 10.1016/j.matpr.2021.10.173

Panuganty, R. (2023). Data Driven Decision Making: Benefits And Challenges. *Machege*. Https://Www.Macheye.Com/Blog/Challenges-And-Benefits-Of-Data-Driven-Decision-Making/

Paredes, R. (2023). What Is A Key Performance Indicator (Kpi)? | Safetyculture. Https://Safetyculture.Com/Topics/Kpi/

Parker, H. (2024). 10 AI Tools for Decision-Making to Tackle Problems Efficiently. *ClickUp*. https://clickup.com/blog/ai-tools-for-decision-making/

Parsons, L. (2020). Ethical Concerns Mount As Ai Takes Bigger Decision-Making Role: Great Promise But Potential For Peril. *Harvard Gazette*. Https://News.Harvard.Edu/Gazette/Story/2020/10/Ethical-Concerns-Mount-As-Ai-Takes-Bigger-Decision-Making-Role/

Partners MBO Blog post. (December 2023). *Soft Skills in the Workplace: Top Skills and How to Improve Them*. https://www.mbopartners.com/blog/how-manage-small-business/why-are-soft-skills-important/

Pelta, R. (2020). *15 Transferable Skills That Companies Want: Examples and Definitions*. https://www.flexjobs.com/blog/post/transferable-skills/

Peng, A. C., & Kim, D. (2020). A meta-analytic test of the differential pathways linking ethical leadership to normative conduct. *Journal of Organizational Behavior*, 41(4), 348–368. DOI: 10.1002/job.2427

PennState Extension. (2023). *Building Trust with Ecosystem Stakeholders* (Part 3). https://extension.psu.edu/building-trust-with-ecosystem-stakeholders-part-3

Perilli, R. (2023). *Importance of inclusion and diversity in communication in the digital workplace*. https://www.simpplr.com/blog/2021/importance-of-diversity-in-communication-in-the-digital-workplace/

Perry, M. (2024). Why Core Values Are Important. *Cooleaf*. Https://Www.Cooleaf.Com/Blog/Why-Core-Values-Are-Important

Pervin, S. (2023). Investigating The Impact Of Ethical Leadership On Student Perceptions Of Ethical Decision-Making In Business Management: Evidence From Bangladesh. *Journal Of Business And Management Studies*. Https://Www.Semanticscholar.Org/Paper/Investigating-The-Impact-Of-Ethical-Leadership-On-Pervin/Ff3676823501f005c9a7f761c679380ab060c2a1

Phukan, P. K. (2023). *Value-Based Decision Making: A Strategic Guide For Executives | Linkedin*. Https://Www.Linkedin.Com/Pulse/Value-Based-Decision-Making-Strategic-Guide-Dr-Pranjal-Kumar-Phukan/

Pietro, M., & Gurpreet, M. (2021). The roles of performance measurement and management in developing and implementing business ecosystem strategies. *International Journal of Operations & Production Management.* https://www.semanticscholar.org/paper/The-roles-of-performance-measurement-and-management-Micheli-Muctor/0c675264d4493fe6fc09842acbf36a0b09600f47

Plack, M. M., & Greenberg, L. (2005). The Reflective Practitioner: Reaching For Excellence In Practice. *Pediatrics*, 116(6), 1546–1552. Https://Doi.Org/10.1542/Peds.2005-0209. DOI: 10.1542/peds.2005-0209 PMID: 16322184

Plečko, S., & Hojnik, B. B. (2024). Sustainable Business Practices and the Role of Digital. Technologies: A Cross-Regional Analysis. *Systems*, 12(3), 97. DOI: 10.3390/systems12030097

Poleski Danielle Blog Post. (March 2023). Why Are Key Performance Indicators Important? *Klipfolio.* Https://Www.Klipfolio.Com/Blog/Kpi-Importance

Polly Blog Post. (n.d.). *8 Ways Employee Feedback Helps Define a Positive Company Culture.* Retrieved August 8, 2024, from https://www.polly.ai/blog/4-ways-employee-feedback-will-help-define-positive-company-culture

Pothineni, S. (2023). The Impact Of Data Strategy And Emerging Technologies On Business Performance. *International Journal of Business Strategy and Automation*, 4(1), 1–19. Https://Doi.Org/10.4018/Ijbsa.334022. DOI: 10.4018/IJBSA.334022

Power, D. M. S. (2020). Why it is important to review policies and procedures. https://www.powerdms.com/policy-learning-center/why-it-is-important-to-review-policies-and-procedures

Pragmatic Institute - Resources. (2024). *10 Data Presentation Tips | Pragmatic Institute.* Https://Www.Pragmaticinstitute.Com/Resources/Articles/Data/10-Ways-To-Communicate-Data-Findings-Effectively/

Premier Agile. (n.d.). *What is Agile Strategic Planning - Process & It's Working.* Retrieved July 15, 2024, from https://premieragile.com/agile-strategic-planning/

Professional & Executive Development | Harvard Dce. (2024). *Ethical Leadership - Professional & Executive Development | Harvard Dce.* Https://Professional.Dce.Harvard.Edu/Programs/Ethical-Leadership/

Provost, F., & Fawcett, T. (2013). *Data Science for Business: What you Need to Know About Data Mining and Data-Analytic Thinking.* O'Reilly Media, Inc.

Pshembayeva, E. S., & Pfeifer, N. E. (2021). Lifelong Learning As A Priority Area And A Condition For Successful Personal Career Development. *Bulletin of Toraighyrov University.Pedagogics Series*, (4), 466–472. DOI: 10.48081/HKOS1842

Psychweb. (2023). *Directive*. Https://Psychweb.Com/Directive/

Pulugurtha, N. (2023). Breaking Barriers: The Stride Framework For Advancing Women Of Color In Product Management. *International Research Journal of Modernization in Engineering Technology and Science*. Advance online publication. DOI: 10.56726/IRJMETS41433

Purnomo, J., & Sri Pudjiarti, E. (2024). Navigasi Kepemimpinan Di Era Digital: Tantangan Dan Peluang Bagi Generasi Mill. Transformasi: Journal of Economics and Business Management.

Purple, B. (2024). *Navigating The Future: Ethical Leadership In The New Era – Guiding Principles For 2024 | Linkedin*. Https://Www.Linkedin.Com/Pulse/Navigating-Future-Ethical-Leadership-New-Era-Guiding-Purple-Group-Z48we/

Purwoko, B. (2024). Diversity and inclusion initiatives: Influence on organizational performance. *Productivity*, 1(3), 461–471. DOI: 10.62207/w5fsnn95

Putra, J., Karundeng, D., Gofur, A., Tresnadjaja, R., Suhara, A., Sukmayadi, S., & Sopyan, A. (2024). Entrepreneurship in the era of society 5.0: Navigating digitalization for innovation and growth. *Journal of Sustainable Tourism and Entrepreneurship*. DOI: 10.35912/joste.v6i1.2224

PwC (2021). *The Workforce of the Future: The Competing Forces Shaping 2030*.

Qualtrics. (2023). *Organizational Core Values: Definition, Benefits, And Examples*. Https://Www.Qualtrics.Com/Experience-Management/Employee/Organizational-Core-Values/

Quärtápa, T. (2024). *Leadership Reimagined: Navigating The Trends At The Intersection Of Technology, Ethics, And Innovation In 2024 | Linkedin*. Https://Www.Linkedin.Com/Pulse/Leadership-Reimagined-Navigating-Trends-Intersection-Ethics-Qu%C3%A4rt%C3%A1pa-Wk6ic/

Radicioni, B. (2023). What Is Inclusive Leadership? Entrepreneurship of All Kinds.

Ragula, A. (2024). Emerging Trends in Cloud Security: Zero Trust and SASE. *International Journal for Research in Applied Science and Engineering Technology*, 12(6), 10–17. DOI: 10.22214/ijraset.2024.62457

Rahman, N. K. A., Yunus, M., Nasri, N. M., & Abd, R. E. (2023). Proficiency Preparedness in Defence Workforce: A Survey of Cadet Officers' English Language Needs. *International Journal of Learning. Teaching and Educational Research*, 22(11), 96–115. DOI: 10.26803/ijlter.22.11.6

Rainey, J. (2024). *Embracing Mistakes in Business: A Guide to Turning Setbacks into Success.* https://jennarainey.com/embracing-mistakes-in-business-a-guide-to-turning-setbacks-into-success/

Rajdeep, D. (2023). Unconscious Bias: Navigating its Impact on Leadership in a Hybrid Work Environment | LinkedIn. https://www.linkedin.com/pulse/unconscious-bias-navigating-its-impact-leadership-hybrid-dutta/

Rajput, S. (2024). *Radiating Excellence: Exploring the Top Trends in the Automotive Radiator Market.* https://www.verifiedmarketreports.com/blog/top-7-trends-in-the-automotive-radiator-market/

Ramadhan, G. J. M., & Niam, S. (2024). Big Data Analytics: Techniques, Tools, And Applications In Various Industries. *Jurnal Ar Ro'is Mandalika (Armada), 3*(2), 56–65. Https://Www.Semanticscholar.Org/Paper/Big-Data-Analytics%3a-Techniques%2c-Tools%2c-And-In-Ramadhan-Niam/E82406e6f77956b992e7b5ec475897662cfa8d5c

Ramalingam, B., Nabarro, D., Oqubay, A., Carnall, D. R., & Wild, L. (2020). *5 Principles to Guide Adaptive Leadership.* https://hbr.org/2020/09/5-principles-to-guide-adaptive-leadership

Rane, N., Choudhary, S., & Rane, J. (2023). Blockchain and Artificial Intelligence (AI) integration is needed to revolutionize security and transparency in finance. SSRN *Electronic Journal.* Advance online publication. DOI: 10.2139/ssrn.4644253

Raz, A. E., Niemiec, E., Howard, H. C., Sterckx, S., Cockbain, J., & Prainsack, B. (2020). Transparency, consent and Trust in the use of customers' data by an online genetic testing company: An Exploratory survey among 23andMe users. *New Genetics & Society*, 39(4), 459–482. DOI: 10.1080/14636778.2020.1755636

Rcademy. (2023). *Effective Communication in Cross-Cultural and Diverse Environments - Rcademy.* https://rcademy.com/effective-communication-in-cross-cultural-and-diverse-environments/

Recklies, D. (2015). *Strategy making in the past and today* – Part 2: Problems with the traditional strategy process. Recklies Management Project GmbH. https://www.themanager.org/2015/08/strategy-making-2-problems-traditional-strategy-process/

Reddit. (2023). *Data-Driven Decision Making: Case Studies: R/Compsci*. Https://Www.Reddit.Com/R/Compsci/Comments/15pub3z/Datadriven_Decision_Making_Case_Studies/

RedHat. (2020). *Understanding open organizational culture*. RedHat. https://www.redhat.com/en/topics/open-culture

Renz, A., Conrad, D. A., & Watts, C. (2013). Stakeholder Perspectives On The Implementation Of Shared Decision Making: A Qualitative Data Analysis. *International Journal of Healthcare Management*, 6(2), 122–131. Https://Doi.Org/10.1179/2047971912y.0000000027. DOI: 10.1179/2047971912Y.0000000027

Revolution, I. T. (2020). *The Five Dimensions of Transformational Leadership - IT Revolution.* https://itrevolution.com/articles/the-five-dimensions-of-transformational-leadership/

Rib Software Blog. (2024). *Why Data Driven Decision Making Is Your Path To Busseness Success*. Https://Www.Rib-Software.Com/En/Blogs/Data-Driven-Decision-Making-In-Businesses

Rider, C. (2023). Building a Partner Ecosystem? 5 Steps to Drive Your Approach. *Impartner*. https://impartner.com/resources/blog/building-a-partner-ecosystem

Ries, E. (2011). *The Lean Startup: How today's entrepreneurs use continuous innovation to create radically successful businesses.* https://theleanstartup.com/casestudies

Roberts, N. F. (2020). The Psychology Of Trust Explains How Institutions Can Regain It Once Lost. *Forbes*. https://www.forbes.com/sites/nicolefisher/2020/09/01/the-psychology-of-trust--how-institutions-can-regain-it-once-lost/

Rockborne Graduates. (2023). *Presenting Data Visualisations And Insights To Business-Minded Stakeholders - Rockborne - Graduates*. Https://Rockborne.Com/Graduates/Blog/Presenting-Data-To-Stakeholders/

Rogers, D.L. (2011). The Network Is Your Customer: Five Strategies to Thrive in a Digital Age.

Rosero-Garcia, J., & Montano-Salamanca, W. (2024). Conceptual model for establishing the relationship between digital transformation and organizational performance in electrical power companies. *International Journal of Management and Sustainability*, 13(2), 253–277. DOI: 10.18488/11.v13i2.3767

Sa. Global U.S. (2023). *Scenario Planning For Adaptable HR*. https://www.saglobal.com/en-us/insights/bringing-in-agility-in-hr-with-scenario-planning.html

Saabye, H., & Powell, D. (2024). Fostering Insights And Improvements From Iiot Systems At The Shop Floor: A Case Of Industry 4.0 And Lean Complementarity Enabled By Action Learning. *International Journal of Lean Six Sigma*, 15(5), 968–996. Https://Doi.Org/10.1108/Ijlss-01-2022-0017. DOI: 10.1108/IJLSS-01-2022-0017

Sahibzada, U., Aslam, N., Muavia, M., Shujahat, M., & Rafi-Ul-Shan, P. (2024). Navigating digital waves: Unveiling entrepreneurial leadership toward digital innovation and sustainable performance in the Chinese IT industry. *Journal of Enterprise Information Management*. Advance online publication. DOI: 10.1108/JEIM-01-2024-0023

Salmon, A. (2021). Inside Amazon's culture of scaling, agility and innovation. Digital Works Consulting. https://digitalworksgroup.com/inside-amazons-culture-of-scaling-agility-and-innovation/

Saloome, S. (2023). Ethical Challenges In Global Business: Navigating Cross-Cultural Dilemmas - Academia World News. *Academia World News*. Https://Academiaworldnews.Com/Ethical-Challenges-In-Global-Business-Navigating-Cross-Cultural-Dilemmas/

Sánchez-García, E., Martínez-Falcó, J., Marco-Lajara, B., & Gigauri, I. (2024). Building the future through digital entrepreneurship and innovation. *European Journal of Innovation Management*. Advance online publication. DOI: 10.1108/EJIM-04-2024-0360

Sankar, S. (N.D.). *Design Your Data Strategy In Six Steps | Ibm*. Retrieved September 6, 2024, From Https://Www.Ibm.Com/Resources/The-Data-Differentiator/Data-Strategy

Sari, E., Anindhita, W., Mulyadi, M., Purwoko, D., Madhakomala, M., & Yatimah, D. (2023). Innovation in Adaptive Leadership Management Model through the Development of Digital Mindset in Activator School Programs. *International Journal of Social Science and Human Research*, 6(12). Advance online publication. https://www.semanticscholar.org/paper/Innovation-in-Adaptive-Leadership-Management-Model-Sari-Anindhita/2091c2d542c06db54415ac421ac4c7a2778bc094. DOI: 10.47191/ijsshr/v6-i12-02

Sarkar, D., & Nath, H. (2024). Embracing Disruption: An Empirical Study On The Accepted Practices And Strategic Responses Of Entrepreneurs To Rapid Technological Advancements. ShodhKosh: *Journal of Visual and Performing Arts*. DOI: 10.29121/shodhkosh.v5.i4.2024.2402

Saurav, G. (2023). The Power of Scenario Planning in Strategic Decision-Making | *LinkedIn*. https://www.linkedin.com/pulse/power-scenario-planning-strategic-decision-making-saurav-goel-o8bff/

Savard, R. (2024). *Preparing for jobs that don't exist yet*. https://www.andover.edu/news/2024/how-to-prepare-for-jobs-that-dont-exist-yetSingh, M. (2024). Digital culture for lean & agile organization. Brazilian Journal of Development.

Sayogo, D. S., Yuli, S. B. C., & Amalia, F. A. (2024). Data-Driven Decision-Making Challenges Of Local Government In Indonesia. *Transforming Government: People, Process And Policy, 18*(1), 145–156. Https://Doi.Org/10.1108/Tg-05-2023-0058

Scala, S. A. (2023). Why Inclusive Communication Matters in the Workplace. Associated Industries of Massachusetts. https://aimnet.org/why-inclusive-communication-matters-in-the-workplace/

Schein, E., & Schein, H. P. A. (2019). *A New Era for Culture, Change, and Leadership*. MIT Sloan Management Review. https://sloanreview.mit.edu/article/a-new-era-for-culture-change-and-leadership/

Schein, E. H. (2017). *Organizational Culture and Leadership*. John Wiley & Sons, Inc.

Schmidt, M., Steigenberger, N., Berndtzon, M., & Uman, T. (2023). Cultural diversity in health care teams: A systematic integrative review and research agenda. *Health Care Management Review*, 48(4), 311–322. DOI: 10.1097/HMR.0000000000000379 PMID: 37615941

Schmocker, D., Tanner, C., Katsarov, J., & Christen, M. (2023). Moral Sensitivity In Business: A Revised Measure. *Current Psychology (New Brunswick, N.J.)*, 42(12), 10277–10291. Https://Doi.Org/10.1007/S12144-021-01926-X. DOI: 10.1007/s12144-021-01926-x PMID: 37215736

Schneeweiß, S., & Glynn, R. J. (2018). Real-World Data Analytics Fit For Regulatory Decision-Making. *American Journal of Law & Medicine*, 44(2-3), 197–217. Https://Doi.Org/10.1177/0098858818789429. DOI: 10.1177/0098858818789429 PMID: 30106649

Schoemaker, P. J. H. (1995). (1995). -Schoemaker Scenario Planning-Tool for Strategic Thinking. *Sloan Management Review*.

Schreiner, E. (2024). What Are The Key Elements Of Ethical Leadership In An Organization? Smith, I. H., & Kouchaki, M. (2021). *Building An Ethical Company*. Harvard Business Review. Https://Hbr.Org/2021/11/Building-An-Ethical-Company

Schwab, K. (2017). *The fourth industrial revolution*. Currency.

Scott, C. (2023). Inclusive Communication: What Is It and Why It Matters. AIHR | Academy to Innovate HR. https://www.aihr.com/blog/inclusive-communication/

ScrumAlliance. (2024). *Agile Manifesto Values and Principles.* https://resources.scrumalliance.org/Article/key-values-principles-agile-manifesto

Searle, R. H. (2022). Counterproductive Work Behaviors. In Searle, R. H. (Ed.), *Oxford Research Encyclopedia of Psychology.* Oxford University Press., DOI: 10.1093/acrefore/9780190236557.013.880

Secker, B. (2013). The Purpose Of The Idea: Ethical Decision-Making Framework.

Seel, J. (2023). How to build a cross-functional team for custom software development.

Segovia-Martín, J., Walker, B., Fay, N., & Tamariz, M. (2020). Network Connectivity Dynamics, Cognitive Biases, and the Evolution of Cultural Diversity in Round-Robin Interactive Micro-Societies. *Cognitive Science*, 44(7), e12852. DOI: 10.1111/cogs.12852 PMID: 32564420

Senadjki, A., Au Yong, H. N., Ganapathy, T., & Ogbeibu, S. (2023). Unlocking the potential: The impact of digital leadership on firms' performance through digital transformation. *Journal of Business and Socio-Economic Development*, 4(2), 161–177. DOI: 10.1108/JBSED-06-2023-0050

Seramount. (2020). Inclusive Employee Resource Groups. https://seramount.com/resources/research-report-inclusive-employee-resource-groups/

Shadbad, M. Z., Hasani, M. T., & Alishahi, A. G. (2017). The Role Of Professional Ethics In Individual And Organizational Outcomes. *Medical Ethics Journal, 11*(40), 53–62. Https://Doi.Org/10.21859/Mej-114053

Sharma, A. (2023). How To Ensure Data Integrity In Your Organization. *Dataversity.* Https://Www.Dataversity.Net/How-To-Ensure-Data-Integrity-In-Your-Organization/

Shillingford, A. (2024). *Building the Cultural Power Ecosystem (SSIR).* https://ssir.org/articles/entry/building_the_cultural_power_ecosystem# Sramek, E. (2023). Partner Incentives: 7 Reward Strategies That Work - *Scaleo Blog*. Scaleo.io. https://www.scaleo.io/blog/partner-incentives-7-reward-strategies-that-work/

Shonk, K. (2024). Consensus-Building Techniques. *Program On Negotiation At Harvard Law School*. Https://Www.Pon.Harvard.Edu/Daily/Dealing-With-Difficult-People-Daily/Consensus-Building-Techniques/

Simplilearn (2020). *What is Agile? Understanding Agile Methodology and Principles in Software Development*. Simplilearn. https://www.simplilearn.com/tutorials/agile-scrum-tutorial/what-is-agile

Singh, A., & Mathur, S. (2019). The Insight of Content Marketing at Social Media Platforms. Adhyayan: A *Journal of Management Sciences*, 9.

Singh, M. (2024). Digital culture for lean & agile organization. Brazilian Journal of Development.

Singh, S., Singh, S., & Dhir, S. (2023). The evolving relationship of entrepreneurship, technology, and innovation: A topic modeling perspective. *International Journal of Entrepreneurship and Innovation*, 14657503231179597. Advance online publication. DOI: 10.1177/14657503231179597

Singletary, L., Koebele, E., Evans, W., Copp, C. J., Hockaday, S., & Rego, J. J. (2022). Evaluating stakeholder engagement in collaborative research: Co-producing knowledge for climate resilience. *Socio-Ecological Practice Research*, 4(3), 235–249. DOI: 10.1007/s42532-022-00124-8 PMID: 36036019

Sinka, H. (2024). Talent Management in Digital Age. *Interantional Journal OF Scientific Research IN Engineering AND Management*, 08(06), 1–5. DOI: 10.55041/IJSREM35730

Sivakumar, P., & Dinesh, E. (2023). Navigating The Modernization Of Legacy Applications And Data: Effective Strategies And Best Practices. *Asian Journal Of Research In Computer Science, 16*(4). Https://Doi.Org/10.9734/Ajrcos/2023/V16i4386

Skyone. (2024). *Data Driven: 4 Challenges In Implementing This Culture*. Https://Skyone.Solutions/En/Blog/Data-Driven-Main-Challenges

Slater, D. (2024). The Imperatives of Customer-Centric Innovation | AWS Executive Insights. https://aws.amazon.com/executive-insights/content/the-imperatives-of-customer-centric-innovation/

Sopact University. (2023). *Actionable Insights: Turning Data Into Dynamic Results*. Https://University.Sopact.Com/Article/Actionable-Insights

Sparrow, G. (2024). *10 Ways to Foster Innovation in Your Company: From Ideas to Impact*. https://www.herox.com/blog/1063-10-ways-to-foster-innovation-in-your-company

Spyre Group. (2024). *Examples of Companies with Successful Innovation Strategies*. https://www.spyre.group/post/examples-of-companies-with-successful-innovation-strategies

Srivastava, Y. C., Srivastava, A., & Granata, C. (2021). *Digitally Enabled Organizations- Leveraging New Age Technologies. On Day 1, Mon, November 15, 2021*. SPE., DOI: 10.2118/207380-M.S

St. John's University Blog Post. (January 2024). *Future-Proof Your Career: The Top 10 Skills Employers are Looking for in 2024*. https://www.stjohns.edu/news-media/johnnies-blog/top-skills-employers-are-looking-for

Standford University. (2024). *Artificial Intelligence Index Report*. Standford University. https://aiindex.stanford.edu/report/

Stephan, U. (2018). Entrepreneurs' mental health and well-being: A review and research agenda. *The Academy of Management Perspectives*, 32(3), 290–322. DOI: 10.5465/amp.2017.0001

Stevens, E. (2021). *The 7 Most Useful Data Analysis Techniques [2024 Guide]*. Https://Careerfoundry.Com/En/Blog/Data-Analytics/Data-Analysis-Techniques/

Stobierski, T. (2020). Emergent vs. Deliberate Strategy: How & When to Use Each. *Harvard Business School*. https://online.hbs.edu/blog/post/emergent-vs-deliberate-strategy

Suar, D., & Khuntia, R. (2010). Influence of Personal Values and Value Congruence on Unethical Practices and Work Behavior. *Journal of Business Ethics*, 97(3), 443–460. DOI: 10.1007/s10551-010-0517-y

Sunitha, B. K. (2024). The Impact Of Data Analytics And Mining. In *Transforming The Decision-Making System – Ijsrem*. Interantional Journal Of Scientific Research In Engineering And Management.

Sun, X., He, Z., & Qian, Y. (2023). Getting organizational adaptability in the context of digital transformation. *Chinese Management Studies*, 18(2), 550–574. DOI: 10.1108/CMS-06-2022-0222

Suresh, J. (2023). Surveillance Technology: Balancing Security And Privacy In The Digital Age. *EPRA International Journal of Multidisciplinary Research*. https://www.semanticscholar.org/paper/Surveillance-Technology%3a-Balancing-Security-And-In-Javvaji/a18d82aa246506494a8510be4f07c507ea8e90ba

Surono, S. (2024). Enhancing Employability Of Professional Self-Employed. In *Business Management Through Mapping Occupational Standards In Entrepreneurship Within The Indonesian Qualification Framework. Jurnal Ekonomi Teknologi Dan Bisnis*. JETBIS.

Sypniewska, B. (2020). Counterproductive Work Behavior and Organizational Citizenship Behavior. *Advances in Cognitive Psychology*, 16(4), 321–328. DOI: 10.5709/acp-0306-9 PMID: 33500742

Tableau. (N. D.). *Guide To Data Cleaning: Definition, Benefits, Components, And How To Clean Your Data*. Retrieved September 4, 2024, From Https://Www.Tableau.Com/Learn/Articles/What-Is-Data-Cleaning

Talin, B. (2023). 4 Most Common Obstacles To Data-Driven Decision-Making And How To Overcome Them – Morethandigital. *Morethandigital Insights*. Https://Insights.Mtd.Info/4-Most-Common-Obstacles-To-Data-Driven-Decision-Making-And-How-To-Overcome-Them/

Tamášová, V. (2015). Professional and Career Development of Vocational Subject Teachers as a Trend in the Lifelong Learning of Teachers. *Acta Technologica Dubnicae*, 5(1), 1–20. DOI: 10.1515/atd-2015-0029

Tan, A. (2023). Partner Ecosystems: why we need them. *Future CFO*. https://futurecio.tech/partner-ecosystems-why-we-need-them

Tangdall, S. (2018). *The Ceo Of Starbucks And The Practice Of Ethical Leadership*. Https://Www.Scu.Edu/Leadership-Ethics/Resources/The-Ceo-Of-Starbucks-And-The-Practice-Of-Ethical-Leadership/

Taqwiem, A., & Arpianto, Y. Faradina, Luthfiyanti, L., & Susanti, P. A. (2024): Cross-Cultural Leadership Models in Global Education Systems Implications for Policy and Practice. In *Intl. J. Rel.* 5 (11), pp. 7343–7353. DOI: DOI: 10.61707/1zwc2a56

Tawil, A. R., Muhidin, M., Schmoor, X., Vlachos, K., & Haidar, D. (2023). *Trends And Challenges Towards An Effective Data-Driven Decision Making In Uk Smes: Case Studies And Lessons Learnt From The Analysis Of 85 Smes*. Http://Arxiv.Org/Pdf/2305.15454

Taylor, A. (2023). *Strategic Plan Examples: Case Studies and Free Strategic Planning Template*. https://www.smestrategy.net/blog/strategic-plan-examples-case-studies-and-free-strategic-planning-template

Taylor, B. (2023). *Nurturing Creativity: Unleashing Innovation and Problem-Solving Skills in the Workplace* | LinkedIn. https://www.linkedin.com/pulse/nurturing-creativity-unleashing-innovation-skills-workplace-taylor/

Team Digitaldefynd. (2024). *15 Business Analytics Case Studies*. Https://Digitaldefynd.Com/Iq/Business-Analytics-Case-Studies/

Technologies, Z. I. N. F. I. Inc. (2024). *Building a Resilient Partner Ecosystem: Strategies Insights.* https://www.zinfi.com/blog/partner-ecosystem-maximizing-strategies/

Terzieva, K. (2023). The Rise Of Ethical Leadership In Modern Business Enterprises. *Forbes.*

The Agile Company. (2023). *Fostering a Culture of Innovation: Lessons from Leading Companies.* https://theagilecompany.org/fostering-a-culture-of-innovation/

The Enterprise World. (2023). *12 Benefits Of Leadership Roles For Next Generation | The Enterprise World.* Https://Theenterpriseworld.Com/Preparing-Generation-For-Leadership-Roles/

The Innovation Mode. (2022). *Design Thinking Grows Up - Welcome to Experience Thinking.* The Innovation Mode. https://www.theinnovationmode.com/the-innovation-blog/design-thinking-grows-up-welcome-to-experience-thinking

The MindTools Content Team. (2024). *Delivering Bad News - Communicating Well Under Pressure.* https://www.mindtools.com/a0byhfl/delivering-bad-news

The National Society Of Leadership And Success. (2022). Why Is Diversity Important in Leadership? https://www.nsls.org/blog/why-is-diversity-important-in-leadership

The World of Work Project. (2019). Edgar Schein's Organizational Culture Triangle: A Simple Summary. *World of Work Project.* https://worldofwork.io/2019/10/edgar-scheins-culture-triangle/

Thinggaard, E., Zetner, D. B., Fabrin, A., Christensen, J. B., & Konge, L. (2023). A Study of Surgical Residents' Self-Assessment of Open Surgery Skills Using Gap Analysis. *Simulation in healthcare. Simulation in Healthcare*, 18(5), 305–311. DOI: 10.1097/SIH.0000000000000694 PMID: 36730862

Thiyagarajan, S., Saldanha, P. R. M., Govindan, R., Leena, K. C., & Vasuki, P. P. (2023). Effectiveness of agile methodology on metacognitive ability, and clinical performance among nursing students-An interventional study. *Journal of Education and Health Promotion*, 12(1), 283. DOI: 10.4103/jehp.jehp_1798_22 PMID: 37849875

Thompson, S. (2023). *What are the best practices for delivering bad news with empathy and honesty? | LinkedIn.* https://www.linkedin.com/pulse/what-best-practices-delivering-bad-news-empathy-honesty-thompson/

Times, A. D. R. (2023). Constructive Conflict: A Positive Catalyst. *ADR Times.* https://www.adrtimes.com/constructive-conflict/

Torelli, C. J., & Rodas, M. A. (2024). *Globally Minded Marketing: A Cultural Approach to Building Iconic Brands*. Springer International Publishing; Imprint Palgrave Macmillan. DOI: 10.1007/978-3-031-50812-7

Torres, R., Reeves, M., & Love, C. (2010). Adaptive Leadership. *BCG Global*. https://www.bcg.com/publications/2010/leadership-engagement-culture-adaptive-leadership

Triangle, I. P. (2023). *10 Trailblazing Companies Leading the Way in Innovative Culture : Triangle I.P.*https://triangleip.com/companies-leading-innovation-culture/

Tripp, D. (2022). Fostering Employee Engagement In The Current Work Environment. Forbes. https://www.forbes.com/sites/forbeshumanresourcescouncil/2022/11/08/fostering-employee-engagement-in-the-current-work-environment/

Tse, C. (2022). *The Best Partnership Ecosystems Learnings of 2022*. https://partnerstack.com/articles/the-best-partnership-ecosystems-learnings-of-2022

Tsou, H., & Chen, J. (2021). How does digital technology usage benefit firm performance? digital transformation strategy and organizational innovation as mediators. Technology Analysis &Amp. *Strategic Management*, 35(9), 1114–1127. DOI: 10.1080/09537325.2021.1991575

Tsvetomira, P. (2022). *Top Data-Driven Companies You Can Learn From*. Https://Www.Slingshotapp.Io/Blog/Top-Data-Driven-Companies

Tulsiani, R. (2023). Overcoming Barriers To Diversity And Inclusion: A Guide For L&D Pros. ELearning Industry Inc. https://elearningindustry.com/overcoming-barriers-to-diversity-and-inclusion-a-guide-for-ld-pros

Tyagi, S. (2023a). *5 Key Benefits: Why Stakeholder Engagement Drives Success -*. ASKEL. https://askelsustainabilitysolutions.com/5-key-benefits-why-stakeholder-engagement-drives-success/

Tyagi, S. (2023b). *7 Strategies for Strong Stakeholder Engagement*. ASKEL. https://askelsustainabilitysolutions.com/7-strategies-for-strong-stakeholder-engagement/

Tynes, B. (2022). The Importance Of Diversity And Inclusion For Today's Companies. Forbes. https://www.forbes.com/sites/forbescommunicationscouncil/2022/03/03/the-importance-of-diversity-and-inclusion-for-todays-companies/

UBC Blog post (September2022). Notes on Brown's Emergent Strategy – You're the Teacher. https://blogs.ubc.ca/chendricks/2022/09/10/brown-emergent-strategy/

Ughulu, J. (2024). Ethical Leadership In Modern Organizations: Navigating Complexity And Promoting Integrity. *International Journal Of Economics, Business And Management Research, 08*(05), 52–62. Https://Doi.Org/10.51505/Ijebmr.2024.8505

Unlit Leadership. (2023). *Mastering Communication in a Diverse Workplace*: A Guide. https://unlitleadership.com/communication-in-diverse-workplace/

Utah Valley University. (2024). *Understanding Technology: Technology and Culture. Understanding Technology.* https://uen.pressbooks.pub/tech1010/chapter/technology-and-culture/

Valerie Kirk Blog Post. (2024, April). What Is Ethical Leadership And Why Is It Important? - Professional & Executive Development | Harvard Dce. Https://Professional.Dce.Harvard.Edu/Blog/What-Is-Ethical-Leadership-And-Why-Is-It-Important/

Valuer (2022). *50 Brands that Failed to Innovate. https*://www.valuer.ai/blog/50-examples-of-corporations-that-failed-to-innovate-and-missed-their-chance

Van Der Merwe, L., & Davey, C. (2024). The Role Of Organisational Culture And Structure In Data-Driven Green Policy And Decision-Making. *Environmental Science & Sustainable Development, 9*(2), 1–7. Https://Doi.Org/10.21625/Essd.V9i2.1085

Van Kuiken, S. V. (2022). *Tech at the Edge: Trends Reshaping the Future of IT and Business: With technological change accelerating, companies must make four fundamental shifts*. McKinsey Digital.

Vandenbroucke, H. (2022). Sense of belonging among UGent Faculty of Economics and Business Administration students. https://libstore.ugent.be/fulltxt/rug01/003/158/502/rug01-003158502_2023_0001_ac.pdf

Veldsman, D. (2022). *Scenario Planning: What HR Needs to Know. AIHR | Academy to Innovate HR*. https://www.aihr.com/blog/scenario-planning/

Verlinden, N. (2018). *5 Reasons Why Diversity Hiring Matters (And How to Go about it). AIHR | Academy to Innovate HR*. https://www.aihr.com/blog/diversity-hiring-reasons-hiring-for-diversity-matters/

Vial, G. (2019). Understanding digital transformation: A review and a research agenda. *The Journal of Strategic Information Systems*, 28(2), 118–144. DOI: 10.1016/j.jsis.2019.01.003

Vincent, T. (2023). Virtue, Utilitarianism, & Deontological Ethics: What Are The Differences? *Just Weighing.* Https://Justweighing.Com/Blogs/Wisdoms-Many-Facets/Virtue-Utilitarianism-Deontological-Ethics-What-Are-The-Differences

Vinod, S., Selvanayaki, S., Vimal, V. R., & Sheik Dhanveer, H. (2023). Screen recording and Sharing over the cloud Platform For Remote Teams And Cross-Functional Teams. In *2023 International Conference on Research Methodologies in Knowledge Management, Artificial Intelligence and Telecommunication Engineering (RMKMATE)* (pp. 1–5). IEEE. DOI: 10.1109/RMKMATE59243.2023.10369912

Vizient Newsroom. (2017). *Adopting an Agile Approach to Strategic Planning*. https://newsroom.vizientinc.com/en-U.S./releases/adopting-an-agile-approach-to-strategic-planning

Vumetric Blog Post. (February 2024). *The Importance Of Cybersecurity For Stakeholders - Vumetric*. Https://Www.Vumetric.Com/Blog/The-Importance-Of-Cybersecurity-For-Stakeholders/

Vu, V., Warschauer, M., & Yim, S. (2019). Digital Storytelling: A District Initiative for Academic Literacy Improvement. *Journal of Adolescent & Adult Literacy*, 63(3), 257–267. DOI: 10.1002/jaal.962

Vyas, D. (2023). *Transparency in the Workplace: What Is It and Why Does It Matter? | LinkedIn.* LinkedIn. https://www.linkedin.com/pulse/transparency-workplace-what-why-does-matter-vyas-l-i-o-n-/

Wade, M., Amit Joshi, A., & Teracino E. A (2021). 6 Principles to Build Your Company's Strategic Agility. *Harvard Business Review*.

Wagner, M. (2024). *Leading With Courage: Navigating Decisions With Confidence And Integrity | Linkedin.* Linkedin. Https://Www.Linkedin.Com/Pulse/Leading-Courage-Navigating-Decisions-Confidence-Integrity-Wagner-Npkgc/

Walacor (2024). 6 Best Practices For Maintaining Data Integrity | Walacor Corporation. *Walacor Corporation*. Https://Www.Walacor.Com/2024/01/24/6-Best-Practices-Maintaining-Data-Integrity/

Wang, C., Wu, S. Y., Nie, Y. Z., Cui, G. Y., & Hou, X. Y. (2022). Open-mindedness trait affects the development of intercultural communication competence in short-term overseas study programs: A mixed-method exploration. *BMC Medical Education*, 22(1), 219. DOI: 10.1186/s12909-022-03281-2 PMID: 35354454

Wang, T., Lin, X., & Sheng, F. (2022). Digital leadership and exploratory innovation: From the dual perspectives of strategic orientation and organizational culture. *Frontiers in Psychology*, 13, 902693. Advance online publication. DOI: 10.3389/fpsyg.2022.902693 PMID: 36176785

Warudkar, H. (2021). What Is Machine Learning And Machine Learning Techniques: A Complete Guide. *Express Analytics*. Https://Www.Expressanalytics.Com/Blog/Machine-Learning-Techniques-Guide/

Watenpaugh, N. (2018). Better Together: The 10 Ingredients Of Successful Partnerships. *Forbes*. https://www.forbes.com/sites/forbessanfranciscocouncil/2018/10/24/better-together-the-10-ingredients-of-successful-partnerships/

Watts, C. (2022). How to Promote Inclusive Communication in the Workplace. https://www.highspeedtraining.co.uk/hub/inclusive-communication-in-the-workplace/

Weinstein, B. (2024). Ai Ethics: 7 Crucial Qualities Of Ethical Leadership. *Forbes*. Https://Www.Forbes.Com/Sites/Bruceweinstein/2024/02/21/Ai-7-Crucial-Qualities-Of-Ethical-Leadership/

Wells, R. (2024, February 15). 8 Leadership Ethics Every Leader Should Live By In 2024. *Forbes*. Https://Www.Forbes.Com/Sites/Rachelwells/2024/02/15/8-Leadership-Ethics-Every-Leader-Should-Live-By-In-2024/

Wells, R. (2024a). 10+ High-Income Soft Skills You Should Learn In 2024. *Forbes*. https://www.forbes.com/sites/rachelwells/2024/06/28/10-high-income-soft-skills-you-should-learn-in-2024/

Wells, R. (2024b). 70% Of Employers Say Creative Thinking Is the Most In-Demand Skill In 2024. Forbes. https://www.forbes.com/sites/rachelwells/2024/01/28/70-of-employers-say-creative-thinking-is-most-in-demand-skill-in-2024/

Wells, R. (2024c, April 15). 3 Critical Thinking Skills You Need In 2024. Forbes. https://www.forbes.com/sites/rachelwells/2024/04/15/3-critical-thinking-skills-you-need-in-2024/

Westover, J. (2024). Finding Your True North: How To Identify And Apply Your Core Values In Leadership. *Human Capital Leadership Review*. Https://Www.Semanticscholar.Org/Paper/Finding-Your-True-North%3a-How-To-Identify-And-Apply-Westover/27816cc440f24916d48dc9866d3af4e3dd162590

Westover, J. (2024). The Invisible Backbone: Leveraging Hidden Teams to Drive Organizational Success. *HCI Consulting*. https://www.innovativehumancapital.com/post/the-invisible-backbone-leveraging-hidden-teams-to-drive-organizational-success

Whitworth, E. (2022). The World Is Flat by Thomas Friedman: Book Overview & Lessons. *Shortform Books*. https://www.shortform.com/blog/the-world-is-flat-by-thomas-friedman/

Wiegand, T., & Brautsch, C. (2022). Digital Technology Deployment in the German Automotive Industry. In Lee, I., & Wynn, M. G. (Eds.), *Handbook of Research on Digital Transformation, Industry Use Cases, and the Impact of Disruptive Technologies* (pp. 249–267). Advances in E-Business Research. IGI Global., DOI: 10.4018/978-1-7998-7712-7.ch014

Wikipedia. (2024). Employee resource group. https://en.wikipedia.org/w/index.php?title=Employee_resource_group&oldid=1198628824

Wikipedia. (2024). *The Third Wave (Toffler book)*. https://en.wikipedia.org/w/index.php?title=The_Third_Wave_(Toffler_book)&oldid=1199447222

Wiley, S. K. (2021). The Grey Area: How Regulations Impact Autonomy in Computational Journalism. *Digital Journalism (Abingdon, England)*, 11(6), 889–905. DOI: 10.1080/21670811.2021.1893199

Wilkinson, J. (2021). Employee Engagement: What It Is and 5 Ways to Foster It. Firespring. https://firespring.com/powered-by-purpose/what-is-employee-engagement-how-to-foster-it/

Williams, A. W. (2016). The Value of Values: The Amplified Role of Authenticity in an Increasingly Transparent World. Journal of Creating Value. https://www.semanticscholar.org/paper/The-Value-of-Values%3A-The-Amplified-Role-of-in-an-Williams/043312b7842b9aa25c386a6161998c70a68e0cf8

Wittrich, A. (2022). Ethical Decision-Making In The Work Of Project Leaders – Why Ethics Gains Importance In Future Project Management. In J. Stankevičienė & V. Skvarciany (Eds.), *International Scientific Conference "Business And Management", 12th International Scientific Conference "Business And Management 2022"*. Vilnius Gediminas Technical University. Https://Doi.Org/10.3846/Bm.2022.820

Wizbowski, R. (2024). *Ethical Leadership: Fostering A Culture Of Integrity From The Top Down*. Https://Www.Diligent.Com/Resources/Blog/Ethical-Leadership

Woliba Market Team. (2024). Why Do Company Core Values Matter? *Woliba*. Https://Woliba.Io/Blog/Company-Core-Values

Wong, K. (2024). Company Core Values: 25 Inspiring Examples. *Achievers*. Https://Www.Achievers.Com/Blog/Company-Core-Value-Examples/

Wong, K. (2024). Diversity and inclusion in the workplace: Benefits and challenges. *Achievers*. https://www.achievers.com/blog/diversity-and-inclusion/

Workhuman Editorial Team. (2023). Barriers to Diversity in the Workplace | Workhuman. https://www.workhuman.com/blog/barriers-to-diversity/

World Economic Forum. (2020). *The Future of Jobs Report 2020*. https://www.weforum.org/reports/the-future-of-jobs-report-2020

World Economic Forum. (2024). These organizations are scaling impactful corporate diversity, equity, and inclusion initiatives. https://www.weforum.org/agenda/2024/01/organizations-impactful-corporate-dei-initiatives/

Wrike (n.d.). project-management-guide.

Writer, A. S. (/2023). *Agile Strategic Planning*. CIOPages.Com. https://www.ciopages.com/agile-strategic-planning/

Wurth, B., Stam, E., & Spigel, B. (2023). Entrepreneurial Ecosystem Mechanisms. *Foundations and Trends® in Entrepreneurship, 19*(3), 224–339. DOI: 10.1561/0300000089

Yakut, E. (2022). Effects of Technological Innovations on Consumer Behavior: Marketing 4.0 Perspective. In Yakut, E. (Ed.), *Industry 4.0 and Global Businesses* (pp. 55–68). Emerald Publishing Limited., DOI: 10.1108/978-1-80117-326-120211004

Yancey, D. (2021). *How Strategic Planning Is Different in a Post-COVID World*. ASAE. https://www.asaecenter.org/resources/articles/an_plus/2021/july/how-strategic-planning-is-different-in-a-postcovid-world

Yan, J., Zhang, S. X., & Hallak, R. (2023). Research Note Mental Health and Wellbeing of Tourism Entrepreneurs During Times of Crisis. *Tourism Analysis*, 28(1), 147–153. DOI: 10.3727/108354223X16729590545180

Yee, L., Chui, M., Roberts, R., & Issler, M. (2024). *McKinsey technology trends outlook 2024 | McKinsey*. https://www.mckinsey.com/capabilities/mckinsey-digital/our-insights/the-top-trends-in-tech#/

Yee, N., Shaffer, L. J., Gore, M. L., & Harrell, R. M. (2021). Expert Perceptions Of Conflicts In African Vulture Conservation: Implications For Overcoming Ethical Decision-Making Dilemmas. *The Journal of Raptor Research*, 55(3), 359–373. Https://Doi.Org/10.3356/Jrr-20-39. DOI: 10.3356/JRR-20-39

York, A. (2024). Transparency In Leadership: Lead Your Team With Class. *Clickup*. Https://Clickup.Com/Blog/Transparency-In-Leadership/

Yousueng, H., & Hong, S. (2019). The Impact Of Accountability On Organizational Performance In The U.S. Federal Government: The Moderating Role Of Autonomy. *Review of Public Personnel Administration*, 39(1), 3–23. Doi.Org/10.1177/0734371x16682816. DOI: 10.1177/0734371X16682816

Zacharias, T., Rahawarin, M., & Yusriadi, Y. (2021). Cultural reconstruction and organization environment for employee performance. *Journal of Ethnic and Cultural Studies*, 8(2), 296–315. Doi.org/10.29333/ejecs/801. DOI: 10.29333/ejecs/801

Zaghmout, B. (2024). Strategic Decision-Making In Startups: The Role Of Data-Driven Insights In Enhancing Business Innovation. *International Journal Of Entrepreneurship And Business Innovation,* 7(3), 76–91. Https://Doi.Org/10.52589/Ijebi-9joy4tvb

Zahoor, N., Khan, Z., Arslan, A., Khan, H., & Tarba, S. Y. (2022). International open innovation and international market success: An empirical study of emerging market small and medium-sized enterprises. *International Marketing Review*, 39(3), 755–782. DOI: 10.1108/IMR-12-2020-0314

Zak, P. J. (2017). *The Neuroscience of Trust.* Harvard Business Review. https://hbr.org/2017/01/the-neuroscience-of-trust

Zaki, J. (2019). *Making Empathy Central to Your Company Culture*. Harvard Business Review. https://hbr.org/2019/05/making-empathy-central-to-your-company-culture

Zaki, A. M., El-Gohary, H., & Edwards, D. J. (2021). Ethical And Sme Internationalisation Determinants. *International Journal of Customer Relationship Marketing and Management*, 12(1), 1–27. DOI: 10.4018/IJCRMM.2021010101

Zhang, W., White, S., & Luo, J. (2020). *How Entrepreneurs Can Build Ecosystems for New Venture Creation*. Social Science Research Network. DOI: 10.2139/ssrn.3713478

Zhao, X., Sun, X., Zhao, L., & Xing, Y. (2022). Can the digital transformation of manufacturing enterprises promote enterprise innovation? *Business Process Management Journal*, 28(4), 960–982. DOI: 10.1108/BPMJ-01-2022-0018

Zheng, X., Sun, C., & Liu, J. (2024). Exploring stakeholder engagement in urban village renovation projects through a mixed-method approach to social network analysis: A case study of Tianjin. *Humanities & Social Sciences Communications*, 11(1), 27. Advance online publication. DOI: 10.1057/s41599-023-02536-7

Zlojutro, S. (N.D.). *Actionable Insights: Translating Research Into Data-Driven Decisions*. Retrieved September 6, 2024, From Https://Thrivable.App/Insights/Actionable-Insights-Translating-Research-Into-Data-Driven-Decisions

Z-Stream Blog. (2019). *What is the agile iterative approach and where is it used?* https://www.zstream.io/blog/what-is-the-agile-iterative-approach-and-where-is-it-used

Zulkifli, Z. (2023).. . *Strategies For Enhancing Zakat Fundraising Through The Utilization Of Social Media And Digital Campaigns*, 1(2). Advance online publication. DOI: 10.56910/ictmt.v1i1.119

About the Author

Amdy Diene leads Touba Digital Consulting as its Chief Executive Officer. With a Doctorate in Strategic Leadership from Liberty University School of Business, he actively contributes to social science research. Dr. Diene's educational background includes a master's degree in leadership and management from Western Governors University and a bachelor's in information technology and security from Campbell University. His professional expertise spans consulting and software development, focusing on hospital patient information systems in the healthcare sector.

Index

A

adaptive 43, 44, 45, 46, 48, 49, 51, 52, 53, 55, 56, 57, 58, 59, 60, 61, 62, 63, 64, 66, 67, 68, 72, 75, 76, 80, 83, 86, 93, 115, 121, 122, 127, 129, 131, 138, 139, 142, 143, 147, 169, 171, 179, 180, 182, 184, 189, 193, 195, 209, 311

analysis 1, 2, 4, 13, 14, 15, 16, 20, 25, 29, 36, 37, 40, 43, 44, 61, 62, 72, 73, 84, 88, 89, 94, 100, 121, 122, 126, 139, 141, 142, 148, 157, 160, 169, 180, 182, 194, 208, 211, 213, 216, 221, 223, 224, 228, 233, 236, 237, 238, 239, 240, 241, 269, 270, 277, 282, 283, 284, 287, 288, 291, 292, 293, 294, 299, 304, 305, 306, 312, 314, 315, 316, 321, 323, 327, 329, 330, 331, 336, 337, 338, 340, 343, 344, 349, 350, 351

B

business 1, 2, 3, 4, 5, 6, 7, 8, 9, 10, 11, 12, 13, 15, 16, 17, 18, 19, 20, 21, 22, 23, 26, 27, 29, 30, 31, 32, 33, 34, 35, 36, 37, 38, 39, 40, 41, 44, 47, 49, 50, 51, 52, 54, 55, 57, 59, 60, 61, 62, 64, 65, 67, 68, 69, 71, 72, 73, 74, 75, 76, 80, 82, 83, 84, 85, 88, 89, 90, 91, 92, 94, 95, 96, 97, 99, 100, 101, 102, 103, 104, 105, 107, 108, 109, 110, 112, 113, 115, 116, 118, 121, 122, 123, 124, 125, 127, 129, 130, 131, 132, 134, 137, 138, 139, 140, 141, 142, 144, 146, 147, 148, 149, 150, 151, 152, 153, 154, 155, 156, 157, 159, 161, 162, 163, 164, 165, 166, 167, 168, 169, 170, 171, 172, 174, 175, 176, 179, 180, 181, 183, 185, 187, 188, 189, 190, 191, 192, 193, 194, 195, 196, 197, 208, 209, 210, 211, 212, 215, 216, 217, 221, 222, 223, 225, 229, 232, 233, 235, 236, 238, 239, 240, 242, 247, 249, 252, 254, 255, 256, 257, 258, 259, 261, 262, 263, 264, 272, 273, 274, 276, 277, 278, 279, 281, 282, 284, 285, 287, 289, 290, 292, 293, 298, 299, 300, 302, 303, 305, 307, 309, 310, 311, 312, 313, 315, 316, 317, 318, 319, 320, 321, 322, 324, 326, 332, 333, 338, 341, 343, 344, 345, 346, 347, 348, 349, 350, 351, 352

C

complex 2, 4, 9, 12, 13, 15, 26, 30, 31, 36, 37, 43, 44, 45, 48, 51, 52, 54, 55, 57, 58, 61, 62, 68, 71, 84, 86, 99, 135, 137, 140, 141, 142, 149, 150, 151, 152, 153, 155, 170, 172, 176, 180, 186, 189, 190, 195, 196, 197, 200, 205, 206, 209, 216, 219, 221, 223, 225, 234, 239, 250, 254, 262, 263, 272, 274, 282, 285, 287, 292, 293, 297, 299, 300, 301, 304, 309, 316, 317, 318, 320, 321, 322, 323, 328, 331, 332, 335, 336, 338, 341, 343, 344

comprehensive 7, 10, 16, 22, 33, 35, 36, 37, 40, 43, 48, 55, 57, 61, 62, 64, 71, 76, 78, 81, 83, 84, 85, 86, 87, 88, 96, 97, 99, 100, 104, 105, 107, 112, 113, 114, 122, 123, 124, 127, 131, 133, 137, 139, 150, 156, 157, 159, 168, 169, 170, 176, 180, 182, 188, 194, 195, 197, 206, 208, 216, 227, 233, 241, 242, 247, 253, 254, 269, 273, 277, 281, 282, 289, 290, 291, 303, 305, 307, 310, 312, 315, 317, 318, 321, 322, 327, 328, 329, 330, 331, 332, 333, 334, 337, 344, 347, 351

consumer 1, 2, 3, 4, 7, 10, 15, 17, 18, 20, 21, 22, 49, 69, 72, 122, 127, 138, 140, 160, 174, 181, 202, 252, 264, 272, 293, 296, 297

convergence 1, 2, 3, 4, 5, 11, 12, 15, 16, 18, 22, 71, 115, 143, 151, 209, 295, 325

corporate 7, 9, 15, 25, 27, 33, 36, 37, 38, 41, 47, 50, 60, 65, 76, 80, 107, 108,

114, 119, 123, 124, 135, 138, 140, 150, 152, 161, 170, 171, 180, 184, 188, 189, 220, 232, 245, 247, 251, 253, 256, 257, 259, 272, 277, 285, 287, 288, 297, 298, 299, 300, 304, 305, 306, 307, 308, 324, 336, 338, 339, 341, 342, 346, 349

create 1, 3, 5, 8, 10, 11, 12, 15, 19, 22, 23, 25, 26, 28, 31, 35, 36, 37, 45, 46, 47, 48, 50, 53, 55, 57, 59, 62, 69, 72, 81, 83, 84, 85, 100, 107, 111, 114, 115, 137, 141, 149, 150, 153, 161, 166, 170, 171, 176, 181, 186, 193, 194, 196, 197, 201, 207, 213, 221, 232, 233, 234, 243, 246, 254, 256, 263, 268, 270, 274, 291, 308, 310, 315, 321, 322, 334, 340, 341

cultural 1, 2, 3, 4, 5, 6, 7, 8, 9, 10, 11, 12, 15, 16, 17, 18, 19, 20, 21, 22, 27, 34, 37, 41, 43, 44, 45, 46, 47, 48, 49, 50, 51, 52, 53, 54, 55, 56, 57, 58, 59, 60, 61, 62, 63, 64, 65, 66, 67, 68, 69, 72, 74, 86, 87, 95, 104, 106, 107, 110, 111, 112, 113, 115, 119, 160, 161, 162, 172, 175, 190, 195, 196, 197, 198, 199, 200, 201, 202, 205, 206, 207, 208, 209, 210, 211, 212, 213, 242, 243, 244, 247, 248, 254, 258, 259, 304, 305, 308, 318, 320, 339, 340, 348

culture 1, 2, 3, 5, 6, 7, 8, 9, 12, 15, 17, 18, 19, 22, 23, 25, 26, 28, 29, 30, 31, 32, 33, 37, 38, 39, 40, 41, 43, 45, 46, 47, 48, 49, 50, 51, 52, 53, 54, 56, 57, 60, 61, 63, 64, 65, 66, 67, 68, 69, 71, 73, 74, 75, 76, 77, 78, 79, 80, 83, 85, 86, 88, 93, 95, 96, 97, 100, 101, 102, 103, 107, 110, 111, 116, 122, 125, 129, 131, 132, 137, 139, 140, 142, 161, 168, 169, 170, 173, 179, 180, 181, 185, 186, 187, 188, 193, 199, 201, 203, 209, 215, 219, 224, 226, 227, 232, 233, 238, 239, 241, 243, 244, 245, 246, 249, 250, 251, 252, 253, 254, 256, 257, 258, 259, 262, 264, 266, 267, 268, 269, 270, 273, 276, 278, 279, 281, 282, 283, 286, 289, 300, 303, 304, 305, 306, 307, 308, 309, 310, 311, 314, 315, 317, 318, 320, 321, 322, 323, 324, 325, 326, 336, 338, 339, 341, 342, 343, 344, 345, 351

D

developing 12, 34, 44, 45, 50, 54, 57, 61, 62, 63, 72, 78, 79, 80, 86, 89, 99, 106, 115, 119, 121, 125, 126, 127, 136, 139, 142, 143, 147, 148, 149, 159, 163, 175, 195, 200, 203, 205, 206, 209, 211, 216, 219, 223, 225, 228, 231, 232, 233, 234, 240, 241, 242, 250, 254, 261, 271, 274, 283, 287, 299, 302, 305, 306, 308, 318, 319, 322, 342, 348

digital 1, 2, 3, 4, 5, 6, 7, 8, 9, 10, 12, 13, 15, 16, 17, 18, 19, 20, 21, 22, 23, 26, 27, 29, 34, 36, 37, 40, 41, 43, 45, 48, 50, 52, 59, 63, 66, 68, 71, 72, 73, 74, 75, 76, 77, 78, 79, 80, 82, 83, 84, 85, 86, 87, 88, 89, 90, 91, 92, 93, 94, 95, 96, 97, 109, 115, 132, 149, 151, 163, 166, 173, 181, 204, 206, 209, 212, 214, 217, 219, 224, 225, 227, 230, 233, 238, 241, 242, 248, 249, 254, 256, 259, 263, 270, 271, 275, 276, 277, 279, 281, 285, 287, 290, 291, 294, 295, 296, 297, 298, 299, 304, 311, 347

diverse 3, 6, 11, 43, 44, 45, 48, 49, 50, 51, 53, 54, 55, 58, 59, 61, 62, 64, 68, 69, 73, 76, 79, 83, 84, 85, 87, 100, 101, 103, 104, 105, 106, 107, 108, 109, 110, 112, 113, 114, 115, 117, 119, 120, 125, 128, 132, 137, 142, 143, 152, 153, 154, 166, 167, 168, 169, 180, 185, 186, 187, 189, 190, 191, 193, 195, 196, 198, 199, 200, 201, 202, 203, 204, 206, 207, 208, 209, 212, 223, 226, 227, 228, 231, 232, 242, 243, 244, 247, 249, 251, 259, 287, 301, 304, 317, 318, 320, 321, 322, 328, 329, 331, 332, 333, 334, 335, 338, 339, 345

drive 3, 6, 8, 9, 12, 22, 25, 26, 28, 29, 32, 34, 36, 37, 39, 49, 50, 51, 54, 55, 60, 62, 65, 67, 73, 81, 83, 85, 91, 96, 99,

102, 111, 115, 149, 150, 153, 164, 169, 170, 171, 175, 176, 179, 181, 185, 189, 192, 193, 195, 204, 216, 217, 229, 234, 252, 274, 281, 282, 292, 296, 317

dynamics 1, 2, 3, 4, 5, 6, 7, 11, 15, 16, 22, 27, 30, 43, 44, 47, 48, 49, 51, 58, 61, 64, 66, 67, 68, 69, 79, 84, 103, 108, 129, 131, 149, 151, 160, 163, 180, 185, 186, 189, 196, 205, 209, 223, 225, 235, 251, 255, 263, 266, 276, 298, 299, 336, 339

E

environmental 25, 27, 32, 33, 34, 36, 37, 41, 61, 69, 88, 122, 141, 148, 172, 173, 180, 182, 183, 193, 203, 231, 247, 248, 251, 254, 259, 272, 274, 296, 315, 319, 329, 339, 349

ethical 16, 25, 26, 27, 28, 29, 30, 36, 37, 39, 40, 41, 42, 71, 72, 73, 74, 75, 77, 84, 86, 201, 211, 228, 229, 234, 236, 241, 242, 243, 244, 245, 246, 247, 248, 249, 250, 251, 252, 253, 254, 255, 256, 257, 258, 259, 262, 264, 271, 272, 298, 299, 307, 308, 309, 317, 318, 319, 320, 321, 322, 323, 325, 326, 327, 328, 329, 330, 331, 332, 334, 335, 336, 337, 338, 339, 340, 341, 342, 343, 344, 345, 346, 347, 348, 349, 350, 351, 352

evolution 1, 2, 3, 4, 5, 15, 16, 33, 37, 44, 45, 49, 67, 80, 85, 86, 87, 92, 112, 115, 121, 123, 141, 142, 143, 144, 150, 151, 160, 164, 165, 167, 170, 171, 182, 188, 197, 209, 216, 222, 228, 233, 235, 237, 273, 274, 282, 305, 308, 309

F

frameworks 2, 15, 16, 26, 27, 33, 37, 44, 50, 72, 81, 84, 86, 96, 107, 121, 122, 143, 171, 180, 189, 190, 196, 216, 227, 228, 233, 234, 247, 248, 262, 266, 268, 271, 272, 274, 275, 309,

317, 318, 320, 321, 322, 328, 331, 335, 336, 337, 338, 339, 340, 344, 347, 348, 351

G

global 1, 2, 3, 4, 5, 6, 8, 11, 12, 15, 17, 18, 19, 20, 21, 22, 37, 43, 44, 45, 48, 49, 51, 52, 54, 55, 57, 60, 61, 62, 63, 67, 74, 85, 99, 100, 102, 106, 110, 111, 115, 119, 122, 127, 136, 146, 150, 152, 153, 159, 165, 166, 167, 168, 170, 174, 181, 187, 190, 195, 196, 198, 199, 200, 202, 208, 209, 211, 223, 236, 241, 242, 243, 247, 248, 254, 258, 259, 296, 318, 319, 320, 321, 340, 347

I

increasingly 1, 3, 11, 15, 22, 27, 33, 37, 44, 45, 48, 50, 51, 52, 54, 61, 63, 72, 95, 96, 99, 107, 115, 121, 125, 127, 129, 138, 139, 140, 141, 142, 149, 150, 151, 152, 153, 164, 165, 167, 169, 171, 179, 180, 189, 190, 195, 199, 200, 206, 209, 215, 216, 219, 220, 221, 223, 225, 226, 231, 233, 240, 241, 251, 252, 254, 262, 270, 272, 274, 275, 281, 285, 295, 298, 305, 309, 318, 320, 321, 331, 336, 344

innovation 1, 2, 3, 5, 6, 7, 8, 9, 11, 12, 13, 15, 19, 22, 26, 27, 28, 32, 34, 36, 37, 41, 43, 44, 49, 50, 51, 52, 53, 54, 55, 56, 58, 60, 61, 62, 63, 65, 66, 67, 69, 71, 72, 73, 74, 75, 76, 77, 78, 79, 80, 81, 82, 83, 84, 85, 86, 87, 88, 89, 90, 91, 92, 93, 94, 95, 96, 99, 100, 102, 103, 105, 107, 109, 110, 111, 112, 115, 119, 121, 123, 142, 147, 149, 150, 151, 153, 154, 156, 159, 160, 161, 163, 164, 165, 166, 167, 168, 169, 170, 171, 174, 175, 176, 179, 180, 181, 183, 184, 185, 186, 187, 188, 189, 190, 191, 192, 193, 195, 196, 198, 202, 203, 204, 206, 207, 208, 209, 212, 216, 217, 219, 220,

417

223, 224, 225, 229, 231, 234, 238, 240, 257, 267, 269, 271, 272, 278, 281, 284, 285, 294, 295, 296, 297, 298, 303, 304, 307, 308, 309, 315, 332, 334

L

leadership 2, 7, 11, 15, 16, 20, 25, 26, 27, 28, 29, 30, 31, 32, 33, 36, 37, 38, 39, 40, 41, 42, 43, 44, 45, 46, 47, 48, 49, 50, 51, 52, 53, 55, 56, 57, 58, 59, 60, 61, 62, 63, 64, 65, 66, 67, 68, 69, 71, 72, 75, 76, 80, 83, 84, 86, 87, 88, 89, 90, 91, 92, 93, 94, 95, 96, 99, 100, 101, 104, 105, 106, 107, 108, 111, 112, 113, 115, 116, 118, 119, 122, 123, 136, 147, 149, 151, 153, 156, 172, 176, 199, 200, 206, 207, 209, 212, 216, 217, 219, 225, 226, 230, 234, 235, 236, 240, 241, 242, 243, 244, 245, 246, 248, 249, 250, 251, 252, 253, 254, 255, 256, 257, 258, 259, 261, 262, 266, 267, 268, 269, 275, 300, 304, 306, 309, 317, 318, 320, 321, 322, 323, 324, 325, 326, 331, 332, 333, 335, 336, 338, 339, 340, 341, 342, 343, 344, 345, 346, 348, 349, 350, 351

M

maintaining 2, 4, 5, 9, 11, 15, 16, 21, 22, 25, 26, 36, 37, 41, 44, 56, 57, 58, 61, 62, 63, 71, 72, 73, 74, 79, 83, 87, 96, 99, 113, 115, 121, 122, 132, 135, 136, 137, 141, 142, 148, 150, 155, 160, 162, 164, 167, 171, 176, 179, 186, 189, 190, 193, 209, 216, 230, 233, 240, 241, 242, 243, 244, 247, 248, 250, 252, 253, 254, 259, 261, 262, 263, 264, 265, 267, 270, 290, 308, 309, 315, 317, 318, 325, 343, 344, 351

market 1, 2, 4, 5, 8, 11, 12, 15, 22, 27, 36, 41, 47, 48, 49, 52, 54, 55, 60, 61, 66, 68, 69, 72, 83, 84, 85, 95, 102, 123, 126, 127, 129, 130, 131, 132, 134, 136, 137, 138, 142, 143, 148, 154, 155, 156, 157, 159, 160, 161, 163, 164, 166, 167, 168, 169, 170, 171, 173, 175, 177, 179, 180, 181, 183, 187, 188, 189, 193, 215, 219, 221, 223, 224, 225, 231, 233, 240, 256, 282, 283, 285, 286, 293, 297, 298, 299, 322, 323, 350

N

navigate 1, 2, 3, 4, 7, 11, 12, 15, 16, 17, 27, 37, 43, 44, 45, 46, 49, 51, 52, 54, 57, 60, 61, 62, 63, 68, 71, 73, 74, 75, 77, 80, 86, 87, 96, 101, 102, 103, 107, 115, 122, 123, 124, 125, 126, 127, 130, 131, 132, 134, 135, 136, 137, 138, 140, 141, 142, 143, 150, 153, 171, 179, 181, 183, 188, 189, 190, 196, 197, 200, 207, 209, 212, 216, 221, 223, 225, 230, 232, 233, 234, 241, 242, 243, 247, 250, 252, 253, 254, 263, 272, 274, 284, 285, 286, 292, 293, 299, 300, 301, 302, 304, 306, 309, 317, 319, 321, 325, 326, 328, 330, 332, 333, 334, 336, 337, 338, 339, 340, 342, 343, 344

non-Western 44, 61, 62

O

organizational 1, 2, 3, 4, 5, 6, 7, 8, 13, 15, 16, 17, 18, 19, 22, 25, 26, 27, 29, 30, 31, 32, 33, 35, 36, 37, 38, 39, 40, 41, 42, 44, 45, 47, 48, 49, 50, 51, 52, 53, 54, 56, 57, 58, 61, 62, 63, 64, 66, 68, 69, 71, 72, 73, 74, 75, 76, 77, 78, 79, 80, 81, 82, 86, 87, 88, 89, 90, 91, 92, 93, 94, 95, 96, 97, 99, 100, 101, 102, 103, 104, 105, 106, 107, 108, 109, 110, 111, 112, 113, 114, 115, 116, 118, 121, 122, 123, 124, 125, 126, 127, 129, 130, 131, 136, 137, 138, 140, 141, 142, 143, 147, 148, 157, 160, 161, 168, 171, 180, 182, 183, 184, 185, 186, 189, 190, 192, 193, 196, 197, 199, 200, 205, 206, 208, 209, 216, 217, 220, 223, 230, 232,

418

233, 234, 236, 240, 241, 242, 243, 245, 246, 248, 249, 250, 251, 252, 253, 254, 255, 256, 257, 259, 265, 267, 268, 269, 270, 271, 273, 274, 279, 281, 282, 283, 285, 286, 287, 288, 289, 290, 298, 299, 300, 301, 302, 303, 304, 305, 306, 307, 308, 309, 315, 317, 318, 320, 321, 322, 323, 324, 325, 326, 328, 330, 332, 333, 334, 335, 336, 337, 338, 339, 340, 341, 342, 343, 344, 345, 348, 350, 351, 352

organizations 1, 2, 3, 4, 5, 6, 7, 15, 16, 18, 22, 23, 26, 27, 29, 30, 31, 33, 34, 35, 36, 37, 41, 43, 44, 45, 47, 48, 49, 50, 51, 52, 53, 54, 55, 56, 57, 58, 59, 61, 62, 63, 66, 67, 68, 71, 72, 73, 74, 75, 76, 77, 78, 80, 81, 82, 83, 85, 86, 87, 88, 89, 90, 94, 96, 97, 99, 100, 101, 102, 103, 104, 105, 106, 107, 108, 110, 111, 112, 113, 115, 119, 121, 122, 123, 124, 125, 127, 129, 130, 131, 132, 135, 136, 137, 138, 139, 140, 141, 142, 143, 148, 149, 150, 153, 156, 158, 159, 160, 161, 163, 164, 169, 170, 171, 172, 176, 179, 180, 182, 183, 184, 185, 186, 189, 190, 193, 194, 195, 196, 197, 198, 199, 202, 203, 204, 205, 207, 208, 209, 213, 214, 215, 216, 217, 219, 221, 222, 223, 224, 225, 226, 229, 232, 233, 234, 237, 241, 242, 244, 246, 247, 249, 250, 251, 252, 253, 254, 257, 258, 261, 262, 266, 268, 269, 270, 272, 273, 274, 275, 281, 282, 283, 284, 285, 286, 291, 292, 293, 294, 295, 299, 300, 301, 302, 303, 304, 306, 307, 308, 309, 318, 319, 320, 321, 322, 323, 324, 325, 326, 333, 335, 336, 338, 339, 344

P

practices 1, 4, 5, 7, 8, 9, 15, 16, 23, 25, 26, 27, 33, 34, 36, 37, 40, 41, 42, 46, 47, 51, 55, 59, 60, 61, 62, 65, 68, 69, 73, 75, 84, 87, 88, 93, 94, 99, 101, 103, 106, 109, 110, 111, 112, 113, 114, 115, 117, 119, 121, 132, 137, 138, 143, 144, 157, 161, 166, 167, 170, 185, 192, 194, 196, 201, 204, 206, 209, 213, 215, 216, 222, 223, 224, 229, 233, 242, 247, 248, 249, 253, 254, 259, 261, 262, 264, 269, 272, 274, 279, 289, 291, 303, 306, 310, 314, 315, 319, 320, 321, 323, 325, 333, 334, 344, 347, 351

S

shifts 2, 3, 6, 7, 15, 19, 36, 37, 43, 44, 45, 46, 47, 48, 49, 50, 51, 52, 53, 54, 55, 56, 57, 58, 60, 61, 62, 63, 69, 82, 84, 85, 110, 123, 126, 129, 134, 140, 160, 161, 230, 243, 309, 336

social 3, 5, 6, 7, 10, 11, 12, 17, 25, 27, 33, 34, 36, 37, 38, 41, 45, 54, 61, 66, 69, 73, 74, 76, 77, 89, 93, 94, 95, 102, 104, 108, 114, 115, 120, 141, 148, 160, 175, 185, 191, 193, 201, 202, 213, 219, 241, 247, 248, 251, 254, 256, 257, 259, 263, 272, 277, 347, 349

successful 1, 2, 3, 5, 6, 9, 11, 12, 15, 19, 23, 26, 28, 29, 31, 34, 36, 37, 44, 46, 47, 49, 54, 56, 58, 62, 65, 72, 75, 76, 83, 86, 99, 100, 111, 112, 115, 121, 138, 149, 155, 157, 158, 159, 162, 165, 166, 167, 169, 172, 173, 174, 175, 179, 180, 187, 189, 191, 192, 196, 204, 208, 224, 238, 239, 242, 254, 261, 274, 285, 308, 312, 339, 341, 343, 344

sustainable 2, 3, 9, 26, 27, 32, 33, 34, 36, 37, 38, 40, 41, 42, 49, 57, 59, 61, 62, 63, 65, 69, 71, 80, 85, 87, 93, 115, 150, 161, 162, 164, 167, 169, 171, 174, 189, 190, 195, 196, 202, 204, 209, 211, 224, 226, 234, 244, 247, 248, 252, 253, 254, 261, 262, 264, 272, 273, 278, 283, 285, 315, 344, 346

T

technological 1, 2, 3, 4, 6, 7, 9, 10, 11, 12, 15, 16, 17, 18, 19, 20, 22, 44, 47, 49, 61, 63, 68, 71, 72, 73, 74, 78, 80, 83, 84, 85, 86, 87, 93, 96, 102, 110, 111, 115, 122, 126, 127, 132, 140, 141, 143, 148, 149, 150, 156, 160, 161, 163, 166, 167, 168, 170, 171, 176, 179, 181, 183, 189, 190, 209, 215, 216, 217, 218, 219, 221, 225, 227, 228, 230, 232, 233, 234, 235, 239, 240, 241, 242, 243, 247, 248, 252, 254, 261, 264, 270, 271, 272, 287, 294, 302, 304, 305, 309, 319, 330

technologies 1, 2, 3, 4, 5, 6, 7, 8, 9, 12, 15, 16, 20, 21, 22, 23, 34, 36, 40, 41, 53, 60, 72, 73, 74, 75, 80, 85, 89, 90, 94, 96, 97, 110, 112, 132, 134, 151, 164, 167, 170, 175, 188, 219, 229, 233, 243, 261, 262, 264, 271, 272, 274, 278, 284, 296, 298, 304, 305, 308, 309, 313, 319, 331

technology 1, 2, 3, 4, 5, 6, 7, 8, 9, 10, 11, 12, 13, 15, 17, 18, 19, 20, 21, 22, 23, 27, 37, 54, 65, 68, 71, 73, 78, 80, 83, 85, 86, 87, 88, 89, 90, 91, 92, 94, 96, 99, 100, 102, 109, 112, 114, 116, 117, 118, 119, 120, 132, 150, 156, 163, 169, 170, 177, 181, 185, 195, 200, 204, 210, 216, 219, 220, 225, 226, 228, 231, 233, 235, 236, 237, 239, 241, 242, 248, 249, 253, 254, 257, 261, 262, 270, 271, 273, 274, 276, 277, 278, 279, 295, 301, 302, 305, 308, 309, 312, 330

transformation 1, 2, 3, 4, 5, 6, 7, 8, 9, 10, 15, 16, 18, 19, 20, 21, 22, 26, 27, 29, 31, 33, 37, 43, 44, 45, 52, 59, 61, 62, 63, 65, 68, 71, 72, 75, 76, 78, 80, 83, 84, 85, 86, 87, 88, 89, 90, 91, 92, 93, 94, 95, 96, 97, 101, 102, 107, 112, 115, 149, 151, 160, 205, 206, 209, 216, 220, 224, 233, 234, 240, 254, 256, 271, 283, 284, 293, 300, 303, 305, 306, 307, 308, 309, 324, 325, 331, 341

transformational 25, 30, 31, 36, 38, 39, 40, 42, 59, 304

U

understanding 1, 2, 4, 5, 10, 11, 15, 19, 21, 22, 26, 30, 31, 32, 33, 37, 44, 46, 49, 51, 58, 59, 61, 62, 63, 68, 72, 84, 87, 99, 103, 109, 143, 146, 147, 150, 153, 155, 159, 161, 168, 171, 180, 186, 195, 197, 198, 199, 200, 201, 203, 206, 207, 208, 209, 212, 216, 233, 242, 244, 247, 250, 254, 259, 262, 265, 269, 278, 279, 282, 287, 288, 290, 292, 297, 298, 301, 302, 303, 304, 312, 319, 320, 321, 322, 323, 326, 328, 331, 334, 340, 341, 342, 343, 346, 347, 351

V

values 7, 11, 13, 14, 23, 25, 26, 27, 28, 29, 30, 32, 33, 34, 35, 36, 37, 38, 39, 41, 42, 43, 45, 46, 47, 48, 49, 51, 53, 58, 61, 68, 71, 72, 73, 74, 76, 77, 78, 80, 81, 82, 83, 85, 86, 87, 92, 94, 95, 96, 97, 102, 103, 107, 112, 113, 115, 131, 138, 142, 146, 149, 168, 169, 183, 186, 198, 200, 201, 206, 207, 209, 213, 216, 223, 226, 242, 247, 250, 252, 257, 259, 265, 267, 291, 309, 317, 318, 321, 322, 323, 324, 325, 326, 332, 333, 334, 336, 337, 338, 339, 340, 341, 342, 343, 344, 345, 347, 348, 349, 350, 351, 352

vision 16, 25, 26, 27, 28, 29, 30, 31, 33, 34, 35, 36, 37, 42, 46, 53, 71, 72, 76, 77, 80, 81, 82, 83, 85, 86, 87, 88, 90, 96, 121, 129, 131, 136, 137, 138, 139, 141, 142, 148, 157, 162, 167, 229, 288, 289, 295, 298, 322, 324

W

while 2, 3, 4, 5, 7, 8, 9, 11, 13, 15, 16, 21, 22, 25, 26, 27, 30, 35, 36, 37, 41, 42, 44, 45, 48, 60, 61, 62, 63, 68, 69, 71, 72, 74, 83, 84, 86, 87, 96, 99, 100,

420

101, 102, 104, 107, 109, 111, 112, 115, 119, 121, 122, 123, 126, 127, 129, 130, 132, 135, 136, 141, 142, 143, 148, 150, 151, 153, 154, 156, 164, 165, 166, 167, 169, 179, 180, 181, 185, 189, 190, 193, 196, 198, 199, 204, 209, 215, 216, 217, 219, 233, 234, 239, 241, 242, 247, 248, 249, 251, 254, 259, 262, 264, 266, 270, 271, 272, 274, 282, 284, 285, 286, 290, 298, 299, 309, 315, 317, 318, 321, 325, 328, 329, 330, 331, 332, 333, 334, 335, 337, 342, 343, 344, 352